Related titles

Pharmaceutical Microbiology: Essentials for Quality Assurance and Quality Control, First edition
(ISBN 978-0-08100-022-9)

Predictive Modeling of Pharmaceutical Unit Operations

Woodhead Publishing Series in Biomedicine:
Number 87

Predictive Modeling of Pharmaceutical Unit Operations

Edited by

Preetanshu Pandey
Rahul Bharadwaj

ELSEVIER

AMSTERDAM • BOSTON • HEIDELBERG • LONDON
NEW YORK • OXFORD • PARIS • SAN DIEGO
SAN FRANCISCO • SINGAPORE • SYDNEY • TOKYO
Woodhead Publishing is an imprint of Elsevier

WP WOODHEAD PUBLISHING

Woodhead Publishing is an imprint of Elsevier
The Officers' Mess Business Centre, Royston Road, Duxford, CB22 4QH, United Kingdom
50 Hampshire Street, 5th Floor, Cambridge, MA 02139, United States
The Boulevard, Langford Lane, Kidlington, OX5 1GB, United Kingdom

British Library Cataloguing-in-Publication Data
A catalogue record for this book is available from the British Library

Library of Congress Cataloging-in-Publication Data
A catalog record for this book is available from the Library of Congress

ISBN: 978-0-08-100154-7 (print)
ISBN: 978-0-08-100180-6 (online)

For information on all Woodhead Publishing visit our website at https://www.elsevier.com

Publisher: Mica Haley
Acquisition Editor: Glyn Jones
Editorial Project Manager: Lindsay Lawrence
Production Project Manager: Omer Mukthar
Cover Designer: Matthew Limbert

Typeset by MPS Limited, Chennai, India

Contents

List of contributors

A. Afolabi New Jersey Institute of Technology, Newark, NJ, United States

A. Aliseda University of Washington, Seattle, WA, United States

M. am Ende Pfizer Worldwide Research & Development, Groton, CT, United States

D. Barrasso Rutgers-The State University of New Jersey, Piscataway, NJ, United States

A. Berchielli Pfizer Worldwide Research & Development, Groton, CT, United States

R. Bharadwaj Rocky-DEM, Houston, TX, United States

E. Bilgili New Jersey Institute of Technology, Newark, NJ, United States

M. Capece New Jersey Institute of Technology, Newark, NJ, United States

S. Chatterjee Food and Drug Administration, Silver Spring, MD, United States

A. Chaudhury Rutgers-The State University of New Jersey, Piscataway, NJ, United States

X. Chen Drug Product Science and Technology, Bristol-Myers Squibb, New Brunswick, NJ, United States

Y. Chen Novast Laboratories, Ltd., Nantong, China

D. Clancy GlaxoSmithKline, Collegeville, PA, United States

J. Cunningham Johnson and Johnson, New Brunswick, NJ, United States

J.C. Cunningham Johnson & Johnson Pharmaceutical R&D, Spring House, PA, United States

P. Doshi Pfizer Worldwide Research & Development, Groton, CT, United States

A. Dubey Aditya Birla Science and Technology Company Pvt. Ltd. (ABSTCPL), New Panvel, India

B. Freireich The Dow Chemical Company, Midland, MI, United States

Y. Guo University of Florida, Gainesville, FL, United States

R. Gupta Celgene, Summit, NJ, United States

M. Horner ANSYS, Inc., Evanston, IL, United States

S. Joshi ANSYS Fluent India Pvt Ltd., Pune, Maharashtra, India

W. Ketterhagen Pfizer Worldwide Research & Development, Groton, CT, United States

K. LaMarche Bristol-Myers Squibb, New York, NY, United States

S. Lee Food and Drug Administration, Silver Spring, MD, United States

Y. Li Abbvie Inc., North Chicago, IL, United States

J.D. Litster Purdue University, West Lafayette, IN, United States

A. Michrafy CNRS-Mines Albi, Albi, France

F. Nikfar Bristol-Myers Squibb, New Brunswick, NJ, United States

T. O'Connor Food and Drug Administration, Silver Spring, MD, United States

P. Pandey Drug Product Science and Technology, Bristol-Myers Squibb, New Brunswick, NJ, United States

D.A. Pohlman Purdue University, West Lafayette, IN, United States

A. Prpich Pfizer Worldwide Research & Development, Groton, CT, United States

R. Ramachandran Rutgers-The State University of New Jersey, Piscataway, NJ, United States

J.M. Rowe Bristol-Myers Squibb, New Brunswick, NJ, United States

G. Tian Food and Drug Administration, Silver Spring, MD, United States

Y. Waghmare Sanofi-Genzyme, Framingham, MA, United States

C.-Y. Wu University of Surrey, Guildford, United Kingdom

X. Yang Food and Drug Administration, Silver Spring, MD, United States

A. Zavaliangos Drexel University, Philadelphia, PA, United States

Predictive modeling of pharmaceutical unit operations

Editors
Preetanshu Pandey (Bristol-Myers Squibb)
Rahul Bharadwaj (Rocky-DEM)

Preetanshu Pandey
Dr. Preetanshu Pandey obtained his Bachelor's degree in chemical engineering from the Indian Institute of Technology, Kanpur, India. He holds M.S. and Ph.D. degrees in chemical engineering from West Virginia University. He is currently working as a Principal Scientist at the Drug Product Science and Technology Department at Bristol-Myers Squibb (BMS). At BMS, he is primarily involved with developing oral solid dosage drug products. Prior to joining BMS, he worked at Schering-Plough/Merck for over 3 years on drug product development of inhalation products. He is actively involved with American Association of Pharmaceutical Scientists (AAPS) and the American Institute of Chemical Engineers (AIChE) organizations and has chaired symposiums and open forums in previous annual meetings. He serves as a reviewer for multiple journals and has authored over 40 peer-reviewed publications, three patent applications, and three invited book chapters.

Rahul Bharadwaj
Dr. Rahul Bharadwaj is the Vice President of Engineering and Business Development at Rocky-DEM, Inc. Dr. Bharadwaj has over a decade of experience in the development, validation, and application of computational tools such as discrete element modeling (DEM), computational fluid dynamics (CFD), and finite element analyses for industries such as pharmaceutical, chemical, agriculture, mining, oil, and gas. He received his M.S. in mechanical engineering from the University of Kentucky in 2003 and his Ph.D. in mechanical engineering from Purdue University in 2006. He has since then held positions as a senior scientist at Pfizer R&D and as a consulting engineer at Jenike & Johanson, Inc. He is also an active member of the American Institute of Chemical Engineers (AIChE), American Association of Pharmaceutical Scientists (AAPS), and is the founder and past-chair of its Process Modeling and Simulation Focus Group.

Xiaodong Chen

Dr. Xiaodong Chen received his Ph.D. from Ohio State University and joined Bristol-Myers Squibb (BMS) in 2012. He works as a Research Investigator in the Drug Product Science and Technology Department. He is developing and implementing innovative computational models to pharmaceutical processes such as powder compaction, freeze drying, and fill/finish manufacturing of late-stage candidates for both oral dosage forms and sterile/nonsterile liquid formulations. Dr. Chen has served as an invited reviewer for many international scientific journals in the area of pharmaceutical science and chemical engineering. He is currently advising two National Science Foundation (NSF)-funded projects and serving as an organizing committee member for international conferences such as American Institute of Chemical Engineers (AIChE) Annual Conference and American Association of Pharmaceutical Scientists (AAPS) National Biotechnology Conference.

Thomas O'Connor

Dr. Thomas O'Connor is currently Manufacturing Science Team Leader for the science staff within the Office of Pharmaceutical Quality. His work at the FDA is focused on regulatory research in the area of emerging technologies such as utilizing models to aid the risk assessment of continuous manufacturing processes. He is an experienced practitioner of advanced process control techniques including statistical process control and holds patents related to the development of statistical monitoring systems for industrial plants. Dr. O'Connor earned his B.S. in chemical engineering from the Cooper Union and his Ph.D. in chemical engineering from Princeton University.

Xiaochuan Yang

Dr. Xiaochuan Yang is a Visiting Associate on the Science Staff Manufacturing Science team on Advanced Manufacturing Technologies. He received his B.S. degree in chemical engineering from Tsinghua University and his M.S. and Ph.D. degrees from the Massachusetts Institute of Technology. His research is mainly focused on crystal/polymorphism, chiral compounds, various analytical tools, novel formulation methods, and advanced manufacturing science.

Geng Tian

Geng Tian joined the FDA as an ORISE fellow in the Office of Pharmaceutical Quality in 2014. He is currently working on modeling of processes for the continuous manufacturing of solid-based pharmaceutical dosage forms. Dr. Tian has worked at Virginia Commonwealth University to develop novel techniques and inhaler devices for the efficient aerosol drug delivery.

Sharmista Chatterjee

Dr. Sharmista Chatterjee is currently serving as the Acting Division Director in Division of Process Assessment II, within the FDA's Office of Process and Facilities (OPF). Chatterjee has been with the FDA since 2006. During her tenure, she served as the CMC lead for Quality by Design (QbD) in the Office of New

Drug Quality Assessment (ONDQA) and as the technical lead for the European Medicines Agency QbD pilot. She is an agency expert in CMC modeling and simulation. In addition to her current responsibilities, she is serving as one of OPF's representatives on the CDER Emerging Technology Team. Prior to joining the agency in 2006, she spent around 10 years in the industry. Her industry experience was primarily in process development and modeling in diverse areas that ranged from consumer goods to pharmaceuticals. She received her Bachelor's degree in chemical engineering from the Indian Institute of Technology and her Ph.D. in chemical engineering with a comajor in biomedical engineering from Iowa State University.

Sau Lee

Sau Lee is a Senior Biomedical Research Scientist and serves as the Associate Director for Science of the Office of Pharmaceutical Quality (OPQ), the Team Leader of the OPQ Botanical Review Team, and the chair of the OPQ Emerging Technology Team. Lee and his OPQ Scientific and Research Staff are leading the effort in advancing OPQ research and in manufacturing science, complex drug substances, and products containing nanomaterials, as well as in developing the regulatory policy, scientific standards, and computational and modeling tools supporting quality review and inspection in OPQ.

Atul Dubey

Dr. Atul Dubey is a Senior Scientist at the Aditya Birla Science and Technology Company Pvt. Ltd., Navi Mumbai, India, and is involved in several R&D activities involving granular materials. He received his doctoral degree in mechanical engineering from Rutgers University in 2007. Since then, his interest has been in the application of mechanistic modeling methods on manufacturing processes involving granular materials. He has authored several peer-reviewed journal articles and book chapters and his work has been presented in several international conferences. His primary focus has been on developing models for the optimization of powder mixing, tablet coating, and material handling with applications in pharmaceutical, cement, mining, food, and confectionary industries.

Abderrahim Michrafy

Dr. Abderrahim Michrafy has an M.Sc. and a Ph.D. in applied mathematics from the University of Bordeaux, France. He has also a Habilitation in the field of mechanical engineering. He joined the CNRS (the French National Center for Scientific Research) as a research engineer in 1989 and worked successively for three French laboratories in chemical and mechanical fields. His research is focused on the development of finite element modeling (FEM) for engineering processes. During the last 15 years. Michrafy spent in the research center of Particulate Solids and Processes of Ecole des Mines (Albi, France), he developed research work on die and rolling compaction processes for pharmaceutical and mineral applications.

Antonios Zavaliangos

Dr. Antonios Zavaliangos is the A. W. Grosvenor Professor of Materials Science and Engineering at Drexel University. He received his Diploma in mechanical engineering from the National Technical University of Athens in 1986, his M.S. from Columbia University in 1987, and his Ph.D. from MIT in 1992. He served as Department Head of Materials Science and Engineering at Drexel from 2007 to 2014. His research interests are in the areas of constitutive modeling of the mechanical behavior of materials, with emphasis in the processing and properties of solids made from powders. Prior work includes reactive sintering, semisolid processing, electric current aided sintering, and pharmaceutical tableting. He has consulted and lectured extensively for several industries, including Merck, J&J/Janssen, Genentech, Amgen, and Corning.

John C. Cunningham

Dr. John C. Cunningham joined Johnson and Johnson in 2005 after working at Merck from 1989 to 2004. He received his B.S. in 1986, M.S. in 1989, and Ph.D. in 2006 in materials science and engineering from Drexel University.

Anwesha Chaudhury

Dr. Anwesha Chaudhury graduated with a Ph.D. in chemical engineering from Rutgers University in 2015. Her doctoral thesis focused on developing mechanistic mathematical models and optimization tools to describe wet granulation processes. She has also developed efficient numerical techniques for solving hyperbolic partial differential equations, e.g., population balance equations. She has worked extensively on building predictive and analytical mathematical frameworks during her research career, and is an expert in systems engineering. She has authored multiple book chapters and journal articles that are published in reputed international peer-reviewed journals. Her doctoral experience has been focused on process systems engineering, but she is currently pursuing her postdoctoral training at Massachusetts General Hospital and Harvard Medical School in the Department of Systems Biology.

Dana Barrasso

Dr. Dana Barrasso completed her Ph.D. in chemical engineering at Rutgers University in 2015. Her doctoral research focused on modeling drug product manufacturing processes, with a particular interest in wet granulation. Her dissertation, titled, "Multiscale modeling of wet granulation processes," involved the development, verification, and application of mechanistic models describing wet granulation processes. In this work, she developed multiscale models combining the capabilities of discrete element method (DEM) models and population balance models, and she applied these hybrid models to simulate twin screw granulation processes. Following her Ph.D., she joined Process Systems Enterprise (PSE) as a consultant on the Formulated Products team.

Daniel A. Pohlman

Dr. Daniel A. Pohlman, Ph.D. is currently a Lead Engineer of Process Development at Alkermes in Waltham, MA. He received his Bachelor's degree in chemical engineering from the University of Notre Dame in 2010, and worked as a research engineer in the Notre Dame Energy Center for one year before starting graduate studies. Dr. Pohlman received his Ph.D. in chemical engineering from Purdue University in 2015 and joined the process development team at Alkermes in 2016.

James D. Litster

Jim Litster is Professor and Head of the Chemical and Bioengineering Department at the University of Sheffield. His research area is particulate products and processes. He is an international leading expert on wet granulation with over 25 years of experience in the field. His key contributions include the development of key regime maps for granulation processes and the development of mathematical models for engineering design and scaling of granulation processes. He is the coauthor of the well-known monograph in this area (*The Science and Engineering of Granulation Processes*) and his approaches are now widely used in engineering practice in the industry. He is the author of over 200 refereed publications. In recognition of his contribution to the field, he was awarded the Achievement Award for Excellence in Granulation Research, 9th International Symposium on Agglomeration in 2009, the Thomas Barron Award in Fluid-Particle Systems from the American Institute of Chemical Engineers (AIChE) in 2012, and the Pharmaceutical Discovery, Development and Manufacturing Award for Outstanding Contribution to QbD for Drug Products from the AIChE in 2015. Jim is a Fellow of the Australian Academy of Technological Sciences and Engineering.

Rohit Ramachandran

Dr. Rohit Ramachandran is currently an Associate Professor in the Department of Chemical and Biochemical Engineering at Rutgers University. His research interests are in modeling, control, optimization, and experimental validation of pharmaceutical and chemical processes. He has published more than 60 peer-reviewed journal articles and has presented his work at numerous national and international conferences, and at invited seminars at various universities and industrial companies. His work is supported by the National Science Foundation, the U.S. FDA, Rutgers University research council, and various industrial sources. He has won several awards such as the NSF Career Award for young faculty, NIPTE Young Investigator Award and the Chemical Engineering Outstanding Faculty Award.

Rajan Gupta

Dr. Rajan Gupta is Principal Investigator at Celgene, Summit, New Jersey. He was formerly with GlaxoSmithKline, Merck, Schering-Plough, and Cargill, where he worked in various pharmaceutical and food product development groups. He received his Ph.D. in chemical engineering from City College of New York. Prior to his Ph.D., he worked at the Computer Aided Design Center at the Indian Institute of Technology in Bombay, India, focusing on modeling of chemical processes. He developed his interest in fluid-bed processes during his B.S. in chemical engineering from Malaviya National Institute of Technology in Jaipur, India, where he modeled and published in the field. Dr. Gupta's current research interests include using modeling approaches in solving drug product formulation and process scale-up problems for fluid-bed granulation and drying processes.

Ecevit Bilgili

Dr. Ecevit Bilgili is an Associate Professor and Associate Chair of the Chemical Engineering Department at the New Jersey Institute of Technology (NJIT). His Particle Engineering and Pharmaceutical Nanotechnology Laboratory conducts research in designing formulations and processes for high-value-added products with enhanced functionalities. Dr. Bilgili has authored 60 peer-reviewed journal articles, three U.S. patents (one recently filed), two provisional patents, and several invention disclosures and delivered more than 70 national/international presentations and more than 20 invited talks. He is currently the leader of Project A1: Particle Formation at the Center for Structured Organic Particulate systems, a National Science Foundation (NSF) Engineering Research Center. Dr. Bilgili is one of the United States editors of the Elsevier journal Advanced Powder Technology. He also served as an elected Executive Committee Member of the Particle Technology Forum of the American Institute of Chemical Engineers (AIChE) and the Chair of AIChE Area 3a: Particle Production and Characterization. He received the Best Ph.D. Thesis in Particle Technology Award from AIChE and NJIT's Excellence in Teaching Award. Dr. Bilgili's research has been funded by the National Science Foundation (NSF), FDA, IFF, and several pharmaceutical companies including Boehringer-Ingelheim and Catalent.

Maxx Capece

Dr. Maxx Capece graduated from the New Jersey Institute of Technology (NJIT) in 2014 with a Ph.D. in chemical engineering. His dissertation, "MultiScale Modeling of Dry Milling Processes: Influence of Mechanical Multiparticle Interactions" won NJIT's Newark College of Engineering Outstanding Dissertation Award. His graduate work resulted in fourteen peer-reviewed journal articles and nineteen international/national presentations. Dr. Capece is now a senior scientist in the Formulation Sciences Department at AbbVie. His research is mainly focused on modeling particulate processes and understanding the relationship between material properties and pharmaceutical formulation manufacturability/performance.

Afolawemi Afolabi

Dr. Afolawemi Afolabi is currently a Visiting Researcher at the Department of Agricultural and Biological Engineering at Purdue University. He was recently a senior engineer and formulation process scientist at Dow Agrosciences LLC. Dr. Afolabi conducts particle science and engineering research on various liquid and dry formulations and their manufacturing processes for food, pharmaceuticals, agrochemicals, chemicals, and electronic materials. Dr. Afolabi has authored/coauthored ten peer-reviewed journal articles and several invention disclosures. He has also delivered more than fifteen peer-reviewed presentations and one invited science and technology showcase newsletter published by American Association of Pharmaceutical Scientists (AAPS). He received awards for his technical presentations at the National Society of Black Engineers (NSBE) and International Society of Pharmaceutical Engineering (ISPE) conferences. Dr. Afolabi has also served as both session chair and cochair at various American Institute of Chemical Engineers (AIChE) conferences in the field of Particle Breakage and Comminution Processes.

Keirnan LaMarche

Dr. Keirnan LaMarche is a Senior Research Investigator for the Drug Product Science and Technology Department of Bristol-Myers Squibb (BMS). He has worked on innovative approaches to formulation and process development for solid dosage forms at BMS since 2008. While at BMS, he has focused on developing material sparing approaches to understand the mechanisms of tablet compaction. Dr. LaMarche received his Ph.D. in chemical engineering from Rutgers University in 2008. While at Rutgers University, he studied the impact of electrostatics on the flow of granular materials. Dr. LaMarche also received his Master's degree in chemical engineering from Rutgers University in 2005 and his Bachelor's degree in chemical engineering from the Cooper Union for the Advancement of Science and Art in 2002.

Jasmine Rowe

Dr. Jasmine Rowe earned her Ph.D. in chemical engineering from the University of Texas at Austin. She is currently a senior research investigator at Bristol-Myers Squibb (BMS), working in the area of drug product development for both small and large molecules. She is an active member of the American Association of Pharmaceutical Scientists, currently serving as the Chair of the Process Development Focus Group.

Faranak Nikfar

Dr. Faranak Nikfar is a Research Fellow in Drug Product Science and Technology at Bristol-Myers Squibb (BMS). She has over 25 years of experience in the pharmaceutical industry and she has been responsible for formulation and process development for small molecules, and evaluation of new drug delivery technologies. She has extensive experience in developing a range of dosage forms such as hard and soft gelatin capsules, film-coated single- and multilayer tablets, and powders for pediatric use. She is a registered pharmacist and earned her Ph.D. in pharmaceutics from the University of Wisconsin-Madison.

Alberto Aliseda

Dr. Alberto Aliseda is Associate Professor of Mechanical Engineering at the University of Washington. Before joining the faculty at the University of Washington in 2006, he completed his Master's degree and Ph.D. in aerospace engineering at the University of California, San Diego in 2000 and 2004, respectively. He also worked as a postdoctoral research associate in the Mechanical and

Aerospace Engineering Department at University of California, San Diego from 2004 to 2006 after obtaining his Ph.D. Dr. Aliseda's research interest and expertise is in fluid mechanics, specifically in the areas of turbulent and multiphase flows, with application to sprays, and biofluid mechanics of the human circulatory system with applications to medical devices for vascular disease and to microbubble-based targeted drug delivery.

Mary am Ende

Dr. Mary am Ende is a Research Fellow in Drug Product Design at Pfizer in Groton, Connecticut. She received her B.S. in chemical engineering from the University of Iowa in 1988 and her Ph.D. in chemical engineering from Purdue University in 1993. Dr. am Ende's research interests are in the field of process development and use of predictive tools to streamline commercial development and scale-up through process modeling. She has published over 20 papers, five patents, and 40 presentations. Her current responsibilities include the development and use of process models and engineering technologies to support dosage form development and commercialization. Dr. am Ende is a member of the American Institute of Chemical Engineers (AIChE).

Alfred Berchielli

Alfred Berchielli is a Senior Principal Scientist at Pfizer in Groton, Connecticut. He has been working at Pfizer in Drug Product Design for 21 years with a total of 26 years of experience in the pharmaceutical industry. He received his M.S. in industrial pharmacy from the Arnold and Marie Schwartz School of Pharmacy at Long Island University, New York. His areas of expertise include development and scale-up of drug delivery systems (e.g., sustained release osmotic and matrix tablets). His new product development work has focused on IR/CR combinations, application of active ingredients in tablet coatings, controlled release functional coatings, and modeling of coating processes.

Pankaj Doshi

Dr. Pankaj Doshi is a Senior Principal Scientist in Drug Product Design at Pfizer in Groton, Connecticut. He received his Ph.D. in chemical engineering from Purdue University in 2003, which was followed by a postdoctoral position at the Massachusetts Institute of Technology. His research interest includes scale-up and modeling of pharmaceutical processes and unit operations, mathematical modeling of fluid and powder flow, polymer processing, and interfacial flows. He has published 25 papers and delivered over 30 presentations.

Ben Freireich

Dr. Ben Freireich is a Research Scientist in Engineering and Process Sciences—Solids Processing at the Dow Chemical Company in Midland, Michigan. He received his B.S. in mechanical engineering from the Milwaukee School of Engineering in 2006, and his Ph.D. in mechanical engineering from Purdue University in 2010. At Dow, he has been involved in many products and processes, with expertise on powder flowability, fluidization, size enlargement, attrition, drying, compaction, mixing, etc. Dr. Freireich is an Executive Committee member of the Particle Technology Forum of the American Institute of Chemical Engineers (AIChE) and Chair of ASTM D18.24 Subcommittee on Characterization of Bulk Solids and Powers.

William Ketterhagen

Dr. William (Bill) Ketterhagen is a Senior Principal Scientist in the Process Modeling and Engineering Technology Group and also leads a Materials Assessment Lab within Pfizer Worldwide Research and Development in Groton, Connecticut. In this role, he works to develop and implement predictive models and engineering solutions in support of pharmaceutical drug product development, leveraging materials characterization and small-scale experimentation to ensure models are parameterized and validated with robust experimental data. He has published 25 peer-reviewed papers and delivered nearly 50 presentations at national and international conferences. Prior to his time at Pfizer, Ketterhagen completed his B.S. in chemical engineering at the University of Wisconsin-Madison and his Ph.D. in chemical engineering at Purdue University.

Andrew Prpich

Andrew Prpich is a Senior Scientist in Drug Product Design at Pfizer in Groton, Connecticut. He received his B.S. and M.S. in chemical engineering in 2005 and 2007, respectively, from the University of Waterloo in Ontario, Canada. Prpich's research interests are in the field of process development, multiparticulate development for pediatric dosage forms, and tablet film coating scale-up through process modeling. His current responsibilities include leading the drug product development efforts for two pediatric multiparticulate programs. He has authored nine publications and presentations.

Yu Guo

Yu Guo received his M.Sc. degree from Tsinghua University in Beijing, China, in 2006 and his Ph.D. from the University of Birmingham, England, in 2010. He was a postdoctoral researcher at the University of Florida in Gainesville, USA, from 2011 to 2014 before he worked as a research engineer at Jenike & Johanson, Inc. in Massachusetts, USA, from 2014 to 2015. Since January of 2016, Dr. Guo has been a Research Scientist in the Department of Chemical Engineering at the University of Florida. Dr. Guo has extensive experience in the development of computational methods (discrete element method (DEM) and computational fluid dynamics (CFD)) for the modeling of complex particulate systems with nonspherical particles, flexible fibers, and fluid-particle two phases. His research work has been published in multiple high-impact scientific journals and presented in many influential conferences.

Chuan-Yu Wu

Dr. Chuan-Yu (Charley) Wu obtained his B.Sc. and M.Sc. from Huazhong University of Science and Technology in China in 1994 and 1997, respectively, and his Ph.D. in finite element analysis of particle impact problems from Aston University in Birmingham, England, in 2002. He worked as a postdoctoral research associate in the Department of Engineering at the University of Leicester in England and at the Pfizer Institute for Pharmaceutical Materials Science under the Department of Materials Science and Metallurgy at the University of Cambridge, England. In 2005, Wu was awarded an EPSRC Advanced Research Fellowship and joined the University of Birmingham. He was appointed as a senior lecturer in the School of Chemical Engineering at the University of Birmingham in 2008 and a professor in chemistry at the University of Surrey in 2013. He has expertise in discrete element analysis, multiscale modeling and simulations, pharmaceutical engineering, particle technology, and granular dynamics. Wu has been working closely with global pharmaceutical companies over the last 10 years and has run industrial collaborative research projects with Pfizer, AstraZeneca, and Sanofi to develop advanced numerical modeling techniques for pharmaceutical application. He is currently coordinating an EU FP7 Initial Training Network (ITN) consortium (€3.8M), IPROCOM, on the development of in silico models for roll compaction, which consists of ten full partners and four associate partners from eight EU countries.

Yanxia Li

Yanxia Li received an M.S. in pharmaceutical sciences from the College of Pharmacy at the University of Illinois at Chicago and an M.S. in physical chemistry from the Chinese Academy of Sciences, China. Her expertise includes formulation and process development and modeling in pharmaceutical packaging. She is currently working at AbbVie, Inc. in formulation sciences, and serving as a subject matter expert on packaging evaluation and selection for drug products.

Yisheng Chen

Dr. Yisheng Chen earned his Ph.D. in 1994 from the College of Pharmacy at the University of Iowa. His expertise includes formulation and process development, material characterization, and modeling of moisture uptake by packaged products. Previously, Dr. Chen worked in Burroughs Wellcome and Abbott Laboratories in new and generic drug product development, and served as an expert member of both the PQRI Container Closure Working Group and the USP <671> Containers—Performance Testing Expert Panel. He is now Vice President of Novast Laboratories, responsible for product development. He has published numerous research articles, book chapters, patents, and patent applications. He is a frequent speaker at various conferences.

Donald Clancy

Don Clancy graduated with his B.S. and M.S. in chemical engineering from Texas Tech University, with a focus in process control and modeling. Clancy's first years of experience were with Mobil Oil doing thermodynamics and flowsheet modeling, and designing membrane units and distillation columns for oil and gas plants near Lubbock, Texas. Clancy then moved to the Hoechst Celanese Corporation in Corpus Christi, Texas, and worked in pharmaceuticals for several years, overseeing ibuprofen reactor operations and developing control models to optimize reactors and crystallizers. A former professor that Clancy had done graduate research work with at Texas Tech invited him to Pennsylvania to work for Cabot Corporation R&D, developing processes to make electronic capacitor materials such as barium titanate, niobium, and tantalum. After six years with Cabot, Don joined GlaxoSmithKline in 2006 and has focused on helping teams develop models of their processes for Quality by Design (QbD), improved yield, process control, or long-term stability predictions.

Marc Horner

Dr. Marc Horner is currently working as Lead Healthcare Specialist at ANSYS, Inc. Dr. Horner joined ANSYS after earning his Ph.D. in chemical engineering from Northwestern University in 2001. Dr. Horner began by providing support and professional services for biomedical and pharmaceutical clients, primarily in the areas of cardiovascular devices, orthopaedic devices, drug delivery, packaging, microfluidics, and fluid mixing. During this time, Dr. Horner developed numerous modeling approaches that can be used to establish the safety and efficacy of medical devices. Dr. Horner now helps coordinate ANSYS business and technology development for the healthcare sector in North America. This includes managing collaborative research projects between ANSYS and industry, academia, and the U.S. FDA. Dr. Horner is a member of the ASME V&V 40 Subcommittee (which is establishing V&V best practices for the medical device industry) and the American Association of Pharmaceutical Scientists (AAPS) Process Modeling and Simulation Focus Group (which focuses on the application of physics-based engineering and mathematical modeling techniques to better understand, control, develop, and improve pharmaceutical manufacturing processes). Dr. Horner is also an Associate Editor of the ASME Journal of Verification, Validation, and Uncertainty Quantification.

Shitalkumar Joshi

Shitalkumar Joshi is currently working as Senior Technology Manager at ANSYS India. He joined ANSYS in 2001 after completing his Master's degree in chemical engineering from the Indian Institute of Science, Bangalore. Joshi has expertise in the field of fluid dynamics and multiphase flows simulations. Joshi has worked extensively with healthcare and pharmaceutical companies in the United States and India to deploy numerical modeling tools in the design process. Over the years, Joshi has developed several numerical methods and best practices aimed at advancing simulation modeling practices of bioreactors and mixers. He also has been instrumental in embedding state-of-the-art modeling methods into easy-to-use software for adoption by a wider biopharmaceutical community.

Yogesh Waghmare

Dr. Yogesh Waghmare, Ph.D., is currently Senior Scientist in the Bioprocess Development Organization at Sanofi. Dr. Waghmare has almost a decade of experience in the field of fluid dynamics and process modeling. He specializes in the application of mathematical modeling tools, including computational fluid dynamics (CFD) for process development, scale-up, and optimization of bio/pharmaceutical processes. Additionally, his research interests include bioreactor characterization and the control and role of modeling in quality by design (QbD). Dr. Waghmare received his Ph.D. in chemical engineering in 2008 from Louisiana State University, researching in the field of mass transfer and multiphase flows. Before joining Genzyme, he was a research chemical engineer at Bend Research Inc., one of the pioneers in using CFD for pharmaceutical process development. He has published several research articles and has presented at a number of conferences in his area of expertise.

Preface

The use of modeling and simulation tools is rapidly gaining prominence in the pharmaceutical industry covering a wide range of applications. Modeling tools can improve fundamental process understanding and provide valuable insights into the manufacturing processes, which can result in significant process improvements and cost savings. With FDA mandating the use of Quality by Design (QbD) principles during manufacturing, reliable modeling techniques can help to alleviate the costs associated with such efforts, and be used to create in silico formulation and process design space. This book is intended to cover the different modeling and simulation techniques and their application to pharmaceutical unit operations related mainly to drug product manufacturing. By way of examples that include case studies, various modeling principles are explained for the nonexpert end users.

The general layout of the book follows a typical drug product manufacturing process train, as explained in Chapter 1, Modeling of Drug Product Manufacturing Processes in the Pharmaceutical Industry. Chapter 1, Modeling of Drug Product Manufacturing Processes in the Pharmaceutical Industry, introduces the various modeling techniques typically used in the pharmaceutical industry and their association with each unit operation. Chapter 2, Quality Risk Management for Pharmaceutical Manufacturing: The Role of Process Modeling and Simulations, discusses the use of process models to support quality risk management in pharmaceutical manufacturing and provides case studies of continuous manufacturing to illustrate the potential role of process models in the implementation of emerging manufacturing technologies. Chapter 3, Powder Flow and Blending, discusses the fundamentals of granular mixing and flow, and the different modeling tools with special attention to mechanistic models. A case study describing the development of a discrete element method (DEM) model for numerical analysis is also included.

Chapter 4, Dry Granulation Process Modeling, presents the state of current research and development on modeling of dry granulation process, specifically, roller compaction. Finite element method (FEM) predictive modeling was shown to provide process insight, guidance, and practical solutions that can be used to optimize formulation design and process development. Chapter 5, Mechanistic Modeling of High-Shear and Twin Screw Mixer Granulation Processes, provides an overview on the current state of high-shear granulation models with the implementation of a systems-based approach. A case study using a coupled population balance model (PBM) and DEM to model a high-shear wet granulation process is also included.

Chapter 6, Fluid Bed Granulation and Drying, discusses the different modeling approaches for fluid bed granulation and drying processes followed by a description of an integrated granulation and drying model, with examples for practical applications in formulation and process development. Chapter 7, Modeling of Milling Processes via DEM, PBM, and Microhydrodynamics, presents the various modeling approaches used for the simulation and design of wet and dry milling processes. Case studies are used to demonstrate the application of microhydrodynamic models in designing wet milling processes, and the use of combined particle scale-ensemble scale-process scale models (DEM-PBM) to simulate the evolution of particle size distribution during dry milling.

Chapter 8, Modeling of Powder Compaction With the Drucker–Prager Cap Model, and Chapter 9, Modeling Approaches to Multilayer Tableting, focus on the modeling techniques used in compaction process for monolayer and bilayer tablets, respectively. Case studies focused on compaction model application (FEM for see chapter: Modeling of Powder Compaction With the Drucker–Prager Cap Model) to pharmaceutical formulations are presented. Chapter 10, Computational Modeling of Pharmaceutical Die Filling Processes, discusses the use of DEM and CFD models in facilitating the analysis and design of die filling systems.

Chapter 11, Modeling Tablet Film-Coating Processes, focuses on process models for a tablet film-coating process and their application to the subprocesses occurring within the main film coating unit operation. Model application is shown in relation to determining the process design space, scale-up, and equipment transfer. Chapter 12, Modeling in Pharmaceutical Packaging, presents the use of sorption-desorption moisture transfer model in selecting containers for moisture protection, so as to reduce cost and cycle time of drug product development and post approval packaging changes. Finally, Chapter 13, Continuous Secondary Process Selection and the Modeling of Batch and Continuous Wet Granulation, and Chapter 14, Process Modeling in the Biopharmaceutical Industry, discuss the usage of modeling in newer and upcoming areas of drug product development such as continuous manufacturing and biologics manufacturing, respectively.

The editors would like to thank the publishers (Harriet Clayton, Glyn Jones, Omer Moosa, Mani Prabakaran) for their involvement and support throughout the development of this book. Special thanks to all the authors for taking the time to share their knowledge, data, and experience via their individual chapters. Finally, the editors would like to thank their corresponding family members for their support, encouragement, and understanding during the preparation of this book.

P. Pandey and R. Bharadwaj

Modeling of drug product manufacturing processes in the pharmaceutical industry

1

P. Pandey[1], *R. Bharadwaj*[2] *and X. Chen*[1]
[1]Drug Product Science and Technology, Bristol-Myers Squibb, New Brunswick, NJ, United States, [2]Rocky-DEM, Houston, TX, United States

1.1 Introduction

The use of modeling techniques is becoming more common in the pharmaceutical industry, covering a wide range of application areas, such as drug discovery, pharmacokinetics and pharmacodynamics, biopharmaceutical (effect of pH, food, etc.), drug substance (chemistry and manufacturing), and drug product. This book primarily focuses on modeling as it pertains to the drug product manufacturing processes, although similar modeling principles and techniques apply to other areas as well. The drug product manufacturing processes spans the entire range that includes the preparation of a formulation to the processing and packaging of the final drug product.

The use of modeling tools enable fundamental process understanding and provide insights into the unit operations, which can lead to significant process improvements and cost savings. With FDA mandating the use of Quality by Design (QbD) principles during manufacturing, the establishment of a formulation and process design space during drug product development is imperative (U.S. Department of Health and Human Services FDA, 2006, 2009a,b; Pandey and Badawy, 2016; Pandey et al., 2006d; Yu et al., 2014) This means that on the formulation end, the effects of variations in input material properties (API and excipients), referred to as potential critical material properties (CMAs), on drug product critical quality attributes (CQAs) have to be studied. A similar effort is needed on the manufacturing process where the effects of potential critical process parameters (CPPs) from each unit operation on drug product CQAs are to be established. Additionally, there is significant interaction between formulation and process components that needs to be characterized.

Given that a typical pharmaceutical formulation has 5–6 different components (API and excipients—filler, disintegrant, binder, flow aid, lubricant), and 5–6 different unit operations (such as blending, granulation, milling, compression, coating, packaging) are involved, studying the effects of variations of each and their interactions can be a tedious and expensive experimental study. Reliable modeling and simulation tools can help tremendously to alleviate such an elaborate effort. Appropriate modeling tools can be used to create both *in silico* formulation and process design space by varying potential CMAs and CPPs and studying their impact

Predictive Modeling of Pharmaceutical Unit Operations. DOI: http://dx.doi.org/10.1016/B978-0-08-100154-7.00001-6

on drug product CQAs. (U.S. Department of Health and Human Services FDA, 2006, 2009a,b) The models can be used to conduct a sensitivity analysis that will in turn reduce the number of variables that need to be studied experimentally. Models can also be used to identify edge of process failure, which can be expensive experimentally. A good process and scale-up model will also allow for more small-scale experiments (cost savings) with limited amount of work required at the larger scale. In an era of "speed to patient," there is often limited availability of API during early development, and certain formulation and manufacturing process selection decisions that could have a long-term impact on the product are required. For example, one may have to choose between wet granulation and dry granulation process with only a limited amount of information on API powder properties. In order to gauge the risk levels appropriately at an early stage, material-sparing tools such as minipiloting and modeling are becoming increasingly important (LaMarche et al., 2014) Therefore, the use of predictive tools is not only important during the later stage of drug product development but also during early stages of development.

In a QbD paradigm, regulators are looking for a risk-based approach towards drug product development. A risk assessment identifies the formulation, process, and any other risks that can affect a drug product CQA and identifies the failure modes, their probability of detection and occurrence, and their severity levels. Once the knowledge gaps are appropriately identified and ranked, a mitigation plan is put in place and executed. A process control strategy is put in place when a certain risk can't be eliminated totally, in which case a residual risk level is identified and monitored. From a regulatory perspective, the use of predictive tools such as modeling and simulation can enable a quantitative risk assessment, facilitating the quality assessment of manufacturing processes. It can also support the evaluation of control strategies by demonstrating system capabilities to handle multiple sources of variability (formulation and process). FDA has provided guidelines that in part discuss the role and usage of models in QbD (U.S. Department of Health and Human Services FDA, 2006, 2009a,b) ICH recommends categorization of models based on their impact to drug product quality. The three categories on the types of models based on impact include high impact, medium impact, and low impact models. A high impact model is defined as one where the model is the sole predictor of the drug product quality, a medium impact is defined as ones which are important for assuring quality of the product but are not the sole indicators of the drug product quality, and low impact models are defined as ones that are used to support formulation and process development type of activity. The high impact models (e.g., chemometric model for drug product assay) are not encountered routinely but when they are they undergo the most scrutiny (given their impact). High impact models require development of appropriate calibration and validation procedures with the ability to discern OOS (out of specification) batches, development of a model monitoring system (model maintenance and updates during the life cycle), and tracking and trending of the process within the Quality system. In order to categorize models based on their mode of implementation, they can be classified into models for supporting analytical methods (e.g., NIR methods), models for supporting process design (e.g., design space and scale-up models such as DEM, CFD, etc.), and models for process monitoring and control (e.g., multivariate statistical models).

The following sections explain some of the modeling methods used in process design/control and also the resources required for implementing them.

1.2 Modeling techniques

The various kinds of modeling approaches currently being used can be broadly classified into two categories, namely physics-based models and empirical models. The physics-based models utilize fundamental first principles (conservation of mass, momentum, and energy) to predict the behavior of the fluid or powder in the process. The more commonly used modeling approach for granular materials is the discrete element method (DEM). Continuum methods for modeling include finite element method (FEM), computational fluid dynamics (CFD), and, more recently, hybrid methods that utilize a combination of one or two other methods.

1.2.1 First principle predictive models

1.2.1.1 Discrete element method

DEM is a powerful predictive tool commonly used in applications that include powder mixing (blending), powder conveying (e.g., hopper discharge, die filling, twin screw extruder feeding, and conveying), milling (by including breakage kernels), granulation, and tablet movement during film coating. A good review of application of process modeling in the pharmaceutical industry using DEM was provided by Ketterhagen et al. (2009).

The discrete element method takes into account the forces acting on each individual particle and then integrates them over time (Newton's laws of motion) to get its velocity and subsequent position. The forces in the model can include gravity, contact, cohesive, and fluid forces. Since pharmaceutical powder size distributions are typically in the micron meter ranges, this approach becomes computationally expensive if the actual size of the powder is used in the model due to large number of particles in the simulation. Hence, it is common practice to scale the particle sizes in the DEM model to study mixing and flow patterns. In addition, particles are generally assumed to be spheres due to the additional complexity that arises by using different non-spherical shape representations in the model.

Particle shapes in DEM have traditionally been represented by a glued-sphere approach where spheres are rigidly glued together to form close to the desired shape (Favier et al., 1999) Although this representation of the shape has various limitations, it is relatively easy to program and implement and hence is available in various commercial software (EDEM, Star CCM, PFC 3D) (Nakamura et al., 2013) Limitations with this method include restrictive computational times, poor representation of shapes with large aspect ratios, and large bulk friction produced due to particle interlocking (due to the bumpy surface) (Suzzi et al., 2012) Another, more recently evolving technique, such as that used in commercial software Rocky DEM, applies a new method using a polyhedral shape representation to overcome the limitations associated with the glued sphere approach. The ability to scan the exact particle shape into Rocky DEM, such as a tablet, enables a virtual design environment for studying scale-up of processes such as tablet coating and blending. Although the contact detection using the polyhedral shape is computationally intensive, the ability to use the graphics processing unit (GPU) with thousands of cores within the Rocky DEM solver, enable practical run times. In addition, most commercial DEM software allow the import of process equipment in native CAD drawing formats which make for efficient comparison between different process equipment performance.

Other challenging aspects for DEM are the ability to incorporate the physics of a liquid being present in the system (e.g., water in granulation), and cohesive forces between particles, although there are existing models (or kernels) in literature that have been used before (Asmar et al., 2002, 2003; Matuttis and Schinner, 2001). Although there are certain limitations with the use of DEM, advances in computer hardware power and technology are making this a practical tool and a well-calibrated DEM model can provide valuable insights into the process (Bharadwaj, 2012; Pandey et al., 2006c; Toschkoff et al., 2013, 2015; Hilton et al., 2013; Kulju et al., 2016).

1.2.1.2 Computational fluid dynamics

CFD is widely used to model fluid flow in a process and finds its pharmaceutical applications in modeling mixing in agitated vessels (API drying, mixing in bioreactors, lyophilization, suspension preparation, etc.), spray drying, and air flow in systems such as fluidized bed, film coaters etc. (van Wachem et al., 2001; Petitti et al., 2013; Alonso et al., 2001; Karlsson et al., 2009). Commercially available software packages. such as Fluent, CFX, are most commonly used for CFD modeling. In CFD, the geometry of process being modeled is first divided into small volumes called computational meshes. The governing equations (e.g., heat, mass, and momentum transfer etc.) and boundary conditions are then applied and solved for each mesh point. The mesh results are recreated in the form of graphical visualizations, which is the most common form of analyzing CFD results. The strength of CFD lies in modeling systems that are dominated primarily by fluid flow, such as spray drying, fluidized beds, inhalation, agitated mixing (Kremer and Hancock, 2005). The use of CFD in the pharmaceutical industry is increasing by the day with a growing focus towards large molecules, where understanding of phenomena such as protein folding and unfolding during mixing is gaining importance.

1.2.1.3 Finite element method

FEM is another numerical approach similar to CFD, where the process is divided into finite elements or volumes and then partial differential equations that conserve mass, momentum, and energy are solved to predict the behavior of the powder. In the pharmaceutical industry FEM is often used for modeling of dry granulation (roller compaction) and powder compaction (tableting or compression) unit operations. Several studies have utilized FEM simulations for compaction using a Drucker-Prager Cap (DPC) compaction model, which has provided tremendous insight into the tableting process. FEM DPC models have the ability to quantitatively predict the distribution of material properties during different stages of tableting (LaMarche et al., 2014; Sinha et al., 2010; Dec et al., 2003; Cunningham et al., 2004; Michrafy et al., 2002) and have been used to investigate tablet capping during tableting (Wu et al., 2008). Similar models were also used to model dry granulation process (roller compaction), where stress and density distributions in ribbons were estimated (Reynolds et al., 2010; Muliadi et al., 2012; Mazor et al., 2016).

1.2.1.4 Hybrid models

DEM, CFD, and FEM approaches all have their individual strengths and limitations in scenarios where they can be applied successfully. More recently, there is a surge in the use of hybrid-model approaches (coupled-models), where a combination of two or more modeling approaches are used (Hilton et al., 2013; Kulju et al., 2016; Barrasso et al., 2014). The system to be modeled is divided into different components and the best-fit modeling approach for each component is applied and integrated. For example, for the modeling of a pan coating process, the process can be broken-down into subcomponents such as tablet movement (pan geometry, tablet shape, size, etc.) and process thermodynamics (air flow, spray dynamics, etc.). DEM modeling approach is more suited to model tablet movement (including pan geometry, baffles, etc.), whereas CFD can model the airflow pattern (Toschkoff et al., 2012). The use of a coupled-model approach for this scenario has shown promising results in developing an integrated coating model (Toschkoff and Khinast, 2013). Another example of a coupled model approach (DEM + FEM) would be the powder compaction of a pharmaceutical tablet. DEM simulations would model the properties of powdered material, such as particle size distribution, Young's modulus, etc., whereas FEM would model tablet geometry, die-wall friction, and other compression process parameters (Munjiza et al., 1995).

1.2.1.5 Empirical models

Another modeling approach is one that is not based on fundamental first principles, but is purely an empirical/semiempirical or statistical approach. This approach involves collecting a large amount of experimental data and forming a model based on that data set. Such modeling methods include artificial neural network (ANN), MVA (multivariate analysis), modeling based on a statistical experimental design (such as design of experiments), Monte Carlo (Pandey et al., 2006a), etc. These approaches work well with predictions within the design space that the experiments are conducted in but often fail to predict outside of that design space or on a different formulation and process equipment due to the lack of underlying physics in the model. However, within the design space of experiments these models work extremely well and are good tools for process monitoring and control. Modeling approaches such as ANN and MVA work best in identifying general trends, and/or outliers when there are large amounts of data (such as from manufacturing plants) with little to no insight on the relevance of the collected data.

Population balance modeling (PBM) can be considered as a semiempirical approach since it often utilizes kernels that have some mechanistic basis. PBM finds its utility when dealing with a large number of populations (such as particles), the size of which may be increasing and decreasing over the course of the process. For example, in wet granulation, PBM is able to model several competing granulation mechanisms (aggregation, consolidation, breakage, etc.) at the same time, and provide information on the particle size and porosity distributions at any given time during the granulation, which can be time-consuming to obtain experimentally (Pandey et al., 2013; Chaudhury et al., 2014). Once the model is developed, it can be used to create *in silico* formulation and process design space and can also identify the edge of process failure, which would be expensive to do experimentally. The factors in the PBM include the equipment geometry, material properties (particle size distribution, Young's modulus, porosity distribution, etc.), and fluid properties (viscosity, spray rate, contact angle, surface tension, etc.). A challenge with PBM is that until the kernels are fully mechanistic, it will require experimental data to estimate some of the unknown constants in the kernels, which makes it empirical in nature (Iveson, 2002; Poon et al., 2009; Liu and Litster, 2002). Also, PBM doesn't provide particle-level information, such as particle velocity, stress, etc. More recently, DEM and other techniques have been used in conjunction with PBM, with DEM feeding particle-level information, such as particle velocities, to the PBM framework. Such a hybrid-model approach has revived the usage of PBM in modeling of unit operation (Sen and Ramachandran, 2013).

Besides empirical and first principle-based modeling methods, there are some engineering principles that can be used as rules of thumbs for providing direction for process understanding, modeling and especially during scale-up. These types of models are typically derived from physics-based models, as is depicted in Fig. 1.1. These would include the use of dimensionless numbers (e.g., Froude number, Reynolds' number, Stokes number, etc.), general thermodynamic principles (Ende and Berchielli, 2005; Ebey, 1987), and heat and mass transfer equations (Srinivasakannan and Balasubramanian, 2008). Often a basic dimensionless analysis is conducted with the process being broken down into the independent variables. The number of dimensionless groups required to completely describe the system is given by Buckingham's pi theorem (Pandey et al., 2006b; Agrawal and Pandey, 2015). The value of dimensionless numbers lie during equipment transfer and scale-up because these numbers by design are independent of these factors (Pandey et al., 2006b; Rowe et al., 2013; Tao et al., 2015).

The modeling techniques discussed so far pertain to modeling one unit operation at a time. While this approach is most commonly used, there is value in "knitting" together all the unit operations required in a particular process train within one modeling framework. An integrated modeling framework will allow for studying the effects of input variables to one upstream process having a certain impact on further downstream. This will become particularly important as a shift from batch to continuous processing is

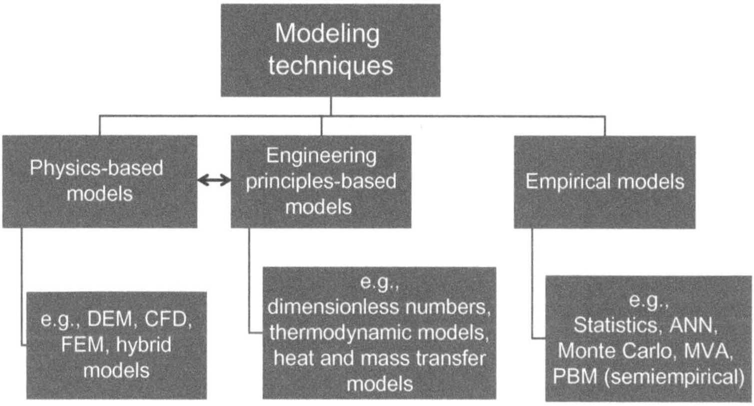

Figure 1.1 Classification of different modeling techniques and some examples of the specific model types that fall into those categories.

observed in the pharmaceutical industry and process control systems have to be put in place. This type of a framework is enabled by modeling tools such as flowsheet modeling, where the individual unit operations are connected in series. Mathematically, the individual unit operation models are combined by taking the outputs from a previous unit operation and using it as the inputs into the next unit operation. Commercially available software packages such as ASPEN Plus, and gPROMS can be used for flowsheet modeling (Boukouvala et al., 2012; Toebermann et al., 2000). An integrated modeling framework will also allow a true risk assessment analysis to be conducted since the impact of each variable to the entire process train (upstream and downstream) can be quantified using such a model. Flowsheet models can aid risk assessment through the use of sensitivity analysis. Some of the challenges associated with flowsheet modeling is that there is a need to identify all the possible manipulated and controlled variables and their interactions, develop models that describe each unit operation, identify "global" operating conditions, and correctly identify the critical connecting properties that communicate across the unit operations. Additionally, as different modeling techniques with varied amounts of complexities and simulation times are utilized for each unit operation, integrating them into a unified process train is not trivial.

1.3 Process modeling in drug product manufacturing

The general workflow of model development is similar across different modeling techniques, although the specific resources and requirements for model development may vary. For example, physics-based models such as first principle-based and engineering-based models require minimum experimental data beyond the input parameters. However, for semiempirical and empirical models, such as PBM and statistical models, experimental data requirements are high in order to develop a good model.

Fig. 1.2 shows the typical stages that are involved in a model development framework. These stages of model development can be broadly classified as: model

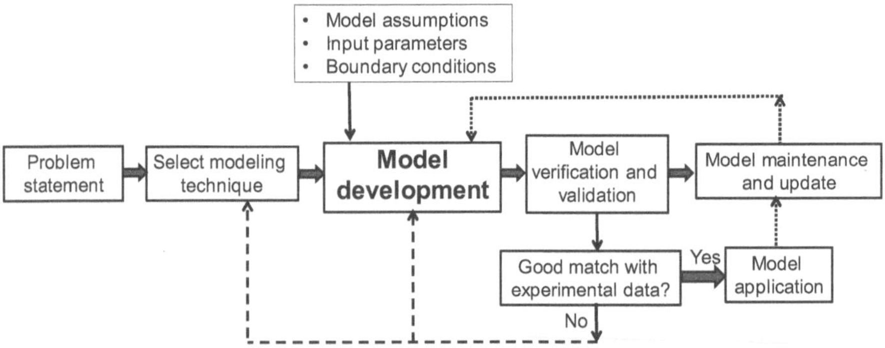

Figure 1.2 Model development framework detailing the typical stages involved in model development.

purpose and desired outcome definition, model technique selection, model building (based on certain assumptions, input parameters and boundary conditions, etc.), model validation and verification, and model maintenance and update. The first step of model development is to have a clearly defined problem statement and desired outcomes, which is important in order to select an appropriate modeling technique. It is equally or more important to ensure the accuracy of the model input parameters and put in place the appropriate test methods to measure those input parameters. This stage may sometimes be referred to as "model calibration" (e.g., for PBM), more so for empirical models. Model verification and validation is one of the final steps before applying a model to any pharmaceutical unit operation, as the accuracy and applicability are essential to the final application. The main purpose of this step is to validate any assumptions that were made during model development. Specifically, "verification" is used to ensure that the numerical solutions are an accurate solution to the computational model, and "validation" refers to the comparison of the model predictions to experiment data. One of the common practices is to compare one or a few key output parameters related to process with experiment results. Another stage of model development that doesn't receive enough attention is the "model maintenance and update" stage. Once a model is built and applied, there is new information that gets generated, both by the model and any ongoing experiments. This information can be fed into the model and be used to improve upon the model accuracy. This doesn't mean that the model that was built before is inaccurate but that the model accuracy can be improved even further as new information becomes available. This is especially true for models that are more empirical in nature such as PBM, ANN, NIR-based models, statistics-based, etc.

Let us consider the model development framework with an example of a tablet film coating unit operation:

1.3.1 Problem statement

To predict the coating uniformity during a pan coating unit operation.

1.3.2 Modeling technique selection

The critical variables in this unit operation are the tablet velocities and the tablet residence time, defined as the time spent by a tablet in its spray zone. There are existing coating uniformity models in literature that require the tablet residence time (or circulation time, defined as the time taken by a tablet to return in the spray zone after a coating event), and tablet velocities in the spray zone as input parameters to predict the coating uniformity (Pandey et al., 2006b; Chen et al., 2010; Joglekar et al., 2007). However, these models do not include the effects of airflow and spray dynamics on the coating uniformity predictions and only tablet motion is taken into account (model assumption). The tablet movement in the coater is influenced by the pan speed and baffle geometry. It is evident that DEM would be a suitable technique for predicting the effects of pan speed and various coating geometries on the tablet velocities and residence times, since the individual tablet velocity and position can be computed. The outputs from the DEM model can then be used as inputs to other models to predict the coating uniformity.

1.3.3 Model development

The properties that affect the tablet motion in the DEM model would be the tablet–tablet and tablet–wall friction, both of which can be determined using existing measurement techniques (Pandey et al., 2006c; Just et al., 2013; Freireich et al., 2015). Although other variables like tablet stiffness will affect the simulation results, the friction and the tablet shape are the most critical parameters.

1.3.4 Model verification and validation

The tablet velocity and residence/circulation times can be determined experimentally using video-imaging techniques for a certain set of process conditions and can be used to verify and validate the model. In this verification step, any assumptions that may have been made during model development (such as for tablet size, shape representation, friction, etc.) can be "validated." For example, using the glued-sphere tablet shape representation, the tablet friction values are tuned to ensure a good match between the model and experiments (Just et al., 2013; Freireich et al., 2015). This tuning of the friction values can be avoided if the shape of the tablet was represented accurately using polyhedral meshes. Once validated, the model is ready for "model application" across different coating conditions and across different scale coaters.

Although the above example covers one unit operation, the methodology followed is applicable for any unit operation in the process workstream. A typical workstream for an oral solids drug product manufacturing process and the commonly used modeling techniques pertaining to each unit operation are shown in Fig. 1.3. The commonly used manufacturing methods include direct compression, dry granulation, and wet granulation. The direct compression process involves the blending of drug substance with other excipients (filler, lubricants, disintegrant, etc.), and compression of this formulation/blend into tablets. Quite routinely, granulation of the formulation is required to improve the flow characteristics of the formulation by increasing its particle size and bulk density. It also helps to minimize segregation risk and offers better content uniformity. The granulation can be done either using dry granulation (e.g., roller compaction), or wet granulation (e.g., high-shear, fluid bed) process, as illustrated in Fig. 1.3. The granulation is then mixed with extragranular components (flow aids, lubricant, antiadherents, etc.), and compressed into tablets on a tableting press. The compressed tablets are film-coated using a pan or a fluid bed coater, either for aesthetic purposes or sometimes for achieving functionality (e.g., enteric, active coating). The coated tablets are finally packaged into appropriate container-closure system (e.g., bottles, blister-packs).

The individual chapters in this book discuss more details about the modeling approaches associated with each of the unit operations and illustrate its application using case studies.

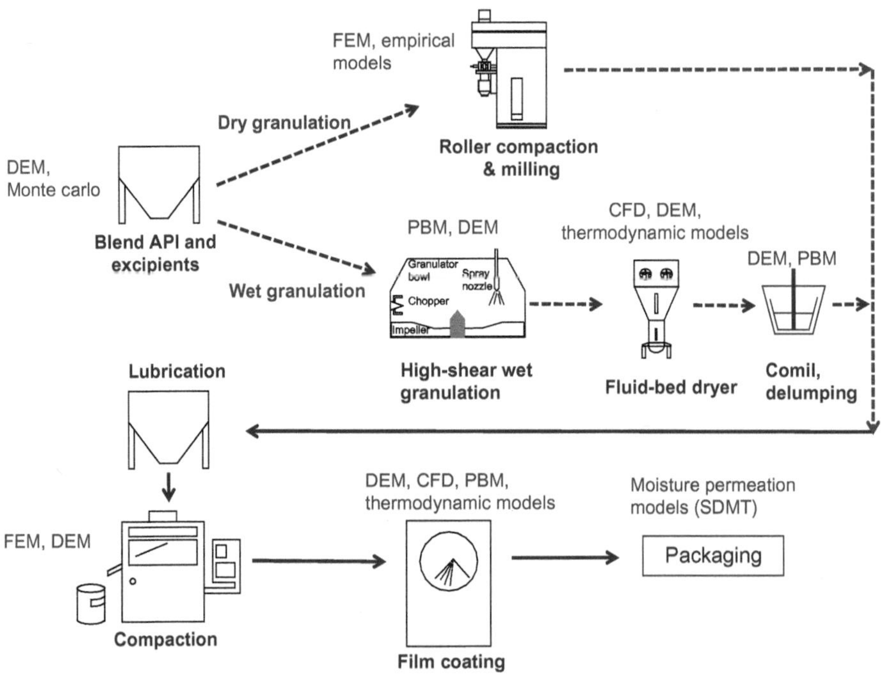

Figure 1.3 A typical drug product manufacturing workstream and most commonly used modeling techniques related to each unit operation. Empirical models and hybrid models are applicable to each unit operation but are not explicitly stated for each one in this figure.

References

Agrawal, A.M., Pandey, P., 2015. Scale up of pan coating process using quality by design principles. J. Pharm. Sci. 104 (11), 3589–3611. Available from: http://dx.doi.org/10.1002/jps.24582.

Alonso, S., Bertrand, F., Tanguy, P.A. A., 2001. CFD assessment of film coating process viscosity models. Can. J. Chem. Eng. 79 (5), 751–759.

Asmar, B.N., Langston, P.A., Matchett, A.J., Walters, J.K., 2002. Validation tests on a distinct element model of vibrating cohesive particle systems. Comput. Chem. Eng. 26 (6), 785–802.

Asmar, B.N., Langston, P.A., Matchett, A.J., Walters, J.K., 2003. Energy monitoring in distinct element models of particle systems. Adv. Powder Technol. 14 (1), 43–69.

Barrasso, D., Tamrakar, A., Ramachandran, R., 2014. A reduced order PBM–ANN model of a multi-scale PBM–DEM description of a wet granulation process. Chem. Eng. Sci. 119, 319–329.

Bharadwaj, R., 2012. Using DEM to solve bulk material handling problems. Chem. Eng. Prog. 54–58.

Boukouvala, F., Niotis, V., Ramachandran, R., Muzzio, F.J., Ierapetritou, M.G., 2012. An integrated approach for dynamic flowsheet modeling and sensitivity analysis of a continuous tablet manufacturing process. Comput. Chem. Eng. 42, 30–47.

Chaudhury, A., Barrasso, D., Pandey, P., Wu, H., Ramachandran, R., 2014. Population balance model development, validation, and prediction of CQAs of a high-shear wet granulation process: towards QbD in drug product pharmaceutical manufacturing. J. Pharm. Innov. 9 (1), 53–64.

Chen, W., Chang, S.-Y., Kiang, S., Marchut, A., Lyngberg, O., Wang, J., et al., 2010. Modeling of pan coating processes: prediction of tablet content uniformity and determination of critical process parameters. J. Pharm. Sci. 99 (7), 3213–3225.

Cunningham, J.C., Sinka, I.C., Zavaliangos, A., 2004. Analysis of tablet compaction. I. Characterization of mechanical behavior of powder and powder/tooling friction. J. Pharm. Sci. 93 (8), 2022–2039.

Dec, R.T., Zavaliangos, A., Cunningham, J.C., 2003. Comparison of various modeling methods for analysis of powder compaction in roller press. Powder Technol. 130 (1–3), 265–271.

Ebey, G.C., 1987. Thermodynamic model for aqueous film coating. Pharm. Technol. (USA). 11 (Apr), 40–50.

Ende, M.T., Berchielli, A., 2005. A thermodynamic model for organic and aqueous tablet film coating. Pharm. Dev. Technol. (USA). 10 (Jan), 47–58.

Favier, J. A.-F.M., Kremmer, M., Raji, A., 1999. Shape representation of axi-symmetrical, non-spherical particles in discrete element simulation using multi-element model particles. Eng. Comput. 16 (4), 467–480.

Freireich, B., Kumar, R., Ketterhagen, W., Su, K., Wassgren, C., Zeitler, J.A., 2015. Comparisons of intra-tablet coating variability using DEM simulations, asymptotic limit models, and experiments. Chem. Eng. Sci. 131, 197–212.

Hilton, J.E., Ying, D.Y., Cleary, P.W., 2013. Modelling spray coating using a combined CFD–DEM and spherical harmonic formulation. Chem. Eng. Sci. 99, 141–160.

Iveson, S.M., 2002. Limitations of one-dimensional population balance models of wet granulation processes. Powder Technol. 124 (3), 219–229.

Joglekar, A., Joshi, N., Song, Y., Ergun, J., 2007. Mathematical model to predict coat weight variability in a pan coating process. Pharm. Dev. Technol. 12 (3), 297–306.
Just, S., Toschkoff, G., Funke, A., Djuric, D., Scharrer, G., Khinast, J., et al., 2013. Experimental analysis of tablet properties for discrete element modeling of an active coating process. AAPS PharmSciTech. 14 (1), 402–411.
Karlsson, S., Rasmuson, A., van Wachem, B., Björn, I.N., 2009. CFD modeling of the Wurster bed coater. AIChE J. 55 (10), 2578–2590.
Ketterhagen, W.R., am Ende, M.T., Hancock, B.C., 2009. Process modeling in the pharmaceutical industry using the discrete element method. J. Pharm. Sci. 98 (2), 442–470.
Kremer, D.M., Hancock, B.C., 2005. Process simulation in the pharmaceutical industry: a review of some basic physical models. J. Pharm. Sci. 95 (3), 517–529.
Kulju, T., Paavola, M., Spittka, H., Keiski, R.L., Juuso, E., Leiviskä, K., et al., 2016. Modeling continuous high-shear wet granulation with DEM-PB. Chem. Eng. Sci. 142, 190–200.
LaMarche, K., Buckley, D., Hartley, R., Qian, F., Badawy, S., 2014. Assessing materials' tablet compaction properties using the Drucker–Prager Cap model. Powder Technol. 267, 208–220.
Liu, X., Litster, J.D., 2002. Population balance modelling of granulation with a physically based coalescence kernel. Chem. Eng. Sci. 57 (12), 2183–2191.
Matuttis, H.-G., Schinner, A., 2001. Particle simulation of cohesive granular materials. Int. J0 Mod. Phys. C. 12 (07), 1011–1021.
Mazor, A., Perez-Gandarillas, L., de Ryck, A., Michrafy, A., 2016. Effect of roll compactor sealing system designs: a finite element analysis. Powder Technol. 289, 21–30.
Michrafy, A., Ringenbacher, D., Tchoreloff, P., 2002. Modelling the compaction behaviour of powders: application to pharmaceutical powders. Powder Technol. 127 (3), 257–266.
Muliadi, A.R., Litster, J.D., Wassgren, C.R., 2012. Modeling the powder roll compaction process: comparison of 2-D finite element method and the rolling theory for granular solids (Johanson's model). Powder Technol. 221, 90–100.
Munjiza, A., Owen, D.R.J., Bicanic, N., 1995. A combined finite-discrete element method in transient dynamics of fracturing solids. Eng. Comput. 12 (2), 145–174.
Nakamura, H., Fujii, H., Watano, S., 2013. Scale-up of high shear mixer-granulator based on discrete element analysis. Powder Technol. 236 (0), 149–156.
Pandey, P., Badawy, S., 2016. A quality by design approach to scale-up of high-shear wet granulation process. Drug Dev. Ind. Pharm. 42 (2), 175–189.
Pandey, P., Katakdaunde, M., Turton, R., 2006a. Modeling weight variability in a pan coating process using Monte Carlo simulations. AAPS PharmSciTech. 7 (4), 83.
Pandey, P., Katakdaunde, M., Turton, R., 2006b. Modeling weight variability in a pan coating process using Monte Carlo simulations. AAPS PharmSciTech. 7 (4), E2–E11.
Pandey, P., Song, Y., Kayihan, F., Turton, R., 2006c. Simulation of particle movement in a pan coating device using discrete element modeling and its comparison with video-imaging experiments. Powder Technol. 161 (2), 79–88.
Pandey, P., Tao, J., Chaudhury, A., Ramachandran, R., Gao, J.Z., Bindra, D.S., 2013. A combined experimental and modeling approach to study the effects of high-shear wet granulation process parameters on granule characteristics. Pharm. Dev. Technol. 18 (1), 210–224.
Pandey, P., Turton, R., Joshi, N., Hammerman, E., Ergun, J., 2006d. Scale-up of a pan-coating process. AAPS PharmSciTech. 7 (4), 102.
Petitti, M., Barresi, A.A., Marchisio, D.L., 2013. CFD modelling of condensers for freeze-drying processes. Sadhana. 38 (6), 1219–1239.

Poon, J.M.H., Ramachandran, R., Sanders, C.F.W., Glaser, T., Immanuel, C.D., Doyle Iii, F.J., et al., 2009. Experimental validation studies on a multi-dimensional and multi-scale population balance model of batch granulation. Chem. Eng. Sci. 64 (4), 775–786.

Reynolds, G., Ingale, R., Roberts, R., Kothari, S., Gururajan, B., 2010. Practical application of roller compaction process modeling. Comput. Chem. Eng. 34 (7), 1049–1057.

Rowe, J.M., Crison, J.R., Carragher, T.J., Vatsaraj, N., McCann, R.J., Nikfar, F., 2013. Mechanistic insights into the scale-up of the roller compaction process: a practical and dimensionless approach. J. Pharm. Sci. 102 (10), 3586–3595.

Sen, M., Ramachandran, R., 2013. A multi-dimensional population balance model approach to continuous powder mixing processes. Adv. Powder Technol. 24 (1), 51–59.

Sinha, T., Bharadwaj, R., Curtis, J.S., Hancock, B.C., Wassgren, C., 2010. Finite element analysis of pharmaceutical tablet compaction using a density dependent material plasticity model. Powder Technol. 202 (1–3), 46–54.

Srinivasakannan, C., Balasubramanian, N., 2008. An analysis on modeling of fluidized bed drying of granular material. Adv. Powder Technol. 19 (1), 73–82.

Suzzi, D. T.G., Radl, S., Machold, D., Fraser, S.D., Glasser, B.J., Khinast, J.G., 2012. DEM simulation of continuous tablet coating: effects of tablet shape and fill level on inter-tablet coating variability. Chem. Eng. Sci. 69 (1), 107–121.

Tao, J., Pandey, P., Bindra, D.S., Gao, J.Z., Narang, A.S., 2015. Evaluating scale-up rules of a high-shear wet granulation process. J. Pharm. Sci. 104 (7), 2323–2333.

Toebermann, J.C., Rosenkranz, J., Werther, J., Gruhn, G., 2000. Block-oriented process simulation of solids processes. Comput. Chem. Eng. 23 (11–12), 1773–1782.

Toschkoff, G., Just, S., Funke, A., Djuric, D., Knop, K., Kleinebudde, P., et al., 2013. Spray models for discrete element simulations of particle coating processes. Chem. Eng. Sci. 101, 603–614.

Toschkoff, G., Just, S., Knop, K., Kleinebudde, P., Funke, A., Djuric, D., et al., 2015. Modeling of an active tablet coating process. J. Pharm. Sci. 104 (12), 4082–4092.

Toschkoff, G., Khinast, J.G., 2013. Mathematical modeling of the coating process. Int. J. Pharm. 457 (2), 407–422.

Toschkoff, G., Suzzi, D., Tritthart, W., Reiter, F., Schlingmann, M., Khinast, J.G., 2012. Detailed analysis of air flow and spray loss in a pharmaceutical coating process. AIChE J. 58 (2), 399–411.

U.S. Department of Health and Human Services FDA, 2006. Guidance for Industry, Q9 Quality Risk Management.

U.S. Department of Health and Human Services FDA, 2009a. Guidance for Industry, Q8 (R2) Pharmaceutical Development.

U.S. Department of Health and Human Services FDA, 2009b. Guidance for Industry Q10 Pharmaceutical Quality System.

van Wachem, B.G.M., Schouten, J.C., van den Bleek, C.M., Krishna, R., Sinclair, J.L., 2001. CFD modeling of gas-fluidized beds with a bimodal particle mixture. AIChE J. 47 (6), 1292–1302.

Wu, C.Y., Hancock, B.C., Mills, A., Bentham, A.C., Best, S.M., Elliott, J.A., 2008. Numerical and experimental investigation of capping mechanisms during pharmaceutical tablet compaction. Powder Technol. 181 (2), 121–129.

Yu, L.X., Amidon, G., Khan, M.A., Hoag, S.W., Polli, J., Raju, G.K., et al., 2014. Understanding pharmaceutical quality by design. AAPS J. 16 (4), 771–783.

Quality risk management for pharmaceutical manufacturing: The role of process modeling and simulations

2

T. O'Connor, X. Yang, G. Tian, S. Chatterjee and S. Lee
Food and Drug Administration, Silver Spring, MD, United States

2.1 Introduction

The quality-by-design (QbD) paradigm for drug development and manufacturing systematically incorporates science- and risk-based principles to ensure that drug products consistently perform according to predefined elements of safety and efficacy promised to the patient in the label (Yu et al., 2014). A major component of the QbD approach to development is the assessment of process risk, whereby process parameters and material attributes that may potentially affect product quality are identified and ranked (Guidance for Industry, 2006). Once the significant parameters are identified, they can be further studied with the purpose of enhancing process understanding and establishing a control strategy to mitigate the identified risks to product quality.

Mathematical models that draw on scientific principles and experimental data can be applied to almost any stage of drug product development and manufacturing. Predictive models can aid process design by estimating the impact of process and equipment parameters and material attributes (i.e., the model inputs) on product attributes (i.e., the model outputs), thereby providing a quantitative framework to assess risk and evaluate risk mitigation approaches. In this chapter, we discuss the application of process models in quality risk management for pharmaceutical manufacturing and scientific considerations regarding model development for such applications. We will also describe case studies of continuous manufacturing to illustrate the potential role of process models in the implementation of emerging manufacturing technologies.

2.2 Quality risk management in pharmaceutical manufacturing

2.2.1 *Managing risk to quality*

Risk is the combination of the probability of occurrence of harm and the severity of that harm (Guidance for Industry, 2006). As some degree of risk is inherent in the

Predictive Modeling of Pharmaceutical Unit Operations. DOI: http://dx.doi.org/10.1016/B978-0-08-100154-7.00002-8

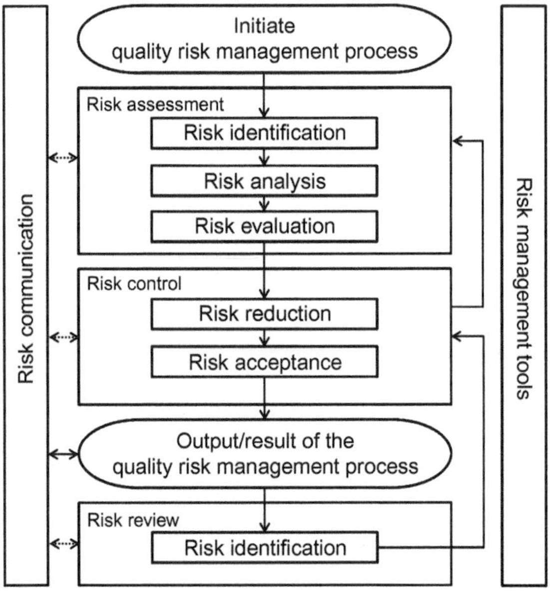

Figure 2.1 Overview of a typical quality risk management process. Quality risk management is a systematic process that incorporates practices for the assessment, control, communication, and review of risks to product quality. In addition, necessary risk management tools are essential.
Source: Reprinted from Guidance for Industry, 2006. Q9 quality risk management.

manufacturing and use of a drug product, it is important to scientifically understand and systematically manage sources of risk. Quality risk management is a broad system of considerations and practices (Fig. 2.1), applied across the drug product lifecycle, that encompasses the assessment, control, and communication of risks to product quality. Effective quality risk management is scientifically grounded and should ultimately link to protecting the patient. It may obviate the need for extensive regulatory oversight because it aligns activities to proactively identify, mitigate, and communicate potential quality issues within a solid culture of continuous improvement (Guidance for Industry, 2006).

The International Committee on Harmonization (ICH) Q9 guidance on quality risk management provides an overview of practices for the assessment, control, and communication of risks to product quality (Guidance for Industry, 2006). Risk assessment consists of the identification of hazards and the analysis and evaluation of risks associated with exposure to those hazards. It addresses the question: "What might go wrong?" Revealing assumptions and reasonable sources of uncertainty will enhance confidence in the output of the risk assessment and/or help identify its limitations. Typical sources of uncertainty include gaps in knowledge regarding process understanding, sources of harm (e.g., failure modes of a process and sources of variability), and probability of detection of issues (Guidance for Industry, 2006). The adoption of process analytical technology (PAT) tools can increase the detectability of some process hazards, as many PAT tools are able to obtain measurements at a high sampling frequency without disturbing the process (Bakeev, 2010).

Hazards identified during the risk assessment should be controlled. Risk control focuses on approaches to mitigate or avoid a quality risk when it exceeds an acceptable level. Risk reduction can include the introduction of controls to mitigate the severity and/or probability of occurrence of harm (Guidance for Industry, 2006). Risk mitigation actions initiated as a result of the quality risk management can be utilized to establish an initial control strategy for the process, however, this strategy should not be viewed as a one-time activity. Throughout the product lifecycle, sources of variation affecting process performance and product quality can be continuously identified and assessed, particularly utilizing the quality risk management process to identify potential continual improvement activities to reduce or control variation that is enhancing product quality and manufacturing capability (Guidance for Industry, 2009a).

Risk communication is the sharing of information about risk and risk management between the decision makers and other stakeholders. The output/result of the quality risk management should be appropriately communicated and documented. Communications among interested parties (e.g., regulators and industry; industry and the patient; within a company, industry, or regulatory authority) can include the nature of the severity and probability of the identified harms, controls established to mitigate the risk, and residual level of risk to quality after the implementation of the control strategy (Guidance for Industry, 2006).

2.2.2 Utilization of models to support quality risk management

Various types of models can be used to support quality risk management, from qualitative models that elicit trends between process parameters and quality attributes of the drug product to quantitative models that can be used to proactively adjust the process in response to the occurrence of a process disturbance. In many cases, process models can provide insights through computer-based simulations of the manufacturing process, supplementing expensive and time-consuming experimentation. Predictive mathematical models can identify potential hazards by estimating the impact of potential variations in the process, equipment conditions, incoming raw materials, or environmental factors (i.e., model inputs) on product quality attributes (i.e., model outputs). The control strategy adopted to mitigate the identified hazards can be incorporated into the process model and the impact of potential variations in model inputs can be reexamined, enabling an evaluation of the control strategy's effectiveness in ensuring product quality. Furthermore, models can provide a formal structure for capturing process knowledge and assumptions, facilitating risk communication among various stakeholders.

2.2.2.1 Sensitivity analysis: a risk assessment tool

Sensitivity analysis is a tool for performing quantitative risk assessments that evaluates the relationships between process parameters, material attributes, and product quality attributes. Parametric sensitivities, $S_{i,j}$, normalized with respect to the average value of the output variable, $\overline{y}_i$ (i.e., quality attributes), and input variable, $\overline{p}_j$ (i.e., process parameters and material attributes), can be defined as noted in the next equation (Saltelli et al., 2000):

$$S_{i,j} = \frac{\frac{\partial y_i}{\partial p_j}}{\left(\frac{\overline{y}_i}{\overline{p}_j}\right)}$$

Normalization enables relative comparisons between similar size variations in input parameters. As an example, the sensitivity of the active pharmaceutical ingredient (API) concentration in the tablet to a 10% change in API particle size and a 10% change in blender mixing speed can then be directly compared. Parametric sensitivities can be determined from process model simulations or design of experiments studies. Predictive process models can facilitate examining the impact of a greater number of parameters over a wider range of conditions than may be experimentally feasible, thus enhancing process knowledge.

Sensitivity analysis can also be beneficial as feedback to the development of the process model by identifying uncertain model parameters that can have a significant impact on the prediction of quality attributes. In the application of sensitivity analysis, model parameters can be treated as model inputs, along with process parameters and material attributes. Model parameters can be based on noisy experimental data, and uncertainty in these fitted model parameters can contribute to the uncertainty in the model outputs. This analysis aids the assessment of whether the parameter estimates are sufficiently precise to produce reliable predictions of the critical product quality attributes. If not, further work can be directed to refining the estimation of the parameters that give rise to the greatest uncertainty in the model outputs (Saltelli et al., 2000). To illustrate this concept, sensitivity analysis was applied to a model of a continuous direct compression process. The population balance parameters for the blending model (e.g., axial, radial, and backward fluxes) were found insignificant in this case study; however, this finding does not mean that these parameters are not important. This result simply denotes that for the chosen model outputs considered, which were related to bulk output stream properties, variations in these model parameters are not significant compared to the 11 process parameter and material attribute model inputs identified (e.g., API bulk density, API mean particle size, mixer rpm (revolutions per minute), feed frame rotation rate) (Boukouvala et al., 2012).

In addition to identifying critical model inputs, the output of a sensitivity analysis can facilitate the design of an active process control system for risk mitigation. The analysis identifies the relationship between variables guiding the selection of pairs of manipulated variables and controlled variables for automated control loops that form the foundation of an active control system. The active control system is then designed to adjust the manipulated variables upon the detection of a process variation to maintain the controlled variable at the desired targets. In this manner, disturbances are rejected and risks to product quality are mitigated (Singh et al., 2013).

Differential sensitivity analysis methods can be applied depending on the situation, and can be broadly categorized as either a local or a global method. Local sensitivity analysis focuses on the local impact of factors on the model (Saltelli et al., 2000), and is considered as a particular case of the one-factor-at-a-time approach, because all other factors are held constant when one is varied. Derivative-based approaches are the most common local sensitivity analysis method. To compute the derivative numerically, the model inputs are varied within a small range around a nominal value. But when it is important to explore a wider span of the input parameter space, or model inputs have combined effects that cannot be reduced to the sum of the individual responses precluding a linear description, a global sensitivity analysis approach should be utilized (Saltelli et al., 2000).

Global sensitivity analysis methods vary all model inputs simultaneously, and the parametric sensitivities are calculated over the entire range of each model input (Saltelli et al., 2000). Monte Carlo analysis is a common approach for global methods. Monte Carlo analysis is based on performing multiple evaluations with randomly selected values of model inputs, and then using the results of these simulations to (1) determine both uncertainty in the prediction of model outputs and (2) assign to each model input its contribution to the variance in model outputs (Saltelli et al., 2000). The general workflow of Monte Carlo approaches is as follows. (1) Select the range and distribution for each model input; the distributions are significant because they reflect the knowledge, or the lack thereof, with respect to the model and its parameterization. (2) Generate a sample from the ranges and distributions specified in the first step. Samples can be generated via random sampling, stratified sampling (e.g., Latin hypercube designs), or correlation sampling (e.g., Gaussian copula) procedures (Sampling Parameters for Sensitivity Analysis, 2015; Deodatis et al., 2013). (3) Evaluate the expected value and variance for the model outputs from the array of sample points. (4) Apportion the variation in the output to the variation in different model inputs. Many techniques are available for this analysis, including visual methods (e.g., scatterplots and three-dimensional plots) and quantitative methods [e.g., linear regression, Sobol's method, and the Fourier amplitude sensitivity test (FAST)] (Saltelli et al., 2008; Sobol, 2001). Sobol's method and FAST can be used to compute higher-order sensitivity indices based on interactions between model inputs in addition to first-order indices (Saltelli et al., 2008; Sobol, 2001).

Global sensitivity analysis methods can be adopted to calculate, in addition to steady-state values, time-dependent sensitivity indices that can provide additional insights. In a case study, Boukouvala et al. calculated the time profile of the model output after a process perturbation was simulated (Boukouvala et al., 2012). Fig. 2.2 illustrates, for a continuous manufacturing process, the time-dependent sensitivities of tablet API concentration to mean particle size of excipient, mean particle size of API, excipient bulk density, and API bulk density. In this example, the sensitivity of tablet API concentration to the mean particle size of the API significantly decreases during the start-up of the process (i.e., before 300 s) prior to

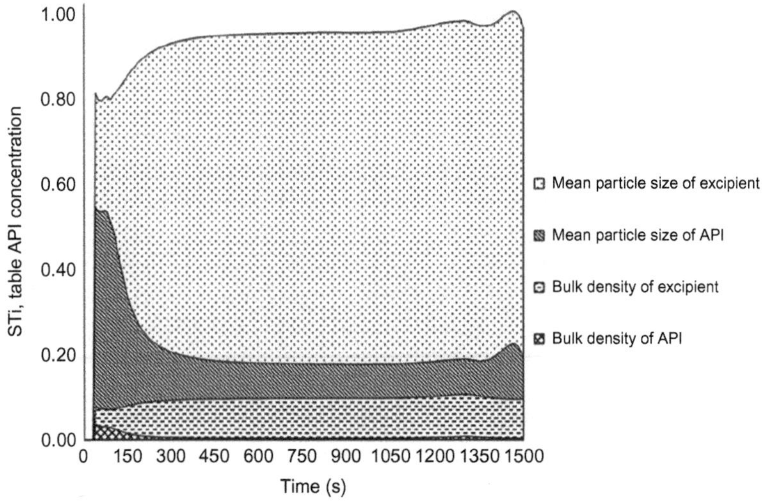

Figure 2.2 Dynamic sensitivity analysis for tablet API concentration. STi represents the time-dependent sensitivity. As time goes on, the sensitivity index of tablet API concentration versus mean particle size of excipient increases and becomes dominant after roughly 300 s; the sensitivity indices of tablet API concentration versus mean particle size of API and bulk density of API decrease significantly; and the sensitivity index of tablet API concentration versus bulk density of excipient increases slightly.
Source: Reprinted from Boukouvala, F., Niotis, V., Ramachandran, R., Muzzio, F.J., Ierapetritou, M.G., 2012. An integrated approach for dynamic flowsheet modeling and sensitivity analysis of a continuous tablet manufacturing process. Comput. Chem. Eng. 42, 40, Copyright 2012, with permission from Elsevier.

reaching a steady-state value, and the mean particle size of the excipient becomes the most influential parameter on tablet API concentration over this time period. The case study illustrates that the parameters identified as having a significant impact on product quality attributes during dynamic operations (e.g., start-up, shut-down) may be different those identified during the steady-state operations.

2.2.2.2 Feasibility analysis: a tool to evaluate risk mitigation strategies

An appropriate control strategy should be established to mitigate the hazards to product quality identified during the risk assessment. Control strategy implementations can consist of establishing ranges for material attributes and process parameters that provide an assurance of product quality. Alternatively, moving beyond such pharmaceutical controls, the control strategy can utilize an active process control system to monitor the quality attributes of materials in real time. In this case, process parameters are automatically adjusted in response to disturbances to ensure that the quality attributes consistently conform to the established acceptance criteria (Yu et al., 2014). Feasibility analysis can be utilized as a tool to evaluate whether a proposed control strategy, with respect to the critical material attributes and critical process parameters (CPPs) identified using sensitivity analysis, is appropriate for ensuring product quality. It is an evaluation of the system to determine the probability of not meeting all the product quality criteria for a given operating point and it can be utilized to locate the boundaries of the multidimensional operating envelope for the process. Feasibility analysis can provide information on combinations of material attributes and process parameters that will produce acceptable product quality, given the uncertainty in the predictions of quality attributes due to measurement variability and/or error in the estimated model parameters (Floudas et al., 2001). The effect of the active process control system to compensate for operational deviations can also be included in the formulation of the system being analyzed. Thus, feasibility analysis can be applied to evaluate control strategy implementations that include pharmaceutical controls, engineering controls (i.e., an active process control system), or a combination of both.

The proposed control strategy can be further assessed by examining the process's ability to mitigate the impact of disturbances (e.g., feeder refills). Such disturbances can move the process outside the bounds of the feasible operating region. Potential process disturbances should be identified during the risk assessment process and the control strategy should be designed to mitigate any risks to quality posed by the potential disturbances. Models can be utilized to simulate the response of the process to such disturbances. These types of modeling approaches can aid the quality risk management process by identifying classes of disturbances that may have a significant impact on product quality and evaluating whether the proposed control strategy is sufficient to mitigate the risk. An example of such approaches related to continuous manufacturing will be discussed in Section 2.4 (Boukouvala et al., 2012).

A number of methods and metrics for quantifying the feasible space for a process have been proposed in the literature (Floudas et al., 2001; Goyal and Ierapetritou, 2002; Straub and Grossmann, 1993). Most of these methods assume the feasibility space can be defined by a convex shape (i.e., a geometric shape where all the edges and curves point outward). Pharmaceutical manufacturing processes are complex and many of them do not conform to the assumption that the feasibility space is convex. A limited number of approaches are available for nonconvex problems (Banerjee and Ierapetritou, 2005). Shape reconstruction, adopted from the field of computer graphics, is one such technique (Banerjee and Ierapetritou, 2005). The feasibility space can be considered analogous to an object, the shape or surface of which can be estimated. The input to any surface reconstruction algorithm needs to be a set of points representing the object. The points can be obtained from simulations of the process model. Optimization techniques are available to increase the efficiency of sampling as, in many processes, the feasible region covers only a restricted area of the entire parameter space (Banerjee and Ierapetritou, 2005). A shape can be constructed that identifies points from the process simulations that lie on the boundary of the feasibility space (Banerjee and Ierapetritou, 2005). These points are then connected, giving rise to a polygon enclosing the feasible region. Finally, whether a set of operating conditions are feasible can be verified by checking if the point lies within the represented polygon.

Another set of techniques appropriate for complex problems with nonconvex feasible regions are surrogate-based methods (Boukouvala and Ierapetritou, 2012).

In surrogate-based methods, a computationally expensive process model is replaced by a reduced-order surrogate approximation. The surrogate approximation can be developed using response surface modeling techniques and model input–output data generated from simulations (Boukouvala and Ierapetritou, 2012). Among these techniques, Kriging, a black-box interpolating technique, is particularly useful, as it can model highly nonlinear, noisy, and dynamic processes (Kleijnen, 2009). This approach can enable accurate mapping of the feasibility space with fewer sampling points. Boukouvala and Ierapetritou (Boukouvala and Ierapetritou, 2012) have demonstrated the use of this surrogate-based approach to identify the feasibility space for a roller compaction process. In this example, illustrated in Fig. 2.3 (Boukouvala, 2013), the feasibility space is established with respect to

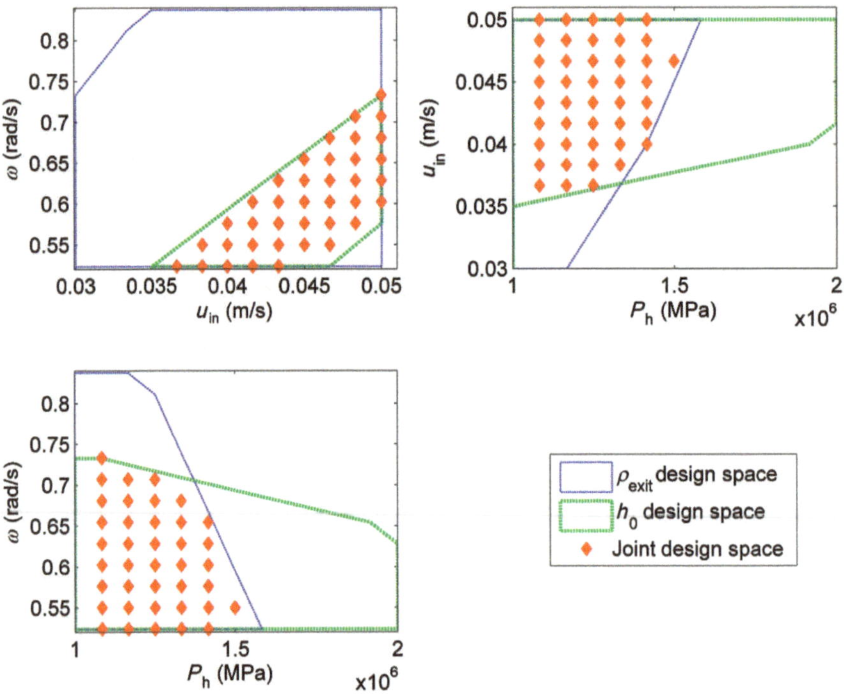

Figure 2.3 Feasible region (i.e., design space) of roller compactor. In this case, the ribbon thickness, h_O, and ribbon density, ρ_{exit}, are the constraints; applied pressure, P_h, powder feed speed, u_{in}, and roll speed, ω, are the control variables; and inlet powder density, ρ_{in}, and the inlet angle, θ_{in}, are the chosen uncertain parameters. The region within blue dashed line represents the set of conditions that lead to acceptable products in terms of the ribbon density, and the region within the green dashed line satisfies the thickness quality constraints. Their intersection defines the feasible region where both specifications are met, which is the design space for the roller compactor.

Source: Reprinted from Boukouvala, F., 2013. Integrated Simulation and Optimization of Continuous Pharmaceutical Manufacturing. Thesis Rutgers University-Graduate School-New Brunswick, Copyright 2013 with permission from the Author.

constraints on the ribbon thickness and ribbon density given uncertainty in the inlet powder density and the inlet angle, an estimated model parameter.

2.3 Scientific considerations in model development for quality risk management

As discussed in the previous section, in the QbD paradigm, models can be very useful in the support of quality risk management, leading to improvements in drug quality. Models are a simplified representation of a system using mathematical terms (ICH). Mathematical models can be formulated based on first-principles, empirical data, or a combination. Models can be utilized to better understand the manufacturing processes, and they may be potentially used to predict and control the behavior of the system. There are multiple options for categorizing models. One viable approach for classifying models is through the model's contribution in assuring the quality of the product: low-impact, medium-impact, and high-impact models. Scientific considerations for model development and maintenance are dependent on the level of impact.

2.3.1 *High-impact models*

High-impact models are models from which predictions are the significant or sole indicators of product quality. Most of the models focused on in this chapter do not fall into this category. Consider a calibration model associated with a near-infrared (NIR) spectroscopy measurement for real-time release testing (RTRT) of tablet assay. RTRT is the ability to evaluate and ensure in-process and/or final-product quality based on process data (Guidance for Industry, 2009b). Skibsted et al. illustrated one example using NIR spectroscopy and process data from a tablet manufacturing process (Skibsted et al., 2007). In this example, a regression model was developed to evaluate API content, one of the critical product quality attributes. To closely monitor the API content in each final tablet, NIR spectroscopy and a regression model were utilized. For each of the six calibration batches, one calibration spectrum was made from the averaging of 120 measured tablet spectra. Each calibration spectrum was then assigned a reference value representing the average API content in the corresponding calibration batch measured offline via high-performance liquid chromatography (HPLC). Finally, a regression model was built between the average calibration spectra and their reference values for tablet assay. Cross-validation demonstrated good agreement between model predictions and offline analytical measurements of mg API per tablets: the root mean square error of cross-validation was 0.066 and the correlation coefficient was 0.9999. As a part of an online measurement and analysis for a critical quality attribute (CQA), the role of this model in the tablet manufacturing process is significant (i.e., of high impact). It is capable of detecting process trends (as shown in Fig. 2.4), thus

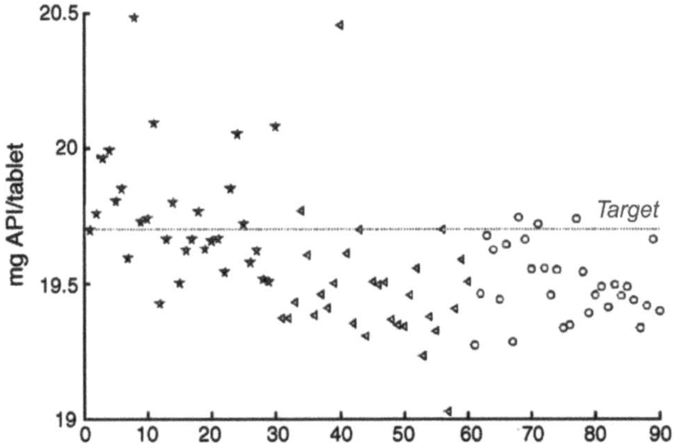

Figure 2.4 Ninety assay predictions from one batch. Thirty data points are from the beginning of the batch (star), 30 data points are from the middle of the batch (triangle), and 30 data points are from the end of the batch (circle). There is a trending that more APIs were in the tablets at the beginning of the batch compared to tablets in the middle or at the end of the batch. The trending is difficult to identify and control if only a few samples are tested as traditional methods.
Source: Reprinted from Skibsted, E.T.S., Westerhuis, J.A., Smilde, A.K., Witte, D.T., 2007. Examples of NIR based real time release in tablet manufacturing. J. Pharm. Biomed. Anal. 43, 1304, Copyright 2007, with permission from Elsevier.

increasing the detectability of potential nonconforming products that may be difficult to identify using traditional end-product testing.

Scientific considerations that may need to be taken into account when implementing such high-impact models include the following. First, high-impact models should demonstrate the ability to discern out-of-specification materials and, additionally, procedures need to be established when a tablet is detected with higher or lower API content than the established range in the drug product specification. Second, during the risk assessment for the commercial manufacturing process, failure modes for the model should be considered because they can affect the detectability of potential risks. Third, a model maintenance program can be established, including routinely monitoring the model to verify its performance and to identify when updates or modifications are required.

2.3.2 Medium-impact models

Medium-impact models are also important to assure product quality but they are not the sole indicators of quality. Fissore et al. demonstrated the utilization of a process model to build the design space for the primary drying stage of a pharmaceutical lyophilization process (Giordano et al., 2011). A simplified monodimensional model of the freeze-dry interface, based on the energy balance for the frozen product and the mass balance for the water vapor inside the dried product,

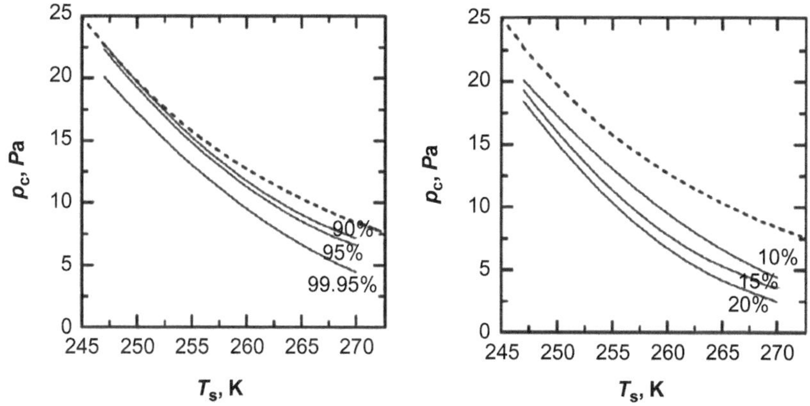

Figure 2.5 Examples of design space when the maximum allowed product temperature is 241K (dashed lines identify the design space boundary when parameter uncertainty is not considered). Upper graph: design space boundaries for various values of probability of success while assuming parameter uncertainty is fixed at 10%. Lower graph: design space boundaries for various values of parameter uncertainty while assuming probability of success is fixed at 99.95%.

Source: Reprinted from Giordano, A., Barresi, A.A., Fissore, D., 2011. On the use of mathematical models to build the design space for the primary drying phase of a pharmaceutical lyophilization process. J. Pharm. Sci. 100, 320, Copyright 2010, with permission from John Wiley and Sons.

was utilized to minimize the computational cost (Velardi and Barresi, 2008). Process simulations with a dynamic parameter estimation algorithm were performed to identify the design space for the process. Parameter uncertainty was taken into account so that boundaries of the design space were determined for a given probability (e.g., 99%, 95%, and 90%) of successfully producing quality product. To explore the design space for the process, all the operating constraints should be fully understood and identified. For example, in this case, the maximum product temperature (241K) has to be maintained under a certain value to preserve the product quality. Fig. 2.5 illustrates the design space of shelf temperature and chamber pressure (below the line). Such design space models define the operating boundaries for the lyophilization process. The control strategy should be designed to mitigate the potential hazards identified during the risk assessment and control the process to operate within this identified region. These models may be utilized during the risk assessment and the evaluation risk mitigation steps as part of the quality risk management system for the commercial manufacturing process. However, because all the analytical testing of final products is still in place for quality assurance, such a type of model would be categorized as medium impact.

Scientific considerations that may need to be taken into account when implementing such medium-impact models include the following. First, it is important to understand the impact of multivariate interactions and potential scale effects at the initial scale, because scale-up may significantly redraw the design space identified during process development. Second, it may be important to factor in process and/or method uncertainty into model predictions. Third, it must be verified that all model assumptions are still applicable at commercial scale to ensure the applicability of the model during commercial production.

2.3.3 Low-impact models

Models to support product and/or process developments are generally low-impact models. One example is a formulation optimization model, which is similar to the sensitivity analysis methods discussed in the previous risk assessment section. For example, Liu et al. built multiblock partial lease square models from historical data (Liu et al., 2011a) using a multivariate statistical software package called ProMV. The impact of many material attributes and process variables on drug product quality attributes were evaluated. As shown in Fig. 2.6, average tablet weight was positively correlated with excipient 9, 10, and 11; cup depth; cup volume; and die-hole area, and negatively correlated with API and vertical feed screw rpm. Other material attributes and process variables seemed to show little impact on the average tablet weight. This optimization model suggests relative magnitudes of the impact for different material attributes and process variables on CQAs. Such knowledge is especially useful for identification and quantification of potential risks to product quality as part of the risk assessment approaches, and may significantly accelerate designing the drug formulation or setting up a new manufacturing line by optimizing process operations and control strategies.

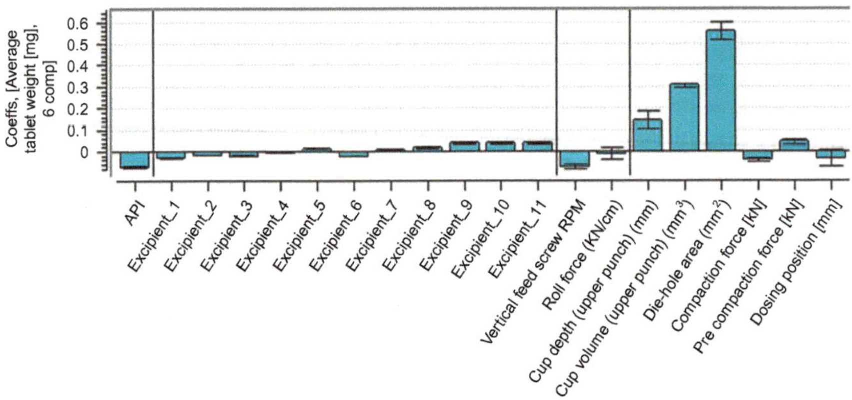

Figure 2.6 The relationship between some material attributes/process variables and quality attribute (average tablet weight). Bigger absolute values represent strong correlations, and positive values indicate proportional correlations. The coefficient is arranged to the blocking of the variables. The bars represent the approximate 95% confidence intervals.
Source: Reprinted from Liu, Z., et al., 2011. Modeling and optimization of a tablet manufacturing line. J. Pharm. Innov. 6, 176, figure number 5, in which the material was originally published with kind permission from Springer Science and Business Media.

A scale-up model of a roller compactor is another example of low-impact models. MacGregor et al. utilized a new latent variable regression methodology for product scale-up from a laboratory-scale roller compactor to a full-scale roller compactor (Liu et al., 2011b). The model was first built with historic data on the two roller compactors, and then correlation between inputs and outputs for the laboratory-scale roller compactor was utilized to estimate the process settings of the full-scale roller compactor to achieve the same quality of product made at the lab scale. The results suggest that this latent variable regression methodology is very useful in providing process settings during scale-up between the two roller compactors. The types of models that support process development but are not utilized during routine commercial production are typically classified as low-impact models. Science-based approaches for model development and validation should still be adopted but additional considerations may not be needed during routine production.

2.4 Using process models to support quality risk management for emerging technologies

The pharmaceutical industry has recognized that the development and implementation of emerging technology is critical for modernized, robust manufacturing processes that possess fewer interruptions in production, fewer product failures (before or after distribution), and greater assurance that the drug products manufactured in any given period of time will provide the expected clinical performance. The development and utilization of process models, therefore, offer valuable opportunities to advance the knowledge base and support the effective implementation of emerging technologies (Boukouvala et al., 2012; Rogers et al., 2013a). Models can be used to design, control, and optimize novel processes. Models can also be used to assess and mitigate risks associated with potential disturbances in the process, equipment conditions, incoming raw materials, or environmental factors (Rogers et al., 2013a). Within the pharmaceutical industry, continuous manufacturing is recognized as an emerging technology that can offer many advantages over traditional batch methods, including flexibility, quality, robustness, and economic improvements (Lee et al., 2015). Continuous manufacturing is not a new technology per se, as it has been extensively utilized in the petroleum, chemical, and food industries, among others, for several decades. However, there is limited experience with implementing this technology within the pharmaceutical industry. Continuous manufacturing is the integration of process operations into a single system, where material(s) and product are, respectively, charged into and discharged from the system on a continuous basis. Continuous manufacturing has attracted the attention of industry and academia for its ability to enable smaller manufacturing facilities; alleviate bottlenecks related to scale-up; provide greater response capacity; eliminate the isolation and storage of intermediate products; shorten manufacturing cycle times; improve control of product quality; reduce the number of manufacturing steps; decrease raw-material and final-product waste; and increase production yields and overall product manufacturing efficiency (Boukouvala et al., 2012; Rogers et al., 2013a; Leuenberger, 2001; Plumb, 2005).

Considerations unique to continuous production may pose challenges in developing and implementing a comprehensive strategy to control process, product, and environmental conditions over time. Process dynamics that ensue from process integration must be considered with respect to process start-ups and shut-downs; flowability as a function of material attributes; and designing appropriate measurement systems for monitoring and control (Boukouvala et al., 2012; Giridhar et al., 2014). The development and utilization of predictive process models can be used to address many of these challenges and to support quality risk management. The case studies presented next, based on recent literature reports, demonstrate how process models can contribute to the identification of CPPs and facilitate quality risk assessments, as well as how they can contribute to the evaluation of control strategies designed to mitigate the identified risks (Rogers et al., 2013a).

2.4.1 Risk assessment case studies for continuous manufacturing

In designing continuous manufacturing systems, while the analysis and optimization of individual process equipment remain important, the primary objective is to identify and evaluate design elements that pose a potential risk to product quality for the fully integrated system. Effective risk management requires sufficient process understanding of all the effects and interactions among unit operations employed in the dynamic transformation of raw materials into the final product. This can be a challenging task, but one that can be aided by the development of integrated process models.

In an integrated process, individual pieces of equipment (i.e., unit operations) are connected in series. In such a process, a train of multiple units, one after the next, is connected via piping to sequentially perform, e.g., powder-to-tablet manufacturing without isolation of intermediates. The output of a preceding unit becomes the input of the subsequent unit, with material continuously flowing from one unit to the next. Mathematical modeling of the integrated process must follow the same logic. The results or outputs from an individual unit operation model become the inputs for the subsequent unit operation model. Integrated flow sheet models include sequential modules for all the necessary unit operations, such as powder feeding, blending, roller compaction, milling, and tablet press, to represent the manufacturing process.

The individual unit operation models can vary from first-principle to empirical models. Fig. 2.7 illustrates a flow sheet model for a continuous direct compression system. Several software packages for flow sheet modeling (e.g., Aspen Plus, CHEMCAD, gPROMS) have been widely used across the chemical and petrochemical industries and have been proven effective for predictive modeling and design of fluid-based processes (Othman et al., 2010). Flow sheet models have been recently developed for continuous pharmaceutical manufacturing schemes and have

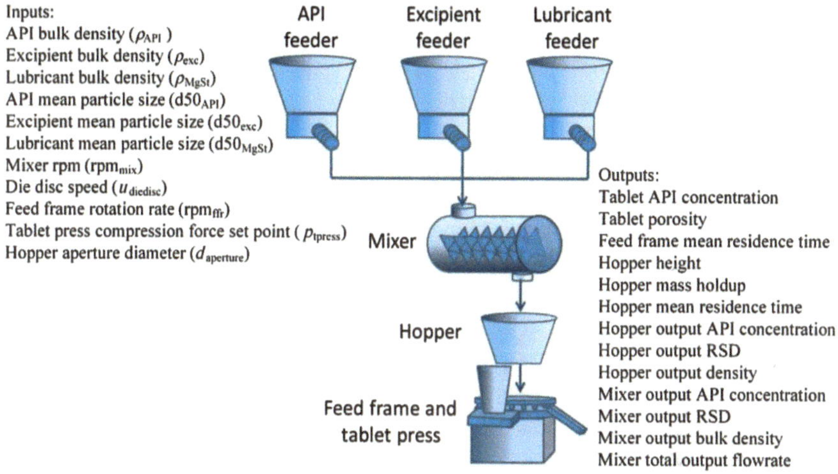

Figure 2.7 Integrated flow sheet model for a continuous direct compaction. The identified inputs are displayed on the left side of the figure. The outputs of intermediate- and final-product properties are displayed on the right side of the figure.
Source: Reprinted from Boukouvala, F., Niotis, V., Ramachandran, R., Muzzio, F.J., Ierapetritou, M.G., 2012. An integrated approach for dynamic flowsheet modeling and sensitivity analysis of a continuous tablet manufacturing process. Comput. Chem. Eng. 42, 36, Copyright 2012, with permission from Elsevier.

been shown to effectively capture integrated process dynamics (Boukouvala et al., 2012; Rogers et al., 2013a). Flow sheet models, such as the one shown in Fig. 2.7, can be used as a tool for process design, optimization (Boukouvala et al., 2013; Sen et al., 2013; Escotet-Espinoza et al., 2015), risk assessment (Escotet-Espinoza et al., 2015; Rogers et al., 2013b), control strategy analysis (Singh et al., 2014a,b), and monitoring of a continuous pharmaceutical process.

2.4.1.1 Continuous direct compression risk assessment: a case study

Our first case study is extracted from a risk assessment of an integrated continuous direct compression process (Boukouvala et al., 2012). The process consists of three feeders that supply materials (API, excipient, and lubricant) into a mixer. The mixture of raw materials is then continuously delivered through a hopper and feed frame to the tablet press (Fig. 2.7). The first step in the quality risk management process is the identification and assessment of risks to address the question: "What might go wrong?" There are more than a hundred inputs for this continuous direct compression process, including design variables, process conditions, and material properties, that could impact product quality. To aid effective risk assessment of this integrated continuous process, a flow sheet model was utilized to conduct a sensitivity analysis. Unit operation models were developed and integrated using gPROMS as a platform to build the flow sheet model.

An initial qualitative sensitivity analysis method was performed to screen the large number of inputs to the flow sheet model. As an output of this initial screening, a total of 11 inputs were identified as important parameters. These inputs include variables related to particle size distributions, bulk densities, flow rates, mixer rpm, and tablet press compaction force and were prioritized to be further assessed utilizing a quantitative global sensitivity analysis method. A summary of the identified inputs are displayed on the left side of Fig. 2.7. The process responses related to particle size distributions, bulk densities, and mass flow rate that were tracked throughout the process across the units up to the final product are listed on the right side of Fig. 2.7. Using Monte Carlo simulations, the sensitivity indices were calculated, and the effects of process parameters and material attributes on the CQAs of the intermediate and final product are shown in Fig. 2.8 (Boukouvala et al., 2012). Mean particle size and bulk density of the raw materials were found to be the most significant sources of variability for this particular continuous manufacturing process, whereas parameters related to the lubricant properties and lubricant feeder did not have a significant impact on product quality (Boukouvala et al., 2012). Thus, sensitivity analysis was used to rank the relative

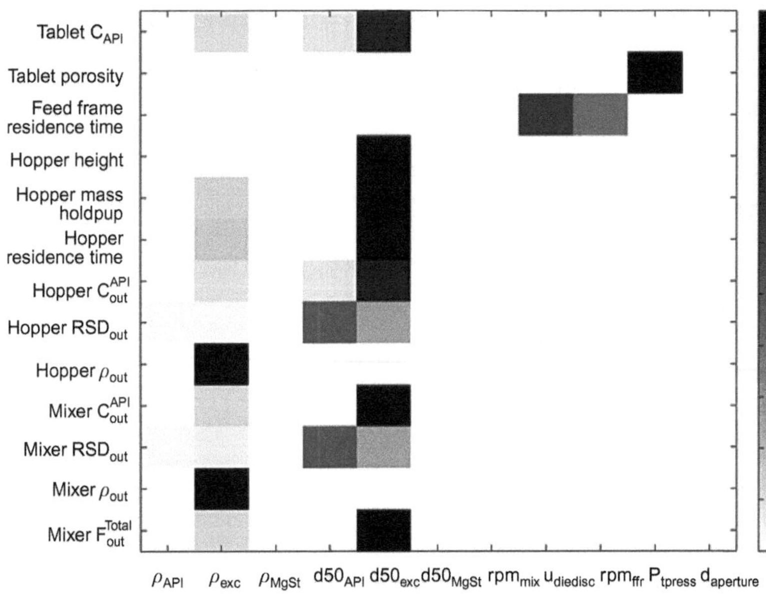

Figure 2.8 Intensity plot of total sensitivity indices of inputs to outputs at steady state. Value of zero indicates no interactions between input parameter and output, whereas value of one indicates strong influence (i.e., tablet porosity is only affected by the compaction pressure).

Source: Reprinted from Boukouvala, F., Niotis, V., Ramachandran, R., Muzzio, F.J., Ierapetritou, M.G., 2012. An integrated approach for dynamic flowsheet modeling and sensitivity analysis of a continuous tablet manufacturing process. Comput. Chem. Eng. 42, 40, Copyright 2012, with permission from Elsevier.

effect of the uncertain inputs on specific outputs, and identify the process parameters and material attributes critical to product quality. Risk control measures can be implemented as part of the control strategy to mitigate hazards related to the identified high-risk areas (e.g., variability in raw material particle size and density) to ensure that product quality is maintained throughout the product lifecycle.

In addition to evaluating the impact of variability in process parameters and material attributes on product quality during normal operations, the flow sheet model can also be utilized to estimate the effects of dynamic disturbances on product quality. One of the considerations unique to continuous production is the need to understand process dynamics, including the transient behavior of potential process disturbances. The refilling of feeders is a typical disturbance during continuous pharmaceutical production; during refilling, the feeders temporarily operate in volumetric mode, without correction for density changes, which can lead to an overshoot in the API flow rate. This can cause variations in the blend composition. The sensitivity indices were recalculated during feeder refilling. The sensitivity indices during normal operation and during the feeding disturbance were compared and it was found that process parameters, such as mixer rotation rate and feed frame speed, become critical for the content uniformity of the API in the produced tablets, and that they overshadow the effect of material properties. The authors of the study attribute this result to the fact that these two process parameters impact the amount of backmixing (i.e., the width of the residence time distribution) present in the process, which controls the spreading out of the overshoot in API concentration and thus the impact on blend and content uniformity (Engisch, 2014). As illustrated, flow sheet models can thus aid the evaluation of the effects of identified risks on final-product quality and can identify process variables (i.e., mixing rotation rate and feed frame speed) that can be optimized with respect to the ability to filter disturbance as part of the control strategy to mitigate the identified risks.

2.4.1.2 End-to-end risk assessment: a case study

A plant-wide dynamic and integrated process model has been developed for an end-to-end continuous pharmaceutical process, and sensitivity analysis has been utilized to identify relationships between CPPs and CQAs for this system (Lakerveld et al., 2013). The model includes the production of API, multistep reactions and purification stages, and solids processing and excipient addition for drug product production. The importance of each model input was assessed by computing the parametric sensitivities utilizing a dynamic simulator (Jacobian, RES Group, Inc.). This systematic risk assessment identified the variations that pose a high risk to product quality and the process parameters that could be manipulated to control the identified risks.

The plant-wide analysis identified that the residual solvent and the API concentration in the tablet (i.e., CQAs) are mainly influenced by the following CPPs: flow rate of reactant C_1, flow rate of solvent S_1 for the first extraction, flow rate of the second excipient, heat input into the flash evaporator, and the purity of the feed stream (Fig. 2.9). These process parameters also have a strong influence on another

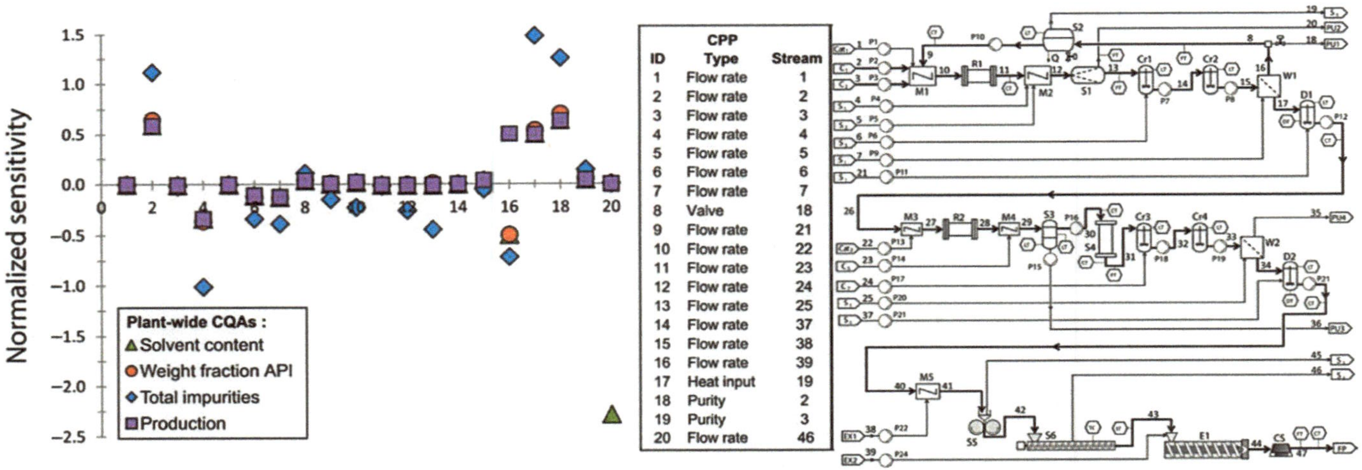

ID	CPP Type	Stream
1	Flow rate	1
2	Flow rate	2
3	Flow rate	3
4	Flow rate	4
5	Flow rate	5
6	Flow rate	6
7	Flow rate	7
8	Valve	18
9	Flow rate	21
10	Flow rate	22
11	Flow rate	23
12	Flow rate	24
13	Flow rate	25
14	Flow rate	37
15	Flow rate	38
16	Flow rate	39
17	Heat input	19
18	Purity	2
19	Purity	3
20	Flow rate	46

Figure 2.9 Steady-state values of the normalized sensitivities of the CQAs with respect to the CPPs. The stream numbers that are used to explain the CPPs refer to the process flow sheet on the right.

Source: Reprinted from Lakerveld, R., Benyahia, B., Braatz, R.D., Barton, P.I., 2013. Model-based design of a plant-wide control strategy for a continuous pharmaceutical plant. AIChE J. 59, 3676, 3682, Copyright 2013, with permission from John Wiley and Sons.

CQA: the total level of organic purities. The purity of the final tablet is significantly influenced by a number of process parameters, as evidenced by Fig. 2.9, which likely makes the control of purity of the final tablets the most challenging risk mitigation task. Sensitivity analysis was then conducted for subsections of the plant to identify relationships between the process parameters that impact API concentration and process parameters in the related subsection. The identified relationships were used to design process control loops (i.e., pairs of manipulated and control variables) as part of the plant-wide control strategy to ensure that product quality attributes were well-controlled. The interactions between production, purification, and formulation operations result in complex, dynamic behavior of the plant. The availability of an integrated process model for the system enables the systematic identification of relationships between CPPs and CQAs and the design of an active process control system that would be potentially too expensive and time-consuming to conduct by experimentation alone.

2.4.2 Risk mitigation case studies for continuous manufacturing

Mitigating the risks identified through the risk assessment process is an important component in the development of a control strategy. Based on the risk assessment using sensitivity analysis, the process parameters and material attributes that are critical to the product quality were identified. Deviations from the established ranges for these critical variables could lead to increased process risk, process failure, and production of an inferior-quality product. Therefore, process parameters and material variables identified through the risk assessment need to be controlled within predetermined multivariate ranges. Continuous processes are designed to operate under a state of control: a condition in which a set of controls consistently provides assurance of continued process performance and product quality (Guidance for Industry, 2009a). Although a control strategy reliant on end-product testing may be feasible for a well-mixed, segregation-resistant continuous manufacturing system, it is unlikely to be operationally feasible for a continuous process with low back-mixing or for high-risk formulations (i.e., low drug content products). Although a high degree of back-mixing may promote process robustness, it may represent a physical limitation to material traceability (Skoglund and Dejmek, 2007). Thus, integrated continuous manufacturing systems naturally lead to the development of active process control strategy to ensure that a quality product is being consistently manufactured.

An active process control system monitors the quality attributes of materials in real time. Process parameters are automatically adjusted in response to disturbances to ensure that the quality attributes consistently conform to the established acceptance criteria. This level of control represents a high degree of product and process understanding, as the design of an engineering control system entails expressing the dynamic relationships among process parameters, raw material, and product attributes in a quantitative and predictive manner. A process control approach can be incorporated in the integrated dynamic model. As such, integrated flow sheet models can facilitate the design, implementation, and tuning of process control systems.

The closed-loop behavior of the process can then be simulated to evaluate the control of risks identified during the risk assessment phase.

Using the continuous direct compression scenario modeled in the previous section, a case study assessing the control system's ability to mitigate a process deviation was conducted (Singh et al., 2013). A flow sheet model of the continuous direct compaction process including the active process control system was developed. The critical controlled variables in the continuous process, including total flow rate, API composition, tablet weight, and tablet dissolution, were previously identified during the risk assessment. To assess whether the process remained within a feasible operating region after process disturbances and set point changes due to control actions, variations in these critical variables were tracked during these transient states. Closed-loop (i.e., with active process control) process simulations were used to tune the process control loops to optimize the system's response during these transient states. Model outputs from closed-loop process simulations were then compared to open-loop process simulations to assess the impact of the control strategy. In this case, a sinusoidal disturbance in the flow rate from the blender was introduced. As shown in Fig. 2.10A, in an open-loop scenario, the flow rate violated the established limits, whereas in a closed-loop scenario, the flow rate was maintained within the specified limits. Fig. 2.10B shows the set point of the API flow rate was being continuously adjusted, demonstrating the active process control system's ability to mitigate risks due flow rate variations. The case study illustrates the

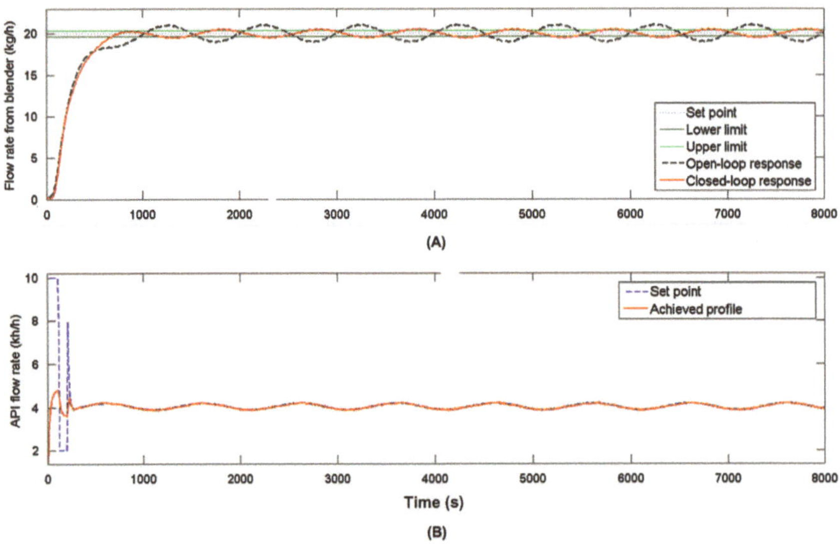

Figure 2.10 (A) Closed-loop control for disturbance rejection and (B) a set-tracking control for a continuous direct compression manufacturing line.
Source: Singh, R., Ierapetritou, M., Ramachandran, R., 2013. System-wide hybrid MPC–PID control of a continuous pharmaceutical tablet manufacturing process via direct compaction. Eur. J. Pharm. Biopharm. 85, 1173, Copyright 2013, with permission from Elsevier.

ability of flow sheet models to facilitate the design, tuning, and evaluation of control systems to reduce process deviations, ensuring that processes remain within their feasibility space.

2.5 Conclusions

This chapter provides a discussion on the potential role of models in supporting quality risk management for the development of pharmaceutical manufacturing processes. The systematic risk management process incorporates practices for the assessment, control, communication, and review of risks to product quality. Risk assessment activities can include conducting sensitivity analysis using a process model to identify high-risk material attributes and process parameters that can significantly affect CQAs. Feasibility studies can then be utilized as a tool to evaluate whether a proposed control strategy is appropriate for mitigating the risks to product quality identified during the risk assessment stage. Process models can also provide a framework for capturing the related scientific knowledge and provide a common approach for risk assessment to facilitate the communication of risk and risk mitigation approaches. Scientific considerations for the development and implementation of process models are dependent on their role within the overall control strategy. The development and utilization of process model tools can be useful in addressing the identified knowledge and experience gaps supporting the implementation of emerging technologies. One such emerging manufacturing technology within the pharmaceutical industry that offers potential flexibility, quality, robustness, and economic advantages over traditional processing methods is continuous manufacturing. Case studies were utilized to illustrate the benefits of using process models to identify risks and evaluate risk control approaches for a continuous direct compaction process and an end-to-end continuous pharmaceutical process. Predictive process models were developed and utilized in these cases to supplement expensive and time-consuming experimentation throughout process development. Furthermore, in the case studies, predictive process models through supporting a quality risk management approach to pharmaceutical development were able to help achieve high process efficiency and to attain the desired product quality.

References

Bakeev, K.A., 2010. Process Analytical Technology: Spectroscopic Tools and Implementation Strategies for the Chemical and Pharmaceutical Industries. Wiley.

Banerjee, I., Ierapetritou, M.G., 2005. Feasibility evaluation of nonconvex systems using shape reconstruction techniques. Ind. Eng. Chem. Res. 44 (10), 3638–3647.

Boukouvala, F., 2013. Integrated Simulation and Optimization of Continuous Pharmaceutical Manufacturing. Rutgers University-Graduate School-New Brunswick.

Boukouvala, F., Ierapetritou, M.G., 2012. Feasibility analysis of black-box processes using an adaptive sampling Kriging-based method. Comput. Chem. Eng. 36, 358–368.

Boukouvala, F., et al., 2012. An integrated approach for dynamic flowsheet modeling and sensitivity analysis of a continuous tablet manufacturing process. Comput. Chem. Eng. 42, 30–47.

Boukouvala, F., et al., 2013. Computer-aided flowsheet simulation of a pharmaceutical tablet manufacturing process incorporating wet granulation. J. Pharm. Innov. 8 (1), 11–27.

Deodatis, G., Ellingwood, B.R., Frangopol, D.M., 2013. Safety, Reliability, Risk and Life-Cycle Performance of Structures and Infrastructures. CRC Press, New York.

Engisch, Jr., W.E., 2014. Loss-in-Weight Feeding in Continuous Powder Manufacturing. Rutgers The State University of New Jersey-New Brunswick.

Escotet-Espinoza, M.S., et al., 2015. Flowsheet models modernize pharmaceutical manufacturing design and risk assessment in-silico design facilitates process optimization and evaluation of process control strategies. Pharm. Technol. 39 (4), 34–42.

Floudas, C.A., Gümüs, Z.H., Ierapetritou, M.G., 2001. Global optimization in design under uncertainty: feasibility test and flexibility index problems. Ind. Eng. Chem. Res. 40 (20), 4267–4282.

Giordano, A., Barresi, A.A., Fissore, D., 2011. On the use of mathematical models to build the design space for the primary drying phase of a pharmaceutical lyophilization process. J. Pharm. Sci. 100 (1), 311–324.

Giridhar, A., et al., 2014. Intelligent Process Management for Continuous Operations in Pharmaceutical Manufacturing. In 24th European Symposium on Computer Aided Process Engineering. Elsevier.

Goyal, V., Ierapetritou, M.G., 2002. Determination of operability limits using simplicial approximation. AIChE J. 48 (12), 2902–2909.

Guidance for Industry, 2006. Q9 quality risk management.

Guidance for Industry, 2009a. Pharmaceutical quality system Q10.

Guidance for Industry, 2009b. Q8(R2) Pharmaceutical development.

ICH, 2011, Quality implementation working group points to consider (R2).

Kleijnen, J.P., 2009. Kriging metamodeling in simulation: a review. Eur. J. Oper. Res. 192 (3), 707–716.

Lakerveld, R., et al., 2013. Model-based design of a plant-wide control strategy for a continuous pharmaceutical plant. AIChE J. 59 (10), 3671–3685.

Lee, S.L., et al., 2015. Modernizing pharmaceutical manufacturing: from batch to continuous production. J. Pharm. Innov. 10 (3), 191–199.

Leuenberger, H., 2001. New trends in the production of pharmaceutical granules: batch versus continuous processing. Eur. J. Pharm. Biopharm. 52 (3), 289–296.

Liu, Z., et al., 2011a. Modeling and optimization of a tablet manufacturing line. J. Pharm. Innov. 6 (3), 170–180.

Liu, Z., et al., 2011b. Scale-up of a pharmaceutical roller compaction process using a joint-y partial least squares model. Ind. Eng. Chem. Res. 50 (18), 10696–10706.

Othman, M.R., et al., 2010. A modular approach to sustainability assessment and decision support in chemical process design. Ind. Eng. Chem. Res. 49 (17), 7870–7881.

Plumb, K., 2005. Continuous processing in the pharmaceutical industry: changing the mind set. Chem. Eng. Res. Des. 83 (A6), 730–738.

Rogers, A.J., Hashemi, A., Ierapetritou, M.G., 2013a. Modeling of particulate processes for the continuous manufacture of solid-based pharmaceutical dosage forms. Processes 1 (2), 67–127.

Rogers, A.J., Inamdar, C., Ierapetritou, M.G., 2013b. An integrated approach to simulation of pharmaceutical processes for solid drug manufacture. Ind. Eng. Chem. Res. 53 (13), 5128–5147.

Saltelli, A., Chan, K., Scott, E., 2000. Sensitivity Analysis Wiley Series in Probability and Statistics. Willey, New York.

Saltelli, A., et al., 2008. Global Sensitivity Analysis: the Primer. John Wiley & Sons.

Sampling Parameters for Sensitivity Analysis, 2015. Available from: <http://www.mathworks.com/help/sldo/ug/sampling-parameters-and-states.html>.

Sen, M., et al., 2013. Flowsheet optimization of an integrated continuous purification-processing pharmaceutical manufacturing operation. Chem. Eng. Sci. 102, 56–66.

Singh, R., Ierapetritou, M., Ramachandran, R., 2013. System-wide hybrid MPC–PID control of a continuous pharmaceutical tablet manufacturing process via direct compaction. Eur. J. Pharm. Biopharm. 85 (3), 1164–1182.

Singh, R., et al., 2014a. A systematic framework for onsite design and implementation of a control system in a continuous tablet manufacturing process. Comput. Chem. Eng. 66, 186–200.

Singh, R., et al., 2014b. Implementation of an advanced hybrid MPC–PID control system using PAT tools into a direct compaction continuous pharmaceutical tablet manufacturing pilot plant. Int. J. Pharm. 473 (1–2), 38–54.

Skibsted, E.T.S., et al., 2007. Examples of NIR based real time release in tablet manufacturing. J. Pharm. Biomed. Anal. 43 (4), 1297–1305.

Skoglund, T., Dejmek, P., 2007. Fuzzy traceability: a process simulation derived extension of the traceability concept in continuous food processing. Food Bioprod. Process. 85 (4), 354–359.

Sobol, I.M., 2001. Global sensitivity indices for nonlinear mathematical models and their Monte Carlo estimates. Math. Comput. Simul. 55 (1–3), 271–280.

Straub, D.A., Grossmann, I.E., 1993. Design optimization of stochastic flexibility. Comput. Chem. Eng. 17 (4), 339–354.

Velardi, S.A., Barresi, A.A., 2008. Development of simplified models for the freeze-drying process and investigation of the optimal operating conditions. Chem. Eng. Res. Des. 86 (1), 9–22.

Yu, L.X., et al., 2014. Understanding pharmaceutical quality by design. AAPS. J. 16 (4), 771–783.

Powder flow and blending

3

A. Dubey
Aditya Birla Science and Technology Company Pvt. Ltd. (ABSTCPL), New Panvel, India

Industrial solids are often multicomponent granular substances and mixing and maintaining their blends poses a daunting challenge for a process designer. Mixing can be an intermediate step in a process chain or it may be aimed at producing the end product of desired quality. In certain specialized processes, a reaction or drying can simultaneously occur. Good understanding of mixing mechanisms and the effect of material, equipment, and processing conditions on blend quality is critical. For this, granular material behavior of not only individual components but also their mutual interaction must be understood. Any environmental factors, such as humidity, that can impact flow and/or chemical properties must be known. The traditional way to design and optimize a powder mixing operation has been to leverage previous experience coupled with manufacturer knowledge about equipment and to perform a series of pilot- and/or production-scale test runs. Pharmaceutical process engineers in particular have relied on time-tested methods using lab- and pilot-scale equipment followed by scaling-up to thc production stagc (Harnby, 2000; Bridgwater, 2010). However, this exercise is time-intensive and capital-intensive and modern day process engineers want to minimize experimentation and the associated material usage. The domain knowledge of mixing has often been regarded as an art rather than a science due to the lack of sound scientific basis.

Extensive experimentally validated modeling work on the mixing of fluids has been performed over the past several decades. Fluid flow is a well-understood field and the underlying physics has been defined using momentum- and energy-based governing equations. Hence, the analysis of a fluid mixing process is often easily done in silico using computer modeling. In many cases, detailed computational fluid dynamics (CFD) modeling is not even required. Empirical equations are sufficient to determine several performance attributes such as mixing time, power consumption, particulate dispersion, heat transfer, and even reaction dynamics. These models are used as effective design and optimization tools to predict factors such as effect of impeller type, location of sparger, cooling jacket design, baffle types, etc. When dealing with solids, however, the challenge is bigger. Depending on certain factors, the granular material may behave as a solid, flow like a liquid, or fluidize like a gas (Jop et al., 2006). Further handling complications arise due to size segregation and density segregation among dissimilar species. Stringent regulatory and quality requirements, especially in the food and pharmaceutical industries, compound the challenge. Early investigations in the subject of granular mixing were published in the 1950s to 1970s (Lacey, 1954; Carley-Macauly and Donald, 1962, 1964; Cooke et al., 1976; Bridgwater, 1976).

Predictive Modeling of Pharmaceutical Unit Operations. DOI: http://dx.doi.org/10.1016/B978-0-08-100154-7.00003-X

The subject has attracted renewed attention from the 1990s onward (Bridgwater, 2010, 2012).

On the modeling front, several techniques have been employed to model granular mixing, from early efforts employing continuum descriptions (Ottino and Shinbrot, 1999; Jenkins and Richman, 1985), kinetic-theory-based models (Jenkins and Richman, 1985), Monte Carlo models (Hopkins and Shen, 1992), and cellular automata (Shinbrot et al., 1997). However, with increasing computational capabilities and new software, mechanistic models like the discrete element method (DEM) have become more popular in the last 15 years (Bertrand et al., 2005).

Based on his decades of experience working on the subject, in 2010 John Bridgwater summarized the history, emerging state-of-the-art techniques (at the time), and future projections in the area of granular mixing (Bridgwater, 2010). He noted that up until about 1950, the mixing equipment and process design were based on observation, intuition, and luck, with very few scientific studies available. He referred to this period as the age of intuition and mechanical design. The 40-year period between 1950 and 1990 saw developments in the process side, though the understanding of the physics of mixing remained poor even in 1990. Bridgwater referred to this period as the age of process design science. Progress in the area accelerated between 1990 and 2010 with the development of several measurement, analytical, and computational methods. Hence, Bridgewater referred to this period as the start of the age of measurement and IT. Major developments in this period have been further elaborated on in his work (Bridgwater, 2012). While the period between 1990 and 2010 saw developments primarily involving small-scale equipment and relatively simple materials, it is expected that research and development on larger, more complex systems will carried out in the period between 2010 and 2030. There are several precursors to this development, such as sensor-equipped improved online sampling methods that produce a lot more measurements as the process is running, analytical and big-data handling systems to process those signals, algorithms for feedback control, continuous manufacturing and the associated paradigm change in scale-up techniques, and mass availability of massively parallel computational hardware. With the industry moving on to new therapeutic areas and more sophisticated products, it is expected that more complex materials will be handled during the mixing operation in the coming decades.

The pharmaceutical industry has shown interest in adopting, customizing, and developing continuous manufacturing techniques in recent years. The manufacturing line could be a direct compression technique, or employ dry/wet granulation. A typical line would involve two or more feeders, continuous mixers, a wet or dry granulator, compression, and coating equipment. There may also be one or more milling steps as per requirements. The paradigm shift from batch to continuous manufacturing requires building up of support knowledge. It is important to develop understanding of individual unit operations, their sequential operation in the manufacturing line, and the impact of upstream process perturbations down the line and eventually on product quality. Continuous mixing of granular materials has been a subject of interest for over 50 years (Rutgers, 1965). Initial developments were based on fluid systems, followed by the use of common granular materials like sand

and sugar (Harwood et al., 1975). In their most prevalent form, continuous powder mixers are comprised of a horizontal cylindrical shell that envelops an axial impeller. The blades on the impeller are designed to induce convective motion to the powder, which is typically fed from the inlet end and conveyed to the outlet end. In some designs, the shell can be tilted or an outlet weir can be included to vary the material residence time. In the pharmaceutical context, the continuous mixing operation has received significant attention from several research groups in the last decade, both in the form of experimental research (Berthiaux et al., 2008; Pernenkil and Cooney, 2006; Portillo et al., 2008) as well as modeling, which we shall discuss in more detail later in the chapter.

3.1 Critical role of the powder blending step in pharmaceutical manufacturing

It is well known that inefficient mixing continues to be a prime factor contributing to losses due to failed batches, recalled products, and added costs due to production delays. Poorly mixed materials cause problems in downstream unit operations as well as adversely impact product quality. Given the tight tolerances and design spaces in the pharmaceutical industry, it is critical that the interplay between the material, equipment, and processing sequence is well understood to minimize risk. The importance of quality-specific mixing (meaning, mix at least as well as is required to maintain the product quality) is high because it is usually one of the initial steps in the process chain. There are operations such as granulation, milling, and tableting that follow the mixing step. If a finished product batch is found to be off-specification, and the problem is to be traced back to the mixing step, the losses involved are likely to be higher. This is because all the material in the downstream unit operations must be discarded and those processes may need to be reoptimized. Furthermore, a pharmaceutical mix does not only contain an active pharmaceutical ingredient (API) and an excipient, but also other elements such as lubricants and glidants. Hence, it is not just the API whose concentration distribution is critical in a batch of blended material. Depending on the properties of the main ingredients, the choice of the type and, very importantly, the amount of lubricant must be made. Once the material gets to the mixing step, the amount of shear, shear rate, residence times etc. must be carefully chosen. It has been shown that mechanical-shear-induced overlubrication in a blend can lead to dissolution problems among the tablets made by those blends (Pingali et al., 2010).

3.2 Common challenges in powder blending

Process designers encounter several challenges when designing the mixing unit operations. Even before one gets to the material, chemical, and physical properties, one needs to ensure there is sufficient knowledge of raw material variability. The planned process design must be robust enough to counter this expected variability. Then comes the selection of the available equipment and design space. Care must be taken if the equipment in the plant is of different design or make than the one in the laboratory or pilot plants. Empirical calculations of the total energy/shear on the material must be performed a priori. Once the material is in process, managing the size- and/or density-based segregation/demixing is the biggest challenge. Often the powders being mixed have vastly different particle size distribution and bulk densities. Such powders have a natural tendency to segregate, as particles can experience different inertial forces during processing. Not surprisingly, segregation has been a subject of intense research studies (Ottino and Khakhar, 2000). Size differential is the primary cause of segregation; however, in cases such as gas fluidization (Groh et al., 2011) or presence of interstitial fluid (Ahmed et al., 2012), the density differential can be the dominating cause. Even when a blending operation is efficient, powders can unmix in subsequent transport and processing steps. When materials are free flowing and of dissimilar sizes (or density), they may flow well but it will be difficult to maintain a uniform mix because they are equally prone to segregation. It has been observed that smaller particles percolate through the interstitial spaces between the larger particles during operations such as storage and transport, and the blend quality deteriorates quickly. There are several different such modes of segregation that have been identified, such as trajectory, sieving, fluidization, and agglomeration segregation (Tang and Puri, 2004).

Blending devices are usually required to impart a certain degree of shear stress on materials. Depending on the mode of application, the constituent powders may respond differently. For example, a high impeller rotation rate in a continuous mixer might fluidize the powder. However, the composition of the fluidized material might not be uniform and one species might get preferentially fluidized. Fluidized material also coats the blender walls, which might change the composition of the output blend. Powder particles can have affinity toward their own or another species. This results in aggregate formation during processing, also termed as agglomerate segregation. The agglomerates behave like larger particles and hence can segregate. The mixing operation has to be effective to break up aggregates of cohesive substances and blend materials with differing cohesiveness uniformly.

There are several challenges other than segregation. These include material aeration, caking on equipment surfaces, variations in atmospheric humidity, equipment abrasion, material overheating and safety hazards, particle damage, uncertainties during starting and stopping of operation, emptying and cleaning the equipment, and scaling-up/-down the process. One finds that a scientifically rigorous scale-up procedure is not available, resulting in time-intensive and material-intensive experimentation. Similar is the case when equipment is replaced with one of a different design or make. Hence, equipment design and process optimization must be performed on a case-to-case basis (Muzzio et al., 1997).

To overcome these challenges, the main questions to be asked in relation to a mixing operation are (1) how is the mixing happening (what mechanism), (2) at what rate is it taking place, and (3) to what extent has it taken place at the given point of observation. The challenge, as identified by many researchers, lies in understanding the kinematics of powder behavior. This includes visualizing internal flow fields and mixing patterns (Hassanpour et al., 2011).

3.3 Granular mixing fundamentals

The best possible mixture, also known as an ideally ordered mixture, is defined as one in which every particle of a species is next to a particle of a different species (Poux et al., 1991). However, such a mix may not be practically achievable and hence other definitions, such as ordered mix (Hersey, 1975) and random mix, have been used. A random mix involves mixing of similar particulates that are free of surface effects such as cohesion. This is akin to handling of free-flowing materials with no significant size or density differentials. Ordered mixing involves particulates with different sizes as well as those having affinities such as cohesion. In a situation in which small particles coat larger ones, such as in a pharmaceutical blend with excipient and active ingredients and/or lubricant, a good mix can be considered an ordered mixture. A completely random mixture has been defined as one that exhibits the same probability of selecting a particle of a given constituent from any location in the system and that the probability is related to the proportion of that constituent (Lacey, 1954). Fig. 3.1 shows examples of a completely segregated

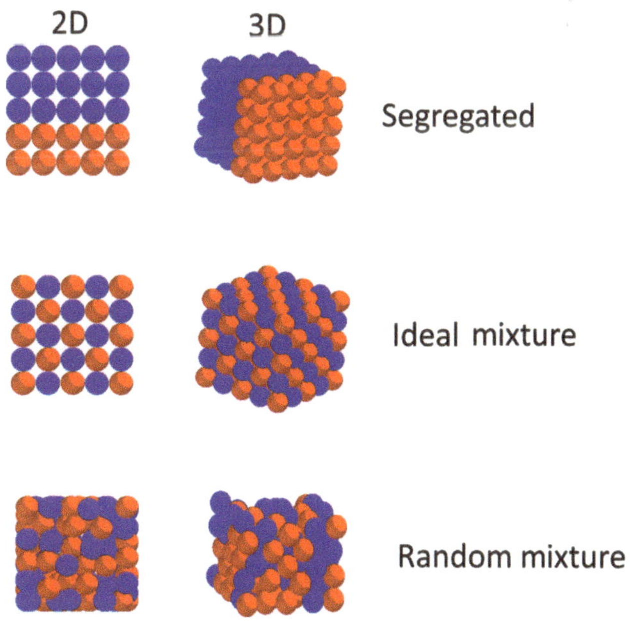

Figure 3.1 2D and 3D descriptions of a segregated mixture, an ideal mixture, and a random mixture of particles.

mix, an ideal mix, and a random mix in two-dimensional (2D) and three-dimensional (3D) descriptions, respectively. The particles were modeled as simple spheres using DEM. It is noticeable that in a random mix, the particles were randomly created within a working space and allowed to settle in a box in an unbiased manner. Hence, the particles do not pack in an orderly fashion as they do for the ideal mixing case and the void spaces between them are bigger and not as orderly.

3.3.1 Mixing mechanisms

Theoretically, mixing is understood to occur using three mechanisms: convection, diffusion, and shear (Lacey, 1954). Most among the vast variety of mixing equipment available exhibit some combination of these three modes. Mixing is carried out by convection when groups of particles are moved relative to each other via, for example, blade or baffle action. As a simple example, consider the paddle or a ploughshare mixer in Fig. 3.2. As the paddle digs through the particle bed and lifts the particles up to displace them elsewhere in the mixer, it is imparting convective motion. Convection leads to fast mixing at a bulk scale. Diffusion (or dispersion), on the contrary, involves motions on the particle-length scale on newly developed surfaces or within the powder bed. As the material in the paddle mixer is thrown up and lands on the surface, the individual particles relocate and find new positions. They diffuse or disperse into other locations. Shear is perceived to be a mode related to convection in which adjacent groups of particles move relative to each other with high velocity gradients (Bridgwater, 1976). In the paddle mixer, the clearance between the paddle and mixer wall is usually very small. The powder that comes in between the two surfaces experiences high shear, which may result in

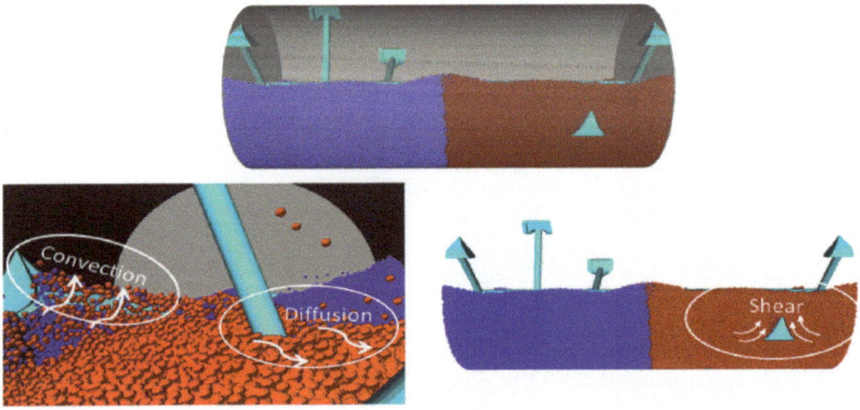

Figure 3.2 Top: A ploughshare mixer in which multiple paddles are used to lift material through on top to induce mixing. Left: Inside view of the mixer with a paddle lifting the material, thereby inducing convective mixing. The material further away from the paddles experiences slow diffusive mixing. Right: Shear induced by the paddle as it traverses through the material.

agglomerate breakage and increased contact area between particles (Bridgwater, 2012). If in a horizontal axis paddle mixer, a flat blade lifts a chunk of material relative to another (convective motion), there is a slip plane across which the velocity differential is present. In free-flowing materials, the plane is not clearly defined and there can be additional diffusive movement as particles fall off the blade. Hence, instead of pure convection or shear, the term often used is convective-shear mixing. Visual observation is the first tool for an analyst to understand the mixing mechanism in a given process. However, when the view is hindered or a combination of mechanisms is at work, other methods, such as tracer tracking, imaging, or computer simulations, to determine the relative contribution of the mechanisms can be employed. Knowledge of the dominant mechanism is important, as it relates to the rate of mixing and can help determine the end-point homogeneity (Gyenis et al., 1999). When looking at mixing vs. demixing of particulates of similar properties, convection is understood to aid mixing action, whereas the other two mechanisms may tend to induce segregation (Kaye, 1997).

3.3.2 Common techniques of mixing powders

There are three primary modes of agitation: shaking, tumbling, and impeller-driven motion (Ottino and Khakhar, 2000). In terms of equipment, powder mixers are broadly classified into two classes: (1) rotating shell type and (2) stationary shell type. In the former, the material is agitated by the rotation of the shell, which can take various shapes such as a simple rotating cylinder, an off-center rotating cylinder, a V-blender, a double cone blender, or a tote blender (Fan et al., 1990). Shear and diffusion usually feature as the dominant mixing mechanisms in this class of devices. In the latter category, the shell remains stationary while the material is moved around using moving blades, e.g., in the ploughshare, ribbon, and certain continuous mixers (Poux et al., 1991). Here, the convection and shear caused by the blade action is dominant. Aside from these a recent development employs resonant frequency vibrations to induce fast movement at the particle scale to induce homogenization in a process termed as resonant acoustic mixing. This technique has been reported to be very effective in mixing small quantities of cohesive API with pharmaceutical materials (Osorio and Muzzio, 2015). The operating parameter, instead of vessel rotation or blade speeds as in traditional blenders, is the acceleration imparted to the particles by the acoustic waves. For mixing highly cohesive nanopowders, magnetic assisted impact mixing has been used (Deng et al., 2013).

3.4 Assessment, measurement, and characterization

3.4.1 Assessment

It is important to establish what determines a good blend. As noted earlier, ideal mixtures are not practically feasible to obtain and hence, random or ordered mixtures are the reality. Whether a blend is good or bad depends on its intended usage.

Hence the term scale of scrutiny was coined (Danckwerts, 1952) with an explanation as "the maximum size of the regions of segregation in mixture which could cause it to be regarded as imperfectly mixed" (Rhodes, 1990). For a pharmaceutical blend for a solid oral dosage product, the scale of scrutiny would be a tablet or a capsule. The requirement is that each individual tablet must contain the same amount of drug even if the drug concentration within the tablet is nonuniform. Similarly, if the product is a detergent powder, the scale of scrutiny would be a scoop of it. As the scale of scrutiny is reduced, the observed quality of the mixture deteriorates.

Once the scale of scrutiny is established, the mixture quality assessment can be performed using an appropriate sampling technique (Gy, 1998, 2004). There are several techniques and sampling equipment available for this purpose and each has its related benefits, issues, and challenges (Muzzio et al., 2003). A process engineer must concentrate on the sampling tools as well as protocols and be wary of misleading results (Muzzio et al., 1997). A common technique involves the use of a thief sampler, which is inserted into the granular bed and a mechanism opens up cavities inside it to collect samples. The sampler can be either a side-filling or end-filling type. In the former, a hollow tube with a number of cavities is inserted in a sleeve that has correspondingly cut slots. When the slots are not aligned with the cavities, they are in a closed state and this setup is inserted in the bed. The tube can then be rotated to align the outer slots with the cavities, allowing the powder to enter. Once filled, the cavities are closed and the thief is withdrawn. In the latter design, only one sampling cavity is present at the end of the sampling tube and can be opened and closed similarly. Segregation during the cavity filling is possible, particularly in the case of freely flowing materials, leading to preferential filling of one particular species. For cohesive materials, it is often challenging to fill the sampling cavity, as the dilated material may not spontaneously flow in. Alternative techniques involving freezing of the particle bed by infiltration with a polymer solution have been developed. It has been inferred that the most important factor is the number of samples chosen.

A theoretically random mixture requires about 30–40 samples to characterize (Devore, 1982). However, for a poorly mixed one, the number can be in the hundreds. An important criterion is that for pharmaceutical blends the sample size must be of the order of three unit dosages provided the mixture is truly random, the sampling technique is bias-free, and the state of powder evaluated after the mixing step is not altered during the downstream processing (Muzzio et al., 1997).

Care must be taken of the disturbances induced in the granular bed during sampling and the associated bias. Inaccurate sampling can lead to erroneous judgment of the quality of mixing with disastrous consequences (Carley-Macauly and Donald, 1962). The golden rules of sampling, as they are known, state that it is best that samples must be taken when the powder is in motion and should be collected uniformly from the entire process stream (Allen, 2003). Precise sampling protocol must be devised, keeping in mind the mixing dynamics of the particular blender and guarding against oversampling and misleading statistical calculations.

The experimentally measured variance σ_e^2 is the sum of the variance produced by the mixing action, σ_m^2, and that due to the sampling, σ_s^2, and analytical errors, σ_a^2. Hence,

$$\sigma_e^2 = \sigma_m^2 + \sigma_s^2 + \sigma_a^2$$

The sampling and analytical variances must ideally be negligible.

3.4.2 Measurement

Several techniques are useful in monitoring and measuring mixing. The previous two decades have seen several important developments in this area owing to advances in digital photography and scanning technologies (Huang and Kuo, 2014). Traditionally, there were two ways of monitoring the extent of mixing: (1) the offline method, in which the material was withdrawn and then analyzed, and (2) the online method, in which the material remained in the process while being analyzed. With a newfound thrust toward continuous manufacturing and process monitoring with an aim of building quality into a product, the inline (Berntsson et al., 2002) and online (Sekulic et al., 1996, 1998) methods of measurement and characterization have gained popularity. A method is considered inline when the measuring equipment, such as probes, is inserted in the path of the material flow and may directly interact with it. This method may be good for a quick analysis of certain key components of the process. When mounted in an online setup, the measurement is also done while the material is in process but without interfering with the process or material. An at-line setup implies that the analytical equipment shares the process floor space, near where the process is taking place. Samples are drawn manually and analyzed quickly so that any corrective measures may be taken right away. The traditional way of taking samples during and after the process and sending them to a separate analytical facility is referred to as the offline method. The offline method would allow for the most detailed analytical information and hence might be most useful during the early stage of process development. The faster inline and online methods involve more monitoring and taking corrective measures in a feedback control fashion rather than characterization of the materials. Depending on the development stage of the process and material types, a suitable combination of these methods may be chosen.

Once samples are drawn, they are analyzed for content uniformity. Typically, one looks for the concentration of a specific species in each of the samples. Several technological advancements, such as in the areas of imaging and image processing, have led to the development of robust analytical methods. While frequency distribution of sample concentrations is the most commonly used indicator, there are other more specialized methods such as phase-space technique, correlation, and fractal analysis (Gyenis, 1999).

Noninvasive measurement by laser Doppler anemometry has been made in loose and transparent particle beds. Light reflection probes and radioactive tracers (Broadbent et al., 1993) have also been used. Such methods are useful in determining velocity profiles and streamlines and can help determine the dominant mixing mechanisms in the process. The profiles can also be used to cross-validate mechanistic models such as DEM. If, for example, the measurements show high temporal variation, this could be an indicator of chaotic mixing mechanisms. On the other hand, if well-defined patterns are observed, it may indicate systematic or ordered mixing. If a method is able to track individual particles and their velocity can be grouped into discrete, identifiable levels, it is an indicator of convective-shear mixing. If random movements at the particle level are observed with no perceived correlation with other particles, it indicates a diffusive mode at work.

Spectroscopic techniques have found extensive usage in characterization of mixing performance, with traditional choices being near-infrared spectroscopy (NIR), infrared (IR), and Raman spectroscopy (Bakeev, 2010). NIR spectroscopy has been an extremely popular technique for characterization in industries such as pharmaceuticals. Image analysis is useful in characterization of blend quality (Obregón and Velázquez, 2007; Wightman et al., 1996). In a recent work, pharmaceutical powder was mixed with iron powder and the cohesive energy was controlled by a magnetic field acting on the iron particles. The iron was later separated using magnetic separation to assess its concentration in the sampled material. The attempt was to correlate the shear energy with the cohesive energy to come up with a mixing rate constant (Shi et al., 2013).

Lately there has been an effort to understand micromixing. Most studies on powder mixing have been concentrated to macromixing, which is mixing of materials at the bulk scale. However, recent studies have found that the interaction at the particle level is also important, especially in the case where ingredients have vastly different properties and small amounts of an ingredient to be dispersed. It has been found that the order of mixing can directly impact the quality of a pharmaceutical product (Pingali et al., 2011), which leads to increasing interest in understanding particle–particle interactions. Near-infrared chemical imaging (NIR-CI) has been found to be a useful tool in this analysis. The technique has now evolved into being used in situ for a real-time noninvasive inline analysis (Osorio et al., 2014; Koller et al., 2011). Calibration methods form an important basis for a spectroscopy-based analytical method. Principal component analysis, partial least square, and now science-based calibration (Marbach, 2005) are used.

3.4.3 Characterization

Besides monitoring of mixing process, characterization of a blend is performed post mixing using sample analysis and statistical tools. It is typical to use a combination of quantities like the sample variance, σ^2, the random sample variance, σ_r^2, and the variance of a fully segregated mixture, σ_0^2. The standard deviation of sample concentrations is usually denoted by σ. It may be noted, however, that the true composition of a mixture may not always be known a priori. Hence, after a number of samples, N_s, has been drawn, the concentration of a given species of interest, c_i, in the i_{th} sample can be estimated using analytical methods. The estimate for that species can be calculated as

$$\bar{c} = \frac{\sum_{i=1}^{N_s} c_i}{N_s} \tag{3.1}$$

With the estimated mean concentration, the standard deviation among the samples can be calculated.

$$\sigma = \frac{\sum_{i=1}^{N_s} (c_i - \bar{c})}{N_s - 1} \tag{3.2}$$

Some fundamentals from the theory of probability form the basis of variance calculation. If a binary mixture is initially segregated and a component has a fractional number concentration denoted by a, then the probability of choosing one particle of that component is a. The probability of not picking it is $(1 - a)$. Then the variance of the segregated system will be given by

$$\sigma_0^2 = a(1 - a) \tag{3.3}$$

Once a random mixing state has been achieved, the variance, now denoted by σ_r^2, is relevant for a set of samples. If a given sample contains N_p particles, the variance is given as

$$\sigma_r^2 = \frac{a(1 - a)}{N_p} \tag{3.4}$$

Segregated mixture variance corresponds to the worst possible state of mixing while the random mixture variance is the target that the sample variance should tend toward. To this end, the Lacey mixing index is defined as (Lacey, 1954)

$$M_L = \frac{\sigma_0^2 - \sigma^2}{\sigma_0^2 - \sigma_r^2} \tag{3.5}$$

M_L can theoretically range between 0 for completely segregated mixtures $(\sigma^2 = \sigma_0^2)$ and 1.0 for completely random mix $\left(\sigma^2 = \sigma_r^2\right)$. However, practically it has been found to range between 0.75 and 1.0. Another mixing index, the Poole, Taylor, and Wall (Poole et al., 1964) index, which uses standard deviation instead of variance, is also used:

$$M_P = \frac{\sigma_r}{\sigma} \tag{3.6}$$

This index would tend to unity as the mixture approaches a random mixing state.

3.5 Modeling techniques for powder mixing

Experts state that the aim of modeling should be to "elucidate engineering principles of general utility" (Bridgwater, 2012). Model-based design strategies need to be developed for both process and equipment design. Modeling can be used to assess the impact of blender design on the rate and magnitude of agitation. This knowledge can be used to make design choices such as the shape and size of the mixer vessel, addition/removal of baffles, and usage of agitator blades. One can also assess the impact of processing variables and, in some cases, the effect of feeding order of ingredients (Xiao et al., 2015). In this section, we first look at the various computational tools that are used, or have previously been used, to study granular mixing. Then we focus in more detail on the DEM and discuss its application. Several examples from published literature are provided that demonstrate how the models help in evolving equipment design, choosing the right process parameters, and assessing the impact on critical quality attributes. The sections that follow this discuss the latest software and hardware developments that make the simulations more efficient and allow modeling of much larger systems, the common computational tools available, and a case study describing how a DEM material model can be prepared.

3.5.1 Development and usage of computational tools

Alongside the advancements in experimental measurement and validation techniques, significant developments have been made in modeling methods and, to date, this area continues to be one of the fastest growing. Here, modeling means that the discussion will be limited to computational modeling. The developments can be classified as due to the following factors:

1. new developments in modeling the underlying physics and processes;
2. improvements in the efficiency of solution methods, algorithms and compute architecture; and
3. advancements in analysis techniques in commercial and open source software.

Prior to exploring these in detail, it is imperative to briefly review some of the recent work that highlights the contribution of modeling techniques, primarily the DEM-based methods, to the field of granular mixing in the context of pharmaceutical manufacturing. This brief overview is by no means exhaustive—the quantum of work is immense, and new research publications increase by the day—but the aim is to focus on the newest work and to cover all major mixing equipment, as much as possible.

Modeling has facilitated the assessment of various mixing devices. Modern computational techniques lead to efficient simulation of mixing processes providing sound qualitative and quantitative assessment. Typically, parameters such as mixing or segregation indices are used to quantify the degree of mixing. Mechanistic modeling allows for the measurement of quantities, such as the number of blade passes and material residence time, that indicate the amount of mechanical agitation experienced by the material. Some experts have classified mixers into three broad categories: gravity-controlled mixers, stirred mixers, and high-shear mixers (Cleary and Sinnott, 2008). Devices such as simple or baffle-equipped rotating drums, V-blenders, double cone blenders, tote blenders, etc. fall under gravity-controlled mixers. The stirred mixers include the ones with agitator blades that can be horizontal, vertical, or inclined. These are commonly found in the form of ploughshare, ribbon, and paddle mixers. High-shear mixers are also bladed but with a high degree of shear agitation, for example, continuous convective mixers.

Flow dynamics and mixing characteristics of a gravity-driven low-shear continuous drum blender; a V-blender; a pan granulator; a ploughshare with single and four blades, respectively; peg mixer; and vertical-bladed high-shear mixer have been analyzed in detail using DEM simulations. In one such study (Cleary and Sinnott, 2008), the quantification was performed by computing the overall degree of homogeneity for the particle bed as well as tracking the centroids of selected particle groups. Furthermore, crucial information regarding particle shape and mixer scale effects was obtained. It was found that mixing in the radial direction in a vertical-bladed mixer reduced as particles became more and more nonspherical. Simulations of mixers of increasing size showed that the mixing time would increase fourfold in the case of a scale-up from the laboratory to a pilot- or small production-scale blender.

A fundamental granular mixing device, the rotating drum, has been studied extensively in the past two decades (Khakhar et al., 1997). Initial efforts used lab-scale equipment and 2D DEM models. With high-performance computing and modern programming tools, the models are bringing new insights into the mixing mechanisms and researchers are able to test different designs in silico. DEM simulation technique is fast moving toward real-time simulation (Xu et al., 2011). High-performance computing using graphical processing units (GPUs) allows faster simulations of large systems at a significantly lower cost on desktop or laptop computers. This allows for the usage of smaller particles in the simulations and hence new insights into material flow can be achieved. For example, the granular flow similarity in rotating drums was studied recently using velocity profiles (Qi et al., 2015). This study highlights the effect of vessel-to-particle diameter ratio (*D/d*) on velocity profiles.

Mechanistic modeling affords access to unique information such as energy spectra, packing fraction distribution, and surface plots of the mixing index. Recent work on rotating drums has shown differences between a cylindrical and a hexagonal shell with respect to mixing efficiency and dead zone creation (Soni et al., 2016). Models are now robust enough to elucidate the remarkable differences between mixing of monodisperse, bidisperse, tridisperse, and polydisperse particles (Alchikh-Sulaiman et al., 2016). In this particular case, the DEM model provided insights regarding the effect of drum rotation speed, particle size, and initial loading pattern on the degree of mixing, all of which were experimentally validated. While mixing is better among monodisperse particles due to lack of segregation effects, the model showed that the mixing among polydisperse ones could be improved by including particles of intermediate sizes.

It is known that segregation or demixing can occur due to percolation in systems of particles with differing size and due to condensation when there is a density differential instead. On these lines, another recent study using DEM models has sought to understand the competition between the two mechanisms and its impact on radial segregation. The results have shown that it is possible to minimize segregation through control of volume and density ratios in a binary particle system (Chen et al., 2016). Researchers have also attempted design changes in mixing devices, and modeling is playing a crucial role here. Simulations have shown that inclusion of a simple centrally mounted axial baffle can greatly enhance mixing in rotating cylinders and models can help recognize the best baffle shape via quantitative comparison (Jiang et al., 2011). Even when dealing with highly cohesive materials, mixing can be greatly enhanced by the use of baffles. It is possible to determine the optimal size and arrangement of baffles mounted on the cylinder walls using validated models prior to fabrication (Zhou et al., 2016). Moving further on with the design, it is well known that axial mixing in most tumbling mixers is a challenge, and a rate-limiting step. New models are helping with the design of equipment with optimal baffle arrangement that imparts convective axial movement as well as enhanced dispersive mixing. Here the parameters are the number and dimensions of the baffles relative to the vessel (Yu et al., 2015). More sophisticated designs such as slant cone mixers with a central agitator have also been studied and the impact of initial loading type and degree of polydispersity (Alchikh-Sulaiman et al., 2015), fill level and agitator rotation relative to that of the vessel (Alian et al., 2015) has been numerically evaluated. There are other notable studies in the area of tumbling blenders such as tote or bin blenders (Arratia et al., 2006; Ren et al., 2013), V-blenders (Lemieux et al., 2008) and double cone blenders (Moakher et al., 2000) performed in the last few years.

While a single-axis tumbling blender is commonly used in batch blending, imparting multi axial motion has been considered to counter the slow axial mixing in the former design. Experimentally validated models of a vessel with biaxial rotation have shown that axial mixing time could be reduced by as much as 90% (Manickam et al., 2010). As a possible improvement over the traditional V-blender, a tetrapodal blender has been analyzed using DEM modeling (Alizadeh et al., 2014). It consists of two V-shells joined at the bottom with one of them twisted by 90 degrees. This configuration facilitates faster axial mixing. In more complex designs, models have captured detail motion of a moving geometry and its impact on granular mixing facilitating direct comparisons between uniaxial, biaxial, and triaxial rotation of a drum (Marigo et al., 2012). A Turbula mixer is a bin moving in repetitive triaxial motion and granular flow in such a complex moving body can be extremely unpredictable. DEM-based models have predicted a transition in flow regime at a critical agitation level, and found that the mixing rate initially decreased with increasing speed and then increased beyond it (Marigo et al., 2011). Experiments with PEPT measurements have confirmed the model predictions (Marigo et al., 2013). The pharmaceutical industry has also adopted this blender, using it primarily in the early stage product development at the lab scale. Scale-up methodologies and a model for lubricant blending have been developed for this blender (Kushner, 2012).

In the area of convective mixing, where the primary mode of mixing is bulk material movement due to impeller blades, modeling has facilitated various studies starting from fundamental designs to production-scale equipment simulations. In a recent study, DEM modeling has been used to study in detail the impact of a single blade on flow dynamics, to begin with (Chandratilleke et al., 2012). Such studies have contributed toward increasing the understanding of design parameters in such bladed blenders. In another work, kinematic insights into material flow mechanisms were obtained using DEM simulations validated with particle image velocimetry (Remy et al., 2010). Simulations captured well the effect of particle and vessel roughness, and the change in flow regime from bumping to roping as the blade speed increased. Particle velocities were found to be proportional to blade tip speed in the bumping regime whereas the proportionality was not found in the roping regime. Further, other studies have elucidated the interaction between the size and density induced segregation tendencies in case of binary mixtures in such bladed vertical mixers (Halidan et al., 2014). This leads to a predictive model that can guide how to utilize the two mechanisms to achieve better mixing. The studies on vertical-bladed mixer can lead to further developments in the field of high-shear wet granulation, which involves similar equipment.

As noted earlier, continuous mixing has gained popularity in the pharmaceutical industry in the last 10–15 years. Naturally, a significant amount of work in the model development for continuous mixing has also been carried out. Some of the DEM models have focused on simulating a periodic slice of a horizontal convective blender, while some have focused on the flow dynamics in entire blenders. Initial work using a periodic slice model elucidated the effect of material fill level and impeller rotation rate in a continuous blender (Sarkar and Wassgren, 2009). The periodic slice simulates the central portion of an idealistic, infinitely long continuous blender, so the inlet and outlet effects can be ignored. The model predicted better mixing at lower impeller speeds at higher fill levels and vice versa. Another study built upon this work to study mixing of cohesive material. The model predicted that mixing will improve when slightly cohesive material is used but will degrade when the cohesion is high (Sarkar and Wassgren, 2010). The applicability of such an approach to continuous mixing process design (Gao et al., 2012) and the correlation between the periodic slice and a full blender simulation was also explored for simple bladed mixers (Govender et al., 2015). More detailed treatment of modeling tools for continuous mixing have also been published (Dubey et al., 2011; Boukouvala et al., 2012). Some researchers have modeled flow dynamics in full blenders from inlet to outlet and characterized their performance based on mixing efficiency and material agitation as a function of flow rate (which relates to the fill level), impeller speed and impeller blade design (Dubey et al., 2012). The study used mean residence time and number of blade passes experienced by the material as quantitative indicators of the agitation received by the material. Further development in the form of a hybrid DEM-population balance method to develop a predictive model has been carried out (Sen et al., 2013). Not all materials can be subjected to high shear by impeller blades. For such materials, a new type of mixer has been designed which is called the continuous tumble mixer (Florian et al., 2014). It consists of a perforated rotating cylinder at the core with an axial material inlet and the perforation allowing the mixed powder to exit on to a hopper. Modeling has been an integral part of the development process (Florian-Algarin and Méndez, 2015).

3.5.1.1 Techniques for modeling the underlying physics and processes

Over the years multiple ways of modeling granular mixing have been developed. Each has its advantages and limitations and they often complement each other. Some early models for predicting mixing performance were based on learning from the field of fluid flow. Hence, methods based on kinetic theory of gases and continuum mechanics were the early entrants in the arena. These methods found success in dilute phase systems or those with simple laminar flow profiles.

A stochastic Markov-chain-based systems approach was used to model a V-blender (Inoue and Yamaguchi, 1969). The approach was also applied for continuous processes to calculate residence time distributions. In this approach, the mixer is modeled as system of interconnecting cells and the Markov chain is used to predict the changes in concentration (Fan et al., 1985).

The continuum-mechanics-based models, as the name suggests, rely on a continuum description of the material, i.e., as a fluid. Hence, the particle level interactions and their impact on the bulk behavior are excluded. This approach is useful when the flow is truly fluid like—when the particles are so many that the discontinuity is negligible, and the particles share similar mass, density etc. across the medium. It is evident that this approach would have limited applicability to many modern day industrial problems.

Among the particulate or discrete methods, an early development was the application of probabilistic Monte Carlo (MC) method (Rosato et al., 1986). Being probabilistic, this method involves displacing particles in a random walk manner and using an energy principle to accept or reject a given displacement. An MC simulation is defined as "a mathematical experiment by which the expected outcome of a stochastic process is estimated by random sampling from the probability density distributions that govern the events making up the process" (Sherritt et al., 2003). However there is no means to incorporate interparticle interactions, which play a central role if most granular mixing scenarios. The method has been found to be applicable in simpler geometries such as rotating cylinder systems when predicting axial mixing. The DEM addresses interparticle interactions and is capable of resolving complex flow and hence mixing dynamics among granular systems. It is arguably the most significant advancement in the modeling of granular mixing in recent years. While it has several advantages, the high computational cost has been a limiting factor. However, this is being mitigated by several advancements in hardware and software. Furthermore it has been shown that if one performs the analogue of grid independence of CFD simulations in a DEM simulations, one might find that increasing the number of particles will only have diminishing advantages

(Hassanpour et al., 2011) in many practical situations. Understanding of the kinematics of the problem at hand remains the key—the particle size (within a certain range) may not have a significant impact on a particular flow system while in problems such as microdynamics of advective flows over blades, it will have a significant role to play (Sarkar and Wassgren, 2015). Given the importance of the DEM in modeling granular mixing, the next section is devoted to providing a more detailed look at it.

The DEM and its application to granular mixing

The DEM, as the name suggests, models the granular material as a set of discrete units, elements, grains or what is generally referred to as particle'. The interactions among the grains and between them and geometry elements are the critical component of this method. For most practical powder mixing applications, it is not feasible to model the elements at the true (mean) particle size as the particles may be very small and the materials being mixed may have vastly different size distribution. Hence, the model elements have to be chosen such that the total number of elements in the simulation is reasonable. The definition of reasonable depends on the computing power and time at hand. Hence, the elemental interaction parameters are chosen such that the bulk flow behavior of the material is faithfully reproduced while keeping the computational cost in check. Traditionally, the DEM considers the elements as spheres. However, nonsphericity is usually achieved by using multi-sphere clusters to form one element (Kruggel-Emden et al., 2008). The individual unit spheres of a clustered element will not have internal interactions between them and will behave as a unit. The center of mass and moment of inertia is also altered accordingly. Natively nonspherical contact models have also been developed for specific applications such as bi-convex tablets (Kodam et al., 2012) and cylindrical elements (Kodam et al., 2010). A commercial software package known as ROCKY allows modeling nonspherical particles without resorting to combined-sphere method.

One aspect to keep in mind while deciding on the model element size is a critical *D/d* ratio where *D* may be a critical length or diameter associated with the equipment and *d* is the particle diameter. For example, in a cylindrical mixer, *D* may be the vessel diameter. For the physical material in a real life application, the *D/d* may range between 100–1000. A modeler has to choose the elemental diameter of the model material keeping in mind the computational efficiency and hence may need to use a *D/d* in the range of 20–50. Intuitive judgment alongside the observation of flow patterns and measurement of velocities to match them with those measured with experimental analysis must be made. In mixing of species with differing mean particle size, the mean particle diameter ratio must also be kept in mind. It may not be possible to maintain the exact ratio in cases where the differences are large (e.g., a pharmaceutical excipient with a 200 μm mean diameter mixed with an API of mean particle diameter of 10 μm).

The contact model dictates the response to a given interelement or element-geometry interaction. The Hertzian contact theory forms the basis of these models as defined by Cundall and Strack (1979). As an initial condition, a certain number of elements are introduced into a working domain which encompasses the equipment geometry and any other areas of interest for the simulation. The new elements may be introduced at a specific location in the domain and could be inducted all-at-once or continuously over time. They may be in a free fall state under gravity or may be introduced with a velocity distribution. The domain is in itself split into subdomains or cells for computational efficiency. The first operation then is to check for collisions. When elements are binned into subdomains, the search for their neighbors is more efficient as elements in faraway subdomains are unlikely to be neighbors to each other. Each element is defined by a center point coordinate and its radius. When the distance between the centers of two elements is equal to or less than the sum of their radii, a collision event has happened. For a plane-element interaction, only the element radius is used. For elements differing in radius and stiffness, effective quantities are computed using Eq. (3.7). The R_{eff} is the effective radius when two elements of radii R_1 and R_2 collide. Similarly the effective shear modulus G_{eff} is computed with the help of the material Poisson ratios ν_1 and ν_2.

$$R_{\text{eff}} = \frac{R_1 R_2}{R_1 + R_2}, \quad \frac{1}{G_{\text{eff}}} = \frac{2-\nu_1}{G_1} + \frac{2-\nu_2}{G_2} \tag{3.7}$$

A small (<5% of effective radius) overlap is allowed, which results in a contact force. There are several contact models available to choose from, and the choice of model must be made based on the desired physics. One of the features of the DEM is that it is amenable to significant changes in the contact models and hence can cover a wide variety of material interactions. Some of the commonly used contact models are the Hertz–Mindlin (Tsuji et al., 1992; Mindlin, 1949), Walton–Braun (Walton and Braun, 1986) and with subsequent add-ons for cohesion with models such as the Johnson–Kendall–Roberts (JKR) cohesion model (Johnson et al., 1971). Based on the forces in the system, equations of motion based on Newton's laws are formulated for every contact. An element may have more than one contact at a given time interval and the equations must compute the normal and tangential force components for each contact. The equations of motion must be solved numerically using a suitable time-stepping scheme to compute the acceleration, velocity and the new position of the element. The element is then moved to the new position and contact detection and all other computations are repeated in the new time step. Typical DEM time steps range in the vicinity of $10^{-4} - 10^{-7}$s. The small time step ensures that the movements between adjacent time steps are small resulting in a quasi-continuous motion and the system stability is maintained.

Once the model material element size is decided upon, certain properties related to the element and interactions must be furnished. For the element and geometry materials, the solid or true density, Young's modulus, and Poisson ratio are required. The shear modulus G is computed as:

$$G = \frac{E}{2(1-\nu)} \tag{3.8}$$

In Eq. (3.8), E and ν are the Young's modulus and Poisson's ratio respectively, of the particle material. Furthermore, the quantities required for modeling the interactions include the coefficients of restitution, static, and rolling friction. Additional parameters such as the cohesion energy density may be required for including additional cohesive forces. Some of the parameters are difficult to measure experimentally; for example, the shear modulus of the material making up a single powder particle, and the particle–particle and particle-geometry coefficient of restitution. Hence, appropriate judgment and fitting of these parameters is made. Some parameters are readily obtained from simple experiments, such as the bulk and tapped density, particle size distribution, shear modulus of geometric elements. The rolling and static friction parameters and intensity of cohesion also must be chosen to reproduce bulk behavior correctly. A measure such as the static angle of repose (AOR) is often used as a validation tool. There are other quantities and parameters such as bulk density, size distribution, and force/torque responses measured from rheometric experiments (Bharadwaj et al., 2010; Hare et al. 2015) which can be used to define a material model.

Several enhancements to the contact models to include additional physics calculations have been made over the years. These include granular heat transfer (Hunt, 1997; Chaudhuri et al., 2006), electrostatic interactions (Yang et al., 2015; Pei et al., 2015), van der Waal forces (Rhodes et al., 2001), and fluid forces (Kruggel-Emden et al., 2007).

3.5.1.2 Improvements in the efficiency of solution methods, algorithms, and compute architecture

Recent years have seen significant advancements in computing hardware, such that a common desktop computer is able to perform calculations that could only have been carried out on large compute clusters just a few years ago. The Compute Unified Device Architecture (CUDA) from NVIDIA was the pioneer in the area of GPU computing (Sanders and Kandrot, 2010). Continuously improving codes and algorithms utilizing message passing interface or OpenMP (Amritkar et al., 2014) have resulted in more efficient utilization of the multicore compute architecture resulting in better predictive models applicable to real-world problems (Shigeto and Sakai, 2011). Furthermore, the use of GPUs as computing devices has made hundreds of compute cores accessible on a desktop computer (Yue et al., 2014). With efficient programming, the CPU-GPU combination (Nishiura and Sakaguchi, 2010) has been proven to be extremely effective in accelerating the solution to most intensive of problems in granular flow and mixing (Ren et al., 2013; Radeke et al., 2010). As noted in an earlier section, in some cases the calculations are so fast that a process can be simulated and visualized almost in real time (Xu et al., 2011; Ye et al., 2011). Typical number of particles simulated on high-end clusters in the 1990s was in the range of 10–20 thousand. It increased about tenfold in the next decade. Now studies are coming out that simulate 4 million particles on a laptop using the GPU at an acceptable speed of 1 h compute time spent per second of simulated time (Govender et al., 2015).

3.5.1.3 Advancement in analysis techniques with commercial and open source software

A number of commercial, academic, and open source software has been developed which is useful in simulations of granular mixing operations. Prominent among commercial tools are EDEM (DEM Solutions Ltd.), PFC (Itasca Consulting Group Inc.) and ROCKY (ROCKY DEM Inc.). One of the popular open source codes is LIGGGHTS (DCS Computing).

Most of these tools allow for one- or two-way interaction with a fluid flow solver which may have application in certain types of mixing processes (Lim et al., 2013). Post processing using these commercial tools or open source tool like Paraview allows visualization of particle trajectories, velocities, stress zones etc. which can be time- and spatially averaged. These tools are continually being further enhanced to compute more properties of interest and are optimized to handle large amount of particle data. Dedicated software for post processing and visualizing DEM simulations has also entered the market (Particle Analytics).

3.5.2 Case study: creating a material model

This case study demonstrates how a material model is created for a real-world application of the DEM. It must be noted that hardware capabilities increase significantly every year and hence some of the approximations made can be relaxed depending on the available hardware and time. Material modeling for DEM-based process simulation is essential to ensure that the material behavior is correctly reproduced in the simulation. As noted in the previous sections, a modeler must work around the limitations imposed by computational cost (hardware and time) as well as the limited knowledge of material properties and physics. To elaborate on the latter, real materials have large variations in particle sizes, shapes, surface roughness, and particle-particle and particle-wall affinities. The exact measure of some of the quantities at that level, for example the van der Waal's or electrostatic forces is usually not available. To build a practicable model, one must restrict the model particles in terms of particle shape, size and its distribution, and often restrict to the use standard contact models with some occasional user defined changes plugged in. Hence, a trial and error type of an approach to optimize the control parameters must be adopted. The parameters to control are classified under particle and contact parameters. The particle parameters are the element size, particle size distribution (PSD), the solid density, the shear modulus, and the coefficient of restitution. The contact parameters for both interparticle and particle-geometry contacts are the two friction coefficients, the intensity of cohesive forces, and when applicable, any other body forces such as magnetic or electrostatic forces. The following step-wise approach can be adopted to create a material model.

1. Determine the bulk density and PSD of the material to be modeled. The model particles' solid density can be adjusted to ensure that the bulk density of the model material matches closely to that of the real material. The element size and PSD should ideally be as close

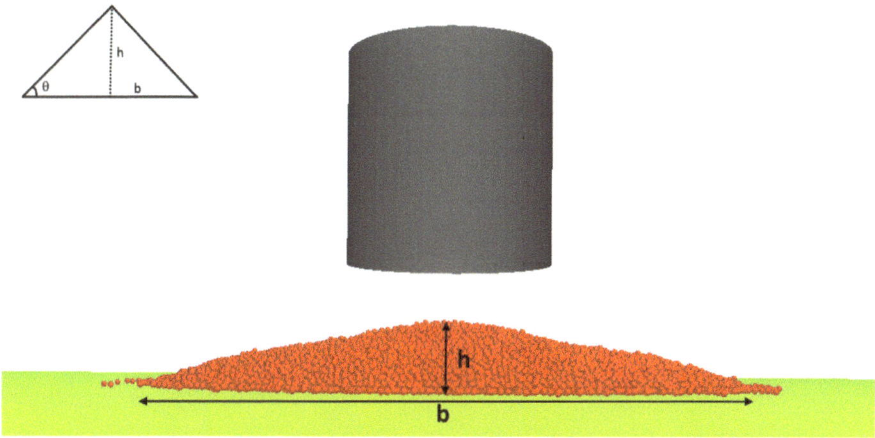

Figure 3.3 Measurement of the AOR using an inverted cup test.

to the real material as possible, but the *D/d*-based approach described in previous section can be adopted to develop a computationally efficient model.

2. Perform a static AOR test in the laboratory. A simple test can be to fill a cup with the material, seal the lid with a piece of paper, and place it upside down on a flat, smooth table. Slide out the paper and gently lift the cup vertically. In case of a conical heap, the base and height of the heap can be measured. A snapshot of a DEM simulation of such a test is shown in Fig. 3.3. The heap angle can then be defined as the arctangent of the ratio of the heap height to half of the base. The test must be repeated multiple times to get an averaged value to minimize errors. In some cases, the heap might not be perfectly conical. In such cases, the angle that the tangent to the heap surface makes near the edges of the heap can be measured using a protractor. If the heap is uneven due to cohesive nature of the material, multiple measurements on radial locations can be taken on a single heap and an average value can be chosen.
3. The control parameters must be adjusted with a number of test simulations in the form of a design of experiment so span the parametric space. Once the modeler develops an understanding of the impact of these parameters, the entire set of simulations does not have to be run repeatedly for modeling a different material. The experience gained helps in reducing the amount of work in successive models.
4. If the simple test is deemed insufficient for calibration, other more sophisticated methods can be adopted. In another method, the AOR tester, consisting of a funnel shaped hopper with a stirrer is simulated. This is particularly useful for powders with poor flowability. The flowing powder is collected on a flat base and the AOR is measured from the heap formed. The other advantage of this technique is that because material is flowing down freely in a dilated state, it packs in an unconfined heap and avoids any marginal bias that may creep in due to the cup-powder interaction and the speed of lifting the cup.

To illustrate the effect of the control parameters on the AOR, a representative study is presented. The coefficient of static friction (COSF), that of rolling friction (CORF) and the JKR cohesion energy density value (JKR-CED) are varied at two levels each; COSF at 0.3 and 0.8, CORF at 0.01 and 0.1, and JKR-CED at 0.0 and 0.1 J/m^2. The JKR cohesion model introduces an additional contact force between

Table 3.1 **Basic material properties**

Property	Particle material	Geometry material
Solid density (kg/m^3)	1500	2500
Shear modulus (Pa)	1.00E+06	1.00E+08
Material Poisson's ratio	0.25	0.25

Table 3.2 **Properties used in the parametric study**

Case #	PP-COSF	PP-CORF	PG-COSF	PG-CORF	PP-JKR-CED	PG-JKR-CED	AOR	Bulk density (kg/m^3)	% Change in BD
1	0.3	0.01	0.3	0.01	0	0	10	959.2	0.00
2	0.8	0.01	0.8	0.01	0	0	12	955.2	−0.42
3	0.3	0.1	0.3	0.1	0	0	18	957.6	−0.17
4	0.8	0.1	0.8	0.1	0	0	27.5	952	−0.75
5	0.3	0.01	0.3	0.01	0.1	0.1	20	952	−0.75
6	0.8	0.01	0.8	0.01	0.1	0.1	22.75	942.4	−1.75
7	0.3	0.1	0.3	0.1	0.1	0.1	24	950.4	−0.92
8	0.8	0.1	0.8	0.1	0.1	0.1	32	937.6	−2.25

interacting entities that is based on the area of contact. A constant parameter, cohesion energy density can be varied in the range of 0.0–0.3 J/m^2. The intensity of the cohesive attraction then depends on the extent of contact.

To keep the study simple, the particle–particle and particle–geometry (P–P and P–G) contacts are given the same values. The cup used in these simulations had a diameter and height of 80 mm each and it was completely filled with 55,000 spherical elements of diameter 2 mm. Simulations were set up using the basic properties listed in Table 3.1.

Table 3.2 shows the parameters used in this set of DEM simulations and the measured values of AOR. Fig. 3.4 shows the snapshots of the heaps formed for each case. It is notable that the shape of the heap changes considerably with the change in parameters.

In the base case (Case 1) with low friction coefficients and no cohesion, the heap is nearly conical and the AOR is 10 degrees. The elements chosen are perfect spheres with a constant size, and hence considerable rolling is expected, resulting in low AOR. This is evident by the following observation. In between Case 1 and Case 2, a relatively small increase in AOR is seen even when the COSF is increased significantly. However when the rolling resistance is increased (comparing Case 1 and Case 3), the AOR increases by about 80%. A similar increase can be observed between Case 3 and Case 4 when the static friction is also increased in addition to the rolling friction. These are rather extreme values chosen to highlight the impact and a modeler can choose a suitable in-between combination of the coefficients to

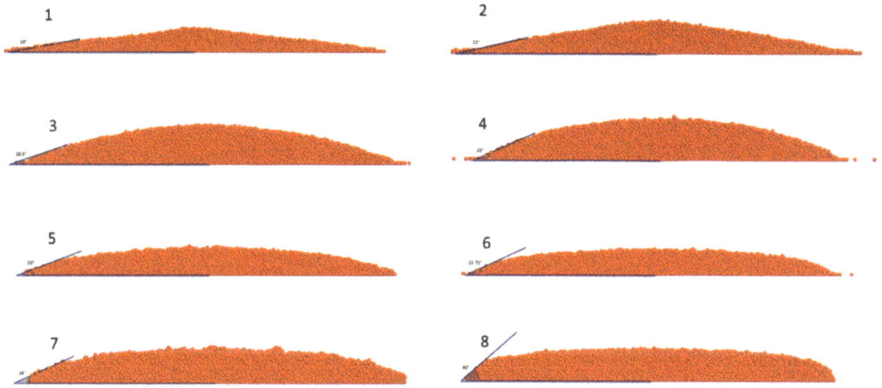

Figure 3.4 A simple method to measure AOR from a DEM simulation and the effect of change in friction and cohesion on the shape and angle of repose. The numbers 1 through 8 correspond to the parameter set listed in Table 3.2.

approach the desired flow behavior. Cases 5−8 are a repetition of the earlier combination with the addition of a moderate amount of interparticle cohesion. No cohesion has been considered between the particle and geometry. In practice, some adhesion can be included which will also resist the movement of particles in contact with the base and may lead to higher AOR. On comparing Case 1 and Case 5, it is evident that the addition of cohesive forces significantly changes the flow behavior and the AOR is doubled. Later combinations show that increasing friction coefficients alongside the cohesion will further add to the trend.

The table also shows the extent of change in the model material bulk density which a modeler must take note of. A particle solid density of 1500 kg/m^3 resulted in the packed bulk density (before the cup is lifted) for the base case of 959.2 kg/m^3. The other cases are evaluated relative to the base case. The variations can be considered to be insignificant until a combination of high factors comes into play, for example, in Case 8. Whether a variation of ~2% is significant or not depends on the problem at hand, but the take away message is that it is a factor to watch out for. The solid density can be scaled down and the calculations run again in case a better match of bulk density is desired.

Typical pharmaceutical powders have AOR values ranging between 25−40 degrees. Using monodispersed spherical elements, one can get AOR up to low 30 degrees. Typically, materials displaying higher values also have high cohesion, wide size distributions, and nonspherical particles. Using a nonspherical element shape, such as one with a combination of two spheres, one can achieve better match with bulk density (as the voidage is higher).

A common approach to add nonsphericity to particles is by defining particles made of two of more overlapping spherical units, often referred to as a glued sphere approach (Kruggel-Emden et al., 2008; Kodam et al., 2009). Using this, we define particles made up of two spheres of diameter 2 mm each, that overlap by 1 mm. Hence, the circumference of one sphere passes through the center of the other and

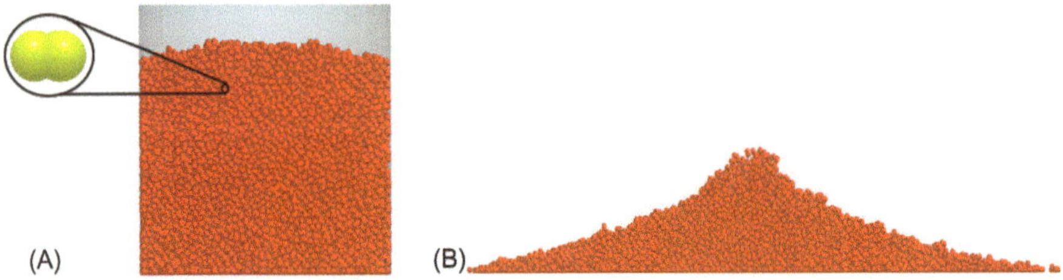

Figure 3.5 Nonspherical particles in a cup-lift experiment for determination of the AOR. Due to significantly lower bulk density and cohesive nature of the material, there is not enough material to carry out the test reliably with this method.

Figure 3.6 A low (15 degrees) AOR can be measured if the number of elements are doubled in the cup-lift experiment with nonspherical elements.

the (length/diameter) aspect ratio is 2.0. If the spherical particles in the same AOR tests are now replaced by these new particles, two challenges appear immediately. Firstly, much less mass of material will fill the same volume, hence the bulk density will be lower; and secondly there might not be enough particles in the system to gauge the AOR correctly (Fig. 3.5). A demonstrates the setup with the new particles in the same 80 mm × 80 mm cup. The inset shows the particle shape in more detail. However, in this case the cup was filled after about 27,000 particles were poured in. Low values of COSF (0.3), CORF (0.01) and JKR-CED (0.1) were used in this set of simulations. After the cup is lifted, a conical heap is formed but the shape is such that measuring AOR would neither be easy nor representative of the material bulk properties. To maintain the same number of elements, the cup length is then increased and 55,000 particles are used in another simulation. The heap obtained is shown in Fig. 3.6. The AOR may now be measured, however the amount of material relative to particle size may still not be enough. To test if this is indeed the true AOR for this material model, more material is slowly poured in on the heap until a steady angle is achieved. It was found that the AOR stabilized at a value of about 35 degrees and the total number of elements in the heap at the time was about 262,000 as shown in Fig. 3.7. When simulations with higher values of JKR-CED were carried out, the material retained the shape of the cup even after the cup was lifted, hence no heap was available.

This learning can now be used to adopt a more reliable calibration technique as demonstrated in Fig. 3.8. A hopper with a central stirrer is placed above a base to resemble a commercially available AOR test equipment. The hopper is filled with 100,000 particles. Material is allowed to fall on to the base as the stirrer is slowly rotated. AOR is measured after the material has consolidated at the bottom. Once

Figure 3.7 When additional material is poured on the heap continuously, a steady AOR is achieved.

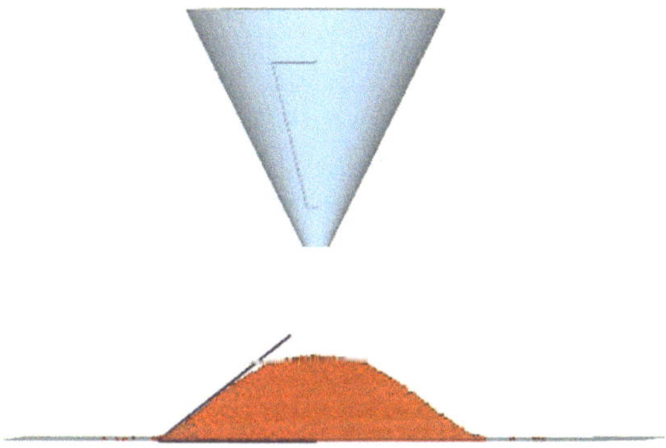

Figure 3.8 New experimental setup with a hopper and a stirrer for gently dropping a specific amount of material to form a heap. The heap is well formed and a steady AOR of 35 degrees is measured.

this method is established, the material solid density can be chosen carefully to achieve the desired bulk density. This illustrative case study describes a general technique for material modeling and determining the impact of model parameters.

3.6 Summary and outlook

Powder flow and mixing are critical for numerous industries. Granular materials, owing to their complexities, pose a daunting challenge when mixing and maintaining their blends. Research and development to increase process understanding, control and risk mitigation have been carried out for the past several decades. Research has provided insights into mixing mechanisms and how to determine the dominant mode of mixing in a particular process. Common techniques of mixing have followed this understanding and various types of mixers have been developed. The developments in visualization and measurement techniques provide more insights into the internal processes in a mixer. The discipline has come a long way, yet a lot more remains to be done. Computational modeling and simulation has added additional dimensions to the understanding of mixing processes.

The aim of modeling is to act as a predictive as well as a design and troubleshooting tool. Most models aim to predict the mixing times and final blend quality thereby enhancing process understanding, minimizing material and time lost in testing and through the process knowledge, reducing risk in situations like scale-up and equipment change. Validated models, however, can also provide enhanced understanding of the equipment-material interaction and expose problem areas such as dead or low velocity zones, high-shear or compaction zones. This can help a process designer keep a check on the amount, rate and distribution of the agitation the material is receiving which can be critical for some formulations. Low velocity or dead zones may indicate areas of poor mixing while if a region is receiving significantly high shear due to equipment design and operation, material in those regions can be adversely impacted with issues such as overlubrication in pharmaceutical blends. Similarly if the material is unduly being compressed in some regions, there can be caking or sticking to equipment walls. This knowledge of internal mechanics can be used to redesign equipment to ensure blend quality.

The future entails development and implementation of more efficient devices, real-time sensor-analytical tools and more efficient and accurate numerical models. Exciting challenges lie ahead in this extremely interesting discipline.

Acknowledgements

The author would like to thank DEM Solutions Inc., creator of the DEM simulation software EDEM, for providing licenses and support and The Aditya Birla Science and Technology Company Pvt. Ltd. for providing hardware support.

References

Ahmed, S., John, S., et al., 2012. Experimental study of density segregation at end walls in a horizontal rotating cylinder saturated with fluid: friction to lubrication transition. Granular Matter. 14 (3), 319–332.

Alchikh-Sulaiman, B., Ein-Mozaffari, F., et al., 2015. Evaluation of poly-disperse solid particles mixing in a slant cone mixer using discrete element method. Chem. Eng. Res. Des. 96, 196–213.

Alchikh-Sulaiman, B., Alian, M., et al., 2016. Using the discrete element method to assess the mixing of polydisperse solid particles in a rotary drum. Particuology. 25, 133–142.

Alian, M., Ein-Mozaffari, F., et al., 2015. Using discrete element method to analyze the mixing of the solid particles in a slant cone mixer. Chem. Eng. Res. Des. 93, 318–329.

Alizadeh, E., Bertrand, F., et al., 2014. Discrete element simulation of particle mixing and segregation in a tetrapodal blender. Comput. Chem. Eng. 64, 1–12.

Allen, T., 2003. Powder Sampling and Particle Size Determination, first ed. Elsevier, Amsterdam.

Amritkar, A., Deb, S., et al., 2014. Efficient parallel CFD-DEM simulations using OpenMP. J. Comput. Phys. 256, 501–519.

Arratia, P.E., Duong, N.-h., et al., 2006. A study of the mixing and segregation mechanisms in the Bohle Tote blender via DEM simulations. Powder Technol. 164 (1), 50–57.
Bakeev, K.A., 2010. Process Analytical Technology: Spectroscopic Tools and Implementation Strategies for the Chemical and Pharmaceutical Industries. second ed. Wiley, Chichester.
Berntsson, O., Danielsson, L., et al., 2002. Quantitative in-line monitoring of powder blending by near infrared reflection spectroscopy. Powder Technol. 123 (2), 185–193.
Berthiaux, H., Marikh, K., et al., 2008. Continuous mixing of powder mixtures with pharmaceutical process constraints. Chem. Eng. Process. Process Intensif. 47 (12), 2315–2322.
Bertrand, F., Leclaire, L.A., et al., 2005. DEM-based models for the mixing of granular materials. Chem. Eng. Sci. 60 (8–9), 2517–2531.
Bharadwaj, R., Ketterhagen, W.R., et al., 2010. Discrete element simulation study of a Freeman powder rheometer. Chem. Eng. Sci. 65 (21), 5747–5756.
Boukouvala, F., Dubey, A., et al., 2012. Computational approaches for studying the granular dynamics of continuous blending processes, 2—population balance and data-based methods. Macromol. Mater. Eng. 297 (1), 9–19.
Bridgwater, J., 1976. Fundamental powder mixing mechanisms. Powder Technol. 15 (2), 215–236.
Bridgwater, J., 2010. Mixing of particles and powders: where next? Particuology 8 (6), 563–567.
Bridgwater, J., 2012. Mixing of powders and granular materials by mechanical means—a perspective. Particuology 10 (4), 397–427.
Broadbent, C.J., Bridgwater, J., et al., 1993. A phenomenological study of a batch mixer using a positron camera. Powder Technol. 76 (3), 317–329.
Carley-Macauly, K.W., Donald, M.B., 1962. The mixing of solids in tumbling mixers—I. Chem. Eng. Sci. 17 (7), 493–506.
Carley-Macauly, K.W., Donald, M.B., 1964. The mixing of solids in tumbling mixers—II. Chem. Eng. Sci. 19 (3), 191–199.
Chandratilleke, G.R., Yu, A.B., et al., 2012. A DEM study of the mixing of particles induced by a flat blade. Chem. Eng. Sci. 79, 54–74.
Chaudhuri, B., Muzzio, F.J., et al., 2006. Modeling of heat transfer in granular flow in rotating vessels. Chem. Eng. Sci. 61 (19), 6348–6360.
Chen, H., Zhao, X.-q, et al., 2016. Radial mixing and segregation of granular bed bi-dispersed both in particle size and density within horizontal rotating drum. Trans. Nonferrous Met. Soc. China 26 (2), 527–535.
Cleary, P.W., Sinnott, M.D., 2008. Assessing mixing characteristics of particle-mixing and granulation devices. Particuology 6 (6), 419–444.
Cooke, M.H., Stephens, D.J., et al., 1976. Powder mixing—a literature survey. Powder Technol. 15 (1), 1–20.
Cundall, P.A., Strack, O.D.L., 1979. A discrete numerical model for granular assemblies. Geotechnique 29 (1), 47–65.
Danckwerts, P.V., 1952. Temperature effects accompanying the absorption of gases in liquids. Appl. Sci. Res., Sect. A. 3 (5), 385–390.
Deng, X., Scicolone, J.V., et al., 2013. Discrete element method simulation of cohesive particles mixing under magnetically assisted impaction. Powder Technol. 243, 96–109.
Devore, J.L., 1982. Probability and Statistics for Engineering and the Sciences, ed. Brooks/Cole, Monterey, CA.
Dubey, A., Sarkar, A., et al., 2011. Computational approaches for studying the granular dynamics of continuous blending processes, 1—DEM based methods. Macromol. Mater. Eng. 296 (3–4), 290–307.

Dubey, A., Vanarase, A.U., et al., 2012. Impact of process parameters on critical performance attributes of a continuous blender—a DEM-based study. AIChE J. 58 (12), 3676–3684.

Fan, L.T., Too, J.R., et al., 1985. Stochastic simulation of residence time distribution curves. Chem. Eng. Sci. 40 (9), 1743–1749.

Fan, L.T., Chen, Y.-M., et al., 1990. Recent developments in solids mixing. Powder Technol. 61 (3), 255–287.

Florian, M., Velázquez, C., et al., 2014. New continuous tumble mixer characterization. Powder Technol. 256, 188–195.

Florian-Algarin, M., Méndez, R., 2015. Blend uniformity and powder phenomena inside the continuous tumble mixer using DEM simulations. AIChE J. 61 (3), 792–801.

Gao, Y., Ierapetritou, M., et al., 2012. Periodic section modeling of convective continuous powder mixing processes. AIChE J. 58 (1), 69–78.

Govender, N., Rajamani, R.K., et al., 2015. Discrete element simulation of mill charge in 3D using the BLAZE-DEM GPU framework. Miner. Eng. 79, 152–168.

Groh, C., Rehberg, I., et al., 2011. Observation of density segregation inside migrating dunes. Phys. Rev. E. 84 (5), 050301.

Gy, P., 1998. Sampling for Analytical Purposes, ed. John Wiley & Sons, Chichester and New York, NY.

Gy, P., 2004. Sampling of discrete materials—a new introduction to the theory of sampling: I. Qualitative approach. Chemom. Intell. Lab. Syst. 74 (1), 7–24.

Gyenis, J., 1999. Assessment of mixing mechanism on the basis of concentration pattern. Chem. Eng. Process. 38, 665–674.

Gyenis, J., Ulbert, Z., et al., 1999. Discrete particle simulation of flow regimes in bulk solids mixing and conveying. Powder Technol. 104 (3), 248–257.

Halidan, M., Chandratilleke, G.R., et al., 2014. Prediction of the mixing behaviour of binary mixtures of particles in a bladed mixer. Chem. Eng. Sci. 120, 37–48.

Hare, C., Zafar, U., et al., 2015. Analysis of the dynamics of the FT4 powder rheometer. Powder Technol. 285, 123–127.

Harnby, N., 2000. An engineering view of pharmaceutical powder mixing. Pharm. Sci. Technol. Today 3 (9), 303–309.

Harwood, C.F., Walanski, K., et al., 1975. The performance of continuous mixers for dry powders. Powder Technol. 11 (3), 289–296.

Hassanpour, A., Tan, H., et al., 2011. Analysis of particle motion in a paddle mixer using discrete element method (DEM). Powder Technol. 206 (1–2), 189–194.

Hersey, J.A., 1975. Ordered mixing: a new concept in powder mixing practice. Powder Technol. 11 (1), 41–44.

Hopkins, M.A., Shen, H.H., 1992. A Monte Carlo solution for rapidly shearing granular flows based on the kinetic theory of dense gases. J. Fluid. Mech. 244, 477–491.

Huang, A.-N., Kuo, H.-P., 2014. Developments in the tools for the investigation of mixing in particulate systems—a review. Adv. Powder Technol. 25 (1), 163–173.

Hunt, M.L., 1997. Discrete element simulations for granular material flows: effective thermal conductivity and self-diffusivity. Int. J.Heat Mass Transf. 40 (13), 3059–3068.

Inoue, I., Yamaguchi, K., 1969. Particle motion in mixer and mixing process-mixing in a two-dimensional V-type mixer. Chem. Eng. 33 (3), 286–292, a1.

Jenkins, J.T., Richman, M.W., 1985. Kinetic theory for plane flows of a dense gas of identical, rough, inelastic, circular disks. Phys. Fluids (1958–1988). 28 (12), 3485–3494.

Jiang, M., Zhao, Y., et al., 2011. Enhancing mixing of particles by baffles in a rotating drum mixer. Particuology 9 (3), 270–278.

Johnson, K.L., Kendall, K. et al. Surface Energy and the Contact of Elastic Solids, Proc. Royal Soc. London A, 324, 1971, 301–313.

Jop, P., Forterre, Y., et al., 2006. A constitutive law for dense granular flows. Nature, 441 (7094), 727–730.

Kaye, B.H., 1997. Powder Mixing. first ed. Springer, The Netherlands.

Khakhar, D.V., McCarthy, J.J., et al., 1997. Transverse flow and mixing of granular materials in a rotating cylinder. Phys. Fluids. 9 (1), 31–43.

Kodam, M., Bharadwaj, R., et al., 2009. Force model considerations for glued-sphere discrete element method simulations. Chem. Eng. Sci. 64 (15), 3466–3475.

Kodam, M., Bharadwaj, R., et al., 2010. Cylindrical object contact detection for use in discrete element method simulations. Part I—contact detection algorithms. Chem. Eng. Sci. 65 (22), 5852–5862.

Kodam, M., Curtis, J., et al., 2012. Discrete element method modeling of bi-convex pharmaceutical tablets: contact detection algorithms and validation. Chem. Eng. Sci. 69 (1), 587–601.

Koller, D.M., Posch, A., et al., 2011. Continuous quantitative monitoring of powder mixing dynamics by near-infrared spectroscopy. Powder Technol. 205 (1–3), 87–96.

Kruggel-Emden, H., Simsek, E., et al., 2007. Review and extension of normal force models for the discrete element method. Powder Technol. 171 (3), 157–173.

Kruggel-Emden, H., Rickelt, S., et al., 2008. A study on the validity of the multi-sphere discrete element method. Powder Technol. 188 (2), 153–165.

Kushner IV, J., 2012. Incorporating Turbula mixers into a blending scale-up model for evaluating the effect of magnesium stearate on tablet tensile strength and bulk specific volume. Int. J. Pharm. 429 (1–2), 1–11.

Lacey, P.M.C., 1954. Developments in the theory of particle mixing. J. Appl. Chem. 4 (5), 257–268.

Lemieux, M., Léonard, G., et al., 2008. Large-scale numerical investigation of solids mixing in a V-blender using the discrete element method. Powder Technol. 181 (2), 205–216.

Lim, E.W.C., Tan, R.B.H., et al., 2013. Mixing behaviors of wet granular materials in gas fluidized bed systems. AIChE J. 59 (11), 4058–4067.

Manickam, S.S., Shah, R., et al., 2010. Investigating mixing in a multi-dimensional rotary mixer: experiments and simulations. Powder Technol. 201 (1), 83–92.

Marbach, R., 2005. A new method for multivariate calibration. J. Near Infrared Spectrosc. 13 (5), 241–254.

Marigo, M., Cairns, D.L., et al., 2011. Developing mechanistic understanding of granular behaviour in complex moving geometry using the discrete element method: Part B: investigation of flow and mixing in the Turbula® mixer. Powder Technol. 212 (1), 17–24.

Marigo, M., Cairns, D.L., et al., 2012. A numerical comparison of mixing efficiencies of solids in a cylindrical vessel subject to a range of motions. Powder Technol. 217, 540–547.

Marigo, M., Davies, M., et al., 2013. Application of Positron Emission Particle Tracking (PEPT) to validate a discrete element method (DEM) model of granular flow and mixing in the Turbula mixer. Int. J. Pharm. 446 (1–2), 46–58.

Mindlin, R.D., 1949. Compliance of elastic bodies in contact. J. Appl. Mech. 16, 259–268.

Moakher, M., Shinbrot, T., et al., 2000. Experimentally validated computations of flow, mixing and segregation of non-cohesive grains in 3D tumbling blenders. Powder Technol. 109 (1–3), 58–71.

Muzzio, F.J., Robinson, P., et al., 1997. Sampling practices in powder blending. Int. J. Pharm. 155 (2), 153–178.

Muzzio, F.J., Goodridge, C.L., et al., 2003. Sampling and characterization of pharmaceutical powders and granular blends. Int. J. Pharm. 250 (1), 51–64.
Nishiura, D., Sakaguchi, H., 2010. High-efficiency algorithm for DEM simulation on GPU. Trans. Jpn. Soc. Comput. Eng. Sci. 2010, 20100007–20100007.
Obregón, L., Velázquez, C., 2007. Discrimination limit between mean gray values for the prediction of powder concentrations. Powder Technol. 175 (1), 8–13.
Osorio, J.G., Muzzio, F.J., 2015. Evaluation of resonant acoustic mixing performance. Powder Technol. 278, 46–56.
Osorio, J.G., Stuessy, G., et al., 2014. Characterization of pharmaceutical powder blends using in situ near-infrared chemical imaging. Chem. Eng. Sci. 108 (0), 244–257.
Ottino, J.M., Khakhar, D.V., 2000. Mixing and segregation of granular materials. Annu. Rev. Fluid Mech. 32 (1), 55.
Ottino, J.M., Shinbrot, T., 1999. Comparing extremes: mixing of fluids, mixing of solids. Mixing 373, 163–186.
Pei, C., Wu, C.-Y., et al., 2015. DEM-CFD modeling of particle systems with long-range electrostatic interactions. AIChE J. 61 (6), 1792–1803.
Pernenkil, L., Cooney, C.L., 2006. A review on the continuous blending of powders. Chem. Eng. Sci. 61 (2), 720–742.
Pingali, K., Mendez, R., et al., 2010. Evaluation of strain-induced hydrophobicity of pharmaceutical blends and its effect on drug release rate under multiple compression conditions. Drug Dev. Ind. Pharm. 37 (4), 428–435.
Pingali, K., Mendez, R., et al., 2011. Mixing order of glidant and lubricant—influence on powder and tablet properties. Int. J. Pharm. 409 (0), 269–277.
Poole, K., Taylor, R., et al., 1964. Mixing Powders to Fine-Scale Homogeneity: Studies of Batch Mixing. UK Atomic Energy Authority Research Group, Harwell.
Portillo, P.M., Ierapetritou, M.G., et al., 2008. Characterization of continuous convective powder mixing processes. Powder Technol. 182 (3), 368–378.
Poux, M., Fayolle, P., et al., 1991. Powder mixing: some practical rules applied to agitated systems. Powder Technol. 68 (3), 213–234.
Qi, H., Xu, J., et al., 2015. Numerical investigation of granular flow similarity in rotating drums. Particuology 22, 119–127.
Radeke, C.A., Glasser, B.J., et al., 2010. Large-scale powder mixer simulations using massively parallel GPUarchitectures. Chem. Eng. Sci. 65 (24), 6435–6442.
Remy, B., Canty, T.M., et al., 2010. Experiments and simulations of cohesionless particles with varying roughness in a bladed mixer. Chem. Eng. Sci. 65 (16), 4557–4571.
Ren, X., Xu, J., et al., 2013. GPU-based discrete element simulation on a tote blender for performance improvement. Powder Technol. 239, 348–357.
Rhodes, M., 1990. Principles of Powder Technology, ed. John Wiley & Sons, UK.
Rhodes, M.J., Wang, X.S., et al., 2001. Use of discrete element method simulation in studying fluidization characteristics: influence of interparticle force. Chem. Eng. Sci. 56 (1), 69–76.
Rosato, A., Prinz, F., et al., 1986. Monte Carlo simulation of particulate matter segregation. Powder Technol. 49 (1), 59–69.
Rutgers, R., 1965. Longitudinal mixing of granular material flowing through a rotating cylinder: Part I. Descriptive and theoretical. Chem. Eng. Sci. 20 (12), 1079–1087.
Sanders, J., Kandrot, E., 2010. CUDA by Example: An Introduction to General-Purpose GPU Programming. ed. Addison-Wesley Professional, Upper Saddle River, NJ.
Sarkar, A., Wassgren, C.R., 2009. Simulation of a continuous granular mixer: effect of operating conditions on flow and mixing. Chem. Eng. Sci. 64 (11), 2672–2682.

Sarkar, A., Wassgren, C., 2010. Continuous blending of cohesive granular material. Chem. Eng. Sci. Available from: http://dx.doi.org/10.1016/j.ces.2010.04.011.
Sarkar, A., Wassgren, C.R., 2015. Effect of particle size on flow and mixing in a bladed granular mixer. AIChE J. 61 (1), 46–57.
Sekulic, S.S., Ward, H.W., et al., 1996. On-line monitoring of powder blend homogeneity by near-infrared spectroscopy. Anal. Chem. 68 (3), 509–513.
Sekulic, S.S., Wakeman, J., et al., 1998. Automated system for the on-line monitoring of powder blending processes using near-infrared spectroscopy: Part II. Qualitative approaches to blend evaluation. J. Pharm. Biomed. Anal. 17 (8), 1285–1309.
Sen, M., Dubey, A., et al., 2013. Mathematical development and comparison of a hybrid PBM-DEM description of a continuous powder mixing process. J. Powder Technol. 2013, 11.
Sherritt, R.G., Chaouki, J., et al., 2003. Axial dispersion in the three-dimensional mixing of particles in a rotating drum reactor. Chem. Eng. Sci. 58 (2), 401–415.
Shi, W., Hajedemos, D., et al., 2013. An energetic approach of powder mixing by manipulating cohesive interaction in a magnetic field. Powder Technol. 235, 400–404.
Shigeto, Y., Sakai, M., 2011. Parallel computing of discrete element method on multi-core processors. Particuology. 9 (4), 398–405.
Shinbrot, T., Khakhar, D., et al., 1997. A simple model for granular convection. Phys. Rev. Lett. 79 (5), 829–832.
Soni, R.K., Mohanty, R., et al., 2016. Numerical analysis of mixing of particles in drum mixers using DEM. Adv. Powder Technol. Available from: http://dx.doi.org/10.1016/j.apt.2016.01.016.
Tang, P., Puri, V.M., 2004. Methods for minimizing segregation: a review. Part. Sci. Technol. 22 (4), 321–337.
Tsuji, Y., Tanaka, T., et al., 1992. Lagrangian numerical simulation of plug flow of cohesionless particles in a horizontal pipe. Powder Technol. 71 (3), 239–250.
Walton, O.R., Braun, R.L., 1986. Viscosity, granular-temperature, and stress calculations for shearing assemblies of inelastic, frictional disks. J. Rheol. 30 (5), 949–980.
Wightman, C., Muzzio, F.J., et al., 1996. A quantitative image analysis method for characterizing mixtures of granular materials. Powder Technol. 89 (2), 165–176.
Xiao, X., Tan, Y., et al., 2015. Numerical investigation on the effect of the particle feeding order on the degree of mixing using DEM. Proc. Eng. 102, 1850–1856.
Xu, J., Qi, H., et al., 2011. Quasi-real-time simulation of rotating drum using discrete element method with parallel GPU computing. Particuology 9 (4), 446–450.
Yang, J., Wu, C.-Y., et al., 2015. DEM analysis of the effect of electrostatic interaction on particle mixing for carrier-based dry powder inhaler formulations. Particuology 23, 25–30.
Ye, J., Chen, J.-X., et al., 2011. Modeling and rendering of real-time large-scale granular flow scene on GPU. Proc. Environ. Sci. 10 (Part B), 1035–1045.
Yu, F., Zhou, G., et al., 2015. Enhanced axial mixing of rotating drums with alternately arranged baffles. Powder Technol. 286, 276–287.
Yue, X., Zhang, H., et al., 2014. Parallelization of a DEM code based on CPU-GPU heterogeneous architecture. Parallel Comput. Fluid Dyn. 405, 149–159.
Zhou, Z., Li, J., et al., 2016. Enhancing mixing of cohesive particles by baffles in a rotary drum. Particuology 25, 104–110.

Dry granulation process modeling

4

A. Michrafy[1], *A. Zavaliangos*[2] *and J.C. Cunningham*[3]
[1]CNRS-Mines Albi, Albi, France, [2]Drexel University, Philadelphia, PA, United States, [3]Johnson & Johnson Pharmaceutical R&D, Spring House, PA, United States

4.1 Introduction

The aim of this chapter is to present the state of current research and development on modeling of the dry granulation process for pharmaceutical applications. First, the roller compaction technology and theoretical background of the process are introduced and second, the significant progress in instrumentations and measurements is reviewed and discussed in light of common problems known in the process. Then, the existing modeling tools are reported and discussed according to their contribution to the process. The approach of finite element method (FEM) of roller compaction process, which is the most performed, is developed. In this context, different simulation techniques for the compaction process are introduced and requirements for FEM implementation of roller compaction are summarized. Experimental validations of two-dimensional (2D) and three-dimensional (3D) FEM for modeling pharmaceutical powders have been attempted to predict density and roll pressure distributions. The current state-of-the-art procedures in this field are discussed. Two case studies are presented with application to pharmaceutical powders. The first case, in two dimensions, demonstrates the capabilities of FEM modeling of roller compaction process to gain greater physical understanding of the process by examination of field variables, for example, stress, strain, velocity, and density distribution of the ribbon. The second, in three dimensions, is about the prediction of pressure and density distributions across the ribbon width. The model predictions are validated using experimental data. Limitations of the model predictions and challenges of the application of modeling are discussed.

4.2 Challenges in dry granulation modeling and recent progress

Dry granulation is a powder agglomeration process used in a variety of industries including pharmaceutical, mineral, and chemical industries. In the pharmaceutical industry, the dry granulation method, which is a continuum process well suited for active pharmaceutical ingredients that are sensitive to water and other solvents, is used to improve the flowability of powders by increasing the particle size. This operation is achieved using a roller press, which can have different

Predictive Modeling of Pharmaceutical Unit Operations. DOI: http://dx.doi.org/10.1016/B978-0-08-100154-7.00004-1

configurations and equipment designs (presented next). In this process, ribbons are formed by the roller press and milled in granules to be processed effectively and efficiently further in the tableting process. The action of the process leads modifications of mechanical properties of powders at particle and assemblies levels with impact on the granule behavior and tablet strength. Progress in experimental investigations has allowed confirming these changes (Freitag et al., 2004), but full understanding of the process remains difficult, in particular for the roller compaction step, which has the most significant effect on the granule properties. The development of a predictive model for roller compaction is promising for providing important insight at the local scale and allowing significant advancement in the understanding, design, optimization, and control of the process.

4.2.1 Roller compaction technology

The roller compaction process is based on feeding powders between two counterrotating rolls; the first is fixed in position, whereas the second is allowed to move in one plane under the action of hydraulic pressure. This pressure, applied evenly across the entering amount of material, causes the material to be compacted into a ribbon that subsequently is reduced in size to granules using an appropriate milling process. The rollers can be mounted so that their axes of rotation are vertical (Alexanderwerk, Komarek), inclined (Gerteis), or horizontal (Fitzpatrick). Fig. 4.1A shows a schematic of a typical roller press with horizontal feeding and a vertical axis. As a general rule, the main process steps are feeding, compaction, and size reduction. Each step is an important factor in the process. Depending on material properties, the feeding devices (hopper and screw feeder) are critical in the control of the material entering into the compaction zone. Indeed, the materials must be presented to the rollers into a continuous and uniform manner in order to achieve a consistent ribbon. To limit the loss of powders from roller sides (Parikh, 1997),

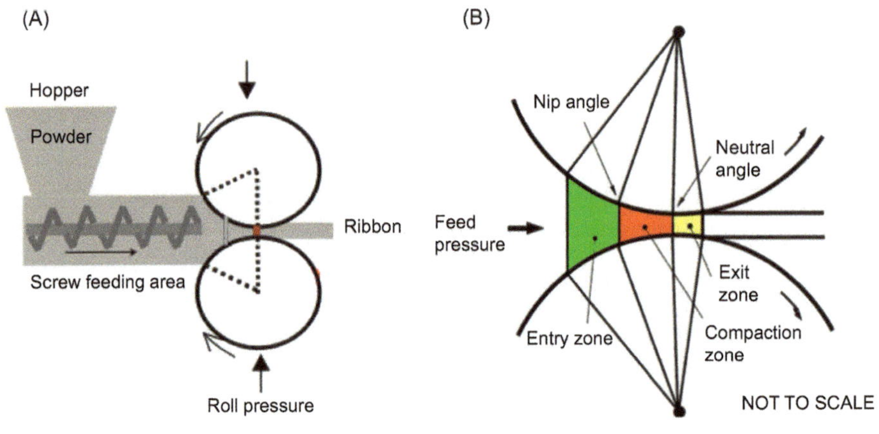

Figure 4.1 (A) Schematic roller press with horizontal feeding and vertical axis and (B) schematic of roller compaction regions and nip angle.

roller presses are generally equipped with a sealing system. Two types of side seals are mainly designed, stationary side seals (cheek plates) that reduce powder loss on roll sides and a rimmed roll that confines the powder during its movement toward the gap (Funakoshi et al., 1977).

In the pharmaceutical industry, different roller press designs are used. Each technology has advantages and weaknesses depending on raw material properties. In general, for noncohesive powders, vertical feed systems, which are dependent on gravity, tend to maintain a uniform powder fill weight into the compaction zone, whereas for light bulk density materials (fine powders), the horizontal or inclined feeding forces the material to be drawn into the compaction zone. However, for poorly flowing powders, a vacuum deaeration system is often used to improve the delivery of material to the rollers.

4.2.2 Theoretical background

As mentioned previously, in the roller compaction process, two parts are combined to work in a coordinated manner. The feeding system leads to improvement of the delivery of raw material to the rollers. Then, the material is drawn toward the narrow space separating the rolls (roll gap) where a high stress is applied to form the ribbon. For horizontal and inclined roller presses, the screw feeder achieving a uniform and continuous flow should be synchronized with the speed of the rollers in order to avoid underfeeding or overfeeding problems (Guigon and Simon, 2003). A correlation between the screw speed and the roller velocity is needed to determine the area of the good compaction rate of the roller press (Simon and Guigon, 2003; Michrafy et al., 2011a,b; Lecompte et al., 2005).

To describe the process by which the granular medium is drawn and compacted between rolls, Johanson introduced the concept of the nip angle, shown in Fig. 4.1B, which defines two contiguous zones. Before the nip angle, the granular medium is transported with relative sliding on the roll. Once the nip angle is reached, the powder is drawn by sticking to the roll surface and is densified by deforming under the high roll pressure.

To predict the powder behavior between rolls, Johanson (1965) introduced a continuous model. The granular medium was considered compressible and cohesive and could be characterized with the Jenike–Shield yield function (Jenike and Shield, 1959). In this model, the granular material is described by the internal friction angle, the wall friction angle, and the compressibility coefficient. Following these assumptions, two equations are used to determine the nip angle and pressure distribution in the compaction area. The merit of the Johanson model is to propose a semianalytic description of the basic properties of a granular material and the rolling process variables. However, this model has limitations (Sommer and Hauser, 2003) and shows discrepancies between calculated and measured values for compressible material. The basic description of the powder behavior and the a priori definition of two zones with two types of properties of contact (slip and stick) to determine the nip angle are the most critical hypotheses. To improve the understanding of the process and to develop a new approach to better predict the final properties of the ribbon, other models of roller compaction were developed for pharmaceutical applications. A review of some was published in Dec et al. (2003).

4.2.3 Common problems of roller compaction and progress

There are several known common problems in the roller compaction process, including heterogeneity of the ribbon's properties, which controls the heterogeneity of granule's quality; air entrapped in fine powders, which may cause instabilities in the feeding system and poor quality of ribbon; and scalability of the process, which currently limits the widespread use of the process in the pharmaceutical industry.

Significant progress has been made over the past two decades in the instrumentation of the process to acquire observations and measurements to better understand the roller compaction process. The heterogeneity of properties over the compacted ribbon width is one of the complex features that has been demonstrated in several experimental investigations. Tundermann and Singer (1969) performed roll compaction of sponge-iron powders MH300 and MH100, and showed nonuniform density over the ribbon width with a distribution that depended on the particle size of the powder. Simon and Guigon (2003) showed the role of the feed screw on the heterogeneity observed on a ribbon of compacted lactose monohydrate mixed with 4% coal. Similarly, in Michrafy et al. (2011a,b), a periodic alternation of darker and lighter zones was revealed in ribbons of microcrystalline cellulose (MCC) using light transmission. In this work, measurements of the density distributions using a mercury porosimeter did not show agreements between the high densities and darker areas. The measured density distribution was higher in the center than at the edges of the ribbon. This profile of density distributions of MCC was also obtained by Miguelez-Moran et al. (2009) using microindentation and x-ray microcomputed tomography and in the work by Muliadi et al. (2013) using a solid displacement pycnometer (GeoPyc-1360).

The heterogeneity of roll pressure was demonstrated in the work by Cunningham et al. (2010) during the roller compaction of MCC powder. Using an instrumented textured roll with five sensors across the width, it was shown that the location of overall maximum roll pressure varied from across the roll width on both sides to the center. The movement of the position of the overall maximum roll pressure across the width was related to the rotating nature of the screw feeder. The heterogeneity of pressure over the roll width was also observed in the work by Nesarikar et al. (2012) during the compaction of a placebo (blend of microcrystalline cellulose and anhydrous lactose with sodium croscarmellose, colloidal silicon dioxide, and magnesium stearate) using an instrumented knurled roll installed on a roll press. It was noted that normal stress values on the roll side were lower than normal stress in the middle and showed greater variability than the measured stress in the middle. This is attributed to heterogeneity of feeding pressure in the last flight of the feed screw. However, in the investigations of Lecompte et al. (2005) on the roll compaction of organic powder using a roll press equipped with large-sized smooth rolls (240 mm diameter and 50 mm width) and a horizontal helical feed screw, the measured maximum pressures for several consecutive rotations did not show variation over the roll width. Moreover, with an increase of feeding rates, the pressure distribution gets more homogeneous. This result was explained by the fact that the screw was positioned further from the rolls.

The air entrapped in the powders is another challenging problem for modeling. Particularly for fine powders, the amount of air can have significant effects in the production. This problem is often emphasized in the literature, but few works on modeling have been addressed. Indeed, compaction creates an air transport away from the compacted zone through the feed zone (Vinogradov and Fedorchenko, 1961). This in turn generates a pressure gradient that can disturb the incoming flow. In the case of gravitational feeding, where particles are only subjected to their own weight, it can even result in the fluidization of the particles, which totally disorganizes the press feeding. The gap starts to increase or decrease as cycles of fluidization/consolidation of the feed arise (Schwechten and Milburn, 1990). Screw feeding allows for greater tolerance to airflow but it is eventually disrupted by the pressure gradient (Johanson and Cox, 1989). Such instabilities are detected by significant fluctuations in gap, roll pressure, and torque, and, in some cases, by vibrations and a popping noise generating rattling in the whole drive system (Dec, 1995). Investigating this multiphysics problem by modeling needs to couple at least two phases of solid–gas analysis. A challenge of interest for the process, and that could be reached at end by modeling, is to establish few operating conditions based on the material properties and process parameters that can lead the operator improving production in good conditions. Some progress of modeling in this area can be found in Johanson and Cox (1989) and Esnault et al. (2013).

The scalability of the process is considered the major obstacle to massive employment of the process in the pharmaceutical industry. Indeed, as the cost of the active ingredients is expensive, it is necessary to develop the product at laboratory scale and then move to the pilot or production scales by ensuring the same quality of the product. However, this operation is often done by trial and error. The development of modeling of this part is an important challenge for pharmaceutical applications. This could be studied through thematic networks with complementary and multidisciplinary skills.

The works cited previously demonstrate significant progress in instrumentations and measurements to better understand the roller compaction process. Current industrial roller compacting practice is largely based on trial-and-error techniques. Although it is possible to achieve the optimum process performance using such techniques, it results in an increase of operating cost and time, especially with high-value materials and quality requirements that are more demanding. An alternative approach is modeling methods to provide necessary information for proper equipment and process design. Johanson's model was the most accessible to understand process operation, but it still has its weaknesses, particularly related to the simplicity of the powder behavior (Johanson, 1965) and the friction conditions between the powder and the roller. In spite of its apparent simplicity, powder compaction in a roller press exhibits nonlinear behavior and interactions that are poorly understood from an analytical model.

4.3 Modeling tools

To meet the industry's challenges related to the development and optimization of the roller compaction process, it is necessary to combine experimental studies and mathematical modeling approaches. Progress of instrumentation in the last 20 years has allowed identifying the complexity of the roller compaction process and characterizing material and process parameters for some specific situations (powder and press). Because of the complex interaction between the powder behavior and process parameters, it is, in general, not easy to extract information from the measurements to be extrapolated to other powder and other press scales or designs. Modeling of the process can provide accurate quantitative results on a material's properties and on press parameters. An appropriate analysis of these results should lead the engineer to gain a better understanding through the process, leading to better design and control.

In particulate solids modeling, there are three main numerical approaches that can be broadly classified as follows: (1) FEM, in which the behavior of particulate solids is modeled as continuum media; (2) discrete element method (DEM), which considers each particle in the assembly as a separate entity that can interact with other particles or surfaces; and (3) multiparticle finite method (MPFEM) or meshed discrete element method, which combines DEM and FEM. Only DEM and FEM are reported next. For MPFEM modeling, refer to the work published in Procopio et al. (2005), Harthong et al. (2009), and Frenning (2010).

4.3.1 DEM modeling

DEM was first proposed by Cundal et al. in 1979. Since then, significant progress has been achieved on the evaluation of particle–particle contact, from the fully elastic Hertzian model for small strain to plastic deformation (Fleck, 1995; Storåkers et al., 1997; Thornton and Ning, 1998). The DEM is now commonly used to investigate various particulate processes involving flow such as in mixing, fluidization, and filling. In the context of dry granulation, the feeding is known as the critical factor in the control of the material entering into the compaction zone. DEM modeling seems more appropriate to simulate particulate solids flow within a feeder. Recent progress has been completed to improve the understanding of conveying particulate material within a screw feeder. In the work by Kretz et al. (in press), DEM simulation allowed computation of the mass flow rate for different screw types and angular velocities of the screw. These results were compared to experimental mass flow rate with less than 10%. Studying the flow of cohesive particles in screw feeders, a numerical investigation based on DEM modeling was developed in Hou et al. (2014). Based on the simulated results, a correlation for the prediction of solid flow rate was formulated as a function of the magnitude of cohesive force and the rotational speed of a screw. The effect of rotational speed of screw, inclination, and the volumetric fill level of the bulk material on the performance of a screw was analyzed in Owen and Cleary (2009) using DEM simulation with periodic boundary conditions. The obtained screw performance was examined in terms of variations of particle speeds, mass flow rate, and energy dissipation according to the operating conditions. These studies showed progress in improving the understanding of the flow of material within a screw. However, they do not consider the presence of the rollers that lead to limiting of the flow rate of material toward the gap due to the DEM procedures that have a poor reproduction of large strains. To overcome this limitation, MPFEM approach can be used. However, this method is computationally expensive.

4.3.2 FEM modeling

Modeling of roller compaction using FEM has been driven by its ability to take into account the nonlinear behavior of powders and its strong dependence on process parameters as well as the interaction between powder and rollers. This ability has been proven in other forming processes such as die compaction, rolling, and drawing. However, its recent implementation for roller compaction of pharmaceutical powders has been challenging due to a number of reasons, including:

- highly compressible behavior of pharmaceutical powders that can reach 80% of densification rate by causing strong distortions of meshes;
- boundary conditions to represent the continuous drawing of powders between rolls and ejection of formed ribbon;
- screw and behavior of powder in it are not modeled in detail;
- interaction between the powder and roll is difficult to quantify experimentally; and
- side seal design (cheek plate or rim).

Currently, FEM modeling is on the brink of becoming a usable tool in roller compaction of powders. Many details require further intensive development work because mechanical behavior of compressible material is numerically more complex to deal with than that of incompressible solids.

Mainly 2D and 3D modeling of roller compaction using FEM were performed for pharmaceutical powders (Dec et al., 2003; Cunningham et al., 2010; Michrafy et al., 2011a,b; Muliadi et al., 2012, 2013). These applications were developed under Abaqus/Explicit software (Abaqus) and simulations of the FEM modeling were solved as a steady-state problem using arbitrary Lagrangian–Eulerian (ALE) adaptive meshing (more details will be given in the next paragraph). The simulation is generally stopped when the stationary conditions are reached.

In these simulations, the feeding system by screw is not directly considered, but represented by an inlet boundary condition as constant or variable velocity and constant stress, for example.

Overall, modeling of the roller compaction process requires knowledge of the following main factors (see Fig. 4.2):

- Geometry of the press: roll dimension, gap, and feeding angle (Fig. 4.2).
- Contact conditions between powder and roll surface and friction coefficient.
- Roll rotating speed.

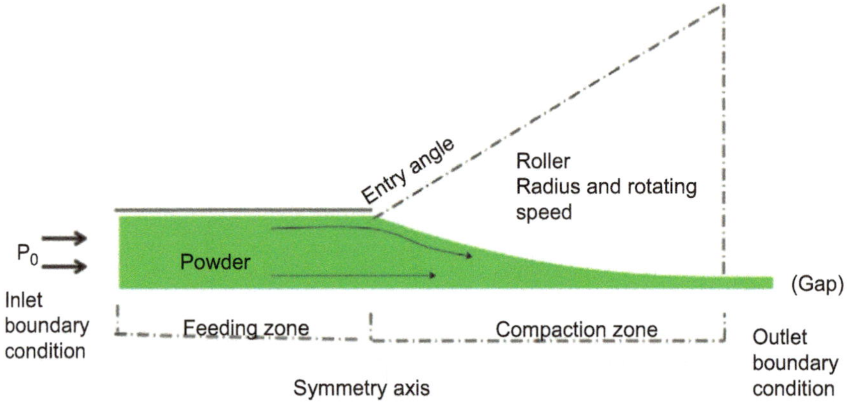

Figure 4.2 Description of factors used in FEM simulation design (case 2D with symmetry axis).

- Boundary conditions: to let powder flow across the boundary at the entry of rolls (inlet boundary condition) and to let free movement the compacted ribbon after the neutral angle (outlet boundary condition).
- Initial conditions: initial density of the powder in the feed zone.
- Constitutive model for powder compaction behavior: the powder is generally considered as continuum and porous elastic plastic material. In this context, Drucker–Prager Cap (DPC) model, described in Chapter 8, Modeling of Powder Compaction with the Drucker Prager Cap Model, is adopted as yield function for admissible stresses. In this modeling, elastic and plastic properties are expressed as functions of the relative density as state variable. This model was extensively employed for die compaction of pharmaceutical powders (Al-Khattat and Al-Hassani, 1987; Michrafy et al., 2002; Sinka et al., 2003; Wu et al., 2005; Kadiri et al., 2005). Its utilization requires reliable accurate input data for the powder properties. For more detailed on experimental procedure to generate input data for DPC, Chapters 5, 6, and 7 in Modelling of Powder Die Compaction, Editors: Brewin, P.R., Tweed, J.H. (Eds.) can be seen.

4.3.3 Simulation technique for the roller compaction process

One of the major problems in FEM modeling of roll compaction of pharmaceutical powders is avoiding the mesh distortion during the mechanical process. The pharmaceutical powder is in fact a porous media, which is highly compressed during the roll compaction process. Basically, there are three different ways to model the roll compaction process in Abaqus/Explicit:

- All the mesh is constructed with Lagrangian elements: the mesh moves and distorts with the physical material: mesh is always full with the single material and deforms as the material deforms. In this case, material boundary coincides with a mesh boundary. This method is widely used because of its ability to track accurately and efficiently material interfaces and incorporates complex material behavior. However, this formulation is very sensitive to distortions resulting a short time step and a possible loss of accuracy. Numerical codes can handle these problems with re-meshing, but this solution can be computationally costly.

- All the mesh is constructed with Eulerian elements: the mesh is fixed in space and the material flows through the mesh that does not deform. This kind of element is generally used for fluid and gas. Free surfaces and material interfaces can move through the fixed meshes, which also brings a partially or completely void mesh. Large deformation does not result in mesh distortions. However, if any Eulerian material moves outside the Eulerian mesh, it is lost from the computation. The Eulerian material can interact with Lagrangian meshes through Eulerian–Lagrangian contact (for multiphases simulation for example). In Abaqus/Explicit, this type of contact is often referred as coupled Eulerian–Lagrangian (CEL) analyses.
- A combination of both Eulerian and Lagrangian elements in the same mesh is called the ALE method, which provides control of mesh distortion. In this analysis, the ALE domain can be completely Lagrangian (nodes move with material motion), completely Eulerian (nodes fixed and material flows through mesh), or between these two extremes. In this type of analysis, some areas of the mesh are considered as Eulerian (usually the inlet/outlet surfaces) and some others as Lagrangian (contact interfaces like contact with roll). The ALE is typically used for steady-state modeling for solids, fluids, and gas and has been generally used in all publications of roller compaction simulations.

4.3.4 Requirements for roller compaction modeling

As previously described, FEM modeling of the roller compaction process is based on key concepts, including the powder behavior model proposal, friction between powder and roll, boundary conditions for input and output material, and initial density. Other information related to the roll press is also needed (roll dimensions, entry angle, and gap). The modeling is conducted with the ultimate goal of producing accurate and credible predictions of the real process. For its implementation, modeling of roller compaction process needs accurate input data for material parameters as elastic and plastic properties, friction conditions and process parameters in the feeding zone.

To achieve implementation of roller compaction simulation, the following will be required:

- Material input data: generation of such material data depends on the material behavior model used. For the Drucker–Prager Cap model, employed in the case studies, a full-instrumented die press is needed at least to determine elastic and plastic properties of the material. Methodology on how to proceed can be found in Chapters 5 and 6 (Modelling of Powder Die Compaction, Editors: Brewin, P.R., Tweed, J.H. (Eds.)).
- Robust finite element software, using a user-friendly graphical interface and allowing one or more continuum models for particulate solids. Currently, most implementations of roller compaction of pharmaceutical powders were performed using Abaqus software.
- Output of the simulation: roller compaction is a steady-state process. Numerically, this state is reached by solving a quasi-static boundary problem that converges to a steady-state solution. The developer has access to information including strain, stress and density distribution, roller force and torque, normal and tangential stresses at contact interface between powder and tooling. Material velocity is also accessible, particularly in the contact zone where the relative movement between material and rollers, leads to determine the nip angle. Overall, the obtained solution is depending on input data (material properties, boundary conditions, and contact-friction conditions).

4.4 Experimental validation

Currently, there is a lack of experimental information under relevant process conditions to improve the quality of predictions. Based on this, only few and partial experimental validations of 2D and 3D FEM for modeling pharmaceutical applications have been attempted (Cunningham et al., 2010; Michrafy et al., 2011a,b; Muliadi et al., 2013). These validations involve the comparison of predictions and measurements including ribbon's density distributions, roller compaction pressure and nip angle. Comparisons of the model predictions with the experimental results are discussed in cases studies 1 and 2. Moreover, experimental data, outlined in previous section but without being explicitly linked to the validation of FEM predictions can also provide information to qualitatively validate tendencies of predictions of the model (Lecompte et al., 2005; Miguelez-Moran et al., 2009).

In the following section, a brief review of experimental techniques used for characterizing density and pressure distribution in roller compaction of pharmaceutical powders is presented. Despite the difficulty in comparing results due to the variety of used roll press designs and the operating conditions, these results concern the ribbon's density and pressure distributions on roll contact surface.

4.4.1 Heterogeneity of density

The density of roller-compacted ribbons is considered as one of the most critical quality attribute which has impact on final product quality because the characteristics of granules are directly dependent on the ribbon density and determines at end the tablet's properties (Malkowska and Khan, 1983; Inghelbrecht and Remon, 1998a,b; Von Eggelkraut-Gottanka et al., 2002; Kleinebudde, 2004).

The nonuniform ribbon's properties are one of the complex features that have been demonstrated in several experimental investigations. Various techniques have been employed for characterizing density distributions of roller-compacted pharmaceutical powders including transmission light, mercury porosimetry intrusion (Simon and Guigon, 2003; Michrafy et al., 2011a,b), microindentation, x-ray microcomputed tomography (Miguelez-Moran et al., 2009), near-infrared chemical imaging in combination with multivariate data analysis (Khorasani et al., 2015) and Terahertz Pulsed Imaging (Lim et al., 2011; May et al., 2013). Most of these investigations showed that using conventional side seal system, the resultant density is not constant and showed higher values in the middle compared to the peripheral parts. However, using a rim roll system the density distribution seems more homogeneous across the ribbon's width (Funakoshi et al., 1977).

To demonstrate the heterogeneity resulting from roller compaction process, ribbons of MCC powder were prepared without lubrication using an instrumented laboratory roll press with a horizontal feed screw (Michrafy et al., 2011a,b). The press was fitted with 100 mm diameter and 38 mm width smooth rolls and two cheek plates to avoid a loss of powder during the process. In this study, the gap is fixed to 2 mm. As the screw speed is a dominant parameter in horizontal feeding

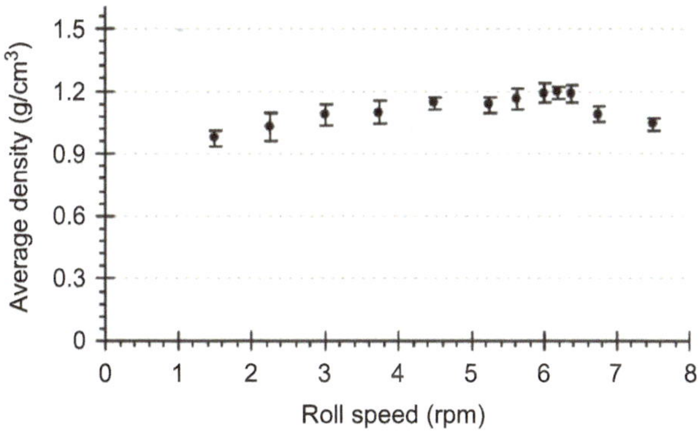

Figure 4.3 Average bulk density of MCC's ribbon according to roll speed with $V_s/V_r = 9.2$.
Source: Reprinted from Powder Technology, Vol. 206, Michrafy, A., Diarra, H., Dodds, J.A., Michrafy, M., 2011a. Experimental and numerical analysis of homogeneity over strip width in roll compaction. Powder Technol. 206, 154–160, copyright © 2016, with permission from Elsevier.

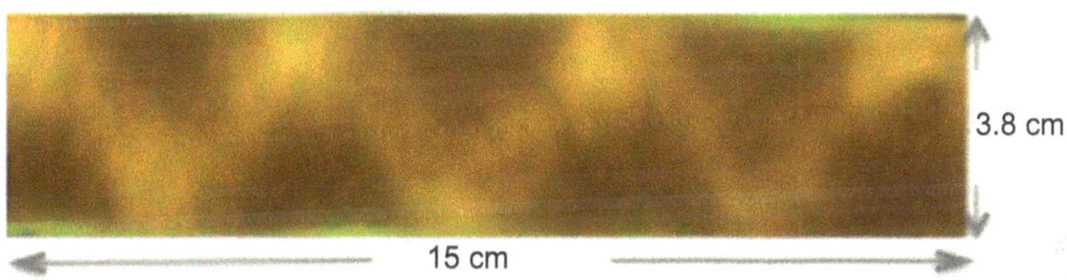

Figure 4.4 Results of light transmission through the depth of MCC ribbon (gap = 2 mm, roll speed = 6.4 rpm, screw speed = 59 rpm).
Source: Reprinted from Powder Technology, Vol. 206, Michrafy, A., Diarra, H., Dodds, J.A., Michrafy, M., 2011a. Experimental and numerical analysis of homogeneity over strip width in roll compaction. Powder Technol. 206, 154–160, copyright © 2016, with permission from Elsevier.

(Guigon and Simon, 2003), a preliminary characterization of the correlation between the screw and roll speeds to obtain a ribbon with good mechanical properties was first determined. Finally, ribbons of MCC were produced with screw-roll speed ratio of 9.2. The bulk densities of the pieces cut from the ribbons were calculated from their mass and volume. Results of the averaged bulk density are plotted in Fig. 4.3 according to the roll speeds. The heterogeneity of ribbon's density revealed by light transmission technique is showed in Fig. 4.4. The observed periodic heterogeneity seems independent on the screw velocity of the used press. Using a numerical microscope (Keyence France), a view of the microstructure of fractured surface through the thickness of MCC ribbon plotted in Fig. 4.5, demonstrates the heterogeneity of microstructure across the depth.

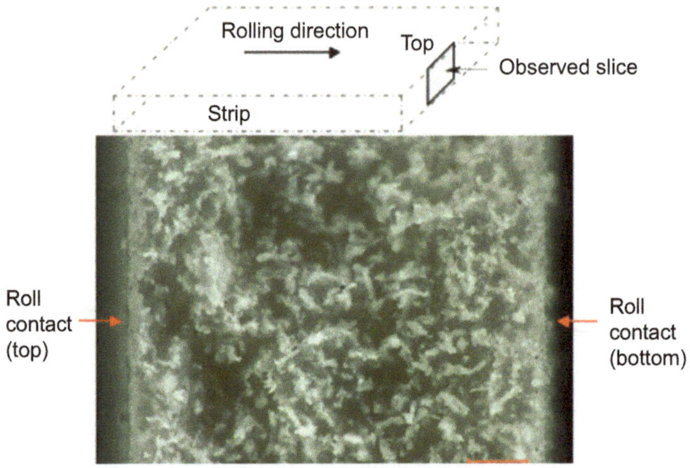

Figure 4.5 Micrograph of fractured surface (plane surface area cut through the thickness) [view obtained using a numerical microscope) (Keyence France)].
Source: Reprinted from Powder Technology, Vol. 208, Michrafy, A., Diarra, H., Dodds, J.A., Michrafy, M., Penazzi, L., 2011b. Analysis of strain stress state in roller compaction process. Powder Technol. 208 (2), 417–422, copyright © 2016, with permission from Elsevier)

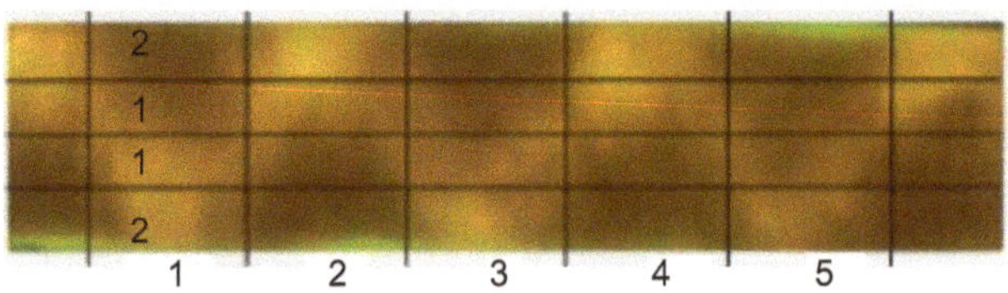

Figure 4.6 Illustration of the method used to cut samples according to the darker and lighter zones.
Source: Reprinted from Powder Technology, Vol. 206, Michrafy, A., Diarra, H., Dodds, J.A., Michrafy, M., 2011a. Experimental and numerical analysis of homogeneity over strip width in roll compaction. Powder Technol. 206, 154–160, copyright © 2016, with permission from Elsevier.

A grid was superimposed according to the alternate lighted and darker zones as shown in Fig. 4.6. Twelve samples (four in the width and three along the rolling direction) were cut from the ribbon. Using a mercury porosimetry technique, the introduced volume of mercury up to 30 MPa was measured for each sample. The introduced volume was considered as an index of the sample's porosity. Results of this analysis are plotted in Fig. 4.7. The samples cut from the center are noted with the symbol 1 and those from the edges with the symbol 2. These results demonstrate:

- The greater is the volume introduced, the higher is the porosity of the sample and hence the lower the density.

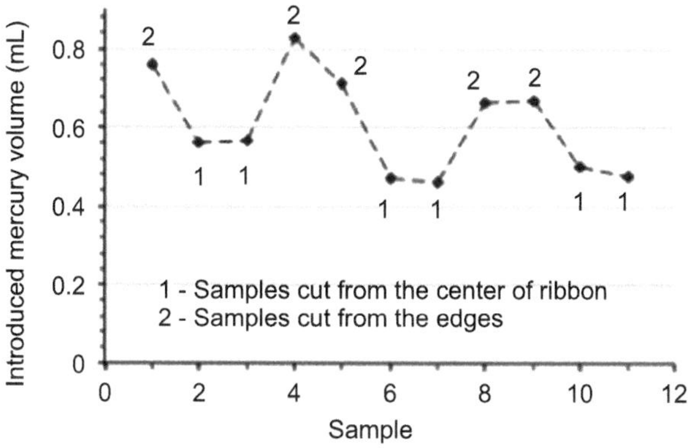

Figure 4.7 Mercury intrusion porosimetry (pressure 30 MPa). Symbols 1 and 2 correspond to those in Fig. 4.6.

- The darker zones do not fit with the denser part of the ribbon. A possible explanation could be related to the fact that the light transmission technique reveals more the texture rather than the density of a fibrous material such as MCC.

Using a vertical roll press equipped with rolls of 200 mm of diameter and 45 mm of width and cheek plates (Miguelez-Moran et al., 2009), ribbons of MCC powder lubricated with magnesium stearate, were produced under different roller compaction conditions (roll gap and roll speed). The density distribution was determined using a micro-indentation and x-ray microcomputed tomography techniques. Results of the density variation along the ribbon width obtained by microindentation are plotted in Fig. 4.8 and show clearly the high density in the middle and the low density at the edges for different process conditions.

4.4.2 Heterogeneity of roll pressure

Variation of maximum roll pressure was also the subject of measurements by various techniques. A vertical roll press with a textured roll (100 mm of diameter and 35 mm of width) and a screw feeding system was instrumented with embedded load cells that measures the contact stresses (Cunnigham et al., 2010). The screw was placed in the center of the roll gap but, because of the helical geometry, the pushing action is not symmetric and the rotation induces a pushing action with a peak that oscillates along the gap width. Moreover, the frictional resistance at the side seal further reduced the flow to the edges. These combined effects (screw and cheek plate effects) are resulting in nonhomogeneous pressure distribution as it is shown in Fig. 4.9.

These observed variations either in pressure or density distributions are analyzed by FEM modeling in case study 2.

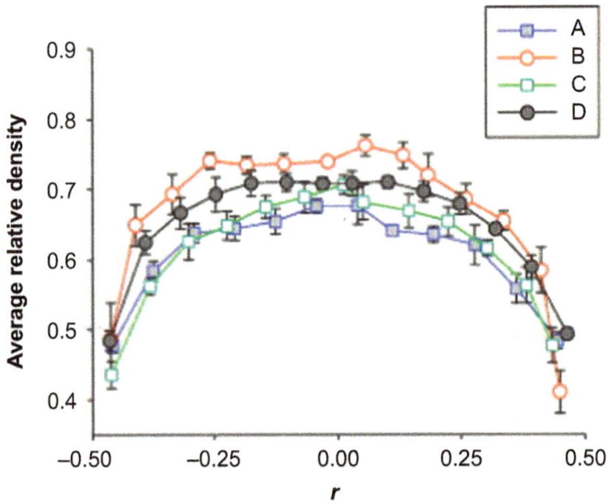

Figure 4.8 Density variation along the ribbon width obtained using micro-indentation with different roll gap (1 mm (A,C,D) and 0.9 (B)) and roll speed (6 rpm (A,B) and 3 rpm (C,D)). *Source*: Reprinted from European Journal of Pharmaceutics and Biopharmaceutics, Vol. 72, Miguelez-Moran, A.M., Wu, C.-Y., Dong, H., Seville, J.P.K., 2009. Characterisation of density distributions in roller-compacted ribbons using micro-indentation and X-ray micro-computed tomography. Eur. J. Pharm. Biopharm. 72, 173, copyright © 2016, with permission from Elsevier.

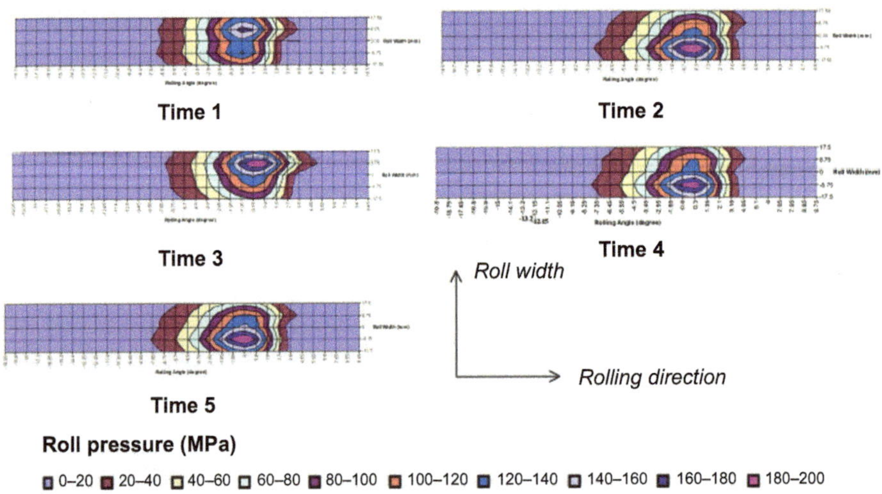

Figure 4.9 Contours of roll pressure with respect to rolling directions and roll width. The middle of the roll along its width is designation of 0 mm. Times 1–5 represent five successive revolutions.
Source: Reprinted from Computers and Chemical Engineering, Vol. 34, Cunningham, J.C., Winstead, D., Zavaliangos, A., 2010. Understanding variation in roller compaction through finite element-based process modeling. Comput. Chem. Eng. 34, 1058–1071, copyright © 2016, with permission from Elsevier.

4.5 Case studies of model application

Two case studies are presented next. Case Study 1 in two dimensions, demonstrates the capabilities of the FEM modeling of roll compaction process to gain greater physical understanding of the process by examination of stress, strain, velocity and density distributions of the ribbon of MCC between rolls. Comparison between predicted and measured density is showed. Effects of material parameters and roll friction on the process variables are also analyzed. Case study 2 presents experimental and numerical analysis to examine the homogeneity of properties over ribbon width of microcrystalline cellulose powder compacted with a laboratory roll press. Predicted and measured density distributions are discussed. The effect of side seal friction and inlet conditions on predictions are analyzed. Case studies 1 and 2 were conducted by assuming that the powder behaves as a single-phase porous media.

4.5.1 Case study 1: 2D finite element modeling

4.5.1.1 Introduction

In this study, the modeling is conducted using the modified Drucker–Prager Cap model, described in Chapter 8, Modeling of Powder Compaction with the Drucker Prager Cap Model. Simulations are conducted using the parameters listed in Table 4.1 and with the hardening function plotted in Fig. 4.10.

Simulations are performed using Abaqus software. The behavior is assumed to be symmetrical between rollers and only half of the domain is considered. As in the experiments, a roll of 100 mm of diameter is assumed as rigid body and rotates with a speed of 6 rpm. The gap is adjusted to 2 mm and the entry height of the material corresponds to approximately 20 degree roll angle. The domain occupied by the powder is meshed with continuum elements CPE4R with reduced integration for plane strain conditions. The initial density is fixed to 0.48 10^3 kg/m^3 corresponding to 0.3 of the relative density. The roll-powder friction coefficient is set to 0.35 (measured from die compaction test). The powder feed system is represented with a uniform feed load (0.1 N, which corresponds to a uniform pressure of 0.046 MPa).

Table 4.1 Material properties used in 2D FEM simulation

Young's modulus (MPa)	Poisson's ratio	Initial cohesion (MPa)	Internal friction (degree)	Eccentricity
5000	0.3	0	65	0.6

Source: Reprinted from Powder Technology, Vol. 208, Michrafy, A., Diarra, H., Dodds, J.A., Michrafy, M., Penazzi, L., 2011b. Analysis of strain stress state in roller compaction process. Powder Technol. 208 (2), 417–422, copyright © 2016, with permission from Elsevier.

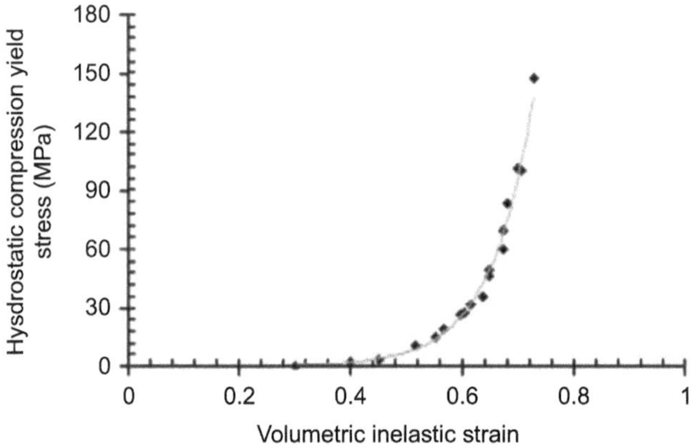

Figure 4.10 Hydrostatic yield stress (hardening function) versus volumetric inelastic strain. *Source*: Reprinted from Powder Technology, Vol. 208, Michrafy, A., Diarra, H., Dodds, J.A., Michrafy, M., Penazzi, L., 2011b. Analysis of strain stress state in roller compaction process. Powder Technol. 208 (2), 417–422, copyright © 2016, with permission from Elsevier.

4.5.1.2 Results and discussion

The predicted density distribution is plotted in Fig. 4.11 as contours (4.11A) and as curves (4.11B) for the density distribution at the contact surface with roll and on the symmetry line.

The predicted density in the gap is in the range of 1050–1110 kg/m^3 and presents a good agreement with the measured bulk density (1000–1200 kg/m^3) presented in previous section for a roll speed of 6 rpm (Fig. 4.3). The maximum density is reached before the 0 degree angle (neutral angle) where the pressure reaches its maximum. The predicted density at the contact zone and center line is identical except before the nip angle (here, 9 degrees). This prediction does not reflect the observation of the internal structure shown in the micrograph of Fig. 4.5.

Fig. 4.12 shows the velocity of the powder at the roll surface and the middle (symmetry line). The predicted velocity of powder in contact shows two zones: a zone where the powder is moving with a velocity lower than the roll speed (slip zone) and a zone where the powder and the roll are moving with the same velocity (stick zone). The nip angle can be easily determined as the angle between the previous two zones. Unlike the Johanson model based on the a priori existence of a nip angle, the FEM model predicts that angle and confirms at the same time, the relevance of this angle in the deeply understanding of transport and densification of powders in roller compaction process.

Material parameters such as cap eccentricity and Young's modulus have notable effects on the predicted nip angle, maximum roll pressure, and relative density. Table 4.2 displays the impact of the eccentricity variation in the range 0.4–1 and by keeping the same hardening function (see more details in Michrafy et al., (2011a,b)). This effect indicated that the increase of the eccentricity causes decrease of the nip angle, maximum pressure, and relative density. These results

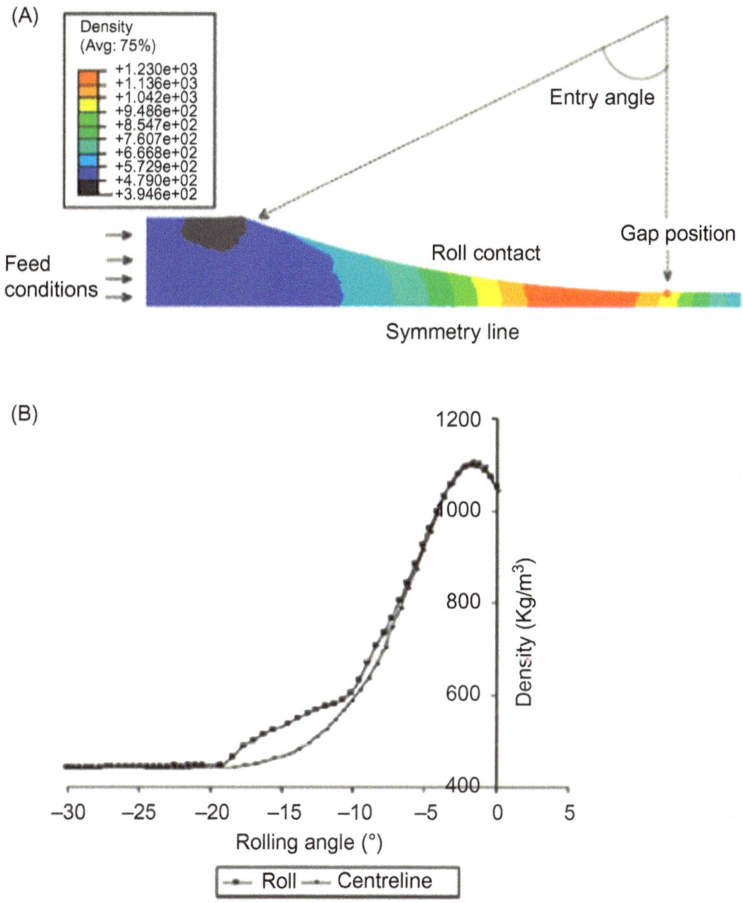

Figure 4.11 (A) Contour plots of density distribution in rolling direction. (B) Density distribution at contact surface with roll and in symmetry line.
Source: Reprinted from Powder Technology, Vol. 208, Michrafy, A., Diarra, H., Dodds, J.A., Michrafy, M., Penazzi, L., 2011b. Analysis of strain stress state in roller compaction process. Powder Technol. 208 (2), 417–422, copyright © 2016, with permission from Elsevier.

are consistent and supported by the general observations where the increase of the nip angle increases the maximum pressure and the density of the ribbon.

Similar conclusions were obtained in Cunnigham et al. (2010) and examination of the sensitivity of results to roll friction and feed stress was undertaken. Results of the effect of roll friction are summarized in Table 4.3. It is showed that increasing the roll friction the nip angle, maximum roll pressure and relative density at the exit increases as well. The effect of a constant feed stress is presented in Fig. 4.13. The increase of the constant feed stress results in increasing the relative density between rolls. However, the nip angle is not affected.

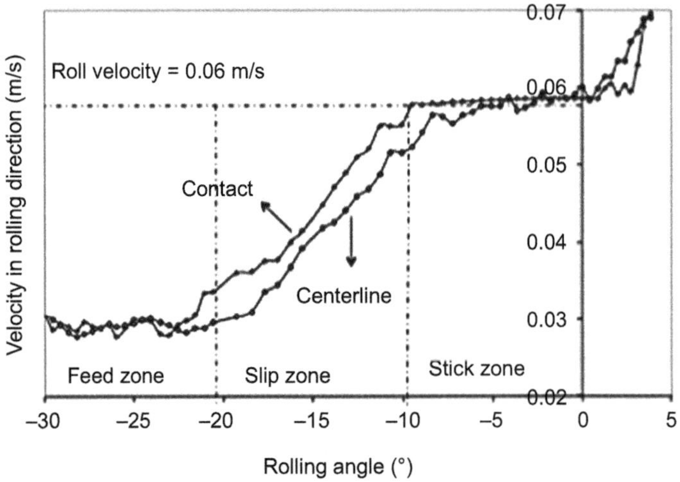

Figure 4.12 Powder velocity at contact surface with roll and in symmetry line versus rotating angle.
Source: Reprinted from Powder Technology, Vol. 208, Michrafy, A., Diarra, H., Dodds, J.A., Michrafy, M., Penazzi, L., 2011b. Analysis of strain stress state in roller compaction process. Powder Technol. 208 (2), 417–422, copyright © 2016, with permission from Elsevier.

Table 4.2 Effect of roll friction coefficient on nip angle, maximum roll pressure, and relative density at exit

Eccentricity (R)	Maximum roll pressure (MPa)	Nip angle (degree)	Maximum relative density
0.4	120.2	12.39	0.81
0.5	78.79	9.55	0.79
0.6	47.2	9.56	0.76
0.7	31.9	8.99	0.74
0.8	23.3	8.43	0.7
0.9	18.5	7.88	0.68
1	16.17	7.35	0.65

Source: Reprinted from Powder Technology, Vol. 208, Michrafy, A., Diarra, H., Dodds, J.A., Michrafy, M., Penazzi, L., 2011b. Analysis of strain stress state in roller compaction process. Powder Technol. 208 (2), 417–422, copyright © 2016, with permission from Elsevier.

4.5.1.3 Concluding comments

The 2D finite element analysis of roller compaction process offers a versatile approach because it takes into account a more representative powder behavior and frictional conditions than Johanson's model, and can include more information for

Table 4.3 Effect of roll friction coefficient on nip angle, maximum roll pressure, and relative density at exit

Roll friction coefficient	Nip angle (degree)	Maximum roll pressure (MPa)	Relative density at exit
0.30	7.0	35	0.71
0.35	8.2	50	0.78
0.40	10.0	75	0.81
0.50	13.5	130	0.89
0.60	14.5	210	0.91

Source: Reprinted from Computers and Chemical Engineering, Vol. 34, Cunningham, J.C., Winstead, D., Zavaliangos, A., 2010. Understanding variation in roller compaction through finite element-based process modeling. Comput. Chem. Eng. 34, 1058–1071, copyright © 2016, with permission from Elsevier.

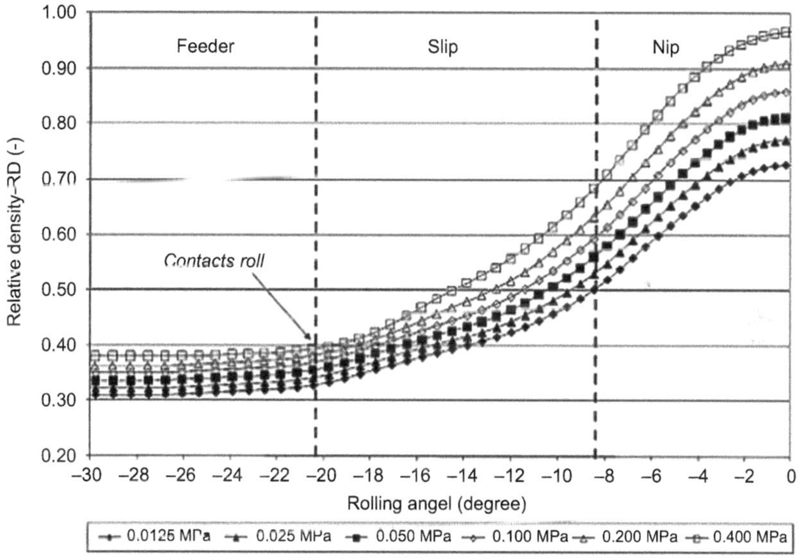

Figure 4.13 Evolution of relative density with rolling angle for various feed stresses (roll friction = 0.35).
Source: Reprinted from Computers and Chemical Engineering, Vol. 34, Cunningham, J.C., Winstead, D., Zavaliangos, A., 2010. Understanding variation in roller compaction through finite element-based process modeling. Comput. Chem. Eng. 34, 1058–1071, copyright © 2016, with permission from Elsevier.

the geometry of the press. This enables to perform realistic computer experiments predicting ribbon density, roll pressure, and nip angle and can lead to an improvement of the design and control of the process. The incorporation of the effect of the screw is one of the remaining challenges.

4.5.2 Case study 2: 3D finite element modeling

4.5.2.1 Introduction

Inhomogeneity of pressure and relative density of roller-compacted microcrystalline cellulose have been revealed by different measurement techniques. It is commonly agreed that the main factors responsible of ribbon heterogeneity are the powder feed system and the powder flow behavior in the compaction area between rolls and side seals. In this case study, numerical simulations are performed in three dimensions to examine the stress and density distributions over the ribbon width of compacted MCC powder using the commercial software Abaqus/Explicit. The powder behavior is described by Drucker–Prager Cap model where material properties are expressed as a function of relative density (details can be found in Michrafy et al. (2011a,b)). Assuming symmetrical behavior between rollers, only the upper half of the domain is considered. The roll of 100 mm of diameter and 38 mm of wide is assumed to be rigid. The powder is meshed with 9690 continuum elements C3D8R with reduced integration (Fig. 4.14). The gap is adjusted to 2 mm and the roll-powder friction coefficient is set to 0.35. The powder feed system is approximated by two conditions: uniform feed velocity and uniform feed pressure (1.0 MPa). As in a 2D case study, Eulerian inflow and outflow boundary conditions are employed to ensure the entry and the exit of the material. The side seals preventing the powder loss from the sides of the rolls are represented either by setting normal displacement of the powder to zero on side seals or by considering two rigid plates with friction condition. To achieve an economical solution for quasi-static simulations, a mass- scaling factor that increases the mass of the model artificially is employed. A rigid surface is created in the feed zone by assuming the friction coefficient as zero. This ensures a uniform velocity profile in the feeder barrel and hence ensures for the powder, at the entrance between rolls, the same velocity than the linear velocity of the roll.

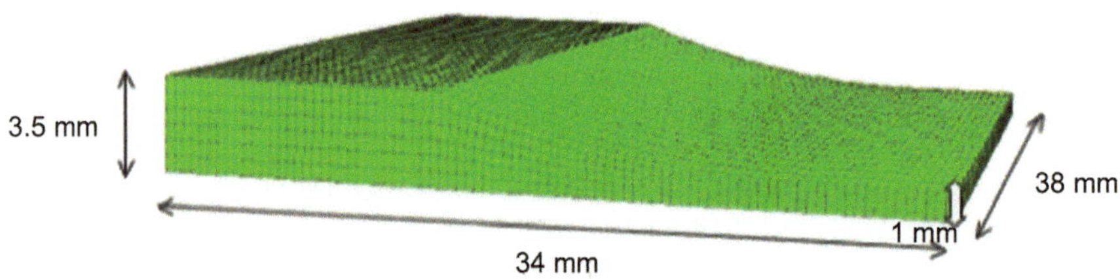

Figure 4.14 Meshed domain with continuum elements (C3D8R continuum element with reduced integration—Abaqus).
Source: Reprinted from Powder Technology, Vol. 206, Michrafy, A., Diarra, H., Dodds, J.A., Michrafy, M., 2011a. Experimental and numerical analysis of homogeneity over strip width in roll compaction. Powder Technol. 206, 154–160, copyright © 2016, with permission from Elsevier.

4.5.2.2 Results and discussion

Fig. 4.15 shows the predicted density distributions across the width of the MCC ribbon for constant feed stress and constant feed velocity. The case of constant feed stress shows a uniform profile of the density across the ribbon's width while results of the density distribution using inlet constant velocity are more in agreement with the measurements from the mercury porosimetry (Fig. 4.7) and the measured bulk density (Fig. 4.8). The decrease of the density near the sides could be explained by a lesser mass of powder in these zones due to the flow of powder.

The effect of side seal friction was examined in Michrafy et al. (2011a,b) by varying the frictional coefficient. The maximum relative density across the ribbon width for side seal friction of 0, 0.20, and 0.35 is plotted in Fig. 4.16. In this simulation, the feed stress was 0.1 MPa. These results show that increasing the side seal friction leads to a lower densification and greater variation in the transverse direction.

It can be noted that both side seal friction and nonuniform feeding contribute to the heterogeneous properties of the ribbon. To distinguish between the effects of these two contributing factors to the heterogeneity, a numerical simulation of roller compaction with a null side seal friction and variable inlet velocity (32 mm/s at the sidewall to 38 mm/s at the center in a linear manner) led to a nonuniform normal and shear stress across the roll width as shown in Fig. 4.17. High pressure and shear, and hence high density are developed in the center of the ribbon due to the high amount of material fed preferentially by the high inlet velocity at the center.

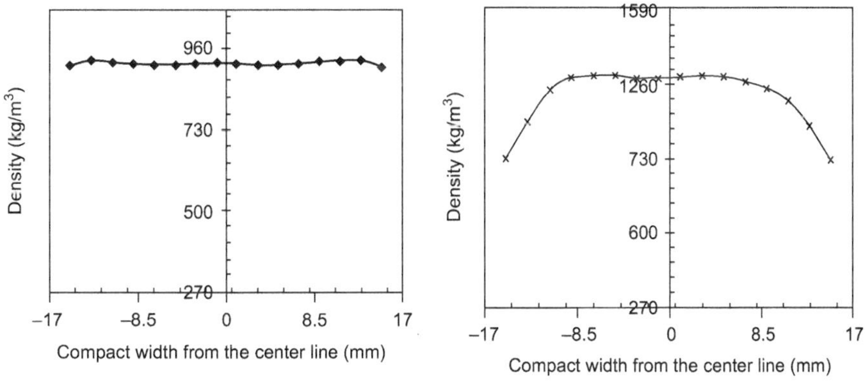

Figure 4.15 Density distribution across ribbon width of MCC, at the gap position: (left) Case of uniform feed pressure; (right) case of uniform feed velocity.
Source: Reprinted from Powder Technology, Vol. 206, Michrafy, A., Diarra, H., Dodds, J.A., Michrafy, M., 2011a. Experimental and numerical analysis of homogeneity over strip width in roll compaction. Powder Technol. 206, 154–160, copyright © 2016, with permission from Elsevier.

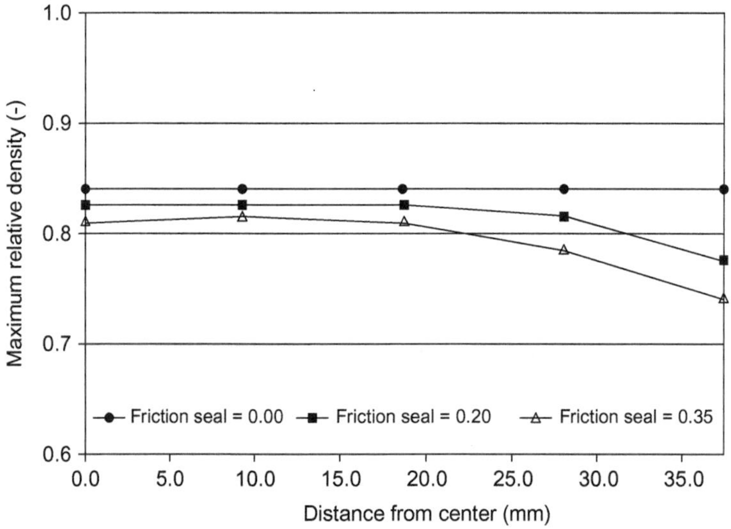

Figure 4.16 Maximum relative density along the transverse direction based on distance from the center (with 0 mm at the center and 37.5 mm at the side seal) for side seal friction of 0, 0.20, and 0.35.
Source: Reprinted from Computers and Chemical Engineering, Vol. 34, Cunningham, J.C., Winstead, D., Zavaliangos, A., 2010. Understanding variation in roller compaction through finite element-based process modeling. Comput. Chem. Eng. 34, 1058–1071, copyright © 2016, with permission from Elsevier.

With the goal to validate the FEM modeling of roller compaction, the helical screw feeder was replaced by a piston using a roll press equipped with a knurled roll (120 mm of diameter and 40 mm in of width) in Muliadi et al. (2013). Experiments of roll compaction of MCC powder were conducted by measuring the feed pressure resulting from the piston action and the corresponding density distribution across the ribbon. The cheek plate friction was also measured. A 3D FEM simulation of the roller compaction was performed using the measured constant feed stress and the Drucker–Prager Cap material data from Cunningham et al. (2010). The roll friction and side seal friction were 0.4 and 0.27, respectively. The comparison between predicted and measured density distributions is plotted in Fig. 4.18. By these results, it is proved again that the presence of cheek plates leads to a nonhomogeneous density across the ribbon's width.

4.5.2.3 Concluding comments

Case study 2 demonstrates the benefits of the practical use of 3D FEM modeling of roller compaction in predicting ribbon properties and process parameters. The preceding examples illustrate well the potential and usefulness of this approach as design tool for the process.

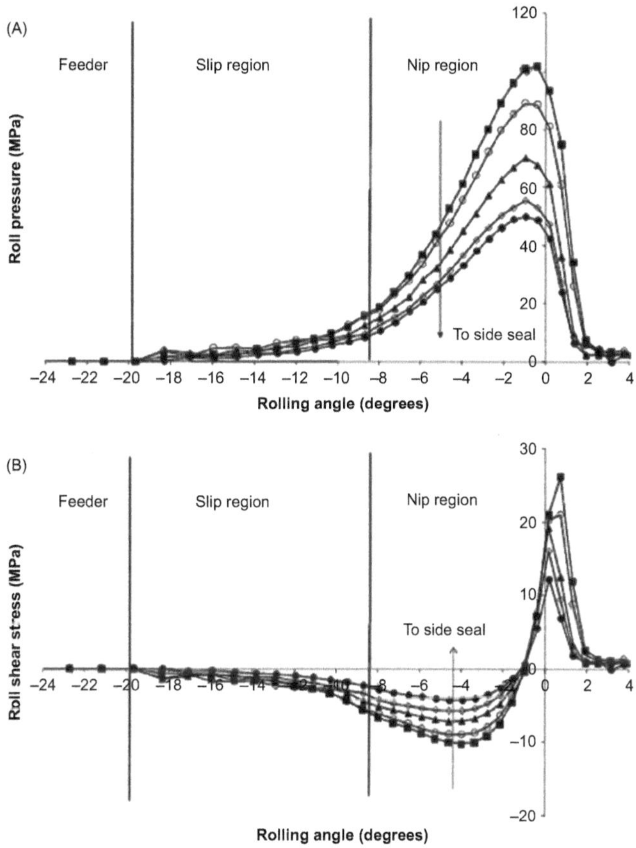

Figure 4.17 (A) Roll pressure versus rolling angle at various positions along the transverse direction from the center; (B) roll shear stress versus rolling angle at various positions along the transverse direction from the center (Inlet condition: noon-uniform velocity, side seal friction coefficient: 0.

Source: Reprinted from Computers and Chemical Engineering, Vol. 34, Cunningham, J.C., Winstead, D., Zavaliangos, A., 2010. Understanding variation in roller compaction through finite element-based process modeling. Comput. Chem. Eng. 34, 1058–1071, copyright © 2016, with permission from Elsevier.

4.6 Conclusions

This chapter has presented the state of current research and development on modeling of dry granulation process for pharmaceutical applications. The existing modeling tools are reported and discussed according to their contribution to the process. Recent progress has been done to improve the understanding of flow behavior of material within a screw feeder using DEM approach. However, the presence of rollers leads to limit the flow rate of material toward the gap due to DEM procedures that have a poor reproduction of large strains. To overcome this limitation, MPFEM method can be used but with an increase of computational cost.

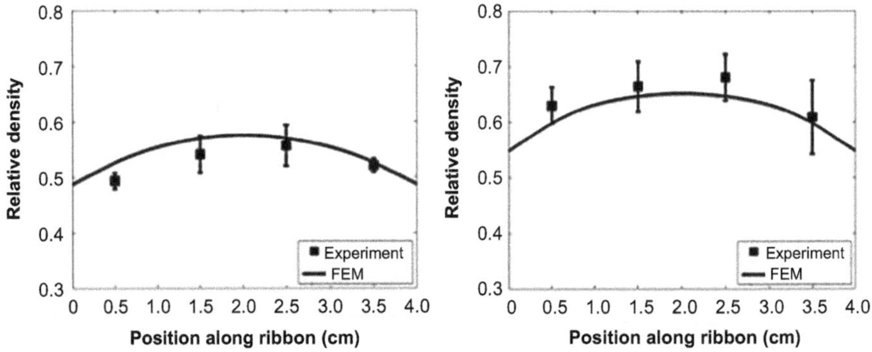

Figure 4.18 Comparisons of FEM-predicted and experimentally measured ribbon density distribution for an inlet stress of 196 kPa. Left and right figures are data corresponding to 5.5 and 9.2 kN of total hydraulic pressure.
Source: Reprinted from Powder Technology, Vol. 237, Muliadi, A.R., Litster, J.D., Wassgren, C.R., 2012. Modeling the powder roll compaction process: comparison of 2-D finite element method and the rolling theory for granular solids (Johanson's model). Powder Technol. 221, 90–100, copyright © 2016, with permission from Elsevier.

The main focus in this chapter was on the modeling of roller compaction process using FEM. The main published research in the topic were reported and discussed. It was showed that this method could provide accurate quantitative results on material properties and on press design because of its ability to incorporate the nonlinear behavior of powders, the design of the press and their strong interactions. Its employment in industry can assist the engineer in product development and the design and control of the process.

Two case studies were presented and showed that, performing FEM simulations in 2D and 3D of roller compaction process can predict many parameters including ribbon's density distribution, material flow, roll pressure, shear stress, and position of nip angle. It was clearly demonstrated that both side seal friction and nonuniform feeding contribute to the heterogeneous properties of the ribbon. It can be concluded that today, FEM modeling of roller compaction process offers insight, guidance, and practical solutions that can be used to optimize formulation design and process development. However, many challenges remain to be overcome to its implementation in industries handling powders. Those include computational problems, lack of materials databases in commercial software as well as multiphysical models taking into account the complexity of powders (effects of air, moisture, static electricity).

References

Abaqus/Explicit, http://www.simulia.com.

Al-Khattat, I.M., Al-Hassani, S.T.S., 1987. Towards a computer-aided analysis and design of tablet compaction. Chem. Eng. Sci. 42 (4), 707–712.

Brewin, P.R., Tweed, J.H. (Eds.), 2008. Modelling of Powder Die Compaction. Springer.
Cundall, P.A., Strack, O.D., 1979. A discrete numerical model for granular assemblies. Geotechnique. 29, 47–65.
Cunningham, J.C., Experimental studies and modeling of the roller compaction of pharmaceutical powders, PhD Thesis, Drexel University, 2005.
Cunningham, J.C., Winstead, D., Zavaliangos, A., 2010. Understanding variation in roller compaction through finite element-based process modeling. Comput. Chem. Eng. 34, 1058–1071.
Dec, R.T., 1995. Problems with processing of fine powders in roll press, In Proceedings of the 24rd Biennial Conference of the Institute for Briquetting and Agglomeration, 24, pp. 199–210.
Dec, R.T., Zavaliangos, A., Cunningham, J.C., 2003. Comparison of various modeling methods for analysis of powder compaction in roller press. Powder Technol. 130, 265–271.
Esnault, V., Heitzmann, D., Michrafy, M., Oulahna, D., Michrafy, A., 2013. Numerical simulation of roll compaction of aerated powders. Chem. Eng. Sci. 104, 717–726.
Fleck, N.A., 1995. On the cold compaction of powders. J. Mech. Phys. Solids. 43, 1409–1431.
Freitag, F., Reincke, K., Runge, J., Grellmann, J.W., Kleinebudde, P., 2004. How do roll compaction/dry granulation affect the tableting behaviour of inorganic materials? Microhardness of ribbons and mercury porosimetry measurements of tablets. Eur. J. Pharm. Sci. 22, 325–333.
Frenning, G., 2010. Compression mechanics of granule beds: a combined finite/discrete element study. Chem. Eng. Sci. 65, 2464–2471.
Funakoshi, Y., Asogawa, T., Satake, E., 1977. Use of a novel roller compactor with a concavoconvex roller pair to obtain uniform compacting pressure. Drug Dev. Ind. Pharm. 3 (6), 555–573.
Guigon, P., Simon, O., 2003. Roll press design—influence of force feed system on compaction. Powder Technol. 130, 41–48.
Harthong, B., Jerier, J.F., Doremus, P., Imbault, D., Donze, F.V., 2009. Modeling of high-density compaction of granular materials by the discrete element method. Int. J. Solids Struct. 46, 3357–3364.
Hou, Q.F., Dong, K.J., Yu, A.B., 2014. DEM study of the flow of cohesive particles in a screw feeder. Powder Technol.
Inghelbrecht, S., Remon, J.P., 1998a. The roller compaction of different types of lactose. Int. J. Pharm. 166, 135–144.
Inghelbrecht, S., Remon, J.P., 1998b. Roller compaction and tabletting of microcrystalline cellulose/drug mixtures. Int. J. Pharm. 161, 215–224.
Jenike, A.W., Shield, R.T., 1959. On the plastic flow of Coulomb solids beyond original failure. J. Appl. Mechan.; Trans. ASME. 26, 599–602.
Johanson, J.R., 1965. A rolling theory for granular solids. ASME J. Appl. Mech. 32, 842–848, Series E.
Johanson, J.R., Cox, B.D., 1989. Fluid entrainment effects in roll press compaction. Powder Handl. Process. 1, 2.
Kadiri, M.S., Michrafy, A., Dodds, J.A., 2005. Pharmaceutical powders compaction: experimental and numerical analysis of the density distribution. Powder Technol. 157, 176–182.
Khorasani, M., Amigo, J.M., Sonnergaard, J., Olsen, P., Bertelsen, P., Rantanen, J., 2015. Visualization and prediction of porosity in roller-compacted ribbons with near-infrared chemical imaging (NIR-CI). J. Pharm. Biomed. Anal. 109, 11–17.

Kleinebudde, P., 2004. Roll compaction/dry granulation: pharmaceutical applications. Eur. J. Pharm. Biopharm. 58, 317–326.

Kretz, D., Callau-Monje, S., Hitschler, M., Hien, A., Raedle, M., Hesser, J., 2015. Discrete element method (DEM) simulation and validation of a screw feeder system. Powder Technol. 287, 131–138.

Lecompte, T., Doremus, P., Thomas, G., Perier-Camby, L., Le Thiesse, J.-L., Masteau, J.-C., et al., 2005. Dry granulation of organic powders-dependence of pressure 2D-distribution on different process parameters. Chem. Eng. Sci. 60 (14), 3933–3940.

Lim, H., Dave, V.S., Kidder, L., Lewis, E.N., Fahmy, R., Hoag, S.W., 2011. Assessment of the critical factors affecting the porosity of roller-compacted ribbons and the feasibility of using NIR chemical imaging to evaluate the porosity distribution. Int. J. Pharm. 410, 1–8.

Malkowska, S., Khan, K.A., 1983. Effect of recompression on the properties of tablets prepared by dry granulation. Drug Dev. Ind. Pharm. 9, 331–347.

May, R.K., Su, K., Han, L., Zhong, S., Elliott, J.A., Gladden, L.F., et al., 2013. Hardness and density distributions of pharmaceutical tablets measured by terahertz pulsed imaging. J. Pharm. Sci. 102, 2179–2186.

Mesarovic, S.D., Fleck, N.A., 2000. Frictionless indentation of dissimilar elastic-plastic spheres. Int. J. Solids Struct. 37, 7071–7091.

Michrafy, A., Ringenbacher, D., Tchoreloff, P., 2002. Modelling the compaction behaviour of powders: application to pharmaceutical powders. Powder Technol. 127, 257–266.

Michrafy, A., Diarra, H., Dodds, J.A., Michrafy, M., 2011a. Experimental and numerical analysis of homogeneity over strip width in roll compaction. Powder Technol. 206, 154–160.

Michrafy, A., Diarra, H., Dodds, J.A., Michrafy, M., Penazzi, L., 2011b. Analysis of strain stress state in roller compaction process. Powder Technol. 208 (2), 417–422.

Miguelez-Moran, A.M., Wu, C.-Y., Dong, H., Seville, J.P.K., 2009. Characterisation of density distributions in roller-compacted ribbons using micro-indentation and X-ray micro-computed tomography. Eur. J. Pharm. Biopharm. 72, 173.

Muliadi, A.R., Litster, J.D., Wassgren, C.R., 2012. Modeling the powder roll compaction process: comparison of 2-D finite element method and the rolling theory for granular solids (Johanson's model). Powder Technol. 221, 90–100.

Muliadi, A.R., Litster, J.D., Wassgren, C.R., 2013. Validation of 3-D finite element analysis for predicting the density distribution of roll compacted pharmaceutical powder. Powder Technol. 237, 386–399.

Nesarikar, V.V., Vatsaraj, N., Patel, C., Early, W., Pandey, P., Sprockel, O., et al., 2012. Instrumented roll technology for the design space development of roller compaction process. Int. J. Pharm. 426, 116–131.

Owen, P.J., Cleary, P.W., 2009. Prediction of screw conveyor performance using the discrete element method (DEM). Powder Techol. 237, 247–248.

Parikh, D.M., 1997. Handbook of Pharmaceutical Granulation Technology. Dekker, New York.

Procopio, A.T., Zavaliangos, A., 2005. Simulation of multi-axial compaction of granular media from loose to high relative densities. J. Mech. Phys. Solids. 53, 1523–1551.

Schwechten, D., Milburn, G.H., 1990. Experiences in dry grinding with high compression roller mills for end product quality below 20 μm. Miner. Eng. 3 (1–2), 23–34.

Simon, O., Guigon, P., 2003. Correlation between powder-packing properties and roll press compact heterogeneity. Powder Technol. 130, 257–264.

Sinka, I.C., Cunningham, J.C., Zavaliangos, A., 2003. The effect of wall friction in the compaction of pharmaceutical tablets with curved faces: a validation study of the Drucker Prager Cap model. Powder Technol. 133, 33–43.

Sommer, K., Hauser, G., 2003. Flow and compression properties of feed solids for roll-type presses and extrusion presses. Powder Technol. 130, 272–276.

Storåkers, B., Biwa, S., Larsson, P.L., 1997. Similarity analysis of inelastic contact. Int. J. Solids Struct. 34, 3061–3083.

Thornton, C., Ning, Z.M., 1998. A theoretical model for the stick/bounce behaviour of adhesive, elastic-plastic spheres. Powder Technol. 99, 154–162.

Tundermann, J.H., Singer, R.E., 1969. Deformation and densification during the rolling of metal powders. Powder Metallurgy. 12 (23), 219–242.

Vinogradov, G.A., Fedorchenko, I.M., 1961. Effect of the gaseous phase on the pressing of powder in rolling. Poroshk. Metall. No. 1, 61–68.

Von Eggelkraut-Gottanka, S.G., Abed, S.A., Muller, W., Schmidt, P.C., 2002. Roller compaction and tabletting of St. John's wort plant dry extract using a gap width and force controlled roller compactor. II. Study of roller compaction variables on granule and tablet properties by a 3x3 factorial design. Pharm. Dev. Technol. 7, 447–455.

Wu, C.-Y., Ruddy, O.M., Bentham, A.C., Hancock, B.C., Best, S.M., Elliott, J.A., 2005. Modelling the mechanical behaviour of pharmaceutical powders during compaction. Powder Technol. 152, 107–117.

Mechanistic modeling of high-shear and twin screw mixer granulation processes

5

A. Chaudhury[1], D. Barrasso[1], D.A. Pohlman[2], J.D. Litster[2] and R. Ramachandran[1]
[1]Rutgers-The State University of New Jersey, Piscataway, NJ, United States, [2]Purdue University, West Lafayette, IN, United States

5.1 Introduction

5.1.1 QbD/Overview/challenges in high-shear granulation modeling

Granulation is a crucial particle design process that is widely used in the pharmaceutical industry to improve the handling of solids, control the dissolution profile of the drug and control the bioavailability of the final oral dosage form (Salman et al., 2007). It is a complex process controlled by various underlying mechanisms such as wetting and nucleation, agglomeration and consolidation, breakage/attrition, and layering (Iveson et al., 2001a,b). Granulation is a process involving particle size enlargement, which is used to modify the flow properties of solids utilized in the pharmaceutical industry. Granulation can be carried out in various equipment such as high-shear mixer, fluid bed granulator, drum granulator (batch mode), or a twin screw granulator (continuous mode). High-shear mixer equipment is popular for granulating fine powder due to its ease of operation and low operating costs. It is typically operated in batch mode and involves the addition of liquid binder to a bed of powder that is agitated within the mixer equipment.

From a pharmaceutical standpoint, the most crucial critical quality attributes (CQAs) of the granulation process include the particle size distribution (PSD), the intragranule porosity, and the bulk density of the granules. Significant work has been performed to investigate the effect of the process parameters on the final properties of the granules. Operating parameters that affect the final process outcome include the impeller speed, the binder viscosity, the amount of the granulation liquid utilized, and the wet massing time (Emady et al., 2011; Pandey et al., 2013).

A model-based design approach requires a fundamental understanding of the effects of the operating parameters. This approach is in alignment with the Quality by Design (QbD) initiative from the US FDA. QbD emphasizes obtaining more detailed information of the process and gaining insights toward its associated risks to

Predictive Modeling of Pharmaceutical Unit Operations. DOI: http://dx.doi.org/10.1016/B978-0-08-100154-7.00005-3

improve process operation and minimize the waste of money and material. It requires the development of a predictive model, which can provide more information about the process outcome/process optimization without having to actually run excessive experimental trials. Keeping these principles in mind, adopting a systems-engineering-based approach seems to be the best approach to abide by QbD.

A significant amount of research has been performed to study and understand the dynamics of granulation in greater detail such that QbD can be built into the process. For instance, wet granulation has been modeled using empirical kernels to describe the underlying mechanisms; however, with the utilization of more mechanistic kernels, a model can be designed to make effective predictions outside the design space as well. A mechanistic submodel links experimental parameters to population balance expressions (often through analysis at granule and macro scales). A well-designed QbD model framework should attempt to describe changes in the model according to process changes and predict similar outcomes. A common practice involves modeling a mixer granulator as a well-mixed system; however, this assumption might lead to oversimplification while modeling. Understanding of the granulation environment, assumptions behind submodel expressions, and solution techniques to the equations is critical to model formulation.

5.1.2 High-shear granulation rate processes/underlying mechanisms

The eventual granule size distribution and other granule properties are predicted through granulation models by representing the fundamental rate processes as terms within the model framework. The rate equations used to mathematically describe these rate processes are summarized in Table 5.1. Once a physical description of the system is well understood, the designer of a population balance model (PBM) can choose a set of rate expressions that describes the dynamic behavior of the system of interest. These phenomena are briefly discussed in the following sections.

5.1.2.1 Liquid distribution

Liquid distribution of binder into the bed of primary particles and granules is characterized by nucleation and wetting (Iveson et al., 2001a,b). Nucleation is the first step in granulation where the powder and liquid first come into contact. If a large drop reaches the powder surface, multiple particles come together to form a nucleus granule. Regime map analysis describes two major types of wetting behavior in granulation: droplet-controlled granulation and mechanical dispersion. If liquid droplets are able to penetrate into the powder quickly enough and are sprayed such that the droplets do not overlap-the behavior is described as the droplet-controlled regime (Hapgood et al., 2002). In droplet-controlled wetting, the basic assumption suggests that each droplet corresponds to a single granule. On the contrary, mechanical dispersion is a result of high effective spray rate or long penetration times. This is predominant in high-shear systems. Under these conditions, the spray distribution is no longer assumed to have a direct relationship to the initial PSD in the

Table 5.1 Qualitative and quantitative description of major mechanisms occurring in high-shear wet granulation

Mechanism	Dimensionless groups	1D PBM equation	1D Monte Carlo rate
Liquid distribution	Birth term of the 1D population balance	$\frac{\partial n}{\partial t} = B^0 \delta(x - x_0)$	$V_s B^0 \delta(v - v_0)$
Layering	In 1D layering growth, the size change can be due to uniform liquid or solid layering	Liquid spray uniform layering: size change term: $\frac{\partial n}{\partial t} = \frac{\partial n}{\partial v}\left[n(v,t)\frac{\partial v}{\partial t}\right]$	$\frac{C_s}{V_s}\sum_i K_{\text{layer}}(v_i)$
Consolidation	The original empirical equation to describe the consolidation of a porous granule is in terms of porosity	$\frac{d\varepsilon}{dt} = k(\varepsilon - \varepsilon_{\min})$	$\frac{C_s}{V_s}\sum_i K_{\text{cons}}(v_i)$
Agglomeration	The agglomeration kernel contains much of the information about growth kinetics in wet granulation	$B_{\text{agg}}(v) = \frac{1}{2}\int_0^v \beta(v' - v, v)$ $n(v - v', t)\, n(v', t)\, dv'$ $D_{\text{agg}}(v) = n(v,t)\int_0^\infty \beta(v, v')n(v', t)dv$	$\frac{1}{2V_s^2}\sum_i\sum_{j\neq i}\beta(v_i, v_j)$
Breakage	The breakage equation	$B_{\text{brk}}(v) = \int_0^\infty K_{\text{brk}}(v)b_{\text{brk}}(v, v')dv'$ $D_{\text{brk}} = K_{\text{brk}}(v)n(v,t)$	$\frac{1}{V_s}\sum_i K_{\text{brk}}(v_i)b_{\text{brk}}(v_i, v_j)$

granulator (Hapgood et al., 2003). Much of the work on PBM for high-shear wet granulation systems define the liquid distribution as uniform growth of liquid on each particle (on the entire surface area), rather than discrete droplets which is only physically realistic for certain specific cases (Hapgood et al., 2004; Reynolds et al., 2004; Smirani-Khayati et al., 2009).

5.1.2.2 Consolidation and growth

Consolidation is the mechanism by which the pore volume within the granules gets compacted due to agitation, thus resulting in an increase in the granule pore saturation. Once enlarged granules make up a significant portion of the population in a granulation system, the interactions between them dominate the process. Granule–granule and granule–impeller impacts can lead to granule consolidation. High-shear granulation systems in particular can cause extensive densification of granular material. This consolidation is typically treated as a slow and continuous process over a high number of impacts (Iveson et al., 1996; Iveson and Litster, 1998a). The consolidation of granules in batch granulation has most often been described using an empirical exponential decay expression that approaches a minimum porosity with respect to the extent of granulation (Iveson and Litster, 1998b; Iveson et al., 2001a,b).

Granule growth is described in two separate ways. If a continuous solid phase of uniform primary powder is assumed, the layering of this fine powder on the outside of relatively larger granules can be treated as a continuous growth (layering) of granules (Tu et al., 2009). Alternatively, growth has also been described as the binary coalescence of two granules. The agglomeration kernel of a population balance mathematically describes this coalescence behavior (Hounslow et al., 1988).

5.1.2.3 Breakage

Breakage of agglomerates and wet mass in a high-shear granulator can also be a dominant or controlling process in granulation. Breakage in granulation is described mathematically through the breakage kernel and the distribution function (Reynolds et al., 2005). The understanding of breakage in high-shear wet granulation modeling is still a subject of active research. While mechanistic descriptions for breakage attempt to relate the relative strength of granules to the average stresses that occur in the granulator, these investigations are still primitive relative to the development of coalescence models that describe growth. Often the breakage distribution function is assumed to be binary and uniform breakage. This is necessary since the exact expression for the distribution of the fragmented particles is difficult to predict or validate (Kumar et al., 2013).

High-shear wet granulation environment is subjected to many, if not all, of these rate processes influencing the granule population simultaneously. While some process conditions and formulations seem to have a dominant set of behaviors in one piece of equipment or scale, it is difficult to predict how different formulations or changes in equipment will affect the final granule attributes. Expressions for both the

PBM term as well as the Monte Carlo rate per unit volume expression are provided for comparison in Table 5.1. This table provides an understanding of how particular rate processes depend on the current population of granules. One-dimensional (1D) expressions are useful in understanding the mathematical framework of both of these population tracking techniques. However, wet granulation rate processes depend directly on granule attributes such as porosity, liquid saturation, and size, which cannot be distinctly tracked with only one dimension (Iveson, 2002).

5.1.3 High-shear granulation equipment

High-shear wet granulation has been traditionally performed in the vertical mixer equipment or the twin screw granulation equipment. The vertical mixer equipment is run in the batch mode, while the twin screw granulator is run in the continuous mode. The geometry and mode of operation for the granulation process influence the final product and thus should be considered while modeling the system. Additional details regarding this equipment are provided next.

5.1.3.1 Vertical high-shear

A high-shear granulation process is often carried out industrially in a vertical mixer. The powder is added to the vessel, wherein binder is added into the system in two modes: dry mixing or wet mixing. The binder is wet mixed into the system by dissolving the solid binder into the solvent (thus increasing its viscosity) before adding it to the powder. In certain instances, the solid binder is mixed with the fine powder to be granulated, followed by the addition of pure water into the system. This case is known as dry mixing of the binder. In a vertical high-shear mixer, the crucial operating parameters are the binder amount, impeller and chopper speed, mode of binder addition, spray dynamics, granulation time, and wet massing time, which play a vital role in shaping the resulting granule physical properties (Pandey et al., 2013). Moisture content and impeller speed significantly affect the consolidation and agglomeration mechanisms. The final granule properties are a result of complex interactions between the various mechanisms that are influenced by the operating parameters.

Iveson and Litster (1998b), Hapgood et al. (2003), and Emady et al. (2011) have used a regime-map-based approach to identify the dynamics of the granulation process using dimensionless numbers. Badawy et al. (2000) investigated the effect of impeller speed on the granule properties and identified the granules to be very dense (with lower propensity of breakage) when granulated under high impeller and chopper speed. This trait is a consequence of increased consolidation due to high agitation within the system. Breakage of granules is also affected by the impeller and chopper speed.

5.1.3.2 Twin screw granulation

Twin screw granulation is a variant of high-shear granulation in which a twin screw extruder is used to granulate the powder. Twin screw granulation has shown particular potential for pharmaceutical manufacturing operations due to its low throughput, design flexibility, and short residence time (Keleb et al., 2004; Vervaet and Remon, 2005). When compared to high-shear mixer/granulators, the twin screw granulator typically produces more porous and irregularly shaped granules. This is due to the lack of coalescence and consolidation in twin screw granulation (Lee et al., 2013). Instead, nucleation, breakage, and layering drive the process.

Fig. 5.1B shows a schematic of the twin screw granulator along with an image of the screws (Dhenge et al., 2012). Two interlocking screws rotate to convey and knead the powder, distributing liquid and producing granules. Powder is fed through the screw barrel at one end, where conveying elements transport the powder toward an inlet where liquid droplets are added. Additional conveying elements feed the powder along the granulator. The powder reaches zones of kneading elements, which break large, wet nuclei into smaller granules and induce layering (see next section for details) and liquid distribution (El Hagrasy and Litster, 2013).

Screw design and configuration is an area of significant research (Keleb et al., 2004; Thompson and Sun, 2010; Vercruysse et al., 2012). The pitch of the conveying elements can vary, and the offset angle between kneading elements is found to have significant effect on the product size distribution as well as the liquid homogeneity of the product. Fig. 5.2 shows a block of kneading elements with five different offset angles (El Hagrasy and Litster, 2013). The forward offset angles have conveying characteristics and tend to push the material in the direction of flow, while reverse configurations tend to counteract the transport of material. These options also influence the residence time in the compartment and the extent of mixing and breakage. Further, many possible screw configurations can be created, with any number, order, and length of conveying and kneading element sections.

Figure 5.1 Schematic of mixer granulators (A) Scheme of batch granulator KG5,1 stainless steel bowl (volume 3.9 L), 2 three-blade impeller, 3 chopper, 4 impact resistant cover, 5 safety screw, 6-material (B) Configuration of the corotating screws with different compartments.

Source: Reprinted from Dhenge, R.M., Cartwright, J.J., Hounslow, M.J., Salman, A.D., 2012. Twin screw granulation: steps in granule growth. Int. J. Pharm. 438 (12), 20–32. Copyright (2012), with permission from Elsevier.

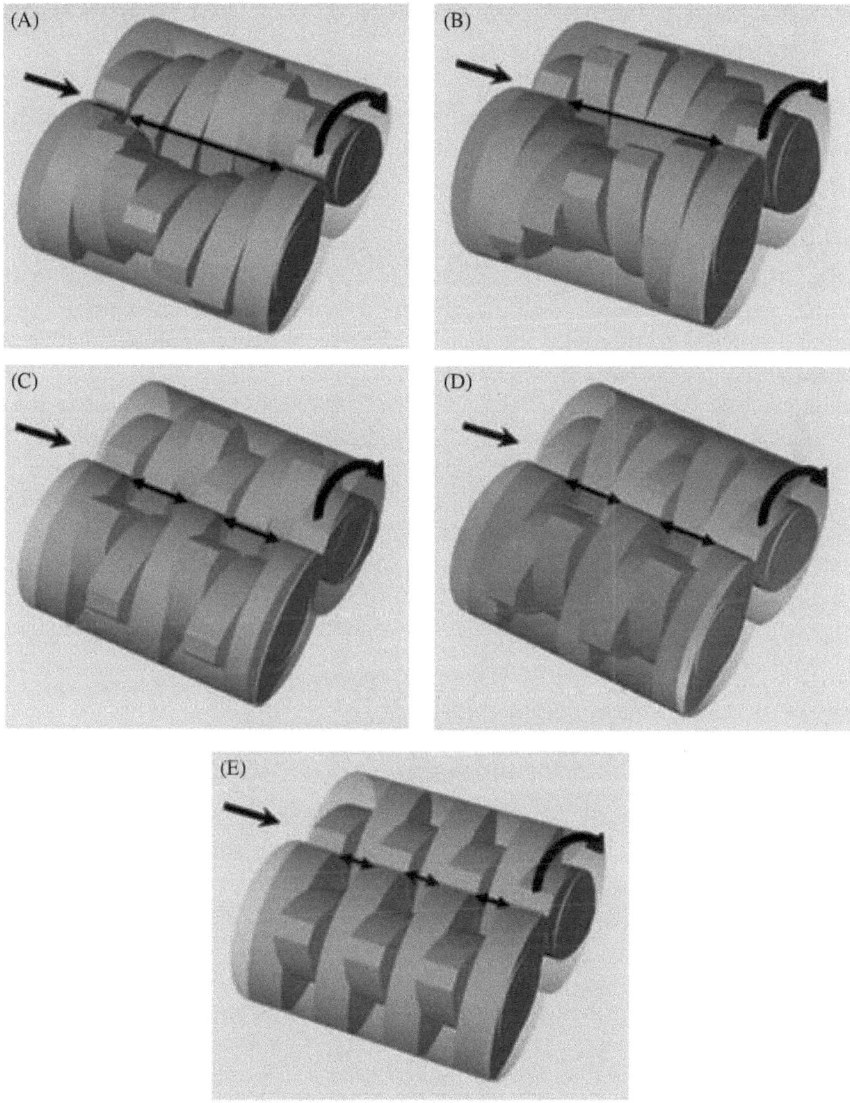

Figure 5.2 Configurations of kneading section using 7 KE at (A) 30°F, (B) 30°R, (C) 60°F, (D) 60°R, and (E) 90°. The curved arrow indicates the direction of rotation of the shafts and the straight arrow depicts the direction of material flow from the CE into the kneading section.
Source: Reprinted from El Hagrasy, A.S., Litster, J.D., 2013. Granulation rate processes in the kneading elements of a twin screw granulator. AIChE J. 59 (11), 4100–4115. Copyright (2013), with permission from John Wiley & Sons.

5.2 Modeling techniques for high-shear wet granulation processes

Modeling of granulation processes can be done using various approaches, including PBMs (Chaudhury and Ramachandran, 2013; Chaudhury et al., 2013a,b), multiscale models discrete element method (DEM), computational fluid dynamics (CFD) (Fries et al., 2011; Gantt and Gatzke, 2006), hybrid models (CFD + DEM, CFD + Volume of Fluid, DEM + PBM) (Stepanek and Rajniak, 2006; Rajniak et al., 2007; Sen et al., 2014; Barrasso and Ramachandran, 2015), and so on. Several researchers have worked toward obtaining a comprehensive high-dimensional PBM to represent the high-shear wet granulation process. Multiscale modeling frameworks have also been used to track the occurrences within the granulation process. DEM provides deep understanding of the microscopic behavior of the process, particle collisions, and the agglomeration tendency based on the amount of liquid available. If DEM is coupled with the PBM framework, the overall process can be better represented while considering the occurrences and outcomes taking place at all scales. Using a multiscale representation of the process is very accurate, however, the computational expenses associated with solving such a framework is significantly high. PBMs are also very effective toward representing particulate systems; however, the associated computational overheads are relatively low.

5.2.1 Population balance modeling

PBMs are a class of hyperbolic partial differential equations that describe the mesoscopic interactions and are extremely effective for representing discrete systems. They utilize information from the microscale and relate them to macroscopic properties of the system. The high-shear wet granulation system can be well-captured using population balance equations, wherein the independent variable consists of an internal coordinate of the system (e.g., particle size, porosity, composition). It seems like particle size is the most crucial attribute that needs to be taken into consideration while modeling granulation, however, porosity and moisture content also play a crucial role in culminating the final granule attributes. Knight et al. (1993); Liu et al. (2000); Osborne et al. (2011) suggested the importance of moisture content in the design of particles through granulation, as it influences the availability of liquid on the surface, thus controlling the agglomeration mechanism. Porosity of the granules also plays a vital role in influencing the amount of liquid that is available on the surface (after filling up the pores). Porous particles also have a higher propensity of breaking initially and agglomerating thereafter to form more dense particles (Annapragada and Neilly, 1996). Earlier, 1D models were more popular owing to their low computational complexity, however Iveson (2002) pointed out the limitations of using low dimensional PBMs. To decouple the effect of various mechanisms on the granule properties, Verkoeijen et al. (2002) described the granulation process using a three-dimensional (3D) PBM with respect to the individual solid, liquid and gas volumes. The 3D PBM can be written as

$$\frac{\partial}{\partial t}F(s,l,g,t)+\frac{\partial}{\partial s}\left[F(s,l,g,t)\frac{ds}{dt}\right]+\frac{\partial}{\partial l}\left[F(s,l,g,t)\frac{dl}{dt}\right]+\frac{\partial}{\partial g}\left[F(s,l,g,t)\frac{dg}{dt}\right]$$
$$=\Re_{\text{nuc}}+\Re_{\text{agg}}+\Re_{\text{break}} \tag{5.1}$$

where $F(s,l,g,t)$ represents the population density function such that $F(s,l,g,t)dsdldg$ is the number of moles of granules with a solid volume between s and $s+ds$, a liquid volume between l and $l+dl$ and a gas volume between g and $g+dg$. The partial derivative term with respect to s accounts for the layering of fines onto the granule surfaces, the partial derivative term with respect to l accounts for the drying of the binder and the rewetting of granules and the partial derivative with respect to g accounts for consolidation, which, due to compaction of the granules, results in an increase in the pore saturation and decrease in the porosity. The aggregation and breakage terms is described in Eqs. (5.2)–(5.7).

$$\Re_{\text{agg}}(s,l,g)=\Re_{\text{agg}}^{\text{form}}-\Re_{\text{agg}}^{\text{dep}}, \tag{5.2}$$

such that

$$\Re_{\text{agg}}^{\text{form}}=\frac{1}{2}\int_0^{s_{\max}}\int_0^{l_{\max}}\int_0^{g_{\max}}\beta(s',s-s',l',l-l',g',g-g')$$
$$\times F(s',l',g',t)F(s-s',l-l',g-g',t)ds'dl'dg' \tag{5.3}$$

$$\Re_{\text{agg}}^{\text{dep}}=F(s,l,g,t)\int_0^{s_{\max}}\int_0^{l_{\max}}\int_0^{g_{\max}}\beta(s',s-s',l',l-l',g',g-g')$$
$$\times F(s',l',g',t)ds'dl'dg' \tag{5.4}$$

where $\beta(s', s-s', l', l-l', g', g-g')$ is the aggregation kernel that governs the rate at which two granules of internal coordinates (s', l', g') and $(s-s', l-l', g-g')$ agglomerate.

$$\Re_{\text{break}}(s,l,g)=\Re_{\text{break}}^{\text{form}}-\Re_{\text{break}}^{\text{dep}}, \tag{5.5}$$

such that

$$\Re_{\text{break}}^{\text{form}}=\int_s^{s_{\max}}\int_l^{l_{\max}}\int_g^{g_{\max}}b(s,l,g,s',l',g')K_{\text{break}}(s,l,g)\times F(s',l',g',t)ds'dl'dg' \tag{5.6}$$

$$\Re_{\text{break}}^{\text{dep}} = K_{\text{break}}(s,l,g)F(s,l,g,t). \tag{5.7}$$

where K_{break} (s,l,g) is the breakage kernel and $b(s,l,g,s',l',g')$ is the breakage distribution function.

5.2.2 Granulation kernels

While the PBM contains the numerical mechanics needed to study particle processes, the values and forms for the rate constants and kernels are the design choices that truly determine model behavior. The granulation kernels can be perceived to act similar to the rate constant for chemical reactions. They quantify the probability of particles to stick together and form an agglomerate upon collision. The extent to which a model is predictive and accurate also depends on these kernels. Empirical kernels that rely on fitting parameters from experimental data are more accurate within a specified design space. Mechanistic kernel forms promise to be more general and predictive, and are functions of measurable properties and physical process parameters. This section focuses on expressions for kernels describing nucleation, aggregation, and breakage mechanisms that represent the physics of wet granulation. Nucleation kinetics of liquid droplets into a powder bed can have vastly different timescales depending on the liquid and powder properties. Hounslow et al. (2009) described both a capillary and a diffusive mechanism for nucleation as functions of material properties, end state boundary conditions, and an effective diffusion coefficient. These two scenarios describe the breadth of interactions within high-shear granulation: (1) quick capillary penetration of spray to viscous binder materials that require high intensity impacts, and (2) nuclei breakage to reach a granular composition in a smaller amount of time.

Aggregation kernels of several forms have been applied to high-shear and twin screw wet granulation with some success. A generic decoupling of the aggregation kernel is developed through understanding that it measures the frequency of successful coalescence events occurring in the control volume. The kernel is thus decoupled into a collision frequency and collision efficiency term in the following equation.

$$\beta(v,v',t) = \beta_0(t) \times \beta^*(v,v') \tag{5.8}$$

Here β^* denotes the collision efficiency between granules of class v and v' while β_0 is the collision frequency. The collision frequency is typically used as a fitting parameter to adjust the concentration of collisions relative to the current population of particles (Adetayo and Ennis, 1997). DEM simulations have also been used to estimate the collision frequency between particles without the need to use a fitting parameter (Gantt et al., 2006). Collision efficiency expressions in their simplest forms are a function of size and adjustable parameters. The physical description of the collision of a pair of granules should determine whether a collision is successful. Mechanistic approaches to kernel formulation attempt to describe the collision efficiency based on measured or estimated values that describe these collisions. Properties and conditions that describe granule collisions include; granule properties (size, surface wetness, granule yield stress, etc.), binder properties (viscosity, surface tension, etc.), and collision information (relative velocity, orientation, etc.). In order to accurately represent some of these properties multidimensional population balances and appropriate kernels are necessary, as attributes like strength and wetness are not simply a function of size (Iveson et al., 2003). Examples of these kernels used to describe high-shear granulation behavior are presented in Kumar et al. (2013). A brief review has also been provided in Tables 5.2–5.4. The kernel developed by Liu and Litster (2002) has also been extended to the multidimensional framework (Pohlman and Litster, 2015). This describes the collision between granules as that of two elastic plastic spheres that can have a uniform liquid layer on the surface. The multidimensional kernels used in the models describing high-shear granulators are fit to expressions that include both granule size, x^3, and granule liquid concentration, c_x. Another form of a semimechanistic kernel is based on the volume of liquid greater than some saturation value.

In previous works by Chaudhury et al. (2014a,b,c), a semimechanistic kernel has been proposed, which captures the effect of the crucial operating conditions on the agglomeration event. The total liquid content of the granules is categorized as internal liquid and surface liquid using an empirical parameter that lies between 0 and 1.

It is assumed that the liquid present on the surface is in the form of a single droplet. As time progresses and liquid begins to get squeezed out to the surface

Table 5.2 Mechanistic Nucleation expressions with applications to population balance equations

Name and equation	Comments
Spray flux: $\psi = \frac{3\dot{V}_k}{2\dot{A}\bar{d}_d}$ and poison nuclei distribution (Hapgood et al., 2009) $P_n(B_{\text{nuc}}) = \exp(-4\psi)\frac{(4\psi)^n}{n!}$	This model takes the dimensionless analysis of the droplet spray and describes a distribution of droplets that could be as a nucleation rate term in a PBM (Hapgood et al., 2009)
Capillary nucleation time relation (Hounslow et al., 2009) $t_{max} = 18.75\frac{\mu h_0^2}{d_p \gamma_{LV}}\frac{(1-\phi_{cp}^{1/3})}{\phi_{cp}^3}$ and $\frac{dv_s}{dt} = \frac{1}{2t_{max}}\frac{v_l^2}{v_s}\left(\frac{1-\phi_{cp}}{\phi_{cp}}\right)^2$	Penetration time and subsequently rate can be derived from this expression describing capillary nucleation
Diffusive nucleation relation (Hounslow et al., 2009) $\frac{d\upsilon_s}{dt} \cong \frac{12\, D_{\text{eff}}\phi_{\text{cp}}^{2/3}}{(3\upsilon_l/4\pi)^{2/3}}\left(\frac{1-\phi_{\text{cp}}}{\phi_{\text{cp}}}\upsilon_l - \upsilon_s\right)$	Expression for the diffusive layering of solid causing granule growth through slow deformations

Table 5.3 Physically based coalescence kernels and descriptions of their mechanisms

Name and equation	Comments
Granule scale collision mechanisms $\beta = \begin{cases} \beta 1, \text{ type I coalescence} \\ \beta_2, \text{ type II coalescence} \\ 0, \text{ rebound} \end{cases}$	This kernel is based on microscale collisions of two elastic plastic, deformable granules with possible liquid layer Type I is liquid layer dissipated coalescence, while type II is coalescence with some deformation of the granule (Liu and Litster, 2002)
Multidimensional function $\beta = \beta_0(x^3 + x'^3) \left[(c_x + c_{x'})^\alpha \left(100 - \frac{c_x + c_{x'}}{2} \right)^\delta \right]^\alpha$	Both size and liquid content are used to evaluate this kernel. Fitted parameters α and δ fit the effect of total concentrations of binder and the average concentrations of binder respectively. α and δ are fitting parameters (Madec et al., 2003)
Mechanistic kernel based on volume of liquid $\beta = \beta_0 \frac{q_{li} - q_{l^*i}}{4\pi\left(\frac{d_i}{2}\right)^2 \frac{q_{si} + q_{li}}{v_i}} - \frac{q_{lj} - q_{l^*j}}{4\pi\left(\frac{d_j}{2}\right)^2 \frac{(q_{sj} + q_{lj})}{v_j}}$	This kernel is a function of granule composition. Here $q_{lj} - q_{l^*j}$ is defined as the volume of liquid on the surface of the granule, similar to a critical saturation value. This effect ties coalescence directly to the consolidation of a granule (Darelius et al., 2006)

Table 5.4 Mechanistic breakage kernels that incorporate granule strength

Name and equation	Comments
Mechanistic breakage kernel $K_{\text{break}}(v) = \sum_{v=1}^{v_1-\text{upper}} \frac{\sigma_{\text{ext}}^{\text{particle}}(v, v')}{\sigma_{\text{int}}(v)} F(v)\, N_u \frac{SA(v')}{SA + WA + IA} + \frac{\sigma_{\text{ext}}^{\text{wall}}(v)}{\sigma_{\text{int}}(v)} \frac{WA}{SA + WA + IA} + \frac{\sigma_{\text{ext}}^{\text{impeller}}(v)}{\sigma_{\text{int}}(v)} \frac{IA}{SA + WA + IA} + \frac{\sigma_{\text{ext}}^{\text{fluid}}(v)}{\sigma_{\text{int}}(v)}$	This model assumes that the breakage of particles in a system will be proportional to the relative surface areas of their possible collision partner times the relative stress each partner impacts on a granule (Ramachandran et al., 2009).
Nuclei granule breakage kernel $K_{\text{break}}(v) = St_{\text{def}}^p u^q$ $b_{\text{break}}(v_i, v_j) = \frac{1}{v_j}$	This model incorporates the stokes deformation number into the form of the semimechanistic kernel (Liu et al., 2013)

(owing to consolidation), the radius and thickness of the droplet increases as more liquid keeps accumulating on the surface. This can be represented as a function of a constant contact angle, θ, and has been shown in Eq. (5.9).

$$R_{\text{wet}} = \sqrt[3]{\frac{3V}{\pi}}\Phi(\theta) \tag{5.9}$$

where

$$\Phi(\theta) = \frac{\sin^3(\theta)}{2 - 3\cos(\theta) + \cos^3(\theta)} \tag{5.10}$$

The depth of the surface liquid, h_0, can be expressed as a function of the volume and the wetted area as

$$h_0(s, l, g) = 1.5 \times \frac{V_{\text{ext}}(s, l, g)}{A_{\text{wet}}(s, l, g)} \tag{5.11}$$

The aggregation kernel can thus be represented as

$$\begin{aligned} &K_{\text{agg}}(s', l', g', s - s', l - l', g - g') \\ &= B_0\Psi(s', l', g', s - s', l - l', g - g') \times A(s', l', g', s - s', l - l', g - g') \end{aligned} \tag{5.12}$$

where $\Psi(s', l', g', s - s', l - l', g - g')$ is a binary variable depicting the Stokes criterion and can be written as expressed in Eq. (5.13) and $A(s', l', g', s - s', l - l', g - g')$ is obtained from the fractional wetted area of the two aggregating particles. $\Psi(s, l', g', s - s', l - l', g - g')$ can be calculated from the Stoke's criterion as

$$\Psi(s', l', g', s - s', l - l', g - g') = \begin{cases} 1, & \text{if } St \leq St^* \\ 0, & \text{if } St \geq St^* \end{cases} \tag{5.13}$$

where the Stokes number, St, and the critical Stokes number, St^*, can be written as

$$\begin{aligned} St &= \frac{8\tilde{m}u_0}{3\pi\mu\tilde{d}^2} \\ St^* &= 2\ln\frac{h_0}{h_a} \end{aligned} \tag{5.14}$$

where $\tilde{m}$ is the harmonic mean of the mass of the two particles, u_0 is the velocity of the particles, μ is the viscosity of the binder, d is the harmonic mean of the diameter of the aggregating particles and h_0 is the depth of the surface liquid on the particle. The factor $A(s', l', g', s - s', l - l', g - g')$ represents the product of the fractional wetted area of the two aggregating particles. Contrary to the monotonic variation in the aggregation kernel with an increase in any of the individual particle volumes, the semi-mechanistic kernel can better capture the effect of the individual (solid, liquid, or gas) volumes on the aggregation propensity. This has also been exhibited in Fig. 5.3.

Mechanistic breakage kernels continue to be developed that include models for the strength of materials and the stresses that populations of granules might undergo in high-shear granulation. The mechanistic kernel developed by Ramachandran et al. (2009) formulates the kernel as a series of ratios between the external stress applied to a granule and the intrinsic strength of a granule of class v. Relative contact areas for each collision type have also been incorporated into the model. The collision types include granule–granule, granule–wall, and granule–impeller breakage events. Each event is weighted according to the stress on the granule and the relative available surface area for the interaction to occur. The intrinsic strength is calculated according to relations for strength of liquid bridges between particles and the possible solid-solid cohesive strength. While extensive assumptions are made to develop the forms that relate breakage to intrinsic strength models and external stresses, this work exemplifies the use of physical understanding of granular systems in kernel design.

A less extensive approach was developed that relates the breakage kernel to the Stokes deformation number.

$$St_{\mathrm{def}} = \frac{\rho_g U^2}{2\tau_y} \tag{5.15}$$

where ρ_g is the granule density, U is the collision velocity of the particles, and τ_y is the yield stress. This dimensionless group is the ratio of the intensity of the

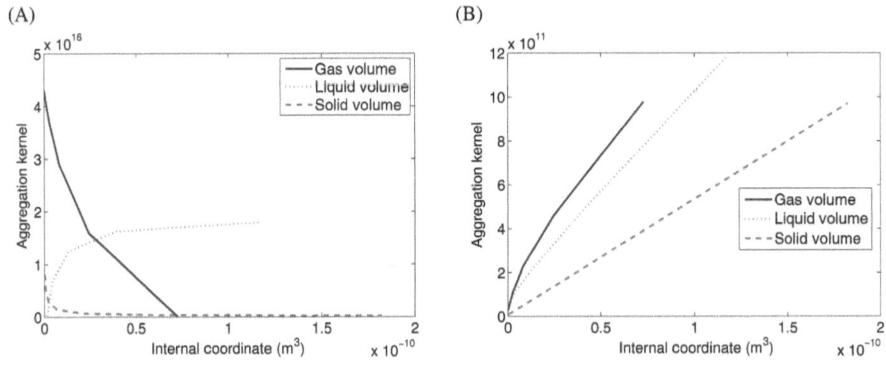

Figure 5.3 Comparison of the behavior of the semimechanistic kernel and the empirical kernels with respect to the individual volumes (β(1, 5, 1, 1, 5, :) for gas, β(1, 1, 1, 1, :, 5) for liquid and β(1, 1, 1, :,1, 1) for solid in both cases). (A) Semimechanistic kernel; (B) empirical kernel.
Source: Reprinted from Chaudhury, A., Wu, H., Khan, M., Ramachandran, R., 2014c. A mechanistic population balance model for granulation processes: effect of process and formulation parameters. Chem. Eng. Sci. 107, 76–92. Copyright (2014), with permission from Elsevier.

granulation to the strength of the granular material. While this single value may be used to characterize a particular system, it contains the same form as the mechanistic kernel discussed prior (Liu et al., 2013). This semimechanistic approach therefore attempts to inform the kernel with physically representative information as a part of the empirical fit.

5.2.3 Discrete element method

The DEM can also be used to simulate wet granulation processes. In contrast to the PBM, DEM considers the position and velocity of each individual granule as it moves through space, colliding with other particles and surfaces. This computationally expensive technique is typically used to simulate particle-scale mechanisms rather than process-level outcomes. This technique has been developed by Cundall and Strack (1979) and has been used extensively in recent years to model particulate pharmaceutical manufacturing processes (Ketterhagen et al., 2009). While PBMs typically simulate rate processes such as aggregation, breakage, and consolidation, DEM has several limitations in these areas. First, the physical contact models used in DEM simulations typically do not account for these rate processes, and the particles themselves remain unchanged before and after each collision. While some studies have simulated breakage and cohesion using DEM simulations, these typically rely on replacing a particle with several fragments or adding a cohesive force to the particles. Because of this limitation, most DEM studies for wet granulation processes focus on flow and velocity behavior rather than particle property changes (Freireich et al., 2009, 2011).

Cleary and Sinnott (2008) used DEM simulations to analyze mixing behavior in various mixing and granulation devices and characterized the effect of particle shape on mixing. In a different study, Hassanpour et al. (2009) studied the effect of operating scale on granule strength using DEM simulations, presenting particle flow and shear stress fields within the granulator and validating these results with experimental data using positron emission particle tracking. Nakamura et al. (2013) also investigated scale-up using DEM simulations, looking at the effects of vessel size on particle flow and collision energy. A different approach has been taken by Hassanpour et al. (2013), who simulated seeded granulation in DEM simulations by creating large seed granules that stick to smaller particles upon contact.

Some studies have used DEM simulations along with fluid modeling techniques, such as CFD, to model drop penetration of a liquid in a powder bed. Washino et al. (2013a) coupled DEM simulations with CFD to capture the capillary forces as a liquid droplet penetrates a particle bed, also applying drag forces on the particles captured by the liquid. Washino et al. (2013b) also used this technique to simulate drop penetration on a dynamic particle bed in a high-shear mixer to characterize the drop penetration time.

5.2.4 Hybrid PBM-DEM techniques

Hybrid PBM-DEM simulations are a new approach to capturing mechanistic details efficiently in a multiscale model. Several attempts have been made to effectively and efficiently combine these approaches. DEM simulations generally have two roles; first, to characterize flow and transport behavior of the particles in the system, and second, to obtain particle-scale collision and velocity data used to evaluate mechanistic rate kernels in the PBM. Ingram and Cameron (2005) presented and compared alternative multiscale modeling frameworks that combine DEM and PBM techniques, and some of these have since been demonstrated in practice.

Coupled with compartmental PBMs, DEM simulations have been used to obtain flow information to evaluate transfer between compartments. Chaudhury et al. (2015) presented a multicompartment PBM for a high-shear granulation process, using DEM data to identify the compartments and fluxes between them. This is meant to avoid the coupling of a PBM with DEM in order to accurately describe the system (and thus reduce the computational overheads). Bouffard et al. (2012) also used DEM simulations to complete a compartmental model of a granulation process.

Alternatively, DEM simulations can provide collision and velocity data as inputs to mechanistic rate expressions in the PBM, as demonstrated by Gantt and Gatzke (2006). Gantt and Gatzke (2006) present a mechanistic aggregation rate kernel as the product of a collision frequency function, or the rate at which two particle types collide, and a collision efficiency, or the likelihood that a collision event results in coalescence. Collision frequency data have been obtained directly from DEM simulations, and velocities have been used within a collision efficiency expression based on particle science theory. Gantt et al. (2006) extended this work to solve a multidimensional PBM. However, this model does not account for changes in collision rates and velocities as the system changes, demonstrating a one-way coupling approach.

Barrasso and Ramachandran (2015) extended this work, solving a PBM within a DEM simulation, using collision frequencies to evaluate agglomeration rates. The DEM simulation proceeds, and at specified time intervals, the DEM simulation pauses and the PBM is solved. As the PSD evolves, particles are removed or injected into the simulation to represent the current results of the PBM. The DEM simulation then proceeds until another evaluation of the PBM. Sen et al. (2014) also used this approach for a fluid bed granulator, coupling the PBM-DEM model with a CFD simulation. Reinhold and Briesen (2012) developed a similar technique using DEM simulations to predict aggregation rate kernels. To overcome the computational expense of the DEM simulations, Barrasso et al. (2014) replaced the DEM step with an artificial neural network trained from DEM data, finding good agreement with the fully coupled model.

Barrasso et al. (2015a,b) also developed a bidirectional coupling algorithm in which a detailed PBM is solved and new DEM simulations are triggered automatically when large changes occur in the particle properties. The DEM simulations provide collision and velocity data used to evaluate mechanistic aggregation, breakage, and consolidation rate expressions. The work of Barrasso et al. (2015a,b) is discussed in detail as a case study in section 4.3.

5.2.5 Compartmental approach for high-shear wet granulation processes

5.2.5.1 Vertical high-shear

The vertical high-shear granulator is usually considered as a single, well-mixed system. It is however an oversimplifying assumption due to the various heterogeneities within the system that exist due to the operation of the granulator under mechanical-dispersion regime (which is a more common observation) (Hapgood et al., 2002). Bouffard et al. (2012, 2013) had presented a procedure for representing the compartments in a rotor-based equipment using a Markov-chain approach. Their works, however, did not consider the change in particle size and number, which is characteristic of granulation processes. Primarily, the inhomogeneities exist with respect to the velocity of the particles and the binder dispersion. In Chaudhury et al. (2015), inhomogeneity with respect to binder is expressed by confining a separate spray zone wherein the liquid wets the particles. The physical experiment is mathematically mimicked by running it within a DEM framework. The granulator geometry is discretized into $15 \times 7 \times 15$ *gridbingroups* and the velocity data are exported over time. The inhomogeneities with respect to particle velocity is however demarcated using an elaborate procedure that utilizes statistical and data analytical tools (Chaudhury et al., 2015). Based on the analysis of the data, the compartment-based model is thus obtained which can successfully represent the mechanical-dispersion regime.

5.2.5.2 Twin screw

Experimental studies have found that, along the length of the granulator, the dominant rate mechanisms vary depending on the screw element (Dhenge et al., 2012; El Hagrasy and Litster, 2013). Further, granules evolve along the length of the granulator, as fine powder is fed at an inlet and larger granules exit from the outlet. As such, it is logical to divide the granulator into axial compartments, where the particles exiting from one compartment enter the next compartment. A residence time relationship can be used to evaluate the rate at which particles leave each compartment, as shown in Eq. (5.16) (Barrasso et al., 2015a,b).

$$\dot{F}_{\text{in}}(x, z_{i+1}, t) = \dot{F}_{\text{out}}(x, z_i, t) = \frac{F(x, z_i, t)}{\tau(z_i)} \tag{5.16}$$

Here, $\dot{F}_{\text{in}}(x, z_{i+1}, t)$ is the inlet particle flow rate in compartment $i+1$, and $\dot{F}_{\text{out}}(x, z_i, t)$ is the outlet flow rate from compartment i. These inlet and outlet particle flow rates can be treated as source terms in the population balance equation, which is solved separately for each compartment. The residence time in compartment i is given by $\tau(z_i)$. The residence time can be estimated from experimental data.

5.3 Numerical techniques

For granulation a population balance equation of a single mechanism (e.g., looking only at aggregation) can be solved analytically, however more complicated systems rely heavily on numerical techniques to find solutions. Typically, the numerical techniques can be divided into deterministic approaches and stochastic approaches. Deterministic approaches include discretization techniques such as cell-average technique, fixed-pivot method, moving pivot method, finite volume method and the finite element method. Monte Carlo techniques fall under the category of stochastic approaches. It gives the solution with a degree of uncertainty rather than a determined numerical solution (Smith and Matsoukas, 1998).

5.3.1 Monte Carlo solution techniques

Monte Carlo simulations calculate the changes in a sample population of granules that undergo discrete events. Because Monte Carlo simulations are event focused; they lend themselves well to the task of tracking the coalescence and breakage of granules as well as other rate processes. Two major types of Monte Carlo simulation exist: time-driven and event-driven simulations. These two types of simulations either progress a certain time after an event is performed (event-driven), or perform any number of events in a given time interval (time-driven). Further distinctions can be made to types of Monte Carlo simulations as to how the total number of particles or the total volume is tracked as the simulation elapses (Zhao et al., 2007). Multidimensional properties of a population of particles can be tracked through each of the possible events in a Monte Carlo simulation and be extrapolated to predict the properties of the population as a whole. For example a multidimensional vector of granule properties could contain solid volume, pore volume, and external and internal liquid volume (Braumann et al., 2010). Processes similar to those in Table 5.1 describe the effects of each of the mechanisms on this particle population. The early stages of a high-shear granulation were investigated using a 2D population balance and solved using a Monte Carlo method (Oullion et al., 2009). By simulating the rate processes of nucleation and growth of the initial granules this work is able to capture complicated dynamic interactions within the stochastic framework.

5.3.2 Lumped-parameter approach for PBM

It is known 1D PBMs are often used to model particulate processes, typically tracking particle distributions with respect to size. However, adopting multidimensional models would be the right approach owing to its ability to track multiple crucial granule attributes.

To reduce the dimensionality of a PBM, but still track these key particle properties, a lumped-parameter approach can be used. The internal coordinate space is described by one or more distributed dimensions, such as size. An assumption is made that every granule in a given size class has the same properties, such as liquid content and porosity. However, these properties can change over time as the particles are subjected to rate process, such as liquid addition and consolidation. In addition to the main population balance equation, a new equation is used to track each lumped property on the distributed domain. Eqs. (5.17) and (5.18) demonstrate this technique.

$$\frac{\partial F(x,t)}{\partial t} + \frac{\partial}{\partial x}\left[F(x,t)\frac{dx}{dt}\right] = \Re_{\text{form}}(x,t) - \Re_{\text{dep}}(x,t) \tag{5.17}$$

$$\frac{\partial M(x,t)}{\partial t} + \frac{\partial}{\partial x}\left[M(x,t)\frac{dx}{dt}\right] = \Re_{M,\text{form}}(x,t) - \Re_{M,\text{dep}}(x,t) \tag{5.18}$$

Here, F is the particle density, and x is the distributed parameter, such as size. $M(x,t)$ is the total mass or volume of the lumped parameter of all particles of size x. $\Re_{M,\text{form}}$ and $\Re_{M,\text{dep}}$ are the formation and depletion rates of the lumped parameter. Expressions for these source terms have been developed for aggregation and breakage (Hounslow et al., 2001).

The lumped-parameter approach was first demonstrated for granulation by Hounslow et al. (2001) to monitor the mass of a tracer in each size class throughout a high-shear granulation process. Biggs et al. (2003) used this technique to track the average liquid content in each size class, using an aggregation rate kernel that depends on particle wetness. Barrasso and Ramachandran (2012) extended this technique to higher dimensions, comparing a fully distributed four-dimensional PBM to PBMs of lower dimensionality with various lumped parameters. Results showed a drastic reduction in computation time using the lumped-parameter approach. However, some models are unable to capture the effects of the lumped parameters on the final size distribution. This limitation is particularly pronounced when the rate kernels depended strongly on the lumped parameters.

5.3.3 Multidimensional cell-average technique

Multidimensional PBMs can be discretized using a linear grid spanning the range for the solid, liquid and gas volume grids. The partial derivatives with respect to the internal coordinates representing the various underlying mechanisms are addressed using finite difference techniques, resulting in ordinary differential equations (ODEs). This final system of ODEs (IVP) is integrated using the first-order Euler technique. Eq. (5.1) can be expressed in the discrete form as shown in Eq. (5.19).

$$\begin{aligned}\frac{dF'_{i,j,k}}{dt} &+ \left(\frac{F'_{i,j,k}}{\Delta s_i}\frac{ds}{dt}\bigg|_{s_i} - \frac{F'_{i+1,j,k}}{\Delta s_{i+1}}\frac{ds}{dt}\bigg|_{s_{i+1}}\right) + \left(\frac{F'_{i,j,k}}{\Delta l_j}\frac{dl}{dt}\bigg|_{l_j} - \frac{F'_{i,j+1,k}}{\Delta l_{j+1}}\frac{dl}{dt}\bigg|_{l_{j+1}}\right)\\ &+ \left(\frac{F'_{i,j,k}}{\Delta g_k}\frac{dg}{dt}\bigg|_{g_k} - \frac{F'_{i,j,k+1}}{\Delta g_{k+1}}\frac{dl}{dt}\bigg|_{g\ k+1}\right) = \Re_{\text{agg}}(s_i, l_j, g_k) + \Re_{\text{break}}(s_i, l_j, g_k)\end{aligned} \tag{5.19}$$

Here $F'_{i,j,k} = \int_{s_i}^{s_{i+1}} \int_{l_j}^{l_{j+1}} \int_{g_k}^{g_{k+1}} F(s,l,g)\, dsdldg$, s_i is the value of the solid volume at the upper end of the ith bin along the solid volume axis, l_j is the value of the liquid volume at the upper end of the jth bin along the liquid volume axis, g_k is the value of the gas volume at the upper end of the kth bin along the gas volume axis. We find Δs_i, Δl, and Δ_{gk} are the sizes of the ith, jth, and kth bin with respect to the solid, liquid, and gas volume axis. Using this technique, the population balance equation is reduced to a system of ODEs in terms of the aggregation ($\Re_{\text{agg}}(s_i, l_j, g_k)$) and breakage ($\Re_{\text{break}}\ (s_i, l_j, g_k)$). The triple integral for the aggregation term can thereby be evaluated by casting it into simpler addition and multiplication terms. This approach can effectively solve PBMs, however the computational expenses associated with the technique is high owing to the large number of grids required to span the volume range (for solid, liquid, gas). The computational overheads for the solution of the PBM can be relieved by discretizing the spatial domain using a nonlinear grid. Because a nonlinear grid is considered for the solution of the PBM, the newborn particle from aggregation/breakage might not exactly lie on the grid, suggesting the need for another technique to circumvent this issue. This particle needs to be reallocated, in certain fractions, to the neighboring grids. The approach similar to that of Kumar et al. (2006) has been utilized, where primarily the third moment, total volume/mass of particles is conserved. For n grid points with respect to each individual volume, there are n^3 ODEs representing the number of particles in each bin (i,j,k).

The average solid volume, $V_{s,i,j,k}$ (also average liquid, $V_{l,i,j,k}$ and gas volume, $V_{g,ij,k}$) are obtained by multiplying the solid volume of the new particle formed (agglomeration-volume of the agglomerate, breakage-volume of the daughter fragment) to the formation term as described in Eqs. (5.3) and (5.6). This is basically obtained by summing the solid volumes s' and $s - s'$ of the colliding particles (in case of aggregation). From this, the average value of each property in cell C_{ijk} can be calculated, as follows (similar formulation can yield $\bar{l}_{i,j,k}$ and $\bar{g}_{i,j,k}$) :

$$\bar{s}_{i,j,k} = \frac{V_{s,i,j,k}}{B_{ijk}} \tag{5.20}$$

In this context, B_{ijk} is the birth of particles due to agglomeration or breakage. For sake of conciseness, $s_{i,j,k}$, $l_{i,j,k}$, and $g_{i,j,k}$ are expressed as s_i, l_j, and g_k. This is the birth that is distributed to the neighboring nodes when the birth does not fall exactly on a representative node (the usual case). For a 3D grid, distribution would occur to eight neighboring nodes. Let us suppose that the particle fractions α_1, α_2, α_3, α_4, α_5, α_6, α_7, and α_8 are distributed to the neighboring nodes $P_{i,j,k}$, $P_{i+1,j,k}$, $P_{i+1,j+1,k}$, $P_{i,j+1,k}$, $P_{i,j,k+1}$, $P_{i+1,j,k+1}$, $P_{i+1,j+1,k+1}$, and $P_{i,j+1,k+1}$, respectively. Then, the particle fractions must satisfy 13 equations, to conserve the total volume as well as the particle number (Chaudhury et al., 2014a,b,c).

This fractionation thus obtained from the conservation equations can cause many births to occur on a single representative point. These births need to be added together to obtain the cell-average birth. This cell-average birth is used in lieu of the birth term in the PBM. No redistribution occurs to obtain a death term, as death is just the disappearance of particles from a representative point. From the method of mathematical induction, it can be noted that for an N-dimensional population balance equation, a particle would distribute into 2^N fractions into its adjacent grid points. The 2^N fractions corresponding to the 2^N neighboring grids can be obtained in a similar way as the 2^3 fractions for the 3D PBM was obtained.

5.3.4 Tensor decomposition method

A reduced order framework can also be obtained for the solution of PBMs with minimal computational overheads. Solving the PBM with fine grid widths help reduce the discretization error in the numerical framework. This results in having to use large number of grids in each dimension of the multidimensional framework so that the entire range of the particle attribute can be spanned. The computation time for solving the PBM increases polynomially as the number of grids thus making the solution to the PBM infeasible. The tensor decomposition method allows the solution of the PBM using large number of linear grids. The curse of dimensionality can be significantly broken by this approach, whereby not only the computation is faster but memory limitations are also overcome.

This approach involves making approximations for the aggregation kernel by separation of variables. The aggregation kernel for a 3D PBM is a 6D array (three dimensions for each independent variable of the colliding particles), which involves large computational time for its calculation and incorporates huge computation overheads into the calculation of the triple integral in the aggregation term. Once the aggregation kernel is approximated, the triple integral in the aggregation term can be treated as a convolution, which can be computed using Fast Fourier transforms. The breakage distribution is also dimensionally reduced using separation of variables followed by iteratively summing (to calculate the integral) the product of the breakage kernel, the breakage distribution function, and the particle density in that bin. The details of this procedure and the equations are provided in Chaudhury et al. (2013b).

The techniques proposed in Chaudhury et al. (2013b) can be individually applied or utilized with a combination of these methods to obtain the computationally fast, reduced memory requiring reduced order model. This approach is more efficient while solving the PBM with larger number of grids. The accuracy obtained from this framework is high, with a relative error in the order of 10^{-13}. The time savings obtained are also significant. While performing numerical experiments, simulating the model for 500 s took $\sim$23 and $\sim$9960 s for 6 grids and 26 grids respectively. On the other hand, the reduced order framework required 3.8 and $\sim$200 seconds for solving the PBM with same number of grids with high accuracy. This establishes the advantage of developing reduced order frameworks using the tensor decomposition technique and motivates the utilization of such approaches in solving high-dimensional PBMs.

5.4 Application of high-shear wet granulation models

5.4.1 Case study of parameter estimation

PBMs can be efficiently used to describe wet granulation processes. A major drawback of using PBMs, is the presence of multiple empirical parameters in the mathematical model. This necessitates the need for employing efficient parameter estimation techniques in order to obtain optimal parametric values to calibrate the model. The calibrated PBM can thus be utilized for predictive purposes. Utilizing a mechanistic model would be a better practice owing to its ability to make predictions beyond the design space of model calibration. Various CQAs are of significant importance in the wet granulation process. The PSD and granule porosity are crucial particle properties that are tailored through the wet granulation process. These finally affect the compatibility of the solid into tablets and are thus vital properties to be controlled.

Utilizing empirical kernels to describe aggregation and breakage can make it computationally less expensive; however, the predictability of the model is limited within the design space. The kernel proposed by Madec et al. (2003) and Soos et al. (2006) for aggregation and breakage respectively is considered in the model to describe the source terms. The parameter estimation can be expressed as a multiobjective optimization problem in the form of an ε-constraint formulation. The problem can be formulated as

$$\Phi(\theta) = \min_{\theta} \sum_{k=1}^{N} (O_k - E_k(\theta))^2 \tag{5.21}$$

$$\theta = [\beta_0 \; \alpha \; \delta \; B \; c \; x_{\text{sat}} \; \varepsilon_{\min}] \tag{5.22}$$

In Eqs. (5.21) and (5.22), θ is the set of adjustable parameters, O_k is the *kth* measurement value, $E_k(\theta)$ is the simulated value of that measurement, and N is the total number of measurements across all experiments used in parameter estimation. The measurements encompass the porosity values of a particular size class as well as the relative volume of each size class in the final PSD. The experimental data are obtained from Pandey et al. (2013).

The readers are also directed to Pandey et al. (2013) or Chaudhury et al. (2014a,b,c) for the design of experiments (DOE) for the estimation. This multiobjective optimization problem is solved using the particle swarm algorithm as proposed by Kennedy and Eberhart (1995). Minor modifications were made to the algorithm (Chaudhury et al., 2014a,b,c), so that the optimization can be efficiently carried out.

The optimization algorithm not only fits the model to the entire experimental PSD but also to the porosity (simultaneously). The fitted CQAs have been shown in Fig. 5.4A, B. Experimentally, the size was analyzed using sieving techniques, which is not a very accurate procedure for particle size analysis due to a large

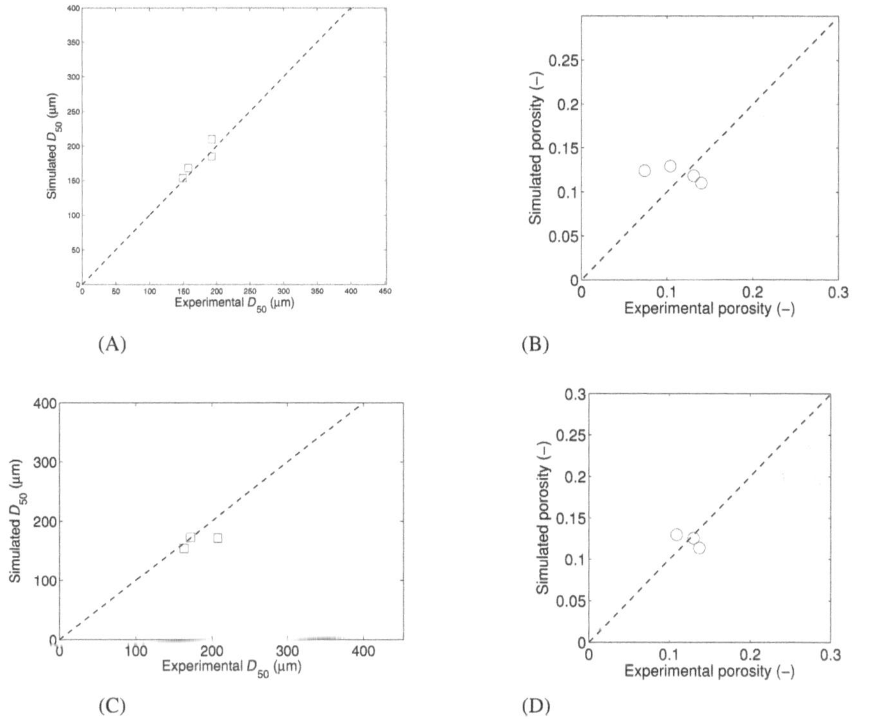

Figure 5.4 Estimated and predicted CQAs from a high-shear granulator using multiobjective parameter estimation: (A) estimated D_{50}; (B) estimated granule porosity; (C) model prediction: D_{50}; and (D) model prediction: granule porosity.
Source: With kind permission from Springer Science + Business Media: Chaudhury, A., Barrasso, D., Pandey, P., Wu, H., Ramachandran, R., 2014a. Population balance model development, validation, and prediction of CQAs of a high-shear wet granulation process: towards QbD in drug product pharmaceutical manufacturing. J. Pharm. Innov. 9 (1), 53–64. Figs. 5.3, 5.4, 5.6, 5.7.

amount of mechanical energy required for the particles to pass through the screen (by overcoming particle–particle and particle–screen interactions). The sums of squared error, *SSE*, between the simulated and the experimental distributions are significantly low. In Fig. 5.4, the 45-degree line in the plot represents complete agreement between the experimental and simulated values. The batches operated at lower impeller speeds have been used for parameter estimation. The model predictions are shown in Fig. 5.4C,D. The predicted PSD shows low error between the simulated and the experimental distributions, and the *SSE* for these predictions are of approximately the same magnitude as those used to calibrate the model (Fig. 5.4C,D). The plots suggest good agreement between the experimental and the simulated/predicted results for the particle size and the porosity.

5.4.2 Case study of compartment model of high-shear granulation

In order to obtain the compartment model, a series of steps involving DEM simulations and data analysis is employed. The variation in particle number and size has been taken into account while running the DEM simulations to mimic the physical process. Multiple short DEM simulations were run with intermediate PSD data for the experiment. The intermediate PSD has been generated using a PBM, which is calibrated using the experimental end point particle size data. The velocity data within the granulator is exported from DEM and is further utilized to identify and implement the compartments. *k*-means clustering technique was employed to identify the various compartments within the high-shear granulator. It involves defining *k* centroids (each representing a cluster) that are placed in a systematic way within the dataset with the common choice being its placement farthest from each other. The next step involves associating all the points within the dataset to the nearest centroid that is a representative of the cluster. An initial cluster is thus obtained, however it is further revised and the obtainment of the final set of clusters is an iterative process involving the minimization of the distance between the points and the centroids. Choosing an optimal value for *k* is also a crucial task. A lower value of *k* might lead to inadequacy with the clustering while a larger value of *k* can lead to overfitting. The sum-of-squares of the variance as a function of the value of *k* is plotted, which is followed by identifying the elbow of the plot Yu et al. (2011) to fix the value of *k* (compartments).

Based on this analysis, the compartments within the granulator have been identified and the size and centroids of the compartments are noted dynamically and as a function of impeller speed and liquid to solid ratio in the system (Fig. 5.5). Regression analysis was performed using Design Expert that yields expressions to describe the size and centroid of each compartment dynamically and across the DOE. The expressions obtained from ANOVA are shown in Table 5.5 and the validation for using these experiments for other experiments within the design space is shown in Fig. 5.6.

The various compartments that have been identified from the preceding analysis leads to the demarcation of four distinct regions within the granulator with respect to velocity and liquid distribution. The spray region, the shear region, and high and low velocity region within the bulk can address the heterogeneities in a lumped manner. The spray region is characterized by the wetting mechanism, the shear zone comprises of breakage while the bulk (high and low velocity) comprise of primarily aggregation and consolidation along with some breakage. The overall granulator can be modeled using four compartments within which a particular mechanism predominates and which also exchange particles between each other in an arrangement similar to parallel electrical circuits. This framework can be represented in the form of a system of partial differential equations as shown in Eqs. (5.23)–(5.26).

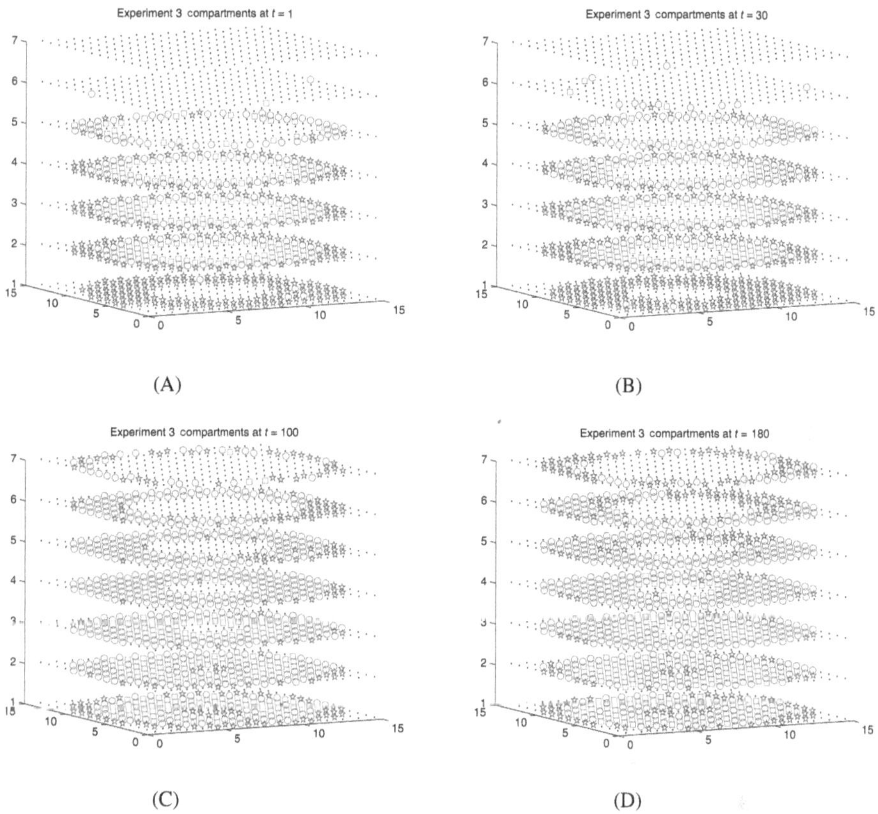

Figure 5.5 Clusters within the granulator at different time instances (· - *compartment* 1, ○ - *compartment* 2, □ - *compartment* 3, * - *compartment* 4). The *X*, *Y*, and *Z* axis depicts the *gridbingroups* in the DEM simulation replicating the granulator. (A) $t = 1$; (B) $t = 30$; (C) $t = 100$; and (D) $t = 180$.

Source: Reprinted from Chaudhury, A., Armenante, M.E., Ramachandran, R., 2015. Compartment based population balance modeling of a high shear wet granulation process using data analytics. Chem. Eng. Res. Des. 95, 211–228. Copyright (2015), with permission from Elsevier.

$$\frac{\partial}{\partial t}F_1(s,l,g,t) + \frac{\partial}{\partial l}\left[F_1(s,l,g,t\frac{dl}{dt}\right] = \mathrm{Flux}_{1,\,\Delta\alpha}(s,l,g,t) + \mathrm{Flux}_{1,\,\mathrm{wet}}(s,l,g,t) \tag{5.23}$$

$$\frac{\partial}{dt}F_2(s,l,g,t) + \frac{\partial}{\partial g}\left[F_2(s,l,g,t\frac{dg}{dt}\right] = \Re_{\mathrm{agg},\,2}(s,l,g,t) + \Re_{\mathrm{break},\,2}(s,l,g,t) + \mathrm{Flux}_{2,\,\Delta\alpha} + \mathrm{Flux}_{2,\,\mathrm{wet}}(s,l,g,t) \tag{5.24}$$

Table 5.5 Polynomials for centroids and sizes developed from ANOVA (where A is Time, B is Liquid Content, C is impeller speed)

Property	Significant terms	Polynomial
Centroid for shear zone	A,C	$-0.64 - 1.08 \times 10^{-3}A + 0.18C + 3.52 \times 10^{-4}AC$
Centroid for low velocity bulk zone	A,C	$-0.88 + 1.20 \times 10^{-4}A + 0.27C$
Centroid for high velocity bulk zone	A,C	$-0.43 - 2.58 \times 10^{-4}A + 0.07C - 3.30 \times 10^{-4}AC + 5.36 \times 10^{-6}A^2 + 0.03C^2$
Size for shear zone	A,B,C	$-366.2 + 11.77A + 11.69B + 101.4C - 0.222AB - 1.95AC - 0.036A^2$ $-0.197B^2 + 7.02 \times 10^{-3}A^2C + 3.73 \times 10^{-3}AB^2 + 1.38 \times 10^{-5}A^3$
Size for low velocity bulk zone	A,B,C	$-390.0 + 4.69A - 9.80B + 133.5C - 0.012A^2 + 0.16B^2$
Size for high velocity bulk zone	A,B,C	$-115.6 + 2.39A + 29.0B - 24.37C - 0.164AC - 3.47 \times 10^{-3}A^2 - 0.48B^2$
Size of spray zone	B,C	$1.585 - 0.022B + 0.11C - 2.45 \times 10^{-3}BC + 3.79 \times 10^{-4}B^2$

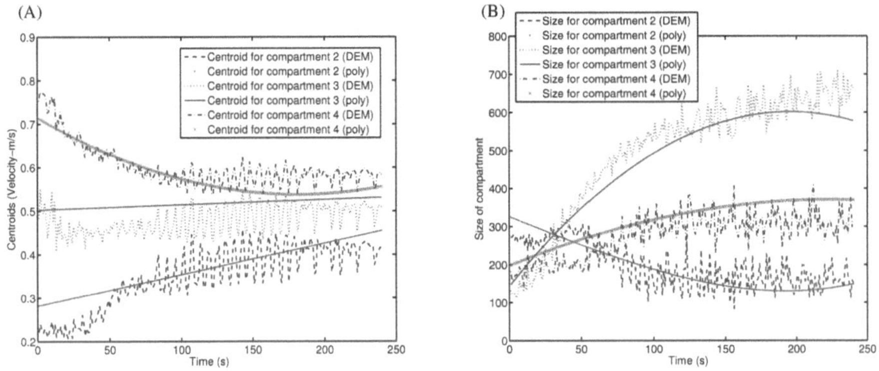

Figure 5.6 Validation results from the regression analysis: (A) centroid values for L/S = 30%, impeller speed = 5.05 m/s; (B) cluster sizes (number of *gridbingroup* belonging to a cluster) for L/S = 30%, Impeller speed = 5.05 m/s.
Source: Reprinted from Chaudhury, A., Armenante, M.E., Ramachandran, R., 2015. Compartment based population balance modeling of a high shear wet granulation process using data analytics. Chem. Eng. Res. Des. 95, 211–228. Copyright (2015), with permission from Elsevier.

$$\frac{\partial}{dt}F_3(s,l,g,t) + \frac{\partial}{\partial g}\left[F_3(s,l,g,t\frac{dg}{dt}\right] = \Re_{\text{agg},\,3}(s,l,g,t) + \Re_{\text{break},\,3}(s,l,g,t) + \text{Flux}_{3,\,\Delta\alpha}(s,l,g,t) + \text{Flux}_{3,\,\text{wet}}(s,l,g,t) \tag{5.25}$$

$$\frac{\partial}{\partial t}F_4(s,l,g,t) = \Re_{\text{break},\,4}(s,l,g,t) + \text{Flux}_{4,\,\Delta\alpha}(s,l,g,t) + \text{Flux}_{4,\,\text{wet}}(s,l,g,t) \tag{5.26}$$

where F_i represents the number of particles enclosed within the ith compartment. The number of particles in the ith compartment is obtained by multiplying the initial size fraction of the ith compartment (size of the ith compartment/sum of sizes of all compartments) to the total number of particles present within the granulator. For the granulation process, because there is an overall change in the particle size and the number of particles involved, mechanistically tracking the fluxes ($Flux_{i,\,\Delta\alpha}$ and $Flux_{i,\text{wet}}$) between the particles becomes complicated. The compartment model presented in this section first isolates the number of particles enclosed within each compartment followed by updating the PBM for the particular compartment that modifies the evolution of a particular property among a number of particles that are present in the compartment. The fluxes, $Flux_{i,\Delta\alpha}$, entering or leaving a compartment is calculated based on the size change of each compartment while $Flux_{i,\text{wet}}$ enables the distribution of wet particles from the spray zone to the various compartments and vice-versa. The variable α_i represents the normalized size of the compartment or the size fraction of a compartment (α_i = *size of compartment i/cumulative size of all compartments* = $V_i/\Sigma_i V_i$). It should be noted that an accurate model for the surface-renewal-theory-based approach has not been implemented for the spray zone. However, in order to account for the renewal of the wet surface in the spray zone, 60% of particles within the spray zone are circulated to other compartments in order to allow distribution of the liquid. Another assumption with the distribution of particles among compartments involves reassigning same volume (based on 60% of the particles in the spray zone) of wet particles within each of the other three compartments. This is however an arbitrary choice for circulating the wet particles and a more accurate modeling approach would require implementing the principles of surface renewal theory (Sherony, 1981).

The primary objective behind formulating a compartment-based model is to be able to successfully track the inhomogeneities within the well-mixed high-shear granulator. Some consequences of considering a well-mixed homogeneous model include the incapability in tracking the mechanical-dispersion regime (Hapgood et al., 2003). A wider PSD is expected when the system is not well-mixed or the binder is not distributed properly across the granulator. Hapgood et al. (2003) correlated the mechanical-dispersion regime as a function of the spray flux. The spray flux can be attributed to the various process parameters such as the viscosity of the binder, the mode of binder addition, the amount of binder added. Using the compartment model presented in this work, not only can these conditions be effectively captured, but the variation in the mechanisms due to changing average velocity can also be accounted for. It is expected that the PSD would be wider for a more heterogeneous case. As a consequence of this approach, the overall PSD within the granulator is wider in case of the compartment model (as shown in Fig. 5.7). However, as time progresses, the system homogenizes and as expected intuitively, the PSD gets narrower. This suggests the capability of the compartment model to be able to capture the mechanical-dispersion regime. The utilization of a compartment model can thus enable better representation of the granulation process taking place in a high-shear granulator.

5.4.3 Case study of PBM-DEM coupling

Barrasso et al. (2015a,b) developed a mechanistic model for a twin screw wet granulation process and bidirectional coupling algorithm using PBM and DEM techniques. A two-dimensional PBM is created, tracking distributions in particle size and liquid content, and the lumped-parameter technique is implemented to track the porosity in each bin. Additionally, a distinction is made between internal and external liquid, so a reduction in particle porosity enhances coalescence. Mechanistic expressions for aggregation, breakage, and consolidation are used, and DEM simulations provided the necessary collision and velocity data to evaluate these rates.

The bidirectional coupling algorithm has been designed and implemented using gPROMS ModelBuilder 4.0 to solve the PBM and automatically execute DEM simulations using STAR-CCM + v9.02. A diagram of the algorithm is presented in Fig. 5.8. When significant changes to the state of the system are observed, such as

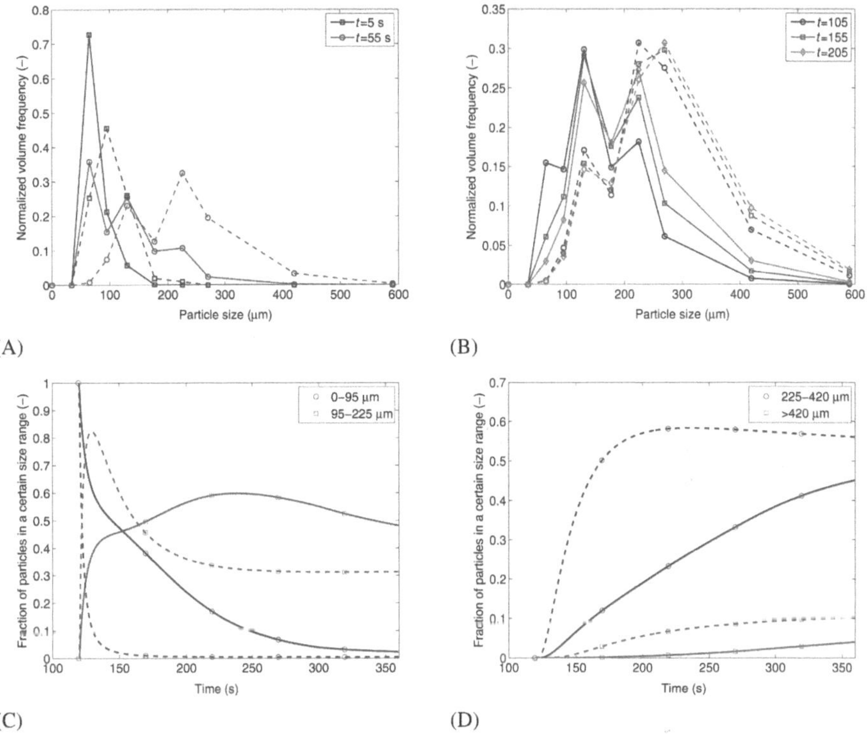

Figure 5.7 Comparison between the single and multicompartment model (time mentioned in the legend is after the onset of liquid addition). (A) PSD for the single and compartment model at initial time instances (single = dashed line, compartment = solid line); (B) PSD for the single and compartment model at later time instances (single = dashed line, compartment = solid line); (C) Evolution of the PSD (for finer particles) over time (single = dashed line, compartment = solid line); (D) Evolution of the PSD (for coarser particles) over time (single = dashed line, compartment = solid line).
Source: Reprinted from Chaudhury, A., Armenante, M.E., Ramachandran, R., 2015. Compartment based population balance modeling of a high shear wet granulation process using data analytics. Chem. Eng. Res. Des. 95, 211–228. Copyright (2015), with permission from Elsevier.

a change in average particle size or liquid content, new DEM simulations are triggered to update the particle-scale collision and velocity data.

The model has been used to model two separate compartments of a twin screw granulator. The first compartment consisted of a conveying screw, while the second comprises of kneading elements with a 90% offset angle. As shown in Fig. 5.9, the two compartments produced different granules. The particles in the conveying screw stayed relatively small, with little aggregation or growth, while some large granules formed in the mixing elements. This result is likely because the particles in the kneading elements collide more frequently and with a wider velocity

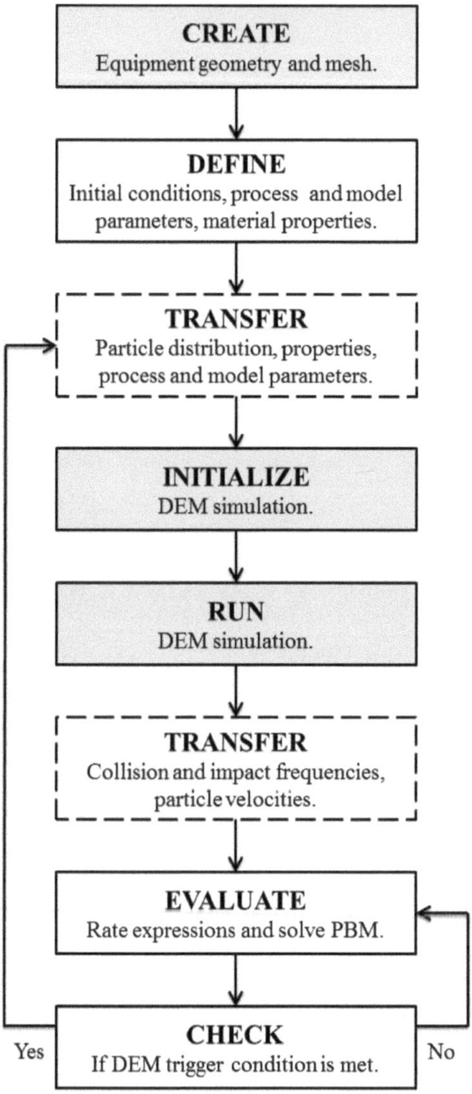

Figure 5.8 Schematic of bidirectional coupling approach. Boxes shaded in gray are executed in STAR-CCM + , and white, solid-lined boxes are executed in gPROMS ModelBuilder. Dashed lines indicate data transfer across software platforms.
Source: Reprinted from Barrasso, D., Eppinger, T., Pereira, F.E., Aglave, R., Debus, K., Bermingham, S.K., et al., 2015b. A multi-scale, mechanistic model of a wet granulation process using a novel bi-directional PBM-DEM coupling algorithm. Chem. Eng. Sci. 123, 500–513. Copyright (2015), with permission from Elsevier.

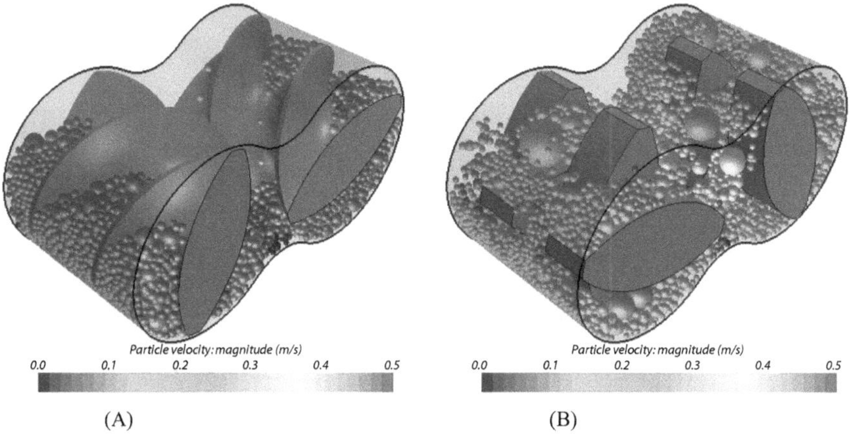

Figure 5.9 Snapshots of coupled PBM-DEM simulations for a compartment of a twin screw granulator after 30 s. (A) Conveying elements; (B) Kneading elements.
Source: Reprinted from Barrasso, D., Eppinger, T., Pereira, F.E., Aglave, R., Debus, K., Bermingham, S.K., et al., 2015b. A multi-scale, mechanistic model of a wet granulation process using a novel bi-directional PBM-DEM coupling algorithm. Chem. Eng. Sci. 123, 500–513. Copyright (2015), with permission from Elsevier.

distribution, resulting in faster coalescence. The geometry used for the DEM simulations was the only difference in the two models, demonstrating the ability of the coupled PBM-DEM model to capture sensitivities to equipment geometry.

Fig. 5.10 shows additional results of these simulations, showing the effects of screw geometry and rotational speed on the product size distribution and evolution of the average diameter, porosity, and external liquid volume over time. The kneading elements produced more large granules than the conveying screw and with lower porosities, indicating that more consolidation occurs in the kneading elements. Further, an increase in screw speed results in larger, denser particles with more surface liquid. These results demonstrate the ability of the coupled model to predict the effects of design parameters on the product attributes, leading to a model-based approach to Quality by Design.

5.5 General discussion and conclusions

It is a well-established fact that wet granulation processes are extremely vital to the processing of pharmaceutical oral dosage forms. Mathematical modeling of wet granulation process can significantly facilitate the operation of this complex, particulate process. The readers are provided with a sample workflow (Fig. 5.11) to derive guidance on how to alleviate inefficient process operation using mathematical models. Various approaches have surfaced in the past few decades that exemplify efficient methods for modeling and operating the granulation process in an improved

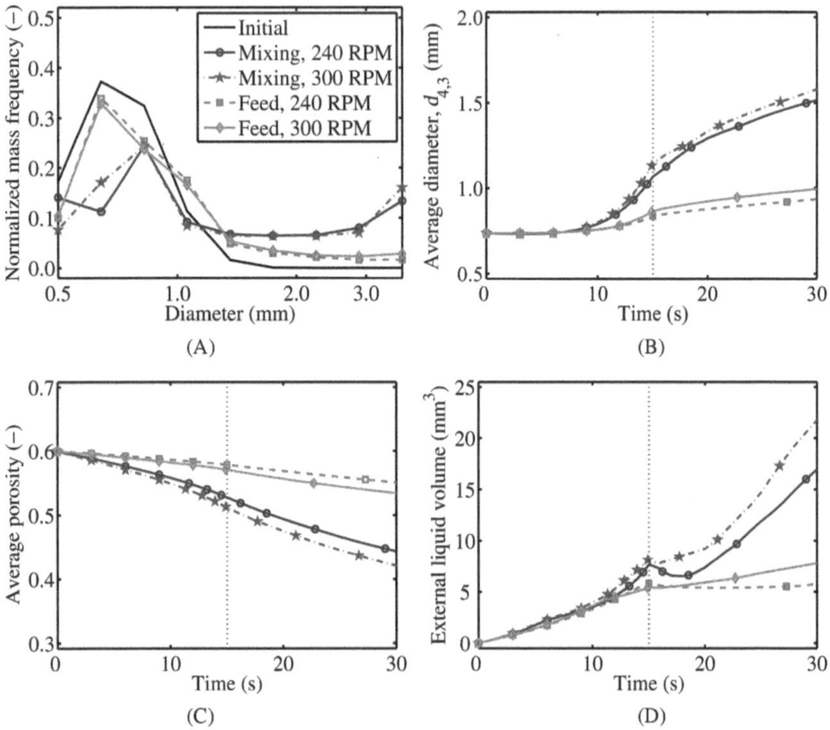

Figure 5.10 PBM-DEM results showing effects of equipment geometry and screw speed on (A) the product size distribution, (B) the average diameter over time, (C) the average porosity over time, and (D) the total volume of external liquid over time. The points on time plots indicate DEM iterations. Vertical lines denote the end of the liquid addition period. *Source*: Reprinted from Barrasso, D., Eppinger, T., Pereira, F.E., Aglave, R., Debus, K., Bermingham, S.K., et al., 2015b. A multi-scale, mechanistic model of a wet granulation process using a novel bi-directional PBM-DEM coupling algorithm. Chem. Eng. Sci. 123, 500–513. Copyright (2015), with permission from Elsevier.

manner. Apart from developing novel modeling techniques, efficient numerical techniques have also been developed which can enable the solution of complex models with greater ease. The modeling techniques utilized for representing wet granulation can be categorized as multiscale or confined to a single scale. While multiscale approaches provide better representation of the unit operation, their computational complexity could be a major issue. In this chapter, various mathematical approaches have been discussed that can facilitate the modeling of wet granulation processes. PBMs are very efficient with the modeling of wet granulation processes due to their discrete nature and reduced computational expense compared to other multiscale models. A detailed discussion is also provided with respect to the various numerical techniques that can be employed for the solution of PBMs. The numerical techniques comprise of reduced order models and other approaches to efficiently solve the PBM while keeping the computational overheads to a minimum.

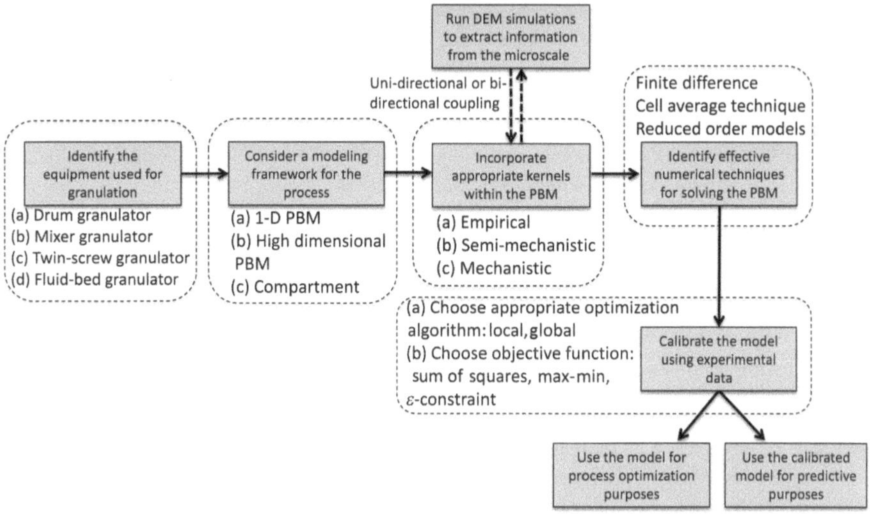

Figure 5.11 Typical workflow to be utilized to build in QbD into process operation.

Various numerical techniques, including reduced order models and other approaches, are used to efficiently solve the PBM while keeping the computational overheads to a minimum. The employment of effective parameter estimation techniques can add a predictive ability to the PBMs. The inclusion of compartments within the granulator and utilizing a separate equation for each of these behaviorally different zones can account for the inhomogeneities within the granulator. A coupled PBM-DEM model illustrates a multiscale model, which can mechanistically represent the dynamics of a wet granulation process, however it is computationally very expensive. There are other approaches which can somewhat help with overcoming this limitation. This chapter provides a comprehensive discussion that illustrates the application of mathematical modeling to wet granulation processes to enable the granulation processes to be better understood scientifically.

References

Adetayo, A.A., Ennis, B.J., 1997. Unifying approach to modeling granule coalescence mechanisms. AIChE J. 43 (4), 927–934.

Annapragada, A., Neilly, J., 1996. On the modelling of granulation processes: a short note. Powder Technol. 89 (1), 83–84.

Badawy, S.I., Menning, M.M., Gorko, M.A., Gilbert, D.L., 2000. Effect of process parameters on compressibility of granulation manufactured in a high-shear mixer. Int. J. Pharm. 198 (1), 51–61.

Barrasso, D., Ramachandran, R., 2012. A comparison of model order reduction techniques for a four-dimensional population balance model describing multi-component wet granulation processes. Chem. Eng. Sci. 80, 380–392.

Barrasso, D., Ramachandran, R., 2015. Multi-scale modeling of granulation processes: bi-directional coupling of PBM with DEM via collision frequencies. Chem. Eng. Res. Des. 93, 304–317.

Barrasso, D., Tamrakar, A., Ramachandran, R., 2014. A reduced order PBM-ANN model of a multi-scale PBM-DEM description of a wet granulation process. Chem. Eng. Sci. 119, 319–329.

Barrasso, D., El Hagrasy, A., Litster, J.D., Ramachandran, R., 2015a. Multi-dimensional population balance model development and validation for a twin screw granulation process. Powder Technol. 270 (Part B), 612–621.

Barrasso, D., Eppinger, T., Pereira, F.E., Aglave, R., Debus, K., Bermingham, S.K., et al., 2015b. A multi-scale, mechanistic model of a wet granulation process using a novel bi-directional PBM-DEM coupling algorithm. Chem. Eng. Sci. 123, 500–513.

Biggs, C., Sanders, C., Scott, A., Willemse, A., Hoffman, A., Instone, T., et al., 2003. Coupling granule properties and granulation rates in high-shear granulation. Powder Technol. 130 (1–3), 162–168.

Bouffard, J., Bertrand, F., Chaouki, J., 2012. A multiscale model for the simulation of granulation in rotor-based equipment. Chem. Eng. Sci. 81 (0), 106–117.

Bouffard, J., Bertrand, F., Chaouki, J., Dumont, H., 2013. Discrete element investigation of flow patterns and segregation in a spheronizer. Comput. Chem. Eng. 49, 170–182.

Braumann, A., Kraft, M., Wagner, W., 2010. Numerical study of a stochastic particle algorithm solving a multidimensional population balance model for high shear granulation. J. Comput. Phys. 229 (20), 7672–7691.

Chaudhury, A., Ramachandran, R., 2013. Integrated population balance model development and validation of a granulation process. Particul. Sci. Technol. 31 (4), 407–418.

Chaudhury, A., Niziolek, A., Ramachandran, R., 2013a. Multi-dimensional mechanistic modeling of fluid bed granulation processes: an integrated approach. Adv. Powder Technol. 24 (1), 113–131.

Chaudhury, A., Oseledets, I.V., Ramachandran, R., 2013b. A computationally efficient technique for the solution of multi-dimensional population balance models of granulation via tensor decomposition. Comput. Chem. Eng. 61, 234–244.

Chaudhury, A., Barrasso, D., Pandey, P., Wu, H., Ramachandran, R., 2014a. Population balance model development, validation, and prediction of CQAs of a high-shear wet granulation process: towards QbD in drug product pharmaceutical manufacturing. J. Pharm. Innov. 9 (1), 53–64.

Chaudhury, A., Kapadia, A., Prakash, A.V., Barrasso, D., Ramachandran, R., 2014b. An extended cell-average technique for a multi-dimensional population balance of granulation describing aggregation and breakage. Adv. Powder Technol. 24 (6), 962–971.

Chaudhury, A., Wu, H., Khan, M., Ramachandran, R., 2014c. A mechanistic population balance model for granulation processes: effect of process and formulation parameters. Chem. Eng. Sci. 107, 76–92.

Chaudhury, A., Armenante, M.E., Ramachandran, R., 2015. Compartment based population balance modeling of a high shear wet granulation process using data analytics. Chem. Eng. Res. Des. 95, 211–228.

Cleary, P.W., Sinnott, M.D., 2008. Assessing mixing characteristics of particle-mixing and granulation devices. Particuology. 6 (6), 419–444.

Cundall, P., Strack, O., 1979. Discrete numerical model for granular assemblies. Geotechnique. 29 (1), 47–65.

Darelius, A., Brage, H., Rasmuson, A., Bjrn, I.N., Folestad, S., 2006. A volume-based multi-dimensional population balance approach for modelling high shear granulation. Chem. Eng. Sci. 61 (8), 2482–2493.

Dhenge, R.M., Cartwright, J.J., Hounslow, M.J., Salman, A.D., 2012. Twin screw granulation: steps in granule growth. Int. J. Pharm. 438 (12), 20–32.

El Hagrasy, A.S., Litster, J.D., 2013. Granulation rate processes in the kneading elements of a twin screw granulator. AIChE J. 59 (11), 4100–4115.

Emady, H.N., Kayrak-Talay, D., Schwerin, W.C., Litster, J.D., 2011. Granule formation mechanisms and morphology from single drop impact on powder beds. Powder Technol. 212 (1), 69–79.

Freireich, B., Litster, J., Wassgren, C., 2009. Using the discrete element method to predict collision-scale behavior: a sensitivity analysis. Chem. Eng. Sci. 64 (15), 3407–3416.

Freireich, B., Li, J., Litster, J., Wassgren, C., 2011. Incorporating particle flow information from discrete element simulations in population balance models of mixer-coaters. Chem. Eng. Sci. 66 (16), 3592–3604.

Fries, L., Dosta, M., Antonyuk, S., Heinrich, S., Palzer, S., 2011. Moisture distribution in fluidized beds with liquid injection. Chem. Eng. Technol. 34 (7), 1076–1084.

Gantt, J.A., Gatzke, E.P., 2006. A stochastic technique for multidimensional granulation modeling. AIChE J. 52 (9), 3067–3077.

Gantt, J.A., Cameron, I.T., Litster, J.D., Gatzke, E.P., 2006. Determination of coalescence kernels for high-shear granulation using dem simulations. Powder Technol. 170 (2), 53–63.

Hapgood, K.P., Litster, J.D., Biggs, S.R., Howes, T., 2002. Drop penetration into porous powder beds. J. Colloid Interface Sci. 253 (2), 353–366.

Hapgood, K.P., Litster, J.D., Smith, R., 2003. Nucleation regime map for liquid bound granules. AIChE J. 49 (2), 350–361.

Hapgood, K.P., Litster, J.D., White, E.T., Mort, P.R., Jones, D.G., 2004. Dimension-less spray flux in wet granulation: Monte-carlo simulations and experimental validation. Powder Technol. 141 (12), 20–30.

Hapgood, K.P., Nguyen, T.H., Hauw, S., Iveson, S.M., Shen, W., 2009. Rewetting effects and droplet motion on partially wetted powder surfaces. AIChE J. 55 (6), 1402–1415.

Hassanpour, A., Kwan, C., Ng, B., Rahmanian, N., Ding, Y., Antony, S., et al., 2009. Effect of granulation scale-up on the strength of granules. Powder Technol. 189 (2), 304–312.

Hassanpour, A., Pasha, M., Susana, L., Rahmanian, N., Santomaso, A.C., Ghadiri, M., 2013. Analysis of seeded granulation in high shear granulators by discrete element method. Powder Technol. 238, 50–55.

Hounslow, M.J., Ryall, R.L., Marshall, V.R., 1988. A discretized population balance for nucleation, growth, and aggregation. AIChE J. 34 (11), 1821–1832.

Hounslow, M.J., Pearson, J.M.K., Instone, T., 2001. Tracer studies of high-shear granulation: Ii. population balance modeling. AIChE J. 47 (9), 1984–1999.

Hounslow, M.J., Oullion, M., Reynolds, G., 2009. Kinetic models for granule nucleation by the immersion mechanism. Powder Technol. 189 (2), 177–189.

Ingram, G.D., Cameron, I.T., 2005. Formulation and comparison of alternative multiscale models for drum granulation. Comput. Aided Chem. Eng. 20, 481–486.

Iveson, S.M., 2002. Limitations of one-dimensional population balance models of wet granulation processes. Powder Technol. 124, 219–229.

Iveson, S.M., Litster, J.D., 1998a. Fundamental studies of granule consolidation part 2: quantifying the effects of particle and binder properties. Powder Technol. 99 (3), 243–250.

Iveson, S.M., Litster, J.D., 1998b. Growth regime map for liquid-bound granules. AIChE J. 44 (7), 1510–1518.

Iveson, S.M., Litster, J., Ennis, B., 1996. Fundamental studies of granule consolidation part 1: effects of binder content and binder viscosity. Powder Technol. 88 (1), 15–20.

Iveson, S.M., Litster, J.D., Hapgood, K., Ennis, B.J., 2001a. Nucleation, growth and breakage phenomena in agitated wet granulation processes: a review. Powder Technol. 117 (1–2), 3–39.

Iveson, S.M., Wauters, P.A., Forrest, S., Litster, J.D., Meesters, G.M., Scarlett, B., 2001b. Growth regime map for liquid-bound granules: further development and experimental validation. Powder Technol. 117 (12), 83–97.

Iveson, S.M., Page, N.W., Litster, J.D., 2003. The importance of wet-powder dynamic mechanical properties in understanding granulation. Powder Technol. 130 (13), 97–101.

Keleb, E., Vermeire, A., Vervaet, C., Remon, J., 2004. Twin screw granulation as a simple and efficient tool for continuous wet granulation. Int. J. Pharm. 273 (12), 183–194.

Kennedy, J., Eberhart, R., 1995. Particle swarm optimization. In: Neural Networks, 1995. Proceedings, IEEE International Conference on, Volume 4, pp. 1942–1948.

Ketterhagen, W.R., am Ende, M.T., Hancock, B.C., 2009. Process modeling in the pharmaceutical industry using the discrete element method. J. Pharm. Sci. 98 (2), 442–470.

Knight, P., Instone, T., Pearson, J.M., Hounslow, M., 1993. An investigation into the kinetics of granulation using a high shear mixer. Powder Technol. 77, 159–169.

Kumar, A., Gernaey, K.V., Beer, T.D., Nopens, I., 2013. Model-based analysis of high shear wet granulation from batch to continuous processes in pharmaceutical production a critical review. Eur. J. Pharm. Biopharm. 85 (3 Part B), 814–832.

Kumar, J., Peglow, M., Warnecke, G., Heinrich, S., Mörl, L., 2006. Improved accuracy and convergence of discretized population balance for aggregation: the cell-average technique. Chem. Eng. Sci. 61 (10), 3327–3342.

Lee, K.T., Ingram, A., Rowson, N.A., 2013. Comparison of granule properties produced using twin screw extruder and high shear mixer: a step towards understanding the mechanism of twin screw wet granulation. Powder Technol. 238, 91–98.

Liu, L.X., Litster, J.D., 2002. Population balance modelling of granulation with a physically based coalescence kernel. Chem. Eng. Sci. 57 (12), 2183–2191.

Liu, L.X., Litster, J.D., Iveson, S.M., Ennis, B.J., 2000. Coalescence of deformable granules in wet granulation processes. AIChE J. 46 (3), 529–539.

Liu, L.X., Zhou, L., Robinson, D., Addai-Mensah, J., 2013. A nuclei size distribution model including nuclei breakage. Chem. Eng. Sci. 86, 19–24.

Madec, L., Falk, L., Plasari, E., 2003. Modelling of the agglomeration in suspension process with multidimensional kernels. Powder Technol. 130 (1–3), 147–153.

Nakamura, H., Fujii, H., Watano, S., 2013. Scale-up of high shear mixer-granulator based on discrete element analysis. Powder Technol. 236, 149–156.

Osborne, J.D., Sochon, R.P., Cartwright, J.J., Doughty, D.G., Hounslow, M.J., Salman, A.D., 2011. Binder addition methods and binder distribution in high shear and fluidised bed granulation. Chem. Eng. Res. Des. 89 (5), 553–559.

Oullion, M., Reynolds, G., Hounslow, M., 2009. Simulating the early stage of high-shear granulation using a two-dimensional monte-carlo approach. Chem. Eng. Sci. 64 (4), 673–685.

Pandey, P., Tao, J., Chaudhury, A., Ramachandran, R., Gao, J.Z., Bindra, D.S., 2013. A combined experimental and modeling approach to study the effects of high-shear wet granulation process parameters on granule characteristics. Pharm. Dev. Technol. 18 (1), 210–224.

Pohlman, D.A., Litster, J.D., 2015. Coalescence model for induction growth behavior in high shear granulation. Powder Technol. 270 (Part B), 435–444, 6th International Workshop on Granulation: Granulation across the length scales.

Rajniak, P., Mancinelli, C., Chern, R., Stepanek, F., Farber, L., Hill, B., 2007. Experimental study of wet granulation in fluidized bed: impact of the binder properties on the granule morphology. Int. J. Pharm. 334 (1–2), 92–102.
Ramachandran, R., Immanuel, C.D., Stepanek, F., Litster, J.D., Doyle III, F.J., 2009. A mechanistic model for breakage in population balances of granulation: theoretical kernel development and experimental validation. Chem. Eng. Res. Des. 87 (4), 598–614.
Reinhold, A., Briesen, H., 2012. Numerical behavior of a multiscale aggregation modelcoupling population balances and discrete element models. Chem. Eng. Sci. 70, 165–175.
Reynolds, G.K., Biggs, C.A., Salman, A.D., Hounslow, M.J., 2004. Non-uniformity of binder distribution in high-shear granulation. Powder Technol. 140, 203–208.
Reynolds, G.K., Fu, J., Cheong, Y., Hounslow, M., Salman, A., 2005. Breakage in granulation: a review. Chem. Eng. Sci. 60 (14), 3969–3992.
Salman, A.D., Hounslow, M.J., Seville, J.P.K., 2007. Granulation. Elsevier.
Sen, M., Barrasso, D., Singh, R., Ramachandran, R., 2014. A multi-scale hybrid cfd-dem-pbm description of a fluid bed granulation process. Processes. 2 (1), 89–111.
Sherony, D.F., 1981. A model of surface renewal with application to fluid bed coating of particles. Chem. Eng. Sci. 36 (5), 845–848.
Smirani-Khayati, N., Falk, V., Bardin-Monnier, N., Marchal-Heussler, L., 2009. Binder liquid distribution during granulation process and its relationship to granule size distribution. Powder Technol. 195 (2), 105–112.
Smith, M., Matsoukas, T., 1998. Constant-number monte carlo simulation of population balances. Chem. Eng. Sci. 53 (9), 1777–1786.
Soos, M., Sefcik, J., Morbidelli, M., 2006. Investigation of aggregation, breakage and restructuring kinetics of colloidal dispersions in turbulent flows by population balance modeling and static light scattering. Chem. Eng. Sci. 61 (8), 2349–2363.
Stepanek, F., Rajniak, P., 2006. Droplet morphologies on particles with macroscopic surface roughness. Langmuir. 22 (3), 917–923.
Thompson, M., Sun, J., 2010. Wet granulation in a twin-screw extruder: implications of screw design. J. Pharm. Sci. 99 (4), 2090–2103.
Tu, W.-D., Ingram, A., Seville, J., Hsiau, S.-S., 2009. Exploring the regime map for high-shear mixer granulation. Chem. Eng. J. 145 (3), 505–513.
Vercruysse, J., Daz, D.C., Peeters, E., Fonteyne, M., Delaet, U., Assche, I.V., et al., 2012. Continuous twin screw granulation: influence of process variables on granule and tablet quality. Eur. J. Pharm. Biopharm. 82 (1), 205–211.
Verkoeijen, D., Pouw, G.A., Meesters, G.M.H., Scarlett, B., 2002. Population balances for particulate processes—a volume approach. Chem. Eng. Sci. 57 (12), 2287–2303.
Vervaet, C., Remon, J.P., 2005. Continuous granulation in the pharmaceutical industry. Chem. Eng. Sci. 60 (14), 3949–3957.
Washino, K., Tan, H., Hounslow, M., Salman, A., 2013a. Meso-scale coupling model of DEM and CIP for nucleation processes in wet granulation. Chem. Eng. Sci. 86, 25–37.
Washino, K., Tan, H., Hounslow, M., Salman, A., 2013b. A new capillary force model implemented in micro-scale cfddem coupling for wet granulation. Chem. Eng. Sci. 93, 197–205.
Yu, S., Liu, X., Tranchevent, L.-C., Glnzel, W., Suykens, J.A.K., De Moor, B., et al., 2011. Optimized data fusion for k-means laplacian clustering. Bioinformatics. 27 (1), 118–126.
Zhao, H., Maisels, A., Matsoukas, T., Zheng, C., 2007. Analysis of four monte carlo methods for the solution of population balances in dispersed systems. Powder Technol. 173 (1), 38–50.

Fluid bed granulation and drying

6

R. Gupta
Celgene, Summit, NJ, United States

6.1 Introduction

Fluid bed processing is a widely used pharmaceutical process in the manufacturing of a wide range of granular products. This process typically works by spraying binder liquid (generally aqueous) onto a bed of fluidized particles, accompanied by drying of the resulting granules using hot fluidizing air. During this process, bed humidity typically increases during spraying and then decreases once the spray is stopped. The granules are then dried to a desired water content. The whole process influences the resulting granule properties (particle size distribution, density, porosity, etc.), which has an impact on downstream processing (e.g., compression or encapsulation). Fluid bed processes are also used on dry granulations produced by high-shear equipment. A typical schematic of fluid bed equipment is provided in Fig. 6.1 (Hu et al., 2008).

To ensure that the granulation is able to deliver the desired finished product quality attributes (assay, content uniformity, dissolution, etc.), the fluid bed process must be adequately developed and controlled throughout the product development stages (e.g., formulation development, scale-up, process robustness studies, etc.). An understanding should be developed of any linkages among raw material attributes, batch parameters, processing conditions, granule attributes, and finished product quality attributes. Table 6.1 lists the main variables affecting the quality of the granules and eventually that of the finished product.

In theory, processing conditions and certain granule attributes can be estimated quantitatively using input variables by applying first-principles. However, this is rarely achieved for pharmaceutical solids due to the following practical reasons:

1. *Complex process*: Limited understanding of granulation kinetics and its dependence upon the many interactions between the input variables and formulation characteristics exists.
2. *Heterogeneous system*: Most models make several assumptions, such as a single component, spherical particles, homogeneous, monodisperse, uniform wetting, etc., to simplify the complex scenarios. In reality, a formulation is generally a heterogeneous mixture of active pharmaceutical ingredient (API) and several excipients. Also, the properties of the API are rarely fully understood, at least during the drug development phase. Further, as these materials have varying properties (particle size, tortuosity, wettability, etc.), they sorb/desorb water differently (this has a significant influence on bed moisture accumulation as described later). Furthermore, the properties of this input material change during the granulation and drying steps, making predictions of these properties complex.

Predictive Modeling of Pharmaceutical Unit Operations. DOI: http://dx.doi.org/10.1016/B978-0-08-100154-7.00006-5

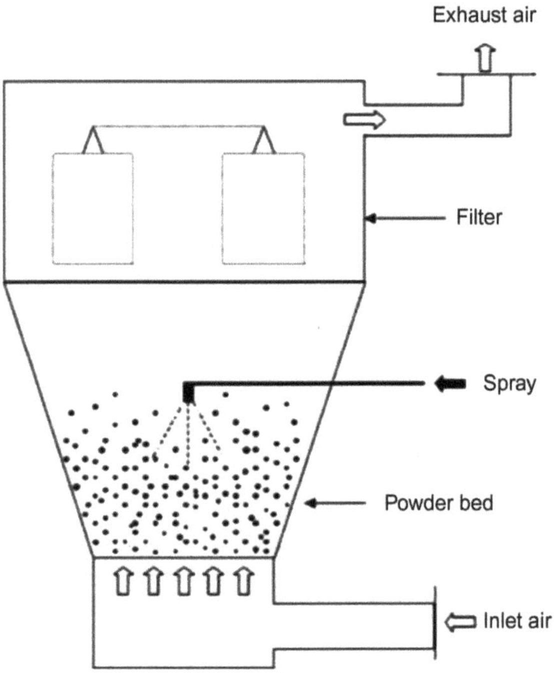

Figure 6.1 Schematic of a typical top spray fluid bed unit.

3. *Equipment aspects*: Heat losses during granulation and drying can have a big impact on processing conditions. The design, make, age, scale, etc. of a piece of equipment are all important. Heat losses can be calculated using well-known heat transfer coefficients. However, during drug development, equipment is commonly changed as the process is scaled-up or transferred. Scientists in the industry rarely have the time or resources to establish heat loss factors for every equipment and processing condition. Even when the compound is mature (e.g., once it is generic) and not much development is needed, it is typically difficult to justify efforts needed to establish heat loss factors for process modeling.
4. *Process dynamics*: The processing conditions can change from subsaturated to saturated [close to 100% relative humidity (RH) exhaust air] and vice versa as the granulation proceeds. The granule properties also change throughout the process (from individual particles to agglomerates). In addition, in an industrial setting, some of the process variables are adjusted during the process (e.g., airflow during initial granulation and final drying stages). A theoretical model must account for all these aspects to make reasonable predictions. This can make the preprogramming of the process a bit complex and impractical, especially for pharmaceutical applications.

Another key challenge is an ability to perform prospective modeling. At times, theoretical models are claimed to give a good or excellent fit to the experimental data. However, upon careful examination, it is realized that either some correction factors or back-fitting from the experimental data was used. As such, this approach

Table 6.1 Linkages among batch parameters, processing conditions, granule attributes, and finished product quality attributes

Input variables	Processing conditions	Granule attributes	Finished product attributes
Fixed variables • Formulation (incoming material particle size distribution (PSD), wettability, etc.) • Batch size • Equipment • Binder concentration Process variables • Spray rate • Airflow[a] • Inlet air temperature • Inlet air humidity • Atomizing air pressure • Filter shake/back-pressure parameters	Granulation • Bed humidity[a] • Product/exhaust temperature[a] • Droplet size • Granulation time • Exhaust RH[a] Drying • Drying time • Product/exhaust temperature[a] • Exhaust RH[a]	Granulation • Particle size distribution[a] • Density/porosity[a] • Granule strength[a] • Moisture content[a] Drying • Particle size distribution[a] • Density/porosity[a] • Granule strength[a] • Blend uniformity[a] • Moisture content[a]	• Assay • Content uniformity • Dissolution/disintegration • Moisture content • Microbiological attributes • Appearance • Friability • Radial tensile strength

RH, Relative humidity.
[a]Typically, a function of time during processing.

may be useful for a specific formulation, processing conditions, or scale (e.g., the food industry commonly uses correction factors for modeling secondary drying), although a more desired way is to use correction factors that work for a variety of formulations, conditions, and scales, but that is indeed difficult.

However, despite the preceding challenges, there are opportunities in modeling pharmaceutical granulation and drying processes. Unlike chemical and other industries, pharmaceutical processes typically do not require very accurate calculations. The focus is mainly on quality of products from the patient perspective, instead of energy savings, maximizing throughputs, or minimizing cycle times. Thus, a compromise can be made in terms of model predictions as long as they are able to provide reasonable and fit-for-purpose estimates.

Based on the preceding context, this chapter is written from an industrial perspective with the goal to provide scientists with practical solutions to model the complex granulation and drying processes. It is recognized that sometimes pharmaceutical scientists prefer a simple and basic model that provides an opportunity to do prospective predictions rather than a highly detailed and rigorous model that requires special programming skills, numerous physical properties of the API and excipients, etc.

Accordingly, this chapter first provides various modeling approaches for granulation (Section 6.2) and drying (Section 6.3), followed by case studies using an integrated granulation and drying model (Section 6.4). The last section, Section 6.5, briefly discusses opportunities for future development in this field.

6.2 Granulation modeling

6.2.1 Granulation conditions

Depending upon the input conditions, the processing environment during granulation can be either saturated or subsaturated. Saturated granulations run with saturated or near-saturated exhaust air, and the product bed temperature operates close to the wet bulb conditions (often ~20–30°C). Here, the amount of liquid sprayed is more than the evaporation capacity, and thus moisture accumulation takes place in the fluidized bed. Typically, peak loss-on-drying (LOD) measurements (a measure of moisture accumulation) range from 5% to 15% LOD, and up to 30% LOD in some cases (e.g., formulations with high percentages of calcium carbonate).

In many cases, the granulation process is operated under subsaturated conditions (e.g., for systems with high solubility such as metformin or moisture-sensitive compounds). Here, the binder spray rate is less than the evaporation capacity of the processing conditions. These granulations accumulate less moisture, with peak LODs generally <5%. The exhaust air is far from being saturated, and the operating temperature is significantly higher than the wet bulb temperature. Subsaturated conditions may also exist during the initial phase of granulation when preheating is provided.

6.2.1.1 Granulation under saturated conditions

Most granulation processes are operated under saturated environmental conditions. The rate of drying is approximately constant during this phase (known as the constant-rate period). Because there is a negligible change in the temperature of the solids, all of the energy is transferred to evaporate the water (mostly the free surface water). Here, the rate of removal of the water is also the rate of mass transfer, from the solid to the ambient air. The mass and heat transfer rates must predict the same rate of drying for a given set of circumstances, as expressed in Eqs. (6.1) and (6.2) (Hlinak and Saleki-Gerhardt, 2000).

$$\text{Mass balance (vapor): } m_{H_2O}^{evap} = m_{air}(\omega_{out} - \omega_{in}) \tag{6.1}$$

$$\text{Heat balance: } m_{H_2O}^{evap} = \frac{m_{air}C_{p,air}(T_{in} - T_{out}) - Q_{loss}}{h_{fg}} \tag{6.2}$$

Here, $m_{H_2O}^{evap}$ is the mass flow rate of water evaporated from the bed, m_{air} is the mass flow rate of air through the dryer, ω_{in} is the inlet humidity, ω_{out} is the outlet humidity, $C_{p,\ \mathrm{air}}$ is the specific heat capacity of air at constant pressure, T_{in} is the inlet temperature of dryer air, T_{out} is the outlet temperature of dryer air, Q_{loss} is the heat loss, and h_{fg} is latent heat of vaporization for water at the dryer outlet temperature. The working assumption in the preceding equations is that the granulator is well-mixed, the bed temperature is equivalent to the exhaust air temperature, and the reference temperature is the temperature of the binder solution.

Now, assuming ideal gas law, m_{air} can be calculated based on the inlet volumetric airflow rate, whereas the humidity ratio, ω, can be estimated using the following relation:

$$\omega = 0.622\frac{p_{\mathrm{H_2O}}}{p_{\mathrm{air}}} \tag{6.3}$$

Here, $p_{\mathrm{H_2O}}$ and p_{air} are the partial pressure of water and air in the dryer, respectively, given as

$$p_{\mathrm{air}} + p_{\mathrm{H_2O}} = P \tag{6.4}$$

The saturated vapor pressure can be calculated using the Antoine equation within a range of 1–100°C:

$$p_{\mathrm{H_2O}}^{\mathrm{sat}} = 10^{8.07131-\frac{1730.63}{244.485+T}} \tag{6.5}$$

where $p_{\mathrm{H_2O}}^{\mathrm{sat}}$ is in mmHg and T is the air temperature in degrees Celsius.

Now, based on the inlet air dew point, the inlet humidity can be calculated from the preceding relations. The outlet humidity can be expressed in terms of the outlet temperature. Assuming heat losses are neglected or estimated separately (discussed later) and exhaust air is at ~100% RH (reasonable assumption for saturated conditions), Eqs. (6.1) and (6.2) can be solved simultaneously to calculate $m_{\mathrm{H_2O}}^{\mathrm{evap}}$ and T_{out} (and thus ω_{out}).

Once the outlet temperature and humidity are known, it is then straightforward to calculate the mass evaporation rate, moisture accumulation (m_{accu}), etc. at any given time based on Eqs. (6.1) and (6.2) and following relations:

$$\text{Mass balance (liquid): } m_{\mathrm{accu}} = m_{\mathrm{spray}}(1-b) - m_{\mathrm{H_2O}}^{\mathrm{evap}} \tag{6.6}$$

$$X_{\mathrm{bed}} = m_{\mathrm{accu}}/(m_{\mathrm{accu}} + m_{\mathrm{bed}}) \tag{6.7}$$

Here, m_{spray} is the spray rate of the binder solution, b is the binder concentration in the binder solution, X_{bed} is the bed moisture fraction, and m_{bed} is the bed mass. Note, the bed mass changes with time due to the addition of a solid binder, and thus should be accounted for.

One of the problems in solving the preceding equations is the exponent factor in Eq. (6.5). If the equations are solved using a sophisticated software or programming language, this is generally not a problem (as iterative loops can be coded); however, solving these simultaneous equations in simple worksheets like Microsoft Excel can be an issue for outlet saturated humidity. To overcome this potential problem, the preceding equations can be simplified for fluid bed granulation for pharmaceutical applications (Gupta, 2012):

$$\omega^{sat} = 0.0387 \cdot T^2 - 0.669 \cdot T + 12.36 \tag{6.8}$$

where ω^{sat} is in g water/kg dry air and T is the air temperature in degrees Celsius.

Eq. (6.8) is considered to be suitable in a temperature range of 16–36°C (with roughly 99% accuracy), which is the typical outlet temperature range for fluid bed granulation under saturated conditions.

The preceding equations were written from a macroscopic view of the granulation process; however, similar mass and heat balances can be written and solved around single particles as well (Wang et al., 2007; Hu et al., 2008). Generally, this approach requires information on particle size, diffusion and thermal coefficients, etc., many of which vary during the process and are generally not easily determined. These equations are typically valid for specific/defined systems and are solved numerically or using similar techniques. Now, because the importance of particle morphology is considered to be minimal for the constant-rate period (as surface water is freely available for saturated conditions) and significant efforts may be needed to solve such equations, a macroscopic solution as presented previously is considered reasonable for most practical applications.

6.2.1.2 Granulation under subsaturated conditions

Very little is reported in the literature on granulation under subsaturated conditions, likely because most granulation processes are run under saturated conditions. However, as pointed out earlier, subsaturated conditions may also exist during the initial phase of granulation when preheating is provided or the entire process may be operated under subsaturated conditions due to the compound needs.

During subsaturated conditions, only a fraction of available water is evaporated, even though (1) air may have enough capacity to hold water and (2) there may be sufficient water present in the system (water sprayed + bed moisture). The bed accumulates remaining water, generally leading to equilibrium conditions as the granulation proceeds. Now, to estimate how much water is evaporated at a given time, t, one needs to consider the sources of water evaporation and their relative contributions.

As such, the source for water evaporation could be from droplets being sprayed (M_{spray}), surface water ($M_{surface}$), or water present inside the granules (referred to here as pore water, M_{pores}). As opposed to the saturated conditions where droplet size and granule water have little relevance, these factors are quite important for the subsaturated conditions. As the water (or binder solution) is sprayed as atomized droplets, these droplets evaporate prior to particle contact or be absorbed on the particles. The absorbed water on the particles can be further categorized as surface water or pore water. The contribution for evaporation from pore water is negligible, as water migration from the granule interior to the surface is mostly by molecular diffusion, which is slow. Thus, the water evaporation is primarily from spray drying of water droplets ($M_{spraydrying}$) and surface water; the relative contribution of these will depend upon the droplet size, environmental conditions, and granule properties.

Based on the preceding understanding, Gupta (2012) proposed that at any given time, t, the total water in the system, M, can be expressed as

$$M|_t = M_{pores}|_{t-1} + M_{spray}|_{\partial t} = M_{pores}|_t + M_{evap}|_t \quad (6.9a)$$

where

$$M_{evap}|_t = M_{surface}|_t + M_{spraydrying}|_t \quad (6.9b)$$

Now, if the fraction of water evaporated relative to total liquid water in the system can be written as

$$\alpha|_t = M_{evap}|_t / M|_t \quad (6.10a)$$

then,

$$M_{pores}|_t = (1 - \alpha|_t)M|_t \quad (6.10b)$$

The key to solving the preceding equations is in estimating α (and as a function of time). In theory, α can be 0% for no spray drying and/or extremely porous/hygroscopic materials to ~100% for extensive spray drying and/or nonporous/nonhygroscopic materials. Because this represents a wide range of environmental conditions and material properties, it is difficult to come up with equations to predict α based on first-principles. To overcome this problem, Gupta (2012) utilized historical industrial batch data and empirically estimated α. It was found that α is generally ~10–30% for typical pharmaceutical solids under subsaturated conditions. Further, it was shown that α is dependent upon the product temperature, given by the following relation:

$$\alpha = 0.7 \cdot T_{out} - 7 \quad (6.11)$$

where T_{out} is in degrees Celsius.

In the preceding relation, it is noted that higher product temperatures result in greater water availability for evaporation. This is expected because higher product temperature in the bed would lead to higher driving potential for water evaporation compared to lower temperatures. In addition, high product temperature is indicative of usage of high inlet air temperature, high airflow, or low spray rate (or a combination of these). These conditions can potentially lead to spray drying of binder droplets, resulting in higher water availability for evaporation, as described previously.

In terms of maximum water availability from a practical perspective, the relation shows that only up to 30% of available water may be evaporated even at an upper end of outlet temperature of 50°C. Finally, it is also recognized that because T_{out} is not constant (generally the case for subsaturated conditions), α will also change as the granulation proceeds.

The preceding relation for fraction of water evaporated can be fine-tuned for more specific formulations and spray conditions. For example, if the composition and granule structure cause a reduction in the surface water availability (e.g., for hydrophilic and/or porous granules), then less water should be available for evaporation and vice versa. In this case, coefficients of Eq. (6.11) can be calibrated against the formulation of interest to obtain more accurate predictions. Similarly, if spray drying is considered important for a particular process, then this equation can be modified to account for various droplet sizes.

Now, to predict bed and outlet conditions, Eqs. (6.1) and (6.2) are used as before. However, because $m_{H_2O}^{evap}$ is estimated directly from Eqs. (6.9a)–(6.11), it makes the rest of the calculations relatively straightforward. The outlet RH is calculated using Eq. (6.12):

$$\mathrm{RH}^{out} = \frac{\omega_{out}}{\omega_{out}^{sat}} \cdot 100 \tag{6.12}$$

where ω_{out}^{sat} is calculated using Eqs. (6.3)–(6.5).

6.2.2 Heat loss

Modeling heat loss is theoretically simple but practically complex for pharmaceutical granulation and drying applications. (This section also covers heat losses during drying, as the concepts are common). As such, the rate of convective heat transfer is equal to an overall heat transfer coefficient, U, multiplied by the transfer surface area, A, and the temperature differential between the average temperature inside the unit, T, and the ambient temperature, T_{amb}.

$$Q_{loss} = UA(T - T_{amb}) \tag{6.13}$$

However, as the temperature of the airstream inside the granulator is a function of both time and space, more complicated equations result. In addition, calculation of the overall heat transfer coefficient requires knowledge of local heat transfer coefficients, thermal conductivities of the materials involved, etc. Solutions to such problems require collection of these values, followed by rigorous computations.

A more practical approach taken by pharmaceutical scientists sometimes is estimating heat losses for empty columns or when the process is in equilibrium e.g., toward the end of drying process when the evaporation rate is negligible (Hlinak and Saleki-Gerhardt, 2000). Using this approach, heat loss is calculated by Eq. (6.14) next, where values on the right-hand side are measurable. Now, knowing the overall heat loss, the value of UA is calculated using Eq. (6.13), which is then used for subsequent applications. Based on the author's personal experience, the temperature drop for empty columns is typically in the range of 5–15°C, and as high as 30°C for some old equipment.

$$Q_{\text{loss}} = m_{\text{air}} C_{p,\text{air}} (T_{\text{in}} - T_{\text{out}}) \tag{6.14}$$

The preceding approach, while useful, is limited to a particular set of conditions (equipment, inlet air temperature, scale, etc.). Further, this approach has the potential to overestimate heat loss. For example, if the inlet air temperature and outlet air temperature for an empty column trial (or process under equilibrium conditions) are 70°C and 60°C, respectively, then, the average temperature in Eq. (6.13) would be ~65°C, leading to $T - T_{\text{amb}} = 40°\text{C}$ (assuming $T_{\text{amb}} = 25°\text{C}$). However, for filled columns with binder spraying, typically the outlet air temperature goes down to the saturation temperature, generally in a range of 20–30°C, due to evaporative cooling. Now, within the fluid bed unit, there would be a temperature differential, but, as explained by Kemp and Sohet (2010), the inlet air temperature would drop sharply within the active layer close to the distributor plate. Thus, the average air temperature inside the filled column would likely be much lower than 60°C for the bulk of the process, except toward the end of the drying step where product temperature rises considerably. Thus, $T - T_{\text{amb}}$ would be much lower than 40°C as otherwise estimated from the empty column or equilibrium trials.

Recently, Gupta (2012) took another approach to estimate the heat loss. Here, the temperature differential, $|T_{\text{in}} - T_{\text{out}}|_{\text{filled}}$, in Eq. (6.14) was defined as the heat loss factor or dT. This heat loss factor was then estimated for filled columns by using the actual batch data of over 40 historical batches on various equipment. It was found that dT is highly dependent on the processing temperatures and equipment age and design (surface area exposed to ambient conditions is dependent on the bowl design). For example, processes operated at lower temperatures of 50°C, along with shallow Glatt WSG columns (less heat loss due to reduced surface area) and newer equipment, were found to have dT as low as 1–2°C. On the other hand, one process using 75°C inlet air temperature and a long Niro column was noted to have dT up to 12°C (the equipment was old, with potential leaks). In general, dT ranged from 4°C to 8°C at typical inlet air temperatures of ~60°C for most equipment. Accordingly, for a new process, it was recommended to assume a dT of 5°C, with adjustments made as further actual batch experience is gained for more accurate predictions (as such, a correction of dT by ±3°C affects bed moisture by just ±1%). This approach, although preliminary, is based on actual industrial data and has been shown to give acceptable results for prospective modeling irrespective of scale, process conditions, etc.

6.2.3 Granule properties

The granulation process as described previously has a significant impact on the resulting granule attributes (particle size, density, flowability, etc.). Several mechanisms have been reported in the literature to explain the complex science behind it, including the pioneering work of Ennis et al. (2000). It is now generally well accepted that granule properties are a result of three sets of rate processes (Iveson et al., 2001):

1. *Wetting and nucleation*: The liquid binder is brought into contact with a dry powder bed via pouring, spraying, or melting, followed by distribution through the bed to lead to nuclei formation of granules.
2. *Consolidation and growth*: Collisions between two granules, granules and feed powder, or a granule and the equipment lead to granule compaction and growth.
3. *Attrition and breakage*: Wet or dried granules break due to impact, wear or compaction in the granulator, or during subsequent downstream processing.

To model granule properties, particularly the particle size distribution, these processes need to be well understood. Wetting and nucleation are primarily a function of wetting thermodynamics, kinetics, and binder dispersion (delivery method, powder mixing, binder distribution, etc.). Although limited research has been done in this area, the nuclei size distribution during this process can be estimated using the nucleation regime map proposed by Hapgood et al. (2003). The granule growth and breakage processes during fluid bed granulation have been widely studied experimentally (Tan et al., 2006; Tardos and Gupta, 1996; Hemati et al., 2003; Zank et al., 2001) and using population balance models (PBMs). For PBMs, the key is to estimate the probability of coalescence, or the coalescence kernel β, when a granule or particle from size interval i collides with a granule or particle of size interval j. These models are extremely complex and require several assumptions for simplification and solving, with limited success as reported recently (Vreman et al., 2009; Faure et al., 2001; Heinrich et al., 2002; Li et al., 2011). Overall, to date, a holistic model that has been shown to prospectively and quantitatively predict granule properties for various formulations, scales, equipment, and granulation conditions does not exist. Accordingly, this chapter does not cover modeling of granule attributes. The interested reader should consult the reviews referred to here for further information.

6.3 Drying modeling

Drying of pharmaceutical solids is typically achieved by fluidizing the aqueous powder bed with a warm inlet air. Here, the energy is continuously added to the fluidized bed, leading to evaporation of the water over a period of time. At the onset of drying, solids have water present as surface water or absorbed water, while the processing conditions are usually saturated, i.e., the exhaust air is close to 100% RH. The surface water is freely available for evaporation and thus it is withdrawn first, typically at a constant rate. This period is referred as the constant-rate period in the literature. As the surface water is evaporated, the remaining moisture must migrate from the interior of the granules through micropores and fissures, or diffuse through the solid to reach the surface before it can be removed by drying air. Here, the drying rate declines substantially and the period is defined as the falling-rate period. The moisture content at which this change of rate occurs is known as the critical moisture content, X_c. The processing conditions are typically subsaturated during the falling-rate period. Finally, if the drying is continued, the moisture content of the granules reaches a thermodynamic equilibrium with the surrounding air and the final water content is determined by the granule temperature and partial pressure of water in the drying airstream. This product moisture content is generally referred to as the equilibrium moisture content. For pharmaceutical solids, the end-point of drying is generally between 1% and 2%.

As the process is of great interest to a wide range of industrial applications in food, pharmaceutical, fertilizers, etc., numerous mathematical models have been developed to estimate the drying kinetics. In general, these models are based on mass and heat transfer balances around a single particle or fluid bed unit, or, in other words, modeling the process at a microscopic or macroscopic level, respectively.

6.3.1 Microscopic models

Single particle models for the constant-rate period are generally based on the assumption that there is no change in the temperature of the material and all the heat energy transferred to solids results in the evaporation of water. Thus, because both mass and heat transfer must predict the same rate of drying, mass and heat model equations can be written around a single particle as represented by Eq. (6.15) (Brooker et al., 1992):

$$\frac{dM}{dt} = \frac{h_c A(T - T_{bu})}{h_{fg}} = \frac{h_m A}{R_v}\left(\frac{P_{vbu}}{T_{bu}} - \frac{P_{v\infty}}{T}\right) \tag{6.15}$$

in which:

h_c—global convective heat transfer coefficient, W/m$^{2\circ}$C
h_m—global convective mass transfer coefficient, m/s
h_{fg}—latent heat of vaporization, J/kg
R_v—universal water vapor constant, 0.462 J/kg K
A—area, m^2
T—drying temperature, α°C
T_{bu}—wet bulb temperature, °C
$P_{v\infty}$—vapor pressure, Pa
P_{vbu}—vapor pressure for wet bulb temperature, Pa
dM/dt—constant drying rate, kg/s

For a given system with known mass and heat transfer coefficients, particle surface area, critical moisture content, etc., the preceding equation in principle can be used to predict the constant-rate drying rate. Drying rates, once predicted from theory or determined experimentally, can then be used to calculate drying times for the constant-rate period assuming the critical moisture content is known (see Broughton, 1945 on how to predict critical moisture content):

$$t = w(X_o - X_c)/(dM/dt)_{\text{const}} \tag{6.16}$$

where w is weight of the granulation material (dry basis).

However, modeling for the falling-rate period is highly dependent upon the particle properties (particle size, tortuosity/porosity, pore size distribution, desorption energies, etc.). As such, the drying rate inside the particle can be estimated by Fick's diffusion equation (Srinivasakannan and Balasubramanian, 2008):

$$\frac{\partial C}{\partial t} = D_{\text{eff}}\left(\frac{\partial^2 C}{\partial r^2} + \frac{2}{r}\frac{\partial C}{\partial r}\right) \tag{6.17}$$

Several researchers have presented solutions to the preceding equation and shown applicability to practical studies (Crank, 1975; Kannan et al., 1994; Sereno and Medeiros, 1990; Fyhr et al., 2009; Wang et al., 2007). As such, this requires detailed knowledge or assumptions of particle properties, diffusion coefficients, etc., followed by complex numerical techniques to solve the equations. Some researchers also attempted to simplify the problem by using a correction coefficient (Hu et al., 2008; Chaudhury et al., 2013) or by estimating the surface water availability, α, by empirically estimating it for particle-based heat and mass transfer. However, as pointed out by Kemp (2011), generally these solutions are restricted to a single material, equipment, or operating conditions, with limited applicability to different situations. Overall, it is difficult to measure the kinetics of the drying process experimentally around a single particle, especially considering impact of scale-up and scale-down on the drying behavior.

6.3.2 Macroscopic models

In general, the drying process can be modeled macroscopically by using the mass and heat balance around the fluid bed unit as described in the previous section (Eqs. 6.1–6.7, 6.13, and 6.14; note, spray rate is zero during drying). As such, retrospective modeling can be easily performed to calculate the drying time, and this has been particularly shown to be very useful for the food industry in which the solid phase properties, processing conditions, etc. are better understood. A similar approach can also be taken for the pharmaceutical applications for established processes. Here, first the drying rate is determined for a given system, leading to a calculation of relative drying rate, f, at various moisture content (Earle and Earle, 2004; see also Fig. 6.2):

$$f = \frac{\text{Actual drying rate}}{\text{Maximum drying rate}} = \frac{dM/dt}{(dM/dt)_{\text{constant rate}}} \tag{6.18}$$

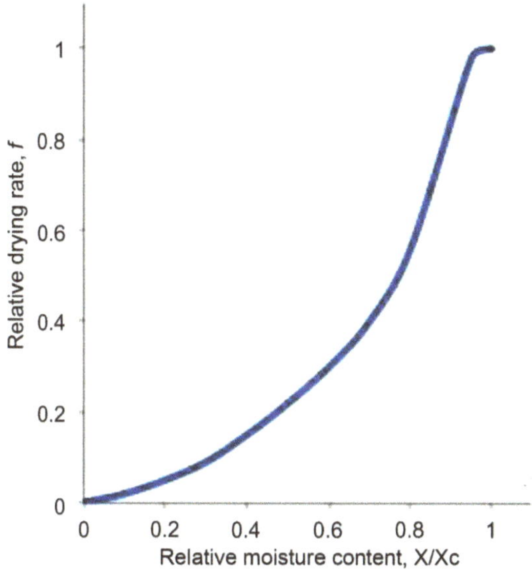

Figure 6.2 Generalized drying curve.

Once the relative drying rate curve is known for a system, then the total drying time during the falling-rate period can be determined by considering sufficiently small differential quantities of moisture content where the drying rate is effectively constant:

$$\Delta t = w(\Delta X)/[f(dw/dt)_{\text{const}}] \quad (6.19)$$

Kemp and Sohet (2010) further developed a range of retrospective models to enable scale-up or scale-down, selection of operating conditions, detection of end-point, and prediction of cycle time. For example, it was shown that if the outlet humidity or temperature is known, then scaling models could be used to back-calculate the drying rate and moisture profile.

Now, the desired state for modeling the drying process is where the drying rate and resulting profiles (bed moisture, product temperature, exhaust humidity, etc. vs time) can be prospectively calculated based on the input batch parameters (airflow rate, inlet air temperature, inlet air humidity, batch size, etc.). Hlinak and Saleki-Gerhardt (2000) successfully evaluated the drying process for a specific formulation and scale while estimating for heat loss from the conditions at equilibrium drying period. Chaudhury et al. (2013) integrated the heat and mass transfer equations with a PBM; however, this required detailed particle properties for calculations. Again, in general, available models are specific to particular systems and rarely differentiate between constant-rate and falling-rate periods. It is widely recognized that modeling for the falling-rate period remains a major challenge, especially for pharmaceutical solids (for the reasons given in Section 6.1). As such, it appears that a more practical approach is one in which first-principle-based equations can be used

Table 6.2 Surface water availability during falling-rate period

Granulation time, min	15	16–45	>45
Surface water availability, γ	20%	10%	5%

while empirically correcting for heat losses and surface water availability based on the actual industrial data, as shown by Gupta (2012).

In Gupta's model, heat and mass balance are based on Eqs. (6.1)–(6.7), while correcting for the heat loss factor as described in the previous section. Now, the surface water availability, γ, is assumed to be 100% during the constant-rate period. For the falling-rate period, γ was found to be ~5–20% for typical pharmaceutical solids by empirically fitting the historical industrial batch data. It was also found that γ depends upon the granulation time; longer granulation times generally lead to lower γ, which is understandable as that allows for more water to diffuse inside the pores. Here, based on an analysis over 20 batches, roughly three time periods were considered as shown in Table 6.2.

In reality, these values would be more continuous than discrete, but are considered suitable for preliminary estimations. This approach, although preliminary, was found to reasonably predict drying rate and profiles for numerous batches prospectively and to work for various systems and scales (discussed in the next section).

6.4 FluidBeG: an integrated granulation and drying model

6.4.1 Model background

An integrated model, fluid bed granulation (FluidBeG), was developed by Gupta (2012) with an aim to prospectively predict granulation and drying processing conditions and process outputs (bed humidity, product temperature, exhaust humidity, moisture evaporation rate, etc.) as a function of time. Here, one of the key goals was to develop a model that could be easily used by pharmaceutical scientists with little or no information on granule properties, heat transfer coefficients, equipment aspects, etc. Accordingly, the following assumptions were made:

1. The granulator is well-mixed, the bed/product temperature is equivalent to the exhaust air temperature, and the reference temperature is 25°C.
2. Heat and mass balances are performed at a macro scale. A default value of 5°C for the heat loss factor, *dT*, is used for the entire granulation and drying phase for a new process. Further adjustments can be made as necessary based on the batch history with that equipment and those processing conditions.
3. The source of water evaporation during subsaturated granulation is assumed to be primarily from spray droplets and surface water, with values of fraction water evaporated, α, as estimated by Eq. (6.11).
4. Surface water availability during constant-rate period is ~100%, whereas during the falling-rate period, it is 5–20%, as per Table 6.2.

5. The process is divided into 1-min intervals. Product temperature and humidity are averaged for the same previous 5 min (there was no firm basis for this assumption, however this helps avoid dramatic changes due to other model assumptions).
6. Calculations are performed at each time-point for both saturated and subsaturated conditions. If the exhaust humidity is predicted to be >100%, then the saturated-case solution is taken, else the process is assumed to be subsaturated for that time-point.
7. The output conditions for each time-point are taken as input conditions for the next time-point.

The model was initially developed in MS Excel, and later adapted to the gSolids platform of Process Systems Enterprise. It has been successfully used at Merck, GSK, and other pharmaceutical companies. Fig. 6.3 shows the typical prediction profiles for bed moisture (%LOD), product temperature, and exhaust humidity

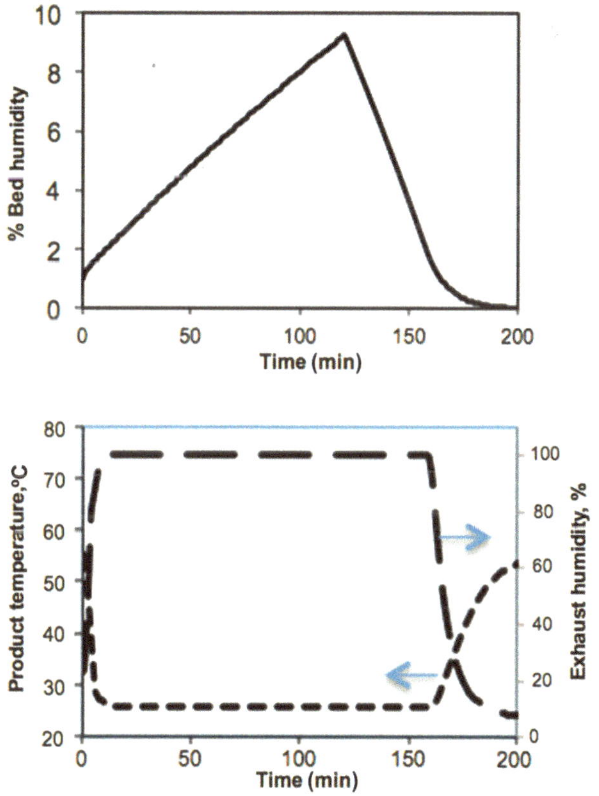

Figure 6.3 Typical profiles using FluidBeG model. (1) Batch parameters—batch size: 100 kg; binder concentration (solids-based): 4%; granulation fluid level: 35 kg/kg of batch (or water amount: 35 kg); and initial bed moisture: 1%. (2) Preheating/drying variables—airflow: 500 cfm; inlet air temperature: 60°C; and inlet air dew *T*: 10°C. (3) Granulation variables—spray rate: 325 g/min; airflow: 500 cfm; inlet air temperature: 60°C; and inlet air dew *T*: 10°C. (4) Assumption—heat loss factor (*dT*): 5°C.

using the FluidBeG model. As expected, bed moisture first increases during spraying and then decreases in the drying phase. The product temperature can be observed to initiate with a high temperature (due to preheating), followed by a constant-rate period, and then ending with a falling-rate period where temperature is observed to increase rapidly. The exhaust humidity profiles show subsaturated conditions at the beginning and end of the process, with a majority of the process under saturated conditions (RH ~100%). It is noted that the model predicts temperature and humidity profiles to undergo sharp transitions, however, in reality, these transitions are relatively smooth due to dynamics and inhomogeneity in the system.

6.4.2 Case studies

Table 6.3 presents a summary of case studies using the FluidBeG model for various product development activities in an industrial setting. One case study on MK-D is discussed in detail to illustrate how prospective modeling can be used for formulation and process development studies.

6.4.2.1 MK-D: DOE studies and scale-up

In this case study, the FluidBeG model was used by Merck scientists for design of experiments (DOE) studies at a lab scale, followed by a scale-up to a pilot and commercial scale (Gupta, 2012). The formulation comprised API (5% drug loading), binder (4%), disintegrant, and standard diluents for an immediate-release formulation. Lab-scale batches were manufactured at a 5-kg scale, whereas pilot- and commercial-scale batches were manufactured at 80-kg and 430-kg scale, respectively. The equipment used for the 5-kg, 80-kg, and 430-kg scales were Fluidair 0020, Niro MP-4, and Niro MP-7, respectively. Bed moisture was measured periodically using the LOD method.

For lab-scale studies, Table 6.4 shows the predicted and measured process outputs for the target batch manufactured at a 5-kg scale, with the detailed bed moisture profile presented in Fig. 6.4. It is observed that the bed moisture profile, exhaust humidity, processing time, and product temperatures match well to the estimated values by the model. The peak LOD is found to be ~16%, with product temperature reaching ~40°C to achieve an end-point LOD of <1.5%. It is also noted that the majority of the batch is processed under saturated or near-saturated conditions (detailed profiles not shown).

The model was then used to design a DOE study. Here, the goal was to understand the impact of key variables on granule attributes. Because bed moisture has a significant impact on the resulting granule properties, it was used as a response factor. Specifically, the model was utilized for the following:

- *Screening studies*: Here, an *in-silico* analysis of various process variables on peak LOD was conducted using the model (one-variable-at-a-time approach; Fig. 6.5 shows an example of impact of spray rate and inlet air dew point on peak bed humidity). It is observed that spray rate can have a significant impact on the bed humidity, whereas the inlet air dew point will have a limited impact on the resulting bed humidity.

Table 6.3 Case studies using FluidBeG model

Case study	Situation	FluidBeG model usage	Results
MK-A[a]	Formulation had insoluble excipients, requiring >20% bed moisture to form adequate granules.	Based on the model, a processing regime to obtain peak LOD of up to 40% was determined.	Batches were processed successfully with a peak LOD range of 25–37%.
MK-B[a]	Need to control bed moisture within <10% to avoid hydrate formation of the drug substance.	The model was used to find suitable batch parameters and prospectively estimate the entire bed moisture profile.	The resulting batches were manufactured with peak LOD range of 5–8%.
MK-C[a]	The drug substance was heat-sensitive, requiring product temperatures to be <40°C.	Simulations were performed to estimate product temperature profile and choose process variables accordingly.	Actual batch data showed that product temperatures were kept <35°C.
GSK-A[b]	Difficult to simulate thc process, likely due to extensive spray drying (see Section 2.1.2).	α in Eq. (6.11) was adjusted to $\alpha = 0.9$. $T_{out} - 7$ to account for potential spray drying of binder droplets.	Batch data matched well for the subsequent batches, leading to a successful scale-up of the process.
MK-D[a]	Needed parameter estimation for DOE studies and scale-up.	Discussed in detail next.	Discussed in detail next.

[a]Gupta (2012)
[b]Van-Milligen et al. (2016)

Table 6.4 Model outputs for case study MK-D

Output variable	Predicted	Measured
Peak bed moisture (LOD)	16%	16%
RH	Peak: ~100% Average: ~88%	80–95%
Processing time	66 min	69 min
Product T (constant rate)	25°C	25°C
Final product temperature (at LOD ~1.4%)	40°C	40°C

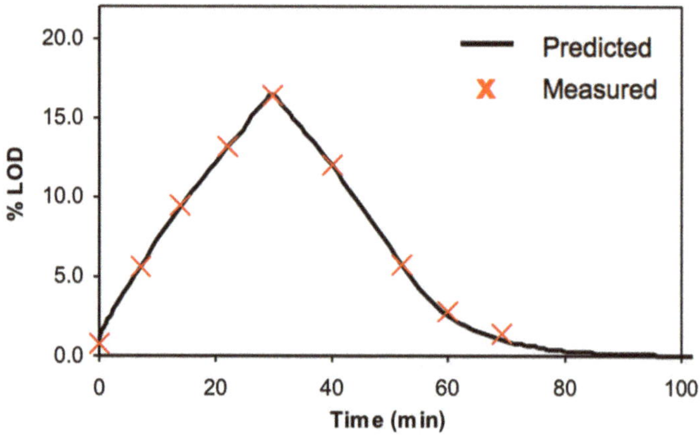

Figure 6.4 MK-D bed moisture profile at 5-kg scale.

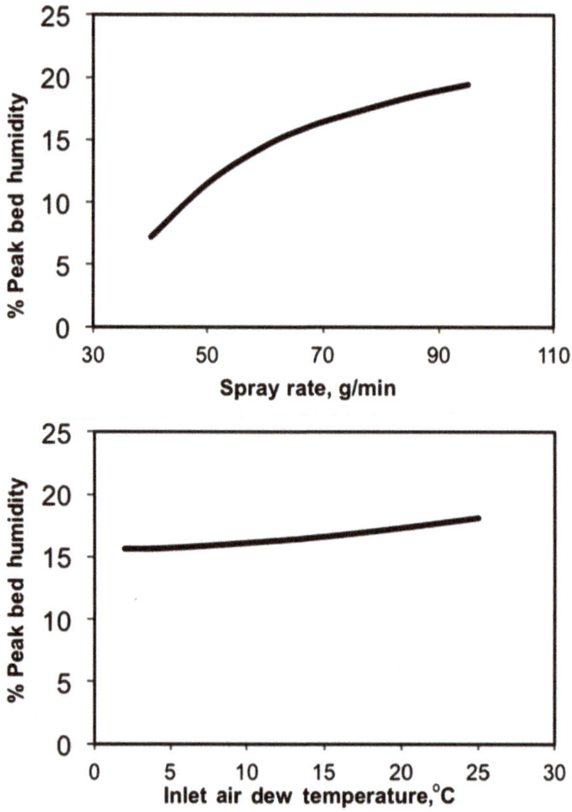

Figure 6.5 Impact of spray rate and inlet air dew temperature on bed moisture.

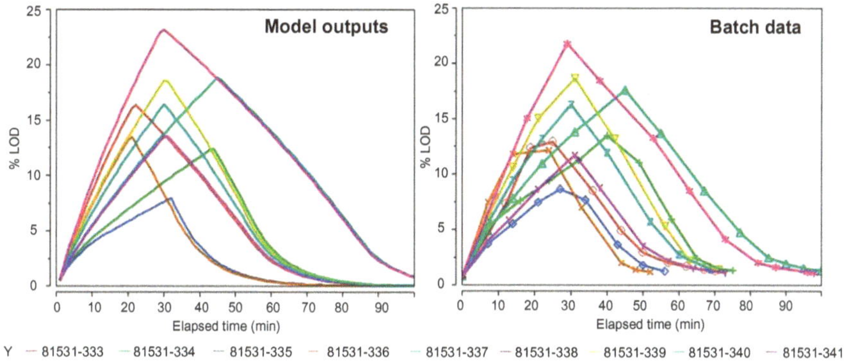

Figure 6.6 Comparison of predicted and measured moisture profiles of MK-D DOE batches.

- *Variable selection for DOE studies*: Based on the preceding screening studies, only certain variables, such as spray rate, inlet air temperature, and granulating fluid level, were selected for further DOE studies.
- *Variable ranges*: The model was then utilized to determine the ranges of various variables for the DOE batches such that the resulting peak LOD was within the 5–25% range (chosen based on the past experience). Here, the model allowed a multivariate analysis on bed humidity prior to actual batch manufacturing.

Fig. 6.6 shows a comparison of predicted and measured bed moisture profiles of the DOE batches. As before, there was a very good agreement between the predicted and the measured values. It is noted that the peak LOD range for all batches was between 8% and 23% as estimated, whereas the overall processing time (granulation + drying time) to achieve an LOD of <1.5% was also within 50–100 min, as predicted. The resulting granules were also found to be acceptable for all these batches (data not shown).

For scale-up studies, the process was then scaled-up to 80 kg (16X) and 430 kg (~5.5X), pilot and commercial scales, respectively. Here, the model was utilized for the following:

- *Scaling-up based on constant peak LOD*: Here, to obtain comparable granule properties, the goal was to maintain a similar bed moisture as observed for the target batch at the 5-kg scale. Accordingly, the peak LOD was targeted to be ~16% (a minor adjustment to 14% was made due to differences in bowl design and ancillary equipment limitations). The processing times were estimated to be longer than the lab scale, as expected.
- *End-point sampling times*: Estimates of processing times and product temperature were made to achieve an LOD <1.5%, allowing efficient sampling.
- *Preliminary recipe design*: The model allowed to design the recipe for pilot- and commercial-scale batches. Based on the estimates on the beginning of the falling-rate period from the model, a more systematic step-down approach for airflow was taken. Generally, airflow rate is lower at the beginning of granulation and toward the end of drying to minimize elutriation of fines.

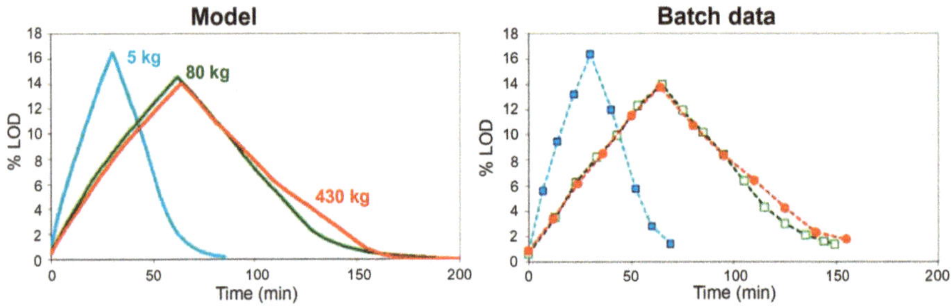

Figure 6.7 Comparison of predicted and measured moisture profiles of MK-D scale-up batches.

Fig. 6.7 shows the bed moisture profile predictions, along with the actual batch data. Again, the agreement between measured and predicted values is found to be fairly good. More importantly, the granule attributes (particle size and density) were found to be within the expected range (data not shown), enabling scientists to achieve the desired quality attributes of the product.

6.5 Future developments

While significant advancement has been made in the understanding and modeling of the granulation and drying processes, there is still a lot of unrealized opportunity in the field. One of the critical needs is an ability to perform quantitative prediction of granule growth (and breakage) behavior. Now, as the particle-level mechanisms are better understood and linked with appropriate meso- or macro-scale models, achieving this state in the future is quite possible. This will most likely require an integration of process and product models. In fact, Chaudhury et al. (2013) recently developed one of the first models in this area. In their work, they integrated a heat and mass model with a PBM of a fluid bed granulation process. This is indeed a major step forward, and it would be very interesting to see a wider use of this model, along with more development in this field. The other approaches including neural network, linguistic equation models, fuzzy logic, simulation systems, etc. are also quite attractive (Juuso, 2007; Werther et al., 2011). Overall, the desired state is where both process and product outputs are estimated prospectively, easily, and for a variety of systems and scales, using the input variables.

The other key opportunity area for fluid bed modeling is in continuous processing. Many pharmaceutical manufacturers are already converting their batch processes to adopt continuous manufacturing, as discussed in Chapter 2, Quality Risk Management for Pharmaceutical Manufacturing: The Role of Process Modeling and Simulations. Now, because the production steps are performed sequentially in a continuous process, it is important to carefully design the system. In this case, the residence time in each unit is important, as the output of one unit becomes the input

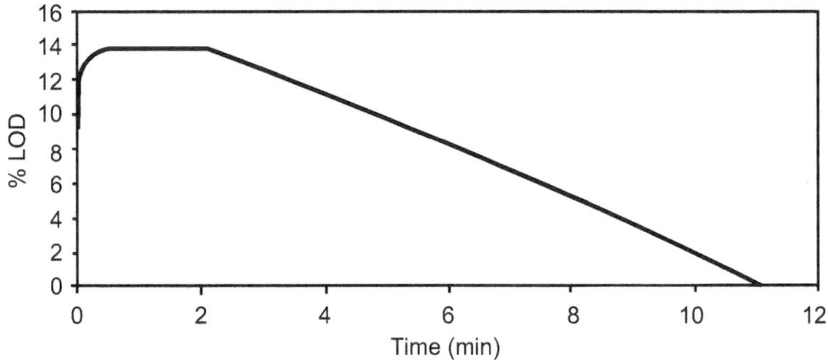

Figure 6.8 Bed moisture profile in a continuous dryer. Batch size: 1.2 kg; initial bed moisture: 20%; granulation charging time: 2 min; airflow per cell: 50 cfm; inlet air temperature: 60°C; inlet air dew *T*: 10°C. Assumption—heat loss factor (*dT*): 5°C.

of the subsequent unit, requiring a higher degree of automation and fewer manual interventions. Here, modeling of fluid bed drying can be very useful to design and optimize the process and product. Fig. 6.8 presents an estimation of a bed moisture profile based on a continuous model developed by Gupta (2016).

Along with the previously mentioned areas and other ongoing developments, one can expect a major progression in the field in coming years. This will also enable scientists to be more confident in using fluid bed models for development activities and even consider models for regulatory filings.

References

Brooker, D.B., Bakker-Arkema, F.W., Hall, C.W., 1992. Drying and Storage of Grains and Oilseeds, vol. 12. Springer Science & Business Media, pp. 450.

Broughton, D.B., 1945. Drying of solids: prediction of critical moisture content. Ind. Eng. Chem. 37, 1184−1185.

Chaudhury, A., Niziolek, A., Ramachandran, R., 2013. Multi-dimensional mechanistic modeling of fluid bed granulation processes: an integrated approach. Adv. Powder Technol. 24, 113−131.

Crank, J., 1975. The Mathematics of Diffusion. second ed. Clarendon Press, Oxford.

Earle, R.L., Earle, M.D. 2004. Unit Operations in Food Processing—Drying, Available from: The New Zealand Institute of Food Science & Technology (Inc.).

Ennis, B.J., Li, J., Tardos, G.I., Pfeffer, R., 2000. The influence of viscosity on the strength of an axially strained pendular liquid bridge. Chem. Eng. Sci. 45 (10), 3071−3088.

Faure, A., York, P., Rowe, R.C., 2001. Process control and scale-up of pharmaceutical wet granulation processes: a review. Eur. J. Pharm. Biopharm. 52, 269−277.

Fyhr, C., Kemp, I.C., Wimmerstedt, R., 2009. Mathematical modelling of fluidised bed dryers with horizontal dispersion. Chem. Eng. Process. 38, 89−94.

Gupta, R., 2012. Modeling of fluid bed granulation process for aqueous systems. Presented in: AIChE Annual Meeting, Pittsburgh.

Gupta, R., 2016. Modeling of fluid bed granulation and drying processes for pharmaceutical applications. Under preparation.

Hapgood, K.P., Litster, J.D., Smith, R., 2003. Nucleation regime map for liquid bound granules. AIChE J. 49 (2), 350–361.

Heinrich, S., Peglow, M., Mörl, L., 2002. Unsteady and steady-state particle size distributions in batch and continuous fluidized bed granulation systems. Chem. Eng. J. 86, 223–231.

Hemati, M., Cherif, R., Saleh, K., Pont, V., 2003. Fluidized bed coating and granulation: influence of process-related variables and physicochemical properties on the growth kinetics. Powder Technol. 130, 18–34.

Hlinak, A.J., Saleki-Gerhardt, A., 2000. An evaluation of fluid bed drying of aqueous granulations. Pharm. Dev. Technol. 5 (1), 11–17.

Hu, X., Cunningham, J., Winstead, D., 2008. Understanding and predicting bed humidity in fluidized bed granulation. J. Pharm. Sci. 97 (4), 1564–1577.

Iveson, S.M., Litster, J.D., Hapgood, K.P., Ennis, B.J., 2001. Nucleation, growth, and breakage phenomena in agitated wet granulation processes: a review. Powder Techno. 117, 3–39.

Juuso, E.K., 2007. Intelligent modelling of a fluidised bed granulator used in production of pharmaceuticals. Paper presented at The 48th Scandinavian Conference on Simulation and Modeling, Göteborg (Särö).

Kannan, C.S., Rao, S.S., Varma, Y.B.G., 1994. A kinetic model for drying of solids in batch fluidized beds. Ind. Chem. Res. 33, 363–370.

Kemp, I.C., 2011. Drying models, myths, and misconceptions. Chem. Eng. Technol. 34 (7), 1057–1066.

Kemp, I.C., Sohet, Q., 2010. Scale-up, optimization, and control of industrial batch fluidized bed dryers using multilevel theoretical models. Drying Technol. 28 (5), 710–722.

Li, Z., Kind, M., Gruenewald, G., 2011. Modeling the growth kinetics of fluidized—bed spray granulation. Chem. Eng. Technol. 4 (7), 1067–1075.

Sereno, A.M., Medeiros, G.L., 1990. A simplified model for the prediction of drying rates for foods. J. Food Eng. 12, 1–11.

Srinivasakannan, C., Balasubramanian, N., 2008. An analysis on modeling of fluidized bed drying of granular material. Adv. Powder Technol. 19, 73–82.

Tan, H.S., Salman, A.D., Hounslow, M.J., 2006. Kinetics of fluidised bed melt granulation I: the effect of process variables. Chem. Eng. Sci. 61, 1585–1601.

Tardos, G.I., Gupta, R., 1996. Forces generated in solidifying liquid bridges between two small particles. Powder Technol. 87, 175–180.

Van-Milligen, A., Djemai, A., Gupta, R., 2016. Unpublished results, GlaxoSmithKline.

Vreman, A.W., van Larea, C.E., Hounslow, M.J., 2009. A basic population balance model for fluid bed spray granulation. Chem. Eng. Sci. 64, 4389–4398.

Wang, H.G., Dyakowski, T., Senior, P., Raghavan, R.S., Yang, W.Q., 2007. Modelling of batch fluidised bed drying of pharmaceutical granules. Chem. Eng. Sci. 62, 1524–1535.

Werther, J., Heinrich, S., Dosta, M., Hartge, E.U., 2011. The ultimate goal of modeling—simulation of system and plant performance. Particuology 9, 320–329.

Zank, J., Kind, M., Schlünder, E.U., 2001. Particle growth and droplet deposition in fluidised bed granulation. Powder Technol. 120, 76–81.

Modeling of milling processes via DEM, PBM, and microhydrodynamics

7

E. Bilgili, M. Capece and A. Afolabi
New Jersey Institute of Technology, Newark, NJ, United States

7.1 Introduction

In the broadest term, milling is defined as a unit operation by which size of particles is reduced by mechanical means, which leads to an increase in both the specific surface area and the total surface area of the particles. Milling is one of the oldest and most widely used processes in a multitude of industries including minerals, ceramics, composites, foods, paints and inks, pharmaceuticals, etc. (Prasher, 1987). It can be carried out dry or wet in various liquids, and the process can be batch or continuous (single pass, multipass, or pendulum mode of operation). The choice of mode of operation and milling medium as well as equipment depends on the specific application in hand. Intended particle size distribution (PSD), end use of the milled particles, sensitivity of the milled materials to high temperature and deformation–stress, and tolerable contamination and product degradation levels play major roles in this selection. In general, size reduction and preparation of fine, active pharmaceutical agent (API) particles enhances the dissolution rate and helps to achieve content uniformity of the solid dosages containing the API. Control of granule PSD via milling or delumping is important to weight control and content uniformity during the tableting. Inhalation applications entail the use of micronized drugs for proper deposition in the lungs. The poor dissolution of the biopharmaceutics classification system (BCS) Class II drugs can be mitigated via preparation of drug nanoparticles with large surface area, which dissolve faster than micronized API. In view of the preceding intended functionalities and/or responses from the APIs or solid dosages, the use of milling in pharmaceutical industry has been quite versatile: size reduction of APIs and control of crystal size distribution (Fisher, 2006), delumping of excipients and APIs (Bilgili et al., 2011), micronization for inhalation applications (Pilcer and Amighi, 2010), preparation of BCS Class II drug nanoparticles for bioavailability enhancement (Afolabi, 2013; Bilgili and Afolabi, 2012; Merisko-Liversidge et al., 2003), size reduction of granules and fine-tuning of the granule PSD (Bilgili et al., 2011; Schenck and Plank, 2008; Verheezen et al., 2004), amorphization (Balani et al., 2010; Caron et al., 2013) and surface modification (Han et al., 2011; 2013). Conical screen mills and hammer mills are used for delumping of excipients–APIs as well as coarse-to-medium size reduction

Predictive Modeling of Pharmaceutical Unit Operations. DOI: http://dx.doi.org/10.1016/B978-0-08-100154-7.00007-7

and fine-tuning of wet and dry granulation PSDs, whereas pin mills, rotor–stator mills, and fluid energy (jet) mills can be used for the preparation of finer API particles. Drug nanoparticles are usually produced by high-pressure homogenizers and wet stirred media mills (WSMMs). Tumbling ball mills, planetary mills, and acoustic vibratory mixer-mills are also used for small-scale formulation and development work.

In any pharmaceutical milling operation, four major concerns must be alleviated via process and formulation design: aggregation of finely milled particles, relatively long cycle times, high energy consumption and associated cost, and possible product contamination due to equipment–media wear and product physicochemical transitions/degradation due to high temperature and/or high-shear rate in the milling environment (Afolabi et al., 2014; Bilgili and Afolabi, 2012; Bilgili et al., 2008; Juhnke et al., 2012; Prasher, 1987). It is well known that milling is an energy-intensive, poorly efficient, and costly process (Kawatra, 2006). Besides experimentation and advanced characterization of the milled product, mathematical modeling can be used for process simulations and design, while allowing for fundamental insight into the resolution of the aforementioned issues. Major approaches used for mathematical modeling of the milling process can be categorized, without being too exhaustive, as follows:

1. Purely data-driven models (Celep et al., 2011; Pradeep and Pitchumani, 2011) and empirical models such as characteristic particle size–milling time correlations (Bilgili et al., 2008; Varinot et al., 1999) and particle size–specific energy correlations (Austin, 1973; Bilgili et al., 2001; Nomura and Tanaka, 2011).
2. Particle-scale mechanistic models, which explicitly incorporate some material properties to explain particle breakage (Gahn and Mersmann, 1999a,b; Ghadiri and Zhang, 2002; Vogel and Peukert, 2003).
3. Mechanistic models such as the discrete element method (DEM), finite element method, or their combination, which account for particle deformation, multiparticle mechanical interactions, and/or collision frequency/energy at the particle ensemble or agglomerate scale (Ahmadian et al., 2011; Antony and Ghadiri, 2001; Bagherzadeh et al., 2011; Rajamani et al., 2000; Thornton and Liu, 2004; Tsoungui et al., 1999).
4. Population balance models (PBMs), which with certain mixing assumptions for the powder/slurry flow (well-mixed, plug-flow, etc.) describe spatial, temporal, or spatiotemporal variation of the PSD during milling (Austin, 1971; Bilgili and Scarlett, 2005a,b,c).
5. Models based on computational fluid dynamics, which describe single and two-phase flows in a comminution equipment (Blecher et al., 1996; Toneva et al., 2011), and its combination with PBM (Fan et al., 2004; Rajniak et al., 2008) or DEM (Teng et al., 2011).

While it may be desirable to report all of the preceding models in detail, due to space limitation, in this chapter we focus only on state-of-the-art modeling techniques including microhydrodynamic models, DEM, and PBM. The discussion of theory is followed by two major cases studies: one on the application of a microhydrodynamic model to the preparation of BCS Class II (poorly water-soluble) drug nanosuspensions in a WSMM and another on the application of a multiscale DEM–PBM approach to tumbling ball milling.

7.2 Microhydrodynamic modeling of wet media milling

Among all top-down approaches such as ball milling, planetary milling, and high-pressure homogenization, WSMM is one of the most commonly used process for producing drug nanoparticles in a stable suspension form (Afolabi, 2013; Bhakay et al., 2011; Merisko-Liversidge and Liversidge, 2011). The so-called nanosuspensions can be further dried into nanocomposites for preparing various solid oral dosage forms such as powders, sachets, capsules, tablets, and strip films (Bhakay et al., 2013, 2014a,b; Sievens-Figueroa et al., 2012; Knieke et al., 2015). Contrary to the bottom-up approaches, WSMM, is considered more universal and promising for large-scale production of BCS Class II drug nanoparticles because of its capability in achieving high drug loading, organic solvent-free processing, continuous operation capability, and ease of scale-up (Merisko-Liversidge et al., 2003; Monteiro et al., 2013).

WSMM is usually considered to be a time-consuming, costly, and energy-intensive process (Kawatra, 2006). As the breakage kinetics determines the cycle time and production rate for a desired fineness, milling process design and optimization entails a good understanding of the breakage kinetics and its controlling process parameters. Process parameters such as stirrer speed, bead loading, and drug loading can significantly affect the breakage rate and milling time required for a desired product fineness. While Peltonen and Hirvonen (2010) and the references cited therein provide great understanding of the impact of stabilization and formulation, little fundamental understanding of the impact of process parameters is available at the beads scale. In a more recent work, Ghosh et al. (2012) presented the effects of stirrer speed, bead size, and drug content on the final milled suspension; however, the impact of these parameters on the breakage kinetics was not investigated. Singare et al. (2010) and Singh et al. (2011) used a statistical design of experiments with a response surface methodology with the goal of optimizing the process parameters including milling speed and time. However, no information regarding the breakage kinetics was presented explicitly. In general, such statistically based designs of experiments do not provide significant process insight as to how the process parameters affect the breakage kinetics because they are devoid of fundamental physics at the beads scale. Unfortunately, in the absence of fundamental knowledge and process insight, valuable development time/resources will be wasted; the process developed will be suboptimal.

It is fair to assert that WSMM has been largely treated as a black box in pharmaceutical literature, and the microhydrodynamics, which is the study of the fluctuating motion of the beads in sheared suspensions, has not been investigated at all until very recently. Based on the kinetic theory of granular flows and the fundamental granular energy balance (Gidaspow, 1994), Eskin et al. (2005a,b) developed a comprehensive microhydrodynamic model to calculate the mean velocity of bead oscillations in a well-mixed slurry. This model was adapted and refined for application to pharmaceutical WSMM (Afolabi et al., 2014; Bilgili and Afolabi, 2012). The power applied by the mill stirrer is uniformly applied throughout the whole

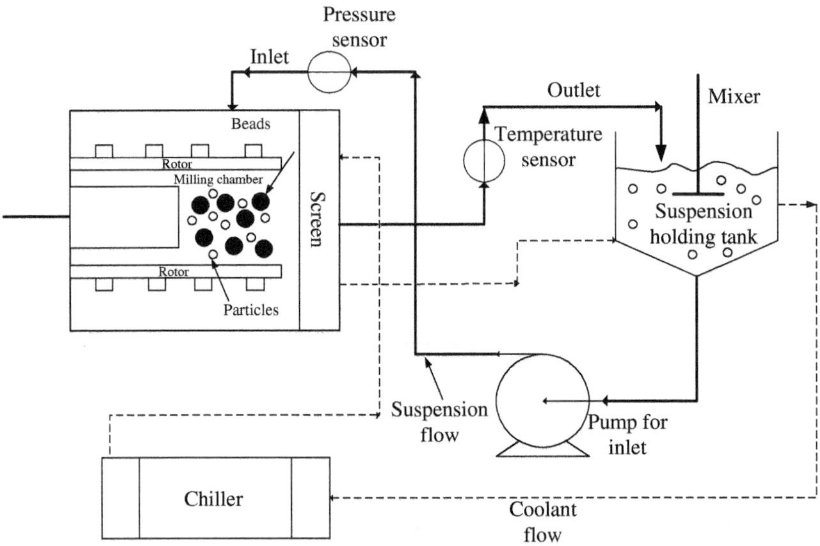

Figure 7.1 Schematic of the Netzsch stirred media mill (Model MicroCer) operating in the recirculation mode of milling. Figure is not drawn to scale.

volume of the slurry (beads and suspension, see Fig. 7.1) and equals the total energy dissipation rate ε_{tot}. This power dissipates through fluctuating motions of the beads at the microscale. Hence, ε_{tot} is described as

$$\varepsilon_{tot} = P_w = \varepsilon_{visc} + \varepsilon_{coll} \tag{7.1}$$

where P_w is the power applied by the rotor per unit volume, ε_{visc} is the energy dissipation rate due to both the liquid–beads viscous friction and lubrication, and ε_{coll} is the energy dissipation rate due to partially inelastic bead–bead collisions. Eq. (7.1) can be used for a suspension undergoing turbulent motion (stirred Reynolds number, Re >35,000) and does not consider the energy dissipation due to friction between liquid layers, which may become especially pertinent in the transition region, i.e., 120 < Re < 35000 (Kawatra, 2006). Therefore, a new term should be added to the right-hand side. Motivated by the work of Eskin and Miller (2008) on slurry flow in fractures, Bilgili and Afolabi (2012) included such a term, ε_{ht}, in the granular energy balance for wet media milling. Here, ε_{ht} is defined as the power spent on shearing equivalent liquid (milled drug suspension) of the slurry at the same shear rate but calculated (or measured approximately) as if no beads were present in the slurry. Then, following Eskin et al. (2005a, 2008), Eq. (7.1) can be modified as

$$P_w = \varepsilon_{visc} + \varepsilon_{coll} + \varepsilon_{ht} \tag{7.2}$$

$$P_w = \frac{54\mu_L c\theta R_{diss}}{d_b^2} + \frac{12}{d_b\sqrt{\pi}}(1-k^2)\left[\frac{1-0.5c}{(1-c)^3}\right]c^2\rho_b\theta^{3/2} + \varepsilon_{ht} \tag{7.3}$$

where μ_L is the apparent shear viscosity of the equivalent liquid and c is the beads volumetric concentration. As commonly assumed in the WSMM literature (refer to Kawatra, 2006), the equivalent liquid was taken as the milled suspension. Here, θ is the granular temperature defined as the bead–equivalent liquid relative mean-square velocity, R_{diss} is the dissipation or effective drag coefficient, d_b is the bead size (taken as the median size), k is the restitution coefficient for the bead–bead collisions, and ρ_b is the density of the milling media (beads). The dissipation coefficient, R_{diss}, is a function of the bead Reynolds number, c, and the nondimensional bead–bead gap thickness at which the lubrication force stops increasing and becomes a constant (refer to Afolabi et al., 2014 for calculation of R_{diss}).

The solution of Eq. (7.3) entails measurement of the equivalent liquid properties, i.e., shear viscosity μ_L and density ρ_L of the drug suspension, the stirrer power per unit volume in the presence of the beads P_w, and the energy dissipation rate for shearing the equivalent liquid ε_{ht} by rheometry and milling experiments (refer to Bilgili and Afolabi, 2012). The shear viscosity obtained at a shear rate of 1000 1/s can be taken as the μ_L value. Although the shear rate in media mills could exceed this value, earlier work (Bernhardt et al., 1999) considered 1000 1/s to be a representative value because the shear viscosity did not change drastically above 1000 1/s and it can be reliably measured by most rheometers. Along with the bead material properties, these measured values are incorporated into Eq. (7.3), which can then be solved for the granular temperature, θ, using any nonlinear equation solver such as Matlab's fsolve function. The average bead oscillation velocity, u_b, and the frequency of single-bead oscillations, ν, are determined using the calculated θ and the following expressions:

$$u_b = \sqrt{\frac{8\theta}{\pi}} \quad \text{and} \quad \nu = \frac{24c}{d_b}\left[\frac{1-0.5c}{(1-c)^3}\right]\sqrt{\frac{\theta}{\pi}} \tag{7.4}$$

In a comprehensive microhydrodynamic model, Eskin et al. (2005a) considered the elastic contact deformation of the beads along with the elastic–perfectly plastic deformation of the particles caught between the beads. While the beads frequently collide due to their fluctuating motions in a slurry, which are characterized by θ, u_b, and ν, the beads capture and compress (deform) the drug particles to be milled. The average maximum normal force, F_b^n, during collision of two identical elastic beads, the radius of the contact circle formed at the contact of two beads, α_b, and the maximum contact pressure at the center of the contact circle, σ_b^{max}, were calculated using

$$F_b^n = 1.96\left(\frac{Y_b}{1-\eta_b^2}\right)^{2/5}\rho_b^{3/5}R_b^2\theta^{3/5} \tag{7.5}$$

$$\alpha_b = \left[\frac{3}{4}\frac{(1-\eta_b^2)}{Y_b}R_bF_b^n\right]^{1/3} \tag{7.6}$$

$$\sigma_{\rm b}^{\rm max} = \frac{3}{2}\frac{F_{\rm b}^{n}}{\pi\alpha_{\rm b}^{2}} \tag{7.7}$$

where $Y_{\rm b}$, and $\eta_{\rm b}$ are the Young modulus and Poisson's ratio of the bead material, $R_{\rm b}$ is the bead radius and was taken as half of $d_{\rm b}$. The probability p of a single particle with radius $R_{\rm p}$ being caught between beads was estimated as the ratio of the volume containing the caught particles to the volume of milled drug suspension falling on a pair of the milling beads and is expressed as

$$p = 0.97\frac{c}{1-c}\left[\frac{\rho_{\rm b}(1-\eta_{\rm b}^{2})}{Y_{\rm b}}\right]^{2/5}\theta^{2/5}\frac{R_{\rm p}}{R_{\rm b}} \tag{7.8}$$

The average frequency of drug particle compressions a was estimated as the product of this probability p and the frequency of single-bead oscillations, ν. The energy dissipation rate resulting from the deformation of the drug particles per unit volume Π characterizes the grinding intensity and is expressed as follows:

$$\Pi = 2.23\frac{c^{2}(2-c)}{(1-c)^{3}}\frac{1}{\pi^{5/2}\varepsilon\sigma_{\rm y}}\left(\frac{Y_{\rm b}}{1-\eta_{\rm b}^{2}}\right)^{18/15}\left(\frac{Y^{*}}{Y_{\rm p}}\right)^{\gamma}\rho_{\rm b}^{4/5}\frac{R_{\rm p}}{R_{\rm b}^{2}}\theta^{13/10} \tag{7.9}$$

where ε, Y^{*}, $Y_{\rm p}$, $\eta_{\rm b}$, $\sigma_{\rm y}$, $R_{\rm p}$, and $R_{\rm b}$, respectively, denote volumetric drug loading in the milled suspension, reduced elastic modulus of the bead–drug particle contact, elastic modulus of the drug particles, Poisson's ratio of the beads, contact pressure in a drug particle captured when the fully plastic condition is obtained, radius of the drug particle, and radius of the bead.

In order to calculate Π using the expressions derived by Eskin et al. (2005a) (Eq. 7.9), one must either find the mechanical properties of the drug particles ($Y_{\rm p}$, $\eta_{\rm p}$, $\sigma_{\rm y}$) from the literature or measure them. In general, it is difficult to find reliable mechanical properties of the drug particles or to measure them reliably. In view of this, Afolabi et al. (2014) factorized Π into a material-dependent factor λ and a process-dependent factor F, which is referred to as the milling intensity factor, to gain insight into the impact of the process parameters as follows:

$$\lambda = 2.23\frac{1}{\pi^{5/2}\sigma_{\rm y}}\left(\frac{Y_{\rm b}}{1-\eta_{\rm b}^{2}}\right)^{18/15}\left(\frac{Y^{*}}{Y_{\rm p}}\right)^{\gamma}\rho_{\rm b}^{4/5}\frac{R_{\rm p}}{R_{\rm b}^{2}} \tag{7.10}$$

$$F = \frac{c^{2}(2-c)}{(1-c)^{3}}\frac{1}{\varepsilon}\theta^{13/10} \tag{7.11}$$

A possible increase/decrease in F corresponds to a proportional increase/decrease in Π in some time- and space-averaged sense because well-mixedness and average power consumption during the milling are assumed, and λ is taken as a constant for a given pair of drug–bead materials. One can then refer to either F or Π while reporting the impact of the process parameters. In a recent study (Li et al., 2015), F was slightly modified to include in the denominator so as to assess the impact of bead size on milling intensity.

7.3 DEM for modeling of dry milling

To study the particle-scale phenomena and micromechanical interactions of particles which produce the complex granular flow and particle fracture behavior in milling processes, the DEM has been utilized (Mishra, 2003a,b; Zhu et al., 2008). While a detailed description of the DEM modeling scheme and numerical methods can be found elsewhere (Cundall and Strack, 1979), a short description is given here. DEM resolves the translational and rotational motion of particles integrating Newton's second law of motion. When particles come into contact with other particles, milling media, or the vessel, contact mechanic models resolve the force and resultant motion of the interaction. The motion of each particle and the forces acting on every particle is resolved and updated every numerical time step of the simulation.

Due to its wide use, the Hertz–Mindlin (no slip) soft particle contact model is detailed next. The Hertz–Mindlin force model is used to resolve particle interactions and is based on the theory of Hertz (1882), Mindlin (1949), and Tsuji et al. (1992). The normal force component F_n shown in Eq. (7.12) is a function of the normal particle overlap δ_n in which the first term on the r.h.s. is the elastic force and the second is a damping force which takes into account the coefficient of restitution e.

$$F_n = \frac{4}{3}E^*\sqrt{R^*}\delta_n^{3/2} - 2\sqrt{\frac{5}{6}}\frac{\ln e}{\ln^2 e + \pi^2}\sqrt{2E^*M^*}(R^*\delta_n)^{\frac{1}{4}}v_n^{\mathrm{rel}} \tag{7.12}$$

Here, v_n^{rel} is the normal component of the relative velocity between two particles at contact and E^*, R^*, and M^* are the equivalent Young's modulus, equivalent radius, and equivalent mass respectively, which are defined as

$$E^* = \left[\frac{1-\nu_{\mathrm{a}}^2}{E_{\mathrm{a}}} + \frac{1-\nu_{\mathrm{b}}^2}{E_{\mathrm{b}}}\right]^{-1}, \quad R^* = \left[\frac{1}{R_{\mathrm{a}}} + \frac{1}{R_{\mathrm{b}}}\right]^{-1}, \quad M^* = \left[\frac{1}{M_{\mathrm{a}}} + \frac{1}{M_{\mathrm{b}}}\right]^{-1} \tag{7.13}$$

where E, R, M, ν are the Young's modulus, radius, mass, and Poisson's ratio of a particle a in contact with particle b. The tangential force F_{t} is modeled by Eq. (7.14) and is based on the work of Mindlin and Deresiewicz (1953). The tangential force is a function of the tangential particle overlap δ_{t} in which the first term on the r.h.s. is the elastic force and the second is a damping force.

$$F_t = -8G^*\sqrt{R^*\delta_n}\delta_t - 2\sqrt{\frac{5}{6}}\frac{\ln e}{\ln^2 e + \pi^2}\sqrt{8G^*M^*}(R^*\delta_n)^{\frac{1}{4}}v_t^{rel} \tag{7.14}$$

Here, G^* is the equivalent shear modulus and calculated from the shear modulus G as shown in Eqs. (7.15) and (7.16).

$$G^* = \left[\frac{1-\nu_a^2}{G_a} + \frac{1-\nu_b^2}{G_b}\right]^{-1} \tag{7.15}$$

$$G = \frac{E}{2(1+\nu)} \tag{7.16}$$

Finally, the torque τ acting on a particle due to contact with a surface is determined by

$$\tau_a = -\mu_r F_n R_a \omega_a \tag{7.17}$$

where μ_r is the coefficient of rolling friction and ω is the angular velocity.

Among the major applications of DEM to model particulate processes (e.g., mixing, conveying, and fluidization), there has been intensive work directed toward understanding the dynamic behavior of milling processes (Weerasekara et al., 2013). Initial DEM milling studies were primarily qualitative comparisons between simulated and experimentally observed granular motion in a mill, but demonstrated the method's validity (Ketterhagen et al., 2009; Mishra, 2003a,b; Zhu et al., 2008). Recently, the method has rapidly developed to predict milling performance and the breakage rate or the breakage rate parameter via simulation of particle interactions obtained by DEM (Bruchmuller et al., 2011; Bwalya et al., 2001; Concas et al., 2006; Datta and Rajamani, 2002; Hoyer, 1999; Kano and Saito, 1998; Kwan et al., 2005; Lee et al., 2010; Mori et al., 2004; Tavares and Carvalho, 2009; Wang et al., 2012). Because the fundamental phenomenon for particle breakage occurs due to a stress-induced event such as a collision of a feed particle with media during media (ball) milling, most studies have sought to relate the impact energy distribution obtained from DEM simulations to the breakage rate.

7.4 PBM for process-scale modeling of milling

Among various approaches to mathematically model and analyze milling processes, PBM has been extensively used for simulating the temporal and/or spatial evolution of the PSD. The general size-discrete, time-continuous PBM given in Eq. (7.18) uses two functions: the specific breakage rate function k, a.k.a. the breakage kernel, which describes the rate at which particles break and the breakage distribution function b, a.k.a. the daughter distribution function, which describes the resultant mass-based PSD of broken particles (Austin, 1971; Austin et al., 1984).

$$\frac{dM_i(t)}{dt} = -k_i(t)M_i(t) + \sum_{j=1}^{i-1} b_{ij}k_j(t)M_j(t) \quad \text{with} \quad M_i(0) = M_{i,\text{ini}} \tag{7.18}$$

Solution of Eq. (7.18), otherwise known as the linear time-variant (LTVAR) PBM, describes the temporal variation of the PSD for well-mixed batch milling processes. The same model can be used for a plug-flow tube mill operating continuously at steady state, where time t refers to a transformed time $t = \tau\eta/L$, where τ is the mean residence time and η is the axial position from the inlet of the mill with length L. In Eq. (7.18), $M_i(t)$ is the mass fraction of particles with size x_i at milling time t. The first term on the r.h.s. is the disappearance rate at which particles of size x_i are broken into smaller particles. The second term on the r.h.s. represents the summed rate at which particles in all size classes $j < i$ are broken into size class i, where i and j are size class indices extending from size class 1 containing the coarsest particles to size class N containing the finest particles usually in a geometric progression. k_i is the size-discrete specific breakage rate parameter and b_{ij} is the size-discrete breakage distribution parameter, which are the discrete counterparts of the size-continuous k and b functions. It is often more convenient to use the cumulative breakage distribution parameter B_{ij}, which defines b_{ij} through $b_{ij} = B_{ij} - B_{i+1j}$ and $b_{nj} = B_{Nj}$ and $b_{ii} = 0$.

In most milling applications, the specific breakage rate constant is assumed time independent ($k_i(t) = k_i$), which reduces Eq. (7.18) to the traditional time-continuous linear PBM (TCL-PBM) in Eq. (7.19):

$$\frac{dM_i(t)}{dt} = -k_iM_i(t) + \sum_{j=1}^{i-1} b_{ij}k_jM_j(t) \quad \textit{with} \quad M_i(0) = M_{i,\text{ini}} \tag{7.19}$$

Although the TCL-PBM is quite elegant and has been widely used in the last 60 years, it has been criticized by several researchers for its restriction to first-order breakage kinetics (see e.g., Meloy and Williams, 1992; Rajamani and Guo, 1992). While first-order breakage kinetics is valid for short-time milling of mono-sized feeds (Austin and Bhatia, 1972; Kotake et al., 2002), non-first-order (i.e., nonlinear) breakage kinetics is frequently observed in dense-phase milling processes in retention-type mills such as ball mills, stirred media mills, vibratory mills, etc., rendering the use of the TCL-PBM restrictive and inaccurate (Austin et al., 1984; Rajamani and Guo, 1992; Verma and Rajamani, 1995). In dense-phase milling, the specific breakage rate or breakage probability of particles of a given size is not solely dependent on the particle size. Particles mechanically interact at the particle ensemble scale transmitting forces among themselves while being broken into smaller ones if the local stresses are sufficiently high. In addition, the distribution of contact forces and the resultant stresses will evolve with the continuously changing population density. Furthermore, impact energy spectra evolve in time as a function of the PSD in dry media milling processes. Because of these evolving multiparticle interactions, one would expect a population dependence to the specific breakage rate thus casting serious doubt about both the validity of first-order breakage kinetics and the predictive capability of the TCL-PBM especially during prolonged milling for the production of fine particles.

To explain and quantify the impact of mechanical multiparticle interactions on the breakage kinetics, Bilgili et al. (2006b) decomposed the specific breakage rate $k(t)$ into a first-order specific breakage rate parameter k_i and a population-dependent functional $\digamma$

$$k_i(t) \equiv k_i \digamma \left[W_{iq} M_q(t) \right] \tag{7.20}$$

$\digamma$ can be expressed via a sum of the weighted interactions of particles in size class i with other particles in generic size class q, i.e., $F_i[\sum_{q=1}^{N} W_{iq} M_q(t)]$. The weighting function W_{iq} expresses the contribution of any size class q to the specific breakage rate of particles in size class i during $i-q$ size class interactions. The nonlinear functional $F_i[\ ]$ describes various non-first-order breakage kinetics due to mechanical multiparticle interactions. It is generally accepted that k_i is more sensitive than b_{ij} to changes in the processing parameters (Austin, 1971; Gutsche and Fuerstenau, 1999; Prasher, 1987). Hence, invariance of b_{ij} to the multiparticle interactions is assumed. Capece et al. (2011a) discussed the importance of the nonlinear functional $F_i[\ ]$ in determining the true breakage kinetics and revealed "falsified" breakage kinetics when multiparticle interactions are neglected. Motivated by the traditional heterogeneous catalysis literature, the functional was referred to as the effectiveness factor (EF) for multiparticle interactions:

$$F_i[] = \frac{\text{Actual (observed) rate of particle breakage in size class } i}{\text{Rate of particle breakage in size class } i \text{ in the absence of multiparticle interactions}} \tag{7.21}$$

Given the preceding definition of the EF, it is immediately apparent that $F_i[\ ] > 1$ and $F_i[\ ] < 1$ signifies an increase (acceleration) and decrease (deceleration) in the specific breakage rate respectively due to multiparticle interactions while $F_i[\ ] = 1$ infers negligible impact of the multiparticle interactions. In this latter case, the specific breakage rate equals the first-order breakage rate and TCL-PBM is recovered as a limiting case.

Motivated by the celebrated review (Austin, 1971), where the PBM for milling was presented in different forms, Table 7.1 presents the general nonlinear PBM framework with the factorization presented in Eq. (7.20) for milling processes via index and matrix formalisms while treating time as a continuous (TCNL-PBM) variable and discrete (DNL-PBM) variable. While the PBM in index notation is particularly amenable to code development, the PBM in matrix notation facilitates the use of sophisticated matrix operations built-in to software like Matlab and Mathematica. Due to the complexity of the multiparticle interactions, Bilgili et al. (2006b) proposed Models A–D with varying mathematical complexity (refer to Table 7.2). For example, neglecting the possible $i-q$ size class interactions for

Table 7.1 Summary of the size-discretized population balance models (PBMs) for nonlinear particle breakage in well-mixed batch milling processes and steady-state, plug-flow continuous milling processes

Model name	Treatment of time[a]	Form	Equation with feed condition[b] and constraints	References
TCNL-PBM	Continuous (rate-based)	Index	$\frac{dM_i(t)}{dt} = -k_iF_i\left[\sum_{q=1}^{N} W_{iq}M_q(t)\right]M_i(t) + \sum_{j=1}^{i-1} b_{ij}k_jF_j\left[\sum_{q=1}^{N} W_{jq}M_q(t)\right]M_j(t)$ $M_i(0)=M_{i0},\quad b_{ij}=B_{ij}-B_{i+1j},\quad B_{ii}-B_{i+1i}=0,\quad B_{N+1j}=0,\quad k_i>0,$ $k_N=0,\quad F_i[\,]>0,\quad F_i[\,]\to 1 \text{ as } \forall M_q(q\neq i,t)\to 0$	Bilgili and Scarlett (2005a)
TCNL-PBM	Continuous (rate-based)	Matrix[c]	$\frac{d\mathbf{M}(t)}{dt} = -(\mathbf{I}-\mathbf{b})\cdot\mathbf{k}\cdot\mathbf{F}[\mathbf{W}\cdot\mathbf{M}(t)]\cdot\mathbf{M}(t)\equiv\mathbf{C}\cdot\mathbf{M}(t)$ with $\mathbf{M}(0)=\mathbf{M}_0$	Bilgili et al. (2006b)
DNL-PBM	Discrete[d] (event-based)	Index	$M_i^{(n)} = \left\{1-P_iF_i\left[\sum_{q=1}^{N} W_{iq}M_q^{(n-1)}\right]\right\}M_i^{(n-1)} + \sum_{j=1}^{i-1} b_{ij}P_jF_j\left[\sum_{q=1}^{N} W_{jq}M_q^{(n-1)}\right]M_j^{(n-1)}$ $n=1,2,\ldots,n_e,\quad M_i^{(n=0)}=M_i^{(0)},\quad b_{ij}=B_{ij}-B_{i+1j},\quad B_{ii}-B_{i+1i}=0,\quad B_{N+1j}=0,$ $0<P_i<1,\quad P_N=0,\quad F_i>0,\quad F_i\to 1 \text{ as } \forall M_q(q\neq i,n)\to 0$	Bilgili and Capece (2011)
DNL-PBM	Discrete[d] (event-based)	Matrix[c]	$\mathbf{M}^{(n)}=\{\mathbf{I}-(\mathbf{I}-\mathbf{b})\cdot\mathbf{P}\cdot\mathbf{F}[\mathbf{W}\cdot\mathbf{M}^{(n-1)}]\}\cdot\mathbf{M}^{(n-1)}\equiv\mathbf{T}^{(n-1)}(\mathbf{M}^{(n-1)})\cdot\mathbf{M}^{(n-1)}$ with $n=1,2,\ldots,n_e,\quad \mathbf{M}^{(n=0)}=\mathbf{M}^{(0)}$	Bilgili and Capece (2011)

[a]Time t refers to $t=\tau\eta/L$ in a plug-flow mill (L, η, and τ stand for length, axial position, and the mean residence time of particles).
[b]Feed condition refers to initial PSD for a batch mill or the inlet PSD for a plug-flow continuous mill.
[c]Same constraints apply regardless of the formalism used to express the equation.
[d]The term discrete or event connotes step, stage, section, passage, and cycle that have been frequently and alternatively used in a multitude of different milling applications. P_i stands for breakage probability parameter.

Table 7.2 General form of the effectiveness factor (EF) with different assumptions for the weighting factor (Models A, B, C, and D)

Model name	Assumption	General form of the EF[a]
Model A	General, nonuniform kinetics	$F_i \equiv F_i[] = F_i\left[\sum_{q=1}^{N} W_{iq}M_q(t)\right]$ for all i-q interactions
Model B	Truncated form (one-way interactions)	$F_i \equiv F_i[] = F_i\left[\sum_{q=i}^{N} W_{iq}M_q(t)\right]$ for all i-q interactions with $q > i$
		$F_i \equiv F_i[] = F_i\left[\sum_{q=1}^{i} W_{iq}M_q(t)\right]$ for all i-q interactions with $q < i$
Model C[b]	Size-separable form	$F_i \equiv F_i[] = F_i\left[\sigma_i \sum_{q=1}^{N} \chi_q M_q(t)\right]$ where $W_{iq} = \sigma_i \chi_q$ for all i-q interactions
Model D[c]	Uniform kinetics (lumped interactions)	$F_i \equiv F_i[] = f\left(\sum_{q=1}^{N} \tau_q M_q(t)\right)$ where f is a function of time

[a]The form specifically refers to TCNL-PBM. $M_q(t)$ is replaced with $M_q^{(n-1)}$ to get the form relevant to DNL-PBM.
[b]Additional size-dependent functions σ_i and χ_q result from the factorization of W_{iq}.
[c]Without loss of generality, f can simply be written as an explicit function of time alone or any PSD statistic that evolves in time.

$q < i$ and assuming a truncated form of W_{iq}, Model B in Eq. (7.22) successfully predicted either the acceleration or the deceleration in batch milling processes (Bilgili and Scarlett, 2005a; Capece et al., 2011b), particle breakage during uniaxial powder compression (Bilgili and Capece, 2012), and steady-state plug-flow continuous milling processes (Bilgili and Scarlett, 2005b).

$$\frac{dM_i(t)}{dt} = -k_i F_i \left[\sum_{q=i}^{N} W_{iq} M_q(t) \right] M_i(t) + \sum_{j=1}^{i-1} b_{ij} k_j F_j \left[\sum_{q=j}^{N} W_{jq} M_q(t) \right] M_j(t) \quad (7.22)$$

with $M_i(0) = M_{i,\text{ini}}$. Motivated by earlier work (Bilgili, 2007), Capece et al. (2013) exposed the absence or delayed attainment of self-similarity in the evolution of the PSD during milling when non-first-order breakage kinetics was prevalent due to multiparticle interactions. While the specific form of the EF can be selected from various mathematical forms presented in Table 7.3, Capece et al. (2012) expressed the EF as a generalized rational function, which can account for any type of nonlinear kinetics and allow for discriminating the best model by statistical analysis. The nonlinear framework in Tables 7.1 and 7.2 has already been adopted by various researchers with modifications (Chakraborty and Ramkrishna, 2011; Kostoglou and Karabelas, 2006; Tuzcu and Rajamani, 2008).

Bilgili and Capece (2011) extended the nonlinear framework to a time- or space-discrete model for event-based milling processes where particles undergo relatively few breakage events or are processed in equipment with short residence times.

Table 7.3 Specific forms of the effectiveness factor (EF) used in model B of TCNL-PBM for nonlinear particle breakage

Code	Specific EF used[a]	References
EF1	$F_i[\,] = \left[1 + \lambda \sum_{q=i}^{N} (1 - x_q/x_i)^{\alpha} M_q \right]^{-1}$	Bilgili and Scarlett (2005b); Bilgili et al. (2006b); Bilgili (2007); Capece et al. (2011a,b); Tuzcu and Rajamani (2008)
EF2	$F_i[\,] = \dfrac{1}{1 + \left[\lambda \sum_{q=i}^{N} (1/x_q - 1/x_i)^{\alpha} M_q \right]^{2}}$	Bilgili and Capece (2011)
EF3	$F_i[\,] = \exp\left[\lambda \sum_{q=i}^{N} \dfrac{M_q}{1 + (x_q/x_i\alpha)^{\beta}}\right]$	Bilgili and Scarlett (2005a); Capece et al. (2011a)
EF4	$F_i[\,] = \dfrac{1 + r_1[\,] + r_2[\,]^2 + \ldots + r_k[\,]^k}{1 + s_1[\,] + s_2[\,]^2 + \ldots + s_u[\,]^u}$ where $[\,] \equiv \sum_{q=i}^{N} (1/x_q - 1/x_i)^{\alpha} M_q$	Bilgili and Capece (2012); Capece et al. (2012)

[a]In the studies cited, M_q was taken as either $M_q(t)$ or $M_q^{(n-1)}$ when TCNL-PBM or DNL-PBM was used, respectively.

A fundamental tenet of the discrete size−time formulation (DNL-PBM) in Table 7.1 is that the breakage or milling process can be adequately described by a series of n breakage events (steps in time or sections in space). The errors associated with the DNL-PBM can be assessed more adequately once details of the breakage process, intended application, and rigor level of the model have been specified. We expect that the DNL-PBM or its linear counterpart (DL-PBM) can be used as follows:

1. *Single breakage event ($n = 1$).* DL-PBM with $n = 1$ was used to model a single particle shatter test (refer to Austin, 1971), a single impact breakage test in which particles are fired against a target (Vervoorn and Austin, 1990), roller milling (Campbell and Webb, 2001; Fistes and Tanovic, 2006), particle bed compression tests (Gutsche and Fuerstenau, 1999), and any single cycle or pass of particles through a mill or breakage tester, or any particle processing equipment in general, where mean residence time is found to be very short: hammer milling (Bertrand et al., 1999; Vogel and Peukert, 2002), high-pressure homogenization (Wong and O'Neill, 1997), and pneumatic conveying (Bas et al., 2011). In these cases, the numerical time-discretization errors are not critical. In fact, TCNL-PBM, if used for rate-based processes, may be regarded as irrelevant, and use of DNL-PBM is justified well. On the other hand, using time-discretized models with $n = 1$ for a comminution process that leads to significant number of breakage events or long residence time is flawed. In such a scenario, the arbitrary lumping of multiple breakage events into a single one (see e.g., Baxter et al., 2004) renders PBM a black-box model with little insight into size dependence of breakage probability and distribution parameters, breakage mechanisms, and multiparticle interactions.
2. *Multiple breakage events ($n > 1$).* This scenario is similar to case 1, but with a relatively small number of breakage events (cycles, passes, compressions, multiple impacts, etc.) in the applications mentioned previously. Although one may not be able to prescribe what constitutes a small number of breakage events, two principles restrict successful use of the DNL-PNM. First, n should either be prescribed by experimental conditions (as in Bas et al., 2011; Vervoorn and Austin, 1990; Wong and O'Neill, 1997) or can be fitted to the experimental data as suggested in Berthiaux (2000) or as performed in Teng et al. (2010). For example, $n = 2-120$ steps for a stirred media mill (Berthiaux, 2000), $n = 1-10$ homogenizer passes (Wong and O'Neill, 1997), $n = 1-20$ cycles during pipe pneumatic conveying (Bas et al., 2011), $n = 1-14$ passes through a single-event fluid mill and up to 140 events in a fluid energy mill (Teng et al., 2010) were considered in the context of DL-PBM. In all these studies, nonrandom deviations from the DL-PBM fit were observed; notable deviations occurred even for dilute-phase systems under some conditions (Bas et al., 2011; Teng et al., 2010). Second, if the residence time is long leading to large number of breakage events or if prescribed number of passes/cycles through equipment is large, then one needs to justify why the DNL-PBM or its linear counterpart (DL-PBM) is used instead of TCNL-PBM in Eq. (7.22). The low-order accuracy of explicit Euler method may become problematic in this case especially when the model parameters need to be calculated from experimental data (inverse problem). Sophisticated ordinary differential equation (ODE) solvers with variable order−variable step-size capability and up to fifth-order accuracy in time are already available in Matlab (Shampine et al., 2003). Their use with TCNL-PBM is much more relevant, efficient, and accurate. In short, when modeling milling processes with long residence time (e.g., in retention-type mills) is concerned, DNL-PBM should be considered as a low-order accurate, limiting case of the more general TCNL-PBM (Bilgili and Capece, 2011).

7.4.1 Calibration of the PBM via parameter estimation (the inverse problem)

Estimation of the parameters of the PBM, i.e., the solution of the inverse PBM problem, for milling processes is a nontrivial problem (refer to Bilgili et al., 2006a; Capece et al., 2011b). Prior to estimation, it is customary to express the PBM parameters, i.e., k_i, b_{ij}, or B_{ij}, and $F_i[\ ]$, as explicit functions of discrete particle sizes. For example, the following power-law function for k_i and a normalized function for B_{ij} have been commonly used in the milling literature (Austin and Luckie, 1972; Klimpel and Austin, 1977):

$$k_i = A\left(\frac{x_i}{x_0}\right)^m \tag{7.23}$$

$$B_{ij} = \phi\left(\frac{x_{i-1}}{x_j}\right)^{\mu} + (1-\phi)\left(\frac{x_{i-1}}{x_j}\right)^{\nu} \tag{7.24}$$

where A, m, ϕ, μ, and ν are the only parameters of the TCL-PBM (Eq. 7.19), and x_0 is a normalizing particle size, which may be taken as the maximum particle size, e.g., 1000 μm. Note that b_{ij} relates to B_{ij} through $b_{ij} = B_{ij} - B_{i+1j}$ and $b_{nj} = B_{Nj}$ and $b_{ii} = 0$. Readers are referred to Prasher (1987) and Diemer and Olson (2002) for other k_i and b_{ij} functions. In case of TCNL-PBM, parameters of the EF F_i have to be estimated additionally (refer to Table 7.3). In the context of LTVAR-PBM (Eq. 7.18), various forms of $k_i(t)$ can be used; the following specific function has been used to account for the deceleration of breakage rate due to presence of fines (Austin et al., 1984):

$$k_i(t) = \kappa(t)k_i = \left[\kappa_0 + \frac{1-\kappa_0}{1+\left(x_{80}/x_{80}^*\right)^{-\Delta}}\right]k_i \tag{7.25}$$

where k_i is the (time-independent) specific breakage rate parameter similar to that in Eq. (7.23), $\kappa(t)$ is a time-dependent deceleration factor, x_{80} is the temporally evolving 80%-passing size of the cumulative PSD, and κ_0, x_{80}^*, and Δ are model parameters to be estimated. The slowing-down factor κ_0 $(0 < \kappa_0 < 1)$ scales the overall deceleration of the breakage rate, while x_{80}^* and Δ modulate the change of $\kappa(t)$ with x_{80}. We note that $\kappa_0 = 1$ reduces the LTVAR-PBM to the TCL-PBM and that Eq. (7.25) is a special form of Model D (refer to Table 7.2).

One can use a back-calculation method with a nonlinear optimization technique so as to find the previously mentioned PBM parameters. In this approach, the sum of squared residuals between the model predictions (solution of the PBM) and the experimental PSD data are minimized by a nonlinear optimizer and the best set of parameters is chosen. Various models can be fit in this way and can be discriminated based on the goodness of fit to the experimental data and the degree of certainty of the fitted parameters. Capece et al. (2011b) and Capece et al. (2012) used the nonlinear optimizer "fmincon," part of the Matlab v7.9 optimization toolbox, to minimize the calculated error between the model and the experimental data. Fmincon uses the algorithm interior-point to solve the nonlinear optimization problem at hand and is suitable for general nonlinear optimization. A simple sum of squared residuals, SSR, seen in Eq. (7.26) can be used as the objective function.

$$\mathrm{SSR} = \sum_{z=1}^{Z} \sum_{i=1}^{N} \left(Q_{zi}^{\mathrm{Exp}} - Q_{zi}^{\mathrm{Mod}} \right)^2 \tag{7.26}$$

Here, Q refers to the cumulative mass fraction undersize distribution, the superscripts Exp and Mod refer to the experimental data and model predicted data respectively, and the subscripts z and i refer to the product size distribution for a particular milling time and the size class respectively. The use of cumulative distribution as opposed to the frequency or density distribution for representing the PSD is mainly motivated by the fact that cumulative distribution of the same data tends to cancel out or mask the random experimental noise (Das, 2001), thus enhancing the precision of the parameters estimated. The inverse method also requires the discretized PBM to be solved multiple times during each optimizer iteration using the ODE integrator, ode15s in Matlab v7.9 with its relative and absolute tolerances set to low values (e.g., 10^{-4} and 10^{-6}, respectively).

In order to discriminate models, the goodness of fit can be assessed based on SSR. To account for the degrees of freedom for the differing models, the standard error of the residuals, SER, presented in Eq. (7.27) is also calculated as follows:

$$\mathrm{SER} = \sqrt{\frac{\mathrm{SSR}}{D - K}} \tag{7.27}$$

where D is the number of comparisons made between the model predictions and the experimental data (i.e., number of experimental data points) and K is the total number of parameters of the model. Moreover, the standard error of the parameter SEP is calculated and evaluated in addition to SSR and SER. While SSR and SER give an indication as to how well the model fits the experimental data, SEP is an important statistic in determining the degree of certainty in the estimated parameters. A high SEP in comparison with the estimated parameter value indicates low certainty of the parameter estimate (or a wide confidence interval), which may be due to a lack of sufficiently accurate dense data set and/or the use of a poor model. SEP is calculated by taking the square root of the diagonals of the parameter covariance matrix, which in turn is calculated by the final optimized Jacobian matrix. The Jacobian matrix is computed at the parameter set determined by the back-calculation method using a first-order finite difference method, as detailed by Aster et al. (2005). The coefficient of variation (*COV*) is simply the expression of the SEP as the percentage of the parameter value. Another measure of the uncertainty of the fitted parameters is the p-value, which can be determined via any statistical package like Minitab 16 using the Student's t-distribution (2-tailed) with a $D-K$ residual degree of freedom and the t-value (parameter value/SEP).

In what follows, our objective is to demonstrate how the aforementioned parameter estimation method can be used to discriminate different PBMs by fitting the experimental data from Austin et al. (1990) on the fine, dry ball milling. Ball milling has been commonly used in the R&D labs in pharmaceutical industry to explore drug amorphization, simultaneous blending–milling, solid dispersions with polymers, etc. (e.g., Caron et al., 2013). Various PBMs were used in the fitting: TCL-PBM (Eq. 7.19), LTVAR-PBM [Eq. (7.18) with Eq. (7.25)], and TCNL-PBM (Eq. 7.22) with two different EFs (refer to EF1 and EF2 in Table 7.3). LTVAR-PBM was also fitted after setting κ_0 to zero because fitted κ_0 was found to be statistically insignificant. Fig. 7.2 illustrates the fit of all models to the experimental data, while Tables 7.4 and 7.5 present the fitted parameters, measures of goodness of fit, and parameter uncertainty, which allows for model discrimination. After 15 min of milling, the most commonly used form of the PBM, TCL-PBM, exhibits marked deviation from the cumulative PSD data (Fig. 7.2), which can also be inferred from the relatively high SSR and SER. Note that even the slightest systematic deviation from experimental data in cumulative representation of the experimental data are regarded significant because cumulative PSDs tend to mask random noise (Das, 2001). TCL-PBM was the least capable of fitting the experimental data among all models. The best fit, i.e., lowest SSR and SER with all statistically significant parameters ($p < 0.05$), was achieved with the nonlinear PBM, TCNL-PBM with EF2 (see Tables 7.4 and 7.5). If 99% confidence level ($p < 0.01$) is intended for the fitted parameters, only the nonlinear PBMs are capable of achieving that objective among all models. The LTVAR-PBM with $\kappa_0 = 0$ also performed well with similar fitting capability to that of TCNL-PBM2. This is not very surprising as the LTVAR-PBM with Eq. (7.25) is actually a specific form of the nonlinear PBM with lumped kinetics known as Model D (Table 7.2). Overall, our results clearly demonstrate the superiority of the nonlinear framework over the traditional TCL-PBM for dense-phase fine milling of materials. Recent multiscale modeling efforts (Capece, 2014; Capece et al., 2015), which will be detailed in the next section, have provided a mechanistic basis for the superiority of the TCNL-PBM for modeling dense-phase dry milling.

Despite the superiority of the nonlinear framework, multiple experiments utilizing different feed PSDs are required in parameter identification with the goal of elucidating uniform versus nonuniform nonlinear breakage kinetics for dense-phase dry milling (Capece et al., 2013). Preferably, a bi-modal feed should also be included to emphasize the impact of nonlinear effects. While a single milling experiment can distinguish between the first-order and non-first-order (nonlinear) breakage kinetics, the use of multiple feed PSDs in the parameter estimation step could elucidate different nonlinear breakage kinetics and allow for more reliable parameter estimates. Moreover, some of the experimental data with different feed PSDs, which have not been used in the parameter estimation, can be used to further assess the predictive capability of the models.

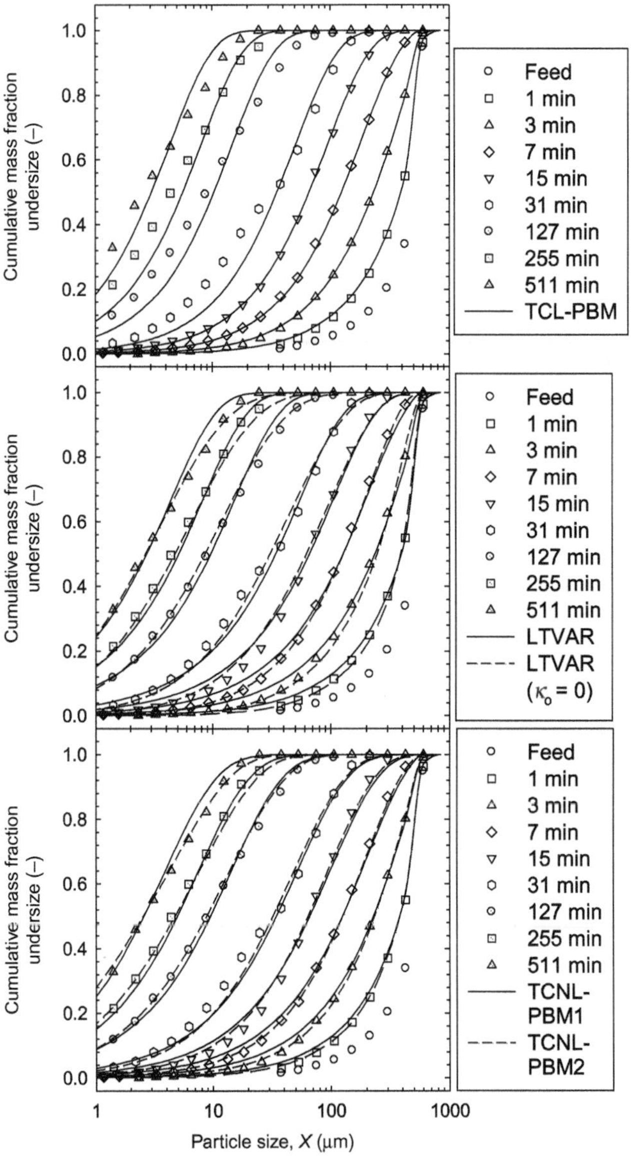

Figure 7.2 Fitting of the experimental ball milling data (Austin et al., 1990) via various population balance models. Fitted parameters are presented in Table 7.4. TCNL-PBM1 and TCNL-PBM2 uses the effectiveness factors EF1 and EF2, respectively, in Table 7.3.

7.4.2 Applications of the PBM for continuous milling

While Eq. (7.19) has been commonly used for modeling batch milling, it can also be used for a continuous mill operating at steady state provided that there is no axial mixing, but perfect transverse or radial mixing in a tubular mill. In this so-called plug-flow continuous milling, time t refers to a transformed time according

Table 7.4 Estimated parameters, *SEP*, *SSR*, and *SER* for various models fit to the batch milling data of Austin et al. (1990)

Parameter	TCL-PBM		LTVAR-PBM		LTVAR-PBM[a]		TCNL-PBM1		TCNL-PBM2	
	Estimated value	*SEP*	Estimated value	*SEP*	Estimated value	*SEP*	Estimated value	*SEP*	Estimated value	*SEP*
A (min^{-1})	1.082	0.342	5.482	1.173	2.551	0.099	1.369	0.277	1.200	0.089
m	1.136	0.012	1.118	0.015	0.316	0.128	1.091	0.015	0.812	0.027
ϕ	0.737	0.267	0.615	0.138	0.313	0.132	0.522	0.187	0.395	0.099
μ	1.053	0.094	0.779	0.074	1.327	0.081	0.816	0.085	0.979	0.031
ν	5.122	2.348	3.151	0.641	7.400	0.202	3.195	0.500	3.768	0.124
α	–	–	–	–	–	–	7.327	2.763	0.320	0.073
λ[b]	–	–	–	–	–	–	3.382	1.307	3.604	0.064
κ_o	–	–	0.155	1.121	–	–	–	–	–	–
Δ	–	–	7.635	1.188	0.969	0.059	–	–	–	–
x_{80}^{*}(μm)	–	–	824.193	0.369	792.580	0.244	–	–	–	–
SSR	1.405×10^{-1}		6.780×10^{-2}		3.477×10^{-2}		5.768×10^{-2}		2.842×10^{-2}	
SER	3.180×10^{-2}		2.233×10^{-2}		1.593×10^{-2}		2.052×10^{-2}		1.440×10^{-2}	

[a]With $\kappa_o = 0$.
[b]λ is dimensionless for TCNL-PBM1 (with EF1) and has units of μm^{α} for TCNL-PBM2 (with EF2).

Table 7.5 ***COV* and *p*-value for various models fit to the batch milling data of Austin et al. (1990)**

Parameter	TCL-PBM		LTVAR-PBM		LTVAR-PBM[a]		TCNL-PBM1		TCNL-PBM2	
	COV (%)	*p* (−)	*COV* (%)	*p* (−)	*COV* (%)	*p* (−)	*COV* (%)	*p* (−)	*COV* (%)	*p* (−)
A (min^{-1})	31.582	0.0019	21.391	< .0001	3.864	< .0001	20.239	< .0001	7.395	< .0001
m	1.070	< .0001	1.301	< .0001	40.441	0.0146	1.351	< .0001	3.371	< .0001
ϕ	36.187	0.0066	22.378	< .0001	42.001	0.0186	35.872	0.006	25.071	0.0001
μ	8.916	< .0001	9.511	< .0001	6.121	< .0001	10.362	< .0001	3.146	< .0001
ν	45.839	0.308	20.344	< .0001	2.731	< .0001	15.663	< .0001	3.285	< .0001
α	–	–	–	–	–	–	37.704	0.009	22.811	< .0001
λ[b]	–	–	–	–	–	–	38.634	0.0107	1.775	< .0001
κ_o	–	–	723.199	0.8902	–	–	–	–	–	–
Δ	–	–	15.565	< .0001	0.766	< .0001	–	–	–	–
x_{80}^{*} (μm)	–	–	0.045	< .0001	0.030	< .0001	–	–	–	–

[a]With $\kappa_o = 0$.
[b]λ is dimensionless for TCNL-PBM1 (with EF1) and has units of μm^{α} for TCNL-PBM2 (with EF2).

to $t = \tau\eta/L$, where τ is the mean residence time and η is the axial position from the inlet of the mill with length L. The inlet PSD, i.e., $M_{i,\text{in}}$, is equivalent to the initial PSD at $t = 0$, i.e., $M_{i,\text{ini}}$. Assuming first-order breakage kinetics ($F_i = 1$), Akkisetty et al. (2010) used Eq. (7.19) to model the milling of API ribbons in a Quadro conical mill without any consideration of the internal classification taking place due to the presence of the internal screen. Similarly, Reynolds (2010) used the same model for modeling of a high-shear wet granulated product in a comil and took the internal classification into account by using a special form of the specific breakage rate function k. A weakness of both models is that the mixing in these mills is closer to perfect mixing than to plug flow, as implied by the DEM simulations (Deng et al., 2015). The following PBM was developed by Bilgili and Scarlett (2005b) to model continuous mills with perfect mixing and nonlinear breakage kinetics at steady state:

$$M_{i,in} - M_i - \tau k_i F_i \left[\sum_{q=i}^{N} W_{iq} M_q\right] M_i + \tau \sum_{j=1}^{i-1} b_{ij} k_j F_j \left[\sum_{q=j}^{N} W_{jq} M_q\right] M_j = 0 \qquad (7.28)$$

The PBM with perfect mixing assumption led to significantly finer product PSD than that with plug-flow assumption, signifying the importance of using the correct mixing model and implying the risk of falsification of breakage kinetics if parameters are to be estimated with incorrect mixing models. Transient version of Eq. (7.28) with first-order kinetics ($F_i = 1$) was used by Barrasso et al. (2013) for modeling the co-milling of roller-compacted Avicel. They also included a classification function to correctly describe the internal classification, unlike previous work, and successfully modeled the product or outlet PSD or M_i and mass hold-up in the mill. A similar transient model without the classification function, which also considered the mixing in a peripheral mixing tank, was used to model the evolution of PSD in a well-mixed WSMM for the manufacture of aerosol particles (Annapragada and Adjei, 1996).

7.5 Multiscale modeling approaches for dry media (ball) milling

In general, traditional PBM is a process-scale model that is devoid of microdynamic or particle ensemble scale information for particles and media, if present, in a mill whereas DEM provides all microdynamic information, but is quite limited in the number of particles that can be realistically simulated (Capece, 2014). Another major issue with the DEM for the simulation of milling is the fact that due to the exponentially increasing number of particles resulting from breakage, the solution via DEM is intractable with the currently available memory and CPU speed of the computers. Hence, novel, judicious use of particle-scale models, DEM, and PBM in a smart multiscale approach could lead to paradigm shift in the modeling of milling.

Despite the aforementioned issues with DEM, it has been widely used to predict some parameters associated with the breakage rate of the particles. The most straightforward approach simply seeks to correlate an experimentally determined breakage rate parameter to the total or average impact energy associated with the collision of grinding media obtained from DEM simulations (Hoyer, 1999; Kano and Saito, 1998; Kwan et al., 2005; Mori et al., 2004). Other methods correlate the impact energy to broken mass of particles which is experimentally determined from powder bed drop-ball tests (Datta and Rajamani, 2002; Wang et al., 2012). A breakage rate is then defined as the total mass of particles broken due to each collision whose energy and frequency is determined by DEM. Despite these developments, they still do not include any fundamental considerations for particle breakage behavior or utilize any fracture mechanics models to predict the specific breakage rate parameter from the microdynamic information. Consequently, these studies are limited in their predictive capacity and in their ability to fully analyze milling processes and the complex breakage behavior. In addition, determination of the breakage rate parameter k_i from DEM simulations is typically performed for the initial milling condition using a coarse sized feed to restrict the number of particles simulated and to reduce computational burden (Wang et al., 2012). It is also common to simulate fine particles as a coarser size (Kwan et al., 2005; Wang et al., 2012) or to omit the feed entirely and only simulate the motion of grinding media (Bwalya et al., 2001; Concas et al., 2006; Datta and Rajamani, 2002; Hoyer, 1999; Kano and Saito, 1998; Lee et al., 2010; Mori et al., 2004; Tavares and Carvalho, 2009).

A novel multiscale modeling framework (Capece, 2014; Capece et al., 2014a,b) that judiciously connects the particle scale, particle ensemble scale, and equipment/process scale is illustrated in Fig. 7.3. In this approach (Capece et al., 2014b), DEM is used to calculate the impact energy spectra inside a ball mill at any milling time for particles of various sizes colliding with each other and vessel wall and milling media (balls). The DEM calculates impact energy spectra, which then allows for the calculation of the potentially time-dependent specific breakage rate $k_i(t)$ through the particle-scale breakage model of Vogel and Peukert (2003). With this $k_i(t)$, the PBM can be solved for a specific milling time, and then the resultant PSD can be fed to the DEM. The DEM with the updated PSD can be invoked subsequently during the evolution of the PSD, and $k_i(t)$ can be updated accordingly. The DEM can be invoked at time intervals of Δt regularly, and depending on the nature of multiparticle interactions, PBM can be solved for prolonged milling without entailing any DEM simulation after a certain milling time. In fact, it is envisioned that a few intermittent DEM simulations may allow for sufficient microdynamic information for estimation of the evolving $k_i(t)$ parameters within the context of the nonlinear PBM, i.e., Eqs. (7.20) and (7.22) in such a way that the evolution of the PSD in a real process with prolonged milling can be solely predicted by the nonlinear PBM that takes into account the microdynamic information at earlier milling times. Hence, the intermittently coupled multiscale model enables the simulation of PSD evolution during the milling effectively, potentially obviating the need to solve the DEM for the entire duration of the milling, which is an elusive and intractable task.

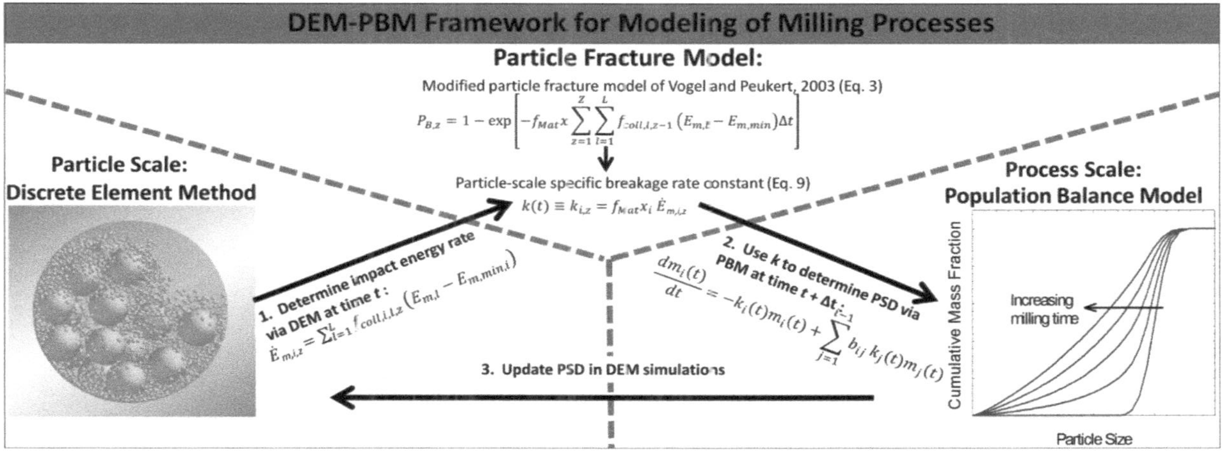

Figure 7.3 Proposed implementation of a unified DEM − PBM framework to predictively model milling process.
Source: Reprinted from Capece, M., Bilgili, E., Dave, R., 2014b. Insight into first-order breakage kinetics using a particle-scale breakage rate constant. Chem. Eng. Sci. 117, 318−330, with permission from Elsevier.

The number of times DEM will be called upon depends on several physical parameters such as the specific milling system, extent of multiparticle interactions, fraction of fines present, presence of dense particle beds, etc. as well as intended cost of numerical implementation and degree of accuracy intended from the simulations. In fact, in the absence of significant multiparticle interactions in dense beds, PBM with first-order breakage kinetics, i.e., constant k can simulate the evolution of PSD during short milling successfully, thus requiring a single DEM simulation for the estimation of k. In the context of the multiscale framework depicted in Fig. 7.3, first-order breakage kinetics imply that k does not have to be updated for different durations of milling, as will be demonstrated in Section 7.7. However, first-order kinetics does not always apply and k evolves in time, thus necessitating the use of the general multiscale framework. The implementation of more frequent DEM simulations allows for more accurate update of the evolving microdynamic parameters in the mill, which in turn allows for more accurate estimation of $k_i(t)$ parameters despite at a higher computational cost with longer simulation time. In view of all these considerations, further research should be directed toward elucidating the right balance between accuracy−numerical cost in the use of the multiscale DEM−PBM framework for specific milling applications. The coupled use of DEM−PBM has already provided significant insight into the origin of nonlinear or non-first-order breakage kinetics in dense-phase milling processes and elucidated when and how nonlinear effects emerge (Capece et al., 2014a,b, 2015).

Let us look into the essential elements of the integrated multiscale framework (Capece et al., 2014b). Based upon fracture mechanics considerations and a complementary similarity analysis, which takes into account various concepts including crack initiation/propagation, pressure distribution (i.e., Hertz's elastic theory), and stress due to particle deformation, Vogel and Peukert (2003) derived Eq. (7.29) for the breakage probability of particles subjected to fracture by impact.

$$P_B = 1 - \exp\left[-f_{Mat} x K \left(E_m - E_{m,min}\right)\right] \tag{7.29}$$

In Eq. (7.29), which has been experimentally verified for a range of materials including glass, limestone, and various polymers, P_B is the breakage probability of a particle subjected to an external load or stress event such as a collision with a mass specific energy E_m, x is the particle diameter, and K is the number of impacts experienced by a particle. The two material properties, f_{Mat} and $E_{m,min}$, in Eq. (7.29) are respectively referred to as the material strength parameter and the threshold impact energy. The former denotes a material's resistance against fracture under an external load and takes into account the particle's relevant fracture and deformation behavior. The latter is also a material property, which gives the impact energy that must be surpassed to initiate fracture through either single or multiple impacts. Below this energy threshold, fracture will never occur regardless of the number of stress events. Since the strain energy that can be stored within a particle depends on its volume, $E_{m,min}$ must be dependent on particle size. While $E_{m,min}$ is a size-dependent material property, Vogel and Peukert (2003) determined that the product $xE_{\mathrm{m,min}}$ is a constant material property.

While Eq. (7.29) is formulated for repeated impact events, which do not explicitly involve time, it is more appropriate to define the total number of impacts in terms of collision frequency f_{coll} and milling time t due to the time-continuous nature of rate processes. In a typical milling process, particles are subjected to a wide distribution of impact energies that are highly dependent upon the evolving PSD. Following Capece et al. (2014a), Eq. (7.29) is modified as

$$P_{\mathrm{B},z} = 1 - \exp\left[-f_{\mathrm{Mat}}x\sum_{z=1}^{Z}\sum_{l=1}^{L} f_{\mathrm{coll},l,z-1}\left(E_{\mathrm{m},l} - E_{\mathrm{m,min}}\right)\Delta t\right] \tag{7.30}$$

where milling time t can be described by $t = z\Delta t$. In Eq. (7.3), z denotes a time index and Δt denotes a short time interval (step) and equals $t_{\mathrm{tot}}/Z_{\mathrm{tot}}$, where t_{tot} is the total milling time and Z_{tot} is the total number of intervals. Impact energy E_{m} has also been discretized into L number of bins as given by the index l for ease of data processing with DEM simulations. While Eq. (7.29) determines the cumulative breakage probability after a succession of K impacts, Eq. (7.30) determines the cumulative breakage probability $P_{\mathrm{B},z}$ at any *specified* milling time t with *specified* time index $z = Z$. Extending the analysis by Vervoorn and Austin (1990), who had formalized the equivalency between the breakage probability and specific breakage rate for milling processes, Capece et al. (2014a,b) derived the following particle-scale or mechanistic specific breakage rate parameter:

$$k(t) \equiv k_{i,z} = f_{\mathrm{Mat}}x_i\sum_{l=1}^{L} f_{\mathrm{coll},i,l,z}(E_{\mathrm{m},l} - E_{\mathrm{m,min},i}) \tag{7.31}$$

The material properties f_{Mat} and $xE_{\mathrm{m,min}}$ in Eq. (7.31) can be determined by fitting Eq. (7.29) to single particle impact test data as in the methodology described by Vogel and Peukert (2003). In general, this is the best approach to calibrate the model, and readers are referred to Vogel and Peukert (2003) for details of implementation. In the absence of such single particle tests, a more practical approach can be devised: f_{Mat} and $xE_{\mathrm{m,min}}$ are identified by fitting Eq. (7.31) to the experimental k data obtained for a given mill operating under a given set of conditions. In the fitting, the impact energy rate $\dot{E}_{\mathrm{m},i,z} = \sum_{l=1}^{L} f_{\mathrm{coll},i,l,z}(E_{\mathrm{m},l} - E_{\mathrm{m,min},i})$ is determined from the impact energy distribution from a DEM simulation. The specific breakage rate constant of a given particle size is proportional to the impact energy rate $(k \propto \dot{E}_{\mathrm{m},})$: $k_{i,z} = f_{\mathrm{Mat}}x_i\dot{E}_{\mathrm{m},i,z}$ and can be used to analyze the milling process and the breakage kinetics. After the calibration, i.e., estimation of f_{Mat} and $xE_{\mathrm{m,min}}$, $k(t)$ for any set of operating conditions can be determined using new DEM simulations for the particular operating conditions. The details of implementation will be given in Section 7.7 as part of a case study, and will not be further elaborated here.

7.6 Case study: application of the microhydrodynamic model to preparation of drug nanosuspensions

The microhydrodynamic modeling presented in Section 7.2 was applied to the WSMM of griseofulvin (GF), a poorly water-soluble (BCS Class II) drug, with the goal of enhancing its bioavailability through higher surface area of the resultant nanoparticles and ensuing higher drug dissolution rate. The baseline process conditions and stabilizers were selected based on earlier work (Bilgili and Afolabi, 2012). An aqueous presuspension of GF (10% at the baseline) in 2.5% hydroxypropyl cellulose (HPC)–0.5% sodium dodecyl sulfate (SDS) was milled in a MicroCer WSMM (Netzsch Fine Particle Technology, LLC., Exton, PA, United States), whose schematic is shown in Fig. 7.1. The combined use of such neutral polymer–anionic pair has synergistic stabilization benefits through electrosteric mechanisms (e.g., Knieke et al., 2013). We used 3200 rpm rotor speed, 126 mL/min suspension flow rate, and 0.388 volume fraction of yttria stabilizer zirconia beads with a median size of 430 μm. Afolabi et al. (2014) investigated the impact of rotor speed, beads volume fraction c, and GF loading on the evolution of median size, which was measured by laser diffraction with Coulter Beckman LS 13 320 and fitted by the following empirical equation (Varinot et al., 1999):

$$d_{50}(t) = d_{\lim} + [d_{50}(0) - d_{\lim}]\exp(-t/\tau_p) \tag{7.32}$$

where $d_{\lim}$ is the limiting median particle size, τ_p is a characteristic time constant of the milling process, and $d_{50}(0)$ is the initial median particle size. A lower τ_p corresponds to faster breakage of the particles and a higher overall apparent breakage rate. To estimate $d_{\lim}$ and τ_p, Eq. (7.32) was fitted to the measured median size data via SigmaPlot's (Version 11) nonlinear regression wizard, which has a built-in Marquardt–Levenberg algorithm for optimization. The equivalent liquid properties, i.e., shear viscosity μ_L and density ρ_L of the drug suspension, the zirconia bead properties, the stirrer power per unit volume in the presence of the beads P_w, and the energy dissipation rate for shearing the equivalent liquid ε_{ht} were all measured and incorporated into Eq. (7.3), which was then solved for the granular temperature θ via Matlab's fsolve function. With this θ, all other microhydrodynamic parameters were calculated using Eqs. (7.4)–(7.11).

The evolution of the median size for various bead loadings is shown in Fig. 7.4A, and the impact of the bead loading on the process time constant, which was obtained from fitting of Eq. (7.32), and the median size at 4 min is shown in Fig. 7.4B. Fig. 7.4 overall shows that an increase in bead loading led to faster breakage and that finer particles were prepared at any given milling time. The impact of the bead size can be explained mechanistically based on the calculated microhydrodynamic parameters: θ, ν, u_b, $\sigma_b^{\max}$, F, and a (see Fig. 7.5). Interestingly, two counteracting effects of an increase in the bead concentration c were observed: θ, u_b, and $\sigma_b^{\max}$ decreased while ν, a, and F increased. In other

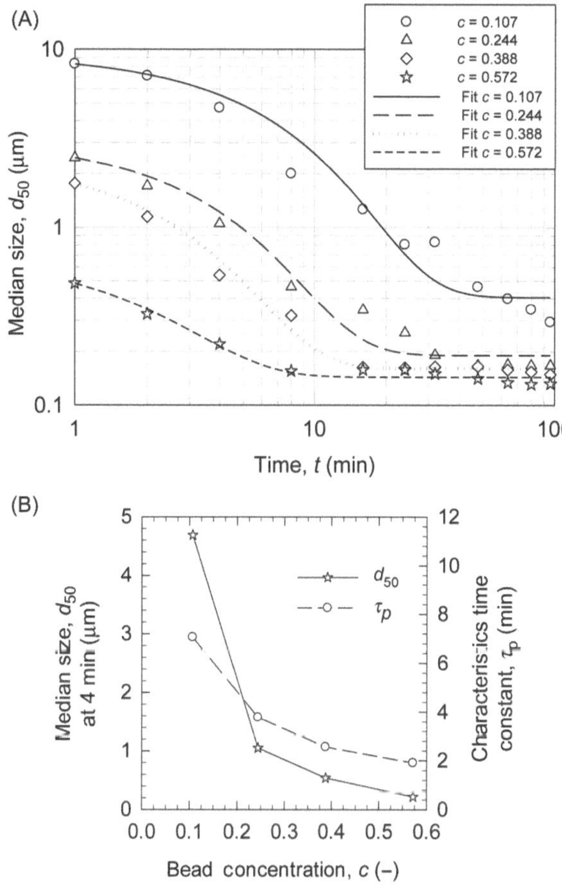

Figure 7.4 Effects of the bead concentration on (A) The time-wise variation of the median size and its model fit by Eq. (7.32) and (B) The median size of GF particles after milling for 4 min and the characteristic time constant. At $t = 0$ min, the GF particles have $d_{50} = 19.65 \pm 1.17$ μm and $d_{90} = 50.88 \pm 6.33$ μm.
Source: Adapted from Afolabi, A., Akinlabi, O., Bilgili, E., 2014. Impact of process parameters on the breakage kinetics of poorly water-soluble drugs during wet stirred media milling: a microhydrodynamic view. Eur. J. Pharm. Sci. 51, 75–86, with permission from Elsevier.

words, the number of stressing events dramatically increased, but their intensity decreased (less impactful collisions and particle compressions). The increase in ν, a, and F seems to be more drastic than the decrease in θ, u_b, and σ_b^{max} in relative terms. Upon an increase in c, the number of the beads increased and the clearance between the beads decreased, leading to a dramatic increase in the bead–bead collisions and the average number of drug particle compressions per unit time (ν and a). On the other hand, despite the increase in the stirrer power and the decrease in the suspension viscosity (not shown for brevity) at the higher bead loading, higher

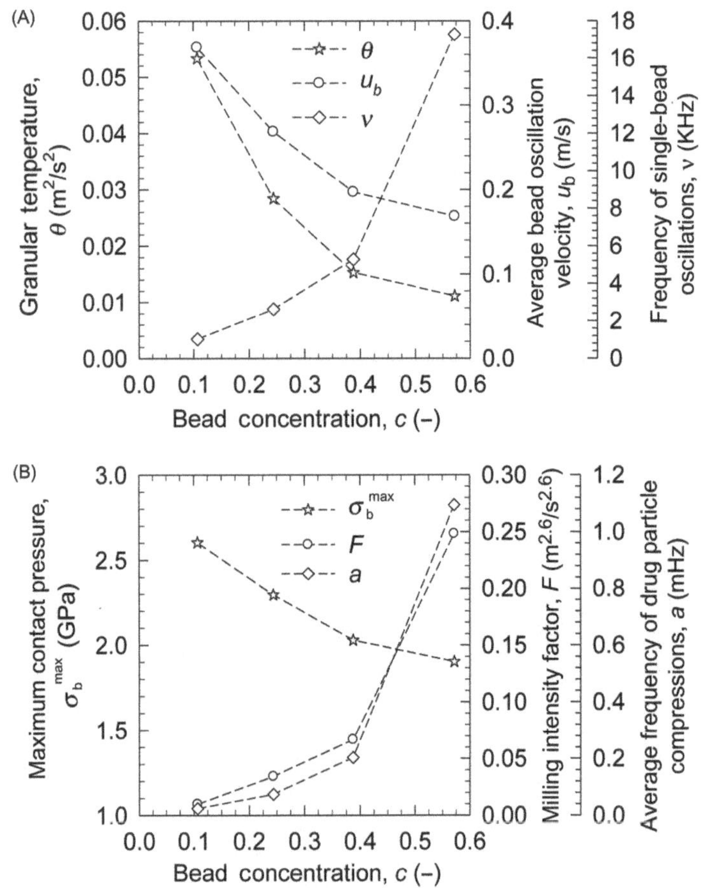

Figure 7.5 Effects of the bead concentration on (A) The granular temperature, the average bead oscillation velocity, and the frequency of single-bead oscillations and (B) The maximum contact pressure, the milling intensity factor, and the average frequency of drug particle compressions.
Source: Adapted from Afolabi, A., Akinlabi, O., Bilgili, E., 2014. Impact of process parameters on the breakage kinetics of poorly water-soluble drugs during wet stirred media milling: a microhydrodynamic view. Eur. J. Pharm. Sci. 51, 75–86, with permission from Elsevier.

number of inelastic bead–bead collisions and liquid-film squeezing events coupled with an increase in the effective drag coefficient R_{diss} led to greater energy dissipation. Consequently, the fluctuating motion of the beads was less vigorous (smaller θ and u_b), which in turn led to smaller bead compression stresses (smaller σ_b^{max}). It is noted that upon an increase in c, both ν and a increased despite the concurrent decrease in θ. This suggests that the microhydrodynamic impact of the decrease in θ was not as pronounced as that of the increase in the number of beads and reduction in the clearance between the beads. Which of the aforementioned two effects will be dominant in explaining the observed increase in the breakage rate upon an increase in c? A comparison of the trends in Fig. 7.4B and Fig. 7.5A and B suggests that upon an increase in the bead loading, the dramatic rise in a was more predominant than the decrease in σ_b^{max}, leading to an increase in the milling intensity factor F, which explains the decrease in τ_p. Recently, similar counteracting effects were observed when bead size was varied (Li et al., 2015), and they were explained thoroughly within the context of microhydrodynamics.

Afolabi et al. (2014) also found that an increase in stirrer (rotor) speed also led to faster breakage as quantified by smaller τ_p values. The stirrer power increased and the viscosity of the milled suspension decreased due to the presence of finer particles upon an increase in the tip speed. Since more mechanical energy was imparted on the slurry and the beads, all microhydrodynamic parameters increased monotonically, as one would expect intuitively. The increase in the overall breakage rate upon an increase in the stirrer speed was simply explained by more bead collisions with greater stressing intensity. In summary, a decrease in τ_p resulted from an increase in the stirrer speed through an increase in F. Unlike the increase in rotor speed and bead loading, the increase in drug loading led to slower breakage as quantified by higher τ_p values, which was explained by the monotonically decreasing values of the microhydrodynamic parameters. Besides guiding process optimization, the analysis rationalizes the preparation of a single high drug-loaded batch (20% or higher) instead of multiple dilute batches despite the slowing-down breakage from an operational efficiency viewpoint.

While all microhydrodynamic parameters provided significant physical insight, only the milling intensity factor F was capable of explaining the influence of all parameters directly through its strong correlation with the process time constant (see Fig. 7.6). Fig. 7.6 also shows that F can explain the impact of all process parameters better than the specific power consumption or specific energy. Since F is a fundamentally derived microhydrodynamic parameter, it is possible that keeping it invariant across different scales can serve as a scale-up criterion, which is yet to be established.

The microhydrodynamic modeling is expected to open a new path to the investigation, design, and optimization of WSMM process in terms of microhydrodynamic parameters as WSMM is affected by the formulation–design–operating parameters. It will help formulators and engineers to develop nanosuspension formulations and select the operating mill parameters in the context of a theoretical framework. In fact, Bilgili and Afolabi (2012) used the microhydrodynamic model to select an optimal nanosuspension formulation considering both the physical stability and the process cycle time. Very recently, Li et al. (2015) developed a microhydrodynamic model-guided process intensification method that led to the production of sub100 nm drug nanoparticles with significantly reduced cycle time and energy consumption while keeping the product contamination at acceptable levels. Overall, these findings suggest that the microhydrodynamic model can be used to streamline pharmaceutical product development involving milling, while reducing cycle time, cost, labor, and materials–energy consumption.

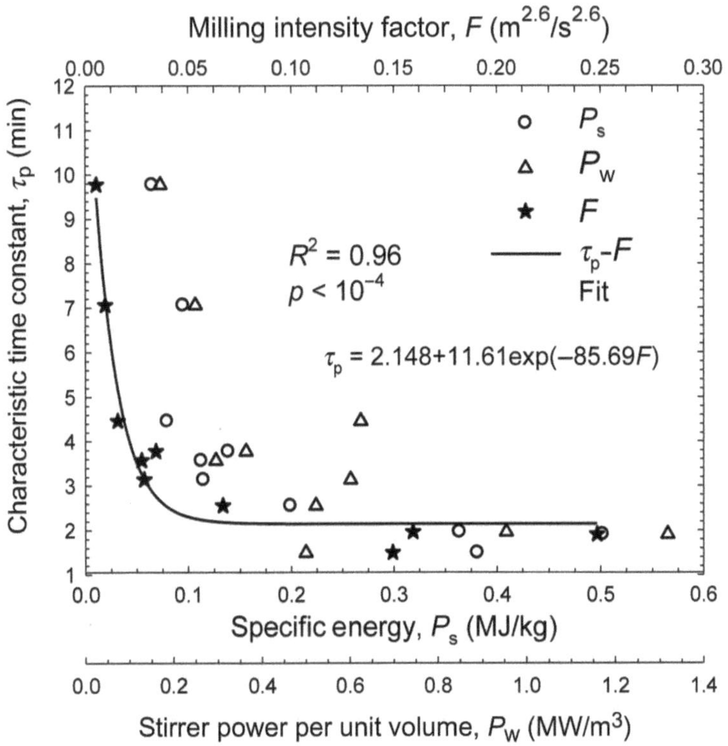

Figure 7.6 Scatter plots for the characteristic time constant versus the specific energy, the milling intensity factor, and the stirrer power per unit volume. Fit: an exponential decay correlation.

Source: Reprinted from Afolabi, A., Akinlabi, O., Bilgili, E., 2014. Impact of process parameters on the breakage kinetics of poorly water-soluble drugs during wet stirred media milling: a microhydrodynamic view. Eur. J. Pharm. Sci. 51, 75–86, with permission from Elsevier.

7.7 Case study: application of the multiscale DEM–PBM approach to rolling ball milling

In this section, we provide how the multiscale DEM–PBM framework presented in Section 7.5 can be used to simulate the rolling ball milling. Again, it is worth-mentioning that ball milling has been commonly used in the R&D labs in pharmaceutical industry to explore drug amorphization, simultaneous blending–milling, solid dispersions with polymers, etc. (e.g., Caron et al., 2013). Hence, the multiscale modeling via DEM–PBM can provide significant process insight. Since the rolling ball mill is frequently studied and simulated using DEM, experimental milling data were taken from a study on the ball milling of silica glass performed by Kotake et al. (2002). The study uses a rolling ball mill in which grinding media (alumina balls) and silica glass particles are contained in a cylindrical vessel whose material of construction is alumina. The vessel rotates along its center axis causing the grinding media and feed to rise and fall resulting in fracture of feed particles. Kotake et al. (2002) specifically investigated the effects of feed particle size and grinding media size on the breakage rate of the silica glass. In this study, the specific breakage rate constant obtained by simulations of various ball–feed sizes in conjunction with use of Eq. (7.31) is first compared to the experimentally obtained specific breakage rate constant to determine the predictive capability of the multi-scale framework. Then, the time dependence of the specific breakage rate parameter is assessed by analyzing the evolution of the impact energy distribution during rolling ball milling by performing PBM–DEM simulations. A slight deviation from the general framework depicted in Fig. 7.3 is that the $k(t)$ of the PBM was not updated at different times because, as will be demonstrated next, for the specific rolling ball mill investigated here, $k(t)$ obtained from DEM simulations at each time turned out to be time-invariant approximately. To be exacting, we could have updated $k(t)$ at each time based on the DEM output exactly, as depicted in Fig. 7.3, but this would not change the results presented next due to the time-invariance of $k(t)$, which is a special case stemming from the short milling time considered in this study. Hence, in general, it is recommended to use the general framework depicted in Fig. 7.3 and elaborated in Section 7.5.

In the first part of this study, we demonstrate the predictive capability of the microdynamically motivated, DEM-based k parameter of the PBM. The rolling ball mill experiments were simulated using 3D DEM with one example being shown in Fig. 7.7 (Feed 1 with 30 mm grinding media). The mill geometry was modeled on a 1:1 basis except for the mill length, which was reduced by half as detailed in Table 7.6. Five different polydispersed feeds were simulated in DEM. These feeds were prepared by first generating a Gaussian distribution with a mean μ of 3 mm and a standard deviation σ of 0.2, 0.4, 0.8, 1.2, or 1.7 mm using the function normpdf in Matlab v8.0. Particle size classes ($N = 160$) used to generate the Gaussian distribution extended from 6 mm with a geometric progression ratio of $2^{1/16}$. The particle sizes (14 total) used to approximate the Gaussian distribution in DEM extended from 0.5 to 6 mm. Feed 1 ($\mu = 3$ mm, $\sigma = 0.2$ mm) was used to approximate the experimental feed PSD, which was specified to contain particles in the size range 2.83–3.36 mm. The remaining four feed PSDs were simulated to theoretically investigate the effects of polydispersity, in this case wider PSDs, on the specific breakage rate constant.

Commercial DEM software, EDEM by DEM solutions Inc., was used to perform the 3D simulations. The Hertz–Mindlin (no slip) soft particle model (refer to Section 7.3) was used to resolve particle interactions with the model parameters given elsewhere (Capece et al., 2014b). Media and feed particles were randomly generated in the milling vessel and allowed to come to rest. The mill was then rotated and allowed to reach a steady state before data collection began. Steady state was determined by the average particle velocity. Impact data were collected for every collision associated with the feed for a total of 10 s of simulated time. This includes Feed – Feed, Feed – Media, and Feed – Vessel type collisions. Impacts collected for a duration of 20 s did not significantly change the impact

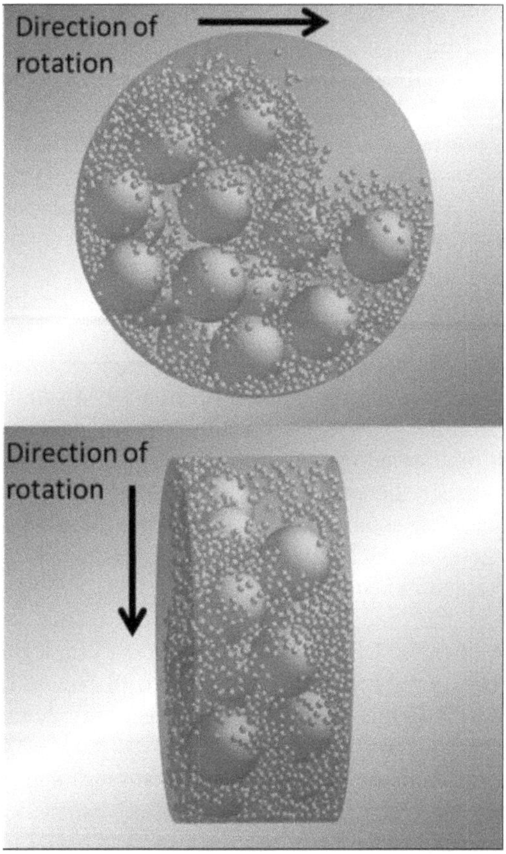

Figure 7.7 Cross-sectional view (top) and bottom view (bottom) of the rolling ball mill simulated by DEM. Feed 1 and 30 mm grinding media processed according to conditions listed in Table 7.6.
Source: Reprinted from Capece, M., Bilgili, E., Dave, R., 2014b. Insight into first-order breakage kinetics using a particle-scale breakage rate constant. Chem. Eng. Sci. 117, 318–330, with permission from Elsevier.

energy distribution, thus 10 s was determined to be sufficient to gain an adequate sample size of impacts. 10 s also results in greater than 90% of the feed left unbroken as determined from experiments. Thus, the impact energy distribution determined by DEM simulation in 10 s should not deviate significantly from the initial condition due to evolution in the PSD caused by particle breakage.

The determination of the specific breakage rate constant from Eq. (7.31) requires the impact energy distribution that is obtained from DEM. The impact energy is often defined by the dissipated energy E_d, which is the energy lost by the inelastic collision of two particles and is commonly used in the modeling of impact milling leading to particle fracture (Datta and Rajamani, 2002; Wang et al., 2012).

Table 7.6 Milling geometry and operating specifications for experimental and DEM simulated ball milling

	Experiment[a]	Simulation
Mill diameter	144 mm	144 mm
Mill length	129 mm	64.5 mm
Vessel material	Alumina[b]	Alumina[b]
Mill rotation speed	108 rpm	108 rpm
Grinding media	2 kg alumina[b]	1 kg alumina[b]
Feed	0.2 kg silica glass[b]	0.1 kg silica glass[b]

[a]Experimental study was performed by Kotake et al. (2002).
[b]Alumina and silica glass have a density of 4000 kg/m^3 and 2150 kg/m^3, respectively.
Source: Adapted from Capece, M., Bilgili, E., Dave, R., 2014b. Insight into first-order breakage kinetics using a particle-scale breakage rate constant. Chem. Eng. Sci. 117, 318–330, with permission from Elsevier.

Dissipated energy is calculated by integrating the normal damping force F_n^{d} and the tangential damping force F_t^{d} with respect to their overlaps over the entire contact period t_{contact} as shown in Eq. (7.33).

$$E_{\mathrm{d}} = \int_0^{t_{\mathrm{contact}}} \left(F_n^{\mathrm{d}} d\delta_n + F_t^{\mathrm{d}} d\delta_t\right) \tag{7.33}$$

The dissipated energy was used to define the impact energy E_{m} which was calculated for every collision and placed into $L = 1800$ bins ranging from 1 J downward with a geometric progression ratio of $2^{1/28}$ and $E_{\mathrm{m},1800} = 10^{-20}$ J.

Eq. (7.31) also requires the material properties f_{Mat} and $xE_{\mathrm{m,min}}$ to be specified. In the absence of single particle impact tests, f_{Mat} and $xE_{\mathrm{m,min}}$ were identified by fitting Eq. (7.31), now with the calculated impact energy distribution from DEM simulations for multiple grinding media sizes with 3 mm silica particles, to the experimental data for k determined by Kotake et al. (2002). Minimization of the sum of squared residuals between the theoretical (Eq. 7.31) and experimental values of k using the optimization routine known as fmincon of the optimization library of Matlab v8.0 led to $f_{\mathrm{Mat}} = 1.09$ kg/J m and $xE_{\mathrm{m,min}} = 2.61 \times 10^{-3}$ J m/kg. Then, with these parameters known, the impact energy rate $\dot{E}_{\mathrm{m},i,z} = \sum_{l=1}^{L} f_{\mathrm{coll},i,l,z}\left(E_{\mathrm{m},l} - E_{\mathrm{m,min},i}\right)$ was determined from the impact energy distribution. Fig. 7.8 shows the specific breakage rate constant for each particle size determined by Eq. (7.31) (data points) along with empirical relationship developed by Kotake et al. (2002) for comparison (solid line), which represents the experimental data and general trends fairly well for the milling conditions in which it was determined. As the empirical expression of Kotake et al. (2002) shows, a maximum in the specific breakage rate constant is obtained at about 3 mm for this particular milling condition using 30 mm grinding media. Particle sizes less than and greater than 3 mm have lower specific breakage rate corresponding to slower breakage. Smaller particles are more difficult to break because fewer flaws (e.g., cracks) are affected by an impact while larger particles are more difficult to efficiently nip between grinding media.

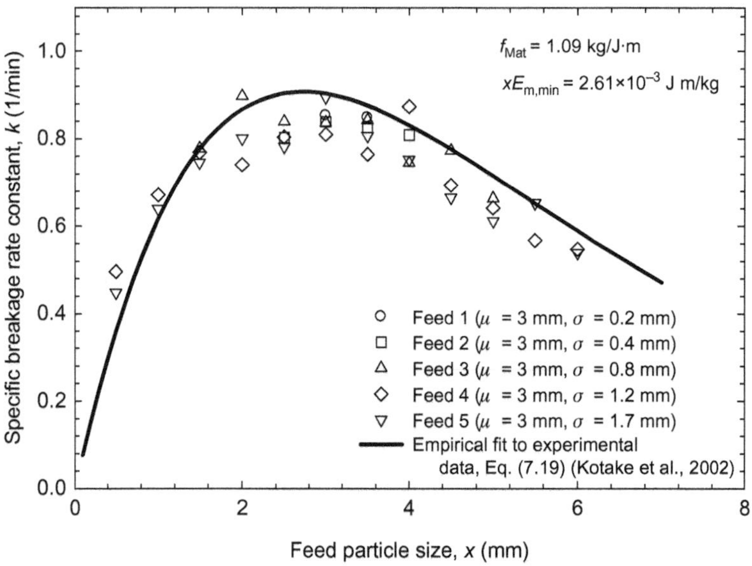

Figure 7.8 Comparisons between the specific breakage rate constant k for all particles sizes within various feed distributions processed with 30 mm grinding media determined by DEM simulations with Eq. (7.31) and by the empirical equation of Kotake et al. (2002). Particle sizes which represented <1 wt% in each feed distribution are omitted.
Source: Adapted from Capece, M., Bilgili, E., Dave, R., 2014b. Insight into first-order breakage kinetics using a particle-scale breakage rate constant. Chem. Eng. Sci. 117, 318–330, with permission from Elsevier.

As seen in Fig. 7.8, the specific breakage rate constants determined by Eq. (7.31) are in close approximation to those determined by Kotake et al. (2002) with some minor variation between feeds. Whereas Kotake et al. (2002) determined the specific breakage rate constant for each particle size by milling narrowly distributed feeds, it is determined here simultaneously and can potentially be determined using single polydispersed feed. These findings suggest that the PBM could be more predictive of the milling process when it is combined with DEM providing the microdynamic information.

To assess the time dependence of the specific breakage rate for ball milling via Eq. (7.31), the evolution of the PSD due to particle breakage was simulated by solving the PBM of Eq. (7.19) assuming first-order breakage kinetics ($k_i(t) = k_i$). As will be demonstrated next, we indeed find from DEM simulations that k is time-invariant during the short milling time (1.5 min) considered here. Hence, slightly deviating from the general framework depicted in Fig. 7.3, we did not update k_i in PBM at different milling times; instead, we generated PSDs at different milling times using the same k_i without updating. While the actual breakage of particles was not simulated in DEM, the PSDs corresponding to different milling times obtained by PBM were simulated in DEM to obtain the motion and mechanical interactions of particles at those times. Hence, this analysis inherently assumed that the daughter particles are spherical like the parent particles. The PSDs at different milling times were generated by solution of the PBM of Eq. (7.19) with the following size-dependent functions for k_i

$$k_i = r_1 d_{\mathrm{M}}^{r_2} x_i^{r_3} \exp\left(-r_4 \frac{x_i}{d_{\mathrm{M}}^{r_5}}\right) \tag{7.34}$$

and Eq. (7.24) for B_{ij}. The function for k is a 5-parameter empirical function developed by Kotake et al. (2002) specifically for the set of milling experiments simulated here. In Eq. (7.34), d_{M} is the grinding media size and $r_1 = 0.24$ 1/min mm$^{1.44}$, $r_2 = 0.39$, $r_3 = 1.05$, $r_4 = 6.7$ 1/mm$^{0.16}$, and $r_5 = 0.84$ were determined in the referenced study. While empirical expressions for the specific breakage rate parameter such as Eq. (7.34) include no fundamental basis for particle breakage and may be limited in a predictive capacity, Eq. (7.34) along with the specified parameters is capable of describing the specific breakage rate constant for the ball milling experiments simulated in this study, as shown by Kotake et al. (2002). Hence, Eq. (7.34) was used in the solution of Eq. (7.19). While Kotake et al. (2002) did not investigate the breakage distribution, a normalized function for b was chosen due to its common use in literature along with parameters $\phi = 0.3$, $\mu = 1.3$, and $\nu = 5.8$ (Austin and Luckie, 1972; Klimpel and Austin, 1977). The PBM of Eq. (7.19) along with Eqs. (7.24) and (7.34) were solved using a stiff ODE solver ode15s in Matlab using $N = 160$ size classes extending from 6 mm with a geometric progression ratio of $2^{1/16}$. The relative and absolute error tolerances for the integrator were set to 10^{-4} and 10^{-6} respectively. Feed 1 was used as the initial PSD, and PSDs at 0.5, 1.0, and 1.5 min obtained via PBM were approximated and simulated in DEM. The impact energy distributions were obtained for the PSDs at each milling time and used to determine the impact energy rate.

Fig. 7.9 shows the PBM-generated PSDs that were then used in DEM for various milling times. As milling continues, the distribution shifts to the left indicating the presence of finer particles due to breakage. Fig. 7.10 (top) shows that the total impact energy rate significantly increases with milling time due to the increased contribution from 3 mm–Feed type impacts when an impact energy threshold is not considered. Fig. 7.10 (bottom), which considers a threshold impact energy ($xE_{\mathrm{m,min}} = 2.61 \times 10^{-3}$ J m/kg), shows a slight decrease in the total impact energy rate by 3% from 0 to 1.5 min, which may be considered negligible. The impact energy rate $\dot{E}_{\mathrm{m},i,z}$ defined as $\sum_{l=1}^{L} f_{\mathrm{coll},i,l,z}\left(E_{\mathrm{m},l} - E_{\mathrm{m,min}}\right)$ remains constant and as an extension, the impact energy distribution above the energy threshold remain the same as the milling progresses to 1.5 min. In view of Eq. (7.31), this finding points to the time-invariance of k_i. The contribution from 3 mm–Media type impacts on the total impact energy rate once again dominates ($\sim$70%), and the contribution from 3 mm–Feed type impacts is less significant ($\sim$15%). This is due to the low feed loading and absence of significant fraction of fine particles in the mill (see Fig. 7.7), which prevents formation of dense particle beds and leads to relatively insignificant mechanical multiparticle interactions among the feed. Such milling

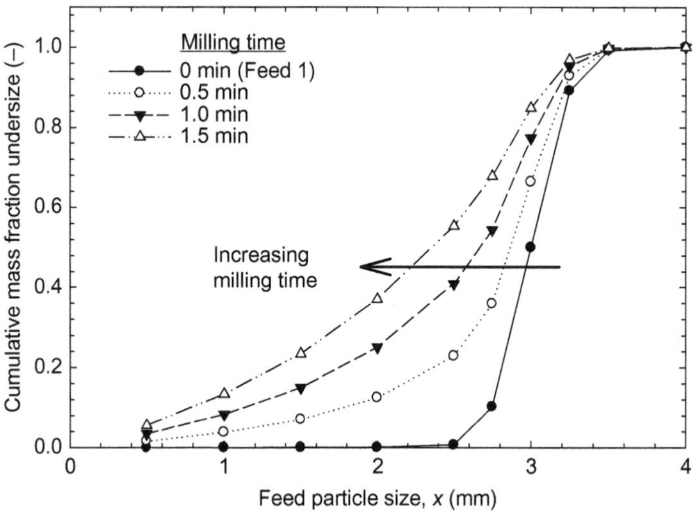

Figure 7.9 Particle size distributions corresponding to various milling times used in DEM simulations. Feed 1 was used as the initial feed distribution.
Source: Reprinted from Capece, M., Bilgili, E., Dave, R., 2014b. Insight into first-order breakage kinetics using a particle-scale breakage rate constant. Chem. Eng. Sci. 117, 318–330, with permission from Elsevier.

conditions seem to be characteristics of a process which results in first-order breakage, explaining the time-invariance of k. While the breakage of particles within the feed distribution produces many low energy impacts and affects the impact energy distribution below the impact energy threshold, they do not influence the impact energy rate or the specific breakage rate constant. Conversely, high energy impacts that contribute to $\dot{E}_{\mathrm{m}}$ the most are insensitive to the feed PSD; hence, as an extension, k remains time-invariant to the extent milling was simulated confirming that first-order breakage kinetics are assured as was observed experimentally by Kotake et al. (2002). Recent work (Capece et al., 2015) suggests that formation of dense particle beds with fine particles leading to significant mechanical multiparticle interactions appears to be the origin of nonlinear particle breakage.

Although the specific breakage rate constant of Eq. (7.31) along with DEM was used for analysis of the milling process simulated by PBM in this section, the methodology presented here naturally lends itself to *prediction* in the evolution of the PSD. One may simulate the initial feed distribution using DEM, determine $k_{i,z}$ for all particle sizes within the distribution using Eq. (7.31) for $z = 0$ ($t = 0$), and solve the PBM of Eq. (7.1) to obtain the PSD for $z = 1$ ($t = \Delta t$). Updating the PSD in DEM and determining $k_{i,z}$ for $z = 1$ ($t = \Delta t$), a fully coupled DEM–PBM scheme can be implemented toward determining the PSD at any milling time, as shown schematically in Fig. 7.3. We slightly deviated from this general framework in this particular case study because of the time-invariance of $\dot{E}_{\mathrm{m}}$ observed from the DEM simulations, and also updating k_i at each time point based on such time-invariant

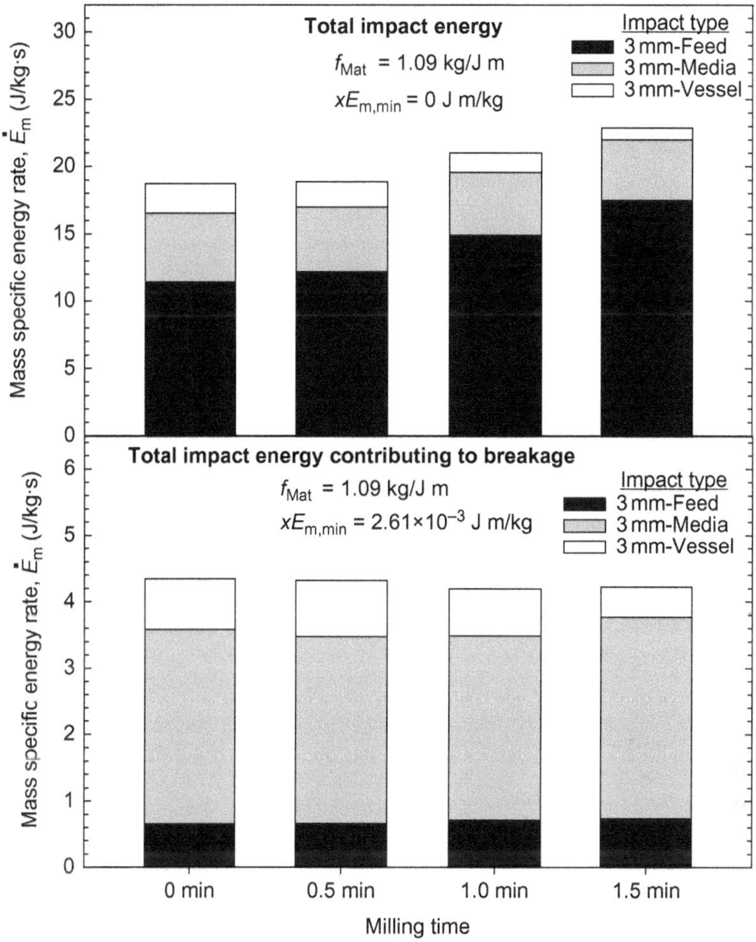

Figure 7.10 Impact energy contributing to the breakage of 3 mm particles by 3 mm − Feed, 3 mm − Media, and 3 mm − Vessel type impacts considering impacts of all energies (top) and impact energy above the threshold xE_{min} (bottom) at various milling times.
Source: Reprinted from Capece, M., Bilgili, E., Dave, R., 2014b. Insight into first-order breakage kinetics using a particle-scale breakage rate constant. Chem. Eng. Sci. 117, 318−330, with permission from Elsevier.

$\dot{E}_m$ would be redundant, as doing so would not change the results. In a future study, the general approach depicted in Fig. 7.3 will be used in its exacting form to simulate the evolution of the PSD for prolonged milling. Another important point to consider is that the solution of the PBM also requires the breakage distribution parameters to be known either from experiments or predicted from fragmentation models combined with DEM (Bruchmuller et al., 2011). Clearly, more work is needed for a complete DEM − PBM unification.

7.8 Concluding remarks

This chapter has presented DEM and PBM approaches for modeling of milling processes as well as microhydrodynamic models for wet media milling. Besides providing ample literature on various pharmaceutical milling processes, we have strived to include all relevant modeling equations, obviating the need for readers to chase alternative resources, with few exceptions for which additional resources have been clearly indicated. In addition, two major case studies have been presented: the microhydrodynamic model was applied to the WSMM of poorly water-soluble drugs, and a multiscale DEM–PBM model was applied to tumbling ball mill. Motivated by the seminal review of Austin (1971), the PBM has been presented in both index and matrix notation while considering time as either a continuous variable or a discrete variable for a multitude of milling processes and breakage tests. Most importantly, this chapter includes the recent developments on nonlinear breakage kinetics and multiscale approaches, which were absent from the review of Austin (1971). It is expected that this unified presentation of the PBM theory for milling processes will not only help pharmaceutical engineers and formulators to find the relevant equations in a single resource, but also enable them to decipher various notation and terminology used in different fields of engineering as applied to minerals, food, ceramics, etc. Finally, we are excited about the multiscale modeling approaches emerging in various engineering fields, which are finding more use in the modeling of pharmaceutical processes including milling. The multiscale modeling approach presented in this chapter is expected to lead the way for the modeling of milling processes until computational power enables DEM approach to simulate the evolution of the PSD during the whole duration of the milling process with ever-diverging number of particles.

Acknowledgments

The authors gratefully acknowledge financial support from the U.S. National Science Foundation Engineering Research Center for Structured Organic Particulate Systems (NSF ERC for SOPS) through the Grant EEC-0540855. The first author (E.B.) is grateful to Professor Rajesh N. Davé for the collaborative work on the multiscale modeling of dry milling processes and stimulating discussions over the last six years. Thanks are extended to Dr. Dmitry Eskin of Schlumberger Inc. for his valuable suggestions on the microhydrodynamic analysis. Last but not least, E.B. thanks all previous and current students/postdocs, Dr. Catharina Knieke, Dr. Mohammad Azad, Dr. Anagha Bhakay, and Ms. Meng Li, just to name a few, who have contributed through their published body of work on the milling processes.

References

Afolabi, A., 2013. Batch and Continuous Production of Stable Dense Suspensions of Drug Nanoparticles in a Wet Stirred Media Mill, PhD Thesis. New Jersey Institute of Technology, Newark, NJ.

Afolabi, A., Akinlabi, O., Bilgili, E., 2014. Impact of process parameters on the breakage kinetics of poorly water-soluble drugs during wet stirred media milling: a microhydrodynamic view. Eur. J. Pharm. Sci. 51, 75–86.

Ahmadian, H., Hassanpour, A., Ghadiri, M., 2011. Analysis of granule breakage in a rotary mixing drum: experimental study and distinct element analysis. Powder Technol. 210, 175–180.

Akkisetty, P.K., Lee, U., Reklaitis, G.V., Venkatasubramanian, V., 2010. Population balance model-based hybrid neural network for a pharmaceutical milling process. J. Pharm. Innovation. 5, 161–168.

Annapragada, A., Adjei, A., 1996. Numerical simulation of milling processes as an aid to process design. Int. J. Pharm. 136, 1–11.

Antony, S.J., Ghadiri, M., 2001. Size effects in slowly sheared granular media. J. Appl. Mech. 68, 772–775, ASME.

Aster, R., Borchers, B., Thurber, C., 2005. Parameter Estimation and Inverse Problems. Elsevier Academic Press, San Diego.

Austin, L.G., 1971. A review: introduction to the mathematical description of grinding as a rate process. Powder Technol. 5, 1–17.

Austin, L.G., 1973. A commentary on the kick, bond and rittinger laws of grinding. Powder Technol. 7, 315–317.

Austin, L., Bhatia, V., 1972. Experimental methods for grinding studies in laboratory mills. Powder Technol. 5, 261–266.

Austin, L., Luckie, P., 1972. Methods for determination of breakage distribution parameters. Powder Technol. 5, 215–222.

Austin, L.G., Bell, D., Rogers, R.S.C., 1984. Incorporation of the slowing down effect into a mill model. Part. Sci. Technol. 2, 135–145.

Austin, L.G., Yekeler, M., Dumm, T., Hogg, R., 1990. Kinetics and shape factors of ultrafine dry grinding in a laboratory tumbling ball mill. Part. Part. Syst. Charact. 7, 242–247.

Bagherzadeh, A., Mirghasemi, A.A., Mohammadi, S., 2011. Numerical simulation of particle breakage of angular particles using combined DEM and FEM. Powder Technol. 205, 15–29.

Balani, P.N., Wong, S.Y., Ng, W.K., Widjaja, E., Tan, R.B.H., Chan, S.Y., 2010. Influence of polymer content on stabilizing milled amorphous salbutamol sulphate. Int. J. Pharm. 391, 125–136.

Barrasso, D., Oka, S., Muliadi, A., Litster, J.D., Wassgren, C., Ramachandran, R., 2013. Population balance model validation and prediction of CQAs for continuous milling processes: toward QbD in pharmaceutical drug product manufacturing. J. Pharm. Innovation. 8, 147–162.

Bas, N., Pathare, P.B., Catak, M., Fitzpatrick, J.J., Cronin, K., Byrne, E.P., 2011. Mathematical modeling of granola breakage during pipe pneumatic conveying. Powder Technol. 206, 170–176.

Baxter, J., Abu-Nahar, A., Tuzun, U., 2004. The breakage matrix approach to inadvertent particulate degradation: dealing with intra-mixture interactions. Powder Technol. 143–144, 174–178.

Bernhardt, C., Reinsch, E., Husemann, K., 1999. The influence of suspension properties on ultra-fine grinding in stirred ball mills. Powder Technol. 105, 357–361.

Berthiaux, H., 2000. Analysis of grinding processes by Markov chains. Chem. Eng. Sci. 55, 4117–4127.

Bertrand, D., Guibert, D., Melcion, J.-P., Duc, G., 1999. Evaluation of the transition matrix for comminuting pea seeds in an impact mill using a linear neural network. Powder Technol. 105, 119–124.

Bhakay, A., Azad, M., Bilgili, E., Dave, R., 2014a. Redispersible fast dissolving nanocomposite microparticles of poorly water-soluble drugs. Int. J. Pharm. 461, 367–379.

Bhakay, A., Azad, M., Vizzotti, E., Dave, R.N., Bilgili, E., 2014b. Enhanced recovery and dissolution of griseofulvin nanoparticles from surfactant-free nanocomposite microparticles incorporating wet-milled swellable dispersants. Drug Dev. Ind. Pharm. 40, 1509–1522.

Bhakay, A., Davé, R., Bilgili, E., 2013. Recovery of BCS class II drugs during aqueous redispersion of core–shell type nanocomposite particles produced via fluidized bed coating. Powder Technol. 236, 221–234.

Bhakay, A., Merwade, M., Bilgili, E., Dave, R.N., 2011. Novel aspects of wet milling for the production of microsuspensions and nanosuspensions of poorly water-soluble drugs. Drug Dev. Ind. Pharm. 37, 963–976.

Bilgili, E., 2007. On the consequences of non-first-order breakage kinetics in comminution processes: absence of self-similar size spectra. Part. Part. Syst. Charact. 24, 12–17.

Bilgili, E., Afolabi, A., 2012. A combined microhydrodynamics–polymer adsorption analysis for elucidation of the roles of stabilizers in wet stirred media milling. Int. J. Pharm. 439, 193–206.

Bilgili, E., Capece, M., 2011. Quantitative analysis of multi-particle interactions during particle breakage: a discrete non-linear population balance framework. Powder Technol. 213, 162–173.

Bilgili, E., Capece, M., 2012. A rigorous breakage methodology for characterization of multi-particle interactions in dense-phase particle breakage. Chem. Eng. Res. Des. 90, 1177–1188.

Bilgili, E., Scarlett, B., 2005a. Population balance modeling of non-linear effects in milling processes. Powder Technol. 153, 59–71.

Bilgili, E., Scarlett, B., 2005b. Numerical simulation of open-circuit continuous mills using a non-linear population balance framework: incorporation of non-first-order effects. Chem. Eng. Technol. 28, 153–159.

Bilgili, E., Scarlett, B., 2005c. Nonlinear effects in particulate processes. Nonlinear Anal. 63, e1131–e1141.

Bilgili, E., Arastoopour, H., Bernstein, B., 2001. Pulverization of rubber granulates using the solid state shear extrusion (SSSE) process: part I. Process concepts and characteristics. Powder Technol. 115, 265–276.

Bilgili, E., Arastoopour, H., Bernstein, B., Hamey, R., 2008. Some novel applications of grinding and milling technologies: milling of soft materials and nanomilling. In: Yekeler, M. (Ed.), Fine Particle Technology and Characterization. Research Signpost, Kerala, pp. 41–67.

Bilgili, E., Hamey, R., Scarlett, B., 2006a. Nano-milling of pigment agglomerates using a wet stirred media mill: elucidation of the kinetics and breakage mechanisms. Chem. Eng. Sci. 61, 149–157.

Bilgili, E., Yepes, J., Scarlett, B., 2006b. Formulation of a non-linear framework for population balance modeling of batch grinding: Beyond first-order kinetics. Chem. Eng. Sci. 61, 33–44.

Bilgili, E., Rosen, L.A., Ko, J.S., Chen, A., Smith, E.J., Fliszar, K., et al., 2011. Experimental study of fluidized bed co-granulation of two active pharmaceutical ingredients: an industrial scale-up perspective. Part. Sci. Technol. 29, 285–309.

Blecher, L., Kwade, A., Schwedes, J., 1996. Motion and stress intensity of grinding beads in a stirred media mill. Part 1: energy density distribution and motion of single grinding beads. Powder Technol. 86, 59–68.

Bruchmuller, J., van Wachem, B., Gu, S., Luo, K., 2011. Modelling discrete fragmentation of brittle particles. Powder Technol. 208, 731–739.

Bwalya, M., Moys, M., Hinde, A., 2001. The use of the discrete element method and fracture mechanics to improve grinding rate prediction. Miner. Eng. 16, 565–573.

Campbell, G.M., Webb, C., 2001. On predicting roller milling performance part I: the breakage equation. Powder Technol. 115, 234–242.

Capece, M.W., 2014. Multi-Scale Modeling of Dry Milling Processes: Influence of Mechanical Multi-Particle Interactions, PhD Thesis. New Jersey Institute of Technology, Newark, NJ.

Capece, M., Bilgili, E., Dave, R., 2011a. Emergence of falsified kinetics as a consequence of multi-particle interactions in dense-phase comminution processes. Chem. Eng. Sci. 66, 5672–5683.

Capece, M., Bilgili, E., Dave, R., 2011b. Identification of the breakage rate and distribution parameters in a non-linear population balance model for batch milling. Powder Technol. 208, 195–204.

Capece, M., Dave, R., Bilgili, E., 2012. A rational function approximation to the effectiveness factor for multi-particle interactions in dense-phase dry milling. Powder Technol. 230, 67–76.

Capece, M., Dave, R., Bilgili, E., 2013. Influence of non-linear breakage kinetics on the attainment of self-similarity for dry milling processes. Chem. Eng. Sci. 97, 96–107.

Capece, M., Bilgili, E., Davé, R.N., 2014a. Formulation of a physically motivated specific breakage rate parameter for ball milling via the discrete element method. AIChE J. 60, 2404–2415.

Capece, M., Bilgili, E., Dave, R., 2014b. Insight into first-order breakage kinetics using a particle-scale breakage rate constant. Chem. Eng. Sci. 117, 318–330.

Capece, M., Davé, R.N., Bilgili, E., 2015. On the origin of non-linear breakage kinetics in dry milling. Powder Technol. 272, 189–203.

Caron, V., Hu, Y., Tajber, L., Erxleben, A., Corrigan, O.I., Mcardle, P., et al., 2013. Amorphous solid dispersions of sulfonamide/soluplus(R) and sulfonamide/PVP prepared by ball milling. AAPS Pharm. Sci. Technol. 14, 464–474.

Celep, O., Aslan, N., Alp, I., Taşdemir, G., 2011. Optimization of some parameters of stirred mill for ultra-fine grinding of refractory Au/Ag ores. Powder Technol. 208, 121–127.

Chakraborty, J., Ramkrishna, D., 2011. Population balance modeling of environment dependent breakage: role of granular viscosity, density and compaction. Model formulation and similarity analysis. Ind. Eng. Chem. Res. 50, 13116–13128.

Concas, A., Lai, N., Pisu, M., Cao, G., 2006. Modelling of comminution processes in Spex mixer/mill. Chem. Eng. Sci. 61, 3746–3760.

Cundall, P.A., Strack, O.D., 1979. A discrete numerical model for granular assemblies. Geotechnique. 29, 47–65.

Das, P.K., 2001. Use of cumulative size distribution to back-calculate the breakage parameters in batch grinding. Comput. Chem. Eng. 25, 1235–1239.

Datta, A., Rajamani, R., 2002. A direct approach of modeling batch grinding in ball mills using population balance principles and impact energy distribution. Int. J. Miner. Process. 64, 181–200.

Deng, X., Scicolone, J., Han, X., Davé, R.N., 2015. Discrete element method simulation of a conical screen mill: a continuous dry coating device. Chem. Eng. Sci. 125, 58–74.

Diemer, R.B., Olson, J.H., 2002. A moment methodology for coagulation and breakage problems: part 3—generalized daughter distribution functions. Chem. Eng. Sci. 57, 4187–4198.

Eskin, D., Miller, M.J., 2008. A model of non-Newtonian slurry flow in a fracture. Powder Technol. 182, 313–322.

Eskin, D., Zhupanska, O., Hamey, R., Moudgil, B., Scarlett, B., 2005a. Microhydrodynamic analysis of nanogrinding in stirred media mills. AIChE J. 51, 1346–1358.

Eskin, D., Zhupanska, O., Hamey, R., Moudgil, B., Scarlett, B., 2005b. Microhydrodynamics of stirred media milling. Powder Technol. 156, 95–102.

Fan, R., Marchisio, D.L., Fox, R.O., 2004. Application of the direct quadrature method of moments to polydisperse gas–solid fluidized beds. Powder Technol. 139, 7–20.

Fisher, E.S., 2006. Milling of active pharmaceutical ingredients. In: Swarbrick, James (Ed.), Encyclopedia of Pharmaceutical Technology, third ed. CRC Press, Boca Raton, pp. 2339–2351., Chapter 170.

Fistes, A., Tanovic, G., 2006. Predicting the size and compositional distributions of wheat flour stocks following first break roller milling using the breakage matrix approach. J. Food Eng. 75, 527–534.

Gahn, C., Mersmann, A., 1999a. Brittle fracture in crystallization processes. Part A. Attrition and abrasion of brittle solids. Chem. Eng. Sci. 54, 1273–1282.

Gahn, C., Mersmann, A., 1999b. Brittle fracture in crystallization processes. Part B. Growth of fragments and scale-up of suspension crystallizers. Chem. Eng. Sci. 54, 1283–1292.

Ghadiri, M., Zhang, Z., 2002. Impact attrition of particulate solids. Part 1: a theoretical model of chipping. Chem. Eng. Sci. 57, 3659–3669.

Ghosh, I., Schenck, D., Bose, S., Ruegger, C., 2012. Optimization of formulation and process parameters for the production of nanosuspension by wet media milling technique: effect of vitamin E TPGS and nanocrystal particle size on oral absorption. Eur. J. Pharm. Sci. 47, 718–728.

Gidaspow, D., 1994. Multiphase Flow and Fluidization: Continuum and Kinetic Theory Descriptions. Academic Press, Boston.

Gutsche, O., Fuerstenau, D.W., 1999. Fracture kinetics of particle bed comminution—ramifications for fines production and mill optimization. Powder Technol. 105, 113–118.

Han, X., Ghoroi, C., To, D., Chen, Y., Davé, R., 2011. Simultaneous micronization and surface modification for improvement of flow and dissolution of drug particles. Int. J. Pharm. 415, 185–195.

Han, X., Jallo, L., To, D., Ghoroi, C., Davé, R., 2013. Passivation of high-surface-energy sites of milled ibuprofen crystals via dry coating for reduced cohesion and improved flowability. J. Pharm. Sci. 102, 2282–2296.

Hertz, H., 1882. On the contact of elastic solids. Journal of reine und angewandte Mathematik. 92, 156–171.

Hoyer, D., 1999. The discrete element method for fine grinding scale-up in Hicom mills. Powder Technol. 105, 250–256.

Juhnke, M., Märtin, D., John, E., 2012. Generation of wear during the production of drug nanosuspensions by wet media milling. Eur. J. Pharm. Biopharm. 81, 214–222.

Kano, J., Saito, F., 1998. Correlation of powder characteristics of talc during planetary ball milling with the impact energy of the balls simulated by the particle element method. Powder Technol. 98, 166–170.

Kawatra, S.K., 2006. Advances in Comminution. Society for Mining Metallurgy.

Ketterhagen, W., Ende, M., Hancock, B., 2009. Process modeling in the pharmaceutical industry using the discrete element method. J. Pharm. Sci. 98, 442–470.

Klimpel, R.R., Austin, L.G., 1977. The back-calculation of specific rates of breakage and non-normalized breakage distribution parameters from batch grinding data. Int. J. Miner. Process. 4, 7–32.

Knieke, C., Azad, M., Dave, R., Bilgili, E., 2013. A study of the physical stability of wet media-milled fenofibrate suspensions using dynamic equilibrium curves. Chem. Eng. Res. Des. 91, 1245–1258.
Knieke, C., Azad, M., To, D., Bilgili, E., Davé, R., 2015. Sub-100 micron fast dissolving nanocomposite drug powders. Powder Technol. 271, 49–60.
Kostoglou, M., Karabelas, A.J., 2006. A study of the collisional fragmentation problem using the Gamma distribution approximation. J. Colloid Interface Sci. 303, 419–429.
Kotake, N., Suzuki, N., Asahi, S., Kanda, Y., 2002. Experimental study on the grinding rate constant of solid materials in a ball mill. Powder Technol. 122, 101–108.
Kwan, C., Mio, H., Chen, Y., Ding, Y., Saito, F., Papadopoulos, D., et al., 2005. Analysis of the milling rate of pharmaceutical powders using the distinct element method (DEM). Chem. Eng. Sci. 60, 1441–1448.
Lee, H., Cho, H., Kwon, J., 2010. Using the discrete element method to analyze the breakage rate in a centrifugal/vibration mill. Powder Technol. 198, 364–372.
Li, M., Yaragudi, N.K.R., Afolabi, A., Dave, R., Bilgili, E., 2015. Sub-100 nm drug particle suspensions with low bead contamination prepared via an intensified wet milling process. Chem. Eng. Sci. 130, 207–220.
Meloy, T.P., Williams, M.C., 1992. Problems in population balance modeling of wet grinding. Powder Technol. 71, 273–279.
Merisko-Liversidge, E., Liversidge, G.G., 2011. Nanosizing for oral and parenteral drug delivery: a perspective on formulating poorly water soluble compounds using wet media milling technology. Adv. Drug Deliv. Rev. 63, 427–440.
Merisko-Liversidge, E., Liversidge, G.G., Cooper, E.R., 2003. Nanosizing: a formulation approach for poorly water-soluble compounds. Eur. J. Pharm. Sci. 18, 113–120.
Mindlin, R., 1949. Compliance of elastic bodies in contact. J. Appl. Mech. 16, 259–268.
Mindlin, R., Deresiewicz, H., 1953. Elastic spheres in contact under varying oblique forces. J. Appl. Mech. 20, 327–344.
Mishra, B., 2003a. A review of computer simulation of tumbling mills by the discrete element method: part I—contact mechanics. Int. J. Miner. Process. 71, 73–93.
Mishra, B., 2003b. A review of computer simulation of tumbling mills by the discrete element method: part II—practical applications. Int. J. Miner. Process. 71, 95–112.
Monteiro, A., Afolabi, A., Bilgili, E., 2013. Continuous production of drug nanoparticle suspensions via wet stirred media milling: a fresh look at the Rehbinder effect. Drug Dev. Ind. Pharm. 39, 266–283.
Mori, H., Mio, H., Kano, K., Saito, F., 2004. Ball mill simulation in wet grinding using a tumbling mill and its correlation to grinding rate. Powder Technol. 143–144, 230–239.
Nomura, S., Tanaka, T., 2011. Analysis of energy–size reduction relationships in batch tumbling ball mills. Powder Technol. 208, 610–616.
Peltonen, L., Hirvonen, J., 2010. Pharmaceutical nanocrystals by nanomilling: critical process parameters, particle fracturing and stabilization methods. J. Pharm. Pharmacol. 62, 1569–1579.
Pilcer, G., Amighi, K., 2010. Formulation strategy and use of excipients in pulmonary drug delivery. Int. J. Pharm. 392, 1–19.
Pradeep, P.R., Pitchumani, B., 2011. Effect of operating variables on the production of nanoparticles by stirred media milling. Asia-Pac. J. Chem. Eng. 6, 154–162.
Prasher, C., 1987. Crushing and Grinding Process Handbook. Wiley, Chichester.
Rajamani, R.K., Guo, D., 1992. Acceleration and deceleration of breakage rates in wet ball mills. Int. J. Miner. Process. 34, 103–118.

Rajamani, R.K., Songfack, P., Mishra, B.K., 2000. Impact energy spectra of tumbling mills. Powder Technol. 108, 116–121.

Rajniak, P., Dhanasekharan, K., Sinka, C., MacPhail, N., Chern, R., 2008. Modeling and measurement of granule attrition during pneumatic conveying in a laboratory scale system. Powder Technol. 185, 202–210.

Reynolds, G.K., 2010. Modelling of pharmaceutical granule size reduction in a conical screen mill. Chem. Eng. J. 164, 383–392.

Schenck, L.R., Plank, R.V., 2008. Impact milling of pharmaceutical agglomerates in the wet and dry States. Int. J. Pharm. 348, 18–26.

Shampine, L.F., Gladwell, I., Thompson, S., 2003. Solving ODEs with MATLAB. first ed. Cambridge University Press, Cambridge.

Sievens-Figueroa, L., Bhakay, A., Jerez-Rozo, I.J., Pandya, N., Romanach, J.R., Michniak-Kohn, B., et al., 2012. Preparation and characterization of hydroxypropylmethyl cellulose films containing stable BCS Class II drug nanoparticles for pharmaceutical applications. Int. J. Pharm. 243, 496–508.

Singare, D.S., Marella, S., Gowthamrajan, K., Kulkarni, G.T., Vooturi, R., Rao, P.S., 2010. Optimization of formulation and process variable of nanosuspension: an industrial perspective. Int. J. Pharm. 402, 213–220.

Singh, S.K., Srinivasan, K., Gowthamarajan, K., Singare, D.S., Prakash, D., Gaikwad, N.B., 2011. Investigation of preparation parameters of nanosuspension by top-down media milling to improve the dissolution of poorly water-soluble glyburide. Eur. J. Pharm. Biopharm. 78, 441–446.

Tavares, L., Carvalho, R., 2009. Modeling breakage rate of coarse particles in ball mills. Miner. Eng. 22, 650–659.

Teng, S., Wang, P., Zhu, L., Young, M.-W., Gogos, C.G., 2010. Mathematical modeling of fluid energy milling based on a stochastic approach. Chem. Eng. Sci. 65, 4323–4331.

Teng, S., Wang, P., Zhang, Q., Gogos, C.G., 2011. Analysis of fluid energy mill by gas-solid two-phase flow simulation. Powder Technol. 208, 684–693.

Thornton, C., Liu, L., 2004. How do agglomerates break? Powder Technol. 143–144, 110–116.

Toneva, P., Epple, P., Breuer, M., Peukert, W., Wirth, K., 2011. Grinding in an air classifier mill—part I: characterisation of the one-phase flow. Powder Technol. 211, 19–27.

Tsoungui, O., Vallet, D., Charmet, J.C., 1999. Numerical model of crushing of grains inside two-dimensional granular materials. Powder Technol. 105, 190–198.

Tsuji, Y., Tanaka, T., Ishida, Y., 1992. Lagrangian numerical simulation of plug flow of cohesionless particles in a horizontal pipe. Powder Technol. 71, 239–250.

Tuzcu, E.T., Rajamani, R., 2008. Analysis of non-linear breakage rates in a batch ball mill. Eleventh International Mineral Proceedings of Symposium, Antalya, Turkey.

Varinot, C., Berthiaux, H., Dodds, J., 1999. Prediction of the product size distribution in associations of stirred bead mills. Powder Technol. 105, 228–236.

Verheezen, J.J.A.M., Maarschalk, K.V., Faassen, F., Vromans, H., 2004. Milling of agglomerates in an impact mill. Int. J. Pharm. 278, 165–172.

Verma, R., Rajamani, R.K., 1995. Environment-dependent breakage rates in ball milling. Powder Technol. 84, 127–137.

Vervoorn, P., Austin, L., 1990. The analysis of repeated breakage events as an equivalent rate process. Powder Technol. 63, 141–147.

Vogel, L., Peukert, W., 2002. Characterisation of grinding-relevant particle properties by inverting a population balance model. Part. Part. Syst. Charact. 19, 149–157.

Vogel, L., Peukert, W., 2003. Breakage behaviour of different materials – construction of a mastercurve for the breakage probability. Powder Technol. 129, 101–110.
Wang, M., Yang, R., Yu, A., 2012. DEM investigation of energy distribution and particle breakage in tumbling ball mills. Powder Technol. 223, 83–91.
Weerasekara, N., Powell, M., Cleary, P., Tavares, L., Evertsson, M., Morrison, R., et al., 2013. The contribution of DEM to the science of comminution. Powder Technol. 248, 3–24.
Wong, H.H., O'Neill, B.K., 1997. A mathematical model for *Escherichia coli* debris size reduction during high pressure homogenization based on grinding theory. Chem. Eng. Sci. 52, 2883–2890.
Zhu, H., Zhou, Z., Yang, R., Yu, A., 2008. Discrete particle simulation of particulate systems: a review of major applications and findings. Chem. Eng. Sci. 63, 5728–5770.

Modeling of powder compaction with the drucker–prager cap model

8

J. Cunningham[1], K. LaMarche[2] and A. Zavaliangos[3]
[1]Johnson and Johnson, New Brunswick, NJ, United States, [2]Bristol-Myers Squibb, New York, NY, United States, [3]Drexel University, Philadelphia, PA, United States

8.1 Introduction

Creating adequately strong compacts from powders is an old, but difficult, problem. A practitioner with extensive experience may be capable of recognizing and solving some problems, but the variety of behavior among different materials and the inherent complexity of the whole problem (including granule/powder production) necessitate a systematic, science-based approach. Fig. 8.1 shows a detailed schematic representation of cause-effect relations in compaction processes starting with the granule and its characteristics as the input and measures of mechanical performance of the compact as the output. Complex interactions of main variables are difficult to represent in such a linear mapping. For example, the presence of high humidity may affect particle flow, die filling, and deformation characteristics of the particles (e.g., Stubberud et al., 1996; Crouter and Briens, 2014). Although experimentation remains the staple of development and troubleshooting in compaction, in the last 10–15 years, computer modeling has offered new insight to compaction and the continuously increasing ability to analyze it offline.

There are two main modeling techniques for compaction of powders:

1. Discrete element method (DEM): Individual particles are modeled by describing their interactions through a specific force-displacement law. DEM offers unique insight and the ability to incorporate complex behavior at the particle level, but its ability to match real results is limited by its inherent assumptions (spherical particles or clusters) (Cundall and Strack, 1979; Heyliger and McMeeking, 2001; Martin et al., 2003; Redanz and Fleck, 2001).
2. Phenomenological continuum mechanics models: The macroscopic behavior of the compacted powder is treated in an averaged manner as a function of the macroscopic stresses and other variables that characterize the state of the compact. These models are calibrated to a limited number of experiments and, if properly designed, can reproduce the behavior of powder compacts over a wide range of geometries and stress conditions (Coube and Riedel, 2000; Michrafy et al., 2002; Sinka et al., 2003; Sinha et al., 2010; Sinka et al., 2004; Cunningham et al., 2004). Due to the practical significance of this type of model, we focus the discussion on it in this chapter.

Predictive Modeling of Pharmaceutical Unit Operations. DOI: http://dx.doi.org/10.1016/B978-0-08-100154-7.00008-9

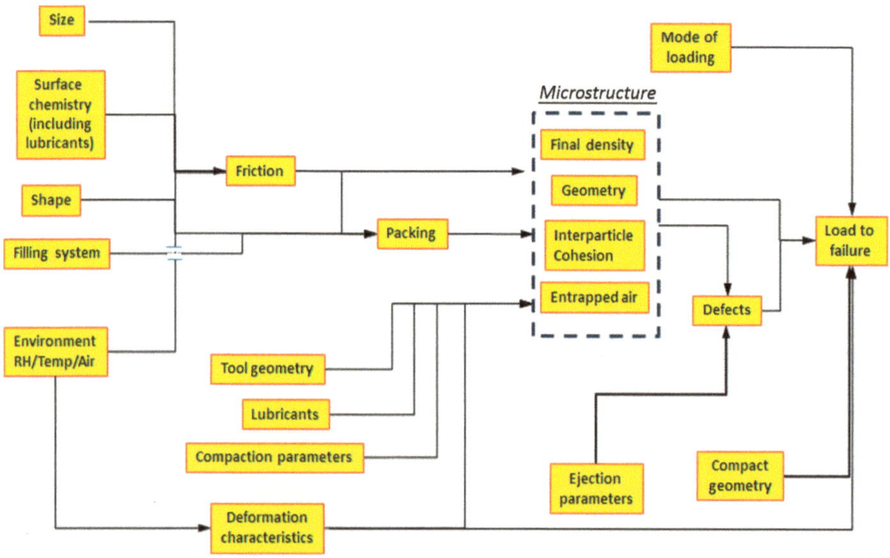

Figure 8.1 Cause and effect diagram for strength of compacts.

8.2 The particulate nature of compacts and the modeling of their behavior

Considering the powder aggregate as a continuum medium seems self-contradictory to the uninitiated, but it is not. The size of the particles is usually more than two orders of magnitude smaller than the dimensions of typical tablets. Therefore, a representative volume element (REV) containing a sufficient number of particles can be defined so that: (1) it can represent the macroscopic response of the material, and (2) its response is insensitive to statistical variations at the particle-length scale. Continuum models relate stresses and strains at the level of the REV. Inside the REV, stresses vary within individual particles and from particle to particle. Averaging such quantities over the REV essentially smooths out their variation to such a degree that a continuum representation is possible. Within this framework, powder compaction is viewed as an irreversible event in which large deformations change the material state from loose packing to near full density.

8.3 Constitutive models

8.3.1 Hydrostatic pressure dependence in compaction

Although hydrostatic pressure cannot induce permanent deformation in most fully dense solids, in porous materials it is the variable responsible for densification.

This concept is reflected in all constitutive models of compaction. The behavior of the material is described in terms of the hydrostatic term, p:

$$p = -\frac{1}{3}(\sigma_{11} + \sigma_{22} + \sigma_{33})$$

which controls the volumetric response of the material and the equivalent Mises stress, q:

$$q = \sqrt{\frac{3}{2}(\sigma_{11} + p)^2 + (\sigma_{22} + p)^2 + (\sigma_{33} + p)^2 + 2\sigma_{12}{}^2 + 2\sigma_{13}{}^2 + 2\sigma_{23}{}^2}$$

which represents the intensity of the deviatoric stress (i.e., the stress that remains after the subtraction of the hydrostatic part), and is related to the distortion of the material.

The limit of elastic deformation of the compact is defined by a yield locus in the p–q space. When a stress state is characterized by a combination of p and q values that are within the limits of the yield locus, the behavior of the material is reversible and can be described by the elastic constants, e.g., Young's modulus of elasticity and Poisson's ratio, and Hooke's law of elasticity. The fact that the higher the density of a compact, the more difficult is to densify it is represented by making the yield locus $F(p, q, \mathrm{RD}) = 0$, function of the relative density, RD. This idea that the yield locus in the p–q space does not depend on pressure for a fully dense material, while it does for a porous compact, as shown schematically in Fig. 8.2A and B, respectively.

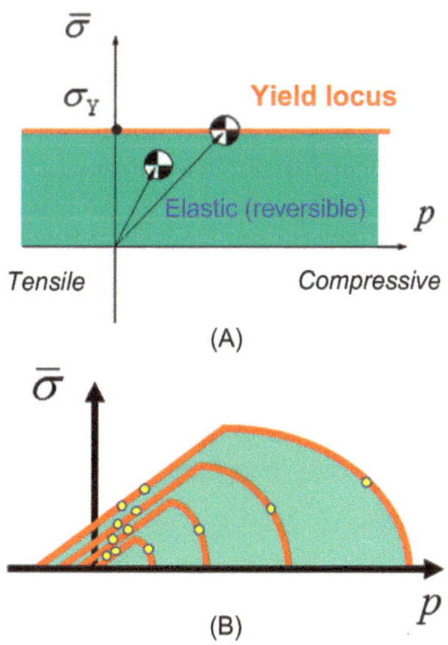

Figure 8.2 Representation of a yield locus for (A) Fully dense solids and (B) Powder compacts. The yield locus of a powder compact is represented by a family of curves, each for a different relative density.

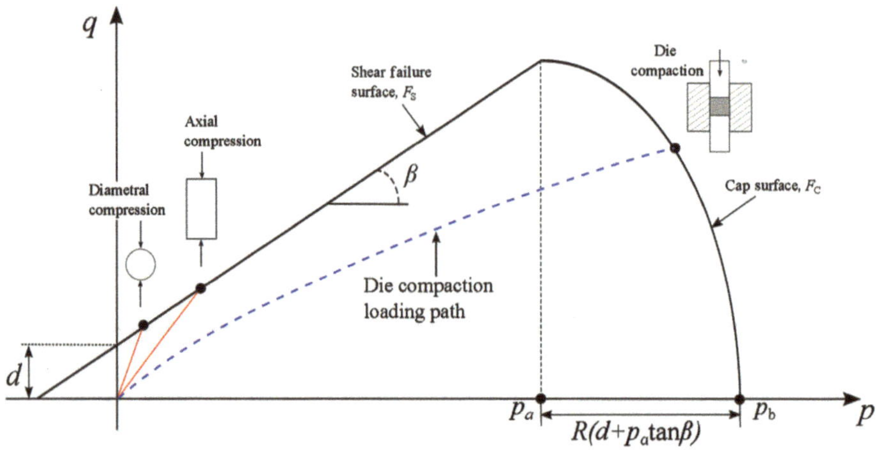

Figure 8.3 Modified Drucker–Prager/cap model: yield surface in the p–q plane.

8.3.2 Drucker–Prager cap (DPC) model

The most accepted plasticity model for powder compacts is the Drucker–Prager cap (DPC) model, which accounts for permanent deformation during compaction and volume dilatancy in shear (i.e., increase in volume) and has its origin in soil mechanics. The yield surface (see Fig. 8.3) is divided into two principal segments: (1) a Drucker–Prager (DP) shear failure (the term failure is traditional terminology from soil mechanics) surface F_s that describes the behavior of the material/powder under low hydrostatic pressure (Drucker and Prager, 2013), and (2) a cap surface F_c that describes the densification of the material/powder under high hydrostatic pressure (DiMaggio and Sandler, 1971). The evolution of the cap and shear failure surfaces are defined in terms the out of die RD $= \rho/\rho_{th}$, where ρ is the density of the compact out of die (fully unloaded material), and ρ_{th} is its theoretical full density. As RD increases, the yield locus expands, i.e., the material effectively hardens.

The shear failure surface in its simplest representation is a straight line:

$$F_s(p, q, \mathrm{RD}) = q - d - p\tan(\beta) = 0 \tag{8.1}$$

where d and β are the cohesion and the internal friction angle, respectively. If the condition (8.1) is met, the material fails in shear.

The cap surface describing the yield surface at high hydrostatic pressures is given by

$$F_c(p, q, \mathrm{RD}) = \sqrt{(p-p_a)^2 + (Rq)^2} - R(d + p_a\tan(\beta)) = 0 \tag{8.2}$$

If the condition Eq. (8.2) is met, the material begins to densify. Eq. (8.2) is an ellipse centered at $(p_a, 0)$ with eccentricity R (vertical over horizontal axis ratio). Here, p_a is called the evolution parameter. In addition to R and p_a, the hydrostatic compressive yield strength, p_b, fully describes the cap surface. Therefore, the overall yield surface of the DPC model is uniquely defined by five parameters*: d, β, R, p_a, and p_b. Note that only four of these parameters are independent because the maximum of the cap ellipse must be on the shear failure line. This condition is satisfied when

$$p_b - p_a = R(d + p_a \tan(\beta)) \tag{8.3}$$

To complete the DPC model, the plastic potential must be defined. This function describes the plastic deformation once the yield condition is met. Traditionally, the deformation increments are assumed to be proportional to the gradient of the plastic potential with respect to stress. The potential is identical with the cap surface F_c in the cap region, while in the shear failure region it is assumed to be an ellipse defined by the two ends of the shear failure line (i.e., the intersections with the cap and the horizontal axis $\sigma = 0$). In this manner, the most compact representation of the plastic potential is defined, because no more material parameters are needed than those describing the yield surface.

8.4 Parameter identification

8.4.1 Compaction simulators

In the pharmaceutical industry, the characterization of the mechanical behavior of powders is achieved with the help of compaction simulators. The name indicates that these testing machines are simulating the actual compaction process. In essence, these are mechanical or hydraulic presses that impose an axial load with the motion of one or two opposing moving pistons that hold the tableting punches. A specified displacement profile is produced by a hydraulic control system, a screw, or a cam mechanism that aims to mimic the motion of the punches in a tableting press. A comparison of the various types of simulators is out of the scope of this chapter. Special reference should be made, however, to the need for specific instrumentation for the proper characterization of the compaction event and the calibration of the DPC model, in particular, and the removal of the machine compliance in the measurements of position. Two load cells are required to capture both upper and lower punch loads, which may be different due to friction. In addition, the dies involved in this type of work must be instrumented with a sensor that provides the magnitude of the wall stress.

8.4.2 Standard procedures for parameter extraction

The calibration of the DPC model is achieved by the determination of the four independent parameters d, β, R, and p_b, [p_a can be determined from these parameters through Eq. (8.3)]. For completeness, we describe briefly the parameter identification process. For more details, see Sinka et al. (2004). Fig. 8.3 shows the necessary experiments in the p–q plane.

Cohesion, d, and internal friction angle, β, for a particular level of RD are obtained via diametral and axial compression strength tests on cylindrical compacts. In the diametral compression strength test, strength is computed based on the transverse tensile stress at the center of the sample estimated by the Hertz (1896) formula:

$$\sigma_T = \frac{2P_T}{\pi Dt} \tag{8.4}$$

where P_{T} is load at failure, D is the diameter of the cylindrical sample, and t is the thickness. The stress state at the center of the disk in the p–q space is given by $p = 2\sigma_{\mathrm{T}}/3$ and $q = \sqrt{13}\sigma_{\mathrm{T}}$. Eq. (8.4) is valid for most cases, except when excessive plastic deformation occurs prior to failure (Procopio and Zavaliangos, 2005).

Similarly, the axial compression strength test is carried out by axially compressing a cylindrical compact having a height to diameter aspect ratio greater than 1 and is given by

$$\sigma_{\mathrm{C}} = \frac{P_{\mathrm{C}}}{A} \tag{8.5}$$

where P_{C} is the load at failure and A is the cross-sectional area of the cylindrical compact. The stress state in the p–q space for axial compression is given by $p = \sigma_{\mathrm{C}}/3$ and $q = \sigma_{\mathrm{C}}$. In principle relatively long samples with a height to diameter ratio of 2 are required for the compression test (Doremus et al., 2001), but the creation of such compacts is rather difficult, if not impossible, for most powders due to the induced density inhomogeneity along the specimen height. Practically, specimens of an aspect ratio of 0.7 to 1 are used, despite the induced error. Lubrication of the specimen faces may improve the estimate of the compression strength.

The cohesion and internal friction are defined in terms of diametral and axial compressive strengths:

$$d = \frac{\sigma_{\mathrm{C}}\sigma_{\mathrm{T}}\left(\sqrt{13} - 2\right)}{\sigma_{\mathrm{C}} - 2\sigma_{\mathrm{T}}} \tag{8.6}$$

$$\beta = \tan^{-1}\left(\frac{3(\sigma_{\mathrm{C}} - d)}{\sigma_{\mathrm{C}}}\right) \tag{8.7}$$

The parameters R and p_{b}, used to define the cap surface, are determined from hydrostatic pressure and equivalent Mises stress measurements in die compaction. This experiment requires a fully instrumented die so that axial, σ_{a}, and radial, σ_{r}, stresses can be measured and the hydrostatic pressure and equivalent Mises stress be estimated as

$$\begin{aligned} p &= \frac{1}{3}(\sigma_{\mathrm{a}} + 2\sigma_{\mathrm{r}}) \\ q &= \sigma_{\mathrm{a}} - \sigma_{\mathrm{r}} \end{aligned} \tag{8.8}$$

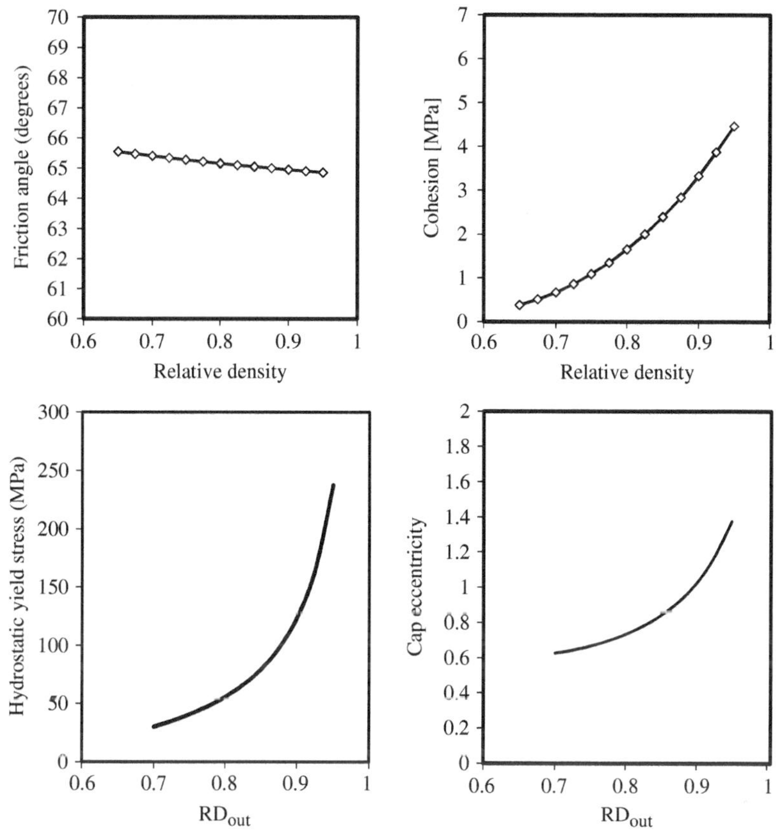

Figure 8.4 DPC parameters for a pharmaceutical excipient. Values shown are only for the range of densities for which a solid tablet can be pressed.

Based on these values, R and p_b can be determined, provided that d and β are known. Assuming a rigid die and low friction at the powder-tooling interfaces, p_b and R can be determined as function of the out of die RD:

$$p_b = p_a + R[d + p_a \tan(\beta)] \tag{8.9}$$

$$R = \sqrt{\frac{2}{3q}(p - p_a)} \tag{8.10}$$

The parameter p_a representing the intersection of the shear and cap surfaces is given by

$$p_a = \frac{-3q - 4d\tan(\beta) + \sqrt{9q^2 + 24dq\tan(\beta) + 8(3pq + 2q^2)\tan^2(\beta)}}{4\tan^2(\beta)} \tag{8.11}$$

Typical values of these parameters are shown in Fig. 8.4. Section 6.2 details the DPC parameter values for several common pharmaceutical excipients.

8.4.3 Extrapolation to low- and high-relative densities

Diametral and axial compression strength tests require intact compacts that can be handled with no damage. This requirement imposes a limit on the lowest density, RD_m that can be achieved. Limits on maximum load on punches pressure on radial wall sensor, or capping and lamination failure also define the upper limit of the RD_f that can be achieved. Therefore, the extraction of DPC parameters is only possible within a range of relative densities. In recent work (Garner et al., 2015), systematic guidelines for the extrapolation of the DPC parameters to low and high densities were presented. If such guidelines are not followed, issues in simulations such as unrealistic results in powder rolling (due to wrong extrapolation to low densities) or the prediction of relative densities above $RD = 1$ in some compaction simulations for high-density extrapolation are possible.

8.4.3.1 High-density extrapolation

The DPC parameters must be extrapolated for high-relative densities $RD_f < RD < 1$. Both the cap eccentricity, R, and hydrostatic yield stress, p_b, should asymptotically approach infinity at $RD = 1$. In other words, the densification cap becomes a degenerated ellipse with an infinite horizontal semiaxis, which corresponds to the yield locus of a fully dense material (see Fig. 8.2A). The extrapolation of p_b can be guided by any porous plasticity model that is consistent with the behavior of porous material at the dilute porosity limit. Here we employ the modified Gurson model (Tvergaard, 1990), but other models are viable. For pure hydrostatic stress, Gurson's model describes the hydrostatic yield stress as

$$p_b = \frac{2\sigma_y}{3q_2}\cosh^{-1}\left[\frac{1+q_1^2(1-RD)^2}{2q_1(1-RD)}\right] \tag{8.12}$$

where σ_y is the strength of the fully dense material, and the parameters q_1 and q_2 are experimentally determined parameters introduced by Tvergaard (1990). At RD_f, these three parameters can be determined from experimental data. Three equations are needed. The first equation is Eq. (8.12) at $RD = RD_f$ with the experimentally determined value of p_b. The second equation is the yield condition based on the Gurson model at $RD = RD_f$. The third equation is obtained by imposing the continuity of slope of p_b versus $\ln(1/(1-RD))$ between the experimentally determined part ($RD < RD_f$) and the model-based part ($RD_f < RD < 1$). The intercept of the latter on the $\ln(1/(1-RD))$ axis is $b = \ln(q_1)$ (Fig. 8.5) and the matching of the slopes is satisfied if

$$q_2 = \frac{2mq_f}{3\sqrt{1+[\exp(b)(1-RD_f)]^2 - 2\exp(b)(1-RD_f)\cosh(mp_f)}} \tag{8.13}$$

where p_f and q_f are the hydrostatic and equivalent Mises stress in compaction at RD_f, and $m = (3/2)(q_2/\sigma_y)$. Once the Gurson model is properly calibrated, then p_b can be obtained from Eq. (8.12) for all relative densities up to $RD = 1$.

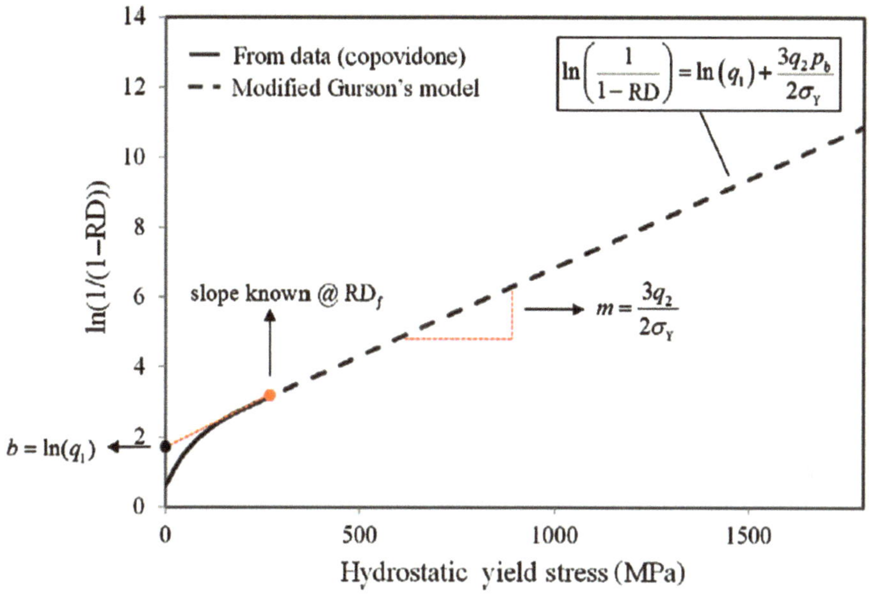

Figure 8.5 Heckel-plot-like graph of 1/(1 − RD), versus hydrostatic stress. The solid curve represents experimental data. The dashed curve is based on the Gurson model.

The extrapolation of cap eccentricity R beyond RD_f is carried out by first extrapolating p_a. The value of p_a at RD = 1 can be found by assuming that the Mises effective stress at RD = 1 is equal to σ_y found from the Gurson model:

$$p_a^{RD=1} \approx \frac{\sigma_y}{\tan \beta} \tag{8.14}$$

Many choices exist for the extrapolation of p_a from its experimentally determined value at RD_f to the limit at RD = 1 given by Eq. (8.14), but a simple second-degree polynomial usually suffices. The extrapolated values for p_a and p_b can be used to determine R from Eq. (8.10).

There is no physical basis to guide the extrapolation of cohesion, d, and internal angle of friction, β, in the range $RD_f < RD < 1$. An exponential form $d = d_0 + K(RD - RD_0)^n$ can be used for cohesion. For most cases, d_0 does not play an important role because of its small value. For the extrapolation of β, a linear extrapolation is possible because it appears consistent with the data (e.g., Fig. 8.4).

8.4.3.2 Low-density extrapolation

At low densities, if the values of β and θ are known, the cap parameters p_b, R, and therefore p_a can be obtained directly from experimental data. In an instrumented die/punch system, axial and radial stresses are recorded continuously. Therefore, the corresponding values of hydrostatic pressure and equivalent stress can be directly obtained. These values, however, are known in terms of in die RD. By establishing a correspondence between in die and out of die density, the cap parameters can be established for the entire low-density region if the values of cohesion and internal angle of friction are known. Therefore, the problem is reduced to the extrapolation of d and β.

A common assumption in the literature (Brewin et al., 2008; Cunningham et al., 2004; Han et al., 2008; Shang et al., 2012) is that cohesion is zero at RD_0. Using this assumption, any nonzero value of the compressive strength, no matter how small, results in an internal friction angle of $\beta = \tan^{-1}(3) = 71.56°$. However, it is preferable to establish connection with experimental data in that range. The ring shear cell test offers an interesting possibility to augment the range of densities probed. A ring-shaped column of powder sheared by a shear stress, τ, is measured under an applied normal stress, σ_n. The column is constrained laterally but the induced lateral stress, σ_{rr}, is not typically measured. The Mohr–Coulomb (MC) model describes the shearing limit by $\tau = c + \sigma_n \tan(\theta)$ independent of the lateral stress. Measurement of the shear stress τ under several values of the normal stress σ_n provides the cohesion, c, and internal angle of friction, θ.

The cohesion value of c and the internal angle of friction θ for the MC model are different from the corresponding d and β from the DPC model, because the condition of shearing for the latter depends on the equivalent stress, q, and the hydrostatic pressure, p, which are related but not identical to τ and σ_n.

Similar to the difference between the von Mises and Tresca yield criteria, the DPC failure surface includes the effect of the intermediate principal stress, whereas the MC does not. By necessity, they only agree along a prescribed set of points in the principal stress space. As a result, cohesion d and friction angle β can be approximated from the MC failure surface but the approximations are not unique. A typical approximation is to assume that the MC hexagonal pyramid in the principal stress space is inscribed within the DP shear failure cone. In that case, the model parameters are related to the MC parameters by (Jiang and Xie, 2011)

$$\tan \beta = \frac{3 \sin \theta}{\sqrt{3} \cos \eta - \sin \theta \sin \eta} \tag{8.15}$$

$$d = \frac{3c \cos \theta}{\sqrt{3} \cos \eta - \sin \theta \sin \eta} \tag{8.16}$$

The angle η is a parameter known as the Lode angle (Lode, 1926) that takes values in the range from $-30°$ to $+30°$. These equations indicate that the correlation between the MC and DPC cohesion and friction angle depends on the stress conditions as determined by the Lode angle. Calculation of the Lode angle requires knowledge of the full stress state, which is commonly not available. To the best of our knowledge, there are no ring shear cells available that can measure the transverse (radial) stress. As a result, we can consider a range of admissible values for β and d as a function of the plausible Lode angles, or further assumptions of the stress state in the shear cell are necessary. By considering viable values of the lateral stress, a range of Lode angle and the corresponding ranges of d and β can be estimated. For example, for the material for which values are shown in Fig. 8.4, the range of d and β at RD_0 is 56–86 Pa and 47° to 58°, respectively. For simplicity, linear or quadratic extrapolations of d and β from RD_0 to the smallest experimentally available data for these parameters can be performed. For more information on these issues, the reader is referred to the work of Garner et al., 2015.

8.5 Finite element modeling

8.5.1 Review of the technique

A mechanical problem involving compaction of powders consists of the following fundamental elements:

1. Equilibrium equations (e.g., partial differential equations that describe the balance of forces transmitted through the material);
2. Geometry of the problem;
3. Constitutive behavior of the powder (e.g., stress–strain behavior);
4. Boundary conditions including loading (e.g., displacement and velocity of the punches or load history) and friction between the tooling and the powder; and
5. Initial conditions (e.g., initial RD of powder, which results from die filling).

FE analysis provides a numerical solution of problems described by partial differential equations. This technique can address complex constitutive models and geometries efficiently, which cannot be dealt analytically, and has become one of the key computational tools in many engineering fields. Today, most commercial finite element programs include a version of the DPC model in their material library. In the case of ABAQUS, which is one of the most common FE programs used, there is a version of the DPC model with constant material parameters, with the exception be dealt analytically of the hydrostatic yield stress, p_b, which is expressed as a function of the plastic volumetric strain. The program offers the opportunity to the user to define a user parameter (namely the out of die RD) which evolves on the basis of the volumetric plastic strain, and then defines the model parameters as a function of the RD. Complexities appear when the initial density varies with position. In that case, a user material must be programmed to address this issue.

8.6 Case studies

8.6.1 Model validation

One of the earlier, but still most instructive, examples of the usage of finite elements in the modeling of compaction is described in the work of Cunningham et al. (2004). Microcrystalline cellulose (MCC) tablets were compacted to the same average RD under two extreme wall friction conditions: (1) low friction achieved by compacting magnesium stearate (MgSt) before the main compaction so that all the tool surfaces are covered by a residual layer of MgSt; and high friction achieved by cleaning the surface of the tools with a solvent. Despite having identical average relative densities, the two tablets have a dramatically different distribution of internal porosity. The experimentally observed density maps are shown in Fig. 8.6A and B and were obtained by an indentation procedure (Cunningham et al., 2004). The nonlubricated tablet exhibits a high-density area in the periphery, while the material in the center is less densified. The lubricated die tablet presents an opposite pattern, with a localized low-density region around the band while the rest of the tablet is densified nearly uniformly. It is evident that the wall lubrication has a significant effect on the local porosity of the tablets.

Finite element predictions of RD are shown in Fig. 8.6C and D for the lubricated and nonlubricated dies, respectively, and are in agreement with the experimental density maps (Fig. 8.6A and B). The numerical simulations of these two cases offer excellent insight into this problem. The concave top punch makes initial contact with the flat surface of the powder bed around the outer periphery and induces densification locally. High values of the friction coefficient restrict the powder movement along the face of the top punch toward the center of the concave cup. The density around the band region becomes progressively higher than the rest of the tablet. The center of the tablet begins to densify initially only mildly due to the transverse motion of the outer ring of the tablet, and practically only after the top punch makes full contact with the top surface of the powder. Low friction coefficient allows relative movement of the powder with respect to the punch. In other words, the material in the periphery can slide easier on the punch rather than densify. The resulting density distribution is essentially inverse of that of the high friction coefficient. The numerical predictions are in excellent agreement with the experimental ones in both cases.

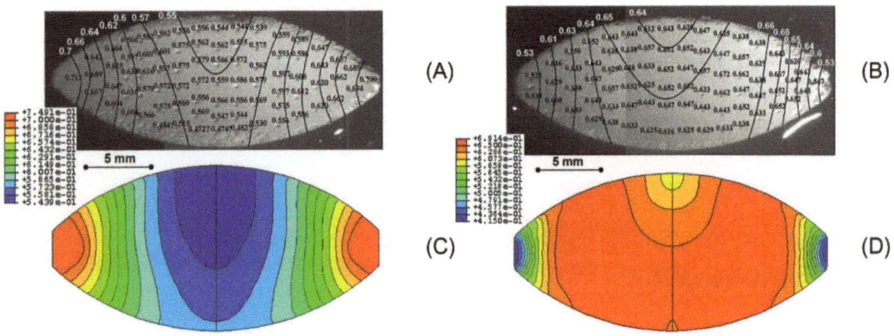

Figure 8.6 Relative density distribution. (A) Experimental map for clean die compaction. (B) Experimental map for lubricated die compaction. (C) Numerical model prediction corresponding to clean die compaction; and (D) Numerical model prediction corresponding to lubricated die compaction (Sinka et al., 2004).

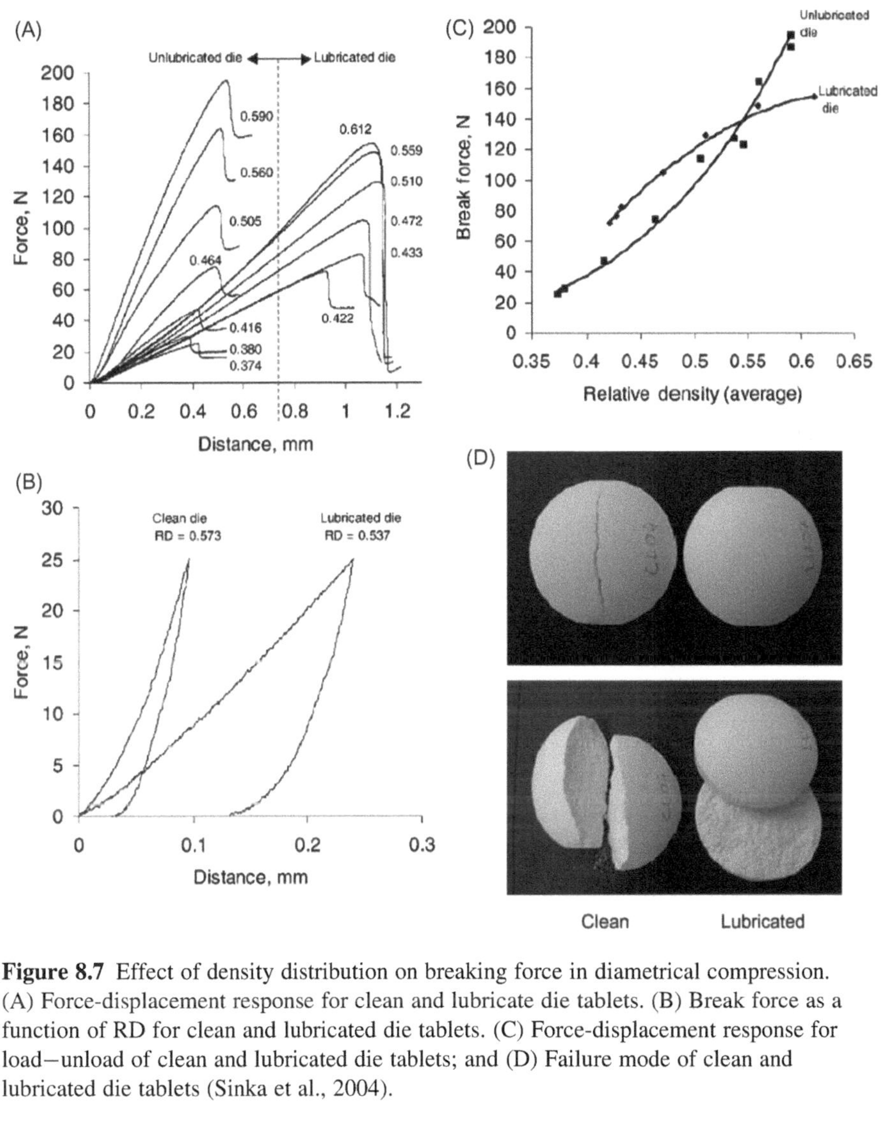

Figure 8.7 Effect of density distribution on breaking force in diametrical compression. (A) Force-displacement response for clean and lubricate die tablets. (B) Break force as a function of RD for clean and lubricated die tablets. (C) Force-displacement response for load–unload of clean and lubricated die tablets; and (D) Failure mode of clean and lubricated die tablets (Sinka et al., 2004).

The differences of the diametrical compression results from the two tablets are also instructive. The force-displacement behavior, fracture loads, and modes of fracture using the results presented in Fig. 8.7. The force-displacement plots for the diametrical compression tests are presented in Fig. 8.7A for different average relative densities. The slopes are increasing with RD and are different for tablets compressed with and without die wall lubrication. This consistent with and can be attributed to the variation of strength and elastic properties of the material with RD. For the same average RD, the lubricated die tablets exhibit much lower slopes and larger displacement to failure. Tablets produced in a lubricated die exhibit low density in their periphery. Therefore, the local deformation at the contacts dominates the diametrical compression test. The lubricated die tablet exhibits larger contact flattening than the unlubricated die tablet. The low density of the lubricated die tablet at the periphery allows for extensive plastic deformation at the contacts under the platens, as can be seen in Fig. 8.7D. Tablets compacted without lubrication have a stiffer exterior and exhibit low deformation at the contact and limited overall plastic deformation The fracture loads as functions of RD for nonlubricated and lubricated die tablets are presented in Fig. 8.7C. This figure shows clearly that the knowledge of the average density is not adequate to characterize the behavior of the tablet. The fracture modes are also dramatically different. Clean die tablets break as normally expected, into two semicylinders (Fig. 8.7D). Lubricated die tablets delaminate across the middle along a plane perpendicular to the axis of symmetry (Fig. 8.7D).

The two types of tablets exhibit also significant differences in friability and abrasion (Fig. 8.8). In both cases, material loss is associated with areas of low density. The lubricated tablet exhibits the highest weight loss in friability because its starts breaking up from the edges while being subjected to impact in the friability cylinder (Fig. 8.8B). Its abrasion resistance is excellent. On the contrary, the abrasion of the unlubricated tablet is considerable and localized at the cup area, where the density is lower, while the edges and the band area remain relatively intact after both friability and abrasion experiments.

There is always a compromise between tablet characteristics and performance under various loading conditions: e.g., the break force of a clean die tablet having $RD > 0.6$ is relatively high (Fig. 8.7C), however it will perform poorly in abrasion (Fig. 8.8B) compared with a lubricated die tablet of same RD. The finite element analysis can highlight possible problem regions in a tablet and aid the optimization of formulation, lubrication, and tablet image design.

8.6.2 Excipient characterization

The previous case study showed the impact that die lubrication can have on tablet properties of a single material. The interaction between the compaction properties of the various excipients and drug blended together in pharmaceutical formulas adds yet another layer of complexity. Each of these excipients exhibits its own compaction behavior, which is reflected in their DPC parameters (LaMarche et al., 2014).

Beyond the active pharmaceutical ingredient (API), a typical formulation will consist of one or two major components, often called fillers, and three to four minor components (Kottke and Rudnic, 2002). Fillers act as bulking agents in low drug load formulations, increasing the size of the tablet so that they can be handled by patients. However, they must also form strong compacts and hold the rest of the ingredients in the tablet together after compaction. This makes the compaction properties of these major excipients very important when selecting a formulation for any given API. In addition, tablets must either break down quickly when

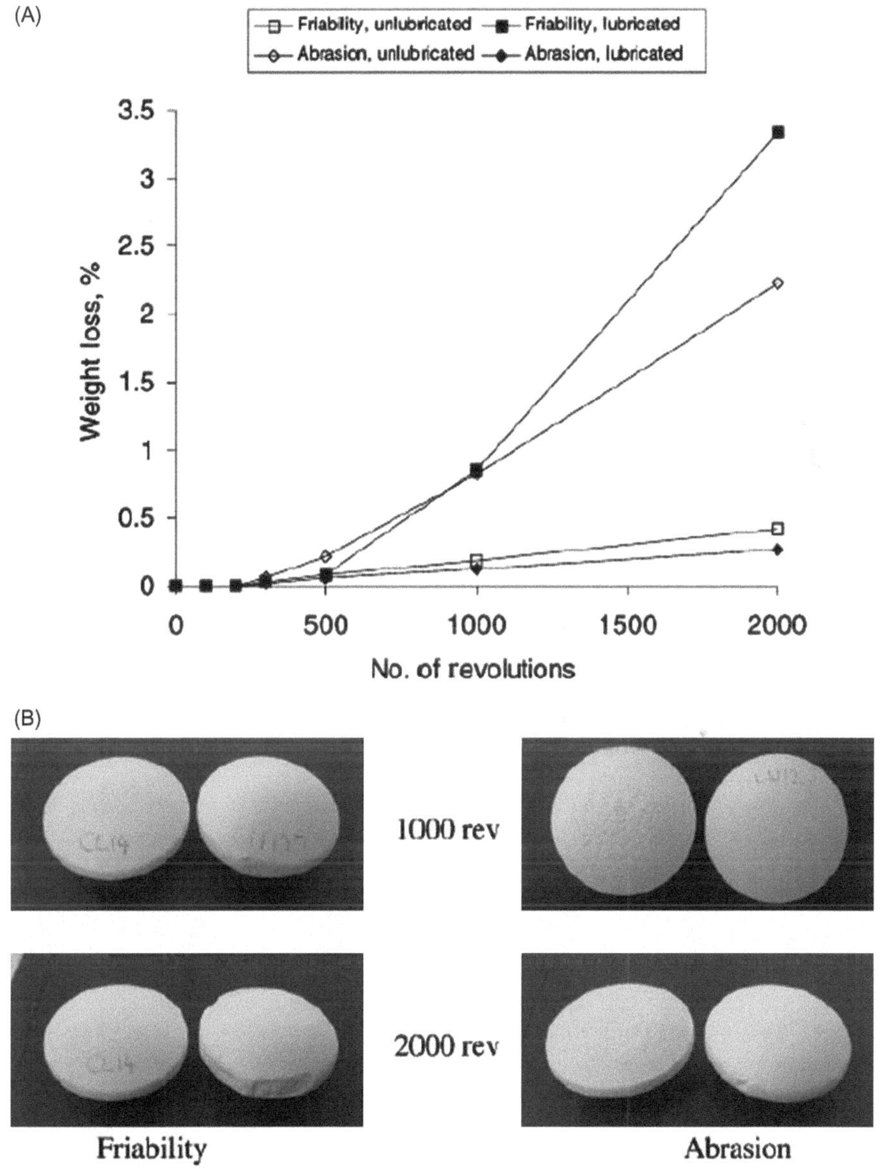

Figure 8.8 Friability and abrasion experiments: (A) Weight loss and (B) Damage to tablets after 1000 and 2000 revolutions (Sinka et al., 2004). In every panel, the tablet on the left is the one from the cleaned tools while the one on the right from lubricated tools.

ingested and release their drug, or release of the drug must be controlled over time. In either case, these excipients need to help facilitate or, at the very least, not hinder that process.

Commonly used filler excipients include MCC, lactose, dicalcium phosphate, or pregelatinized starch. The particles of MCC are known to undergo significant plastic flow when compacted (Jivraj et al., 2000). MCC is used in many formulations due largely to its ability to form strong bonds under compaction. Pregelatinized starch also undergoes plastic flow during compaction (Jivraj et al., 2000). It has the ability to absorb water readily, causing the starch particles to swell, which allows tablets containing starch to break down quickly when ingested. However, this material also expands greatly after compaction (Kottke and Rudnic, 2002). Therefore, it is difficult to make tablets with high quantities of starch that reach a high density and a high strength. Lactose can be obtained in either an anhydrous or monohydrated state. Particles of both forms are known to undergo brittle fracture during compaction (Jivraj et al., 2000; Ilic et al., 2009). The fragmentation of the lactose crystals is the primary mechanism by which bonds are formed as this material is compacted. Lactose has desirable compaction properties, forming strong tablets, and because it is water soluble, it also aids in the breakup of tablets when ingested (Kottke and Rudnic, 2002). Dicalcium phosphate (dical) is available in either an anhydrous or dihydrated form. Dical is a nonorganic salt that is largely insoluble in water. It is commonly used in direct compression formulations due to its ability to flow easily (Kottke and Rudnic, 2002). Like lactose, dical is a material that densifies by brittle particle fracture (Jivraj et al., 2000).

These excipients are produced by several manufactures and grades. Their properties are optimized to meet the various possible needs of a given formulation. Some examples of the properties that can be varied are the hydration state of the compound (in the case of lactose or dicalcium phosphate), the free water content, the particle size, flowability, and the crystal/amorphous content of the material. Each of these properties can potentially affect the compaction behavior of these materials. Therefore, the variation of properties between grades and manufacturers of these excipients is very important when selecting the components of formulation.

These differences in compaction properties can be observed when looking at the DPC parameters and elastic parameters (LaMarche et al., 2014). The elastic properties of tablets of a material, Young's modulus, E, and Poisson's ratio, ν, can be obtained during the same calibration experiments as the DPC parameters (LaMarche et al., 2014; Cunningham et al., 2004). The larger a material's Young's modulus, the more difficult it is to deform elastically. The Poisson's ratio of a material determines the amount of induced deformation in a direction transverse to the main deformation direction.

To explore some of the differences in the common filler materials, the DPC parameters of several filler excipients were determined using the calibration methodology described in Section 4.2. A more detailed description of the methods used can be found in LaMarche et al.'s work (2014). Each excipient grade and their manufacturer are listed in Table 8.1. The two grades of MCC, Avicel PH-102 and

Table 8.1 **Excipients tested in this analysis and their sources**

Excipient	Abbreviated name	Grade	Vender source
Pregelatinized starch	Starch	1500 partially pregelatinized maize starch	Colorcon (West Point, PA, United States)
Microcrystalline cellulose	MCC PH-102	Avicel PH-102	FMC Biopolymer (Newark, DE, United States)
Microcrystalline cellulose	MCC PH-200	Avicel PH-200	FMC Biopolymer (Newark, DE, United States)
Lactose monohydrate	Lactose 310	310 NF Lactose	Foremost Farms (Norwich, NY, United States)
Lactose anhydrous	Lactose DT	Lactose anhydrous DT	Kerry Bio-Science (Norwich, NY, United States)
Dicalcium phosphate dihydrate	Dical–Emcompress	Emcompress	JRS Pharma (Patterson, NY, United States)
Dicalcium phosphate anhydrous	Dical–Fujicalin	Fujicalin	Fuji Chemical Industries Co. (Kamiichi, Toyama, Japan)

Avicel PH-200, differ primarily in their nominal particle size: 100 and 180 μm, respectively. The grades of lactose include a monohydrate form, lactose 310 NF, and an anhydrous form, lactose DT. The grades of dical include Fujicalin, which is an anhydrous form that is prepared by spray drying (Schlack et al., 2001). This produces roughly spherical granules. The other grade, Emcompress, is a dihydrate crystalline material. Both grades of dical were lubricated with 0.5% MgSt by weight before testing to reduce wear on the die. One grade of pregelatinized starch is examined here: starch 1500.

The DPC parameters for each of the excipients are plotted as functions of tablet out of die RD in Figs. 8.9–8.12. There are clear differences between the materials, while subtler differences can be seen between the excipient grades. Immediately apparent are the differences in the RD of the tablets produced for each material. For example, tablets of dical Fujicalin were produced at an out of die density of between 0.45 and 0.70, while lactose DT was produced over a range of 0.63–0.89. For lactose and dical, the maximum RD that could be achieved was limited by the maximum pressure that could be applied in these experiments. Both materials simply became too difficult to compress to higher RD. On the other hand, both MCC and starch reach an apparent RD of about one when under pressure in the die.

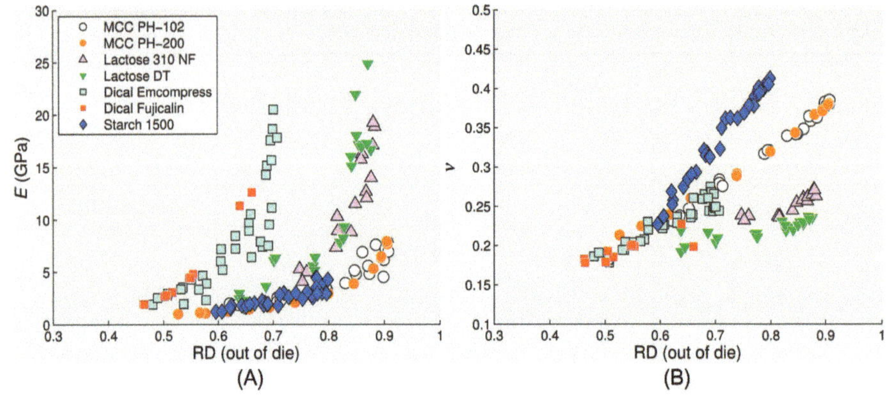

Figure 8.9 Excipient elastic properties: (A) The relationship between tablet's Young's modulus and the relative density and (B) Poisson's ratio of tablets as a function to relative density.

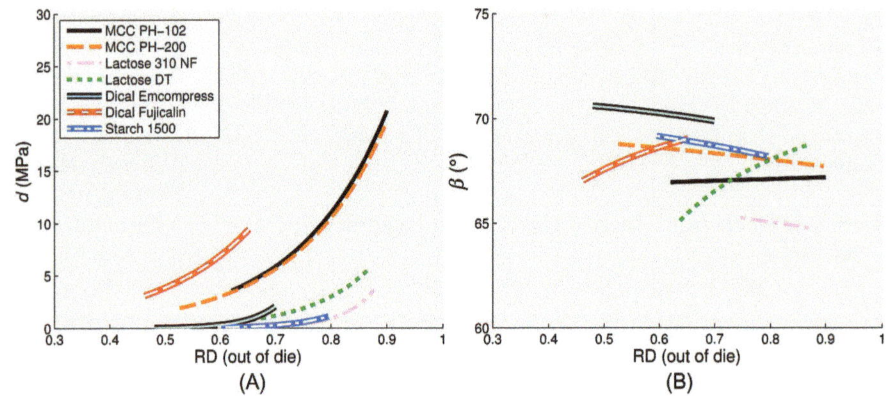

Figure 8.10 The dependence of the cohesion (A) and internal friction angle (B) parameters for the excipients on tablet relative density.

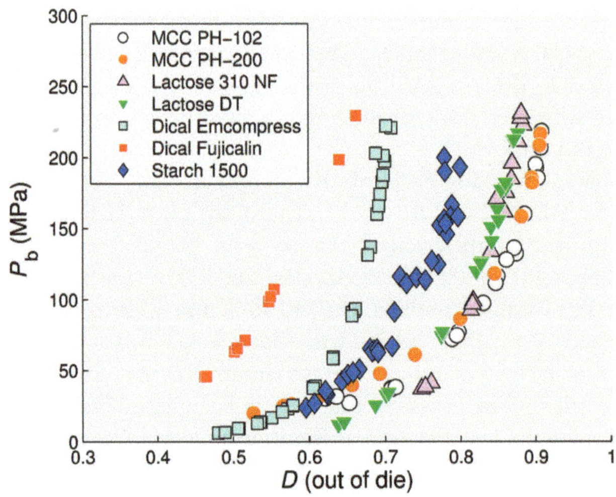

Figure 8.11 The hydrostatic yield stress of excipients.

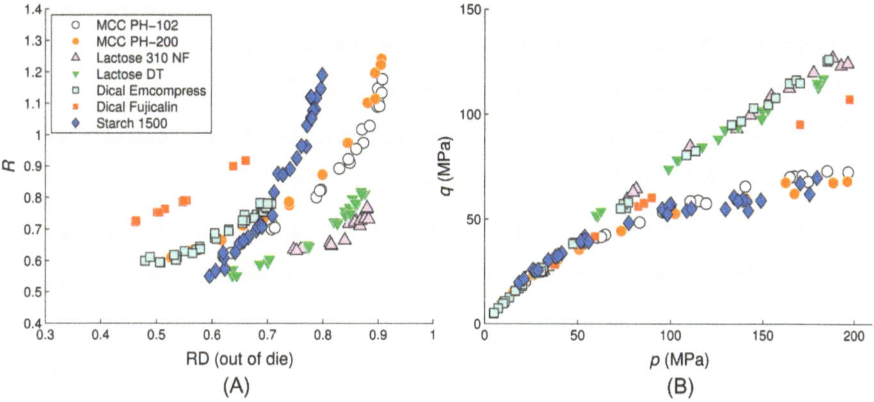

Figure 8.12 Cap eccentricity and the stress state during compaction: (A) Shows the dependence of the excipients' cap eccentricity with relative density and (B) Shows the equivalent Mises and hydrostatic stress acting on a the tablets of each excipient as it reaches its maximum compaction force.

As the pressure is relieved from the tablet during unloading and ejection, the tablets relax and their apparent RDs decrease. Both grades of MCC relaxed a similar amount, bringing the maximum achieved out of die RD to slightly above 0.9. Starch, however, relaxed to a much larger extent. Even though its maximum in die apparent RD reached 0.99, its maximum out of die density is only 0.80. In the case of dical and lactose, it is likely that a higher pressure would result in denser tablets, but for the grades of MCC and starch, even higher pressures would not increase the out of die RD further.

These compaction behavior differences can be better understood by examining the materials' DPC and elastic parameters. From Fig. 8.9, it can be seen that both MCC grades and starch have low Young's modulus, which allows them to deform to a greater extent elastically when under stress than compared to dical or lactose. The Young's modulus of the dical and lactose grades rise quickly as their tablets' RD increases. The Poisson's ratio increases roughly linearly with RD for each material. The Poisson's ratio of starch is larger than any other material. The MCC grades reach similar values to starch at high RD and have a similar value as dical at low RD. The Poisson's ratios of the lactose grades are lower than the other materials. There is little difference between the grades of excipients in either elastic parameter. The most noticeable difference is the slightly lower Poisson's ratio of anhydrous lactose than that of the monohydrate.

What is clear is that the materials that reached high density during compaction and relaxed to a great extend during the tablet ejection, starch and the MCC grades, have similar elastic properties. Starch has the lowest Young's modulus and highest Poisson's ratio of the materials studied here and it recovered to the greatest extent. MCC has a slightly higher Young's modulus and lower Poisson's ratio, and it recovered to a smaller extent than starch. Dical and lactose are much stiffer and have large Young's moduli and small Poisson's ratios. These materials recovered only slightly during ejection.

The differences between the grades are more obvious in Fig. 8.10. Here the cohesion and the internal friction angle show clear differences between the grades of dical and smaller differences between the lactose grades. The grades of MCC appear quite similar. No data points are shown in this figure. As per Eqs. (8.7) and (8.8), both cohesion and friction angle are calculated from separate experiments. Their dependence on RD must be calculated rather than measured directly. Interestingly, the Fujicalin dical has the highest cohesion at the relative densities that could be achieved for that material. The Emcompress dical has a much lower cohesion. Both MCC grades have almost identical cohesion and have the highest achievable cohesion. The lactose grades and starch have much lower cohesion than the other materials. The anhydrous lactose's cohesion is somewhat higher than the monohydrate.

From Fig. 8.10, it is apparent what makes MCC such a popular excipient choice for tablet formulations. It is able to form strong tablets. MCC tablets at a RD of about 0.9 have cohesion is two to three times higher than what is possible for other materials. Interestingly, the difference in particle size between MCC does not noticeably impact this parameter. However, Fujicalin dical's cohesion is considerably higher than Emcompress's. The spray dried preparation of Fujicalin may be the major contributing factor in its different properties (Schlack et al., 2001), but further study of dical's compaction properties dependence on hydration state and particle size is need.

The values of friction angle for each material are all fairly similar at around $65^\circ-71^\circ$ with little dependence on RD. These values are typical for both pharmaceutical powders as well as the compaction of metal powders (Brewin et al., 2008). The internal friction angle is determined from Eq. (8.7) and requires a straight line to pass through a material's diametric and axial breaking strengths in the $p-q$ space. Because the axial strength is much larger than the diametric strength for almost all materials, the value of β is determined largely by the stress distribution during the axial compression strength test (Brewin et al., 2008).

The hydrostatic yield stress is given in Fig. 8.11. The yield stress of each material increases rapidly as their RD approach the maximum that could be achieved in these tests. As was discussed for the elastic parameters, MCC and starch both approach a fully dense state during compression and relax to their out of die RD. The other materials could conceivably achieve higher densities if higher stresses could be applied during compaction. However, very large stresses would be needed to densify the compacts further. The curves in Fig. 8.11 are well described by exponential functions (LaMarche et al., 2014) and the yield stress would become extremely large if one were to extrapolate the shown curves to even slightly higher densities.

The cap eccentricity, R, for the excipients is shown in Fig. 8.12A. Across all the materials and densities, the cap eccentricity varies from about 0.5 to about 1.3. The eccentricity of some materials only weakly increases with increasing RD, while others show a much greater dependence on the density. Interestingly, the materials' densification mechanism is the primary difference. Dical and lactose are both recognized for densifying through brittle fracture, and, as can be seen, both materials have a slight linear increase in *R* as the density of their tablets increase. Starch and MCC, on the other hand, are known compact though plastic flow. These materials' *R* show a much stronger dependence on RD. These materials are able to approach full density during compaction. As discussed in Section 4.3.1, a material with no remaining volume to be closed should not be able to attain greater densities permanently. Any increase in density due to the pressure of the punches should be reversed as the pressure is relieved. In the DPC model, as a material approaches a fully dense state, its eccentricity and hydrostatic yield stress should approach infinity. From Fig. 8.12A, the eccentricity of both starch and MCC appear to be increasing asymptotically as they reach their highest densities. This agrees well with what is expected of materials that approach RD = 1 during compaction.

The behavior of these materials is also interesting to consider in terms of the stress state during compaction. Fig. 8.12B shows the maximum hydrostatic and equivalent Mises stresses experienced by the tablets of each material as they are compacted. The difference in behavior between the brittle fracture and the plastic flow materials is now quite obvious. All the materials begin their compaction with a similar stress state. As the stress increases, along with the density of the tablets, the stress states of MCC and starch curve and appear to approach a maximum shear stress; the lactose and dical grades continue to increase in shear stress. This can be thought of in terms of Fig. 8.2A and B. As the material approaches fully dense, its stress state approaches that of a nonporous material.

The compaction behavior of these materials is likely playing a role in this pattern. It should not be expected for all materials to end up on, or necessarily near, these two paths (LaMarche et al., 2014). It is more likely that some coincidence is involved with the close grouping of these excipients. However, the clear difference in behavior between the materials with densification mechanisms does suggest that they play an important role in the stress path. The only material that does not fall on top of the others is Fujicalin dical. This material experiences slightly lower equivalent Mises stress than Emcompress dical or the lactose grades. It is likely that the spherical shape of the particles may play a role in increasing the stress transfer to the walls, reducing the equivalent Mises stress.

The properties of the excipients examined here vary greatly, but several common themes emerge from their DPC behavior. The density ranges and whether the material could reach a nearly fully dense state during compaction determined much about their cap parameters. The differences between the excipients seem to be their compaction mechanism. The excipients become denser through the fracture or plastic flow of particles. The elastic parameters influence the amount of density relaxation that occurs for tablets during unloading and ejection. The cohesion of MCC and Fujicalin dical are much higher than the other excipients. The friction angle is similar for each of these materials, which is typical of other materials including metal powders (Brewin et al., 2008), and is the result of the relatively low cohesion of all these powders (i.e., the simple compressive strength is much larger than the cohesion, which brings the internal friction angle close to $\tan^{-1}(1/3)$). The hydrostatic yield stress increases rapidly for all of the excipients as the compacts approached their maximum RD. The cap eccentricity increases rapidly for those materials that approached fully dense during compaction. Its increase was much smaller, and approximately linear, for the dical and lactose grades. The stress state during compaction was strikingly different between the excipients with different densification mechanisms. Plastic flow materials transmit more stress to the walls and therefore experience less shear during compaction. The compaction behavior of each of the materials is reflected in its DPC parameters.

References

Brewin, P.R., Coube, O., Doremus, P., Tweed, J.H., 2008. In: Derby, B. (Ed.), Modelling of Powder Die Compaction (Engineering Materials and Processes). Springer-Verlag, London.

Coube, O., Riedel, H., 2000. Numerical simulation of metal powder die compaction with special consideration of cracking. Powder Metall. 43 (2), 123–131.

Crouter, A., Briens, L., 2014. The effect of moisture on the flowability of pharmaceutical excipients. AAPS PharmSciTech. 15 (1), 65–74.

Cundall, P.A., Strack, O.D., 1979. A discrete numerical model for granular assemblies. Geotechnique. 29 (1), 47–65.

Cunningham, J.C., Sinka, I.C., Zavaliangos, A., 2004. Analysis of tablet compaction. I. Characterization of mechanical behavior of powder and powder/tooling friction. J. Pharm. Sci. 93 (8), 2022–2039.

DiMaggio, F.L., Sandler, I.S., 1971. Material model for granular soils. J. Eng. Mech. Div. 97 (3), 935–950.

Doremus, P., Toussaint, F., Alvain, O., 2001. Simple tests and standard procedure for the characterisation of green compacted powder. Nato Science Series Sub Series III Computer And Systems Sciences. 176, 29–41.

Drucker, D.C., Prager, W., 2013. Soil mechanics and plastic analysis or limit design. Q. Appl. Math. 10.

Garner, S., Strong, J., Zavaliangos, A., 2015. The extrapolation of the Drucker–Prager/cap material parameters to low and high relative densities. Powder Technol.

Han, L.H., Elliott, J.A., Bentham, A.C., Mills, A., Amidon, G.E., Hancock, B.C., 2008. A modified Drucker–Prager cap model for die compaction simulation of pharmaceutical powders. Int. J. Solids Struct. 45 (10), 3088–3106.

Hertz, H., 1896. Über die berührung fester elastischer Körper (On the contact of rigid elastic solids). Miscellaneous Papers. Jones and Schott, London.

Heyliger, P., McMeeking, R., 2001. Cold plastic compaction of powders by a network model. J. Mech. Phys. Solids. 49 (9), 2031–2054.

Ilic, I., Kasa Jr., P., Dreu, R., Pintye-Hodi, K., Srcic, S., 2009. The compressibility and compactibility of different types of lactose. Drug Dev. Ind. Pharm. 35 (10), 1271–1280.

Jiang, H., Xie, Y., 2011. A note on the Mohr–Coulomb and Drucker–Prager strength criteria. Mech. Res. Commun. 38 (4), 309–314.

Jivraj, M., Martini, L.G., Thomson, C.M., 2000. An overview of the different excipients useful for the direct compression of tablets. Pharm. Sci. Technol. Today. 3 (2), 58–63.

Kottke, M.K., Rudnic, E.M., 2002. Tablet dosage forms. In: Banker, G.S., Rhodes, C.T. (Eds.), Modern Pharmaceutics. Marcel Dekker, Inc., New York, pp. 437–510.

LaMarche, K., Buckley, D., Hartley, R., Qian, F., Badawy, S., 2014. Assessing materials' tablet compaction properties using the Drucker–Prager cap model. Powder Technol. 267, 208–220.

Lode, W., 1926. Versuche über den Einfluß der mittleren Hauptspannung auf das Fließen der Metalle Eisen, Kupfer und Nickel. Zeitschrift für Physik. 36 (11–12), 913–939.

Martin, C., Bouvard, D., Shima, S., 2003. Study of particle rearrangement during powder compaction by the discrete element method. J. Mech. Phys. Solids. 51 (4), 667–693.

Michrafy, A., Ringenbacher, D., Tchoreloff, P., 2002. Modelling the compaction behaviour of powders: application to pharmaceutical powders. Powder Technol. 127 (3), 257–266.

Procopio, A.T., Zavaliangos, A., 2005. Simulation of multi-axial compaction of granular media from loose to high relative densities. J. Mech. Phys. Solids. 53 (7), 1523–1551.

Redanz, P., Fleck, N.A., 2001. The compaction of a random distribution of metal cylinders by the discrete element method. Acta Mater. 49 (20), 4325–4335.

Schlack, H., Bauer-Brandl, A., Schubert, R., Becker, D., 2001. Properties of Fujicalin, a new modified anhydrous dibasic calcium phosphate for direct compression: comparison with dicalcium phosphate dihydrate. Drug Dev. Ind. Pharm. 27 (8), 789–801.

Shang, C., Sinka, I.C., Pan, J., 2012. Constitutive model calibration for powder compaction using instrumented die testing. Exp. Mech. 52 (7), 903–916.

Sinha, T., Curtis, J.S., Hancock, B.C., Wassgren, C., 2010. A study on the sensitivity of Drucker–Prager cap model parameters during the decompression phase of powder compaction simulations. Powder Technol. 198 (3), 315–324.

Sinka, I., Cunningham, J., Zavaliangos, A., 2003. The effect of wall friction in the compaction of pharmaceutical tablets with curved faces: a validation study of the Drucker–Prager cap model. Powder Technol. 133 (1), 33–43.

Sinka, I., Cunningham, J., Zavaliangos, A., 2004. Analysis of tablet compaction. II. Finite element analysis of density distributions in convex tablets. J. Pharm. Sci. 93 (8), 2040–2053.

Stubberud, L., Arwidsson, H.G., Larsson, A., Graffner, C., 1996. Water solid interactions II. Effect of moisture sorption and glass transition temperature on compactibility of microcrystalline cellulose alone or in binary mixtures with polyvinyl pyrrolidone. Int. J. Pharm. 134 (1), 79–88.

Tvergaard, V., 1990. Material failure by void growth to coalescence. Adv. Appl. Mech. 27 (1), 83–151.

Modeling approaches to multilayer tableting

9

J.M. Rowe and F. Nikfar
Bristol-Myers Squibb, New Brunswick, NJ, United States

9.1 Introduction

Fixed dose combination (FDC) products combine two or more active pharmaceutical ingredients (APIs) into a single dosage form (Desai et al., 2012; Woodcock et al., 2011). The combination of multiple medications into a single dose benefits patients by providing convenience, reduced dosing burdens, and often cost savings (Desai et al., 2012; Abebe et al., 2014). These benefits tend to translate into increased patient compliance. FDCs are also appealing to drug manufacturers because they have the potential to reduce manufacturing costs and they open up opportunities for intellectual property and patent extension (Bangalore et al., 2007; Simon, 2006). In light of the numerous advantages that FDCs have to offer, their popularity has increased over the last couple of decades, especially in disease areas that require large pill burdens and/or chronic dosing, such as diabetes, HIV/AIDS, cardiovascular disease, and hypertension (Desai et al., 2012; Simon, 2006).

FDC products can come in several different packages. In cases where the coadministered APIs are chemically incompatible or where multiple release profiles are desired, layered tablet formulations are preferred. Layered tablet formulations composed of two layers are referred to as bilayer tablets. Layered tablet formulations can conceivably contain multiple layers, i.e., trilayer (three layers); for the sake of simplicity, this chapter will use bilayer tablets as the model for layered tablet formulations. The production of bilayer tablets consists of sequentially compacting layers of different drug formulations atop one another, as illustrated in Fig. 9.1. Briefly, the first layer material is added to the die and a first layer compaction force, F1, is applied. Typically, the magnitude of F1 is relatively low, as F1 often serves solely as a tamping force to minimize mixing between the first and second layer and to provide an even surface for the second layer material. The second layer material is added to the die, atop the first layer, and a second layer compaction force, F2, is applied to form the tablet. For the remainder of the chapter, the general notation of bilayer tablet composition will be as follows: first layer (bottom) material/second layer (top) material.

At first glance, bilayer compaction appears to be no more complicated than monolithic compaction. However, the addition of a second compaction event to the tableting process introduces an extra degree of complexity that scientists have yet

Predictive Modeling of Pharmaceutical Unit Operations. DOI: http://dx.doi.org/10.1016/B978-0-08-100154-7.00009-0

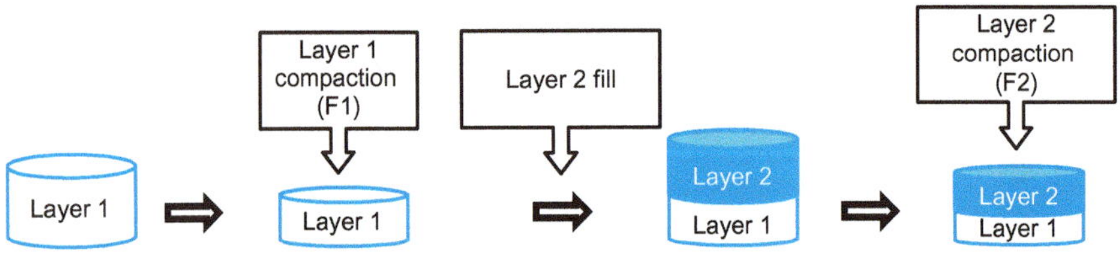

Figure 9.1 Illustration of bilayer compaction process.

to master. Because layered tablet dosage forms are often selected when chemical incompatibilities between APIs have been identified (or when different release profiles are desired), a sufficient physical separation between the APIs in the first and second layers is imperative. Throughout the remainder of the text, the term interface will refer to the boundary between the first and second layers of the tablet.

An abundant number of studies has been conducted to draw relationships between experimental factors and tablet delamination, including assessments of lubricant levels, compaction forces (Dietrich et al., 2000), tablet interface topographies (Inman et al., 2007; Inman et al., 2009; Kottala et al., 2012), elastic mismatch (Anuar and Briscoe, 2009; Anuar and Briscoe, 2010), critical stress intensity factors (Podczeck, 2011), thermal stresses and strains (Podczeck, 2011), coating conditions (Breech et al., 1988; Zacour et al., 2014), and the probing of mechanical properties using air-coupled acoustics (Akseli et al., 2010). Each of these studies sheds insight into important aspects of the bilayer compaction process and highlights desirable characteristics of successful bilayer tablets. However, a strong mechanistic understanding of the bilayer compaction process has not been elucidated from these observations and a robust approach to bilayer compaction has not been established. This chapter will discuss efforts that have been taken to increase the industry's understanding of the bilayer compaction process, with an emphasis on modeling efforts.

9.2 Models

In its simplest form, the bilayer compaction process may be separated into two distinct events: tablet compaction and tablet relaxation. Applying this perspective, the manufacture of robust bilayer tablets, i.e., tablets possessing strong interfaces, may be achieved by a couple of different approaches: (1) maximizing layer adhesion during the compaction step and/or (2) minimizing interfacial stresses during tablet relaxation (Fig. 9.2). Several models have been proposed to predict bilayer tablet performance and these models tend to fall into one of these categories, focusing either on maximizing layer adhesion or minimizing interfacial stresses. To date, there is no known model that encompasses both events of the bilayer compaction process. Therefore, none of these models independently accounts for all aspects of bilayer compaction, nor have they been rigorously tested in terms of material selection and operating conditions. However, these models have provided a rational scientific framework to

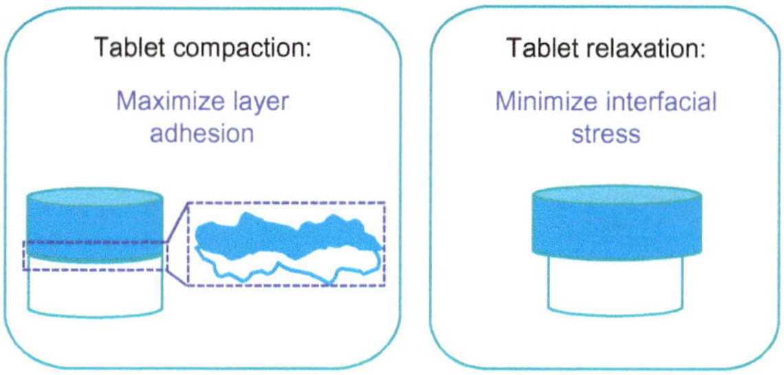

Figure 9.2 Bilayer compaction process may be divided into two events: compaction and relaxation. To make robust tablets, focus can be applied toward maximizing layer adhesion during tablet compaction and/or minimizing interfacial stresses between the layers during tablet relaxation.

probe underlying mechanisms that drive the operation and have improved our understanding of the relative importance of the process's multiple interrelated input factors, including material, equipment, and process considerations.

9.2.1 Theories focusing on understanding layer adhesion/layer strength

9.2.1.1 Empirical correlations: use of mixing rules to estimate bilayer tablet strength

A simple predictive model, based on the Ryshkewitch–Duckworth (R–D) equation (Ryshkewitch, 1953; Duckworth, 1953), has been used to predict the tensile strengths, σ_T, of multicomponent compacts based upon material properties:

$$\ln(\sigma_T) = (RD - 1)\sum_{1}^{n} k_i\zeta_i + \ln\left(\sum_{1}^{n} \sigma_i^*\zeta_i\right) \tag{9.1}$$

where i denotes an individual component, n is the number of total components, RD is the compact's relative density, k is a material constant representing bonding capacity, σ^* is the material's tensile strength at zero porosity (RD = 1), and ζ is the volume fraction of the constituent powder. The parameters k and σ^* are determined from uniaxial compression tests on the individual materials. Therefore, the R–D equation assumes that compactability parameters linked to tablet strength, such as bonding capacity and maximum tensile strengths, are additive properties. Previously, the R–D equation had been shown to effectively predict tensile strengths of monolithic multicomponent tablets (mixture of two or more APIs compressed into a monolithic tablet) (Wu et al., 2005; Michrafy et al., 2007; Wu et al., 2006). Wu and Seville (2009) demonstrated the applicability of the R–D equation to bilayer tablets. The strengths of microcrystalline cellulose (MCC)/lactose monohydrate bilayer tablets (80/20 and 20/80 w/w) were well-modeled by the R–D equation, accurately predicting tensile strengths of tablets with RDs ranging from 0.6 to 0.9. Furthermore, for a given

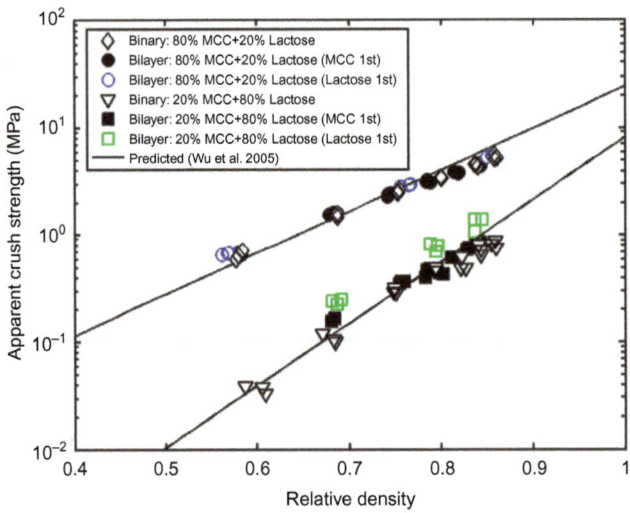

Figure 9.3 Variation of apparent crush strength, as a function of relative density, for both binary and bilayer tablets. The points on the graph represent experimental data and the lines indicate the R–D predictions. Both binary and bilayer tablets adhere to the R–D equation (Wu and Seville, 2009).
Source: Copyright © 2009, with permission from Elsevier.

compact RD, bilayer tablets demonstrated a comparable strength to binary tablets of the same composition (Fig. 9.3). In the study, tablet strength, determined using a hardness tester, was referred to as apparent crush strength, as the failures were not necessarily purely diametrical. Regardless of layer sequence and the layer weight ratio, the bilayer tablets strengths were well-predicted by the R–D equation and possessed comparable strengths as that of monolithic tablets composed of the same formulation.

This observation may suggest that a small degree of mixing between the materials in the different layers occurs during the compaction process. Hence, the interface of a bilayer tablet, which is generally the weakest portion of the tablet, would be expected to possess similar strength to a binary tablet of the same composition. It should be noted, however, that the tablets in this study were manufactured using a manual press and a first layer compression force, F1, was not applied. Application of a first layer tamping force is typical practice during commercial tablet manufacture to minimize mixing between the two layers and thus is necessary if the two APIs are chemically incompatible. From the literature, it is well known that varying the extent of F1 significantly impacts the interface strength bilayer tablets (Desai et al., 2012; Kottala et al., 2012; Vaithiyalingam and Sayeed, 2010). Because an F1 was not applied in this study, the degree of mixing between the first and second layers is likely to be greater than that of commercially manufactured tablet and thus this model would likely overestimate the strengths of commercial bilayer tablets. Belda and Mielck (2005, 2006) utilized a similar approach, except that the compaction behavior of layered compacts was used to predict the compression behavior of powder mixtures. In this work, a double-layer model, based on parameters extracted from Heckel plots and layered tablet strengths, was proposed as an alternative to arithmetic additivity rules, such as the R–D equation, to predict the tablet strengths of blended mixtures. The strengths of compacted blends were reported to be better predicted using the proposed double-layer model compared to predictions from additivity rules.

9.2.1.2 Application of fracture mechanics concepts

Tablet fractures result from the propagation of a crack, or several cracks, within a sample. Tablet fractures are typically categorized under two groups: lamination and capping. Lamination results when internal cracks within the tablet weaken its strength. Capping occurs when the top of a tablet separates from the rest of the body. The mechanisms that cause capping have been likened to those driving the delamination of bilayer tablets (Inman et al., 2007). To better understand the forces that drive delamination, concepts from fracture mechanics have been applied. The field of fracture mechanics studies the propagation of cracks in materials, applying the physics of stress and strain, and concepts from solid mechanics to calculate the driving force on a crack and a material's resistance to fracture. Three modes of loading are defined in fracture mechanics (Fig. 9.4):

1. Mode I: Opening mode, tensile stress normal to the crack.
2. Mode II: Sliding mode, shear stress acting parallel to crack plane and perpendicular to crack front.
3. Mode III: Tearing mode, shear stress acting parallel to crack plane and parallel to crack front.

The mode of fracture within a tablet is dependent upon tablet geometry and interfacial topography; fracture mechanics parameters have been defined as a method to quantify and compare fracture behavior. The use of fracture mechanics parameters to describe failure behavior in monolithic pharmaceutical tablets has been reported (Hancock et al., 2000; Mashadi and Newton, 1987; Mashadi and Newton, 1988; Roberts and Rowe, 1989; Roberts et al., 1993; York et al., 1990), although the results have been highly variable over a range of studies. Table 9.1

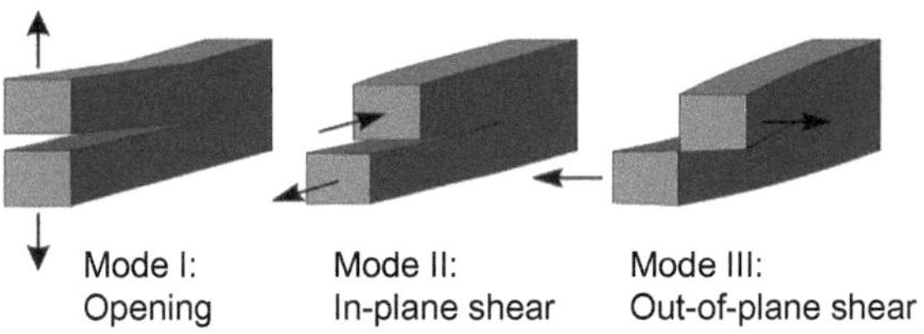

Figure 9.4 Schematic of the three fracture modes.
Source: Courtesy of Wikimedia Commons (https://commons.wikimedia.org/wiki/File:Fracture_modes_v2.svg).

Table 9.1 Reported values of the critical stress intensity factor, K_{1C0}, at zero porosity

Material	K^1_{IC0} (MPa m$^{0.5}$)	Characterization test	Notch type	References
Avicel PH101	2.98/2.24	Radially edge crack disk (compression)	Precrack	Roberts and Rowe (1989)
Avicel PH101	1.81	Double torsion	Precrack	Mashadi and Newton (1988)
Avicel PH101	1.21	Four-point SENB[a]	V	Mashadi and Newton (1988)
Avicel PH101	0.87	Four-point SENB[a]	Straight	York et al. (1990)
Avicel PH102	0.76	Four-point SENB[a]	Straight	York et al. (1990)
Avicel PH101	0.76	Three-point SENB[a]	Razor	Roberts et al. (1993)
Avicel PH102	0.72	Axial tensile test	V	Inman et al. (2008)
Avicel PH101	0.69	Three-point SENB[a]	Sawn	Roberts et al. (1993)
Avicel PH101	0.46	Three-point SENB[a]	V	Hancock et al. (2000)
Acetylsalicylic acid	0.37	Three-point SENB[a]	Sawn	Podczeck (2001)
Lactose Monohydrate	0.49	Three-point SENB[a]	Sawn	Podczeck (2001)

[a]*SENB*, single-edge notched beam.

lists reported values for the fracture mechanic parameter K_{1C0}, which provides an indication of a material's brittleness at zero porosity, for several materials. The variability in calculated K_{1C0} values have been attributed numerous factors:

- porosity of tablets complicates determination of input parameters, i.e., crack length (Roberts and Rowe, 1989);
- sensitivity to sample preparation, accurate input parameters i.e., notch type (Inman et al., 2008), measurement of notch lengths (Roberts and Rowe, 1989), method of data fitting (Mashadi and Newton, 1987; Mashadi and Newton, 1988; Roberts et al., 1993); and
- sensitivity to fracture test used to obtain fracture data (Inman et al., 2008).

These results demonstrate the importance of accurate, robust characterization methods when developing models intended to describe phenomenological behavior.

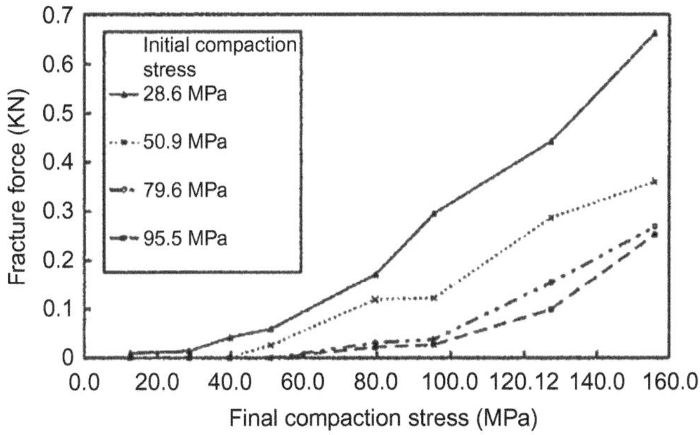

Figure 9.5 Fracture force of bilayer tablets of MCC. Each data set represents an initial compaction force, F1, with increasing final compaction force, F2. Error bars represent one standard deviation (Inman et al., 2007).
Source: Copyright © 2007, with permission from Elsevier.

To date, however, characterization methods for the assessment of bilayer tablets have not been standardized. In fact, the application of fracture mechanics to bilayer compaction has been primarily qualitative thus far. The compaction process consists of the application of stress to a powder bed by a tablet punch, generally possessing a smooth stainless steel surface, which has been suggested to smooth out surface asperities of the powder bed. In a study by Inman et al. (2009), the average rough ness parameter, R_a, as determined by laser profilometry, of the surface of a powder bed that has undergone compaction was shown to decrease as compaction force was increased (Inman et al., 2009). This relationship seems plausible, as higher compaction forces would be more likely to smooth out surface asperities, resulting in lower roughness parameters. Correspondingly, the fracture force, as determined by an axial tester, was found to decrease as the first layer compaction stress, F1, increased (Fig. 9.5; Inman et al., 2007), which is in accordance with other published studies (Kottala et al., 2012).

The results from these studies clearly demonstrate that interfaces possessing a higher degree of roughness (i.e., R_a and R_q) are stronger, thus requiring higher forces to fracture the tablet compared to tablets with smoother interfaces. Asperities on the surface of the first layer of a bilayer tablet are hypothesized to provide sites for second layer material particles to nest or interlock, which not only increases the contact area between the second layer particles to the first layer surface, but also promotes mechanical interlocking of particles. Mechanical interlocking between particles creates a more tortuous path between the two layers, which is more likely to result in failure by mixed modes. Mixed mode failures are more energetically demanding than single failure modes alone, making the resultant tablet more robust against delamination. In contrast, as the roughness of the first layer surface is reduced, second layer particles are more inclined to sit atop the surface, limiting interactions between the two layers due to small contact areas (Inman et al., 2007; Inman et al., 2009; Kottala et al., 2012; Inman et al., 2008).

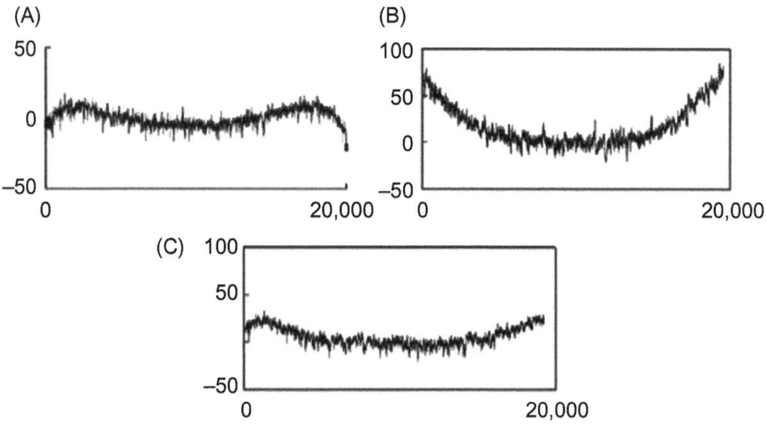

Figure 9.6 Radial profiles of the surfaces of (A) A monolithic MCC tablet and (B) The first and (C) Second layers of a MCC/MCC bilayer tablet. The compaction stress applied to the monolithic tablet was 50.9 MPa. The first, F1, and second layer, F2, compaction stress of the bilayer tablet was 50.9 MPa. All axes are in micron units (Inman et al., 2009).
Source: Copyright © 2009, with permission from Elsevier.

This line of thought is consistent with experiments that compare tablets manufactured using a single compression step versus a double compression process. The addition of a second compression step significantly impacts tablet properties, where the weakest region of the tablet is generally found at the interface. This observation is true regardless of whether or not the first and second layers consist of the same material. The application of multiple compression forces and the resultant creation of new interfaces drastically influence particle bonding within the tablet. To demonstrate this point, radial topographical profiles of MCC tablets manufactured by a single and double compression step are shown in Fig. 9.6 (Inman et al., 2009). From this work, it can be implied that the generation of an interface (after the application of F1), especially one that will be inherently uneven due to die wall friction effects, creates a region of weakness in bilayer tablets. Strong die wall frictional forces do not allow material in contact with the die wall to relax to the same extent as material farther from the die wall, creating nonuniform stress during relaxation and nonuniform volume expansion. When another layer of material is further compressed atop such a nonideal base, nonhomogeneity of strain energy gradients throughout the tablet is magnified, leading to uneven dissipation of stored elastic energy at the interface. These strain energy gradients across a tablet interface are exacerbated during unloading of the punch through tablet ejection, causing an increase in the tendency for tablets to fracture and lead to delamination. As such, robust bilayer tablets require high levels of mechanical interlocking between interfacial particles so that the energy required to fracture the compact exceeds the strain energy generated by nonuniform expansion. This concept will be further discussed later in the chapter. Case study 1 demonstrates the use of fracture mechanics analysis to assess delamination risk of bilayer compacts.

9.2.2 Theories focusing on understanding the role of material relaxation on delamination

Elastic mismatch is another driver for delamination in bilayer tablets. Elastic mismatch is defined as the difference in the elastic properties of the two layers and is hypothesized to facilitate stress concentrations and complex loading conditions near the tablet interface (Podczeck, 2011; Panos and Zavaliangos, 2007). The effects of elastic mismatch are not isolated to post-compaction events, and may be evident during the compaction process, impacting the interfacial topography as discussed in the previous section. Post-compaction, accumulation of elastic mismatch stresses tends to propagate in the form of residual stresses, which affect tablet behavior during relaxation and ejection events. For instance, as a tablet is ejected, the powders expand in the radial direction. If the bilayer tablet is composed of materials that possess different elastic properties, then those two layers are likely to expand at different rates and to different extents. In addition to exhibiting differential expansion, the two layers are also likely to have accumulated different levels of residual wall stresses after unloading. These factors potentially lead to internal stresses within the tablet that may cause spontaneous delamination upon ejection or the formation of cracks (which may not necessarily be visible to the eye) that can significantly reduce the tablet's strength (Panos and Zavaliangos, 2007).

Material mismatch has been difficult to quantify and analyze because of its dependency on RD, which varies throughout the compact, especially in the case of bilayer tablets. As such, the link between elastic mismatch and bilayer tablet delamination has been primarily qualitative. Inman et al. reported nonhomogeneous topographical profiles of interfacial surfaces of MCC/MCC bilayer tablets after the tablets were fractured by axial testing, which were attributed to the uneven dissipation of stored elastic energy that built up during the compaction process. The release of this stored energy during the unloading stage through the ejection process was hypothesized to weaken the mechanical strengths of tablets, leading to delamination (Inman et al., 2007; Inman et al., 2009; Inman et al., 2008). To further establish the link between elastic mismatch and tablet integrity, elastic relaxation at the interface of bilayer tablets was quantified using a laser micrometer to continuously measure the dimensions (axial and radial) of MCC/MCC bilayer tablets as they were being ejected from a die (Anuar and Briscoe, 2010). Interfacial regions of the tablet were detected by a sudden change in tablet diameter (i.e., difference in relaxation behavior between layers).

To better quantify observations of elastic mismatch, Mazel et al. (2012, 2013) investigated which material properties most influenced the elastic behavior of pharmaceutical materials. Traditionally in the ceramics and polymer industries, elastic behavior of materials is often quantified using mechanical properties, such as Young's modulus and Poisson's ratio. Adaptation of these mechanical property descriptors to the pharmaceutical industry has not been trivial due to their dependency on porosity. Several approaches have been proposed to address this gap, including the extrapolation of these mechanical properties to zero porosity [i.e., E_0 = Young's modulus at zero porosity

(Bassam et al., 1990; Kachrimanis and Malamataris, 2004; Roberts and Rowe, 1987)] and the modification of classical equations and terms to make them more appropriate for pharmaceutical materials (Kachrimanis and Malamataris, 2004; Han et al., 2008; LaMarche et al., 2014). Caution should be used when using mechanical property values that have been extrapolated to zero porosity, as the specific value depends on the chosen mathematical model and the zero porosity level is not representative of the elastic behavior of pharmaceutical compacts. A more appropriate approach has been the use of modified methods to calculate Young's modulus and Poisson's ratio as a function of porosity (Mazel et al., 2012; Mazel et al., 2013; Kachrimanis and Malamataris, 2004; Han et al., 2008). Strategies for calculating Young's modulus and Poisson's ratio values have included the use of novel calibration procedures using an instrumented die (Han et al., 2008; LaMarche et al., 2014), a double compaction method using an instrumented die (Mazel et al., 2012), and the use of experimentally determined radial elastic recovery data to estimate relevant values (Kachrimanis and Malamataris, 2004).

When trying to correlate elastic behavior to the mechanical strength of compacts, much of the literature has focused on the use of Young's modulus (Podczeck, 2011; Bassam et al., 1990; Kachrimanis and Malamataris, 2004; Roberts and Rowe, 1987; Busignies et al., 2004; Kerridge and Newton, 1986). Podczek (2011) reported associations between thermal stresses generated during the compaction of layered beams to their tensile strengths. When thermal stresses were greater than typical tensile stresses of the beams (2−3 MPa), delamination was predicted. Because stiffer materials (i.e., materials with higher Young's modulus) tend to produce larger thermal stresses during compaction, these materials were hypothesized to be more prone to delamination. This correlation, however, was only demonstrated for bilayer combinations of lactose monohydrate and acetylsalicylic acid. Further work has not been conducted to qualify this correlation, especially not for compacts produced under relevant commercial manufacturing conditions (i.e., rotary press). In general, conclusive relationships between Young's modulus and tensile strength have not been established. Even Podczek's study (Podczeck, 2011) implied that elastic mismatch between layers played a more dominant role in delamination compared to thermal stresses generated during the compaction process, an observation later confirmed in another study that reported bilayer beams composed of materials with more similar elastic recovery behavior possessed higher tensile strengths (Busignies et al., 2013).

Despite the lack of traction in linking Young's modulus and elastic mismatch to tensile strength, few studies have attempted to make correlations to Poisson's ratio, likely due to the experimental tediousness required to calculate Poisson's ratio values, which require numerous precise measurements (Roberts et al., 1994). In fact, Poisson's ratio values of pharmaceutical materials are commonly assumed to be constant, at a value of 0.3, which is the value determined for MCC (Roberts et al., 1994). On the contrary, Poisson's ratio values can vary significantly for different materials and is highly dependent upon porosity. An example of how drastically the Poisson's ratio values can change as a function of both material and porosity is shown in Fig. 9.7 (Mazel et al., 2012), where the profile of a plastic material (MCC) is compared to that of a more brittle material (anhydrous calcium phosphate).

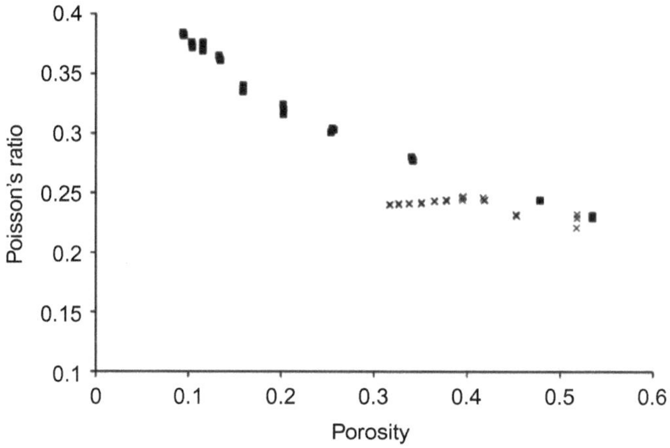

Figure 9.7 Poisson's ratio profile, as a function of porosity for (x) anhydrous calcium phosphate and (■) MCC (Mazel et al., 2012).
Source: Copyright © 2012 by John Wiley & Sons, Inc. Reprinted by permission of John Wiley & Sons, Inc.

Mazel et al. characterized the elastic behavior of four materials (MCC, anhydrous calcium phosphate, ibuprofen, and mannitol) using elastic recovery ($\%ER_t$), which was defined as (Mazel et al., 2013):

$$\%ER_t = \frac{V_f - V_{min}}{V_{min}} \times 100 \tag{9.2}$$

where V_f is the final volume of the tablet (directly after ejection) and V_{min} is the minimal volume of the tablet (during compaction). A correlation was not observed between $\%ER_t$ and Young's modulus, E; however, a clear relationship was apparent between $\%ER_t$ and Poisson's ratio, v, which was represented in the form of the bulk modulus, K (Mazel et al., 2013). Busignies et al. further examined the use of $\%ER_t$ as an appropriate quantifier for the elastic behavior of bilayer tablets, extending its correlation to tablet tensile strengths. In the case of bilayer compacts, elastic mismatch is a result of the difference in the elastic behavior of the two layers. Thus, the difference of total elastic recovery, DER_t, was defined as (Busignies et al., 2013; Busignies et al., 2014)

$$DER_t = |\%ER_{t,1} - \%ER_{t,2}| \tag{9.3}$$

where $\%ER_{t,1}$ and $\%ER_{t,2}$ are the total elastic recovery of the materials of layer 1 and layer 2, respectively. Fig. 9.8, which incorporates data from multiple bilayer combinations, clearly illustrates that material combinations with lower DER_t possess higher tablet strengths, where strengths were measured using a novel technique described in Busignies et al. (Busignies et al., 2014).

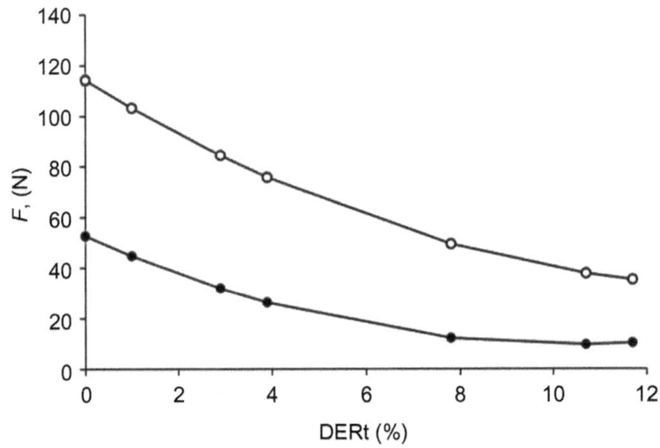

Figure 9.8 Effect of DER_t and compaction pressure on the strength of bilayer tablets (● second layer compaction pressure = 100 MPa; ○ second layer compaction pressure = 250 MPa; 11.28 mm round, flat-faced tooling). Measurements conducted for bilayer tablets manufactured for all permutations of the following materials: calcium phosphate (dihydrate), microcrystalline cellulose, lactose monohydrate, hydroxypropyl methylcellulose. First layer compaction pressures ranged between 10–50 MPa. Tablets that delaminated immediately upon ejection were not included in the analysis (Busignies et al., 2014). *Source*: Copyright © 2014, with permission from Elsevier.

An alternative approach to using DER_t to quantify elastic mismatch within a bilayer tablet is to focus only on the difference between the Poisson's ratios of the two layers. In a study by Rowe et al. (2014, 2015), robustness of bilayer tablets correlated well with the difference in Poisson's ratios of the two layers, Δv

$$\Delta v(\%) = \frac{2 \times |v_1 - v_2|}{v_1 + v_2} \times 100 \qquad (9.4)$$

where v_1 and v_2 are the Poisson's ratios of layer 1 and layer 2, respectively. Bilayer tablets were manufactured using a compaction simulator. Poisson's ratio profiles for each of the materials were determined using previously described methods (Han et al., 2008; LaMarche et al., 2014). In this work, it was observed that tablets did not delaminate when $\Delta v < 25\%$ for over 4 weeks of storage at room conditions, suggesting that bilayer tablets formulated such that $\Delta v < 25\%$ are more likely to remain intact. Furthermore, this study suggests that the use of Poisson's ratio sufficiently describes material elastic behavior in bilayer tablets to provide an indication of delamination; therefore, when the Poisson's ratios of the two layers are within 25% of each other, the relaxation behavior of the layers are similar enough to minimize delamination tendencies.

Table 9.2 lists experimentally measured shear and axial strengths for additional bilayer tablet combinations (compressed using F1 = 0.7 kN; F2 = 18 kN). Despite the high degree of variability observed in the axial strengths, which is consistent with previous studies (Inman et al., 2008; Akseli et al., 2013; Franck et al., 2013), it still provides an

Table 9.2 Shear strength, axial strength, and $\Delta\nu$ values for bilayer tablets

Layer 1/2	Shear strength (MPa), $n = 6$	Axial strength (N), $n = 3$	$\Delta\nu$ (%)	Delaminated at 4 wks
DCP/MCC	4.11 ± 0.38	68 ± 39	17	No
DCP/Starch	2.01 ± 0.15	51 ± 13	24	No
Starch/DCP	2.45 ± 0.11	42 ± 12	20	No
MCC/DCP	3.89 ± 0.27	36 ± 27	21	No
MCC/LAC	2.00 ± 0.45	22 ± 8	26	Yes
LAC/DCP	1.23 ± 0.26	9 ± 9	21	No
MCC/Starch	1.44 ± 0.78	0	28	Yes
Starch/MCC	2.17 ± 0.05	3 ± 2	28	Yes
DCP/LAC	0.64 ± 0.54	3 ± 2	24	No
Starch/LAC	0.46 ± 0.15	2 ± 2	41	Yes (weak at ejection)
LAC/Starch	0.19 ± 0.10	0	43	Yes (weak at ejection)
LAC/MCC	0	0	36	Yes (at ejection)

MCC, Microcrystalline cellulose.
LAC, lactose.
DCP, Dicalcium phosphate.
Starch, pre-gelatanized starch.
Tablets manufactured using an ESH compaction simulator and 3/8 diameter, round, flat-faced tooling (500 mg total weight; 250 mg per layer; F1 = 0.7 kN; F2 = 18 kN). Visual examination for tablet delamination performed at 4 weeks of storage at room conditions.
Source: Reprinted with permission from Rowe et al. (2014).

indication of which combinations possessed adequate strength versus those that had a high tendency to delaminate. Additionally, the majority of the bilayer combinations examined demonstrated reasonable correlations between shear strengths and axial strengths. However, it is clear that shear and axial strengths are not interchangeable, as demonstrated in the case of MCC/starch combinations where reasonable shear strengths were achieved, but the axial strengths were extremely weak. The axial strengths were more representative of the robustness of the tablets, as tablets composed of the MCC/starch combination delaminated when light pressure was applied to the tablet by squeezing it between one's fingers. Thus, delamination observations of tablets stored at room conditions correlated well with the guidance that combinations where $\Delta\nu > 25\%$ tend to delaminate.

To extend the knowledge gained from analyzing the Poisson's ratios of a bilayer system, Rowe et al. (2014, 2015) presented a method to predict the probability of delamination using a Poisson's ratio map. A Poisson's ratio map is a contour chart that plots $\Delta\nu$ values for a material combination as a function of the RD of each of the layers. An example of a Poisson's ratio map is shown in Fig. 9.9. The combination of layer RDs that results in $\Delta\nu$ values less than 25% are shaded blue; those that result in $\Delta\nu$ values between 25% and 50% are shaded red. Thus, Poisson's ratio maps consolidate and facilitate visualization of Poisson's ratio data with respect to tablet robustness. They can be used to highlight compaction conditions at which differences in Poisson's ratio, and thus relaxation behavior, between the two layers is

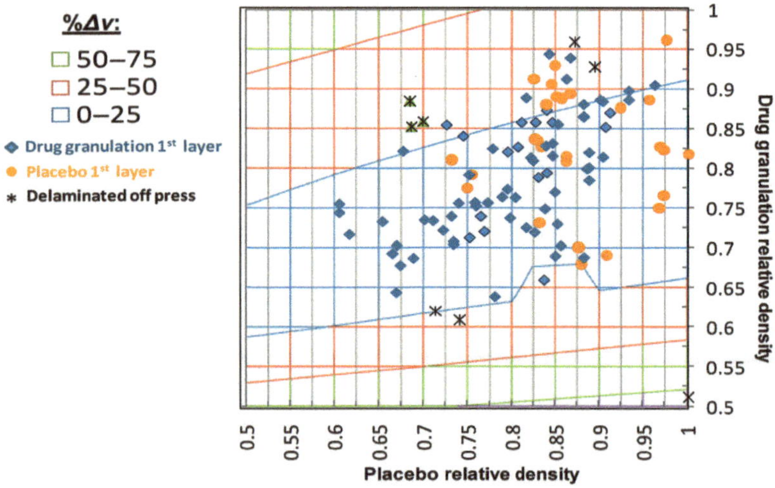

Figure 9.9 Values of Δv plotted as a function of the relative densities (RDs) of each of the layers to create Poisson's ratio maps. Poisson's ratio maps of bilayer tablet compositions consisting of a placebo blend and an active blend, (♦) intact tablets where the active blend was used as the first layer, (●) intact tablets where the placebo blend was used as the first layer, and (*) delaminated tablets.
Source: Reprinted with permission from Rowe et al. (2014).

minimized. In other words, tablets that lie in the blue region are not expected to delaminate. Outside of the blue region, tablets are expected to be more likely to delaminate. To test the accuracy of the Poisson's ratio maps, bilayer tablets composed of a placebo and active blend (~30% drug load, wet granulated) were manufactured under different compaction forces and are indicated as points on the maps. As seen in the figure, the map provided relatively good predictions of bilayer tablet delamination. The solid points on the plot represent intact tablets that were manufactured with either the placebo or the active blend serving as the first layer, while the asterisks represent tablets that delaminated directly off the press. The Poisson's ratio map provided reasonable guidance regarding delamination tendencies and generation of Poisson's ratio maps requires little material, on the order of 30 grams per layer, and does not require the manufacture of a single bilayer tablet because Poisson's ratios are determined for individual materials, not bilayer combinations. Case Study 2 demonstrates the utility of Poisson's ratio maps to guide efficient bilayer tablet formulation development activities from small scale (compaction simulator) to pilot and commercial scale (rotary press).

9.2.3 Numerical simulation

Limited studies have been reported on the numerical simulation of the bilayer compaction process due to challenges with defining appropriate boundary conditions, specifically due to the ever-changing interfacial region during both compaction and ejection events.

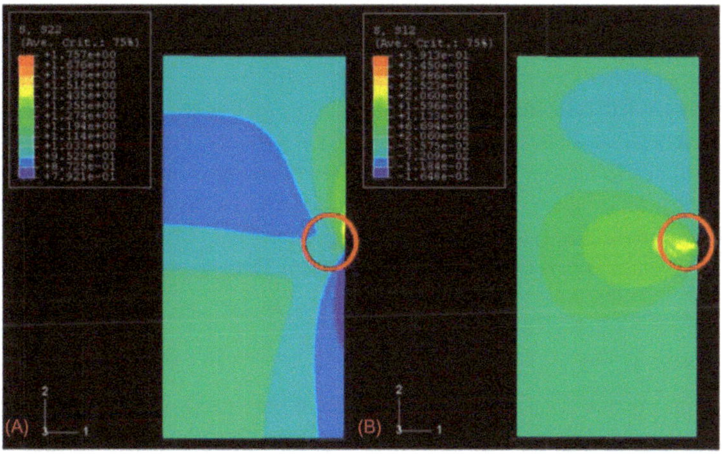

Figure 9.10 Finite element method (FEM) model of a half-tablet (axisymmetric around vertical axis) during tension of a two-layer specimen. Dundurs parameters: $\alpha = 0.54$, $\beta = 0.31$. Stress singularities exist in S22 and S12 at the interface, as highlighted by the red circles.
Source: Reprinted with permission from Sexton et al. (2008).

Sexton et al. (2008) developed a finite element method (FEM) model to understand stress distributions along the interface of a bilayer tablet, allowing the points at which the interface meets the free surface to exist as stress singularities. Local stress fields were defined using Dundurs parameters (Bogy, 1970; Dundurs, 1967). The FEM analysis, shown in Fig. 9.10, indicated the existence of high stress areas, depicted as singularities, along the interfacial region of a bilayer tablet. The primary objective of this work was to understand the evolution of shear stresses within a bilayer tablet when subjected to a shear test. The singularities detected at the interface of a nonstressed bilayer tablet were about seven orders of magnitude weaker than the predicted singularities of a tablet undergoing shear testing. Experimental validation of the FEM simulations was not performed.

FEM simulations have also been used to study the impact of tamping, i.e., F1, the direction of compaction on delamination, and the impact of using one-sided compression versus two-sided compression. Results suggested that simultaneous compaction is desirable to achieve a more even interface for bilayer tablets. All of the simulations performed also showed that the stresses in a bilayer tablets are focused at the interface, and, in this particular case, larger stresses occur in the DCP layer versus the MCC layer. These results were consistent with x-ray transmission data, where crack formation was seen to initiate in the DCP layer, eventually leading to delamination. Additional modifications to the modeling strategy are ongoing to better approximate yield strengths of the powder.

9.3 Conclusions

Modeling the compaction process of layered tablets is still in its infancy, as many questions and uncertainties still exist regarding whether the appropriate tools and methods have been identified to accurately simulate this complex process. However, this chapter highlights the primary schools of thought regarding current modeling approaches for the multilayer compaction, including theories focused on predicting layer adhesion during the compaction process and those concentrating on predicting relaxation behavior. While the majority of the models is still in the early stages, valuable mechanistic knowledge has been generated on multilayer compaction that has served to enhance development activities and validate empirical heuristics, as illustrated in several case studies. Clearly, the continued development of these tools and models are an integral part to the growing success of FDC dosage forms.

Case Study 1: Use of Fracture Mechanics to Predict Delamination

This section is based on a study reported by Podczeck (Podczeck, 2011).

Materials and methods

Materials

The following materials were used:

- Acetylsalicylic acid (ASS)
- Lactose monohydrate (LM)

Beam manufacture

Bilayer beams were manufactured ($45 \times 9 \times 5$ mm^3) using a split die and compaction forces applied using a hydraulic press. Notched beams were manufactured for the determination of far field stress intensity factors. A pull saw was used to produce sharp notches of 100 μm in width. Notch depths for ASS and LM beams were 800 and 600 μm, respectively, based on known depths that yield stable, controlled crack propagation for these materials (Podczeck, 2001). The following compact orientations were manufactured:

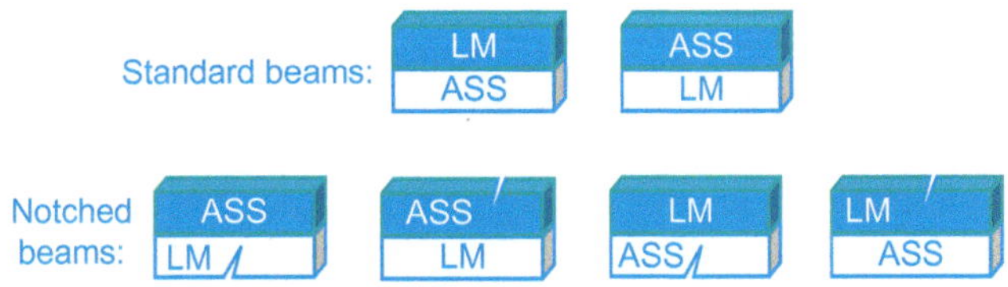

Determination of breaking load

A three-point bending test, using a universal strength tester, test speed of 1 mm/min, and a 5-kg load cell, was employed. The notched beams were tested such that the notched face was oriented downward.

Fracture mechanics calculations

The critical stress intensity factor, K_{IC}^{1}, was calculated as follows:

$$K_{IC}^{1} = Y\frac{6Ma^{0.5}}{bt^2}, \quad \text{where} \quad M = \frac{Pl}{4} \quad \text{and}$$

$$Y = C_0 + C_1\left(\frac{a}{t}\right) + C_2\left(\frac{a}{t}\right)^2 + C_3\left(\frac{a}{t}\right)^3 + C_4\left(\frac{a}{t}\right)^4$$

where M is the bending moment, a is the notch depth, b is the beam width, t is the beam thickness, P is the load applied to the beam that causes failure, l is the distance between the beam supports, and Y is a calibration term defined by Gross and Srawley (1965) and Podczeck (1998).

Far field stress intensity factor (K_{IC}^{∞}) was calculated using

$$K_{IC}^{\infty} = \frac{K_{IC}^{1}}{p}, \quad \text{where} \quad p = \sqrt{\frac{1-\alpha_D}{1-\beta_D}}$$

where p is an elastic mismatch constant and α_D and β_D are Dundurs parameters (Dundurs, 1967). Values of p for ASS and LM were determined to be 0.884 and 0.733, respectively.

$$K_{IC0}^{\infty} = K_{IC}^{\infty} e^{\mathrm{bf} \times \mathrm{por}}$$

where bf is an experimental constant and por is porosity, which was determined in two manners: BP = overall beam porosity or LLP = porosity of the lower layer.

Critical stress intensity factor of the interface in mode I, K_{IC}^{IF}, was calculated using

$$K_{IC}^{IF} = \sigma_{\text{upper layer}}\sqrt{h_{\text{upper layer}}}\,\Omega(\alpha_D, \lambda_0)$$

where $\sigma_{\text{upper layer}}$ is the residual stress in the upper layer, $h_{\text{upper layer}}$ is the thickness of the upper layer, and Ω is a decohesion number.

Critical strain energy release rate of the interface (far field solution), G_{IC}^{∞}, was determined by

$$G_{IC}^{\infty} = \frac{\left(K_{IC}^{\infty}\right)^2}{E'} \quad \text{where} \quad E' = \frac{E_{\text{upper layer}}}{\left(1-\nu_{\text{upper layer}}\right)}$$

where E is the Young's modulus and ν is the Poisson's ratio of the unnotched layer.

(Continued)

(cont'd)

Results

A summary of the results from the fracture mechanics analysis of ASS and LM compacts is shown next:

Material	K^1_{IC0} (kPa m$^{0.5}$)	K^{IF}_{IC} (kPa m$^{0.5}$)	K^{∞}_{IC0} (kPa m$^{0.5}$)	G^1_{IC} (N/m)	G^{∞}_{IC} (N/m)
ASS	366 ± 12	–	–	66.2	–
LM	493 ± 32	–	–	74.0	–
ASS/LM	–	160	–	–	–
LM/ASS	–	53	–	–	–
ASS/LM(n)	–	–	175.5 ± 11.1 (BP) 172.9 ± 13.7 (LLP)	–	11.88
ASS(n)/LM	–	–	498.9 ± 38.3 (BP) 453.6 ± 31.2 (LLP)	–	66.59
LM/ASS(n)	–	–	428.1 ± 22.6 (BP) 450.1 ± 35.5 (LLP)	–	49.03
LM(n)/ASS	–	–	186.9 ± 7.8 (BP) 171.3 ± 13.2 (LLP)	–	13.48

n denotes the layer in which the notch was placed.

Compacts are likely to delaminate when:

1. G^{∞}_{IC} (unnotched layer) $<0.25 * G^1_{IC}$. This predicts delamination for test configuration when ASS is the unnotched layer, where G^1_{IC} is the critical strain energy release rate for a material undergoing mode I stress; G^1_{IC} values for ASS and LM were reported by Podczeck (1998).
2. When $K^{IF}_{IC} < K^{\infty}_{IC0} < K^1_{IC0}$. This predicts delamination in all cases.

Overall conclusions of stress intensity factor analysis suggest delamination likely for layered compacts composed of ASS and LM; experimental observations confirm predictions, regardless of which material was in the upper layer. Beams consisting of ASS in the upper layer were stronger than beams where LM was in the upper layer.

Case Study 2: Use of Poisson's Ratio Map to Predict Impact of Formulation Changes on Bilayer Tablet Integrity

This section is based on a study reported by Rowe et al. (2014, 2015).

Background/objective

Drug granulation A, a wet granulation product, exhibited poor flow properties upon scale-up, impacting bilayer compaction operations. An increase in water levels during the wet granulation process was proposed as a mitigation strategy to improve flow. The impact of this change on the robustness of the bilayer tablet formulation was unknown. The objective of this work was to determine if Poisson's ratio analysis was sensitive enough to detect changes to the formulation and capable of predicting its impact on bilayer tablet integrity.

Materials and methods

Materials

The following materials were used:

- Drug granulation final blend A (wet granulation, >30% drug load)
  - Wet granulation at low water content (for which poor flow was observed)
  - Wet granulation at high water content: 6% higher than the low water content level (acceptable flow)
- Drug granulation final blend B (dry granulation, >30% drug load)

Tablet manufacture and determination of tablet strength

Bilayer tablets were manufactured at small scale using an compaction simulator in conjunction with round, flat-faced tooling (500 mg total press weight). Tablets were manufactured at commercial scale using a Hata rotary press (55 stations) in conjunction with shaped tooling (>1000 mg total press weight). Bilayer tablet strengths were measured by an axial tester.

Results

A significant difference was not apparent in the compaction profiles between granulations manufactured using different levels of water (dried material possessed comparable levels of water). The Poisson's ratio map captures the difference in bilayer tablet formulations using Drug A granulations manufactured using different levels of water. Points on the plot represent tablets manufactured under multiple compaction pressures. The diamonds (♦) represent intact tablets; the crosses (x) represent tablets that delaminated off the press; and the stars represent commercial manufacturing conditions (for which tablets remained intact through accelerated stability testing). The predicted target operating range (blue region) for the bilayer formulation using the high water amount for the Drug A granulation shifted and was more narrow compared to that for the low water amount granulation.

There was good correlation between predictions from the Poisson's map and experimental observations, especially with regard to the edges of failure. For bilayer tablets comprised of the higher water amount Drug A granulation, delaminated tablets were indicated using x on the Poisson's ratio map. Design space for the lower water amount for the Drug A granulation predicted to be wider than that for the higher water amount granulation. At commercial-scale manufacture, bilayer tablet formulations using the lower water amount Drug A granulation were found to possess a wider acceptable operating range, further confirming predictions from Poisson's ratio map. Also, commercial manufacturing conditions produced tablets that lie near center of target region (blue region), which allows for small levels of process drift without significant impact to

(Continued)

(cont'd)

delamination risk. Tablet strengths, measured by axial testing, correlated well with Poisson's ratio analysis. An increase in water level during the granulation of Drug A tended to push $\Delta\nu$ values closer to the edge of failure, and thus, may suggest that those tablets would possess lower tablet strengths.

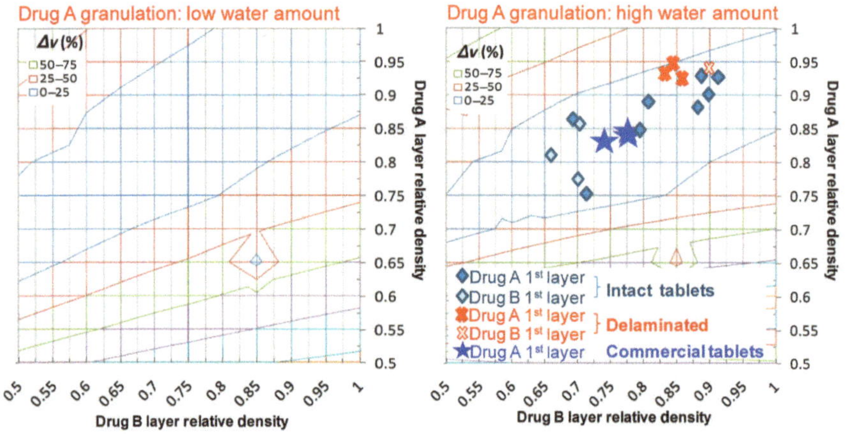

Conclusions

Compaction profiles do not provide sufficient insight as to their behavior in a bilayer tablet formulation; they could not differentiate between the different Drug A granulations manufactured using different levels of water. Poisson's ratio analysis was capable of predicting the impact of Drug A granulation conditions on the overall integrity of the product. The Poisson's ratio map provides knowledge regarding edges of failure for bilayer tablet formulations. They should be used to guide the direction of product development activities and are not meant to provide exact predictions of bilayer tablet strengths.

In this study, Poisson's ratio maps were used to assess the risk of making formulation changes to one layer of a bilayer product to mitigate manufacturing challenges in an area external to tablet compaction. Even with the narrower design space for the final product, compaction conditions could be adjusted to meet target properties, enabling appropriate mitigation of flow challenges without sacrificing robustness of the bilayer tablet. Poisson's ratio maps enabled more confidence regarding changes made to bilayer formulations because they provide a better understanding of where the edges of failure lie as different options are explored, something that has previously been difficult to assess without performing numerous experiments, including long-term stability experiments.

References

Abebe, A., et al., 2014. Review of bilayer tablet technology. Int. J. Pharm. 461 (1–2), 549–558.

Akseli, I., Dey, D., Cetinkaya, C., 2010. Mechanical property characterization of bilayered tablets using nondestructive air-coupled acoustics. AAPS PharmSciTech. 11 (1), 90–102.

Akseli, I., et al., 2013. Mechanistic characterization of bilayer tablet formulations. Powder Technol. 236, 30–36.

Anuar, M.S., Briscoe, B.J., 2009. The elastic relaxation of starch tablets during ejection. Powder Technol. 195 (2), 96–104.

Anuar, M.S., Briscoe, B.J., 2010. Interfacial elastic relaxation during the ejection of bi-layered tablets. Int. J. Pharm. 387 (1–2), 42–47.

Bangalore, S., et al., 2007. Fixed-dose combinations improve medication compliance: a meta-analysis. Am. J. Med. 120 (8), 713–719.

Bassam, F., et al., 1990. Young's modulus of powders used as pharmaceutical excipients. Int. J. Pharm. 64 (1), 55–60.

Belda, P.M., Mielck, J.B., 2005. The difficulty in the assessment of the compression behaviour of powder mixtures: double-layer tablets versus arithmetic additivity rule. Eur. J. Pharm. Biopharm. 60 (1), 133–145.

Belda, P.M., Mielck, J.B., 2006. Considerations about the theoretically expected crushing strength of tablets from binary powder mixtures: double-layer tablets versus arithmetic additivity rule. Eur. J. Pharm. Biopharm. 64 (3), 343–350.

Bogy, D.B., 1970. On the problem of edge-bonded elastic quarter-planes loaded at the boundary. Int. J. Solids Struct. 6 (9), 1287–1313.

Breech, J.A., Lucisano, L.J., Franz, R.M., 1988. Investigation into substrate cracking of a film-coated bilayered tablet. J. Pharm. Pharmacol. 40 (4), 282–283.

Busignies, V., et al., 2004. Compaction of crystallographic forms of pharmaceutical granular lactoses. II. Compacts mechanical properties. Eur. J. Pharm. Biopharm. 58 (3), 577–586.

Busignies, V., et al., 2013. Role of the elasticity of pharmaceutical materials on the interfacial mechanical strength of bilayer tablets. Int. J. Pharm. 457 (1), 260–267.

Busignies, V., et al., 2014. Development of a new test for the easy characterization of the adhesion at the interface of bilayer tablets: Proof-of-concept study by experimental design. Int. J. Pharm. 477 (1–2), 476–484.

Desai, D., et al., 2012. Formulation design, challenges, and development considerations for fixed dose combination (FDC) of oral solid dosage forms. Pharm. Dev. Technol. 18 (6).

Dietrich, P., Bauer-Brandl, A., Schubert, R., 2000. Influence of tableting forces and lubricant concentration on the adhesion strength in complex layer tablets. Drug Dev. Ind. Pharm. 26 (7), 745–754.

Duckworth, W., 1953. Discussion of ryshkewitch paper. J. Am. Ceram. Soc. 36, 68.

Dundurs, J., 1967. Effect of elastic constants on stress in a composite under plane deformation. J. Compos. Mater. 1 (3), 310–322.

Franck, J., et al., 2013. Axial strength test for round flat faced versus capsule shaped bilayer tablets. Pharm. Dev. Technol. 1–7.

Gross, B., and Srawley, J.E., 1965. Stress-intensity factors for three-point bend specimens by boundary collocation. Technical note D-3092, NASA.

Han, L.H., et al., 2008. A modified Drucker–Prager cap model for die compaction simulation of pharmaceutical powders. Int. J. Solids Struct. 45 (10), 3088–3106.

Hancock, B.C., Clas, S.D., Christensen, K., 2000. Micro-scale measurement of the mechanical properties of compressed pharmaceutical powders. 1: the elasticity and fracture behavior of microcrystalline cellulose. Int. J. Pharm. 209 (1–2), 27–35.

Inman, S.J., Briscoe, B.J., Pitt, K.G., 2007. Topographic characterization of cellulose bilayered tablets interfaces. Chem. Eng. Res. Des. 85 (A7), 1005–1012.

Inman, S.J., et al., 2008. Axial tensile fracture of microcrystalline cellulose compacts. Int. J. Pharm. 349 (1–2), 172–179.

Inman, S.J., et al., 2009. The non-uniformity of microcrystalline cellulose bilayer tablets. Powder Technol. 188 (3), 283–294.

Kachrimanis, K., Malamataris, S., 2004. "Apparent" Young's elastic modulus and radial recovery for some tableted pharmaceutical excipients. Eur. J. Pharm. Sci. 21 (2–3), 197–207.

Kerridge, J.C., Newton, J.M., 1986. The determination of the compressive Young's modulus of pharmaceutical materials. J. Pharm. Pharmacol. 38 (S12), p. 79P–79P.

Kottala, N., et al., 2012. Influence of compaction properties and interfacial topography on the performance of bilayer tablets. Int. J. Pharm. 436 (1–2), 171–178.

LaMarche, K., et al., 2014. Assessing materials' tablet compaction properties using the Drucker–Prager cap model. Powder Technol. 267, 208–220.

Mashadi, A.B., Newton, J.M., 1987. The characterization of the mechanical properties of microcrystalline cellulose: a fracture mechanics approach. J. Pharm. Pharmacol. 39 (12), 961–965.

Mashadi, A.B., Newton, J.M., 1988. Determination of the critical stress intensity factor (KIC) of compacted pharmaceutical powders by the double torsion method. J. Pharm. Pharmacol. 40 (9), 597–600.

Mazel, V., et al., 2012. Measurements of elastic moduli of pharmaceutical compacts: a new methodology using double compaction on a compaction simulator. J. Pharm. Sci. 101 (6), 2220–2228.

Mazel, V., et al., 2013. On the links between elastic constants and effective elastic behavior of pharmaceutical compacts: importance of Poisson's ratio and use of bulk modulus. J. Pharm. Sci. 102 (11), 4009–4014.

Michrafy, A., et al., 2007. Predictions of tensile strength of binary tablets using linear and power-law mixing rules. Int. J. Pharm. 333 (1–2), 118–126.

Panos, P.C., Zavaliangos, A., 2007. Understanding the interfacial strength of bilayer pharmaceutical tablets. Adv. Powder Metall. Part. Mater. 1-25–1-35.

Podczeck, F., 1998. Particle-Particle Adhesion in Pharmaceutical Powder Handling. Imperial college press, London.

Podczeck, F., 2001. Investigations into the fracture mechanics of acetylsalicylic acid and lactose monohydrate. J. Mater. Sci. 36 (19), 4687–4693.

Podczeck, F., 2011. Theoretical and experimental investigations into the delamination tendencies of bilayer tablets. Int. J. Pharm. 408 (1–2), 102–112.

Roberts, R.J., Rowe, R.C., 1987. The Young's modulus of pharmaceutical materials. Int. J. Pharm. 37 (1–2), 15–18.

Roberts, R.J., Rowe, R.C., 1989. Determination of the critical stress intensity factor (KIC) of microcrystalline cellulose using radially edge-cracked tablets. Int. J. Pharm. 52 (3), 213–219.

Roberts, R.J., Rowe, R.C., York, P., 1993. The measurement of the critical stress intensity factor (KIC) of pharmaceutical powders using three point single edge notched beam (SENB) testing. Int. J. Pharm. 91 (2–3), 173–182.
Roberts, R.J., Rowe, R.C., York, P., 1994. The Poisson's ratio of microcrystalline cellulose. Int. J. Pharm. 105 (2), 177–180.
Rowe, J.M., et al., 2014. Leveraging Pre-Formulation Results to Commercial Manufacture: A Materials Science Approach to Layered Tablet Formulations. American Association of Pharmaceutical Scientists, San Diego, CA.
Rowe, J.M., Pandey, P., Nikfar, F., 2015. A Materials Science Approach to Bilayer Tablet Compaction Pt 2: Formulation Impacts. American Association of Pharmaceutical Sceintists, Orlando, FL.
Ryshkewitch, E., 1953. Compression strength of porous sintered alumina and zirconia: 9th communication to ceramography. J. Am. Ceram. Soc. 36, 65–68.
Sexton, M., Procopio, A., Zavaliangos, A., 2008. Strength characterization of bilayer compacts. Advances in Powder Metallurgy & Particulate Materials. Taylor and Francis, pp. 220–230.
Simon, F., 2006. The trouble with making combination drugs. Nat. Rev. Drug Discov. 5 (11), 881–882.
Vaithiyalingam, S.R., Sayeed, V.A., 2010. Critical factors in manufacturing multi-layer tablets-Assessing material attributes, in-process controls, manufacturing process and product performance. Int. J. Pharm. 398 (1–2), 9–13.
Woodcock, J., Griffin, J.P., Behrman, R.E., 2011. Development of novel combination therapies. N. Engl. J. Med. 364 (11), 985–987.
Wu, C.-Y., Seville, J.P.K., 2009. A comparative study of compaction properties of binary and bilayer tablets. Powder Technol. 189 (2), 285–294.
Wu, C.-Y., et al., 2005. A simple predictive model for the tensile strength of binary tablets. Eur. J. Pharm. Sci. 25 (2–3), 331–336.
Wu, C.-Y., et al., 2006. Predicting the tensile strength of compacted multi-component mixtures of pharmaceutical powders. Pharm. Res. 23 (8), 1898–1905.
York, P., et al., 1990. Fracture mechanics of microcrystalline cellulose powders. Int. J. Pharm. 66 (1–3), 143–148.
Zacour, B.M., et al., 2014. Correlating bilayer tablet delamination tendencies to micro-environmental thermodynamic conditions during pan coating. Drug Dev. Ind. Pharm. 40 (6), 829–837.

Computational modeling of pharmaceutical die filling processes

10

Y. Guo[1] and C.-Y. Wu[2]
[1]University of Florida, Gainesville, FL, United States, [2]University of Surrey, Guildford, United Kingdom

10.1 Introduction

Die compaction is a typical powder processing route and has been employed to manufacture a wide range of products, such as pharmaceutical tablets, powder metallurgy parts, ceramics, detergent tablets and foodstuffs. The process of die compaction generally consists of three stages (Wu and Cocks, 2004): die filling, compaction, and ejection. In the die filling stage, the powder is delivered from a reservoir hopper through a hose into a movable container (i.e., feed shoe), and then the shoe moves over a confined cavity (i.e., a die), thereby depositing the powder into it. After die filling, the deposited powder is compressed under high pressures to form a coherent compact. Finally, the compact is ejected from the die.

In general, a consistent and uniform die filling process is always desirable. Heterogeneity during die filling can propagate through the subsequent processes and finally lead to serious product defects, such as cracking, low strength, distortion, and shrinkage. On the other hand, a fast filling process is preferable to improve the productivity. Understanding the die filling process can provide essential guidelines to optimize materials, equipment and processes in terms of uniformity and productivity (Sinka and Cocks, 2009). This has motivated increasing interest in the study of die filling. Since Cocks et al. (2001) identified the scientific issues involved in die filling, his coworkers have undertaken a series of experimental studies and the effects of powder characteristics, apparatus features, and some operating conditions on the powder flow behavior during die filling have been explored (Wu et al., 2003a; Schneider et al., 2005, 2007).

For a better understanding of die filling, computational methods (for instance, the discrete element method (DEM) and computational fluid dynamics (CFD)) have also been used to model this process and the results are very promising (Wu and Cocks, 2006; Wu, 2008; Guo et al., 2009a,b; Bierwisch et al., 2009). Computational modeling can provide transient particle-scale information, e.g., individual particle velocities, trajectories, and interaction forces, which is usually very difficult, if not impossible, to obtain in the physical experiments. Such particle-scale information is essential to identify the major factors that influence the macroscopic granular flow

Predictive Modeling of Pharmaceutical Unit Operations. DOI: http://dx.doi.org/10.1016/B978-0-08-100154-7.00011-9

behavior by examining the individual particle movement and interaction. Due to the ease of access to such information, the analysis process is also facilitated. Another advantage of computational modeling over the experimental investigation is that it is much easier to undertake the parametric study in computational simulations because the system parameters (particle properties, die geometry, shoe speed etc.) can be prescribed freely.

In this chapter, the research background of pharmaceutical die filling is introduced before the discussion is focused on the computational modeling of die filling. The basic principles of coupled DEM–CFD method are presented and the computational setup for the die filling simulations is described, and thereafter, several examples are provided to illustrate how the computational modeling can help understand the mechanical behavior of powders in die filling processes.

10.2 Background of pharmaceutical die filling

The studies on die filling can be categorized into three subject areas: powder flow from a shoe, powder packing inside a die, and segregation during die filling. The current research status and challenges are summarized next for these subject areas.

10.2.1 Powder flow from a shoe

The powder flow behavior during die filling is governed by a combination of a number of factors: powder characteristics (particle size, size distribution, density, shape, and surface properties), apparatus features (shoe and die design), and operating conditions (shoe kinematics, the absence or presence of air, suction, vibration, agitation, aeration, humidity, and temperature). Understanding the effects of these factors is crucial for the selection of operating parameters and the control of the filling process.

Wu et al. (2003b) developed a model die filling system to investigate the powder flow behavior during die filling, as shown in Fig. 10.1. The system consists of a transparent die and a transparent shoe that allow the die filling process to be observed and recorded by using a high-speed video system. By adopting this system, systematic studies on powder flow behavior during die filling were conducted (Wu et al., 2003a,b; Wu and Cocks, 2004, 2006; Schneider et al., 2005, 2007; Jackson et al., 2007; Sinka et al., 2009; Sinka and Cocks, 2009) and two types of powder flow were identified: nose flow and bulk flow, as illustrated in Fig. 10.2. When the shoe with a fixed mass of powder translates over the die, the initial acceleration of the shoe and friction between the bottom of the powder mass and the base plate forces the powder toward the back of the shoe, forming a nose-shaped profile. The powder from the top region of the shoe can then be delivered into the die by cascading down the upper surface of the nose. This type of flow is referred to as nose flow. As the tip of the nose moves across the die opening, the powder is delivered into the die by detaching from the bottom surface of the powder mass.

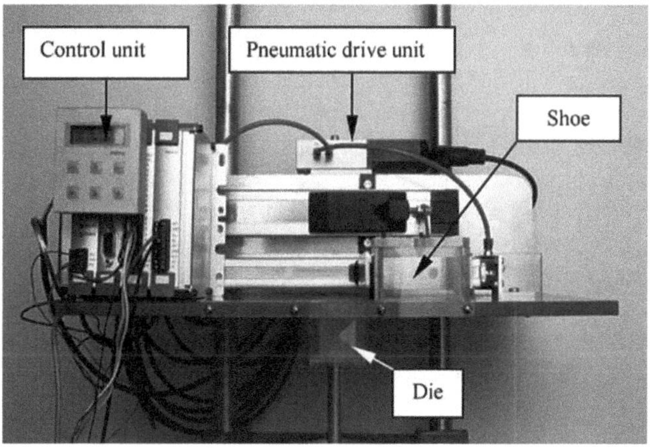

Figure 10.1 A model die filling system (Wu et al., 2003b).

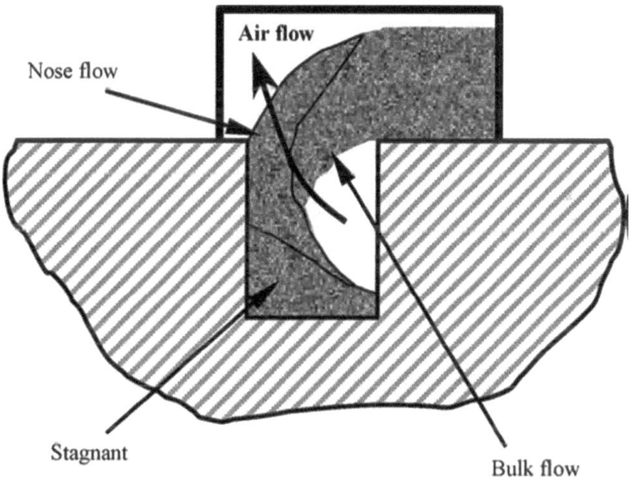

Figure 10.2 Illustration of powder flow patterns in die filling (Wu et al., 2003b).

This type of flow is referred to as bulk flow. Wu et al. (2003b) found that nose flow promotes fast air evacuation and rapid free surface flow so that a high flow rate can be achieved, and the powder detaching rate in bulk flow is low due to the combined effects of the entrapped air and interlocking of the particles. Nose flow and bulk flow are two primary flow patterns during die filling with free-flowing powders. Moreover, for cohesive powders, such as most pharmaceutical powders, Sinka et al. (2004) and Schneider et al. (2007) observed a third flow mechanism, intermittent flow, in which the powder is deposited into the die in the form of a discrete release of large chunks of agglomerated powder.

As argued by Sinka et al. (2004) and Wu and Cocks (2004), a lot of experimental techniques can be used to characterize the flow properties of powders. However, different measurement techniques can produce a different rank order of flowability for a given powder. It is therefore important that the flow characterization is carried out using a device that captures the physical phenomena involved in the process under consideration. Thus, from the die filling point of view, the characterization of powder flow requires a facility that can mimic the real industrial die filling process, such as the model die filling system shown in Fig. 10.1. When the shoe moves over the die at a low velocity, the die cavity can be completely filled. As the shoe velocity increases, the die cavity is just partially filled due to the reduction of filling time and the increase in the interlocking of particles at the acceleration stage. Therefore, there exists a maximum shoe velocity at which the die is completely filled. This maximum velocity is referred to as critical filling velocity (Wu et al., 2003b). The higher the critical filling velocity, the better the powder flows. Therefore, the critical filling velocity can be used to quantify the flowability of powders for die filling.

A number of experimental and numerical studies on the powder flow in die filling have been performed to explore the effects of particle material properties (Sinka et al., 2004; Schneider et al., 2007; Wu, 2008), particle shape (Wu and Cocks, 2006; Wu, 2008; Pei et al., 2015), airflow (Wu et al., 2003b; Schneider et al., 2007; Guo et al., 2009b), shoe kinematics (Sawayama and Seki, 1999; Wu et al., 2003b), shoe design (Cocks et al., 2001; Hashimoto et al., 2002; Zahrah et al., 2001), and die geometry and orientation (Wu et al., 2003b; Schneider et al., 2005; Wu and Cocks, 2004; Sinka et al., 2009).

10.2.2 Powder packing inside a die

After the powder is delivered into a die, consistent weight, uniform density distribution, and minimized segregation of the material in the die cavity are desirable to achieve the required product quality. Many studies have been conducted to evaluate the effects of some factors on powder packing inside a die cavity. The boundary effect on the density distribution was recognized in previous work. Experimental work by Bocchini (1987) using rectangular dies of various widths showed that sparse boundary layers were present at the die walls and across these boundary layers, the apparent density increases from a low value to the bulk value in the middle of the die cavity. Due to the presence of the boundary layers, the fill density decreased as the die width decreased. When the die width was sufficiently large, the fill density tended to be constant as the boundary effect became negligible. These results are consistent with the previous experimental observations using a set of circular dies of different diameters by Rice and Tengzelius (1986), who found that the fill density decreased with decreasing die diameter and it remained constant when the die diameter was sufficiently large. A simple theory was proposed by Bocchini (1987) to describe the fill density as a function of the hydraulic radius of the die opening and the thickness of the boundary layer for different die geometries; and the theoretical predictions were in good agreement with the experimental results.

Die orientation with respect to the direction of shoe motion also has an impact on the fill density. For die filling with a long-narrow die opening, a higher fill density is obtained when the shoe moves in the direction orthogonal to the long axis of the die compared to in the direction parallel to the long axis of the die (Bocchini, 1987; Wu and Cocks, 2004). Bocchini (1987) argued that this is because filling orthogonal to the long die axis produces more frequent particle rebounds from wall to wall as the powder flows into the die and this leads to a densification due to the particle rearrangement. Haskins and Jandeska (1998) used computed tomography to examine the spatial powder distribution and found that the powder density distribution depends on the die shape and the orientation of the die with respect to the direction of shoe motion. The powder density appeared to be higher near the concave die surfaces than near the convex die surfaces in die filling with a core rod inside the die cavity. For a die with slots, teeth, and other geometric discontinuities, higher powder densities were obtained in the regions oriented along the axis of the shoe motion than in the regions off the axis. When filling a ring-shaped die, Hjortsberg and Bergquist (2002) observed that the powder density was generally higher in the sections parallel to the direction of shoe motion.

The kinematics of the shoe have a significant impact on powder flow during the die filling process, and consequently, they also have an influence on the powder packing behavior inside the die. A systematic experimental study was conducted by Hjortsberg and Bergquist (2002) to investigate the effect of shoe motion on density variations after die filling with a ring-shaped die. They found that the powder density increased as the shoe speed increased. During die filling, the kinetic energy of moving particles can be partially transferred into the die cavity, in which it causes rearrangement of the particles and compaction. The increase of shoe speed results in an increase of kinetic energy of particles and hence in an increased densification in the die.

A pressure deposition tester (PDT) was developed by Xie and Puri (2007a,b, 2008) to analyze the uniformity in die deposition. This device is based on the principle that an anisotropic fill density distribution would result in an uneven particulate vertical pressure distribution on the bottom surface of the die (Xie and Puri, 2007a). As a result, the uniformity of the packed power in the die can be evaluated by measuring the pressure distribution at the bottom of the die. Using the PDT, Xie and Puri (2007a,b) tested die depositions with various feed shoe speeds and with dies of different shapes. They found that feed shoe speed did have an effect on pressure distribution and therefore on uniformity. However, this effect depended on the die shape; for instance, the highest feed shoe speed considered in their studies led to the most uniform pressure distribution for the cylindrical dies, but led to the most nonuniform pressure distribution for the toroidal. Higher momentum possessed by particles at higher shoe speed was expected to contribute to relatively uniform filling by minimizing arching and allowing rearrangement of particles.

10.2.3 Segregation during die filling

During die filling, powder blends consisting of particles of different physical properties such as density, size, and/or shape are commonly used. The difference in particle properties can cause segregation, which is referred to as a homogeneous powder blend becoming spatially nonuniform in such a manner that the particles having the same properties congregate in one part of the mixture during handling and processing (Rhodes, 1998). Segregation in die filling may influence product quality by causing variations in filling density and compound concentration from compact to compact. Therefore, segregation is a typical problem and needs to be minimized.

Thirteen segregation mechanisms of granular mixtures were identified by de Silva et al. (2000) as follows: trajectory, air current, rolling, sieving (or sifting), impact, embedding, angle of repose, push-away, displacement, percolation, fluidization, agglomeration, and concentration-driven displacement. By combining similar mechanisms (such as sifting and displacement being special cases of percolation) and dismissing some infrequently occurring mechanisms (such as embedding or push-away), Ketterhagen et al. (2008) argued that these mechanisms have been subsequently condensed to four primary mechanisms: percolation (or sifting) segregation, angle of repose segregation, trajectory segregation, and fluidization segregation. During die filling, all four types of segregation may occur. When a mixture of different sized particles is used, segregation with an excess of fines at the bottom can occur due to the percolation of fines through the void space in the structure of coarse particles. The segregation due to different angles of repose may also occur when particles of different shapes are packing inside the die cavity. When the powder is delivered into the die cavity along a free surface, for instance, in nose flow, the large particles tend to flow over the top of small ones on the top surface and then cascade into the die. Under this condition, segregation occurs due to the different trajectories of large and small particles upon the free surface flow. When air is present during die filling, the airflow can influence the distribution of small and/or light particles by entraining them.

Segregation during die filling was experimentally investigated by Lawrence and Beddow (1968a,b) and their experimental results showed that the size-induced segregation occurred with a higher concentration of fine particles at the bottom of the die and a higher concentration of coarse particles in the periphery of the die cavity, due to the filtration of fines through the flowing powder mass. However, the difference in particle densities was not found to have a significant impact on segregation (Lawrence and Beddow, 1968a). By using a vibrating die (Lawrence and Beddow, 1968b), the radial segregation was reduced, because the inner mound of fines tended to be leveled off, whereas the vertical segregation was found to depend on the amplitude and frequency of the vibration. When the die was oscillated at low or high amplitude, the powder mass was quiescent or bouncing and the vertical segregation was minimized; when the die was oscillated at intermediate amplitude and high frequency, the churning of powder mass occurred and the vertical segregation increased. In recent years, the computational methods, such as DEM and CFD, have been employed to study the segregation in die filling processes (Guo et al., 2009a, 2011a,b), which will be discussed later in this chapter.

10.3 Computational setup of die filling

The coupled DEM–CFD method was developed to simulate the gas–particle two-phase flow in fluidized beds (Tsuji et al., 1993; Kafui et al., 2002). In this method, the motion and interactions of solid particles are modeled using the DEM, and the flow of gas is modeled using CFD. The gas–particle interaction and two-way coupling of particle phase and gas phase are considered. Using this numerical approach, Guo et al. (2009a,b, 2011a,b) studied the powder flow, packing, and segregation during the die filling processes in the presence of air.

10.3.1 Coupled DEM–CFD method

The translational and rotational motions of each particle are governed by Newton's equations of motion:

$$m_i \frac{\mathrm{d}\mathbf{v}_i}{\mathrm{d}t} = \mathbf{f}_{ci} + \mathbf{f}_{\mathrm{ap}i} + m_i\mathbf{g} \tag{10.1}$$

$$I_i \frac{\mathrm{d}\boldsymbol{\omega}_i}{\mathrm{d}t} = \mathbf{T}_i \tag{10.2}$$

in which m_i, I_i, $\mathbf{v}_i$, and $\boldsymbol{\omega}_i$ are the mass, moment of inertia, linear velocity, and angular velocity, respectively, of the particle i. Further, $\mathbf{g}$ is the gravitational acceleration, $\mathbf{f}_{ci}$ is the interparticle contact force, $\mathbf{f}_{\mathrm{ap}i}$ is air–particle interaction force, and $\mathbf{T}_i$ represents the torque arising from the tangential components of the contact force. The particles considered in this study are assumed to be elastic and frictional, and the interparticle interactions are defined by algorithms based on classical contact mechanics (Thornton and Yin, 1991), in which the theory of Hertz is used to determine the normal force and the theory of Mindlin and Deresiewicz is used for the tangential force. The air–particle interaction force can be described in the form

$$\mathbf{f}_{\mathrm{ap}i} = -\,v_{\mathrm{p}i}\nabla p + v_{\mathrm{p}i}\nabla \cdot \boldsymbol{\tau} + \varepsilon \mathbf{f}_{\mathrm{d}i} \tag{10.3}$$

where $v_{\mathrm{p}i}$ is the volume of particle i, and p, $\boldsymbol{\tau}$, ε, and $\mathbf{f}_{\mathrm{d}i}$ are local air pressure, viscous stress tensor, void fraction, and drag force, respectively. The air is treated as a continuum and modeled using CFD, in which the continuity and momentum equations

$$\frac{\partial(\varepsilon\rho_{\mathrm{a}})}{\partial t} + \nabla \cdot (\varepsilon\rho_{\mathrm{a}}\mathbf{u}) = 0 \tag{10.4}$$

$$\frac{\partial(\varepsilon\rho_{\mathrm{a}}\mathbf{u})}{\partial t} + \nabla \cdot (\varepsilon\rho_{\mathrm{a}}\mathbf{u}\mathbf{u}) = -\,\nabla p + \nabla \cdot \boldsymbol{\tau} - \mathbf{F}_{\mathrm{ap}} + \varepsilon\rho_{\mathrm{a}}\mathbf{g} \tag{10.5}$$

are solved to give air velocity, $\mathbf{u}$, air pressure, p, and air density, ρ_a. In Eq. (10.5), the fluid–particle interaction force per unit volume, $\mathbf{F}_{ap}$, is obtained by summing up the fluid–particle interaction forces, $\mathbf{f}_{api}$, acting on all the particles in a fluid cell, n_c, and dividing by the volume of the fluid cell, ΔV_c, thus

$$\mathbf{F}_{ap} = \left(\sum_{i=1}^{n_c} \mathbf{f}_{api}\right) / \Delta V_c \tag{10.6}$$

10.3.2 Numerical model of die filling

The DEM simulation models of die filling from a stationary shoe and a moving shoe are sketched in Figs. 10.3A and B, respectively. The simulated die filling system is composed of a top container, which is generally referred to as a shoe, and a bottom container, which is the die. For die filling from a stationary shoe

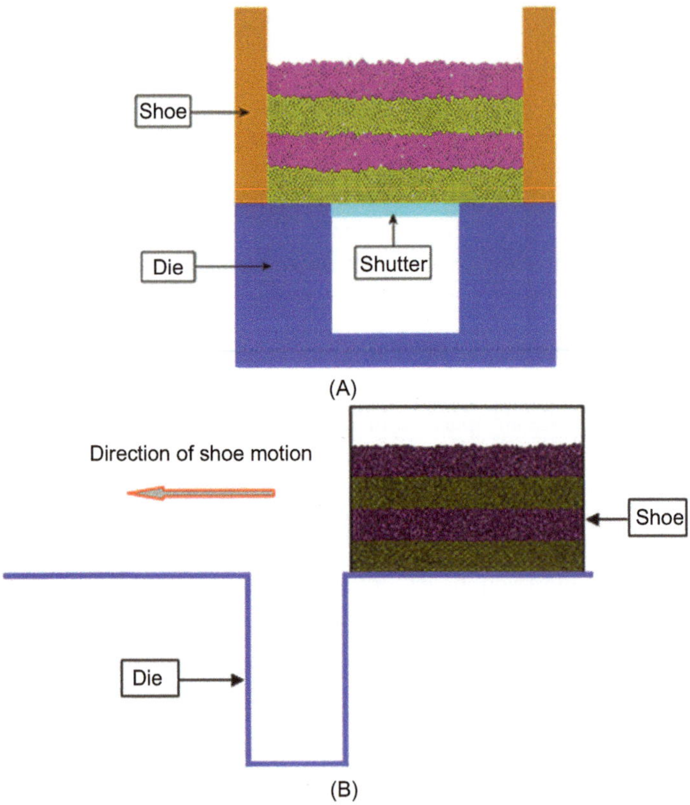

Figure 10.3 The numerical models for die filling from (A) a stationary shoe and (B) a moving shoe.

(Fig. 10.3A), a shutter is set at the top of the die to hold the powder prior to die filling. Initially, a specified number of particles were randomly generated in the shoe, then deposited under gravity in the absence of air until they settled to a steady state with negligible kinetic energy. The powder bed is then color-banded so that the macroscopic flow patterns can be visualized. For die filling from a stationary shoe, the filling process is started by suddenly removing the shutter so that the powder starts to flow into the die under the influence of gravity. For die filling from a moving shoe (Fig. 10.3B), the powder is delivered into the die when the shoe translates over the die opening from the right-hand side to the left-hand side at a constant velocity.

The inputs for the DEM modeling of granular systems include particle size distribution, particle density, friction, coefficient of restitution, elastic modulus or contact stiffness, Poisson's ratio, and cohesive parameters. If these input parameters can be experimentally measured, the measured values should be used as the inputs. If an input parameter is difficult to obtain (e.g., coefficient of restitution), the sensitivity of simulation results to this parameter may be examined. In the sensitivity test, a series of die filling simulations with a range of the magnitudes of the uncertain parameter can be run and compared with the experimental results. The value of the parameter that gives the best agreement with the experimental results should be used as the calibrated input for the subsequent simulations. Spherical particles are frequently used in the DEM modeling due to the simplicity, although the particle shape in reality is usually nonspherical. Fortunately, the DEM simulations of die filling with nonspherical particles can also be performed. As shown in Fig. 10.4, based on the x-ray CT scanned image of a real particle in three dimensions, a model nonspherical particle can be generated using a cluster of rigidly bonded spheres (Fig. 10.4B) for the DEM simulations. Due to the introduction of a large number of constituent spheres in a clustered particle, the computational cost of modeling nonspherical particles can be much higher than that of modeling spheres.

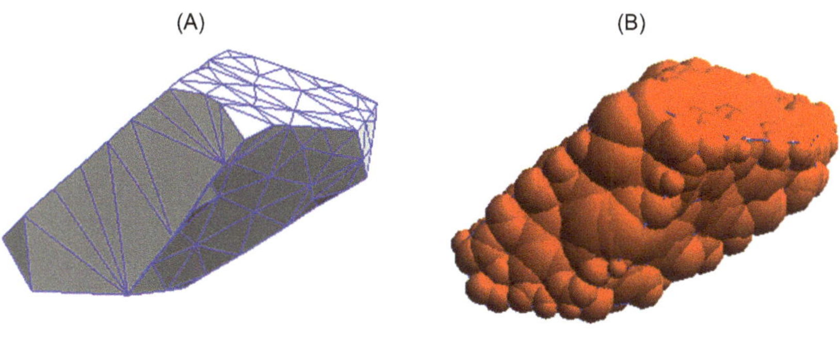

Figure 10.4 Representation of a real particle using a cluster of rigidly bonded spheres in DEM: (A) x-ray CT scanned particle in 3D and (B) model particle.
Source: For (A) Courtesy: X. Jia, Leeds.

To consider the effect of air on the powder flow, air initially fills the void space in the shoe and die regions at uniform pressure (no pressure gradients). The computational fluid cells and boundary conditions for the die filling from a stationary shoe and a moving shoe are schematically shown in Figs. 10.5A and B, respectively. The computational domain for the gas phase (i.e., air) is uniformly discretized with interior fluid cells (1), the solid boundaries are treated as impermeable with no slip boundaries (3) for airflow, and the top of the shoe is modeled using continuous gas outflow wall cells with free slip boundaries (6). All quantities, such as air pressure and air velocity, are averaged in the fluid cells, and the void fraction of each cell is defined by the total volume of particles inside the cell. As argued by

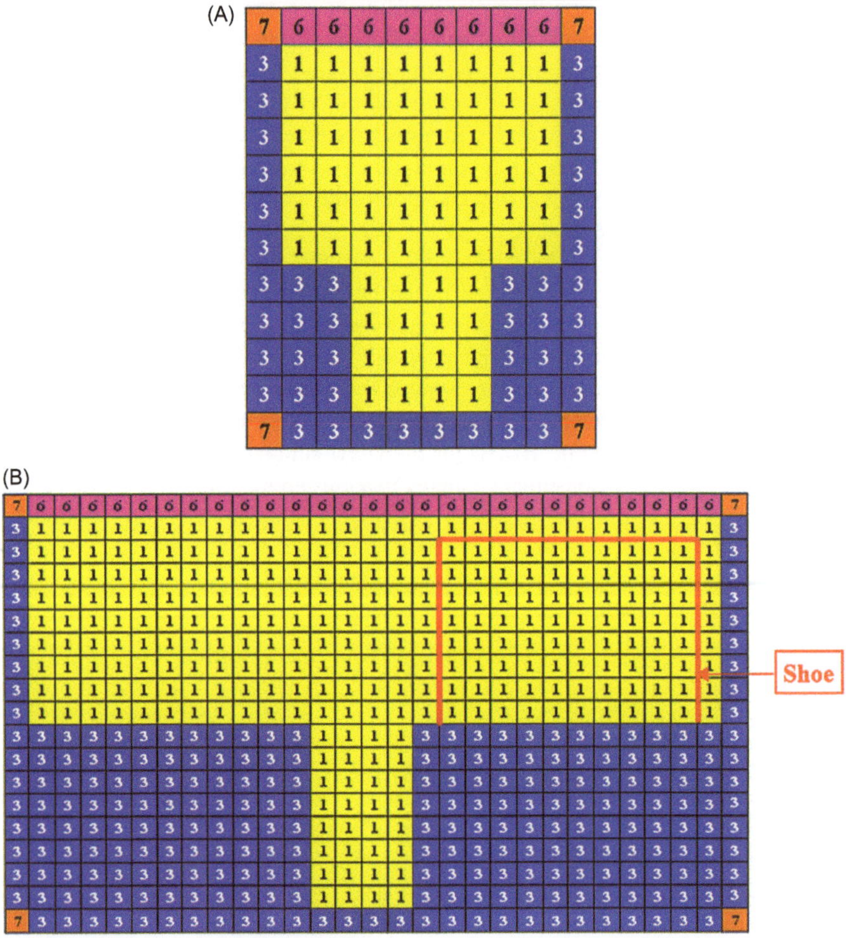

Figure 10.5 Schematic diagrams of the computational fluid cells and boundary conditions for die filling from (A) a stationary shoe and (B) a moving shoe. (1: interior fluid cell; 3: impermeable wall, no slip boundaries; 6: continuous gas outflow wall cell, free slip; 7: corner cell).

Tsuji et al. (1993), the size of the fluid cells should be smaller than the macroscopic motion of bubbles (to simulate the evolution of bubbles and the detailed fluid flow inside the bubbles) but larger than the particle size (to avoid zero void fractions). As typically adopted in simulations of fluidized beds (Tsuji et al., 1993), the size of the fluid cells is set in the range of 3–5 times the average particle diameter in this study. Initially, air with standard atmospheric pressure (1.01325×10^5 Pa) and a viscosity of 1.8E-5 kg $m^{-1}s^{-1}$ was uniformly distributed in the void space and was assumed to be static. Once the particles start to move, the air flows accordingly. The temperature of air is normally assumed to be fixed at the room temperature of 293 K during the die filling process.

10.4 Computational analysis of die filling

The computational simulations produce a lot of data, which can be used to analyze the die filling process. Three examples are provided next to illustrate how the computational modeling helps improve our understanding of die filling processes.

10.4.1 Effect of air on powder flow

The presence of air can have a significant impact on the flow patterns of fine and/or light particles during die filling. As shown in Fig. 10.6, the air can be entrapped inside a die, resisting the delivery of particles into the die. The die fill rate is therefore reduced by the entrapped air. The permeability of the bulk materials also has an influence on the powder flow in die filling. The polydispersed particle system has a smaller void fraction and poorer permeability than the

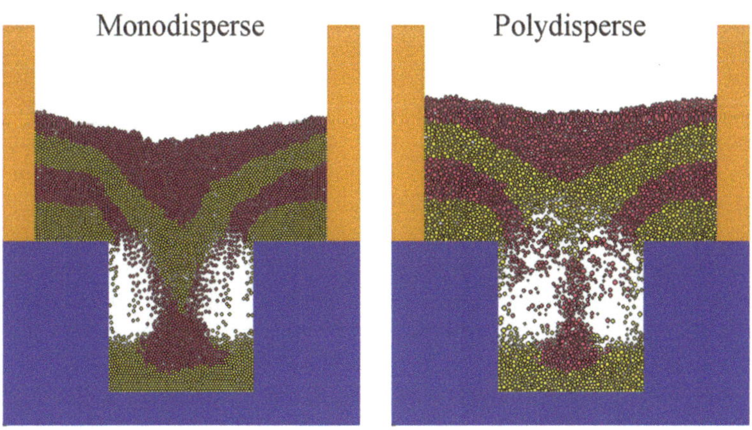

Figure 10.6 Simulated powder flow patterns at the same moment in time during die filling with the monodisperse and polydisperse powder systems in the presence of air. The two powders have the same average particle diameter of 130 μm (Guo et al., 2009b).

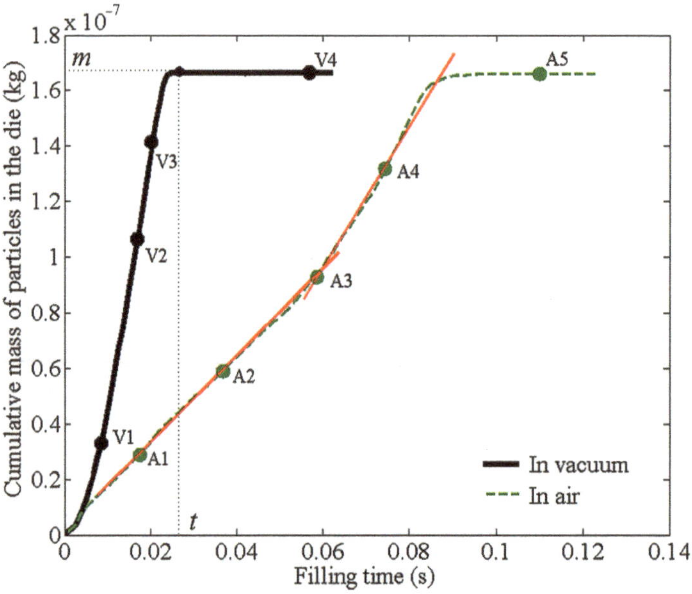

Figure 10.7 Cumulative mass of particles deposited into the die as a function of the filling time for die filling in a vacuum and in air (Guo et al., 2009b).

monodispersed system. Thus, it is more difficult for the air to escape from the die and a larger air bubble can be formed with the polydispersed particle system than with the monodispersed system (Fig. 10.6).

Fig. 10.7 shows the time history of the mass of particles fed into the die for die filling in a vacuum and in air. It is found that for die filling in a vacuum the flow of powder into a die is accelerated from the initial steady state. A relatively low mass flow rate is observed at the very early stage of the process immediately after the shutter is removed (say $t < 0.005$ s). The flow rate increases very sharply thereafter and remains constant during most of the filling process until the die is almost completely filled when a deceleration stage is then observed. For die filling in air, it is also observed that there is an acceleration stage at the beginning of die filling and a deceleration stage when the die is almost completely filled. However, the powder flow process in air can be divided into two distinct regimes: a slow flow regime at the early stage of die filling up to the instant A3 (as labeled in Fig. 10.7) and a fast flow regime thereafter. It is evident that the die is filled much more slowly in air than in a vacuum. This is due to the counterflow of the air against the direction of the powder flow.

By performing the simulations of die fillings with particles of different sizes and densities, Guo et al. (2009b) found that the flow characteristics for die filling in air can be classified into two regimes. There is an air-inert regime in which the particle size and density are sufficiently large that the effect of airflow becomes negligible and the dimensionless mass flow rate is essentially identical to that obtained for die filling in a vacuum. There is also an air-sensitive regime, for smaller particle sizes and lower particle densities, in which the dimensionless mass flow rate increases as the particle size and density increase.

10.4.2 Suction filling

Conventionally, the flow of powder into a die is driven by gravity when the shoe moves over the die. This die filling method is referred to as gravity filling. However, in a rotary tablet press, the effect of suction becomes a key element of the die filling process (Jackson et al., 2007). In this process, the die cavity is initially occupied by a movable punch and this punch moves downwards when the shoe moves across the die opening (see Fig. 10.8). The motion of the punch 'sucks' the powder into the die by creating a partial vacuum below the powder. This die filling method is referred to as suction filling. In suction filling, air is not entrapped to hinder the flow of powder into the die. On the other hand, the formation of the vacuum below the powder induces a large pressure difference between the top and bottom of powder bed, and this pressure difference forces the powder into the die. As a result, a high filling rate is expected under the influence of suction.

Using the coupled DEM−CFD method, the suction filling of powder into a die was simulated by Wu and Guo (2012). The fundamental mechanisms of suction filling have been explored. According to the simulation results, in suction filling the downward motion of the punch induces a low air pressure environment below the powder mass and hence a pressure gradient across the powder bed, which augments the flow of powder into a die. The pressure distributions, which may be difficult to measure in experiments, can be easily obtained from the simulation, as shown in Fig. 10.9. It can be seen the air pressure decreases gradually from the shoe region into the die region and the lowest pressure occurs at the bottom of die region.

Simulated gravity filling processes in a vacuum and in air and suction filling processes with two different punch velocities are shown in Fig. 10.10. During the

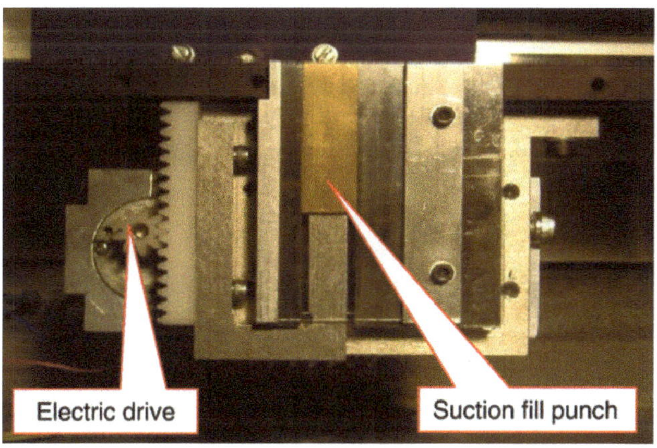

Figure 10.8 A suction filling system (Sinka et al., 2009).

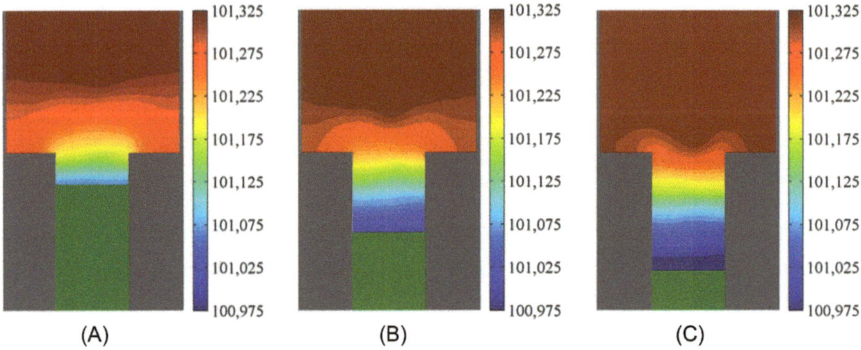

Figure 10.9 Air pressure distributions at various time instants during suction filling with a punch velocity of 100 mm/s. Red represents high pressure and blue represents low pressure. (Wu and Guo, 2012). (A) $t = 8.5$ ms, (B) $t = 21.3$ ms, and (C) $t = 31.5$ ms.

gravity filling, a thin stream of particles is deposited into the die as the shoe passes the die opening. A smaller amount of particle flow is eventually delivered into the die cavity in the presence of air than in a vacuum, due to the resistance effect of the entrapped air in the die. In suction filling, the powder is fed into the die as a column spanning the whole die width. In general, the suction can promote the powder flow. However, if the speed of punch is too low, the delivery of powder into the die can be prevented (Fig. 10.10C). An optimal speed of punch should be chosen to maximize the die filling level and avoid the turbulent flow of powders.

10.4.3 Segregation

The DEM simulations have been performed to investigate the segregation in die filling due to the difference in particle sizes (Guo et al., 2011a) and particle densities (Guo et al., 2009a, 2011b). When a binary mixture of particles of different sizes flew into the die, as shown in Fig. 10.11, the sifting segregation occurred that the fine particles sank to the lower region and coarse particles moved to the surface. If the powder from the free surface could be delivered into the die (see Fig. 10.11), a higher concentration of coarse particles was observed on the leading side of the die (which the shoe moves toward), and a higher concentration of fines was achieved on the trailing side of the die.

From the DEM simulations, the position of each particle at any time can be easily obtained. Thus, the horizontal and vertical concentration distributions of fine particles in the die region were plotted in Fig. 10.12, where x_i is the local fines concentration and x_f is the average fines concentration of the whole particle system. Fig. 10.12A, in which x represents the horizontal position and w is the width of the die, shows that the fines concentration is lower on the leading side of the die and it is higher on the trailing side. This fines concentration profile is consistent with the observation in Fig. 10.11. Significant segregation also occurs in the vertical direction, as shown in Fig. 10.12B, in which y is the vertical position and h is the height

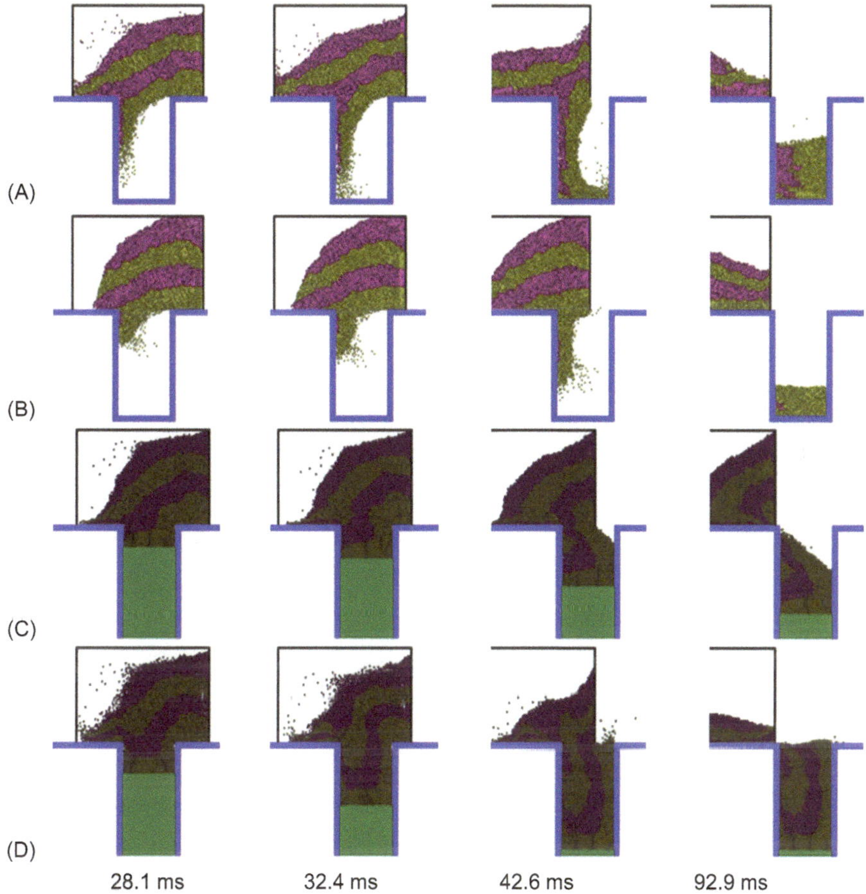

Figure 10.10 Simulated power flow patterns during (A) gravity filling in a vacuum, (B) gravity filling in air, (C) suction filling with a punch velocity of 100 mm/s, and (D) suction filling with a punch velocity of 276 mm/s. The shoe velocity is set to 140 mm/s. The labels indicate the elapsed time from the start of die filling (Wu and Guo, 2012).

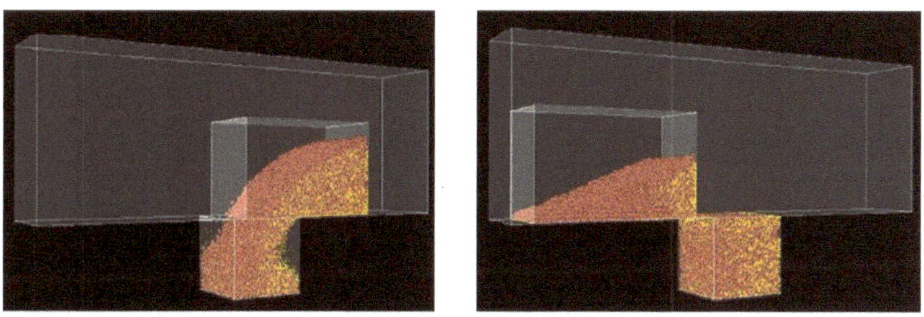

Figure 10.11 Simulated die filling processes with a binary mixture of different sized particles. Coarse particles are red and fines are yellow (Guo et al., 2011a).

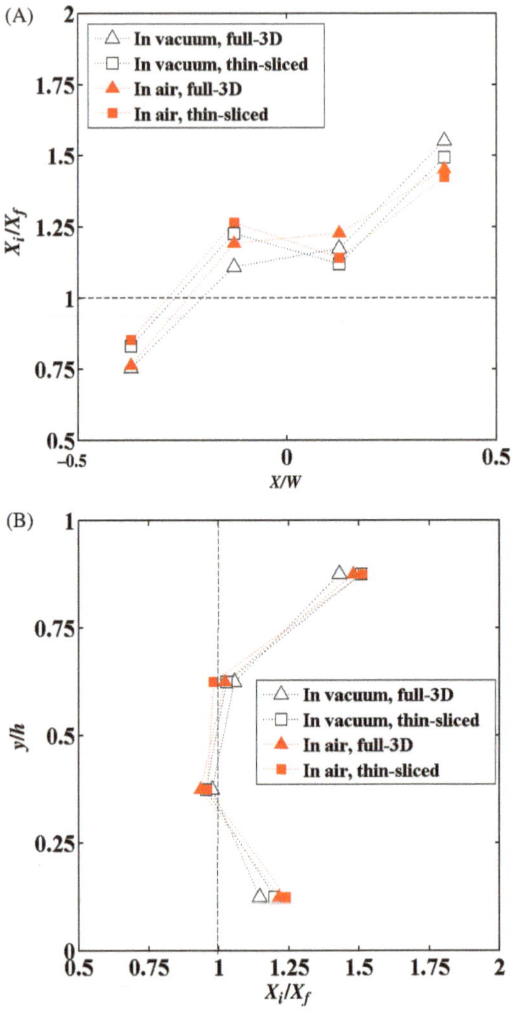

Figure 10.12 (A) Horizontal and (B) vertical concentration distributions of the fine particles in the die after die filling (Guo et al., 2011a).

of the die. Higher fines concentration is observed in the lower region of the die due to the sifting mechanism, which is easy to understand. Interestingly, the highest fines concentration is obtained in the upper region of the die. This may be counter-intuitive at first glance. However, the die filling process (Fig. 10.11) shows that as the particle bed in the shoe moves across the die opening, the top of the die is fed by the fine particles from the bottom of the shoe. The shearing between the particle bed in the die and the particle bed in the shoe promotes the percolation of fines into the die region. As a result, the top region of the die has the highest fines concentration (Fig. 10.12B).

Density-induced segregation may be less significant compared to size-induced segregation in die filling. However, the heavier particles tend to sink to the lower region of die and lighter particles immigrate to the upper region. Numerical simulations (Guo et al., 2011a,b) also showed that airflow can have an impact on the segregation of mixtures with fine and/or light particles. In die filling, airflow opposes the powder flow. As a result, the fine particles and light particles are prevented to reach the lower region of the die. The air can be easily entrapped in the corner regions and small cavities. Thus, lower fines concentration is observed in the corner regions and small cavities in the die.

10.5 Summary

Consistent and uniform die filling process is essential for manufacturing high quality powder compacts. The outcomes of die filling are determined by the powder flow and packing, which are significantly affected by the particle characteristics (particle size, density, and shape), shoe and die geometries, and operating conditions (shoe kinematics and powder level in the shoe). To quantify how well the material can flow in die filling, the flow characterization should be performed using a device that can capture the major features of the real die filling processes, e.g., the model die filling system (Fig. 10.1).

Computational modeling, based on the DEM and CFD, has shown great potential in facilitating the analysis and design of die filling systems. Some important observations have been obtained from the simulations: (1) The air can be entrapped in the die, opposing the flow of fine powders into the die; (2) the use of suction filling can avoid the air entrapment in the die and promote the filling rate; and (3) the differences in particle size, particle density and air sensitivity can cause segregation in die filling. According to the computational analysis, some useful recommendations have been made to optimize the die filling process. For instance, using suction filling for very fine powders can help reduce the effect of air, and promoting dense flow stream, restraining relative particle movement, and reducing the impact of powder stream on the boundaries and deposited powder bed can alleviate segregation. Therefore, the computational modeling makes the design process easier by providing more insights to the particle flow and packing behavior in die filling. In addition, the computational modeling can also be used to verify a design by examining the performance of a proposed die filling system.

References

Bierwisch, C., Kraft, T., Riedel, H., Moseler, M., 2009. Three-dimensional discrete element models for the granular statics and dynamics of powders in cavity filling. J. Mech. Phys. Solids. 57, 10–31.

Bocchini, G.F., 1987. Influence of small die width on filling and compacting densities. Powder Metall. 30 (4), 261–266.

Cocks, A.C.F., Dihoru, L., Lawrence, T., 2001. Proc. PM2001, Nice, France, EPMA, pp. 255–260.

de Silva, S., Dyrøy, A., Enstad, G.G., 2000. Segregation mechanisms and their quantification using segregation testers. In: Rosato, A.D., Blackmore, D.L. (Eds.), IUTAM Symposium on Segregation in Granular Flows. Kluwer Academic Publishers, Boston, pp. 11–29.

Guo, Y., Wu, C.-Y., Kafui, K.D., Thornton, C., 2009a. Numerical analysis of density-induced segregation during die filling. Powder Technol. 197, 111–119.

Guo, Y., Kafui, K.D., Wu, C.-Y., Thornton, C., Seville, J.P.K., 2009b. A coupled DEM/CFD analysis of the effect of air on powder flow during die filling. AIChE J. 55, 49–62.

Guo, Y., Wu, C.-Y., Kafui, K.D., Thornton, C., 2011a. 3D DEM/CFD analysis of size-induced segregation during die filling. Powder Technol. 206 (1–2), 177–188.

Guo, Y., Wu, C.-Y., Thornton, C., 2011b. The effects of air and particle density difference on segregation of powder mixtures during die filling. Chem. Eng. Sci. 66 (4), 661–673.

Hashimoto, Y., Murakami, M., Seki, Y., 2002. 'Whizz' solutions agitate for a better-filled die. Metal Powder Rep. 57 (12), 26–29.

Haskins, J.J., Jandeska, W.F., 1998. Powder flow and die filling studies using computed tomography. In: Int. Conf. on Powder Metallurgy and Particulate Materials, Las Vegas, NV, USA, 31 May 4 June 1999, pp. 10.77–10.87.

Hjortsberg, E., Bergquist, B., 2002. Filling induced density variations in metal powder. Powder Metall. 45 (2), 146–153.

Jackson, S., Sinka, I.C., Cocks, A.C.F., 2007. The effect of suction during die fill on a rotary tablet press. Eur. J. Pharm. Biopharm. 65, 253–256.

Kafui, K.D., Thornton, C., Adams, M.J., 2002. Discrete particle–continuum fluid modelling of gas-solid fluidised beds. Chem. Eng. Sci. 57, 2395–2410.

Ketterhagen, W.R., Curtis, J.S., Wassgren, C.R., Hancock, B.C., 2008. Modeling granular segregation in flow from quasi-three-dimensional, wedge-shaped hoppers. Powder Technol. 179, 126–143.

Lawrence, L.R., Beddow, J.K., 1968a. Powder segregation during die filling. Powder Technol. 2, 253–259.

Lawrence, L.R., Beddow, J.K., 1968b. Some effects of vibration upon powder segregation during die filling. Powder Technol. 2, 125–130.

Pei, C., Wu, C.-Y., Adams, M., 2015. Numerical analysis of contact electrification of non-spherical particles in a rotating drum. Powder Technol. Available from: http://dx.doi.org/10.1016/j.powtec.2015.05.050.

Rhodes, M.J., 1998. Introduction to Particle Technology. John Wiley& Sons Ltd, Chichester, England.

Rice, E.R., Tengzelius, J., 1986. Die filling characteristics of metal powders. Powder Metall. 29 (3), 183–194.

Sawayama, T., Seki, Y., 1999. The effect of filling conditions on die filling. Adv. Powder Metall. Particul. Mater. 1 (2), 61–72.

Schneider, L.C.R., Cocks, A.C.F., Apostolopoulos, A., 2005. Comparison of filling behaviour of metallic, ceramic, hardmetal and magnetic powders. Powder Metall. 48, 77–84.

Schneider, L.C.R., Sinka, I.C., Cocks, A.C.F., 2007. Characterisation of the flow behaviour of pharmaceutical powders using a model die-shoe filling system. Powder Technol. 173, 59–71.

Sinka, I.C., Cocks, A.C.F., 2009. Evaluating the flow behaviour of powders for die fill performance. Powder Metall. 52, 8–11.

Sinka, I.C., Schneider, L.C.R., Cocks, A.C.F., 2004. Measurement of the flow properties of powders with special reference to die fill. Int. J. Pharm. 280, 27–38.

Sinka, I.C., Motazedian, F., Cocks, A.C.F., Pitt, K.G., 2009. The effect of processing parameters on pharmaceutical tablet properties. Powder Technol. 189, 276–284.

Thornton, C., Yin, K.K., 1991. Impact of elastic spheres with and without adhesion. Powder Technol. 65, 153–165.

Tsuji, Y., Kawaguchi, T., Tanaka, T., 1993. Discrete particle simulation of two-dimensional fluidized bed. Powder Technol. 77, 79–87.

Wu, C.-Y., 2008. DEM simulations of die filling during pharmaceutical tabletting. Particuology. 6, 412–418.

Wu, C.-Y., Cocks, A.C.F., 2004. Flow behaviour of powders during die filling. Powder Metall. 47, 127–136.

Wu, C.Y., Cocks, A.C.F., 2006. Numerical and experimental investigations of the flow of powder into a confined space. Mech. Mater. 38 (4), 304–324.

Wu, C.-Y., Cocks, A.C.F., Gillia, O.T., 2003a. Die filling and powder transfer. Int. J. Powder Metall. 39, 51–64.

Wu, C.-Y., Dihoru, L., Cocks, A.C.F., 2003b. The flow of powder into simple and stepped dies. Powder Technol. 134, 24–39.

Wu, C.-Y., Guo, Y., 2012. Numerical modelling of suction filling using DEM/CFD. Chem. Eng. Sci. 73, 231–238.

Xie, X., Puri, V.M., 2007a. Simultaneous deposition of powder in three parallel-oriented cylindrical dies. Particul. Sci. Technol. 25, 247–259.

Xie, X., Puri, V.M., 2007b. Powder deposition in three parallel-oriented dies of different shapes. Particul. Sci. Technol. 25, 507–518.

Xie, X., Puri, V.M., 2008. Modeling of simultaneous deposition of powder in three parallel-oriented cylindrical dies. Particul. Sci. Technol. 26, 563–573.

Zahrah, T.F., Rowland, R., Gasbarre Jr., G., 2001. Fluidized fill shoe for uniform die filling. Key Eng. Mater. 189–191, 288–295.

Modeling tablet film-coating processes

11

W. Ketterhagen[1], *A. Aliseda*[2], *M. am Ende*[1], *A. Berchielli*[1], *P. Doshi*[1], *B. Freireich*[3] *and A. Prpich*[1]
[1]Pfizer Worldwide Research & Development, Groton, CT, United States, [2]University of Washington, Seattle, WA, United States, [3]The Dow Chemical Company, Midland, MI, United States

11.1 Introduction

Film coats are applied to tablet cores for a number of functional and/or esthetic reasons. Coating materials may modify or control the release of the active pharmaceutical ingredient (API) from the tablet core or, in the case of active coatings, may contain an API. Coatings are also used to mask the taste, color, or odor of the tablet core, which can help improve patient compliance. They also can provide physical or chemical protection of the tablet core and API from the environment. Finally, coatings are often used to apply a color coat to improve the elegance and aid identification.

The tablet-coating process can be conducted in either a batch process or continuous process. While there is increasing attention on developing continuous tablet-coating processes, the focus of this chapter is on batch-coating processes as they are more commonly used in commercial-scale manufacturing. However, the same concepts presented here can also be applied to continuous coating processes. Most batch-coating processes are conducted in rotating pans as shown schematically in Fig. 11.1. There are a number of different physical phenomena occurring in the pan, each highlighted with a capital letter. The coating pan has perforated walls to permit the flow of drying air through the flowing tablet bed to quickly dry the tablets (A). One or more spray nozzles positioned along the central axis of the pan atomize the coating formulation into fine droplets (B) that are sprayed toward the cascading tablet bed and may dry to some extent (C). Most droplets impact the tablet bed and spread across the surface of a tablet (D). While still in a liquid phase, there may be transfer of coating between tablets (E) before the coating dries on the tablet surface (F). Coating pans also typically contain a number of baffles intended to improve tablet mixing (G) and the uniformity of the coating.

While all of the phenomena depicted in Fig. 11.1 affect the coating process and the quality of the finished coated tablets to some extent, three of these tend to be more important than the others: the thermodynamics of the system (influenced by both the drying air and spray conditions), the spray atomization, and the tablet mixing. In instances where the thermodynamic and spray atomization parameters are not satisfactory, issues with overwetting or overdrying may arise. These issues affect tablet quality through increased occurrence of twinning, sticking and picking,

Predictive Modeling of Pharmaceutical Unit Operations. DOI: http://dx.doi.org/10.1016/B978-0-08-100154-7.00010-7

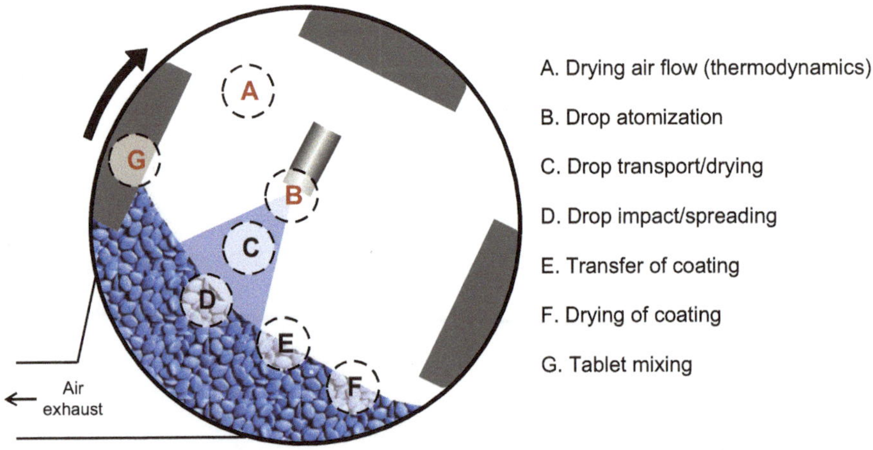

Figure 11.1 A schematic image of a typical batch tablet-coating processes where several different physical phenomena are indicated by the capital letters.

and roughness on the film surface. Insufficient tablet mixing, which is affected by a number of process parameters and equipment design factors, will lead to poor uniformity of the coating on the tablets. The impact of these issues can include process inefficiencies, variability in dissolution performance, and potential batch failure.

In efforts to avoid the aforementioned quality issues, computational models can be used to gain enhanced understanding of the relationships between equipment design, process parameters, and material properties on the quality attributes of the finished coated tablets. These models can then be used to explore what if scenarios, guide experimental efforts, facilitate technology transfer and scale-up, or design a new coating process. While one approach to model the coating process may attempt to include all the physical phenomena described in Fig. 11.1, it is typically customary and advantageous to focus modeling efforts on the key phenomena and add additional physics to the model as needed.

In this chapter, modeling approaches for three key aspects of all tablet-coating processes—the thermodynamics, the spray atomization, and the tablet mixing—are described. In the following sections, the framework for each of the models, along with the key assumptions and limitations, are described and the experimental data required as inputs are specified. In addition, each section focuses on one or more example problems and/or case studies to illustrate how the models are used in industrial applications. Finally, the outlook for developing a single, unified model for film-coating processes is presented.

11.2 Thermodynamic modeling

11.2.1 Description and motivation

Thermodynamic film-coating models have been widely used over the past 20 years to support transfer and scale-up of the process (Table 11.1). These computational

Table 11.1 Overview of published thermodynamic film-coating models for tablets and their applications

References	Application					Predicted outlet parameters	
	Mass balance	Energy balance	Aqueous coatings	Organic coatings	Coating pan(s)	Air exhaust stream	Tablet bed
Reiland et al. (1983)	√	√	√		Accela-Cota 24	Vaporization efficiency (E)	
Stetsko et al. (1983)	√		√		Accela-Cota 48	Water removal efficiency (WRE)	
Ebey (1987)[a]	√	√	√		Accela-Cota	Environmental equivalency (EE)	Tablet rate of drying
Porter et al. (1997)	DOE not thermo model		√		O'Hara technologies labcoat II 24"	$T_{air, out}$	Coating uniformity, LOD, surface roughness, gloss
am Ende and Berchielli (2005)	√	√	√	√	Vector LDCS-20, HCT-30, HCT-60, HC-130L; compulab 36; Accela-Cota 48	$T_{air, out}$ $RH_{air, out}$	
Strong (2009)	√	√	√		Theoretical, no experimental results	Environmental equivalency (EE)	Tablet rate of drying
Prpich et al. (2010)	√	√	√	√	Glatt GC 1250; GC 1500	√	
Choi (accessed 2015)	√	√	√	√	Vector coating pans	$T_{air, out}$ $RH_{air, out}$ Lower explosion limit	Weight uniformity, assay uniformity
Page et al. (2006a,b)	√	√	√		Bohle Lab-Coater	$T_{air, out}$ $RH_{air, out}$	$T_{product}$ Product moisture
Pandey et al. (2006b)	√	√		√	Vector HC-60; HC-130	Scaling rules (inlet parameters to achieve same product): Pan load, pan speed, spray rate, droplet size	
García Muñoz et al. (2011)	√	√	√	√	Vector LDCS-20, HCT-30, HCT-60, HC-130L; compulab 36; Accela-Cota 48	$T_{air, out}$ $RH_{air, out}$ Uncertainty in estimated parameters	
García Muñoz et al. (2012)	√	√	√	√	Vector LDCS-20	Dynamic Conditions: $T_{air, out}$ $RH_{air, out}$	Process end: $T_{product}$ Product moisture

[a] Thermodynamic analysis of aqueous coating (TAAC), computer model by Thomas Engineering.

process tools use mass and energy balances to characterize specific coating types (aqueous or organic) and coating pan equipment (am Ende and Berchielli, 2005; Ebey, 1987). While the majority of modeling applications have been demonstrated for aqueous film coatings, there has been growth in the development of models for organic-based coating systems. The models based on thermodynamics aid in establishing environmental similarity during transfer or scale-up of the formulation and process, whether the term is the water removal efficiency, or environmental equivalency, or stated in terms of outlet conditions of the exhaust and tablets. This approach allows laboratory or pilot-scale experimental results to establish the proven acceptable range, or design space, of environmental conditions (temperature and humidity/solvent levels) for the tablets that can be matched upon transfer and scale-up. Two more recent advances in thermodynamic modeling of the film-coating process include adding parameter estimation to aid in risk management (García Muñoz et al., 2011) and dynamic modeling of the process (García Muñoz et al., 2012).

11.2.2 Model framework

The film-coating process can be considered an adiabatic evaporative cooling process in which the thermodynamic environment is governed by the First Law of Thermodynamics. The am Ende and Berchielli (2005) model is a validated, semi-empirical approach which uses material and energy balances around the tablet bed control volume for the components involved in the process (water and air for aqueous coatings, and solvent(s) and air for organic coatings). The energy balance includes enthalpy expressions for sensible heating as well as latent heat of vaporization of the components. Heat loss from the pan to the surroundings is accounted for through an empirical heat loss factor (HLF) which is directly related to the heat transfer coefficient and the pan surface area. The driving force for fluid evaporation of the coating solution from the tablets is a combination of the drying airflow rate through the pan, the system temperature, and the moisture content of the air. The rotating tablet bed defines the control volume over which the material and energy balances are performed. The inlet streams consist of the drying air, the film-coating solution sprayed from the nozzle, and the compressed air stream used to atomize the coating solution (latter factor neglected due to minimal contribution of <5%). The outlet stream consists of the exhaust air, where the model predicts the temperature and relative humidity of the air exiting the coating pan. The full form of the thermodynamic film-coating model is given as:

$$T_{\text{air,out}} = \frac{\begin{array}{c} m_{\text{air,in}} C_{p,\text{air}} T_{\text{air,in}} + x_w m_{\text{coat}} C_{p,w} T_{\text{coat}} - x_w m_{\text{coat}} \Delta \hat{H}_{\text{vap},w} \\ + x_{\text{org}} m_{\text{coat}} C_{p,\text{org}} T_{\text{coat}} - x_{\text{org}} m_{\text{coat}} \Delta \hat{H}_{\text{vap,org}} + HLF \times T_{\text{RT}} \end{array}}{m_{\text{air,in}} C_{p,\text{air}} + x_w m_{\text{coat}} C_{p,w} + x_{\text{org}} m_{\text{coat}} C_{p,\text{org}} + HLF} \qquad (11.1)$$

where $T_{\text{air,out}}$, $T_{\text{air,in}}$, T_{coat}, and T_{RT} are the temperatures of the exhaust air, inlet air, coating solution, and room temperature, respectively; $m_{\text{air,in}}$ and m_{coat} are the mass flow rates of the inlet air and coating solution; $C_{p,\text{air}}$, $C_{p,w}$, and $C_{p,\text{org}}$ are the specific heat capacities of air, water, and the organic component in the coating solution, respectively; x_w, and x_{org} are the mass fractions of water and organic in the coating solution; $\Delta\hat{H}_{\text{vap},w}$ and $\Delta\hat{H}_{\text{vap,org}}$ are the latent heats of vaporization for water and organic; and *HLF* is the empirical heat loss factor. For aqueous coatings, such as that in the case study in Section 11.2.3.1, the model simplifies to

$$T_{\text{air,out}} = \frac{m_{\text{air,in}} C_{p,\text{air}} T_{\text{air},in} + x_w m_{\text{coat}} C_{p,w} T_{\text{coat}} - x_w m_{\text{coat}} \Delta\hat{H}_{\text{vap},w} + HLF \times T_{\text{RT}}}{m_{\text{air},in} C_{p,\text{air}} + x_w m_{\text{coat}} C_{p,w} + HLF} \tag{11.2}$$

To utilize the model's predictive capabilities, a value for the HLF must be determined for the specific film coater. The HLF for a given coater can be calculated based on a set of experimental data where the exhaust air temperature is known. The HLF is used as a variable fitting parameter to minimize the residual sum of squared error between the experimental data and the model predicted exhaust air temperature. The least squares estimate of the HLF can then be used to predict the exhaust air temperature for the given film coater based on specific inputs to the model, or to determine the set of process conditions that will give a desired exhaust temperature. Once the exhaust air temperature is known, the relative humidity of the outlet air can be calculated based on a material balance for water around the film coater control volume.

11.2.2.1 Similarity of tablet bed and exhaust air conditions

An assumption in the model framework described previously is that the conditions of the exhaust air (temperature and relative humidity) are representative of those in the tablet bed. This was tested in a study where Pyrobutton (Opulus Ltd., Philadelphia, PA) sensors were placed in the exhaust plenum, behind the spray gun, and in the tablet bed during an aqueous film-coating process in the LDCS-30 (2.5 kg scale). As shown in Fig. 11.2, the tablet bed temperature trends with the temperature sensor on the perforated pan as well as the exhaust air temperature at steady state. The relative humidity detected during the coating process responded to changes in temperature and cleaning (Fig. 11.3). The relative humidity near the spray gun was relatively consistent and smaller than the average relative humidity of the tablet bed or exhaust plenum (13–15%RH). This compares well with the predicted value of 18%RH using the thermodynamic model. These remote sensor findings are consistent with previous results demonstrating the tablet bed temperature was essentially equivalent to the exhaust air temperature measured by an infrared gun.

11.2.3 Model verification and application

This model has been extensively verified experimentally across a range of coating formulations and process scales. In Fig. 11.4, the predictive capabilities of this

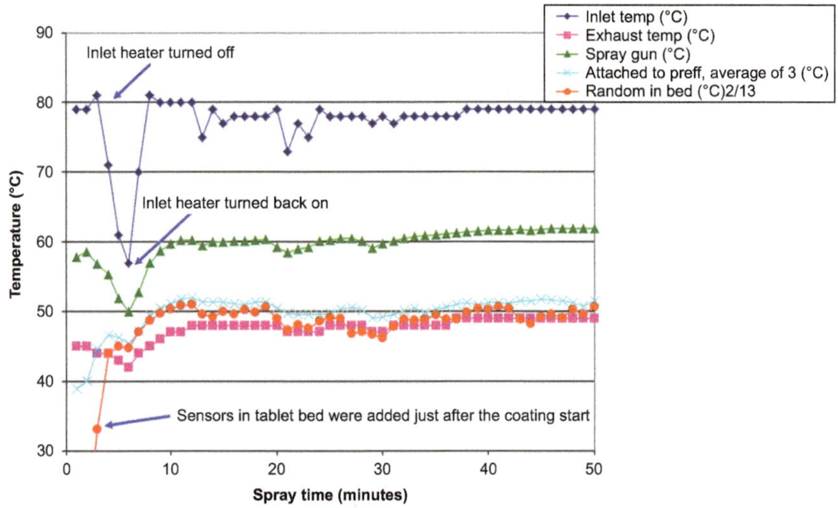

Figure 11.2 Temperature measurement during film coating in a Vector LDCS-30 pan for the given locations in the system.

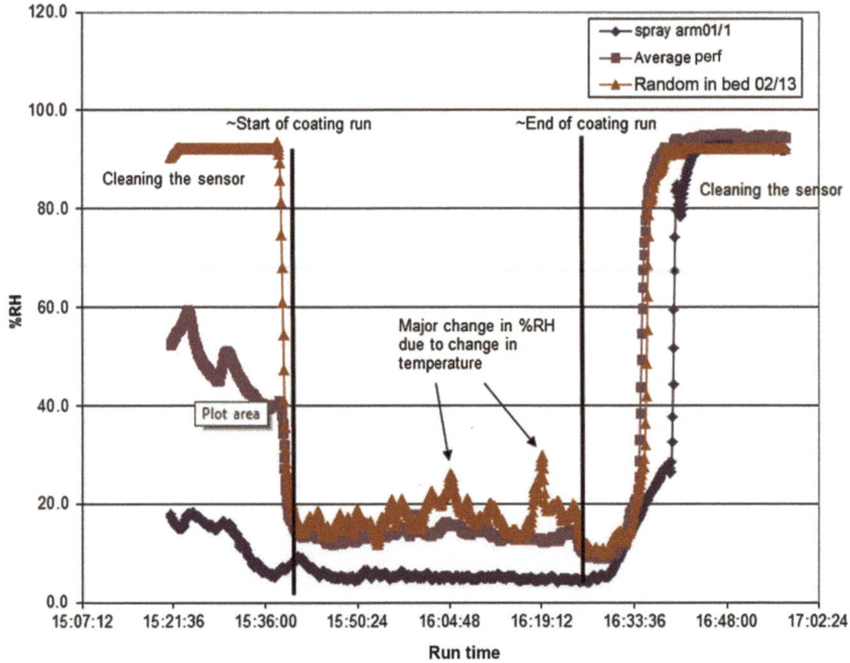

Figure 11.3 Effect of sensor location on measured relative humidity during film coating in a Vector LDCS-30 pan.

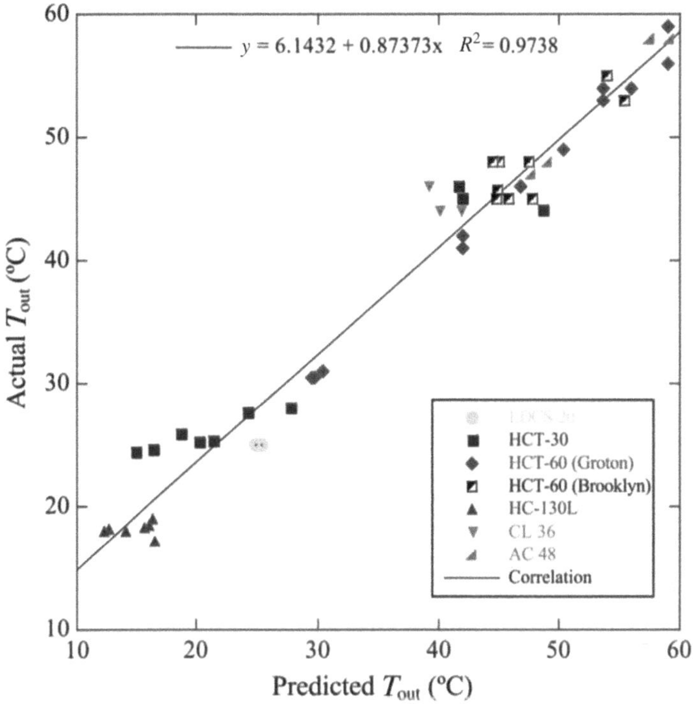

Figure 11.4 Comparison of model predictions with experimental measurements of outlet temperature for both aqueous and organic coatings and process scales ranging from 1 to 220 kg. *Source*: Reprinted from am Ende and Berchielli (2005), with permission from Taylor & Francis Ltd. (http://www.tandfonline.com).

model are shown for six different coating pans (ranging in scale from 1 to 220 kg), two different manufacturing sites, and both aqueous and organic coating formulations. In nearly all cases, good agreement with outlet temperatures within a few degrees is observed.

Example 1: A pilot-scale, aqueous-coating process is to be run in an HCT-60 coating pan with HLF = 700 cal/min°C. The coating formulation consists of 12 wt% solids (88 wt% water), has equilibrated to room temperature of 20°C, and is to be sprayed at 60 g/min. Assuming an inlet air temperature of 68°C, what should the drying airflow rate be set to (in units of CFM) in order to reach an exhaust (bed) temperature of 45°C?

Solution: Using the thermodynamic film-coating model for aqueous formulations (Eq. 11.2), and looking up physical properties of water and air in a handbook, the airflow rate is calculated to be 300 CFM.

11.2.3.1 Case study: immediate release film coating of Drug A tablets

An aqueous-based coating system containing an iron oxide is applied to tablets to enhance photostability and product elegance (García-Muñoz and Gierer, 2010). Coating uniformity is a critical quality attribute due to the ability to provide photostability to Drug A, which without would fail the ICH Q1B guidance for photostability testing requirements. Film-coating spray rate and pan load have been designated as key process parameters and this is a direct relationship with coating uniformity and the number of passes through the spray zone. As the spray rate increases, coating time decreases and leads to a reduced number of times each tablet passes through the spray zone. A compilation of data from development and clinical manufacturing, modeling assessments and prior knowledge was utilized to develop the film-coating-proven acceptable range or design space.

The initial clinical tablet-coating process was developed using plain standard round-, convex-, and oval-shaped tablets coated with a White Opadry II and Clear Opadry coating systems. Tablets were successfully coated in the O'Hara Labcoat II-X and Glatt GC 1000 pan coater units at a scale of 3.5–60 kg. The commercial tablet images were switched to triangular- and oval-shaped tablets coated with an iron oxide containing Opadry II coating systems. These tablets were successfully coated in the Glatt GC 750 and Glatt GC 1000 pans at a scale of 30 and 60 kg, respectively.

The thermodynamic model described previously was used to correlate the thermodynamic operating space to the process parameter ranges for the pan coaters to assist in defining the design space. The HLF was first generated for the Glatt GC 1000 utilizing historical Drug A tablet film-coating data. The predicted and actual exhaust temperatures for the Glatt GC 1000 coater correlated well as shown in Fig. 11.5. Batch data and modeling was then utilized to generate a coating process design space shown in Fig. 11.6. The design space is expressed as a thermodynamic operating space, which is independent of any specific equipment. The thermodynamic model also provided acceptable ranges of specific operating parameters for the Glatt GC 750 coater, a coater that has also been used for clinical supplies manufacture. The HLF for Glatt GC 750 was established using historical coating process data from other products manufactured in the same facility and equipment, using a similar aqueous film-coating system. The four points of the operating spaces for the GC 750 and GC 1000 are based on the thermodynamic modeling data and the central region summarizes the ranges typically used during actual manufacture. Table 11.2 summarizes the acceptable ranges of coating parameters based on thermodynamic consideration for maintaining constant exhaust air temperature between scales, although a multitude of solutions for the inlet variables is possible to meet the same exhaust conditions.

11.2.3.2 Case study: immediate release film coating of Drug B tablets

An aqueous-based coating system was applied to Drug B tablet cores to enhance elegance and provide product differentiation. The water content of the coated

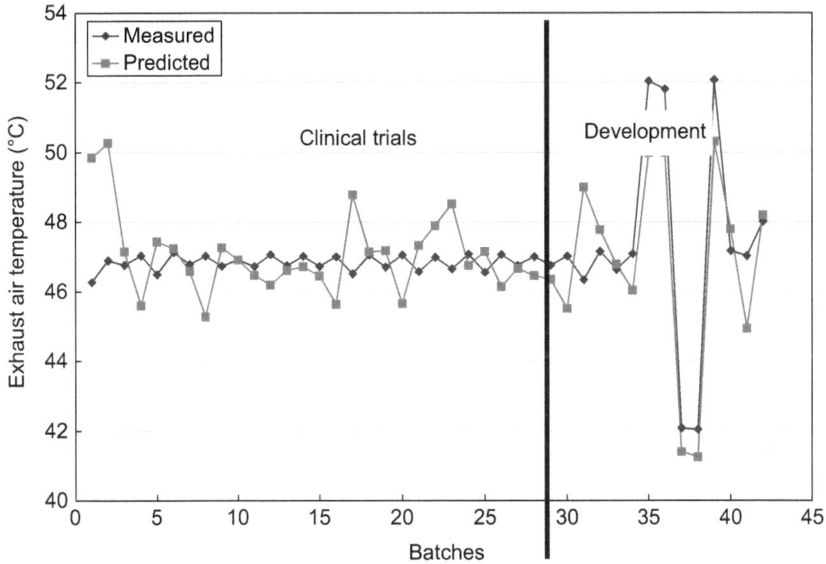

Figure 11.5 Comparison of predicted exhaust air temperature from the thermodynamic model to process data for Drug A from the manufacturing site.

tablets is limited to levels less than 5.5% at release to ensure long-term stability. The film-coating process parameters were evaluated for the impact on tablet appearance and tablet water content. For all coating trials with a wide range of process conditions, tablet water content was found to be less than 5.0%.

To define the acceptable film-coating process parameter operating ranges at commercial scale, a thermodynamic model was used to analyze results collected from the placebo film-coating study and Drug B batch manufacturing. This model accounts for the impact that the process parameters (spray rate, inlet air temperature, airflow rate, and inlet air moisture) and their interactions have on the film-coating operation. As shown in Fig. 11.7, the predicted exhaust air temperature values from the model are in good agreement with the actual Drug B process data, demonstrating the predictive capabilities of this model.

The thermodynamic model was used to delineate the film-coating process knowledge space for Drug B tablets, which is expressed in terms of exhaust air temperature and exhaust air humidity, as shown in Fig. 11.8. Trials with placebo tablets and other similar products have been successfully executed at the boundaries of the operating space using the GC 1000 coater. Points A, C, and D are representative of three of the experimental trials from the placebo film-coating study. Point B corresponds to development trials for another product with similar formulation characteristics. The data from actual Drug B tablet manufacturing trials were also analyzed and were shown to scatter around the center and within the boundaries of the thermodynamic space.

The thermodynamic operating space shown in Fig. 11.8 is independent of the coating equipment used, according the principles of the model. The operating

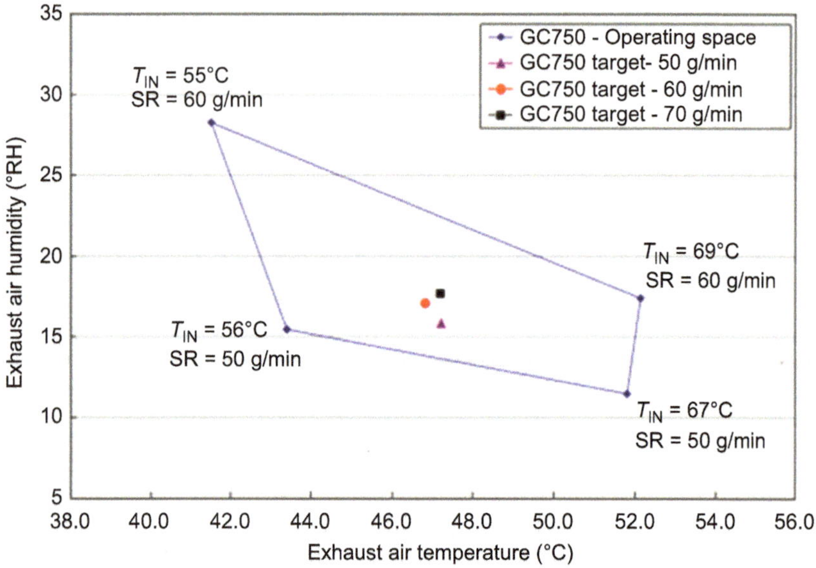

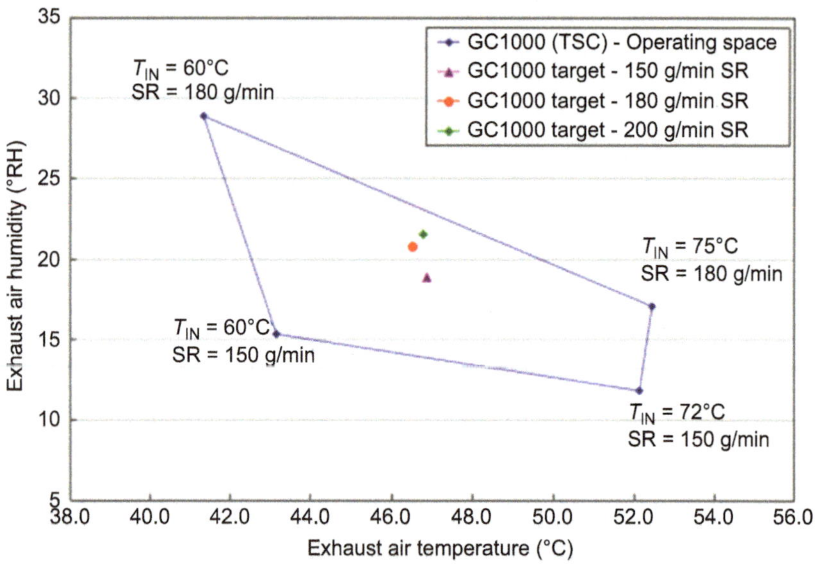

Figure 11.6 Thermodynamic operating space for the Drug A film-coating process in (A) a Glatt GC 750 coating pan and (B) a Glatt GC 1000 coating pan.

parameters equivalent to the acceptable thermodynamic space for GC 1500 coater were defined using the model, and these operating parameters together with the corresponding thermodynamic parameters are listed in Table 11.3.

Over 50 batches of Drug B tablets, including the commercial formulation made with the proposed commercial process, have been successfully coated using the

Table 11.2 Acceptable ranges of coating process parameters based on the coating thermodynamic model

Coating process parameter	Glatt GC 750	Glatt GC 1000
Exhaust temperature (°C)	42–52	42–52
Exhaust humidity (%RH)	10–30	10–30
Inlet air temperature (°C)	55–70	60–75
Drying airflow rate (CFM)	470	860–900
Spray rate (mL/min)	50–70	140–200

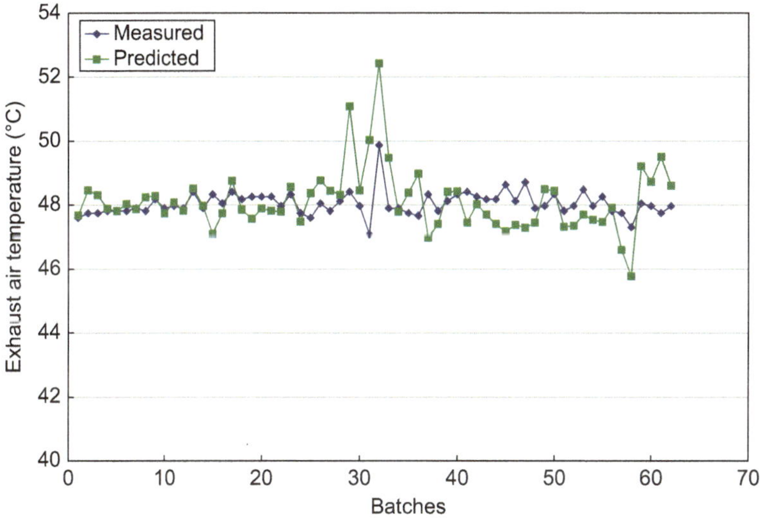

Figure 11.7 Comparison of predicted exhaust air temperature from the thermodynamic model to Drug B tablet process data from the GC 1500 coater.

Glatt GC 1000 and Glatt GC 1500 pan coaters at a range of process conditions. The majority of these batches were coated at the proposed commercial scale (~300 kg). Although the coating spray rate and pan load were varied over wide ranges for these batches, the measured tablet water content values were all found to be below the specification limit. The ranges of the process parameters and the tablet water content measured by loss on drying (LOD) and Karl Fischer (KF) methods are summarized in Table 11.4.

The water content of the coated tablets ranged from 2.9% to 4.1% by LOD method when measured as part of in-process testing, and from 3.9% to 5.0% by KF method when tested at release. These results demonstrate that the film-coating process consistently generates tablets with water content below the release limit of less than or equal to 5.5% by KF, despite the variations in spray rates and pan loads, and confirms the noncritical designation for the spray rate and pan load process parameters.

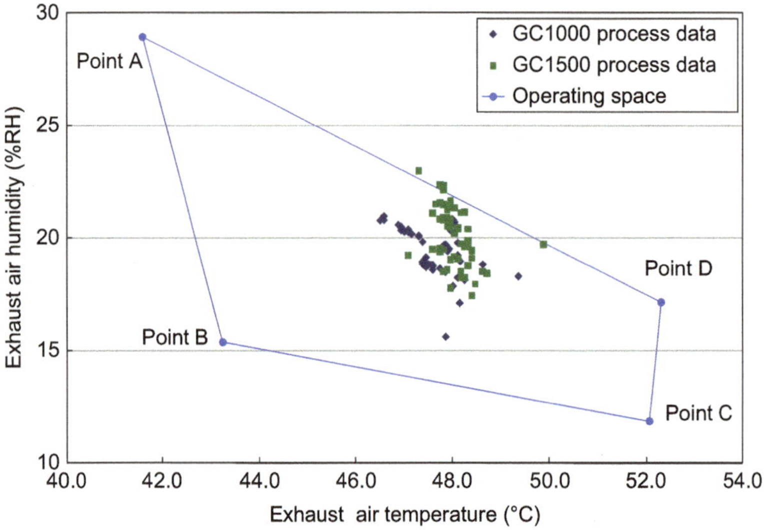

Figure 11.8 Acceptable thermodynamic operating range for Drug B tablet-coating process.

Table 11.3 Examples of coating parameters at target and boundary of the acceptable thermodynamic space

Location	Thermodynamic parameters		GC 1500 operating parameters			
	Exhaust air temperature, °C	Exhaust air humidity, %	Spray rate, g/min	Inlet temperature, °C	Airflow rate, m^3/h	Inlet air moisture, g/kg
Center point	48.0	17.8	500	61.0	5000	7.5
Center point	47.7	22.1	800	68.0	5000	7.5
Point A	41.6	29.1	800	61.0	5000	6.8
Point B	43.5	15.2	500	56.0	5000	3.5
Point C	52.4	11.7	500	66.0	5000	5.0
Point D	52.0	16.9	800	73.0	5000	6.6

11.3 Spray atomization modeling

11.3.1 Description and motivation

Spray atomization models may be used to provide understanding of the spray droplet size, typically an unmeasured process attribute (Aliseda et al., 2008; Mueller and Kleinebudde, 2007; Müller and Kleinebudde, 2006; Tobiska and Kleinebudde,

Table 11.4 Ranges of coating process parameters and tablet water content of Drug B tablets made at pilot/production scale

Coating pan	Pan load (kg)	Pan fill[a] (%)	Set spray rate (g/min)	Tablet water content,% (by LOD)	Tablet water content, % (by KF)
Glatt GC 1000	49–60	51–63	150–200	2.9–4.0	3.9–4.7
Glatt GC 1500	256–369	66–95	500–800	3.1–4.1	4.1–5.0

[a]The percentage of pan fill is based on the brim volume of the pan and tablet bulk density of 0.8 g/cc.

2003). In turn, the drop size predictions can help to design the initial process or provide guidance for scale-up with reduced need for trial-and-error experiments. This section of the book chapter will show how a modeling approach can be used to select the atomization process conditions based on the formulation, process parameters, and equipment design.

Three main factors influence the droplet size created by spray guns. These include (1) the rheological properties of the fluid, (2) the geometry of the spray atomization nozzle, and (3) the process conditions including the fluid spray rate and rates of atomization and pattern airflows. Any of these factors may change during scale up or even from coater to coater at a given scale, due to different vendor and site purchasing preferences.

The rheology of the coating fluid is dependent on the formulation components and plays an important role in determining drop size during atomization. The use of polymers such as hypromellose (HPMC) or polyvinyl alcohol (PVA) for film formers in immediate release color coatings has mostly replaced the use of sugar coatings. Key fluid properties such as viscosity, density, and surface tension for HPMC- and PVA-based coatings are given in Table 11.5 as a function of solids content.

A variety of spray nozzle geometries exists with different fluid nozzle and air orifice diameters. An example spray gun schematic for a Spraying Systems setup is shown in Fig. 11.9. Spray nozzles can be selected along with process parameters to achieve different performance factors related to the droplet size, spray zone shape, and area of coverage. The coating fluid is supplied through a nozzle at a relatively low speed as a process gas (typically air) is introduced around the liquid at very high speed where it atomizes the coating fluid into droplets. These atomizers give precise control of the fluid and atomizing air rates, and associated droplet size. Pattern air may also be applied to shape the spray allowing for better spray coverage in the axial direction across the tablet bed.

Historically, the atomization condition was selected based on previous experience or vendor recommendation, but not adjusted systematically based on the actual formulation properties or equipment/process capability. Generally, adjustment would only be made if there were severe issues during initial development of the coating process or as part of range finding studies.

Physics-based atomization models allow for more rational process design where coating fluid properties (mainly viscosity) and process parameters (mainly

Table 11.5 Summary of material properties for various coating formations with the given solids concentration

Coating no.	Coating type	Percent solids	Viscosity of coating fluid @ 25°C and 1048 s^{-1} (kg/ms)	Density of coating fluid (g/cc)	Surface tension of coating fluid (dynes/cm)
1	Opadry II White (Y-30-18037) HPMC/Lactose/ TiO_2/Triacetin/ Water	15	0.098	1.05	47.0
2	Opadry II White (85F18422) PVA/ PEG/Water	20	0.039	1.07	43.9
3	Opadry II White (OY-LS-28914) HPMC/Lactose/ TiO_2/Triacetin	10	0.095	1.02	48.2
3	Opadry II White (OY-LS-28914) HPMC/Lactose/ TiO_2/Triacetin	12	0.181	1.03	47.7
3	Opadry II White (OY-LS-28914) HPMC/Lactose/ TiO_2/Triacetin	15	0.419	1.04	46.7

atomization airflow rate) can be selected based on spray gun geometry and the desired spray rate to achieve a target primary droplet size. This droplet size can then be maintained or changed as desired during scale-up or technology transfer.

11.3.2 Model framework

It has been well documented (Aliseda et al., 2008; Varga et al., 2003) that the liquid breakup process follows a sequence of Kelvin–Helmholtz instability disrupting the liquid jet and forming liquid ligaments, followed by a Rayleigh–Taylor instability resulting in the breakup of the liquid ligaments into individual droplets. The Kelvin–Helmholtz instability develops in the annular shear layer that exists between the low speed liquid injection and the high-speed coaxial gas jet (Joseph et al., 2002; Lasheras and Hopfinger, 2000; Mansour and Chigier, 1995). Once the liquid has been displaced from its axisymmetric position, it suffers a sudden acceleration as a result of the drag imposed by the gas flow and a Rayleigh–Taylor instability at the interface ensues.

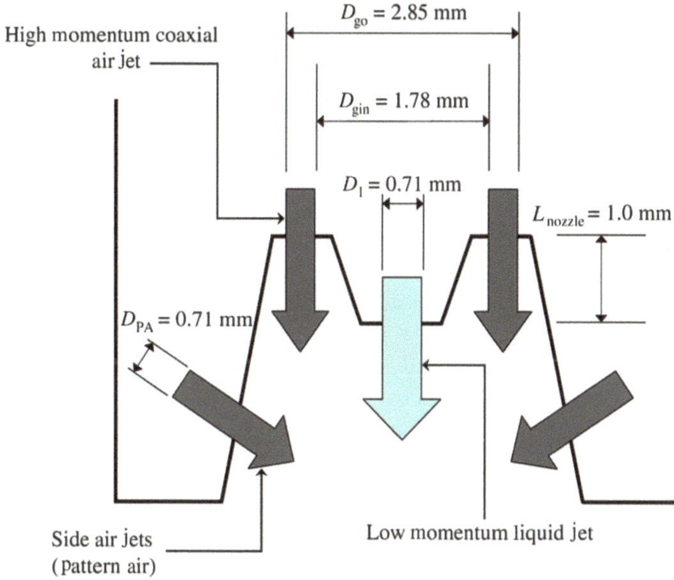

Figure 11.9 Diagram showing the side view of a laboratory scale, Spraying Systems fluid nozzle and air cap setup for tablet coating.
Source: Reprinted from Aliseda et al. (2008), with permission from Elsevier.

As shown previously (Aliseda et al., 2008), a model for the drop diameter, namely the Sauter mean diameter (SMD), can be expressed as

$$\frac{\text{SMD}}{D_l} = C_1(1+m_r)\left(\frac{b_g}{D_l}\right)^{1/2}\left(\frac{\rho_l/\rho_g}{Re_{b_g}}\right)^{1/4} \times \frac{1}{\sqrt{We_{D_l}}}\left\{1 + C_2\left(\frac{D_l}{b_g}\right)^{1/6}\left(\frac{Re_{b_g}}{\rho_l/\rho_g}\right)^{1/12} We_{D_l}^{1/6} Oh^{2/3}\right\} \tag{11.3}$$

where D_l is the liquid orifice diameter, C_1 and C_2 are empirical parameters, ρ_l and ρ_g are the liquid and gas densities, respectively, and the following dimensionless numbers defined as

Weber number: $We_{D_l} = \dfrac{\rho_g(U_{\text{Gas}} - U_c)^2 D_l}{\sigma}$

Ohnesorge number: $Oh = \dfrac{\alpha_l}{\sqrt{\rho_l \sigma D_l}}$

Reynolds number: $Re_{b_g} = \dfrac{U_{\text{Gas}} b_g}{\nu_g}$

Massflux ratio: $m_r = \dfrac{\rho_l U_{\text{Liquid}} A_l}{\rho_g U_{\text{Gas}} A_g}$

Momentum ratio: $M_r = \dfrac{\rho_g U_{\text{Gas}}^2}{\rho_l U_{\text{Liquid}}}$

where U_{Gas} and U_{Liquid} are the velocities of the gas and liquid streams, respectively, U_c is the convective velocity of the liquid tongues, σ is the surface tension, α_l is the effective shear viscosity of the liquid, b_g is thickness of the gas jet, ν_g is kinematic viscosity of the gas, A_l and A_g are areas of the liquid and gas nozzle exit sections, respectively.

While the SMD in Eq. (11.3) is nondimensionalized with the liquid orifice diameter D_l, it should be emphasized that the drop diameter does not depend on the liquid orifice diameter but rather on the gas boundary layer thickness at the nozzle exit. This has been clearly demonstrated by Marmottant (2001) where the liquid orifice diameter was changed by a factor of 3 and the drop diameter remained practically identical for the same gas flow conditions.

The mass loading effect in the form $(1 + m_r)$ is obtained from energy arguments previously outlined by Mansour and Chigier (1995), where $m_r = m_l/m_g = \rho_l U_{Liquid} A_l / \rho_g U_{Gas} A_g$ and A_l and A_g are the areas of the liquid and gas nozzle exit sections, respectively. Furthermore, this equation indicates a dependency of the SMD on $U_{Gas}^{-5/4}$ and $\sigma^{-1/2}$.

The coefficients C_1 and C_2 in Eq. (11.3) are order 1 and values for both coefficients are determined from experiments. The value of C_1 depends on the gas nozzle geometry in general, and on the contraction ratio in particular, because for a given nozzle size the gas boundary layer thickness at the liquid nozzle discharge depends strongly on the contraction ratio. C_2 characterizes the viscosity dependence of the critical wavenumber in the Rayleigh–Taylor instability, compared to the surface tension dependence. This value is associated to the additivity and linearity of both cohesive effects, surface tension and viscosity, which determine the growth rate of the instability. The validity of the linear theory for Rayleigh–Taylor instability has been confirmed for a wide parameter range via qualitative observation of the jet breakup process.

Another important parameter, which does not appear explicitly in Eq. (11.3), is the dynamic pressure, or momentum, ratio M that determines the rate of atomization and hence the intact length of the liquid stream (Lasheras and Hopfinger, 2000). This ratio is defined as

$$M = \frac{\rho_g U_{Gas}^2}{\rho_l U_{Liquid}^2} \tag{11.4}$$

The dimensionless intact length of the liquid stream can be defined as $L/D_l \approx 6/\sqrt{M}$ and in coaxial injectors used under usual tablet-coating processes, M is typically large (of the order 100). The gas potential cone length is approximately $6b_g$. For efficient atomization, it is desirable that the gas potential cone length be equal to or larger than the liquid intact length so that the primary atomization is completed before the gas velocity starts to decrease. This requirement is expressed by

$$\frac{b_g\sqrt{M}}{D_l} > 1 \tag{11.5}$$

It is worth noting that for the flow rates and atomizers utilized in pharmaceutical tablet coating, Eq. (11.5) is satisfied easily, with values typically exceeding 10, strongly suggesting that atomization is typically quite rapid and efficient.

Finally, the fluid jets under the conditions of interest here are laminar at the injector nozzle but would potentially become turbulent if the flow rates are significantly increased or the gas contraction ratio decreased. Turbulent conditions of the liquid stream at the nozzle discharge plane would have little effect on the atomization process, while turbulent conditions in the high-speed gas stream would require altering the exponent of Re_{b_g} in Eq. (11.3).

11.3.2.1 Effect of pattern air on liquid breakup

The model presented previously is derived for two coaxial streams of liquid and air, without taking into account the effect of pattern air on the liquid breakup. The effect of pattern air can be included in the model in two different ways depending on whether the pattern air is involved in the atomization process.

In spray guns where the pattern air nozzles are oriented such that the jets impinge on the spray axis at a distance from the atomization nozzle at which liquid breakup is already underway, the effect of pattern air on droplet size is minor. Because the droplet size is set by the wavelength of the secondary Rayleigh–Taylor instability, pattern air does not modify it when the instability is already growing. Therefore, for this type of atomizer, only the gas flow through the atomization nozzle affects the breakup.

In spray guns where the position and orientation of the pattern air nozzles result in the pattern air jets impinging on the spray axis in the region where the instability of the liquid jet is still developing, the impact of the pattern air jets on the atomized droplet size is very strong. This effect can be modeled by considering that the atomizing air and the pattern air mix while the liquid jet is breaking up. The resulting air stream has axial momentum equal to the sum of all the jets but no radial momentum as the two pattern air side jets have equal but opposite values that cancel when the two streams mix. One can implement this into the previously derived model by computing the gas jet as the mean air velocity of the two streams, $U_g = (m_{\text{atom}} U_{\text{atom}} + m_{\text{pattern}} U_{\text{pattern}} \cos\theta)/(m_{\text{atom}} + m_{\text{pattern}})$, where θ is the angle between the pattern air jet axis and the atomizing air jet axis. Although there are a number of approximations underlying this model, most importantly that the air streams mix instantly and that the instability is not modified by the lack of axial symmetry induced by the pattern air, it has been proven to provide accurate predictions for the droplet size under typical pharmaceutical coating conditions.

In atomizers where the pattern air is supplied by the same line as the atomizer air, the effect of pattern air is simply to reroute some of the available gas from the atomizing nozzle to the side jets, therefore reducing the atomizing airflow rate and the exit velocity. To account for these cases where the pattern air does not have independent flow control and measurements, it is easiest to measure the cross-sectional area of both the atomizing nozzle and the pattern air and to prorate the total flow rate into the two air streams according to the pressure loss across the two nozzles (which is proportional to the diameter to the fourth power). The atomizing air is the value that is input into the model to determine U_g and, consequently, the Weber number and the gas Reynolds number.

11.3.2.2 Materials characterization

It is important to measure the coating fluid material properties, in particular the viscosity, at conditions (i.e., temperature, shear rate) similar to those near the nozzle tip. The viscosity behavior of commonly available coating systems at different shear rates is shown in Fig. 11.10. In a typical atomization process, the shear rate is well above 200 s^{-1} (Aliseda et al., 2008). For simplification, it is suggested to measure viscosity at a sufficiently high-shear rate (e.g., 1000 s^{-1}) because there is typically little variation in viscosity in the range of large shear rates. Similarly, it is also important to measure the viscosity at a temperature similar to that where breakup occurs at the nozzle tip. Viscosity is plotted as a function of temperature for three common coating systems in Fig. 11.11. Another consideration is to stay below the thermal gelation point of the coating fluid to avoid semisolid formation, which may be unsprayable (Cole et al., 1995).

A key factor controlling viscosity is the type and level of film former. Depending on the molecular weight (viscosity grade) and amount of the film former in the formulation (weight percent in the dry formulation and solids loading percent in the fluid), very different viscosity values can be achieved. An example can be seen in Fig. 11.12 where viscosity dramatically increases over the normal range of formulations spanning solids loadings of 10–15%. This change leads to a large difference in droplet sizes.

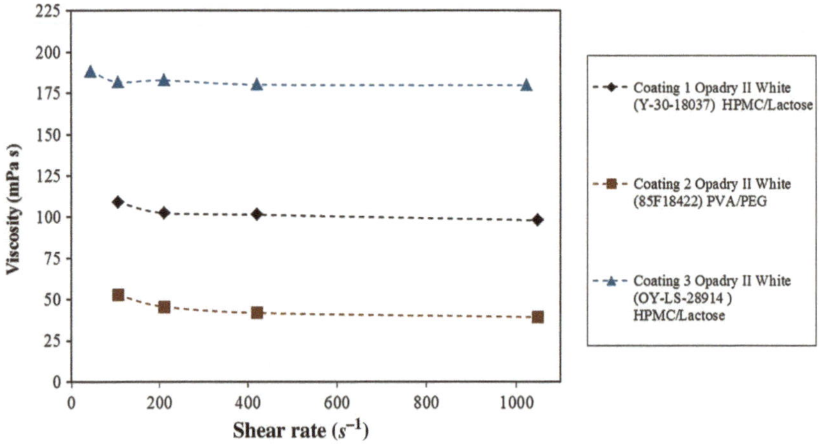

Figure 11.10 Effect of shear rate on viscosity for four coating formulations at 25°C.

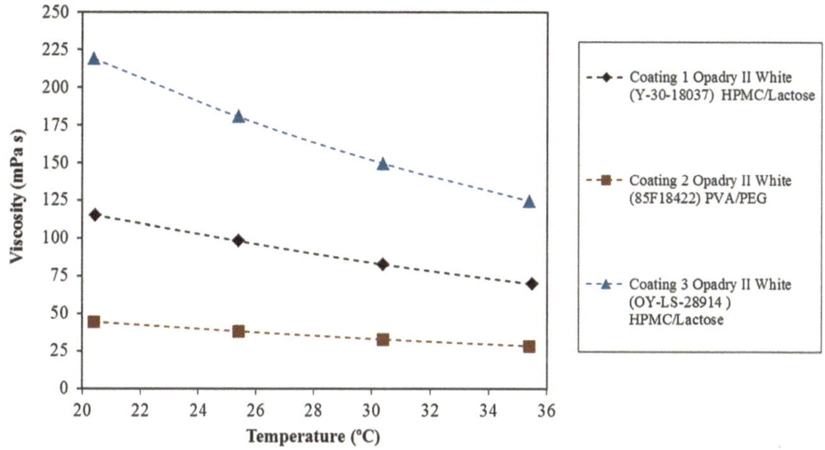

Figure 11.11 Effect of temperature on viscosity for three different coating formulations at a shear rate of 1000 s^{-1}.

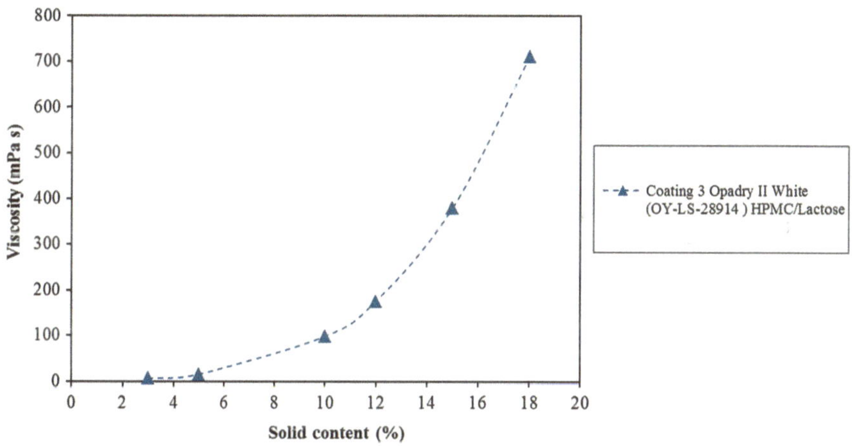

Figure 11.12 Effect of solids content on coating fluid viscosity for Opadry OY-LS-28914 at 25°C and a shear rate of 1000 s^{-1}.

11.3.3 Model verification and application

Droplet size distributions can be measured by a number of instruments that rely on light scattering to determine the droplet size unintrusively. The most widely used measurement technique, Phase Doppler Particle Analysis (PDPA), is based on light interferometry to evaluate the phase shift introduced by a scattering spherical droplet on the point illumination created by the convergence of coherent light from two laser beams with slightly different wavelengths. This phase difference measured in the signal from three photomultipliers, forming two pairs, is linearly dependent on

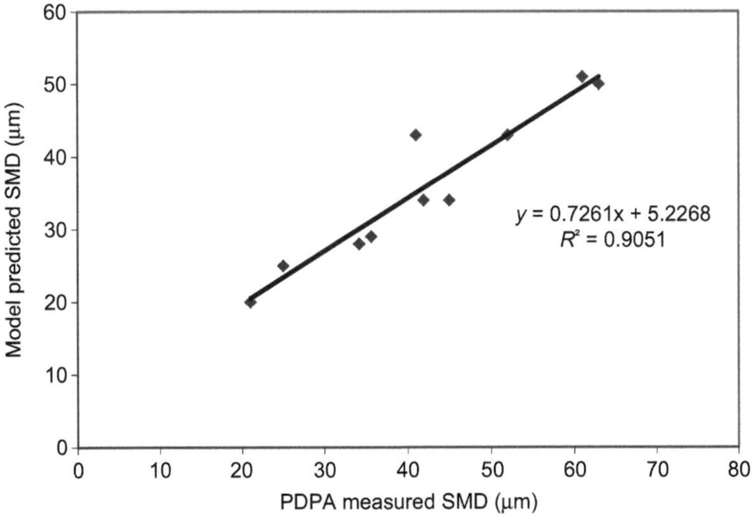

Figure 11.13 Comparison of model predictions and PDPA measured mean drop size SMD for both Spraying Systems and Schlick ABC spray guns.

the scatterer's diameter. A much more detailed description of the measurement principle was published by Bachalo (1994). Utilizing PDPA, droplet size measurements allow for comparison with the model predicted droplet sizes. Fig. 11.13 shows good agreement between the measured and predicted droplet sizes for cases using two different spray gun types (Spraying Systems and Schlick ABC) producing droplets over a typical range of values.

Example 1: Using the atomization model described previously, calculate the Sauter Mean Drop size for a film-coating process using a 15 wt% solids, HPMC-based coating Y-30-18037. The coating formulation properties are given in Table 11.5 and the process conditions and spray nozzle geometry are listed in Table 11.6. How would the drop size be affected if a 20 wt% solid, PVA-based coating 85F18422 were to be used instead? How could one adjust the process conditions to change the drop size of the PVA-based coating to match that of the HPMC-based coating?

Solution: Given the material properties in Table 11.5, coating #1, and the process parameters in Table 11.6, Example 1-1, the atomization model in Eq. (113) predicts a droplet size SMD of 49.9 μm. If the same process were used for a PVA-based formulation (material properties in Table 11.5, coating #2), the predicted droplet size would be ~34% smaller, as shown in Table 11.6, Example 1-2. This may not be intuitive because the solids content was increased in the PVA example, but due to the lower viscosity of the PVA-based formulation, the droplet size will decrease. One approach to match the droplet size of the HPMC-based coating in Example 1-1 (HPMC Process A) is to reduce the atomization air, as shown in Table 11.6 for the lower viscosity PVA coating, Example 1-3 (PVA Process B).

Table 11.6 Impact of coating formulation polymer type (HPMC vs PVA) on droplet size and selection of atomization airflow rate to achieve a similar droplet size

Spray formulation, parameters, and variables	Example 1-1 HPMC based Y-30-18037 (15% solids)	Example 1-2 PVA based 85F18422 (20% solids)	Example 1-3 PVA based 85F18422 (20% solids)
Process type	Process A	Process A	Process B
Coating type	Coating 1	Coating 2	Coating 2
Action taken	None Base process	Base process with new coating	Atomizing gas decreased to match droplet size of process A Coating 1
Spray pattern type	Ellipse	Ellipse	Ellipse
Fluid nozzle part #	PF28100	PF28100	PF28100
Air cap part #	PA110228-45	PA110228-45	PA110228-45
Input parameters:			
Inner diameter of liquid nozzle (mm)	0.71	0.71	0.71
Outer diameter of the atomizing gas cap (mm)	2.79	2.79	2.79
Inner diameter of the atomizing gas cap (mm)	1.78	1.78	1.78
Diameter of the pattern air side orifices (mm)	0.71	0.71	0.71
Liquid surface tension (mN/m)	47.0	43.9	43.9
Liquid density (kg/m^3)	1050.0	1070.0	1070.0
Infinite shear rate viscosity (kg/ms)	0.098	0.039	0.039
Spray rate (grams/min/spray gun)	10	10	10
Atomizing and pattern gas volumetric flow rate (m^3/s)	9.44E-04	9.44E-04	6.63E-04
Calculated values used in model:			
Atomizing gas outlet velocity (m/s)	213.7	213.7	150.1
Model output:			
Sauter mean diameter (μm)	49.9	33.1	49.9

Example 2: The coating process using the HPMC-based coating Y-30-18037, described in Example 1, is modified by changing the spray gun to a Schlick ABC antibearding cap design with dimensions given in Table 11.7. If the same atomization airflow rate is used without pattern air, what will be the mean droplet size for this new process? If the atomization air is set to a volumetric rate equivalent to the atomization air, how would the mean droplet size change? How should the air atomization and pattern air be adjusted, maintaining a 1:1 ratio of the volumetric flow rates, to reach a mean drop size of 49.9 μm?

Solution: Given the material properties in Table 11.5, coating #1, and the process parameters in Table 11.5, Example 2-1, the atomization model in Eq. (11.3) predicts a droplet size SMD of 33.9 μm due to differences in spray gun geometry. The addition of independent pattern air of equal volume (a relatively high setting) further reduces the droplet size to 27.4 μm due to the pattern air contribution to atomization, which was discussed earlier in the chapter (Table 11.7, Example 2-2). To meet a target droplet size of 49.9 μm, the atomization model can be used to back-calculate the necessary airflow rates, assuming a 1:1 volumetric ratio, with inputs given in Table 11.7, Example 2-3. With this spray nozzle, the airflow rates must be reduced to 5.28E-04 m^3/s to reach the target drop size of 49.9 μm.

11.3.4 Global sensitivity analysis

The atomization model described in previous sections is dependent on several input parameters. The reliability of this model's prediction could depend on the source of uncertainty in the input parameters. Therefore, it is important to carry out a sensitivity analysis (SA) of the model to both quantify the impact of this variability on the output as well as rank order the importance of various input parameters. SA has been succinctly defined by Saltelli et al. (2004) as "the study of how the uncertainty in the output of a model can be apportioned to different sources of uncertainty in the model input." Various techniques to carry out SA can be broadly classified into local and global strategies. Local SA is concerned with individual input − output relationships. It typically involves the calculation of partial derivatives of output with respect to various input parameters. The term local refers to the fact that all derivatives are taken at a single point. This kind of analysis cannot evaluate the effect of multiple inputs acting in concert on the output. In global sensitivity analysis (GSA), all inputs are varied simultaneously to evaluate the effect of individual inputs as well as the cooperative effect of multiple inputs on the output. This rich information content from global SA typically requires a large Monte Carlo sampling study, and could be numerically expensive depending on the model at hand (Homma and Saltelli, 1996; Sobol, 2001).

In the current work, because a single invocation of the spray atomization model in Matlab takes less than one second, GSA is being carried out. The goal of this analysis is to determine the impact of two operating parameters, atomization airflow rate and coating fluid spray rates, along with three material parameters, viscosity, surface tension, and density, on the mean drop size. There are several

Table 11.7 Impact of spray gun type and pattern air effect on droplet size for the Schlick ABC setup

Spray formulation, parameters, and variables	Example 2-1 Spray gun 2 Schlick ABC Y-30-18037 (15% solids)	Example 2-2 Spray gun 2 Schlick ABC Y-30-18037 (15% solids)	Example 2-3 Spray gun 2 Schlick ABC Y-30-18037 (15% solids)
Action taken	No pattern air	High volume of pattern air	Change in process to give 49.9 μm droplets to match Example 1-1
Spray pattern type	Circular	Ellipse	Ellipse
Fluid nozzle part #	10 w44019	10 w44019	10 w44019
Air cap part #	27 w44183	27 w44183	27 w44183
Input parameters:			
Inner diameter of liquid nozzle (mm)	1.00	1.00	1.00
Outer diameter of the atomizing gas cap (mm)	2.70	2.70	2.70
Inner diameter of the atomizing gas cap (mm)	1.85	1.85	1.85
Diameter of the pattern air side orifices (mm)	1.50	1.50	1.50
Liquid surface tension (mN/m)	47.0	47.0	47.0
Liquid density (kg/m^3)	1050.0	1050.0	1050.0
Infinite shear rate viscosity (kg/ms)	0.098	0.098	0.098
Spray rate (grams/min/spray gun)	10	10	10
Atomizing gas volumetric flow rate (m^3/s)	9.44E-04	9.44E-04	5.28E-04
Pattern gas volumetric flow rate (m^3/s)	0	9.44E-04	5.28E-04
Calculated values used in model:			
Atomizing gas outlet velocity (m/s)	310.8	310.8	173.8
Model output:			
Sauter mean diameter (μm)	33.9	27.4	49.9

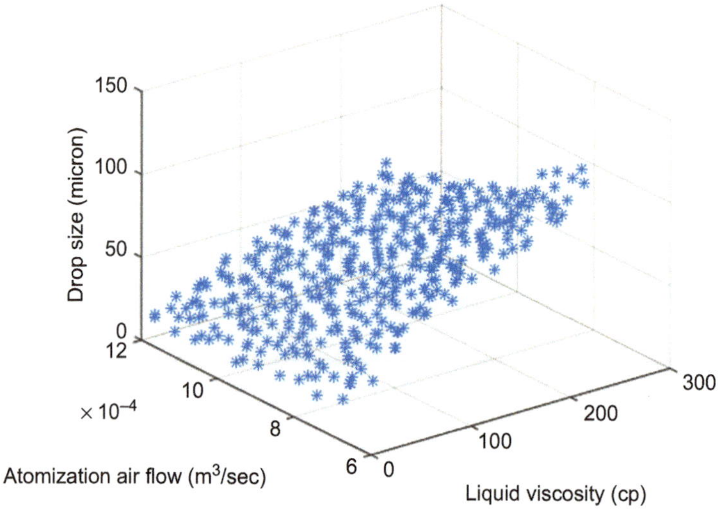

Figure 11.14 Mean drop diameter plotted against atomization airflow rate and liquid viscosity.

methods to carry out GSA, one that is chosen is the Sobol (2001) approach based on ANOVA decomposition. Cannavó (2012) has developed a Matlab-based toolbox, GSAT, to carry out GSA. This toolbox was obtained from Matlab central repository and appropriately modified to analyze the output of atomization model. It uses the algorithm developed by Homma and Saltelli (1996) to compute first-order and higher-order sensitivity indices. The nominal values of five input parameters were chosen as shown in Table 11.6 for coating 1 and process A and GSAT software computed (25-1) sensitivity indices. Fig. 11.14 shows the results of Monte Carlo sampling of 1000 runs when five input parameters were varied between 30% of their nominal values using a pseudorandom distribution. The scatter plot shows that the mean drop size varies between 10 to 120 μm, and it increases with the liquid viscosity, and decreases with the atomization airflow rate. Fig. 11.15 shows the histogram representing the distribution of mean drop size. It is clear from this figure that distribution is asymmetric about mean and is skewed toward larger drop size, emphasizing the nonlinearity of the model. Fig. 11.16 shows the first-order sensitivity indices for the five input parameters. The dominant effects are contributed by atomization airflow rate and liquid viscosity, with sensitivity indices of 0.81 and 0.17, respectively. The remaining three other parameters along with all the higher-order indices have negligible impact on the output. SA clearly shows these two parameters should be closely monitored during atomization process design. As shown in Fig. 11.12, the coating liquid viscosity exhibits large variation with increasing solids fraction. To account for this variability, SA is carried out where liquid viscosity was allowed to vary between 75% of its nominal value, whereas the variability of other four parameters was

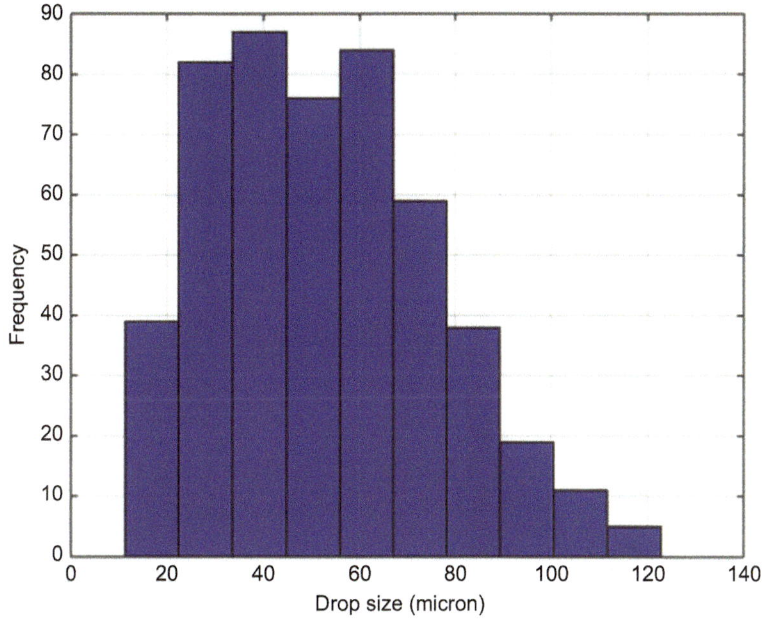

Figure 11.15 Histogram showing the distribution of mean drop size when five input parameters are varied within 30% of their nominal values. This distribution is obtained from a Monte Carlo sample of 1000 elements.

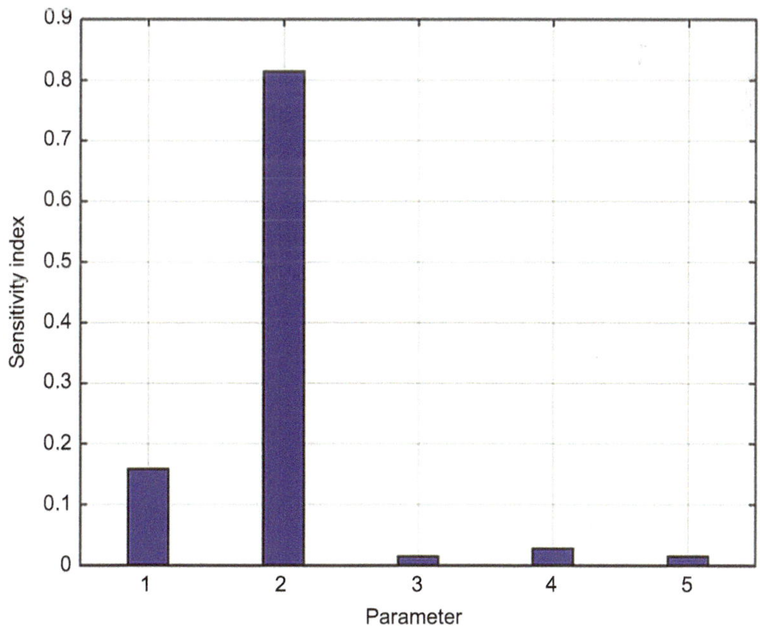

Figure 11.16 First-order sensitivity indices for five input parameters when they are allowed to vary within 30% of their nominal values. Parameters are defined as 1- coating fluid viscosity, 2- atomization airflow rate, 3- spray rate, 4- coating fluid surface tension, and 5- coating fluid density.

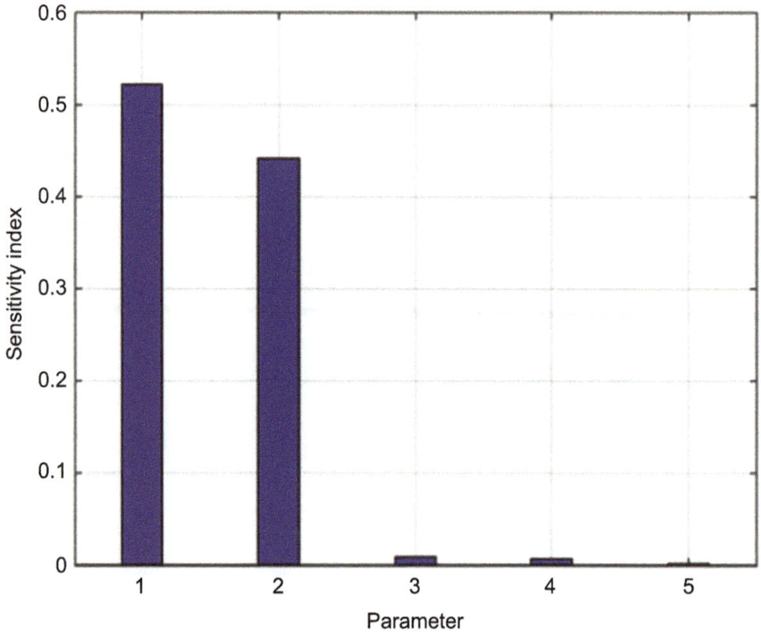

Figure 11.17 First-order sensitivity indices for five input parameters. Here, coating solution viscosity is allowed to vary between 75% of the nominal value, whereas, remaining four input parameter vary within 30% of their nominal values. Parameters are defined as 1- coating fluid viscosity, 2- atomization airflow rate, 3- spray rate, 4- coating fluid surface tension, and 5- coating fluid density.

kept at 30%. Fig. 11.17 shows the first-order indices for the five input parameters. It is clear from this figure that liquid viscosity and atomization airflow rate still make the dominant contributions to the variability of the output. However, now the fluid viscosity assumes the role of most dominant input parameter. So, for the coating process, which uses liquid with high solids fraction, fluid viscosity should be properly controlled and monitored.

11.4 Tablet mixing modeling

11.4.1 Introduction

The focus of the preceding sections of this chapter has been on predicting film drying conditions and the mean droplet size during spray atomization. However, if the coating spray deposits preferentially on a subset of the tablets, or only on preferred faces of the tablets, the coating operation may not meet specifications due to a lack of sufficient uniformity. Therefore, we need means for understanding and limiting intertablet-coating variability (i.e., minimizing the difference of coating mass accumulated between tablets) and intratablet-coating variability (i.e., minimizing the difference of coating mass on the surface of individual tablets). The following sections examine these phenomena in more detail.

11.4.2 Intertablet mixing models

11.4.2.1 Description and motivation

Intertablet-coating mass variability is described via a histogram of coating mass accumulated per tablet. The degree of coating uniformity is typically determined via the coefficient of variation ($\mathrm{CoV_{inter}}$), i.e., the standard deviation divided by the mean, of coating mass. Mathematically, if we express the coating mass accumulated on tablet i as m_i, the mean, standard deviation, and $\mathrm{CoV_{inter}}$ of coating mass are given, respectively, as,

$$\mu = \frac{1}{N}\sum_{i=1}^{N} m_i, \quad \sigma = \sqrt{\frac{1}{N}\sum_{i=1}^{N} (m_i - \mu)^2}, \text{ and } \mathrm{CoV_{inter}} = \frac{\sigma}{\mu} \tag{11.6}$$

where N is the total number of tablets. In general, a coating operation strives to minimize $\mathrm{CoV_{inter}}$. While μ is easily determined via a mass balance on the total coating applied (accounting for process inefficiencies such spray dried droplets, coating of the pan itself, etc.) and number of tablets, σ is not as trivially known. To predict σ one must understand the processes that control the variability in m_i between tablets.

Variability in m_i values can come from a number of sources. Tablets that have visited the spray area of the coater more frequently will have more coating. Of those tablets, ones that have visited the spray for longer duration (per visit) will receive even more coating. Furthermore, tablets that visit portions of the spray with higher coating mass flux will receive yet more coating. For a given amount of total coating, the presence of tablets with excess coating implies that there are also tablets with a shortage of coating. It is clear to see that these inherent variabilities are probabilistic in nature; hence, the modeling techniques are probabilistic themselves.

General tablet motion

Before we delve into more detailed modeling techniques, there are a few simple calculations that can be performed to insure proper tablet motion at any scale and during scale-up. For the most part, a priori prediction of velocity fields of particulate systems is not possible today. However, for the simplified geometry of unbaffled rotating drums multiple researchers have identified useful scaling rules for predicting tablet velocity fields (Alexander et al., 2002; Chen et al., 2010). Although pan coaters are typically baffled, or at least have antislip bars or lifters, the insight gained from the wealth of knowledge for unbaffled rotating drums is still valuable.

Mellmann (2001) developed very useful regime maps of granular materials tumbling in rotating drums. The regime maps provide information on selection of rotation speed and appropriate scaling parameters for rotating drum particle dynamics. In general, the rolling-cascading regimes are preferred for tablet coating. These regimes provides sufficient mixing, a near level bed surface, and minimize mechanical stresses on the tablets. For the rolling to cascading regime, the Froude number Fr should be in the range 10^{-4} to 10^{-1} where

$$Fr \equiv \frac{\omega R^2}{g} \tag{11.7}$$

where ω is the angular speed of the pan, R is the radius of the pan, and g is the acceleration of gravity; and the fill level should exceed 10% of the volume of the drum. For $Fr > 10^{-1}$, the bed will cataract rather than roll or cascade, causing unnecessary stress on the tablet cores. For $Fr < 10^{-4}$ the bed may just slump back and forth, with minimal mixing. These values allow one to choose typical operating speed, as well as scale pan speed with the pan's physical size.

11.4.2.2 Model frameworks

Existing tablet-coating modeling techniques have varying levels of abstractions. In order of increasing abstraction, they are discrete element modeling (DEM), Monte Carlo–coating modeling, population balance modeling (PBM), and renewal theory modeling. In these models, the bed is conceptually divided into at least two separate regions: a region where coating is applied and a region where mixing/drying occurs (i.e., regions D and G from Fig. 11.1). The techniques vary in how those regions are identified, but more importantly in how exchange happens between them (i.e., mixing).

DEM models

Pan coating of tablets is possibly the application for which DEM is most aptly suited. Using DEM, individual tablets are modeled a discrete entities. Contacts between tablets are tracked, and the forces between those contacts are resolved using simplified contact laws (e.g., Zhu et al. (2008)). Typically, DEM simulations must falsely limit the number of tablets simulated as compared to the full-scale operation. In laboratory and pilot-scale tablet-coating operations, however, the true number and size of tablets may be simulated directly for the full coating process duration. The two remaining challenges for modeling a full tablet-coating operation in DEM are (1) accurate prediction of the spray itself, (2) sufficient fidelity of the tablet shape, and (3) prediction of contact parameters.

Rather than explicitly modeling droplets impinging on tablets in DEM (although this has been done, e.g., Toschkoff et al. (2013)), the spray is frequently tracked as a region in space where spray is applied. The rate of coating mass accumulated is then just a function of a tablet position in the pan coater. The spray region can be identified by simply tracking a static region in space (e.g., Toschkoff et al. (2013)), via identification of the free surface by ray tracing (e.g., Freireich et al. (2011b)) or density gradients (e.g., Kalbag et al. (2008)) then specifying a spray region on the free surface, or via line of site from an imagined spray nozzle (e.g., Kumar et al. (2015)). The advantage of these schemes is that the DEM simulation may be run independently of the spray tracking algorithm. Therefore, multiple spray locations or patternations may be studied from a single, much more costly, DEM simulation. The method then reduces to writing all of the tablet positions from DEM simulations at fixed time internals to intermediate files. These files are then postprocessed by a function that determines whether the tablet is in the spray or not. If the tablet is in the spray, the function increments the coating mass variable for that tablet according to the spray flux at that location. The duration between file writing should be chosen frequent enough such that the movement of the fastest tablet is less than the diameter of a tablet, but not so frequent that the writing events become too computationally expensive or hard disk space becomes a limitation. The resulting output of the postprocessing is the coating mass on each tablet for each time stop postprocessed. This highly detailed level of information can be used to compute a full empirical distribution function of coating mass, or just CoV_{inter}, as necessary.

Although DEM simulations are the highest fidelity of all coating operation modeling techniques, they still come with some limitations. Firstly, the fidelity comes at a higher computational cost. Secondly, truc tablet shapes are difficult to model exactly, without using simplifying modeling assumptions such as the glued sphere approach (e.g., Favier et al. (1999), Kodam et al. (2009)). Further discussion of approximating tablet shape is discussed later in "DEM models" section on DEM modeling of intratablet mixing. Third, contact parameter estimation is nontrivial. Methods for contact parameter estimation in DEM simulation of tablet coating have been presented by Just et al. (2013). There are also more detailed references on sliding friction (Hancock et al., 2010), rolling resistance (Ketterhagen et al., 2010), and coefficient of restitution (Bharadwaj et al., 2010). Regarding the importance of contact parameter estimation, it is well known that the most significant contact parameter for accurate predictions of dense particulate flow is the particle–particle friction coefficient (Freireich et al., 2009). Throughout a coating operation, the coating itself can drastically alter the friction between tablets. Because DEM simulations typically model the motion and coating operations in serial rather than parallel (to avoid prohibitively high computational cost), the evolving particle–particle friction is consequently ignored. The degree to which these missing physics alter the resulting predicted coating mass distribution is currently unknown.

Monte Carlo models

Using the DEM approach by itself, one must simulate the full coating operation to achieve the full endpoint coating distribution. The Monte Carlo method requires either short simulations or short experiments to collect relevant information about sources of coating variability. This information is then combined in such a way as to predict the coating distribution at arbitrarily long coating times. In this method (originally developed by Pandey et al. (2006a,b) for pan coating and KuShaari et al.

(2006) for fluid bed coating) experiments (or DEM simulations) can be conducted to sample intermediate distributions of tablet appearance location in the spray, velocity distribution within the spray, projected area exposed to the spray, and spray accumulation as a function of position in the spray. With these statistical distributions, a Monte Carlo scheme can be developed, generating trajectories and coating histories of many tablets very rapidly in a simple computer simulation. The coating statistics of those tablets then combine all of the simulated sources of variability. While this method is very attractive once the relevant variability source statistics have been acquired, acquiring them must be done for each process change. These shorter duration experiments are done with particle tracking video and spray patternation measurement test equipment.

Population balance modeling

The probabilistic nature of coating accumulation on tablets lends itself very well to the PBM approach (Hulburt and Katz, 1964; Ramkrishna, 2000). In this method, the evolution of the distribution of coating mass is tracked via a differential equation. The equations are formulated by assuming idealized flow patterns of various regions, or compartments, within the pan coater. For example, the spray and mixing regions can be modeled as any combination of perfectly mixed regions or plug-flow regions (Denis et al., 2003; Wnukowski and Setterwall, 1989). Furthermore, in order to incorporate poor mixing effects, a dead zone may also be added to the mixing region (Kumar et al., 2015; Maronga and Wnukowski, 1997).

No matter the method, the network of idealized compartments results in a system partial differential equations describing the distribution of coating mass on tablets in each compartment. In practice, it is not necessary to know the full distribution of coating mass, but rather only its standard deviation. Therefore, the system of partial differential equations may be integrated to result in a system of ordinary differential equations (ODEs) in the first two moments of the coating mass distribution (Kumar et al., 2015). These ODEs can be readily solved by conventional means.

In this approach, the mixing and flow has been abstracted into a network of idealized flow compartments. The abstraction allows a significantly lower computational burden, the cost of which is the necessity of converting process parameters (e.g., fill level, drum speed, baffle arrangement) into the new model parameters (e.g., the network of idealized flow regions, the sizes of those regions, and the exchange rates between them). The conversion may be accomplished from pan coater velocity field predictions, DEM simulations (see "Hybrid models and suggestions" section), or practitioner experience and knowledge.

Renewal theory modeling

By far the most abstract tablet-coating modeling technique is renewal theory. This theory (originally derived in Mann (1983)) is built on the premise that the coating of a tablet behaves as a renewal process, where the coating per visit to the spray and time between visits to the spray are independent random variables. The mathematics of renewal theory (Cox, 1977) show that under these assumptions the coating mass distribution is asymptotically Gaussian (after many visits) with coefficient of variation,

$$\mathrm{CoV_{inter}} = \sqrt{\frac{\mu_C}{t}\left[\left(\frac{\sigma_W}{\mu_W}\right)^2 + \left(\frac{\sigma_C}{\mu_C}\right)^2\right]} \tag{11.8}$$

where μ_C and σ_C are the mean and standard deviation of time between visits to the spray (i.e., the cycle time), μ_W and σ_W are the mean and standard deviation of coating mass accumulated on a single visit to the spray, and t is the total coating time. Note, as was shown in Kumar et al. (2015), if significant dead zones exist in the pan coater, the time to reach the asymptotic limit when Eq. (11.8) applies can be much longer than the mean cycle time. For cases where dead zones are not significant, the solution of the compartmental models for long coating times discussed in the previous section can be determined directly from the network of idealized mixing vessels (Freireich and Li, 2013). Furthermore, the renewal theory provides a framework for immediately combining variability due to multiple sources (as with the Monte Carlo approach) in a single equation such as Eq. (11.8). For example, the asymptotic $\mathrm{CoV_{inter}}$ due to variable cycle time, spray zone residence time, and projected area presented to the spray results in (for a derivation see Freireich and Li (2013)),

$$\mathrm{CoV_{inter}} = \sqrt{\frac{\mu_C}{t}\left\{\left[\left(\frac{\sigma_A}{\mu_A}\right)^2 + (1-2\alpha)\right]\left(\frac{\sigma_S}{\mu_S}\right)^2 + \left(\frac{\sigma_A}{\mu_A}\right)^2 + \left(\frac{\sigma_C}{\mu_C}\right)^2\right\}} \tag{11.9}$$

where μ_A and σ_A are the mean and standard deviation of tablet projected area presented to the spray, μ_S and σ_S are the mean and standard deviation of duration in the spray upon a signal visit, and α gives the fraction of tablets in the spray zone. The advantage of expressions like Eq. (11.9) is that variation due to multiple sources can be easily compared. If variability needs to be reduced, such a comparison can be used to focus on the most impactful sources of variation.

The difficulty, of course, comes from the fact that inherent variability from each of the multiple sources must be known in order for the renewal theory expression to be of any use. However, the same can be said for the Monte Carlo and PBM techniques. The most significant result of the renewal theory approach is that asymptotically all coating processing must result in a decay of $\mathrm{CoV_{inter}}$ as a negative one half power law of coating time. That is, for a system without significant dead zones, the $\mathrm{CoV_{inter}}$ will decrease by a factor of two if the coating time is quadrupled. If intermittent sampling is used, the coating endpoint can be easily found via this rule.

Hybrid models and suggestions

Each of the preceding approaches has their own pros and cons as summarized in Table 11.8. Therefore, it is possible to combine them in such a way to take advantage of their strengths, and diminish the impact of their weaknesses. For example, Freireich et al. (2011b) combined the strengths of DEM and PBM by using PBM to

Table 11.8 Pros and cons for each of the modeling methods presented in Section 11.4.2.2

	Pro	Con
DEM	Full tablet history is known at all simulation times	Computationally expensive
Monte Carlo	Relatively fast computationally, intermediate computations are very straightforward, captures variability from many sources	Requires intermediate distributions which are difficult to obtain experimentally
Population balance	Very fast computationally, full distribution over time can be predicted	Idealized flow network must be known, theoretical development is more laborious (i.e., PDEs must be solved)
Renewal theory	Simple analytical expression for comparing influence of variability sources	Only applies asymptotically, knowledge of probability theory is required for theoretical development

extrapolate data gathered from short duration DEM simulations. The extrapolation was accomplished by extracting single visit spray zone and bed residence time distributions from short duration DEM simulations and generating idealized compartment models of each region to match the extracted residence time distributions. The compartment models then were used to develop PBMs for long duration predictions. Similarly, Kumar et al. (2015) used short duration DEM simulations to extract CoV_{inter} versus time curves, and matched them to the output of a PBM based on a network of ideal compartments. In both cases a more abstract technique, PBM, was used to extrapolate the more detailed but expensive technique, DEM. A Monte Carlo scheme or renewal theory could similarly be used to extrapolate a DEM simulation, although this is approach is not currently present in the literature. Following Table 11.8, Monte Carlo, PBM, and renewal theory are all fast, but require intermediate model parameters (e.g., appearance frequency distribution, idealized flow network and exchange rates) rather than process parameter inputs (e.g., fill level, tablet geometry, pan speed). These hybrid techniques use the DEM simulations to extract the intermediate parameters that can be used with the more abstract techniques to extrapolate to longer times.

11.4.2.3 Model verification and application

Chen et al. (2010) assumed the pan could be divided into a very small plug-flow spray section, with a well-mixed drying section. Interestingly, this is opposite to the configuration assumed by Denis et al. (2003). Regardless, in either model Eq. (28) of Freireich and Li (2013) and Eq. (26) of Chen et al. (2010) predict $CoV = T^{-1/2}$, where T is the average number of visits to the spray zone. The average number of visits to the spray zone is simply the total time t divided by the mean cycle time.

In the limiting case of very small sprays, the mean cycle time is equal to the mean time in the drying zone. The mean time in the drying zone is simply the number of particles in that zone N (i.e., the total number of particles because we have assumed a small spray) divided by the number exchange rate between the drying and sprays zones. Finally, the number exchange rate is equal to the product of the number of particles in the spray per spray area ρ, the velocity through the spray v and the spray width w. The resulting expression is,

$$\mathrm{CoV}_{\mathrm{inter}} = \sqrt{\frac{N}{t\rho v w}} \tag{11.10}$$

The model parameters, ρ, v, and w can be determined via process parameters such as spray conditions (e.g., nozzle distance to the bed), pan speed, pan loading level, and tablet size. Chen et al. (2010) showed that this modeling approach predicted relative standard deviations of active coating content uniformity to within $\pm 2\%$ when compared to experimental data at multiple batch sizes with different pan coaters (Fig. 11.18).

Example 1: A pilot-scale tablet-coating operation has run for 10 min. A sample of 10 tablets reveals a mean and standard deviation of coating mass accumulation per

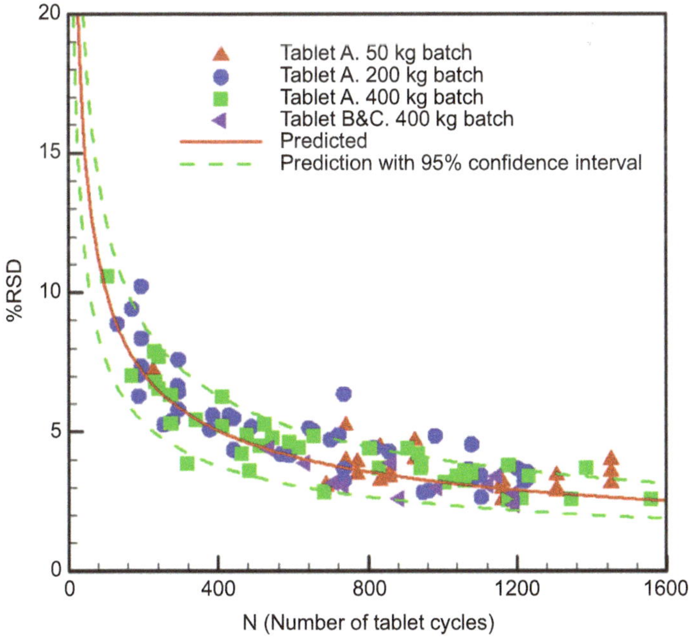

Figure 11.18 Comparison of model predictions and experimental data from Chen et al. (2010). *Source*: Reprinted from Chen et al. (2010), with permission from Elsevier.

tablet of 10 mg and 2 mg, respectively. The target of this coating operation is to add 20 mg total of coating per tablet with a CoV < 0.1. Using renewal theory, comment on whether you expect this coating operation to meet the specification limit.

Solution: The CoV at 10 min is 2/10 = 0.2. If 10 mg has been added in 10 min, then the coating is being applied at an average rate of 1 mg/min. Therefore, for a total accumulation of 20 mg per tablet, 20 min will be required. Renewal theory states that for a sufficiently well-mixed system, the CoV will fall as the coating duration to the − ½ power. Therefore, doubling the time results in 0.71 times the CoV. That is, at 20 min we expect a CoV of 0.14. This value is above the threshold of 0.1, so the coating operation is expected to not meet the uniformity specification limit.

Example 2: In the coating operation described in Example 1, what is the range of weight gain over which 95% of the coating accumulation is expected to occur after an average coating accumulation of 20 mg per tablet is achieved?

Solution: From the solution to Example 1, we know that at 20 mg the CoV is expected to be approximately 0.14, so that the standard deviation of coating mass accumulated per tablet is 2.8 mg. Because renewal theory states that the coating mass distribution is approximately Gaussian, 95% of the tablets will fall within two standard deviations of the mean on either side of the mean. Therefore, 95% of the tablets are expected to have accumulated coating mass between 17.2 to 22.8 mg.

11.4.3 Intratablet mixing models

11.4.3.1 Description and motivation

Intratablet-coating mass variability is described as the distribution of coating mass accumulated over the surface of an individual tablet. The degree of intratablet-coating uniformity can be determined by comparing the ratio coating mass thickness between two locations (e.g., the face and the band, Perez-Ramos et al. (2005)), or by computing the coefficient of variation (CoV_{intra}), i.e., the standard deviation divided by the mean, of coating thickness. Mathematically, if we express the coating thickness accumulated on a patch of area dA on the surface of a tablet as h, the mean, standard deviation, and CoV_{intra} of coating thickness are given, respectively, as,

$$\mu = \frac{1}{A}\int h dA, \quad \sigma = \sqrt{\frac{1}{A}\int (h-\mu)^2 dA}, \quad \text{and} \quad CoV_{intra} = \frac{\sigma}{\mu} \tag{11.11}$$

where A is the total area of an individual tablet. Like with CoV_{inter}, a coating operation should strive to minimize CoV_{intra}. While μ is easily determined via a mass balance on the total coating applied (accounting for process inefficiencies such spray dried droplets, coating of the pan itself, etc.) and surface area of a tablet, σ is not as trivially known. In order to predict σ one must understand the processes that control the variability in thickness over the surface of individual tablets. Note also that with intertablet variability, CoV_{inter} is a single number for the whole batch. Here, there is a separate CoV_{intra} value for each tablet. These individual values may be averaged to give a single batch CoV_{intra} via multiple methods as in Freireich et al. (2015).

Variability in film thickness can come from a number of sources. Points on a tablet that have visited the spray area of the coater more frequently (due to the position and orientation of the tablet) will have more coating. Of those points, ones that have visited the spray for longer duration (per visit) will receive even more coating. Furthermore, points on the tablet surface that visit portions of the spray with higher coating mass flux will receive yet more coating. For a given amount of total coating, the presence of surface elements with excess coating implies that there are also surface elements with a shortage of coating. It is clear to see that these inherent variabilities are probabilistic in nature; hence, the modeling techniques are probabilistic themselves.

11.4.3.2 Model frameworks

Intratablet-coating variability can only occur via preferential coating of a subset of points on a tablets surface. Tablet surface elements can only be preferred for coating because (1) the tablet preferentially rotates about a particular axis, (2) the tablet has preferred orientations while exposed to the spray, or (3) the tablet is preferentially shielded on some surface points due to neighboring tablets while in the spray zone. While mechanism (1) can occur even for spherical tablets if sufficient mixing is not applied in the pan coater (Freireich and Wassgren, 2010), mechanisms (2) and (3) occur only for nonspherical tablet shapes. Therefore, modeling schemes for predicting and interpreting intratablet-coating variability must explicitly account for tablet shape. As with intertablet-coating variability, there are DEM, Monte Carlo, and probabilistic modeling techniques for intratablet-coating variability.

DEM models

Most DEM simulations estimate particles as spheres. However, except for cases of extremely poor mixing (i.e., a pan coater with no baffles), intratablet-coating variability is strongly tied to tablet shape. Therefore, the main challenge of modeling intratablet-coating variability in DEM is modeling of nonspherical tablet shapes.

Nonspherical tablet shapes can be accommodated in DEM via approximating the tablet as an ellipsoid, super-quadric, polyhedron, or an assembly of glue spheres. The latter is by far the most common method, and is implemented in several commercial DEM software packages. However, it has been shown that the glued sphere approach has several drawbacks (Kodam et al., 2009; Kruggel-Emden et al., 2008). Firstly, the simulated surface is inherently bumpy, unless the tablet surface is approximated by many subspheres. This bumpiness results in an effectively higher interparticle frictional behavior, and must be accommodated in tablet parameter selection. Second, unless the subsphere stiffness is strategically decreased, the multiple subsphere contacts occurring at each tablet contact point can result in an effective overly stiff contact.

Assuming the tablet geometry has been adequately modeled in DEM, there is still the additional problem of modeling the spray deposition process. As with intertablet-coating variability, DEM simulations modeling intratablet variability rarely attempt to simultaneously model the tablet motion and spray deposition simultaneously. Instead, the DEM simulation is run independently of the spray tracking algorithm. Therefore, multiple spray locations or patternations may be studied from a single, much more costly, DEM simulation. The method is identical to that used for intertablet-coating variability, but here tablet positions *and orientations* must be written to intermediate files. The orientations are necessary, because which face of a tablet is exposed to the spray is just as important as which tablet is exposed to the spray. The amount of coating applied to each portion of the surface is most easily tracked by first discretizing the surface into a conformal knit of panels. Determining which panels are in the spray region can be performed similarly to how tablets are located in the spray region when studying intertablet-coating variability. However, because the number of panels is larger than the number of tablets, the more sophisticated imaging schemes (e.g., Kumar et al. (2015)) are recommended. For accounting purposes, the position of each of these panels is most easily stored and managed via a frame of reference attached to the tablet. Then as the tablet moves through the bed, the position of a particular panel can be found by knowing the position of the tablet, the orientation of that tablet, and the panel's position in the tablet fixed reference frame.

While tablet positions are easily interpreted as displacement vectors from a common origin, tablet orientations are must less intuitive. There are multiple means for encoding and computing orientations, but they all boil down to the same principle: the orientations encode the rotation of positions measured in the tablet's local frame of reference relative to those measured in the global frame of reference. For clarity, Fig. 11.19 shows two methods for describing a point on the surface of at tablet.

The vector x_G describes a point on the surface of a tablet (e.g., a discretized panel), with the components of the vector in the global coordinate system with basis ($\mathbf{E}_x$, $\mathbf{E}_y$, $\mathbf{E}_z$). The vector X_G describes the center of mass of the tablet, with the components of the vector in the same global coordinate system. The point on the

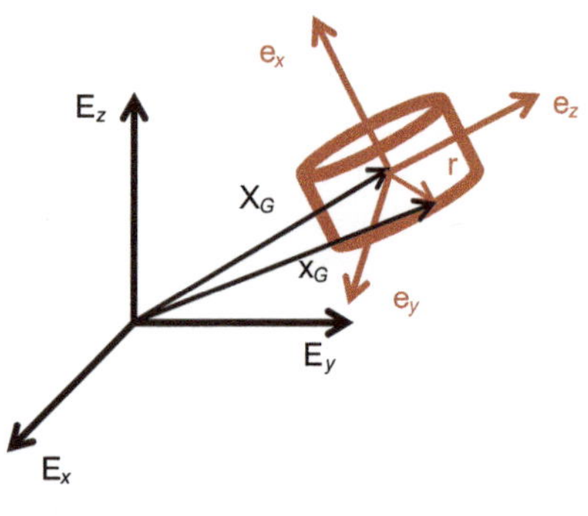

Figure 11.19 Definition of the local frame of reference.

surface is given relative to the center of mass of the tablet via the vector $\mathbf{r}_L$, with the components of the vector in the local coordinate system with basis ($\mathbf{e}_x$, $\mathbf{e}_y$, $\mathbf{e}_z$). Note that as the tablet rotates, the basis vectors ($\mathbf{e}_x$, $\mathbf{e}_y$, $\mathbf{e}_z$) rotate as well, while the basis vectors ($\mathbf{E}_x$, $\mathbf{E}_y$, $\mathbf{E}_z$) never change. The two bases are related via the rotation matrix $\mathbf{R}_{GL}$, i.e.,

$$\lfloor \mathbf{E}_x \quad \mathbf{E}_y \quad \mathbf{E}_z \rfloor^T = \mathbf{R}_{GL} \cdot \lfloor \mathbf{e}_x \quad \mathbf{e}_y \quad \mathbf{e}_z \rfloor^T \tag{11.12}$$

where $\mathbf{R}_{GL}$ is a 3×3 orthonormal matrix encoding the transformation of the local coordinate system to the global coordinate system. We then have the relation,

$$\mathbf{x}_G = \mathbf{X}_G + \mathbf{R}_{GL} \cdot \mathbf{r}_L \tag{11.13}$$

Likewise, the components of a unit normal vector on the surface of a tablet in the local bases $\hat{\mathbf{n}}_L$ can be converted to the global components via,

$$\hat{\mathbf{n}}_G = \mathbf{R}_{GL} \cdot \hat{\mathbf{n}}_L \tag{11.14}$$

Relation (14) is important for noting the amount of spray flux applied to a given surface element. That is, the rate of deposition on the element is proportional to

$$-(\mathbf{R}_{GL} \cdot \hat{\mathbf{n}}_L) \cdot \hat{\mathbf{u}}_G \tag{11.15}$$

when $\hat{\mathbf{u}}_G$ is the unit vector pointing in the direction of the spray in with components in the global basis.

Note that because $\mathbf{R}_{GL}$ gives information about rotating the local basis to the global basis it implicitly captures the orientation of the tablet as well. Therefore, the orientation of the tablet and its respective $\mathbf{R}_{GL}$ are equivalent. Conveniently, of the nine components of the 3×3 orientation matrix $\mathbf{R}_{GL}$, only three are independent. While those three components may be interpreted directly in terms of components of the rotation matrix (i.e., direction cosines), sometimes they are described via Euler angles or quaternions.

The method then reduces to writing all of the tablet positions and orientations for DEM simulations at fixed time intervals to intermediate files. These files are then postprocessed by a function that determines whether or not surface panel of a tablet is in the spray or not. If a panel is in the spray, the function increments the coating mass variable for that panel according to the spray flux at that location (proportional to Eq. (11.15)). The duration of file writing should be chosen frequent enough such that the movement of the fastest panel is less than the characteristic size of the panels. The resulting output of the postprocessing is the coating mass on each panel of each tablet for each time step postprocessed. This highly detailed information can be used to compute a full empirical distribution function of coating mass of all panels, $\text{CoV}_{\text{intra}}$ for each tablet, or some batch averaged $\text{CoV}_{\text{intra}}$, perhaps according to one of the schemes suggested by Freireich et al. (2015).

Monte Carlo—DEM

While DEM simulations give a very rich data set, both the simulation and postprocessing can be computationally expensive when studying intratablet-coating variability. As with intertablet-coating variability, a full coating operation must be simulated to achieve the full endpoint intratablet-coating distribution. In this section, we will outline another Monte Carlo scheme that allows data from short-time DEM simulations to be extrapolated to predict intratablet-coating behavior at longer coating durations (for details, see Freireich et al. (2011a) and Freireich and Wassgren (2010)).

To begin, we assume that intratablet-coating variability is due solely to the randomness of orientations which tablets tend to present themselves to the spray. The DEM data are postprocessed, and the orientation of every tablet in the spray is recorded at each time step. Because the scheme logs only orientations of tablets, the postprocessing routine does not need to track panels, but only tablets. The DEM simulation must be run long enough to insure that the recorded sample of orientations is sufficient to represent the population of orientations over a full coating operation. Next, a separate Monte Carlo analysis is run in which individual tablets are artificially coated by choosing orientations from the sample population.

A significant drawback to this scheme is that the influence of neighboring tablets cannot be accounted for, because the Monte Carlo coating is conducted on individual tablets. To avoid this drawback, instead of recording orientations of tablets in the spray, the panels that are in the spray can be recorded (for more details see Freireich et al. (2015)). Any panels that are shielded from the spray by their neighbors will automatically be ignored. Once the sample of panel spray occurrences has been recorded, a separate Monte Carlo analysis is run in which individual panels are artificially coated by choosing panels from the sample population. The, negligible, drawback to this scheme (as compared to the previous scheme) is that the postprocessing routine must track tablet panels as well as tablet locations.

Both of the preceding schemes require that the coating operation progress as number of coating trials rather than duration of the coating operation. Establishing a link between these two ideas is not clear. That said, the asymptotic nature of either scheme gives comparable results (Freireich et al., 2015).

Probabilistic models

The Monte Carlo models of the previous section can be further abstracted by directly considering their probabilistic nature. That is, rather than collecting the sample population of occurrence frequency of individual panels, we can gain significant mathematical footing by simple postulating that some frequency exists. For clarity, consider that a panel i has a probability p_i of being coated on a particular coating trial, and m of M total panels get coated on each trial. From these assumptions alone, it can be shown that (Freireich and Wassgren, 2010),

$$\mathrm{CoV}_{\mathrm{intra}} = \sqrt{\frac{1}{f}\left[\frac{1}{N}(1-\Pi)+\Pi\right]-1} \tag{11.16}$$

where

$$f = \frac{m}{M} \quad \text{and} \quad \Pi = \frac{1}{m}\sum_{i=1}^{M} p_i^2 \tag{11.17}$$

and N is the number of coating trials. Here f describes the fraction of a particle's surface coating during each trial, and Π is a parameter describing the variability of coating between panels. The most significant result from Eq. (11.16) is that $\text{CoV}_{\text{intra}}$ has an asymptotic value as $N \to \infty$ for all $\Pi \neq f$. It can be shown that $\Pi = f$ if, and only if, all panels are equally likely to enter the spray (a sphere with uniformly random orientations and no shielding). Therefore, unlike for intertablet variability, where $\text{CoV}_{\text{intra}}$ limits to zero for long coating duration, there is a lowest possible $\text{CoV}_{\text{intra}}$ specified by the probability that each tablet enters the spray.

We may also use Eq. (11.16) to project a predicted asymptotic $\text{CoV}_{\text{intra}}$ from an in-process coating operation, DEM simulation, or Monte Carlo model. Squaring both sides of Eq. (11.16) results in a linear relationship between the square of $\text{CoV}_{\text{intra}}$ and N^{-1}. Although the relationship between the coating accumulation and number of fictitious coating trials is unknown, we can assume with some level of confidence that they are proportional. Therefore, the square of $\text{CoV}_{\text{intra}}$ and the reciprocal of the coating accumulation are also linear, and the line's y-intercept value corresponds to the square of the asymptotic $\text{CoV}_{\text{intra}}$. This result can be used to extrapolate early process $\text{CoV}_{\text{intra}}$ measurements to longer times. If the projected asymptotic $\text{CoV}_{\text{intra}}$ value is inadequate for the application, the process can be stopped short.

11.4.3.3 Model verification and application

Due to the inherent difficulty of making measurements of intratablet-coating variability, there is a dearth of experimentally verified computational models. Recently, Freireich et al. (2015) performed DEM simulations, tablet-coating experiments, and terahertz pulsed imaging measurements of select tablets. These data could be used to directly compare the experimental measurements and computational models. However, even in this study, due to the limited number of tablets measured, the comparison was still mostly qualitative. Fig. 11.20 shows a side by side comparison of a triangular tablet measured from experiments and the simulation of the same model from Freireich et al. (2015). Qualitatively the distribution of coating mass is very similar. The faces have more coating than the band, and the small radius portions of the band have less coating than the large radius portions of the band. The experiments and simulations differ in the center of the faces, but simulations did not account for the embossing features on the actual tablet.

Example 1: At 10 min into a 60-min coating operation, 10 tablets are extracted and terahertz pulsed imagining is performed reporting values according to Table 11.9. Based on this data, is $\text{CoV}_{\text{intra}} < 0.1$? If not, what would you change going forward?

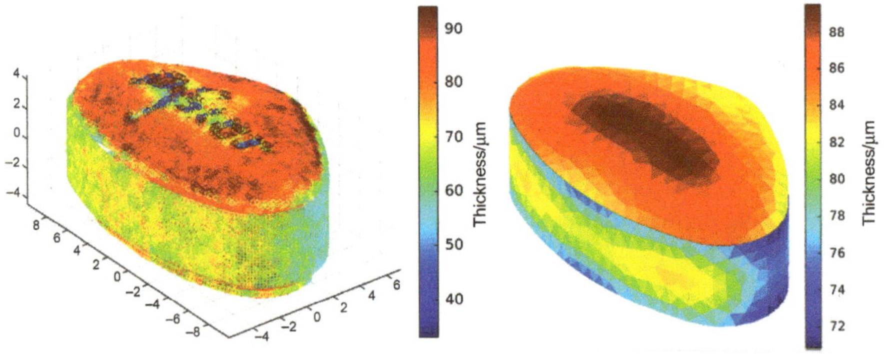

Figure 11.20 Comparison of coating thickness measurements between experiments (left) and simulations (right).
Source: Reprinted from Freireich et al. (2015) under the terms of the Creative Commons Attribution License (CC-BY).

Table 11.9 Tablet data for Example 1 in Section 11.4.3.3

Coating mass (mg)	19.5	9.4	18.9	13.9	19.6	23.8	19.2	33.5	57.1	28.8
CoV_{intra} (−)	0.540	0.703	0.539	0.719	0.478	0.510	0.530	0.425	0.277	0.435

Solution: According to Eq. (11.16), the square of CoV_{intra} should increases linearly with the reciprocal of the coating mass, assuming the "number of coating trials" scales proportionally to the coating mass accumulated. The *y*-intercept of that regression corresponds to the minimum achievable CoV_{intra} value. Performing a least squares linear regression of the data in Table 11.9 returns $(CoV_{intra})^2 = 5.05^*$ $(\text{Coating Mass})^{-1} + 0.023$. Therefore, $CoV_{intra} \approx 0.023^{1/2} \approx 0.15$, and the coating operation is not expected to meet the requirement of $CoV_{intra} < 0.1$. More uniformity may be achievable via a slower coating mass addition and more passes through the spray. Also, a more uniformly random orientation distribution should decrease CoV_{intra}. This may be achieved via a more symmetric tablet shape or more tablet mobility (i.e., more vigorous mixing).

11.5 Prospects for an integrated film-coating process model

In the preceding sections of this chapter, mathematical models governing three important physical processes occurring in a typical film-coating process are presented in great detail. The development of these models in the literature has evolved almost in isolation without much reference to the interconnectedness. For example, the tablet mixing models presented in Section 11.4 are able to capture the movement of tablet bed quite accurately; however, the description of fluid spray is idealized and does not account for drop size distribution. So these models, although capable of predicting variation of coating thickness RSD, are generally impervious to the coating microenvironment and will not be able to predict overwetting and its negative effects. Similarly, the thermodynamic and atomization models are capable of predicting temperature, relative humidity, and mean drop size, but they do not predict the optimum process conditions, which will enable smooth coating with minimum defects. Therefore, for realization of a fully predictive model, different submodels should be connected and work in tandem. Additional physical processes that will enable this integration include drop-tablet impact, spreading, transfer, and drying. Yarin (2006) has thoroughly reviewed the varying drop impact dynamics leading to film formation on dry surfaces. Further understanding of the wetting, spreading, and drying dynamics of isolated droplets on a static tablet surface has begun to emerge through work of Bolleddula et al. (2010). Suzzi et al. (2010) have made further advances in this area using a multiphase computational fluid dynamics approach to model the generation of liquid film on a tablet due to the impact of a population of sprayed droplets. This computational model predicted the flow of droplets and liquid film on the surface of a single, static tablet for varying droplet size and impact velocity, coating viscosity, and temperature. These are critical advances required to build an integrated model encompassing the multitude of physical processes depicted in Fig. 11.1. However, further work should (A) continue to progress understanding of the effects of different tablet shapes, orientation, and surface properties, (B) account for the tumbling of tablets and transfer of coating through contact with neighboring tablets and integrate with the tablet mixing models of Section 11.4, and (C) link the predicted film spreading and drying dynamics to experimental measures of coating quality and elegance defect rates. An integrated tablet film-coating model should be able to predict the most optimum process conditions, which will result in a smooth and uniform coating with minimum variation in intertablet and intratablet thickness.

References

Alexander, A., Shinbrot, T., Muzzio, F.J., 2002. Scaling surface velocities in rotating cylinders as a function of vessel radius, rotation rate, and particle size. Powder Technol. 126 (2), 174–190.

Aliseda, A., Hopfinger, E.J., Lasheras, J.C., Kremer, D.M., Berchielli, A., Connolly, E.K., 2008. Atomization of viscous and non-Newtonian liquids by a co-axial, high-speed gas jet. Experiments and droplet size modeling. Int. J. Multiph. Flow. 34, 161–175.

am Ende, M.T., Berchielli, A., 2005. A thermodynamic model for organic and aqueous tablet film coating. Pharm. Dev. Technol. 1, 47–58.

Bachalo, W., 1994. Experimental methods in multiphase flows. Int. J. Multiph. Flow. 20, 261–295.

Bharadwaj, R., Smith, C., Hancock, B.C., 2010. The coefficient of restitution of some pharmaceutical tablets/compacts. Int. J. Pharm. 402 (1–2), 50–56.

Bolleddula, D.A., Berchielli, A., Aliseda, A., 2010. Impact of a heterogeneous liquid droplet on a dry surface: application to the pharmaceutical industry. Adv. Colloid Interface Sci. 159 (2), 144–159.

Cannavó, F., 2012. Sensitivity analysis for volcanic source modeling quality assessment and model selection. Comput. Geosci. 44, 52–59.

Chen, W., Chang, S.Y., Kiang, S., Marchut, A., Lyngberg, O., Wang, J., et al., 2010. Modeling of pan coating processes: prediction of tablet content uniformity and determination of critical process parameters. J. Pharm. Sci. 99 (7), 3213–3225.

Choi, M., accessed 2015. PCTS, Inc. on-line literature.

Cole, G., Aulton, M.E., Hogan, J.E., 1995. Pharmaceutical Coating Technology. Taylor & Francis.

Cox, D., 1962. Renewal Theory. Methuen, London.

Denis, C., Hemati, M., Chulia, D., Lanne, J.Y., Buisson, B., Daste, G., et al., 2003. A model of surface renewal with application to the coating of pharmaceutical tablets in rotary drums. Powder Technol. 130 (1–3), 174–180.

Ebey, G.C., 1987. A thermodynamic model for aqueous film-coating. Pharm. Technol. 11 (4), 40–50.

Favier, J., Abbaspour-Fard, M., Kremmer, M., Raji, A., 1999. Shape representation of axi-symmetrical, non-spherical particles in discrete element simulation using multi-element model particles. Eng. Comput. 16 (4), 467–480.

Freireich, B., Li, J., 2013. A renewal theory approach to understanding interparticle coating variability. Powder Technol. 249, 330–338.

Freireich, B., Wassgren, C., 2010. Intra-particle coating variability: analysis and Monte Carlo simulations. Chem. Eng. Sci. 65 (3), 1117–1124.

Freireich, B., Litster, J., Wassgren, C., 2009. Using the discrete element method to predict collision-scale behavior: a sensitivity analysis. Chem. Eng. Sci. 64 (15), 3407–3416.

Freireich, B., Ketterhagen, W.R., Wassgren, C., 2011a. Intra-tablet coating variability for several pharmaceutical tablet shapes. Chem. Eng. Sci. 66 (12), 2535–2544.

Freireich, B., Li, J., Litster, J., Wassgren, C., 2011b. Incorporating particle flow information from discrete element simulations in population balance models of mixer-coaters. Chem. Eng. Sci. 66 (16), 3592–3604.

Freireich, B., Kumar, R., Ketterhagen, W., Su, K., Wassgren, C., Zeitler, J.A., 2015. Comparisons of intra-tablet coating variability using DEM simulations, asymptotic limit models, and experiments. Chem. Eng. Sci. 131, 197–212.

García-Muñoz, S., Gierer, D.S., 2010. Coating uniformity assessment for colored immediate release tablets using multivariate image analysis. Int. J. Pharm. 395 (1), 104–113.

García Muñoz, S., Ende, M.T.A., Pinto, M.A., 2011. Model-Based Characterisation of Organic and Aqueous Tablet Film Coating Processes: Parameter Estimation and Risk Management. Paper presented at the AIChE Annual Meeting, Minneapolis, MN.

García Muñoz, S., Moreno, M., Cano, A., Leyland, S., 2012. Modeling the Dynamics of the Film Coating Operation for Pharmaceutical Tablets. Paper presented at the AIChE Annual Meeting, Pittsburgh, PA.

Hancock, B.C., Mojica, N., St John-Green, K., Elliott, J.A., Bharadwaj, R., 2010. An investigation into the kinetic (sliding) friction of some tablets and capsules. Int. J. Pharm. 384 (1–2), 39–45.

Homma, T., Saltelli, A., 1996. Importance measures in global sensitivity analysis of nonlinear models. Reliab. Eng. Syst. Saf. 52 (1), 1–17.

Hulburt, H.M., Katz, S., 1964. Some problems in particle technology: a statistical mechanical formulation. Chem. Eng. Sci. 19 (8), 555–574.
Joseph, D., Beavers, G., Funada, T., 2002. Rayleigh-Taylor instability of viscoelastic drops at high weber numbers. J. Fluid Mech. 453, 109–132.
Just, S., Toschkoff, G., Funke, A., Djuric, D., Scharrer, G., Khinast, J., et al., 2013. Experimental analysis of tablet properties for discrete element modeling of an active coating process. AAPS. PharmSciTech. 14 (1), 402–411.
Kalbag, A., Wassgren, C., Sumana Penumetcha, S., Pérez-Ramos, J.D., 2008. Inter-tablet coating variability: residence times in a horizontal pan coater. Chem. Eng. Sci. 63 (11), 2881–2894.
Ketterhagen, W.R., Bharadwaj, R., Hancock, B.C., 2010. The coefficient of rolling resistance (CoRR) of some pharmaceutical tablets. Int. J. Pharm. 392 (1–2), 107–110.
Kodam, M., Bharadwaj, R., Curtis, J., Hancock, B., Wassgren, C., 2009. Force model considerations for glued-sphere discrete element method simulations. Chem. Eng. Sci. 64, 3466–3475.
Kruggel-Emden, H., Rickelt, S., Wirtz, S., Scherer, V., 2008. A study on the validity of the multi-sphere discrete element method. Powder Technol. 188 (2), 153–165.
Kumar, R., Freireich, B., Wassgren, C., 2015. DEM-compartment-population balance model for particle coating in a horizontal rotating drum. Chem. Eng. Sci. 125, 144–157.
KuShaari, K., Pandey, P., Song, Y., Turton, R., 2006. Monte Carlo simulations to determine coating uniformity in a Wurster fluidized bed coating process. Powder Technol. 166 (2), 81–90.
Lasheras, J., Hopfinger, E., 2000. Liquid jet instability and atomization in a coaxial gas stream. Annu. Rev. Fluid. Mech. 32 (1), 275–308.
Mann, U., 1983. Analysis of spouted-bed coating and granulation. 1. Batch operation. Ind. Eng. Chem. Process Des. Dev. 22, 288–292.
Mansour, A., Chigier, N., 1995. Air-blast atomization of non-Newtonian liquids. J. Nonnewtonian Fluid Mech. 58 (2), 161–194.
Marmottant, P., 2001. Atomisation d'un liquide par un courant gazeux, Grenoble, INPG.
Maronga, S., Wnukowski, P., 1997. Modelling of the three-domain fluidized-bed particulate coating process. Chem. Eng. Sci. 52 (17), 2915–2925.
Mellmann, J., 2001. The transverse motion of solids in rotating cylinders--forms of motion and transition behavior. Powder Technol. 118 (3), 251–270.
Mueller, R., Kleinebudde, P., 2007. Comparison of a laboratory and a production coating spray gun with respect to scale up. AAPS PharmSciTech. 8 (1), E21–E31.
Müller, R., Kleinebudde, P., 2006. Comparison study of laboratory and production spray guns in film coating: effect of pattern air and nozzle diameter. Pharm. Dev. Technol. 11 (4), 425–433.
Page, S., Baumann, K.-H., Kleinebudde, P., 2006a. Mathematical modeling of an aqueous film coating process in a Bohle Lab-Coater, Part 1: development of the model. AAPS PharmSciTech. 7 (2), E79–E86.
Page, S., Baumann, K.-H., Kleinebudde, P., 2006b. Mathematical modeling of an aqueous film coating process in a Bohle Lab-Coater: part 2: application of the model. AAPS PharmSciTech. 7 (2), E87–E94.
Pandey, P., Katakdaunde, M., Turton, R., 2006a. Modeling weight variability in a pan coating process using Monte Carlo simulations. AAPS PharmSciTech. 7 (4), E1–E10.
Pandey, P., Turton, R., Joshi, N., Hammerman, E., Ergun, J., 2006b. Scale-up of a pan-coating process. AAPS PharmSciTech. 7 (4), E125–E132.

Perez-Ramos, J.D., Findlay, W.P., Peck, G., Morris, K.R., 2005. Quantitative analysis of film coating in a pan coater based on in-line sensor measurements. AAPS PharmSciTech. 6 (1), E127–E136.

Porter, S.C., Verseput, R.P., Cunningham, C.R., 1997. Process optimization using design of experiments. Pharm. Technol.1–7, October 1997.

Prpich, A., am Ende, M.T., Katzschner, T., Lubczyk, V., Weyhers, H., Bernhard, G., 2010. Drug product modeling predictions for scale-up of tablet film coating—a quality by design approach. Comput. Chem. Eng. 34 (7), 1092–1097.

Ramkrishna, D., 2000. Population Balances: Theory and Applications to Particulate Systems in Engineering. Academic Press, San Diego, CA.

Reiland, T., Seitz, J., Yeager, J., 1983. Aqueous film-coating vaporization efficiency. Drug Dev. Ind. Pharm. 9 (6), 945–958.

Saltelli, A., Tarantola, S., Campolongo, F., Ratto, M., 2004. Sensitivity Analysis in Practice: A Guide to Assessing Scientific Models. John Wiley & Sons, The Atrium, Southern Gate, Chichester, West Sussex, England.

Sobol, I.M., 2001. Global sensitivity indices for nonlinear mathematical models and their Monte Carlo estimates. Math. Comput. Simul. 55 (1), 271–280.

Stetsko, G., Banker, G., Peck, G., 1983. Mathematical modeling of an aqueous film coating process. Pharm. Technol. 7, 50–62.

Strong, J.C., 2009. Psychrometric analysis of the environmental equivalency factor for aqueous tablet coating. AAPS PharmSciTech. 10 (1), 303–309.

Suzzi, D., Radl, S., Khinast, J.G., 2010. Local analysis of the tablet coating process: impact of operation conditions on film quality. Chem. Eng. Sci. 65 (21), 5699–5715.

Tobiska, S., Kleinebudde, P., 2003. Coating uniformity: influence of atomizing air pressure. Pharm. Dev. Technol. 8 (1), 39–46.

Toschkoff, G., Just, S., Funke, A., Djuric, D., Knop, K., Kleinebudde, P., et al., 2013. Spray models for discrete element simulations of particle coating processes. Chem. Eng. Sci. 101, 603–614.

Varga, C., Lasheras, J.C., Hopfinger, E., 2003. Initial breakup of a small-diameter liquid jet by a high-speed gas stream. J. Fluid Mech. 497, 405–434.

Wnukowski, P., Setterwall, F., 1989. The coating of particles in a fluidized bed (residence time distribution in a system of two coupled perfect mixers). Chem. Eng. Sci. 44 (3), 493–505.

Yarin, A.L., 2006. Drop impact dynamics: Splashing, spreading, receding, bouncing. Vol. 38. Annual Review of Fluid Mechanics, pp. 159–192.

Zhu, H., Zhou, Z., Yang, R., Yu, A., 2008. Discrete particle simulation of particulate systems: a review of major applications and findings. Chem. Eng. Sci. 63 (23), 5728–5770.

Modeling in pharmaceutical packaging

12

Y. Li[1] and Y. Chen[2]
[1]Abbvie Inc., North Chicago, IL, United States, [2]Novast Laboratories, Ltd., Nantong, China

12.1 Introduction

Drug product shelf life is determined based on the time scale over which a product remains chemically and physically stable. Product stability depends on the chemical property of the drug substance, formulation, and the environmental conditions for storage such as temperature, oxygen, and moisture. Sensitivity to environmental conditions, hence the need for protection, is identified during product development. Protective methods are developed based on the need to address the specific degrading element for each product if the product is not stable. There may be multiple approaches to stabilize a product. The discussion of this chapter will be limited to the topic of moisture protection for solid pharmaceutical products.

Moisture can affect drug product stability in many ways. It can change active pharmaceutical ingredient (API) crystal forms, hydration or dehydration, excipient functionality, product dissolution, tablet hardness, tablet color, capsule shell cross-linking, and physical appearance. Loss of moisture for liquid products during storage may also lead to a change in product quality (Ahlneck and Zografi, 1990).

The humidity-corrected Arrhenius equation (Eq. 12.1) relates drug product stability to moisture content for small molecule drugs in solid dosage forms (Waterman et al., 2007).

$$\ln k = \ln A - \frac{E_a}{RT} + B(\mathrm{RH}) \tag{12.1}$$

where k is the degradation rate, A is the Arrhenius collision frequency, E_a is the energy of activation for the chemical reaction, R is the gas constant, T is the temperature in Kelvin, and B is the sensitivity constant for relative humidity (RH).

Eq. (12.1) indicates that API degradation increases exponentially with an increase in RH (relative humidity inside the package that the drug product experiences).

Currently, the most commonly used containers for finished solid oral pharmaceutical products are plastic bottles as multiple-unit containers and blisters as unit

Predictive Modeling of Pharmaceutical Unit Operations. DOI: http://dx.doi.org/10.1016/B978-0-08-100154-7.00012-0

dose containers. These commonly used containers for finished products, such as high-density polyethylene (HDPE), polyethylene terephthalate, and polypropylene bottles, and the thermoformed blisters, as well as the low-density polyethylene bags and fiber drums for bulk products, are permeable to moisture. Therefore, it is important to select an appropriate package container with respect to moisture protection to study moisture uptake of the packaged products during shelf life storage.

Packaging selection and justification for a new product is studied during product development stages. Traditionally, real-life stability trials are conducted to support packaging selection. For stability study, the drug product is packaged in selected primary package for long-term storage under varied climatic zone conditions (25°C/60%RH, 30°C/65%RH, 30°C/75%RH) and accelerated condition (40°C/75% RH). Appropriate analytical tests are performed for each interval to evaluate if the product remains chemically and physically stable to meet quality requirements for the target shelf life. If studies indicate that the containers tested could not provide adequate protection, new studies will have to be repeated using different containers/ materials. Because the rate of chemical degradation in solid state is generally slow, stability study may take several months to reveal if the product is stable or not. It is clear that packaging selection by stability study is time- and resource-intensive. Hence, an ability to predict the moisture uptake of packaged product during storage under varied conditions will be helpful for reducing the cost and cycle time of drug product development. It is particularly useful for evaluating container equivalency for postapproval packaging changes.

Several researchers have conducted studies to predict the moisture uptake during storage and published their studies in the literature. Labuza et al. (1972) used a simple iterative approximation method to predict the moisture uptake of a single component in the container. Nakabayashi et al. (1980) used a more sophisticated computation method by iteration with shorter time duration for prediction of shelf life for square tablets. Zografi et al. (1988) developed a sorption–desorption moisture transfer (SDMT) model to predict the moisture transfer among different components in closed systems. The SDMT model has been used to simulate the product moisture content during storage (Kontny et al., 1992; Badawy et al., 2001). A theoretical model has also been developed by linking the drug product property with container moisture permeability for prediction of product moisture uptake during storage (Chen and Li, 2003). More recently, a mechanistic model for predicting in-use moisture uptake by a packaged product was developed by Remmelgas et al. (2013).

Factors governing moisture uptake of packaged product include water vapor transmission rate (WVTR) of container, moisture sorption isotherm, and initial moisture content of packaged product, product quantities, and environmental conditions. This chapter will focus on the review of methods for determination and estimation of container WVTR, product moisture sorption isotherm, as well as on modeling of moisture uptake by a packaged product. Case studies for the modeling and/or the estimation approaches will also be presented.

12.2 Container WVTR of pharmaceutical packaging

12.2.1 Moisture permeation

Plastic containers such as HDPE bottles and thermoformed blisters are permeable to moisture vapor. For well-sealed plastic containers without gross defects, the mechanism of moisture permeation into the containers is mainly diffusion of water molecules through the container wall and through the seal (Barry et al., 2005). If the container wall is approximated as a homogeneous planar barrier with a constant diffusion coefficient D of water vapor at constant temperature, and if it is assumed that the concentration of water at the surface of the outside wall is kept at a constant level of C_o, the concentration at the inside wall surface is kept at essentially zero or a sink condition, and the initial concentration of water in the wall material is uniform at a level of C_i, moisture permeation into the container can be determined by either measuring the quantity of water permeating through the wall into the sink, or by monitoring the amount of water entering the outer surface of the wall material (Chen and Li, 2008).

If the quantity of water permeating through the wall is measured, Eq. (12.2) can be used to describe the permeation process (Crank, 1986).

$$Q_{t,d} = \frac{DC_o}{h}\left(t + \frac{C_i h^2}{2DC_o} - \frac{h^2}{6D}\right) - \frac{2hC_o}{\pi^2}\sum_{n=1}^{n=\infty}\frac{(-1)^n}{n^2}\exp\left(-\frac{n^2\pi^2 Dt}{h^2}\right) - \frac{4C_i h}{\pi^2}\sum_{m=0}^{m=\infty}\frac{1}{(2m+1)^2}\exp\left(\frac{-(2m+1)^2\pi^2 Dt}{h^2}\right) \tag{12.2}$$

where $Q_{t,d}$ is the amount of moisture diffused through the unit area of the wall at time t, D is the diffusion coefficient of water in the wall, h is the wall thickness, and C_o and C_i represent the water concentration at the outside surface of the wall and the initial concentration in the wall, respectively.

If the amount of water entering the outer surface of the wall material is measured, such as the measurement of weight gain of containers per the previous editions of USP, such as USP29 chapter <671>, the measured quantity per unit surface area, $Q_{t,\mathrm{wg}}$, includes the amount of water absorbed by the wall and the backing material in the closure, and the amount of water diffused through the wall into a sink created by desiccants. In this case, Eq. (12.3) can be used to describe the permeation process.

$$Q_{t,\mathrm{wg}} = \frac{DC_o}{h}\left(t - \frac{C_i h^2}{2DC_o} + \frac{h^2}{3D}\right) - \frac{2hC_o}{\pi^2}\sum_{n=1}^{n=\infty}\frac{1}{n^2}\exp\left(-\frac{n^2\pi^2 Dt}{h^2}\right) + \frac{4C_i h}{\pi^2}\sum_{m=0}^{m=\infty}\frac{1}{(2m+1)^2}\exp\left(\frac{-(2m+1)^2\pi^2 Dt}{h^2}\right) \tag{12.3}$$

WVTR is commonly used to characterize moisture permeability of packaging containers. Obtaining reliable container WVTR is critical to ensure the accuracy of subsequent moisture uptake modeling and appropriate packaging design.

12.2.2 Determination of WVTR

12.2.2.1 Single weight gain method for WVTR determination

The single weight gain method for determination of container WVTR is described in the USP < 671 > (USP38) for classification of multiple-unit container systems. Results obtained by this method may be highly variable. For example, data in the literature shows that the WVTR obtained at 25°C/75%RH was higher than at 40°C/75%RH (Taborsky and Grady, 2001) in one case. A high variability in the data renders little scientific value either for packaging design or for justification of post-approval container changes.

Theoretically, the high variability of WVTR measurement using the single weight gain method can be attributed to material variability, and more importantly, to the initial condition of container walls. Eqs. (12.2) and (12.3) show that the moisture permeation profiles are not linear with time at the early stages because the exponential terms in the equations are nonnegligible at short times. Eqs. (12.2) and (12.3) also show that the moisture permeation profiles are affected by the initial water concentration in the wall material, regardless of the method of determination. The dependency of initial weight gain on the initial wall condition is further depicted in Fig. 12.1.

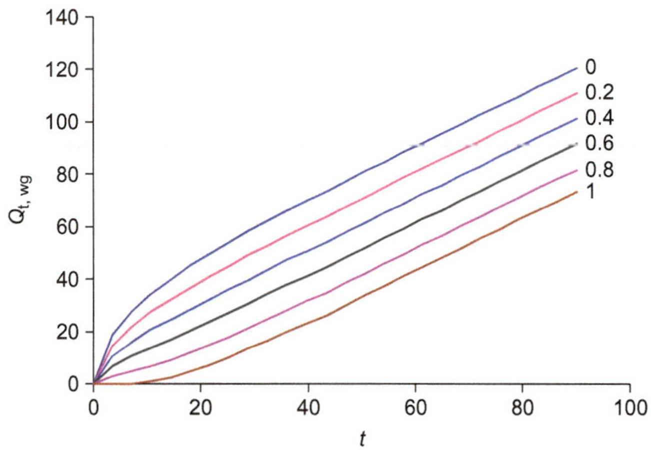

Figure 12.1 Schematic of weight gain curves of containers filled with desiccants and stored at constant temperature and humidity. Numbers at the end of the curves are the values of C_i/C_0. The x- and y-axis are in arbitrary scales.

Source: Reprinted from Chen, Y., Li, Y., 2008. Determination of water vapor transmission rate (WVTR) of HDPE bottles for pharmaceutical products. Int. J. Pharm. 358, 137–143, with permission from Elsevier. (C_i represents initial water content in container wall, C_0 represents water content in environment).

The initial weight gain profiles range from a burst when the wall is initially dry ($C_i = 0$) to a delay when the wall is initially equilibrated with environmental condition ($C_i = C_o$). Therefore, permeability cannot be reliably determined at an early time point by a single weight grain measurement (Chen and Li, 2008).

12.2.2.2 Steady-state method for WVTR determination

From Fig. 12.1, it can be seen that, if the permeation process proceeds for a sufficiently long time to achieve steady-state permeation, the rate of permeation in the later time points (the steady state) is the same regardless of the initial wall conditions, as long as temperature and driving force remain unchanged.

Taking the weight gain method as an example, in the first case where $C_i = 0$, and at $t \to \infty$ when steady state is achieved, weight gain in Eq. (12.3) can be simplified to

$$Q_{t,\mathrm{wg}} = \frac{DC_o}{h}\left(t + \frac{h^2}{3D}\right) \tag{12.4}$$

In the second case where $C_i = C_o$, and at $t \to \infty$, weight gain in Eq. (12.3) can be simplified to

$$Q_{t,\mathrm{wg}} = \frac{DC_o}{h}\left(t - \frac{h^2}{6D}\right) \tag{12.5}$$

Using steady-state data, container WVTR can be determined using the simplified Eq. (12.4) or Eq. (12.5), regardless of the initial water concentration in the wall. Studies showed that the steady-state weight gain method could provide reproducible WVTR results for HDPE bottles. Data in Table 12.1 show that results obtained by steady-state method are consistent, while results obtained by the single weight gain method are highly variable (Chen and Li, 2003 and 2008). The steady-state method is recognized and used by pharmaceutical research scientists including PQRI (Product Quality Research Institute) Container-Closure Working Group in recent

Table 12.1 Moisture permeability of HDPE bottles

Temperature (°C)	$k \times 10^3$ (mg/(day•bottle•% H), mean (SD)			
	1.5 ounce		3.0 ounce	
	Single point method	Steady-state method	Single point method	Steady-state method
40	24.9 (6.5)	13.5 (0.4)	37.5 (10.0)	17.1 (0.3)
30	5.5 (1.7)	8.7 (0.4)	9.2 (3.5)	13.0 (0.9)
25	2.1 (2.5)	4.7 (0.1)	6.3 (2.8)	5.7 (0.2)

years (Barry et al., 2005). The widely used USP <671> general chapter has been updated recently in the USP38 edition to include the steady-state method for testing the WVTR for pharmaceutical containers.

12.2.3 Estimation of container WVTR

Taking the container surface area into consideration, it can be shown that WVTR through the container wall during steady state can be calculated by differentiation of either Eq. (12.4) or Eq. (12.5). The result can be represented by Eq. (12.6).

$$\mathrm{WVTR} = \frac{AdQ_{t,\mathrm{wg}}}{d_{\mathrm{t}}} = \frac{ADC_0}{h} \tag{12.6}$$

where A is the surface area, D is the diffusion coefficient of water vapor in the container wall, h is container wall thickness, and C_0 is water concentration on the outer surface of the container wall.

In practice, water concentration on the outer surface of the container wall, C_0, is not measured. Instead, C_0 can be assumed to be proportional to the equilibrium external water concentration in the air C_{air} by partition theory, as shown in Eq. (12.7).

$$C_0 = KC_{\mathrm{air}} = K\frac{18,000 \times P_{\mathrm{a}}}{RT} = K\frac{180 \times P_{\mathrm{s}} \times \%\mathrm{RH}}{RT} \tag{12.7}$$

where K is the partition coefficient of water vapor in the container wall material, P_{a} and P_{s} (Pa) are the actual and the saturated water vapor pressure in the air at temperature T, respectively, R is the gas constant, and %RH is the percent relative humidity. The value of 18,000 is the molecular weight of water in mg/mol.

Apply Eq. (12.7) into Eq. (12.6) to obtain Eq. (12.8)

$$\mathrm{WVTR} = \frac{A \times P \times \%\mathrm{RH}}{h} \tag{12.8}$$

where $P = \frac{D \times K \times 180 \times P_{\mathrm{s}}}{RT}$ represents the apparent moisture permeability of the packaging material with a unit of $\mathrm{mg \cdot cm/(day \cdot \%RH \cdot cm^2)}$.

The response of the apparent moisture permeability data to temperature follows the Arrhenius rule as expressed in Eq. (12.9).

$$\ln P = a\left(\frac{1}{T}\right) + b \tag{12.9}$$

where a and b are constants.

The apparent moisture permeability, P, can be calculated from the WVTR, surface area, and thickness of the packaging material using Eq. (12.10).

Table 12.2 Experimental and calculated container WVTR of some HDPE bottles

Bottle size (oz)	Surface area (cm^2)	Wall thickness (cm)	WVTR (Exp.)	WVTR (Calc.)	WVTR (Exp.)	WVTR (Calc.)	WVTR (Exp.)	WVTR (Calc.)
			25°C/60%RH (mg/day/bottle)		30°C/65%RH (mg/day/bottle)		40°C/75%RH (mg/day/bottle)	
0.75	69.1	0.096	0.17	0.20	0.28	0.32	0.71	0.81
1.0	87.1	0.104	0.21	0.23	0.34	0.37	0.92	0.94
1.5	101.5	0.102	0.27	0.28	0.41	0.44	1.02	1.12
3.0	157.5	0.132	0.36	0.33	0.53	0.53	1.28	1.35
4.0	195.2	0.103	0.59	0.53	0.93	0.84	2.36	2.14
5.0	228.2	0.103	0.68	0.62	1.12	0.98	2.82	2.50

Apparent moisture permeability of HDPE material, $P \times 10^6$(mg · cm/day · %RH · cm^2): 4.63 (2°C), 6.79 (30°C), 15.04 (40°C).

$$P = \frac{\text{WVTR} \times h}{A \times \%\text{RH}} \tag{12.10}$$

The apparent moisture permeability, P, is a material property, and is expected to be constant under constant temperature. For some commonly used polymeric materials, the respective P may be available in literature. With an existing P, Eq. (12.8) can be used to estimate container WVTR at any desired storage condition based on surface area, wall thickness of the container of the same type of packaging material. The apparent moisture permeability of the packaging material can be obtained from the vendor, or can be calculated using Eqs. (12.9) and (12.10) based on WVTRs of raw material (Chen and Li, 2008).

The comparison of experimentally measured and calculated WVTR for some square HDPE bottles are presented in Table 12.2. It shows that the calculated container WVTR is comparable to the experimental results. Comparable experimental and calculated WVTR values were also obtained for some blister packages.

12.3 Moisture sorption isotherm of pharmaceutical products

12.3.1 Moisture sorption isotherm

The relationship between equilibrium moisture content and RH (water activity) of a material at a given temperature is commonly described in a graphical curve called moisture sorption–desorption isotherm. The moisture sorption isotherm of a product can be used to study moisture uptake of the packaged product by relating the equilibrium moisture content of the product to the RH in the package. Temperature in the range of International Committee on Harmonization (ICH) conditions has minimal effect on moisture sorption isotherm. Moisture sorption isotherm generated at 25°C is comparable or slightly higher than at 40°C.

12.3.2 Determination of moisture sorption isotherm

Equilibrium moisture sorption isotherm of pharmaceutical powders and granules can be determined using a dynamic moisture sorption microbalance (DMSM) method or a desiccator method. The samples are equilibrated under controlled RH and temperature conditions. Weight gain of samples is determined at different humidities, and results can be plotted as moisture sorption isotherm.

For the DMSM method, the samples need to be dried sufficiently using an inline drying method prior to the equilibrium study, or, the initial moisture content of the samples is determined prior to the equilibrium study for the final calculation after the study. The DMSM method is automated and is flexible for controlling humidity and temperature. Moisture equilibrium for powders and granules at any given humidity by this method can usually be achieved within a few hours. It is convenient to use for formulation screening purposes (Dalton and Hancock, 1997).

Because different desiccators can provide different humidities at the same time (Nyqvist, 1983; Greenspan, 1977), the desiccator method with loss on drying (LOD) measurement is another convenient method to study the moisture isotherms of products, especially for tablets. The rate of moisture sorption or desorption of compressed tablets is substantially lower than that of powders and granules. The time needed for tablets to reach equilibrium at a given humidity in a desiccator is approximately 1–2 weeks. The tablets can also be ground into powders or granules, so that the DMSM method can be used to determine the moisture sorption isotherm.

The DMSM and desiccator methods can generate comparable equilibrium moisture content of samples, unless the material contains a significant amount of tightly bonded hydration water, which cannot be easily removed using the DMSM drying method. In such cases, LOD or other moisture measurement techniques should be used to determine moisture content before and after moisture equilibrium.

Common manufacturing processes such as blending, granulation, compression, and coating within a reasonable range of conditions may not alter the moisture sorption capacity of a material significantly. As shown in Fig. 12.2, the moisture sorption isotherms of granules, uncoated, and coated tablets are basically identical to the physical mixture for a model drug product. In the figure, the isotherms for tablets were generated by desiccator method, and the isotherms for granules and physical mixture were generated by DMSM. The slight lower moisture contents of the physical mixture and granules compared with the coated and uncoated tablets was probably due to the insufficient drying in DMSM method (Li and Chen, 2003).

12.3.3 Estimation of moisture sorption isotherm

Equilibrium moisture sorption isotherm of a product is a key factor governing the rate of moisture uptake by a packaged product, besides the container WVTR and

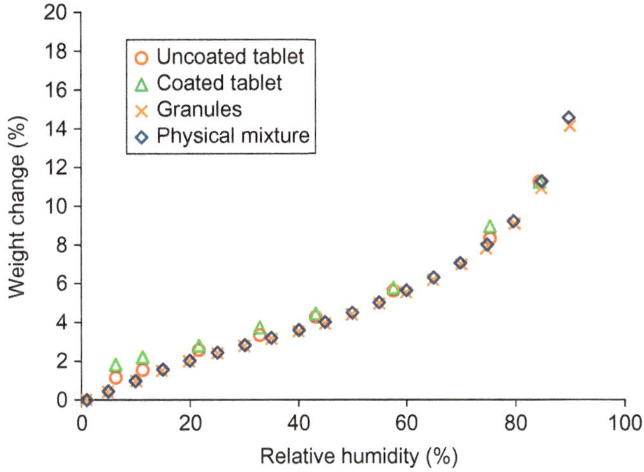

Figure 12.2 Moisture sorption isotherms of tablets, granules, and physical mixture for the model drug product at 25°C.

environmental conditions. Therefore, it would be beneficial if the moisture sorption isotherm of a product could be predicted at the early stage of formulation development. Such a prediction can guide the excipient selection in formulation design to increase the efficiency of product development (Li and Chen, 2003).

Moisture sorption isotherms can be described using a mathematical equation by fitting the equilibrium moisture content with respect to RH into equations using an Excel spreadsheet or other software.

Any equations that would give a good fit over the entire range of humidities can be used to represent the moisture sorption isotherms of pharmaceutical excipients and products for the purpose of the current application. In general, an empirical polynomial equation is more versatile for curve fitting than a theoretical equation such as the Guggenheim–Anderson–de Boer (GAB) or Brunauer–Emmett–Teller (BET) equations, although the polynomial equation has no physical meaning. In addition, the polynomial equation permits simple differentiation and integration in applying the isotherms to predict the moisture uptake by packaged products, which will be discussed in Section 12.4.

The general format of the polynomial equation is described in Eq. (12.11)

$$f_i(\mathrm{RH}) = y_0 + a \times \mathrm{RH}^{0.5} + b \times \mathrm{RH} + c \times \mathrm{RH}^2 + d \times \mathrm{RH}^3 + e \times \mathrm{RH}^4 + g \times \mathrm{RH}^5 + h \times \mathrm{RH}^6 \ldots \quad (12.11)$$

where the symbol $f_i(\mathrm{RH})$ indicates the equilibrium moisture content as a function of the percentage of RH. The symbol of % was omitted from the equation for simplification purposes. Not all the terms in the preceding equation need to be used for a particular material. Fewer terms can be used as long as a good fit can be obtained.

Assuming that there is no significant interaction, and that the solid phase transition of ingredients during the manufacturing process does not occur, the moisture sorption isotherm of a drug product can be estimated from the moisture sorption isotherms of the individual ingredients in the product using Eq. (12.12) (Dalton and Hancock, 1997; Li and Chen, 2003):

$$f_{\mathrm{prod}}(\mathrm{RH}) = \sum_{i=1}^{i=n} x_i f_i(\mathrm{RH}) \tag{12.12}$$

where $f_{\mathrm{prod}}(\mathrm{RH})$ and $f_i(\mathrm{RH})$ represent the moisture sorption isotherms of the product and the ith ingredient in the product, respectively; x_i is the weight fraction of ith ingredient, and RH represents the percent relative humidity.

This predictive approach may be used as a convenient tool for excipient selection and formulation design to protect moisture-sensitive compounds, provided that there is no substantial polymorphic conversion during process.

12.4 Moisture uptake modeling of packaged pharmaceutical products

12.4.1 Overview of moisture uptake modeling

Moisture uptake of packaged product in storage is governed by several factors such as container WVTR, moisture sorption isotherm, environmental condition, packaging configuration, and initial moisture content of the packaged product. The rate of moisture permeation through a container usually decreases over time as the humidity in the container increases due to the accumulation of moisture in the container. The effect of all these factors must be considered in order to predict the rate of moisture uptake in real-life situations.

A simple model was employed by Labuza et al. (1972) to calculate the moisture uptake by a single component in storage. In 1980, an iterative approximation model using sophisticated computation procedure was used by Nakabayashi et al. to estimate the moisture uptake of some packaged products. Later, an SDMT model was developed by Zografi et al. (1988) to predict the moisture transfer among pharmaceutical excipients in closed systems via vapor phase transfer employing the GAB equation. The SDMT model also requires tedious computation procedures to carry out the stepwise approximation through periodical adjustment of internal humidity and permeation rate for each time increment.

Based on the vapor transfer theory and Fick's first law, a new moisture uptake model using polynomial equations was developed (Chen and Li, 2003) by linking the drug product property with container moisture permeability for the prediction of moisture uptake in packaged products during storage. The use of polynomial equations allows a simple operation for differentiation and the subsequent integration in model application.

While it is important to demonstrate that the product remains stable during storage, sometimes, it is also desirable to show that the product remains stable during use. A mechanistic model for predicting in-use moisture uptake by packaged product was developed by Remmelgas et al. (2013). The mechanistic model considers moisture uptake by the product both when the bottle is closed and when it is open.

12.4.2 Moisture uptake model using polynomial equations for packaged product in storage

By using a polynomial equation to describe moisture sorption isotherm of packaged material, the moisture uptake model can predict moisture content of one component or multiple components simultaneously with simple mathematical differentiation and integration.

The model was developed based on the following assumptions:

1. Moisture content of a product is a function of the equilibrium humidity.
2. Moisture permeation through the container is the rate-limiting step.
3. Lag time for moisture diffusion through the container is negligible compared to the shelf life of the product.
4. Moisture permeability of the container is constant at a given temperature.

These assumptions describe the characteristics of the commonly used packaging systems, and therefore are not difficult to satisfy. However, the model is not applicable if product moisture content does not change with humidity, or if the moisture permeation through container is not the rate-limiting step. Pinholes and gross defects are not accounted for by this model.

Under constant temperature and external humidity, the rate of moisture permeation through a container at quasi-steady can be expressed as

$$\frac{d_{\mathrm{w}}}{d_{\mathrm{t}}} = k(\mathrm{RH_{out}} - \mathrm{RH}) \tag{12.13}$$

where $d_{\mathrm{w}}/d_{\mathrm{t}}$ is the rate of moisture permeation through the container, k represents the moisture permeability of the container $\left(k = \frac{\mathrm{WVTR}}{\mathrm{RH_{out}}}\right)$, $\mathrm{RH_{out}}$ and RH represent the percent relative humidity outside and inside the container, respectively.

Assuming that the moisture content of any unit component in the container, w_i, is a function of the equilibrium humidity

$$w_i = f_i(\mathrm{RH}) \tag{12.14}$$

The total amount of moisture of n components in the container, w, can be expressed as

$$w = \sum_{i=1}^{i=n} q_i f_i(\mathrm{RH}) \tag{12.15}$$

where q_i is the quantity of the ith component in the container.

Differentiation of Eq. (12.15) with respect to RH leads to

$$\frac{d_{\mathrm{w}}}{d_{\mathrm{RH}}} = \frac{d}{d_{\mathrm{RH}}}\left(\sum_{i=1}^{i=n} q_i f_i(\mathrm{RH})\right) \tag{12.16}$$

Rearranging and substituting Eq. (12.13) into Eq. (12.16), the rate of moisture permeation through the container can be related to the quantities and the moisture isotherms of all components in the containers, as described by Eq. (12.17).

$$k(\mathrm{RH}_{\mathrm{out}} - \mathrm{RH})d_{\mathrm{t}} = \frac{d}{d_{\mathrm{RH}}}\left(\sum_{i=1}^{i=n} q_i f_i(\mathrm{RH})\right)d_{\mathrm{RH}} \tag{12.17}$$

Rearranging Eq. (12.17) results in

$$d_{\mathrm{t}} = \frac{\frac{d}{d_{\mathrm{RH}}}\left(\sum_{i=1}^{i=n} q_i f_i(\mathrm{RH})\right)}{k(\mathrm{RH}_{\mathrm{out}} - \mathrm{RH})}d_{\mathrm{RH}} \tag{12.18}$$

The t-RH profile inside the container can be calculated by integrating Eq. (12.18). This leads to Eq. (12.19).

$$t = \int_{\mathrm{RH}_0}^{\mathrm{RH}_{\mathrm{t}}} \frac{\frac{d}{d_{\mathrm{RH}}}\left(\sum_{i=1}^{i=n} q_i f_i(\mathrm{RH})\right)}{k(\mathrm{RH}_{\mathrm{out}} - \mathrm{RH})}d_{\mathrm{RH}} \tag{12.19}$$

The RH_0 can be determined from total initial moisture content of the components prior to packaging and the moisture sorption isotherms using Eq. (12.15). The water content of each individual component, as a function of time, can be estimated by substituting the RH at time t into the corresponding moisture sorption isotherm of the component using Eq. (12.14), on the availability of the t-RH profile from Eq. (12.19) (Chen and Li, 2003). The RH at time t can also be substituted into Eq. (12.1) to calculate chemical degradation rate on the availability of associated parameters and constant (Waterman and Macdonald, 2010).

The application of the polynomial moisture uptake model involves a simple computational process. Commonly available software, such as Excel or SigmaPlot, is suitable for curve fitting and the subsequent calculations.

The model has been developed based on the diffusion theory and mass balance principles. It can be used for all packaging systems such as bottles, blisters, bags or drums, as long as the systems satisfy the assumptions listed previously.

The significant advantage of the polynomial moisture uptake model over other existing methods is that the polynomial model does not require any simplification in application. Modeling of moisture uptake by packaged products can be carried out using the standard differentiation and integration procedures upon the availability of the polynomial isotherms and the initial moisture contents of each component in the package.

12.5 Case studies

12.5.1 Estimation of equilibrium moisture sorption isotherm of a tablet formulation

The equilibrium moisture sorption isotherm of a tablet formulation for a model drug was estimated using Eq. (12.12) based on the moisture sorption isotherms of individual ingredients in the formulation. The formulation compositions are presented in Table 12.3. The moisture sorption isotherms of individual ingredients are presented in Fig. 12.3. The equilibrium moisture sorption isotherms were measured using the DMSM method. The polynomial equation coefficients for the isotherms determined by curve fitting the equilibrium moisture sorption data with respect to humidity using SigmaPlot software (Version 7, SPSS Inc.) are presented in Table 12.3. Assumptions made for the prediction include that there will be no interfering chemical–physical interactions between the excipient–excipient and drug–excipient, and that there is no polymorph conversion of individual ingredient during manufacturing process, which would change the moisture sorption properties of the ingredients. Fig. 12.4 shows that the predicted moisture sorption isotherm of the tablet formulation agreed very well with the experimental data. In the figure, the experimental isotherm of the formulation was also generated using the DMSM method.

12.5.2 Moisture uptake modeling for a packaged tablet product in storage

A tablet product contains a drug compound that has been found to be susceptible to degradation over time in the presence of moisture. Therefore, suitable packaging configuration is required to protect the product against potential moisture gain during storage.

Four tablet formulations with different dose strength (listed in Table 12.4) were developed and manufactured. Tablet A is a marketed product and is used as a reference in the study. Tablets B, C, and D are new strengths developed for post marketing application. A new drug application (NDA) stability study on the reference Tablet A packaged in 1-ounce HDPE bottle (3 tablets with 1.1 g silica gel and 9 g cotton) showed that the total moisture content in the packaged tablets is about 1.1% after 6 months storage under 40°C/75%RH condition and the product still remains acceptable. Therefore, 1.1% moisture content in tablets is used as a criterion for packaging selection to ensure acceptable shelf life is achieved for the new strengths of tablets.

Table 12.3 Formulation compositions and polynomial equation coefficients for moisture sorption isotherms

Ingredients	Composition (% w/w)	Polynomial equation coefficients							
		y_0	*a*	*b*	*c*	*d* ($\times 10^{-4}$)	*e* ($\times 10^{-6}$)	*g* ($\times 10^{-8}$)	*h* ($\times 10^{-10}$)
Microcrystalline cellulose	17.2	−3.2397	3.2412	−0.7588	0.0290	−8.8282	15.562	−13.950	4.9873
Hydroxypropyl cellulose	2.9	0	0	0	0.0096	−5.4397	14.442	−17.1420	7.6473
Crospovidone	3.9	−12.833	12.547	−3.0926	0.0987	−23.013	32.502	−24.856	8.2355
Magnesium stearate	0.5	0	0	0	0.0037	−1.7721	3.9205	−4.0570	−1.5881
Croscarmellose sodium	17.2	−5.9531	7.0457	−2.3219	0.1239	−40.910	73.107	−66.100	24.083
Sodium dodecyl sulfate	1.9	0	0	0	0	−0.0036	0.0226	−0.0446	0.0278
Opadry II blue	3.2	−17.389	17.385	−5.0205	0.1661	−44.692	70.943	−59.074	19.925
Model drug	53.2	0.0152	−0.0004	0	1.2×10^{-6}	0	0	0	0

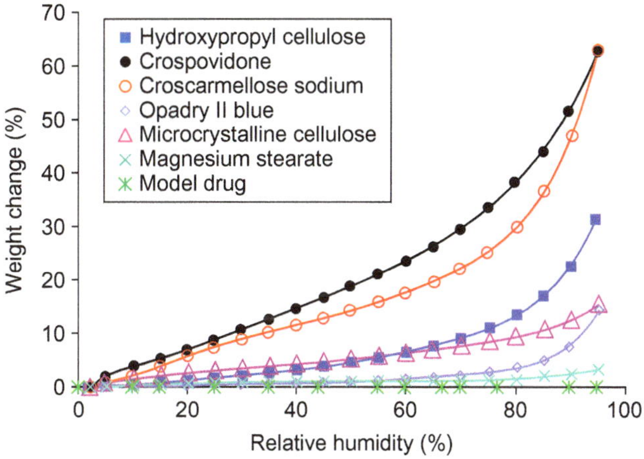

Figure 12.3 Moisture sorption isotherms of individual ingredients in the model drug tablet formulation at 25°C.

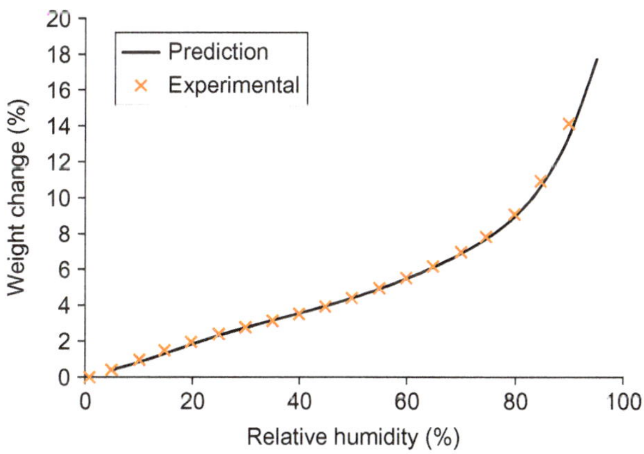

Figure 12.4 Predicted and experimental moisture sorption isotherm of the tablet formulation at 25°C.

Table 12.4 **Tablets with varied dose strength**

Tablet ID	Tablet weight (mg)	Tablet volume (ml)
Tablet A (reference)	792.7	1.0
Tablet B	811.5	1.2
Tablet C	1585.6	2.3
Tablet D	1623.5	2.8

The packaging configurations proposed for the new strengths of tablets B, C, and D are 7 tablets/1-ounce HDPE bottle for physician samples, and 30 tablets/3-ounce HDPE bottle for commercial product supply. During product development, an experimental packaging configuration of 90 tablets/8.5-ounce HDPE bottle was also evaluated. Varied amount of desiccant (silica gel) was used in the containers to minimize moisture uptake during storage.

The polynomial moisture uptake model was used to predict moisture content of the packaged tablets during storage under ICH conditions, and to justify packaging selection for physician samples and commercial products. The objective of the modeling was to select packaging systems that can provide enough protection to ensure tablet moisture content below 1.1% during shelf life storage. Modeling for prediction was carried out using an Excel spreadsheet (Microsoft Excel 2010).

Container WVTR of the HDPE bottles is listed in Table 12.5. The WVTR values were estimated using the mathematical method described in Section 12.2.3.

The moisture sorption isotherms generated by the DMSM method for the formulations, silica gel, and cotton are shown in Fig. 12.5. The corresponding polynomial equation coefficients obtained by curve fitting using SigmaPlot for the isotherms,

Table 12.5 Containers used for the tablet product

HDPE bottle ID	Bottle wall thickness (cm)	Bottle surface area (cm^2)	Bottle overflow volume (ml)	WVTR (mg/day/bottle)	
				25°C/ 60%RH	40°C/ 75%RH
1.0 ounce	0.104	87.1	41.7	0.23	0.94
3.0 ounce	0.132	157.5	114.2	0.33	1.35
8.5 ounce	0.074	308.6	283.5	1.13	4.64

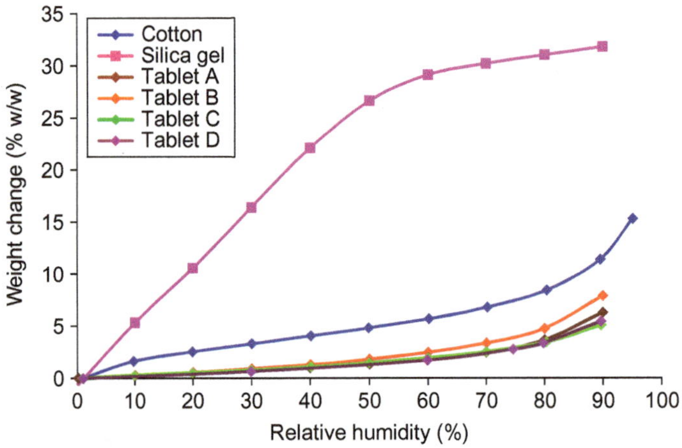

Figure 12.5 Moisture sorption isotherm of tablets, cotton, and silica gel at 25°C.

and the average initial moisture content of the tablets, silica gel, and cotton used in the study are listed in Table 12.6. In reality, the initial moisture content of each material could be different due to lot-to-lot variation. Besides the typical initial moisture content of 1.0% in the new strengths of tablets, a high initial moisture content of 2.0% for the tablets was also evaluated in the modeling to provide a limit for in-process control during tablet manufacturing.

In order to verify that the moisture modeling is reliable and can be used to support packaging selection and shelf life justification for new strengths of tablets, modeling data was compared with actual stability data for Tablet D packaged in 8.5-ounce bottle with and without silica gel. The initial tablet moisture content was 1.0%. As shown in Fig. 12.6, the equilibrium moisture content in the tablet from actual stability study matched very well with the modeling data.

Table 12.6 Initial moisture content and polynomial equation coefficients for tablets, cotton, and silica gel

Material ID	Initial moisture content (%)	*b*	*c*	*d*	*e*
Tablet A (reference)	0.8	6.0816E-02	−1.8267E-03	2.1247E-05	0
Tablet B	1.0, 2.0	6.1934E-02	−1.6614E-03	2.1259E-05	0
Tablet C	1.0, 2.0	4.3309E-02	−9.0192E-04	1.1575E-05	0
Tablet D	1.0, 2.0	0	1.6625E-03	−3.8377E-05	3.0468E-07
Silica gel	5.4	5.8619E-01	0	−2.9493E-05	0
Cotton	5.8	2.2500E-01	−4.8959E-03	4.3500E-05	0

Polynomial equation: $f_i(\text{RH}) = b\text{RH} + c\text{RH}^2 + d\text{RH}^3 + e\text{RH}^4$.

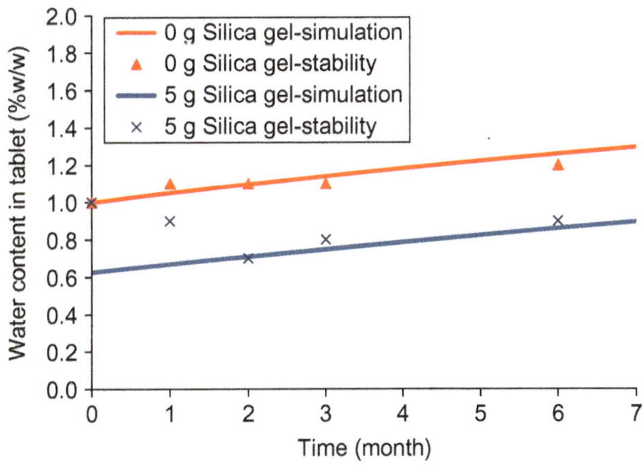

Figure 12.6 Comparison of actual stability data with modeling data for Tablet D packaged in an 8.5-ounce bottle (90 tablets/bottle) with and without silica gel and stored at 40°C/75%RH.

The modeling is used to evaluate the effect of cotton on moisture uptake of packaged tablets. Cotton can provide physical protection to a packaged product during shipping, but, due to its hygroscopicity, it may increase the RH in the packaging system, and therefore may adversely affect the chemical stability of the product. As shown in Fig. 12.7, the predicted equilibrium moisture content of the packaged tablet without cotton is substantially lower compared to the package with 9 g cotton included. Therefore, it is recommended that no cotton be used in packaging systems for the new strengths of tablets.

The proposed commercial package for the new strengths of tablets is 30 tablets per 3-ounce HDPE bottle with 3 g silica gel. There will be no cotton used in the package. Fig. 12.8 shows that with initial tablet moisture content as high as 2.0%,

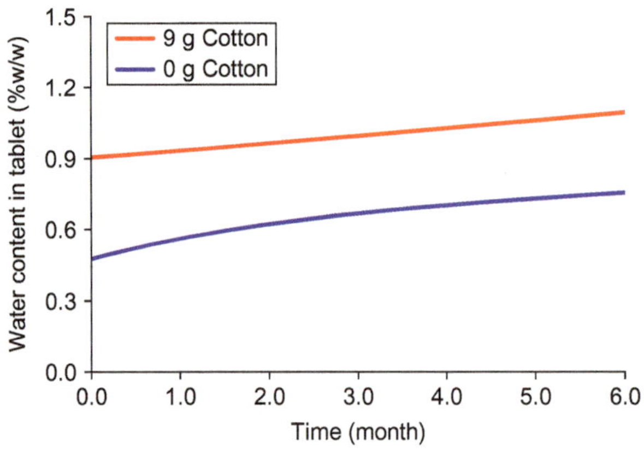

Figure 12.7 Modeling of reference Tablet A packaged in 1-ounce bottle (3 tablets with 1.1 g silica gel), with and without cotton, stored at 40°C/75%RH.

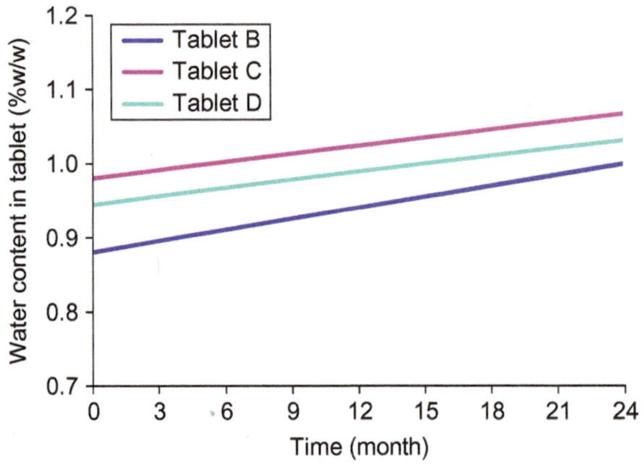

Figure 12.8 Moisture modeling for new strengths of tablets with 2.0% initial moisture content, packaged in 3-ounce HDPE bottle (30 tablets with 3 g silica gel) and stored at 25°C/60%RH.

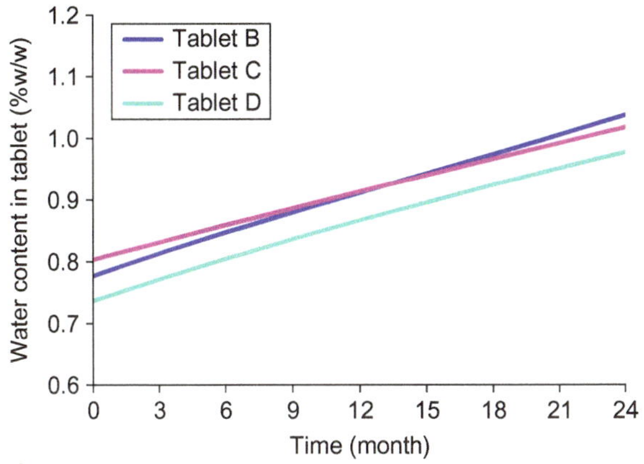

Figure 12.9 Moisture modeling for new strengths of tablets with 2.0% initial moisture content, packaged in 1-ounce HDPE bottle (7 tablets with 1.1 g silica gel) and stored at 25°C/60%RH.

the moisture content in the packaged tablets stored at 25°C/60%RH will be less than 1.1% during storage. The modeling data indicates that the proposed commercial packaging system is suitable for maintaining acceptable product stability over 2 years.

The container for the proposed physician sample of the new strengths of tablets is 7 tablets in a 1-ounce HDPE bottle with 1.1 g silica gel. There will be no cotton used in the package. Fig. 12.9 shows that with initial tablet moisture content as high as 2.0%, the moisture content in the packaged tablets stored at 25°C/60%RH will be less than 1.1% during storage. The modeling data indicates that the proposed packaging for physician's samples is suitable for maintaining acceptable product stability over 2 years.

It should be noted that, in addition to material controls, the manufacturing conditions, such as the environmental humidity and the exposure time of the desiccant during packaging into the bottles, can have a significant effect on the actual protection capability of the desiccant. Exposure of desiccant to room environment can result in adsorption of moisture by the desiccant from room air, leading to a partial or complete loss of the desiccant effect for the product. Therefore, the environmental condition and the process of using desiccant for the product must be carefully controlled.

12.5.3 Moisture uptake modeling for a packaged capsule product in storage

A capsule product containing a combination of two active compounds was developed for commercial manufacturing. Studies showed that both compounds are sensitive to moisture. Therefore, suitable packaging configuration is required to protect the product against moisture during storage.

The two compounds were formulated separately before encapsulation. Compound one was formulated into a powder blend, and compound two was formulated into minitablets. Varied quantities of powder blend and minitablets were filled into a capsule shell. The capsule volume, weight, and initial moisture content are listed in Table 12.7. Previous studies showed that with 5% moisture in the total capsule contents, both compounds still have acceptable stability. Therefore, 5% moisture content was used as a criterion for packaging selection.

The packaging configurations proposed for the product are 1 capsule/Ultrx 2000 blister for physician samples, and 90 capsules/6.4-ounce HDPE bottle for commercial product. To ensure sufficient protection for the capsules, thick-wall (0.135-cm average wall thickness) HDPE bottles were selected for packaging. These bottles have a minimum wall thickness ~1.5 times that of the regular bottles. The thick-wall bottles have a reduced rate of moisture permeation, thereby providing better protection to the product during storage.

The polynomial moisture uptake model was used to predict moisture content of the packaged product during storage under ICH conditions and to justify packaging selections for physician samples and commercial product. All packaging systems selected should provide enough protection to ensure moisture content in capsule contents does not exceed 5.0% during storage.

Container WVTR of the blister and HDPE bottle were estimated using the method described in Section 12.2.3, and are listed in Table 12.8.

Table 12.7 Capsule weight, volume and initial moisture content

Capsule volume (ml)	Weight of a capsule shell (mg)	Amount of powder blend filled in capsule (mg)	Amount of minitablet filled in capsule (mg)	Initial moisture content in capsule contents (%w/w)	Initial moisture content in capsule shell (%w/w)
0.5	76	75	104	3.3	13.0

Table 12.8 Containers used for the capsule product

Package ID	Average container wall thickness (cm)	Container surface area (cm^2)	Container overflow volume (ml)	WVTR (mg/day/bottle)	
				25°C/ 60%RH	40°C/ 75%RH
6.4-ounce HDPE bottle	0.135	229.03	204	0.46	1.89
Ultrx 2000 blister (0.5-ml capsule)	0.0094	6.57	1.5	0.01809	0.1074

The moisture sorption isotherms of the powder blend, minitablets, and hard gelatin capsule shell obtained using desiccator method are shown in Fig. 12.10. The corresponding polynomial equation coefficients are listed in Table 12.9.

In order to verify that the moisture modeling data are reliable and can be used to justify packaging selection for the capsule product, modeling data was compared with actual stability data. The initial moisture content in capsule shell and capsule contents used for modeling was 13% and 3.3%, respectively. As shown in Fig. 12.11, except for the initial time point, the moisture content from actual stability study matched fairly well with the modeling result. The modeling data are initially higher than the actual stability data because the formulation will absorb some moisture from capsule shell after encapsulation until equilibrium moisture distribution is achieved. The moisture modeling is based on the assumption that equilibrium moisture distribution among all components in package is established at time zero after packaging, hence the part of moisture absorbed from capsule shell is accounted for in the modeling. However, the actual equilibrium was not yet

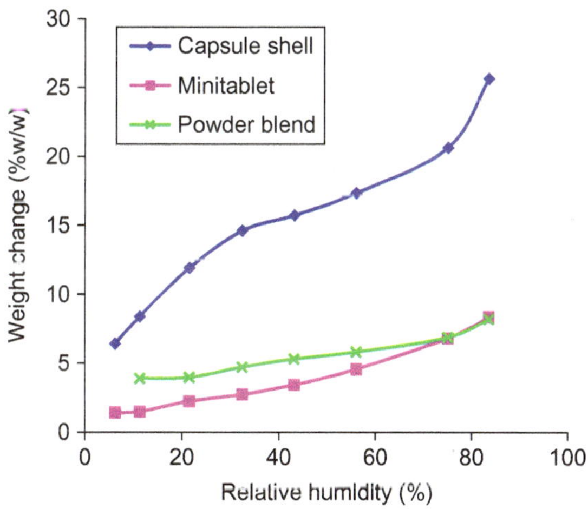

Figure 12.10 Moisture sorption isotherms of capsule product at 25°C.

Table 12.9 Polynomial equation coefficients for the capsule product

Material ID	*a*	*b*	*c*	*d*	*e*	*g*	*h*
Minitablet	0	1.5775E-01	−2.9187E-03	2.6786E-05	0	0	0
Powder blend	3.3468	4.0629E-02	0	0	0	0	3.9393E-12
Capsule shell	3.7142	4.3355E-01	0	−1.3935E-04	1.3718E-06	0	0

Polynomial equation: $f_i(\text{RH}) = a + b\text{RH} + c\text{RH}^2 + d\text{RH}^3 + e\text{RH}^4 + g\text{RH}^5 + h\text{RH}^6$.

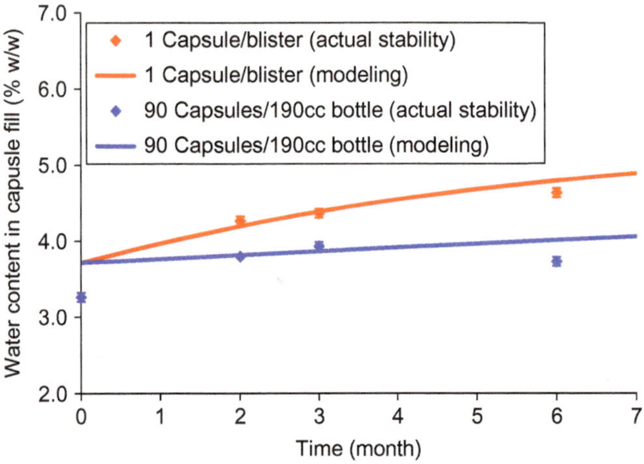

Figure 12.11 Predicted and actual moisture content in capsule contents for capsule product packaged in different packaging systems and stored at 40°C/75%RH.

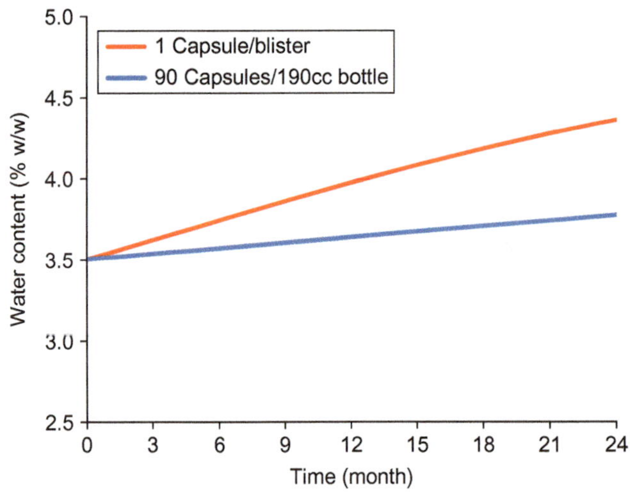

Figure 12.12 Moisture modeling for capsules packaged in Ultrx 2000 blister and 190cc bottle (90 capsules/bottle) and stored at 25°C/60%RH.

established when the samples were tested for the initial time point hence the test results was lower for the initial time point. Since the purpose of moisture uptake modeling is to predict long-term stability for packaged product, the initial discrepancy between the actual and prediction is not important.

The proposed commercial product packaging is 90 capsules/6.4-ounce bottle. Fig. 12.12 shows that, with initial moisture content in capsule shell as 13% and initial moisture content in capsule contents as 3.3%, the moisture content of the

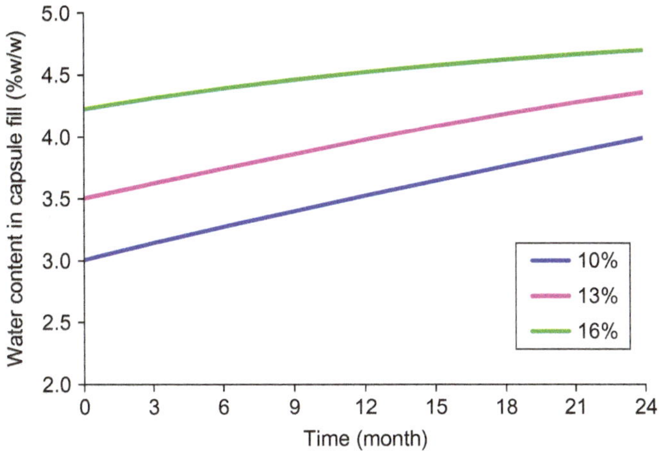

Figure 12.13 Moisture modeling for capsules with varied initial moisture content in capsule shell, packaged in Ultrx 2000 blister and stored at 25°C/60%RH.

capsule contents packaged in the proposed commercial package will not reach 5.0% within 2 years of storage at 25°C/60%RH.

The proposed physician sample packaging is one capsule per Ultrx 2000 blister. Fig. 12.12 also shows that, with initial moisture content in capsule shell as 13% and initial moisture content in capsule contents as 3.3%, the moisture content of the capsule contents packaged in blister will not reach 5.0% within 2 years of storage at 25°C/60%RH.

In order to evaluate the effect of initial moisture content in capsule shell on moisture uptake of the packaged product, the initial moisture content in capsule shell was varied from 10% to 16% in the modeling. The predicted equilibrium moisture content in capsule contents packaged in blister and stored at 25°C/60%RH is shown in Fig. 12.13. With initial moisture content in capsule shell being as high as 16%, the moisture content of capsule contents can be kept below 5% during 2 years storage.

The modeling data indicates that the proposed physician's sample and commercial product packaging systems are suitable to ensure that the moisture content of capsule contents does not exceed 5.0% during storage. The modeling results on Ultrx 2000 blister package for physician's sample and 90 capsules/6.4-ounce bottle for commercial product supported a 2 years shelf life as long as the initial moisture content in capsule contents is controlled to be or less than 3.3%, and the initial moisture content in capsule shell is controlled to be or less than 13%.

12.6 Summary

The container WVTR, moisture sorption isotherm, and the moisture uptake of a drug product during storage can be estimated using mathematical methods based on moisture diffusion theory and mass balance principles. With reliable container

WVTR and moisture sorption isotherm of the product, the moisture content of packaged product during storage can be accurately predicted using the polynomial moisture uptake model. These prediction methods can be used to design formulations, evaluate the selected packaging materials, design packaging configurations, and determine the appropriate amount of desiccant and cotton to be used for a product. These predictive methods can greatly facilitate drug product development.

Acknowledgments

The authors would like to thank Dr. Todd McDermott and Dr. Michael Mackaplow of NCE-FS Abbvie for their scientific review, discussion, and revision in writing the chapter.

References

Ahlneck, C., Zografi, G., 1990. The molecular basis of moisture effects on the physical and chemical stability of drugs in the solid state. Int. J. Pharm. 62, 87–95.

Badawy, S.I.F., Gawronski, A.J., Alvarez, F.J., 2001. Application of sorption–desorption moisture transfer modeling to the study of chemical stability of a moisture sensitive drug product in different packaging configurations. Int. J. Pharm. 223, 1–13.

Barry, J., Bergum, J., Chen, Y., Chern, R., Hollander, R., Klein, D., et al., 2005. Basis for using moisture vapor transmission rate per unit product in the evaluation of moisture-barrier equivalence of primary packages for solid oral dosage forms. Pharmacopeial Forum. 31, 262–269.

Chen, Y., Li, Y., 2003. A new model for predicting moisture uptake by packaged solid pharmaceuticals. Int. J. Pharm. 255, 217–225.

Chen, Y., Li, Y., 2008. Determination of water vapor transmission rate (WVTR) of HDPE bottles for pharmaceutical products. Int. J. Pharm. 358, 137–143.

Crank, J., 1986. The Mathematics of Diffusion. Clarendon Press, Oxford.

Dalton, C.R., Hancock, B.C., 1997. Processing and storage effects on water vapor sorption by some model pharmaceutical solid dosage formulations. Int. J. Pharm. 156, 143–151.

Greenspan, L., 1977. Humidity fixed points of binary saturated aqueous solutions. J. Res. Natl. Bur. Stand. 1, 89–96.

Kontny, M., Koppenol, S., Graham, E.T., 1992. Use of the sorption–desorption moisture transfer model to assess the utility of a desiccant in a solid product. Int. J. Pharm. 84, 261–271.

Labuza, T.P., Mizrahi, S., Karel, M., 1972. Mathematical models for optimization of flexible film packaging of foods for storage. Trans. ASAE. 15, 150–155.

Li, Y., Chen, Y., 2003. A study on moisture isotherms of formulations: the use of polynomial equations to predict the moisture isotherms of tablet products. AAPS PharmSciTech. 4 (4), Article 59.

Nakabayashi, K., Shimamoto, T., Mima, H., 1980. Stability of packaged solid dosage forms. II. Shelf-life prediction for packaged sugar-coated tablets liable to moisture and heat damage. Chem. Pharm. Bull. 28, 1099–1106.

Nyqvist, H., 1983. Saturated salt solutions for maintaining specified relative humidities. Int. J. Pharm. Tech. Prod. Mfr. 4, 47–48.

Remmelgas, J., Simonutti, A., Ronkvist, A., Gradinarsky, L., Lofgren, A., 2013. A mechanistic model for the prediction of in-use moisture uptake by packaged dosage forms. Int. J. Pharm. 441, 316–322.

Taborsky, C.J., Grady, L.T., 2001. Water vapor permeation of prescription vials. Pharmacopeial Forum. 27, 2417–2427.

Waterman, K.C., Carella, A.J., Gumkowski, M.J., Lukulay, P., MacDonald, B.C., Roy, M.C., et al., 2007. Improved protocol and data analysis for accelerated shelf-life estimation of solid dosage forms. Pharm. Res. 24, 780–790.

Waterman, K.C., Macdonald, B.C., 2010. Package selection for moisture protection for solid, oral drug products. J. Pharm. Sci. 99 (11), 4437–4452.

Zografi, G., Grandofi, G.P., Kontny, M.J., Mendenhall, D.W., 1988. Prediction of moisture transfer in mixtures of solids: transfer via the vapor phase. Int. J. Pharm. 42, 77–88.

Continuous secondary process selection and the modeling of batch and continuous wet granulation

13

D. Clancy
GlaxoSmithKline, Collegeville, PA, United States

13.1 Paradigm shift to continuous processing for solid dose manufacture

Continuous manufacture of solid dosage forms has been receiving increasing attention from pharmaceutical companies over the past decade. Novartis, Pfizer, GSK, and universities such as MIT, Purdue, and Rutgers have been actively developing expertise in this area since approximately 2004. A review of most of the possible continuous manufacturing options being considered has been summarized by Pfizer in 2004 (Mollan, 2004). In 2007, Novartis funded a $65 million 10-year partnership with MIT to develop a continuous pharmaceutical manufacturing process from input chemicals to final dosage form (Wallack, 2007). In 2012, the Novartis-MIT Center of Continuous Processing announced successful demonstration of a complete continuous process for manufacture of tablets, starting from API synthesis (Trafton, 2012).

The reasons for strategically heading toward continuous processing include reduced operating costs, footprint, lower cost of poor quality, ease of scale-up, and improvement in overall product quality performance. A complete economic analysis and process description for the Novartis-MIT continuous process has been published with the conclusion estimating a 29% savings in drug product cost compared to conventional manufacture (Wilburn, 2010).

Manufacturing cost has historically not been a strong determining factor for process selection. Maximizing quality and minimizing development complexity are typically favored factors and will likely continue to be so for new drug products since they typically enjoy healthy margins. In these cases continuous processing is still favored for high volume products due to real time quality determination and feedback process control. Continuous processing has another advantage in that less scale-up experimentation is needed as development experiments can be run on equipment representative of the full scale thus shortening development time and uncertainty.

Predictive Modeling of Pharmaceutical Unit Operations. DOI: http://dx.doi.org/10.1016/B978-0-08-100154-7.00013-2

13.2 Selection of the appropriate process based on powder flow and compressibility

Continuous processing requires the powder to flow from one piece of equipment to another; therefore, powder flow is the first critical attribute to consider when determining if a powder is eligible for a particular process route. Compressibility, or the ability of the powder to irreversibly deform under pressure and make hard compacts, is the next most important factor to consider. An evaluation of powder flow utilizing shear cell and compressibility utilizing compaction simulation can provide a rational for first intent manufacturing selection using the qualitative diagram shown in Fig. 13.1.

Dry processing routes are preferred as they offer lower cost, lower complexity, and have no need to dry the material, which reduces the risk of prolonged heat and moisture exposure. If the drug product blend has both good powder flow, and good compressibility then continuous blending and tablet compression can be utilized (Route 1). Drug product blends that do not flow well enough to enable direct compression require granulation prior to compression, and roller compaction is the preferred process (Route 2), or twin screw granulation (4).

Alternatively if the drug product blend flows well, but is not suitable for compression, continuous capsule filling can be utilized (Route 3).

If the drug product blend is not compressible then a binder is needed to form granules and wet granulation on a twin screw extruder is required (Route 4), or batch high shear granulation (Route 5). Selection between batch versus continuous wet granulation is primarily determined by powder flow and assessing how robust the formulation is to granulation variation. An evaluation of the impact of powder flow on twin screw granulation variation will be described later in this chapter.

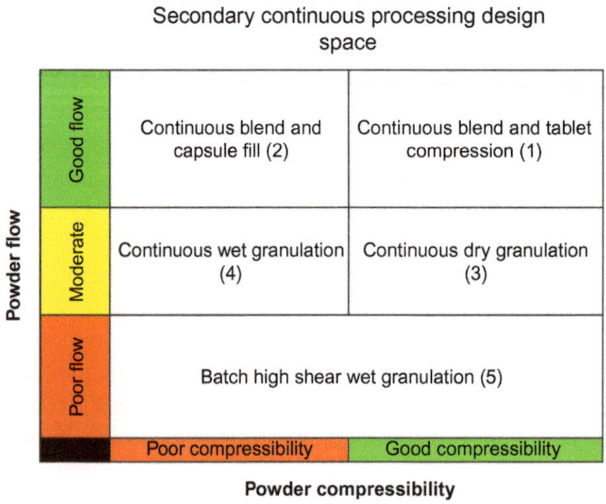

Figure 13.1 Pharmaceutical secondary process selection based on powder compressibility and powder flow—qualitative diagram.

There are inevitably going to be some exceptions to the design space shown in Fig. 13.1. Materials that tend to segregate during blending or discharge may not achieve the content uniformity needed and will also need to granulated. In the case of poorly soluble and poorly wettable (hydrophobic) API, the dissolution can often be significantly improved by coating the API with hydrophilic binder, in which case a wet granulation route would be preferred in secondary processing (von Orelli and Leuenberger, 2004).

Work has been done to put numbers to the powder flow requirements for each unit operation shown in Fig. 13.1 utilizing a shear cell. The resulting design space from this investigation within GSK is shown in Fig. 13.2. Most pharmaceutical processing equipment is fairly small and does not generate the kind of internal stresses observed in large silos, thus it was found that shear cell data at low consolidation stresses between 1 and 6 KPa was typically most predictive of the failure limits for each unit operation.

Typically shear cell powder flow data is reported in literature as the "Flow Function at 10 KPa." Within GSK experimentation it's been found that the inverse of the flow function, which is known as the "Flow Index" tends to provide a linear relationship to the flow variance being observed. Thus the diagram shown in Fig. 13.1 was inverted, as better flowing powder has a lower flow index. Some complexity exists in that different consolidation stresses are needed to describe the failure limits of each unit operation, so the scaling to 1-KPa consolidation stress shown in Fig. 13.2 is primarily for visual purposes to get an idea of the relative size of the space where each unit operation can operate. The specific failure limits for each unit operation are underlined in Fig. 13.2 if they need a different consolidation stress than 1-KPa.

The limits shown in Fig. 13.2 are general guidelines as there are special cases where other dimensions come into play. For example tablet compression up to a flow index of 0.2 at 10 KPa has been demonstrated to result in tablet RSD less than

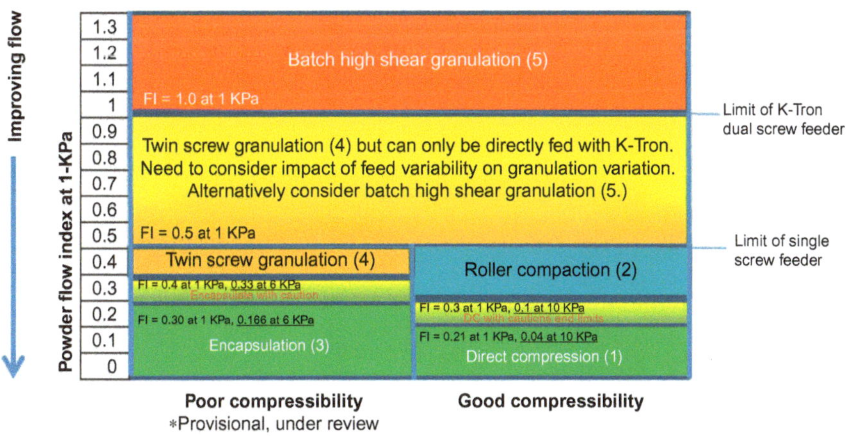

Figure 13.2 Guidelines for secondary process selection based on shear cell assessment of powder flow index.

3% for 600 to 800 mg tablets, whereas the guidelines shown above were developed to allow acceptable RSD for 150 mg tablets. Larger dosage forms can accommodate more poorly flowing materials.

13.3 Introduction to modeling batch high shear granulation

Useful predictive models for batch and continuous granulation utilize many of the same concepts, and it's constructive to understand batch high shear granulation prior to continuous twin screw granulation. Batch high shear granulation has been explored more extensively, and in some ways is less complex than continuous. The models that have been found to be most useful to date are a combination of first principles mechanistic linked with linear regression to predict an outcome such as granule particle size distribution, milled granule density, or tablet dissolution. The prediction in each case is going to be product specific, but the first principle nature of the mechanistic terms utilized in the linear regression models is shown to hold true across multiple drug products.

Most pharmaceutical high shear granulation processes granulate for a specified amount of time, or specify a maximum motor impeller power or torque before stopping the granulation process. Since most products aren't particularly sensitive to granulation endpoint, this simple control methodology is often adequate. Sometimes though, products can be particularly sensitive to changes in granulation extent. As an example, drug product "P" is a micronized hydrophobic API with 80% drug content in the granule. Relatively small changes in granule porosity and density have significant impacts on resulting tablet dissolution, and tablet breaking force. For this reason, the "Work" control model shown as Eq. (13.1) that integrates both power and time was first developed and applied to drug product "P" and has controlled its commercial manufacture. (Clancy, 2010).

From a first principles perspective, "work done" is the instantaneous power applied to the system multiplied by the time the power was applied. Since power varies over time in granulation, the integral of power with respect to time needs to be considered. Typically the power measured in granulation is the power flow to the motor, and some power is lost due to the motor and power train inefficiencies. It's useful to subtract a baseline power (P_0) which is associated with the power usage needed by the motor and drive mechanism from the overall power used by the impeller, as shown in Eq. (13.1).

$$\text{Work} = \int_0^t (Power_{\text{Impeller}} - P_0)\,\mathrm{d}t \tag{13.1}$$

where "$Power_{\text{Impeller}}$" is the measured power of the main impeller during granulation, and P_0 is the steady state baseline power measured prior to start of the granulation process with nothing in the bowl.

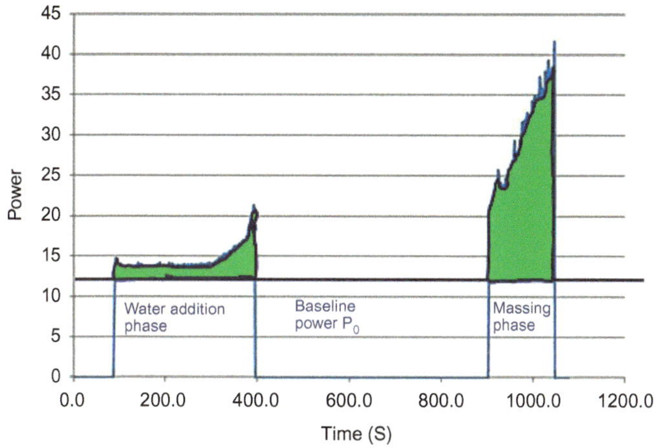

Figure 13.3 Calculation of granulation work corresponds to shaded area.

Graphically what Eq. (13.1) is calculating is the net work done, which is the cumulative amount of power added above baseline, as the shaded in area shown in Fig. 13.3.

Calculation of a definite integral isn't generally possible or convenient, thus Eq. (13.1) is approximated using numeric integration and rapid time slicing. Eq. (13.2) is the actual numeric calculation utilized to calculate the integral shown in Eq. (13.1).

$$W_i = (P_i - P_0)\cdot \Delta t + W_{i-1} \tag{13.2}$$

W_i is the work calculated at the ith time slice, P_i is the impeller power at the ith time slice, Δt is the time difference measured in seconds between "i" and "$i - 1$" time slices. The output from the above equation is integrated over time of the granulation once water input has started.

Work done per unit dry powder mass, water fraction added, and tablet thickness at a constant tablet mass can be used as parameters for empirical linear regression models to predict tablet dissolution. Examples of this are shown for three different drug products in Figs. 13.4–13.6.

The dissolution of tablets from drug product "P" can be modeled as a four-dimensional surface of tablet dissolution as a function of work, water fraction, and tablet thickness, as shown in Fig. 13.4. The empirical model for dissolution in this case is a 10-term linear regression model as a function of work, water, tablet thickness, and their cross-products with an R2 value of 92%. The data to form this model comes from a 10-batch response surface DoE as function of work and water, and split to five levels of compressed tablet thickness to make 50 subbatches in a split plot experimental design. The raw data for this design is available in Appendix A, Table 13.1.

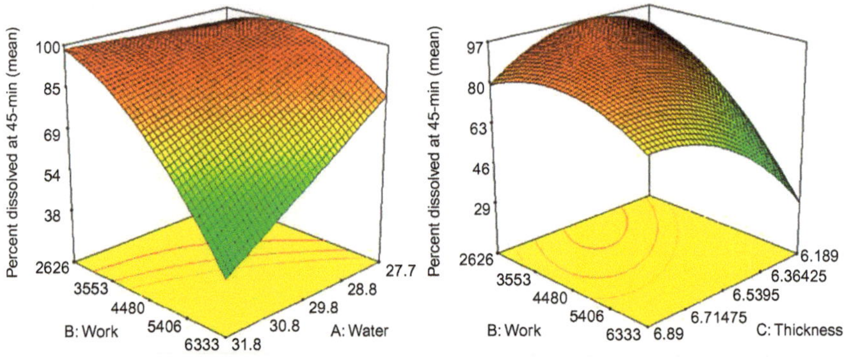

Figure 13.4 Percent tablet dissolved at 45-min for drug product "P" at constant target tablet thickness (left) or constant target granulation water fraction (right).

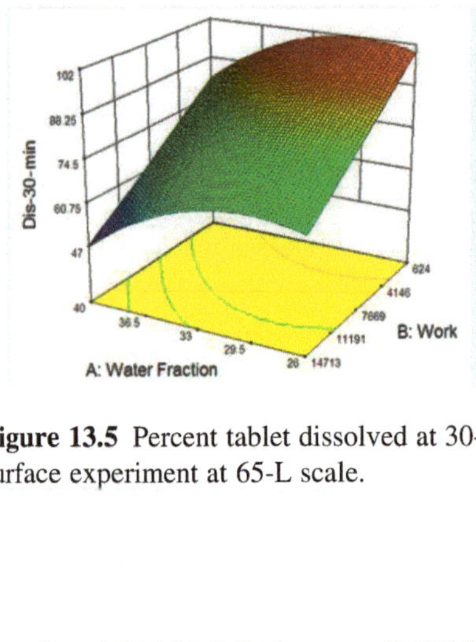

ANOVA for Response Surface Reduced Quadratic Model

Analysis of variance table [Partial sum of squares - Type III]

Source	Sum of Squares	df	Mean Square	F Value	p-value Prob > F	
Model	3160.72	3	1053.57	136.42	< 0.0001	significant
A-Water Fraction	177.52	1	177.52	22.99	0.0049	
B-Work	328.35	1	328.35	42.52	0.0013	
A²	130.80	1	130.80	16.94	0.0092	
Residual	38.61	5	7.72			
Cor Total	3199.33	8				

Std. Dev.	2.78	R-Squared	0.9879
Mean	78.56	Adj R-Squared	0.9807
C.V. %	3.54	Pred R-Squared	0.9654
PRESS	107.37	Adeq Precision	28.065

Figure 13.5 Percent tablet dissolved at 30-min for drug product "D" from 9-batch response surface experiment at 65-L scale.

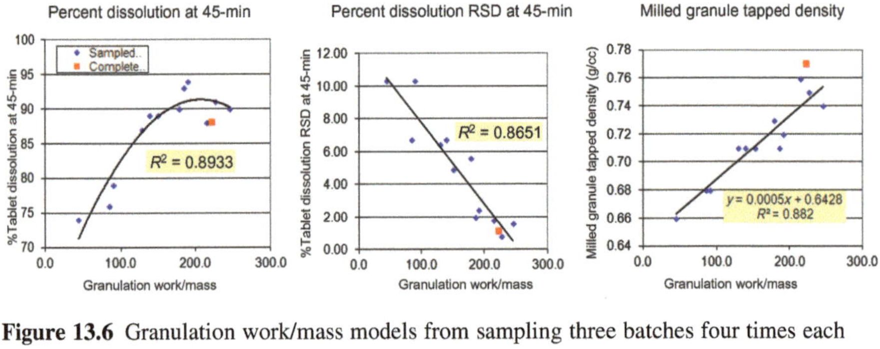

Figure 13.6 Granulation work/mass models from sampling three batches four times each compared to a nonsampled batch.

If tablet thickness is held constant, granule dissolution and tablet hardness can be predicted as a three-dimensional surface as a function of granulation work and water fraction. An example surface for drug product "D" from a nine-batch response surface DoE is shown in Fig. 13.5. In this case the tablet dissolution can be predicted from a simple four-term empirical linear regression model considering work, work-squared, and water with an R2 value of 99%. The DoE data from this experiment is available in Appendix A, Table 13.2.

13.4 Modeling batch high shear granulation by sampling during granulation

The concept has been explored of sampling from high shear granulation at varying time points and using the results from sampled batches to predict the behavior of whole batches on basis of work done per unit mass. To accomplish this, the power input per unit mass needs to be integrated with respect to time to calculate a work done per unit mass for each sample. The equation used for calculation is shown as Eq. (13.3).

$$W_i = \left(\frac{P_i - P_0}{mass_i}\right) \cdot \Delta t + W_{i-1} \qquad (13.3)$$

where "$mass_i$" is the mass of powder remaining in the bowl at the ith time point on a dry weight basis, and W_i is now scaled as the work done per unit of mass.

Use of sampling can have the useful outcome of reducing the material requirements to produce a granulation model by a factor of three to five. Sampling should be used with the caution that there is some power needed to restart the motor and impeller. For smaller or newer granulators this restart power appears to be less significant than with larger or older electric motors. In a typical sampling experiment 20 to 25% of the batch is removed at each of four or five time points, and work done per unit of dry powder mass is calculated at each time point.

An example of sampling three batches at constant water level at 300-L scale for drug product "P," compared to dissolution of a nonsampled batch is shown in Fig. 13.6. Each of three batches was sampled at varying time points to make four samples per batch with each sample 25% of the batch. The results of the 12 subsampled batches at varying work/mass was used to calculate an optimum granulation endpoint that minimized the dissolution RSD while providing close to optimum mean dissolution. The results of the complete batch were within the standard error of prediction for dissolution mean and RSD for models built on the sampled batches.

There is some evidence that models built from sampling will slightly overestimate the optimum granulation work/mass, for example the milled granule tapped density of the nonsampled batch shown in Fig. 13.6 is slightly higher than anticipated from a model built from the sampled batches. This has been attributed to the

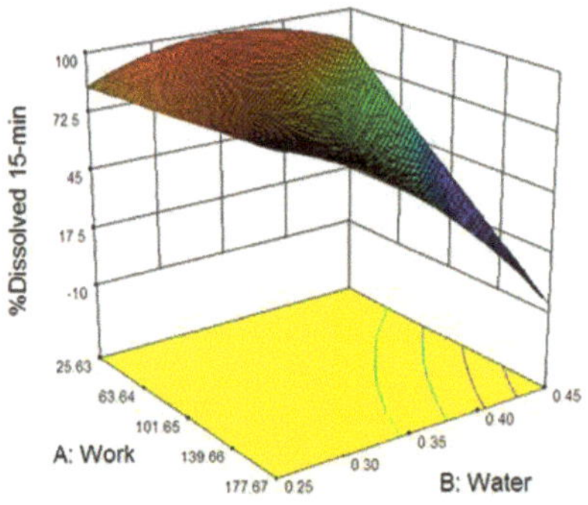

ANOVA for Response Surface Reduced Quadratic Model

Analysis of variance table [Partial sum of squares - Type III]

Source	Sum of Squares	df	Mean Square	F Value	p-value Prob > F
Model	3408.42	4	852.10	26.44	< 0.0001
A-Work	1244.67	1	1244.67	38.62	< 0.0001
B-Water	1467.69	1	1467.69	45.54	< 0.0001
AB	626.50	1	626.50	19.44	0.0010
B²	528.56	1	528.56	16.40	0.0019
Residual	354.52	11	32.23		
Cor Total	3762.94	15			

The Model F-value of 26.44 implies the model is significant. There is only a 0.01% chance that a "Model F-Value" this large could occur due to noise.

Std. Dev.	5.66	R-Squared	0.9058
Mean	79.06	Adj R-Squared	0.8715
C.V. %	7.18	Pred R-Squared	0.7680
PRESS	872.92	Adeq Precision	18.778

Figure 13.7 Response surface of drug product "S" dissolution at 15-min to granulation work/mass and water fraction in granulation from sampled experimentation at 25-L scale.

power needed for startup and shutdown. For this particular 300-L granulator there is an initial power spike as the power is turned on, and some mathematical exploration was done that if this initial power spike were removed, the models improved. The initial power spike varies from equipment scale and motor, with some older motors having too large and variable of an initial power spike to allow meaningful sampling experimentation to occur. The reproducibility and size of the initial power spike and overall stability of the baseline power (P_0) should be looked at carefully if a sampled batch granulation model is desired. In some cases the initial startup power spikes can be reduced or eliminated by warming the motor up for 20 to 30 min prior to adding the granulation mixture to the bowl, and ensuring all moving components are lubricated.

Given the caveat about ensuring use of a granulator motor without a large initial power spike, sampling during granulation can be a useful strategy in R&D to allow modeling and assessment of how robust a formulation is to variation in granulation. Fig. 13.7 shows an example of a 20-point experiment at 25-L scale for product "S" composed of four batches of varying water level each sampled five times. This sampled 20-point experiment was useful for the drug product team in defining the optimum work and water levels needed for subsequent production of clinical batches at 25-L scale. The data table from this experiment is available in Appendix A, Table 13.3.

13.5 Impact of raw material particle size and surface area changes on high shear granulation modeling

As material is milled into finer particle size it requires more granulation work to achieve the same endpoint characteristics. A good example experiment was done at 65-L scale with drug product "P" that illustrates this relationship.

As material is milled to a finer size, a variety of physical properties change—the particle size distribution (PSD) becomes finer, specific surface area (SSA) increases, and bulk density decreases. A challenge is getting a good representative number describing the entire batch as there are typically significant sampling and replication variances for PSD and SSA. A novel technique was developed on a Freeman Powder Rheometer that provided the best signal to noise ratio of these techniques when comparing the RSD of replicate measurements and samples within batches.

A powder Rheometer is simply a very sensitive torque instrument mounted on a mixing blade. The mixing blade can be set to a specified RPM, then travels vertically with the rotating blade tracing a helix into and then out of a powder sample. The methodology established placed 30 grams of dry powder (corresponding to approximately 100 mL of volume) into the 200-mL sample apparatus. Tip speed was set to 300 mm/s with a downward and upward helix angle of traverse of 5°. This rotation should fluidize the powder bed upwards as the blade traverses downwards through the bed. Ten traverses were done to "condition" the powder to remove affects of sample history. Twenty more replications were done, and the instantaneous work done by the impeller at 1-cm height from the bottom of the sample was then measured and called "Rheometer Work" measured in milliJoules (or milliNewton*meters) per 30 grams.

Rheometer work of the dry API powder was found to correlate to the particle size distribution X90 and the specific surface area of the API for drug product "P" as shown in Fig. 13.8.

Specific surface area had an RSD of replicate measurements on a sample of 6%, PSD X90 had an RSD of replicate measurement of 4%, and the measurement of "Rheometer Work" had replicate measurement RSD of 2%. Sampling variance was also a significant concern, and the powder Rheometer uses 60 times as much sample as SSA and PSD testing, significantly reducing the impact of sampling variation.

To evaluate the impact of variation in API milling, a lot of drug product "P" API was micronized to three differing micronization work done of 60, 180, and 280 kJ/kg, resulting in three lots of API with particle size X90 of 6.8, 11.0, and 12.2 microns. These three lots of API were then tested on the Powder Rheometer, resulting in Rheometer Work values of 6.8, 11.0, and 12.2 mJ/30 grams, respectively.

The three lots of API were then granulated at 65-L scale with a constant water amount, and sampled at four different time points during granulation. For this drug

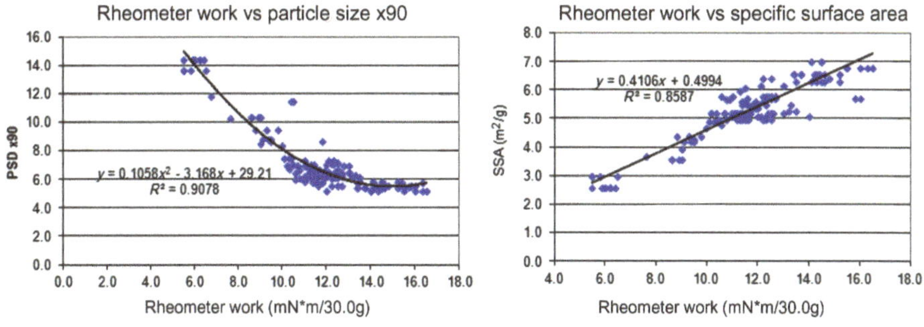

Figure 13.8 Relationship of API surface area and particle size X90 to Powder Rheometer work.

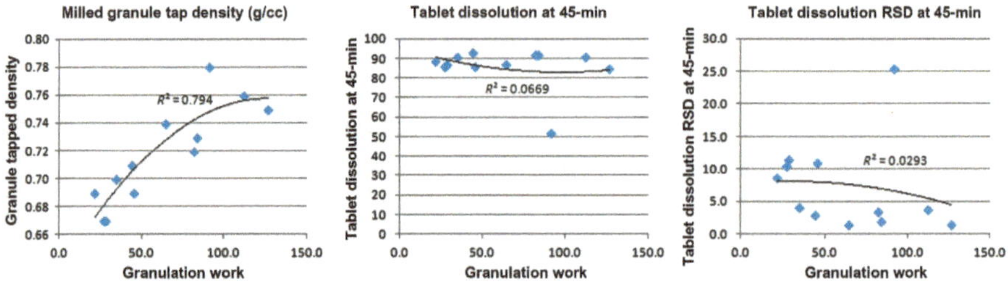

Figure 13.9 Poor correlation of granulation work/mass to output granule and tablet characteristics.

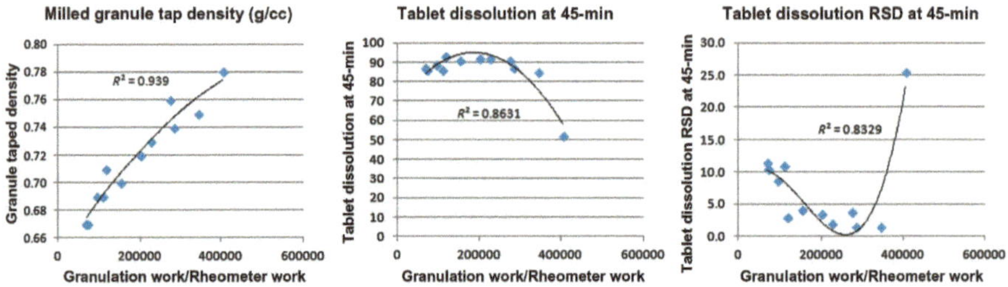

Figure 13.10 Correlation of (granulation work/mass)/rheometer Work to output granule and tablet characteristics.

product, the API is 80% of the granulation mixture, with the remainder consisting of 5.9% PVP binder, 12.4% microcrystalline cellulose, and 1.7% sodium starch glycolate. The granulation work per unit mass was calculated for each sample as described in the previous section. The DoE data from this experiment is available in Appendix A, Table 13.4.

If granulation work per unit mass is then used to correlate the resulting milled granule density, tablet dissolution, and tablet dissolution RSD, poor correlations are observed (Fig. 13.9). Clearly there was a significant impact of the changes in API particle size distribution.

If the granulation work per unit mass is then normalized by dividing by the Powder Rheometer work done on 30 grams of dry sample, then the characteristic models for drug product "P" can be resolved. Milled granule tapped density, tablet dissolution, and tablet dissolution RSD can then be predicted by polynomial fits with goodness of fit ranging from 94 to 83% (Fig. 13.10).

There was a linear relationship noted between Rheometer Work and the API specific surface area, thus the (Granulation Work/Rheometer Work) term could be expressed as a "Granulation Work per unit surface area" basis with similar results. From the perspective of modeling, the most precise measurement was chosen to be utilized, thus this experiment prompted work to qualify a Freeman Powder Rheometer for GMP purposes.

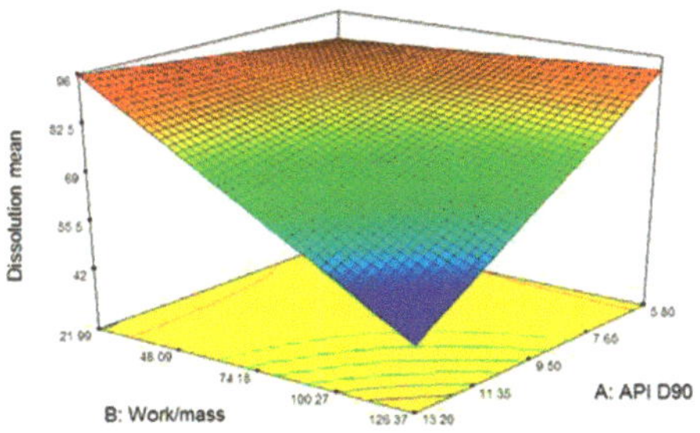

Std. Dev	6.80	R-Squared	0.7400
Mean	85.92	Adj R-Squared	0.6425
C.V. %	7.68	Pred R-Squared	-0.3298
PRESS	1780.46	Adeq Precision	9.298

A negative "Pred R-Squared" implies that the overall mean is a better predictor of your response than the current model.

"Adeq Precision" measures the signal to noise ratio. A ratio greater than 4 is desirable. Your ratio of 9.298 indicates an adequate signal. This model can be used to navigate the design space.

Factor	Coefficient Estimate	df	Standard Error	95% CI Low	95% CI High	VIF
Intercept	-11525.43	1	3348.10	-19246.15	-3804.70	
A-API D90	-16808.12	1	4436.60	-27038.95	-6577.29	2.983E+006
B-Work/mass	-11622.30	1	3351.94	-19351.88	-3892.71	1.41
AB	-16820.35	1	4441.64	-27062.79	-6577.90	2.982E+006

Figure 13.11 Correlation of granulation work/mass and particle size D90 to output tablet dissolution.

It was also possible to model this experiment as a response surface of granulation work per unit mass and API D90 value. This model had significantly lower goodness of fit for the prediction of dissolution mean (74%), and problems with variance inflation in the estimation of model parameters. This response surface model is shown in Fig. 13.11.

Evidence suggests that major changes in raw material particle size and surface area have a significant impact on the granulation process. Finer powder of higher surface area is likely to require more granulation work to achieve a similar endpoint. Since measurements of PSD and SSA have challenges of reproducibility and sampling variance, a more precise model can potentially be developed by examining how much work it takes for a Rheometer blade to traverse a dry sample while fluidizing the powder. This work found that dividing the granulation work by the Rheometer Work resulted in a dimensionless parameter that was predictive of endpoint variation.

13.6 Models describing scale-up and equipment transfer of batch high shear granulation

Research has been done to understand how to transfer the granulation process between different granulators of varying impeller geometry or scale when "work/mass" is being utilized as the control model. The main impeller blade angle and rotations per minute (RPM) have significant impacts on the amount of water needed to start the granulation process, and therefore affect the total amount of water and work needed. Correlations were developed relating the work and water requirements to main impeller Froude number or RPM, diameter, and blade angle (Clancy et al., 2011). With changes in impeller angle, a GSK designed 6-L granulator was made by FluidAir that mimics the performance of a 300-L granulator used in production (Clancy et al., 2011).

Scale-up of high shear granulation is generally accomplished by ensuring similar geometry at each scale, and ensuring the main impeller tip speed is held constant across scale, typically at 5.5 m/s. The main impeller tip speed has significant impacts on granule consolidation and breakage and needs to be fixed at a constant value. Low tip speed for example can result in runaway granule growth, resulting in low density granules the size of golf balls. High tip speed can effectively mill the granules to the point where little granule growth occurs at all, though the granules that do form and survive will be small and highly dense.

It's impossible to fix all the important factors to consider when moving across scale. Fixing the impeller tip speed results in changes of g-forces as RPM and blade diameter are changed. Thus, the key to understanding scale-up of high shear granulation is to realize that the amount of water needed at each scale is not necessarily constant. One possible explanation is that the spread of water among surfaces of the mixture is affected by the g-forces being applied by the main impeller blade. Use of absorbent materials such as microcrystalline cellulose and super-disintegrants within the granulation mixture may amplify this affect as some of the water can be absorbed and will be released as these ingredients are subjected to g-forces.

An observation of impeller load behavior as water is added in granulation for drug product "P" is shown in Fig. 13.12 for four different equipment scales. As the equipment scale was increased more water was need to invoke a power response where the impeller power started rising.

Initially, the impeller power decreased due to hysteresis effects and the time for the impeller motor to warm up then rises at a later point due to commencement of the granulation process. The amount of water added at the point of inflection in the impeller power indicates the beginning of densification in the granulation process and is called "X_{sat}" in this analysis.

X_{sat} can be found using one of two mathematical techniques. The first technique is to find the point where the impeller load mean value for 10 s is 3-sigma higher than the previous 30 s worth of data. A second way is to find the amount of water added at a point of minima of the following function.

$$\text{Objective\_Function} = (Power_{15\text{ s}} - P_0)/Mass_{H_2O} \tag{13.4}$$

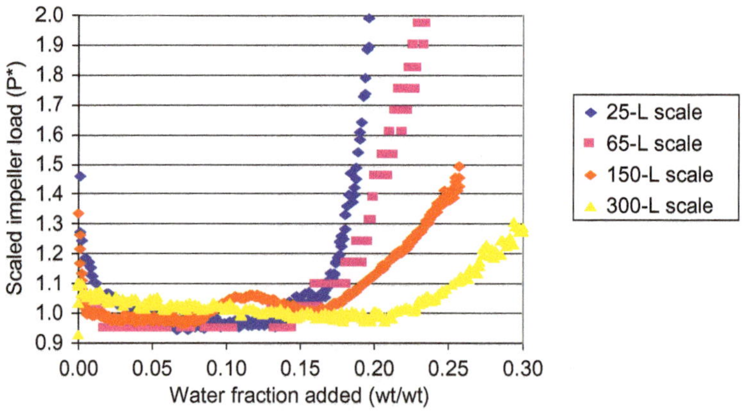

Figure 13.12 Change in impeller power during water addition as granulation scale is changed.

$Power_{15\ s}$ is the 15-s backwards data averaging of the impeller power. 15-s backwards data averaging is used to smooth the impeller load data to prevent extraneous noise from providing a false minimum. The amount of backwards averaging needed will depend on the noise in the impeller power data. At 300-L scale, only 5-s of backwards averaging was used as the signal observed had a higher signal to noise ratio. The variable $Mass_{H_2O}$ is the amount of water added. The two methodologies for X_{sat} determination agree with an R^2 of 90% for the data presented in this paper. The minima approach is chosen and utilized in this paper because it is simpler and more robust to calculate in a Programmable Logic Controller (PLC) than the statistical technique, and is not affected as strongly by signal noise, thus provides better models. An example of what taking the minimum of the objective function looks like during water addition is shown in Fig. 13.13.

Observation was that an incremental approximately 2% more water was needed for each scale from 25-L, to 65-L, to 150-L, and 300-L in order to get an impeller power increase. Optimal granulation was consistently found using water amount of 8% to 10% in excess (X_s) of the point where impeller power starts to increase (X_{sat}), see Fig. 13.14. The optimal water added at 300-L scale is 30%, or 9% in excess.

Centrifugal force is necessary for accelerating the powder bed into toroidal (roping) flow, which is the predominant flow pattern at the later stages in granulation. The centrifugal force also creates a compressive force pressing the powder bed toward the inner walls of the bowl. Thus Froude Number (Fr) (Eq. 13.5) is a hypothesized scaling criteria for granulation, and can be thought of as a measure of the centrifugal forces being applied to the power.

$$Fr = \frac{4\pi^2 RN^2}{60^2 g} \tag{13.5}$$

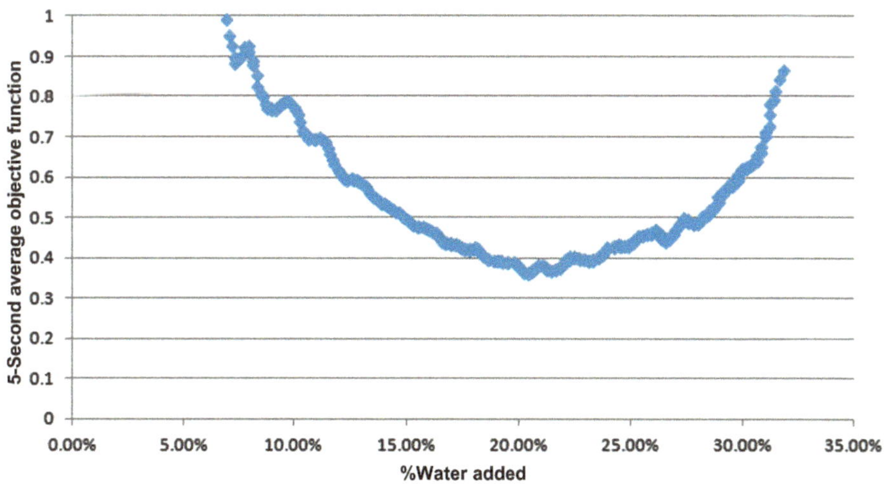

Figure 13.13 Calculation of an X_{sat} of 20% water as the minimum of Eq. (13.4).

Granulator scale (L)	Average X_{sat} values at tip speed 5.5 m/s	Optimal water requirement	Water required in excess of X_{sat}
25	14.7%	23%	8.3%
65	16.0%	26%	10.0%
150	19.4%	28%	8.6%
300	21.1%	30%	8.9%

Figure 13.14 Optimal water requirement at the various granulator scales to achieved X_{sat} and suitable granules for drug product "P."

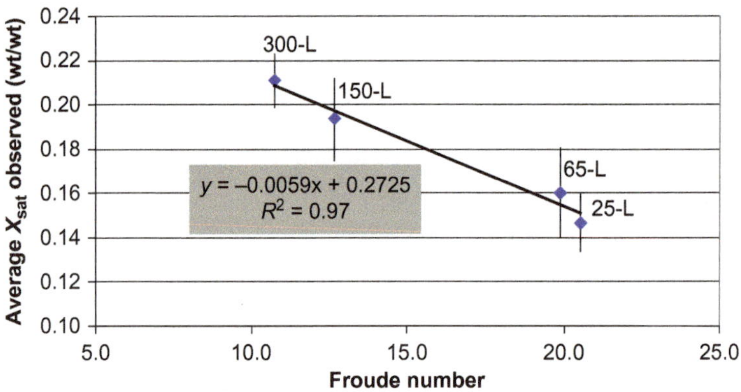

Figure 13.15 A plot of average X_{sat} values versus Froude Number for the various fielder granulator scales at constant tip speed.

where N is the impeller rotational speed (rpm), R is the impeller radius (m), and g is the gravitational constant (9.81 m/s^2).

X_{sat} was noted to be linearly related to impeller Froude Number when granulators of dimensionally similar bowl (blade height/bowl height) are utilized at the same tip speed. In Fig. 13.15, a plot of the average X_{sat} determined at each scale against Froude Number is presented. The linearity between X_{sat} and Froude Number is measured by the high correlation coefficient ($R^2 = 0.97$), which suggests that for dimensionally similar bowl at constant tip speed, possibly the Froude Number may be a reasonable predictor of water or work requirements. This may explain why Froude Number has been postulated as potential scaling factor; however, subsequent experimentation utilizing impellers of differing design and tip speeds suggests this relationship is limited to dimensionally similar blades at same tip speed.

Subsequent experimentation found that X_{sat} can be manipulated by RPM at fixed tip speed (scale), and also by the blade angle. A lower angle blade at smaller scale and higher RPM can replicate the results of a higher angle blade at larger scale and lower RPM. Studies across multiple scales from 6-L, 25-L, 65-L, 150-L, and 300-L were then pursued, with details of the studies documented elsewhere (Clancy et al., 2011).

If the desire is to mimic the behavior of a large-scale granulator using small-scale equipment it's useful to predict the correct blade angle. When a linear regression analysis was carried out on all the data generated from the studies conducted during the scale-up of drug product "P" process, impeller speed and blade angle gave the best fit model of X_{sat} with a 94.4% prediction coefficient. The three-term model is as follows:

$$X_{sat} = 0.797 - 3.25 \times 10^{-4} \times N - 1.85 \times \sin(\theta) + 1.53 \times \sin(\theta)^2 \tag{13.6}$$

Fig. 13.16 shows the plot of actual X_{sat} against the predicted X_{sat} for the different granulator scales. No correlation to Froude number was observed once dissimilar blade angles and differing tip speeds were utilized in the study. Also, when the data is limited to geometrically similar blades to Fielder granulators (eliminating a flared tip 45-degee blade standard to FluidAir), the above correlation fits the data with a 99% coefficient. None of the other possible squared terms or cross products was significant at the 95% confidence interval, suggestive that the inflection point changes linearly with impeller speed and nonlinearly with sine of the blade angle.

Another potential physical explanation for the trend observed in Figs. 13.15 and 13.16 comes from the observation that it appears to be important to maintain the same distribution of coverage of water spraying from the nozzle onto the powder surface passing below. If the geometry of the blade is held constant the powder bed at small scale passes below the spray nozzle many more times during water addition, thus achieving better spray distribution at small scale relative to large scale. The number of passes the powder takes below the spray nozzle for a given time period should be proportional to RPM × $\sin^2$(theta). A plot of

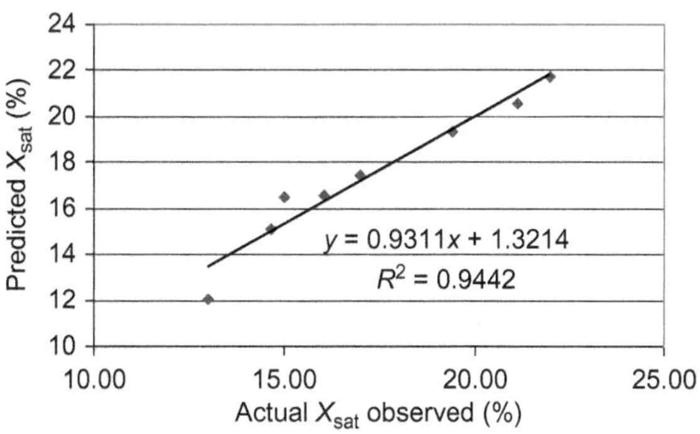

Figure 13.16 Actual X_{sat} observed versus predicted X_{sat} from impeller speed and blade angle model (Eq. 13.6).

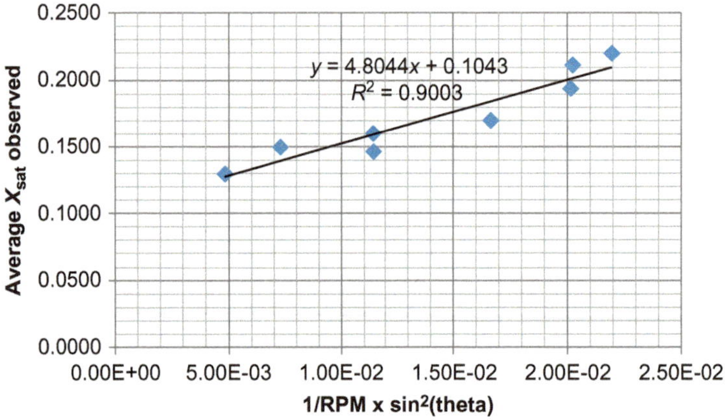

Figure 13.17 Actual average X_{sat} observed versus scaling factor of 1/(RPM × $\sin^2$(theta)).

1/(RPM × $\sin^2$(theta)) creates a linear line of nearly the same goodness of fit as the above fitted statistical trend, and can also be used to estimate the appropriate angle of the blade (Fig. 13.17).

The scaling factor of RPM × $\sin^2$(theta) may already be designed into some Fielder granulators. The 25-L and 65-L granulator used in this study was a fixed-speed unit with two bowls built into the same piece of equipment. It is noted that the blade angle between bowls and the fixed impeller speed between bowls was varied in the design with result that RPM × $\sin^2$(theta) was held constant between the two bowls. Similarly the 150-L and 300-L granulators had slight variation in blade angle such that this potential scaling factor was also held constant between those two machines; however, at a different value compared to the 25/65-L granulator. RPM × $\sin^2$(theta) was the criteria utilized to design an experimental custom blade for the 6-L granulator utilized in this study. RPM × $\sin^2$(theta) appears to be a less-perfect approximation compared to Eq. (13.6), but may provide a close enough approximation for use with engineering the blade angle for use in scaling up of most products.

13.7 Evaluating the significance of work, X_{sat} and the amount of water added within scale

Observation of the impeller power inflection point "X_{sat}" proved to be quite useful when explaining scaling differences, and also shows significant use in monitoring drug products controlled by the work model at constant scale. As an example, for drug product "P" manufactured on a 300-L Fielder granulator, a total of 40 granulation batches were manufactured and presented as data in Table 13.4. The first 10 batches were part of the experimental DoE described with the response surface shown in Fig. 13.3. The next 30 batches were produced using the optimum granulation work and water amount found from the DoE. Dissolution profiles of the film coated tablets were used as an assessment of end product quality. The 40-batch data set with work endpoints and film-coated tablets dissolution are tabulated in Appendix A, Table 13.5.

For this drug product held at constant tablet thickness and tablet weight, granulation work and granulation water amount are good predictors of dissolution performance. It is possible to use a quadratic model to define a region of proven acceptable quality such that if the work, water, and thickness are controlled, acceptable dissolution performance will be achieved. Thus for this drug compound, work, water, and thickness are utilized as effective control parameters to ensure passing dissolution.

Monitoring of 30 batches following the DoE showed there was variation in impeller load inflection point during water addition, and dissolution below 90% was noted to occur at water excess (X_s) values of less than 8% (Fig. 13.18). This drug product has an undergranulation failure mode resulting in reduced dissolution mean and increased dissolution RSD at lower extents of granulation.

The general conclusion was that even at constant scale, there may be variation in the amount of water needed to start the granulation process (X_{sat}) which causes variation in the impeller load during water addition. If the drug product is sensitive to granule variation, the variation in excess water (X_s) can result in small to moderate changes in granule tapped density and drug dissolution. This is a risk factor that will need to be considered when establishing models and process control based on a granulation work model, and might prompt need for a more complex model such as the Saturated Weighted Work (SaWW) model described in the next section. However, it should be noted that even for drug product "P," the Work control model has been used for 700 + granulations to date of this writing with no failures below specification of 75% dissolution. Need for a more complex control model beyond "granulation work," such as the "SaWW" model discussed in the next section, is only for cases where a finer degree of control is needed.

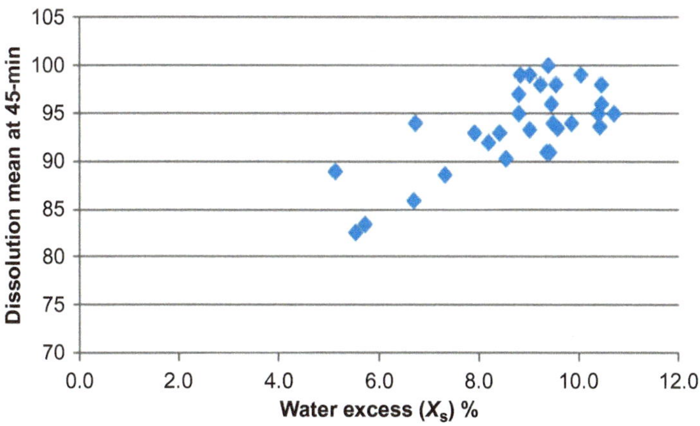

Figure 13.18 Variation in water excess and tablet dissolution for drug product "P" in 30 runs at optimum work and water setting at 300-L scale.

13.8 A single equation to model granulation—SaWW model

The scale-up development work and also monitoring granulation batches at 300-L scale suggested it's not the absolute amount of water added, but the amount of water added above the critical point where an increase is observed in the main impeller power. This led to development of the "SaWW" equation which can be used to predict granulation endpoint across equipment blade angle changes, water amount changes, X_s, or work changes. The SaWW equation describes the granulation process using the idea that water in excess of a certain critical amount and work input can be integrated together to create a single predictive equation.

$$\text{SaWW} = \int_0^t (Power_{\text{Impeller}} - P_0) \cdot X_s \mathrm{d}t \tag{13.7}$$

where X_s is the amount of water above the saturation point, which is defined as follows:

$$X_s = (X_{H_2O} - X_{\text{sat}}) \tag{13.8}$$

X_{H_2O} is the fraction of water added at that point of time. X_{sat} is defined as the fraction of water needed at the point the impeller power begins to increase, indicating onset of granulation. X_{sat} changes with scale, and also with raw material physical property changes, and can be found using Eq. (13.4) described in the previous section discussing scale-up.

The SaWW model, or a model that calculates the appropriate work for a given water excess (X_s) could potentially be used as an improved control methodology when programmed into a PLC, but recommendation at this time is to use the work model by first intent as most drug products are not as sensitive to granulation as drug product "P" and online measurement of X_{sat} may unnecessarily increase the complexity of the control code and control model.

SaWW, or work and X_s were found to provide better model fits compared to work and water as predictive model terms for production and DoE data evaluated, and offers the advantage of reducing the number of factors needed to estimate to fit a linear regression model. As an example, for drug product "P," the 50-point DoE data available in Table 13.1 illustrated in Fig. 13.4 as a complex four-dimensional surface from a 10-factor linear regression model can be reduced to a three-dimensional surface and a six-term linear regression model with a similar goodness of fit ($R^2 = 90\%$). The response surface of SaWW and compressed tablet thickness is shown in Fig. 13.19. For the production monitoring data set in Table 13.5, the resulting tablet dissolution can be correlated to a single polynomial line as shown in Fig. 13.20.

The observation of the SaWW model describing the water and work interactions into a single parameter is not limited to just drug product "P," but has applied to all of them discussed in this chapter. For instance the SaWW model applied to drug

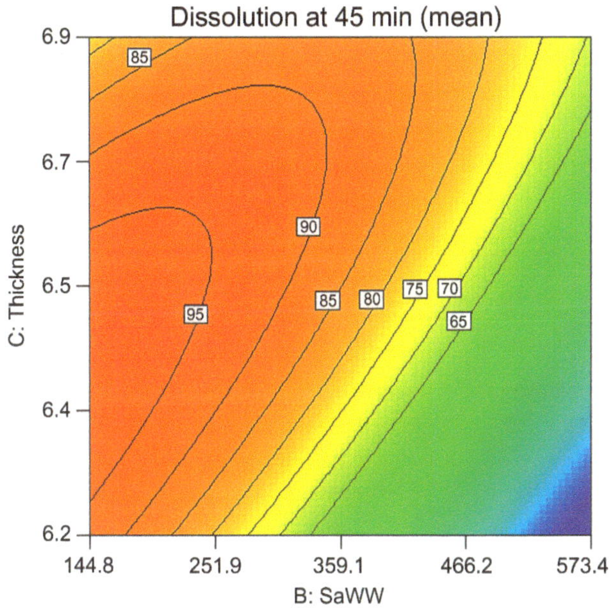

Figure 13.19 Drug product "P" data from 10-batch DoE with five compression levels to 50 observations, dissolution modeled as a single three-dimensional surface using SaWW model with $R^2 - 90\%$.

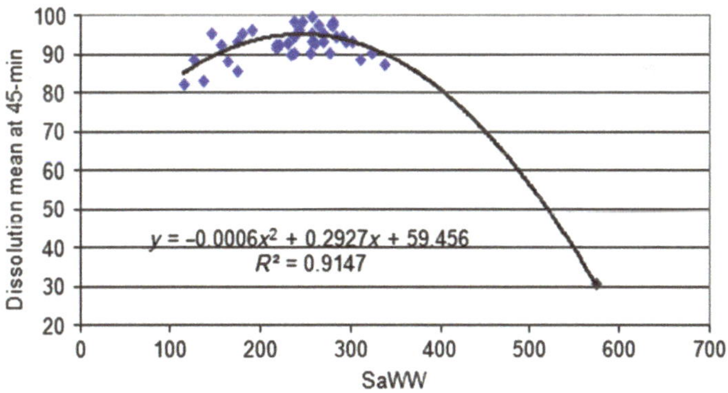

Figure 13.20 Drug product "P" data from 10-batch DoE at constant target tablet thickness, plus 30 subsequent batches, dissolution modeled as a single two-dimensional plot using SaWW model.

products "D" (Figs. 13.21 and 13.22), finds the same observation of the prediction being reduced to a single characteristic line. This single line is different for each drug product, but the underlying mechanistic equation used for prediction is the same.

Drug product "S" (data Table 13.3) is modeled versus the SaWW model in Fig. 13.23. This particular DoE examined water addition over a much larger range

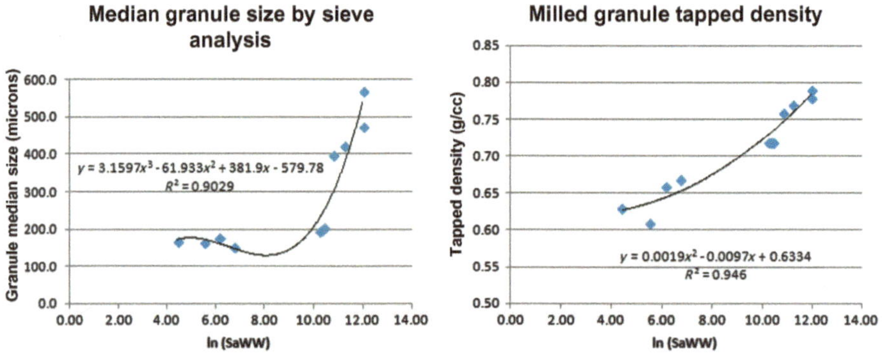

Figure 13.21 Drug product "D," response of tapped density, granule size to the natural log of SaWW.

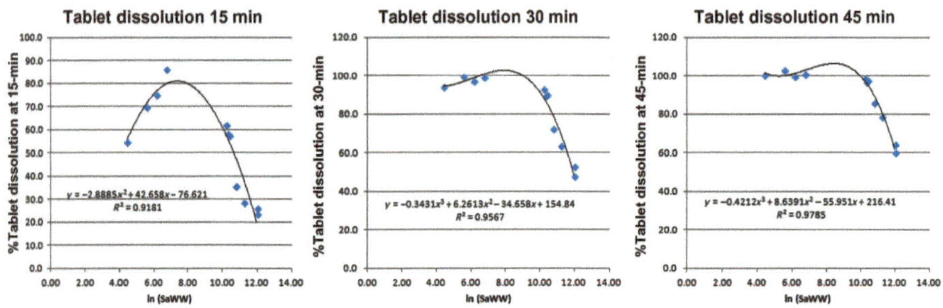

Figure 13.22 Drug product "D," response of tablet dissolution to the natural log of SaWW.

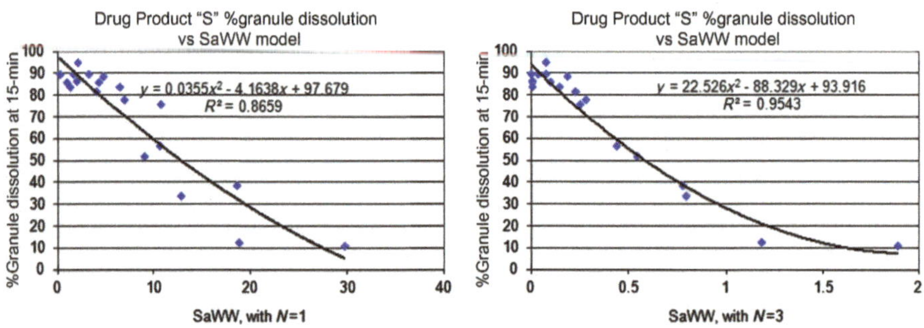

Figure 13.23 Drug product "S" data from 20-batch sampled DoE at constant target tablet thickness, dissolution modeled as a single two-dimensional plot using SaWW model, $N = 1$ on left, and $N = 3$ on right.

than typical from 25 to 40% water. This allows an examination if the impact of water excess is truly linear over a wide range. The model equation used was Eq. (13.9) to test the significance of an exponent "N" on the water excess term. The model results with $N = 1$ or $N = 3$ is shown in Fig. 13.23.

$$\text{SaWW} = \int_0^t (Power_{\text{Impeller}} - P_0) \cdot (X_s)^N \text{d}t \tag{13.9}$$

The fits to granule dissolution data were notably improved using $N = 3$ rather than $N = 1$, indicating changes in water amount over a very broad range, may show a nonlinear impact of water excess, and Eq. (13.9) is recommended.

The power of the SaWW model is that the characteristic lines for a given product can be found with very few experiments. It only takes three to four observations to define a nonlinear line. Testing this line at multiple work and water levels then allows observation of reproducibility of the model prediction. Fewer linear regression terms are needed to fit the models, thus giving much higher capability to estimate the error distribution.

The strength and weakness of the SaWW model will lie in the capability to measure X_{sat}, the point of impeller inflection, as precisely as possible. If X_{sat} is significant and measured precisely, then the SaWW model will provide better model fits compared to models based on work and water amounts alone. As long as X_{sat} can be measured in a robust fashion, and is significant, then use of SaWW to control the process directly is likely to provide improved levels of process control compared to use of the work equation.

13.9 Modeling twin screw continuous wet granulation

Twin screw extrusion has been extensively studied and developed in the polymer industry since the 1950s. The first application to large scale OTC pharmaceutical granulation began in the 1970s and 1980s, primarily by GSK for antacid production. More recently, starting in 2002 twin screw extrusion came under more intensive study as an efficient and continuous means of replacing high shear wet granulation (Keleb et al., 2002). Use of "kneading" mixing elements (Fig. 13.24) in the screw conveyer improves the granule flow, and is the primary source of granule consolidation (Djuric, 2008).

An excellent publically available data set that illustrates many of the principles for fitting a model to twin screw granulation data is from work done at

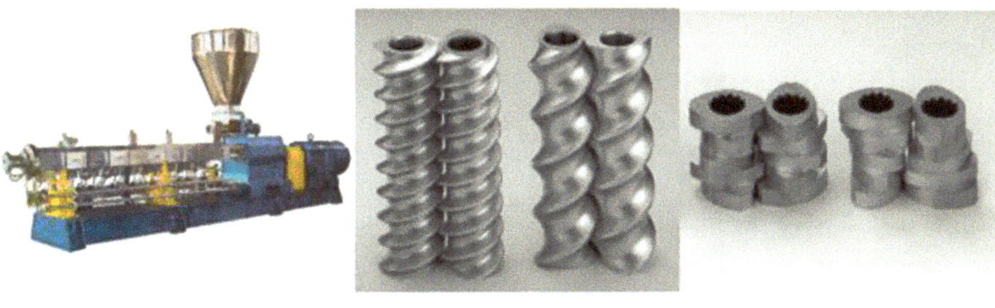

Figure 13.24 Twin screw extruder (left) with conveying elements (center) and kneading elements (right).

Response Yield (Percent Granules between 150-1400 micron)

Actual by Predicted Plot

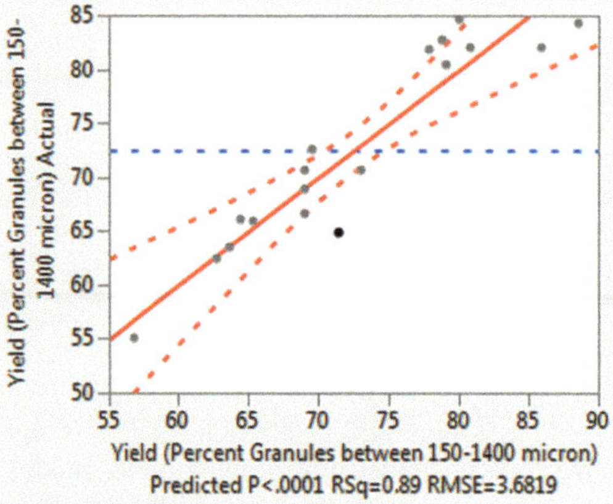

Summary of Fit

RSquare	0.885191
RSquare Adj	0.837354
Root Mean Square Error	3.681898
Mean of Response	72.52778
Observations (or Sum Wgts)	18

Parameter Estimates

Term	Estimate	Std Error	t Ratio	Prob>|t|
Intercept	44.971531	7.06944	6.36	<.0001*
Throughput (kg/hr)	-0.209037	0.127923	-1.63	0.1282
Screw Speed (RPM)	0.0080413	0.005482	1.47	0.1682
Kneading Elements	1.6275576	0.20184	8.06	<.0001*
Barrel Temp (°C)	0.4616674	0.128307	3.60	0.0037*
(Throughput (kg/hr)-17.9167)*(Screw Speed (RPM)-784.722)	0.0019671	0.000736	2.67	0.0203*

Figure 13.25 Regression model of twin screw theophelline DoE.

Ghent University (Vercruysse et al., 2012). The experiment granulated a theophylline mixture in a six-parameter DoE. The relevant data analyzed utilizing the first principle equations described in this section is shown in Appendix A, Table 13.6.

The signal that can be best correlated from the granulation data is the observed granule yield, defined as material between 150 microns and 1400 microns in size. Too little granulation extent reduces yield due to increased fines, but too much granulation results in yield loss due to granules larger than 1400 microns in size. Regression analysis of the DoE parameters to predict granule yield finds the most significant terms are the number of kneading elements, and the barrel temperature. There's a possible cross product of throughput and screw speed that also appears to be significant. A regression model constructed from these parameters is shown in Fig. 13.25 with impacts of factors shown in Fig. 13.26.

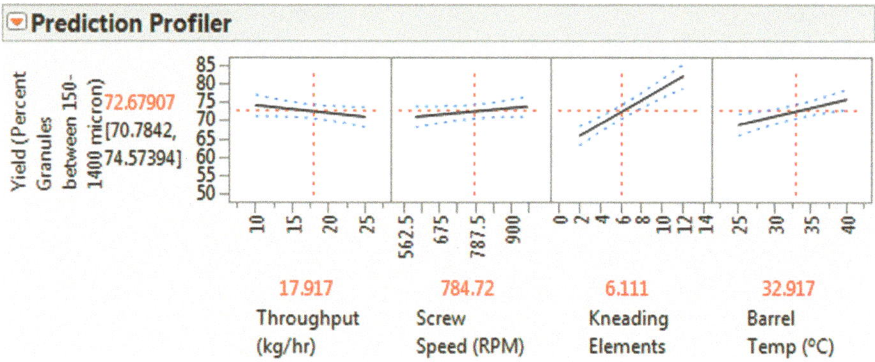

Figure 13.26 Factor prediction profiler for DoE parameters for fit granule yield.

Alternatively, it's possible to construct a model for twin screw granulation using first principles and the knowledge developed for high shear granulation, discussed earlier in this chapter. From first principles, the power input into the powder mixture is a function of torque and RPM as shown in Eq. (13.10).

$$\text{Power} = Torque \cdot \frac{RPM \cdot 2 \cdot \pi}{60} \tag{13.10}$$

High shear granulation was best modeled as power per unit dry powder mass, thus the above power term needs to be divided by the mass throughput measured in grams per second.

$$\text{Power\_per\_mass} = Torque \cdot \frac{RPM \cdot 2 \cdot \pi}{60 \cdot throughput} \tag{13.11}$$

There's an effect of temperature where higher temperature is noted to drive the granulation further. This effect is hypothesized to be due to changes in rheology. A mixture that requires more energy to overcome viscous forces or surface area interactions will require more power to reach an equivalent endpoint. Thus the impact of temperature is hypothesized to reduce the viscosity of the binding liquid thus allowing easier deformation and consolidation of the wet granules. The power per unit mass in the above equation is divided by the liquid viscosity at the granulation temperature resulting in Eq. (13.12).

$$\text{Power\_per\_mass\_viscosity} = Torque \cdot \frac{RPM \cdot 2 \cdot \pi}{60 \cdot throughput \cdot u} \tag{13.12}$$

Plots of power per unit mass, and then power per unit mass divided by viscosity are shown in Fig. 13.27. Use of viscosity to describe the temperature effect is noted to improve the correlation coefficient. The resulting model provides a better correlation coefficient ($R^2 = 90\%$) than that achieved with linear regression, and only needs to estimate two fitted parameters.

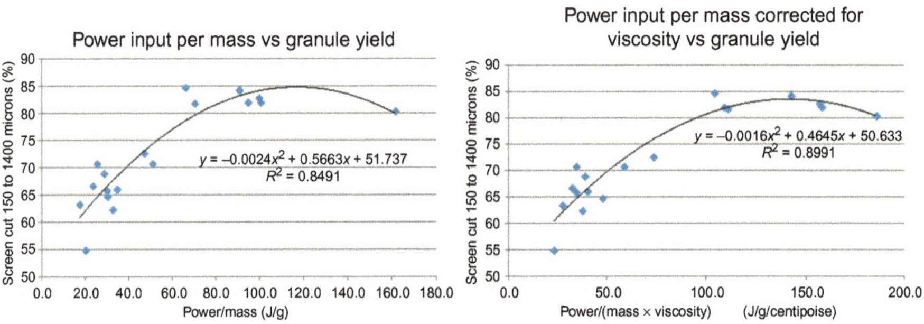

Figure 13.27 Prediction of granule yield from first principle equations.

The same relationship to power is noted to be valid for both high shear granulation and twin screw granulation. If the twin screw granulation has motor power measured instead of torque then power per unit mass can be calculated as:

$$\text{Power\_per\_mass} = \frac{(P - P_0)}{throughput} \tag{13.13}$$

where P is the measured power, and P_0 is the baseline power needed to turn the impeller without solids present. The resulting units from Eq. (13.13) are J/g, which is equivalent to the work/mass models described in the description of batch high shear granulation modeling.

13.10 The impact of feeder variability on twin screw wet granulation

Continuous operations make the assumption that the flow into the equipment is continuous, and unfortunately powders that need to be granulated do not tend to flow in a continuous fashion. It is useful to consider the impact of granulation variation induced by variation in inlet powder flow to the twin screw granulator. If drug product tablet dissolution is sensitive to changes in granulation extent, the impact of feed variation is in-batch variation of granulation extent, resulting in increased in-batch variation in granule properties, and potentially reduced dissolution mean with higher RSD. In cases of very poorly flowing powders, the observation is that the tablet dissolution properties achieved from twin screw granulation is not as good as those observed in high shear granulation. The situation can be improved by improving the powder flow of the mixture being granulated, through use of flow aids like fumed silica, or by limiting the region of operation of the powder hopper feeding the twin screw granulator.

Example hoppers used for feeding dry powder into twin screw granulation are manufactured by K-Tron, or Brahbender (Fig. 13.28), and utilize either dual or single helical impellers (Fig. 13.29).

Figure 13.28 K-Tron hopper (left) and Brahbender hopper (right).

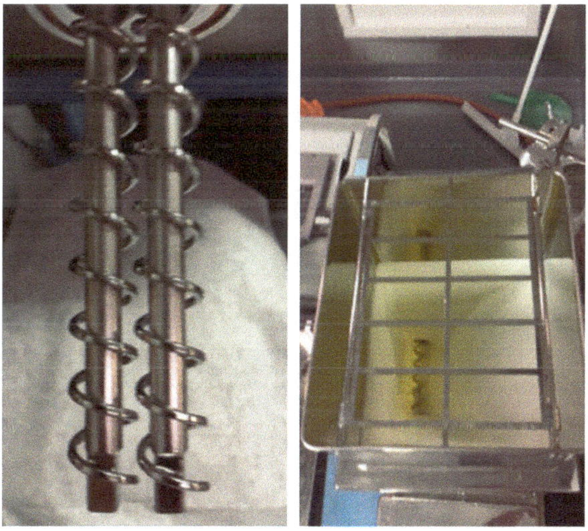

Figure 13.29 Dual helical impeller of K-Tron hopper (left) and single helix of the Brahbender hopper (Right).

Fig. 13.30 shows two different powders being fed from a K-Tron dual screw hopper. The freely flowing powder on the left comes out as nearly a continuous stream, whereas the poorly flowing powder on the right exits the hopper in cohesive packets.

To examine the variability of powder flow from hoppers, 10 different powders were analyzed using a 6-inch Brookfield PFT shear cell, with resulting density and flow index analytical data shown in Fig. 13.31.

Figure 13.30 Freely flowing powder from K-Tron hopper (left), very cohesive powder (right).

Rank #	Material Name	Flow Function Slope	Flow Function Intercept	Fill Bulk Density (kg/m^3)	Flow Index at 0.5 KPA	Flow Index at 1 KPA	Flow Index at 2.4 KPA	Flow Index at 5 KPA	Flow Index at 10 KPA	Type of Flow at 1 KPA
1	Manitol Pearlitol 200SD	0.03	0.002	484.4	0.034	0.032	0.031	0.0304	0.0302	Free Flowing
2	Avicel PH102	0.14	0.04	367.3	0.22	0.18	0.157	0.148	0.144	Easy Flowing
3	Avicel PH101	0.22	0.023	303	0.266	0.243	0.230	0.2246	0.2223	Easy Flowing
4	HPMC Pharmacoat 603	0.22	0.116	401.7	0.452	0.336	0.268	0.2432	0.2316	Cohesive
5	Improved 6% API Formulation	0.06	0.277	378.8	0.614	0.337	0.175	0.1154	0.0877	Cohesive
6	Improved 12% API Formulation	0.14	0.338	332.9	0.816	0.478	0.281	0.2076	0.1738	Cohesive
7	Manitol Pearlitol 160C	0.16	0.366	585.3	0.892	0.526	0.313	0.2332	0.1966	Very Cohesive
8	6% API Formulation	0.19	0.555	378.8	1.3	0.745	0.421	0.301	0.2455	Very Cohesive
9	12% API Formulation	0.23	0.561	332.9	1.352	0.791	0.464	0.3422	0.2861	Very Cohesive
10	100% API lot 76	0.16	0.835	134.9	1.83	0.995	0.508	0.327	0.2435	Very Cohesive

Figure 13.31 Shear cell analysis of 10 powders utilized in hopper study.

Each powder was then loaded into the K-Tron hopper, and the feedrate setting was varied over values of 10%, 15%, 25%, 50%, 75%, and 99% of maximum RPM. After powder flow was established, data recording was enabled on a Mettler Toledo scale, collecting dynamic weight measurement at eight measurements per second, with data averaging for 3 s per weight observation. The average feedrate for the trial was recorded, as well as the 3-s relative standard deviation (RSD) of the powder flow rate. Example data for Manitol 200 SD is shown in Fig. 13.32, and this process was repeated for the nine other powders resulting in a total of 126 observations.

At a fixed RPM, 25% for example, a correlation is observed between the shear cell flow index at 1 KPa, and the 3-s hopper flow RSD (Fig. 13.33). Correlations were attempted at shear cell consolidation stresses ranging from 0.5 KPa to 10 KPa, with the conclusion that the RSD data is best fit to shear cell data at 1 KPa consolidation pressure.

Name	Hopper Mass	Feed setting	Feed Rate (grams/sec)	Flow RSD% for 3 second time interval
Manitol 200SD	2.8	99%	5.472	1.35%
Manitol 200SD	2.55	75%	4.113	1.59%
Manitol 200SD	2.99	50%	2.587	2.00%
Manitol 200SD	3.2	25%	1.092	2.57%
Manitol 200SD	1.92	99%	5.404	2.89%
Manitol 200SD	1.53	75%	4.133	0.70%
Manitol 200SD	1.73	50%	2.623	2.54%
Manitol 200SD	1.26	25%	1.136	2.25%
Manitol 200SD	0.97	15%	0.541	5.59%
Manitol 200SD	2.147	15%	0.527	5.53%
Manitol 200SD	2.33	10%	0.215	14.93%

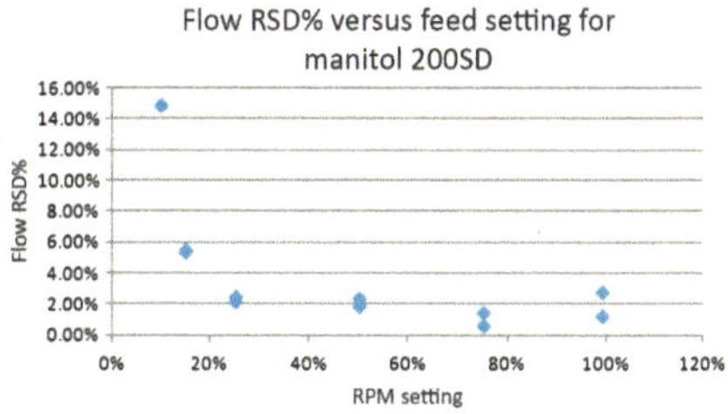

Figure 13.32 K-Tron flow data for Manitol 200 SD (left), observed relationship between RPM setting and flow RSD% (right).

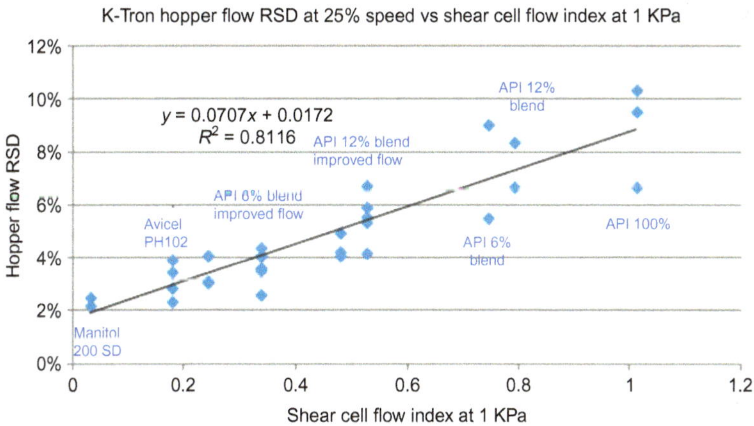

Figure 13.33 K-Tron hopper flow RSD at 25% feed setting versus shear cell flow index at 1-KPa.

Modeling all the data collected on the K-Tron hopper at all the RPM settings results in a five-term linear regression model built from 126 observations. The response surface is best fit to the reciprocal of feeder RPM, measured as seconds per feed screw revolution. The model for the K-Tron hopper, parameter estimates, and the resulting response surface predicting RSD fraction is shown in Fig. 13.34.

The K-Tron hopper is remarkably robust, and was able to successfully feed powder up to a flow index of 0.995 at 1 KPa, albeit with increasing levels of variation measured every 3-s. The disadvantage of the K-Tron in this particular configuration is that even for very good flowing powders, such as Manitol 200 SD, there was still a significant relationship between hopper speed setting and the observed RSD of flow. It should be noted there is also an impact of screw pitch, a finer pitch impeller is able to have more discharge events per second thus lower RSD, but cannot handle as well poor flowing of powders.

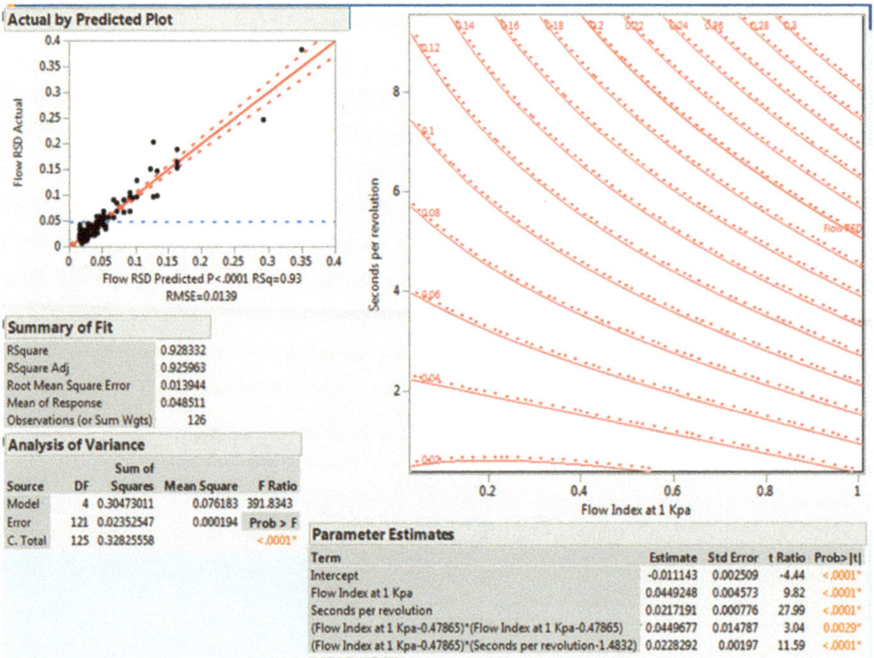

Summary of Fit

RSquare	0.928332
RSquare Adj	0.925963
Root Mean Square Error	0.013944
Mean of Response	0.048511
Observations (or Sum Wgts)	126

Analysis of Variance

Source	DF	Sum of Squares	Mean Square	F Ratio
Model	4	0.30473011	0.076183	391.8343
Error	121	0.02352547	0.000194	Prob > F
C. Total	125	0.32825558		<.0001*

Parameter Estimates

Term	Estimate	Std Error	t Ratio	Prob>|t|
Intercept	-0.011143	0.002509	-4.44	<.0001*
Flow Index at 1 Kpa	0.0449248	0.004573	9.82	<.0001*
Seconds per revolution	0.0217191	0.000776	27.99	<.0001*
(Flow Index at 1 Kpa-0.47865)*(Flow Index at 1 Kpa-0.47865)	0.0449677	0.014787	3.04	0.0029*
(Flow Index at 1 Kpa-0.47865)*(Seconds per revolution-1.4832)	0.0228292	0.00197	11.59	<.0001*

Figure 13.34 K-Tron twin-screw hopper powder flow RSD fraction model, response surface to powder flow index at 1-KPa, and number of seconds per feed screw rotation.

The same experimental procedure was also applied to the Brahbender hopper, though fewer powders could be fed through this hopper. Powders above a flow index of 0.5 to 0.6 at 1 KPa have a probability of forming cohesive arching resulting in starving the impeller screw of powder. The Brahbender hopper was able to poorly feed a powder with a flow index of 0.75 at 1 KPa, but with numerous observations of cohesive arching and powder flow entirely stopping for seconds. Only six test powders could be fed through the Brahbender, resulting in 72 observations for the experiment. The resulting model to predict powder flow RSD fraction and response surface diagram is shown in Fig. 13.35.

The significant advantage the Brahbender hopper has is that for powders that flow well, up to a flow index of approximately 0.4, there is comparatively less impact of feed rate (RPM) variation compared to the K-Tron hopper, as illustrated by the response surface in Fig. 13.35. This makes the Brahbender hopper the preferred choice for feeding materials that flow well, such as excipient mixtures. The K-Tron should be chosen if the flow index is greater than 0.4 to 0.5 at 1 KPa consolidation stress.

To this point, the response surfaces shown are the RSD relative to a 3-s measurement of mass discharge. Three seconds is an arbitrary number which was decided upon based on the settling time of the scale. As the time period of measurement is reduced, the RSD will increase, so it's important to consider what the residence time is of the powder underneath the powder feed point and the water input point. The input ports where the water and powder enter the granulator require 3.66

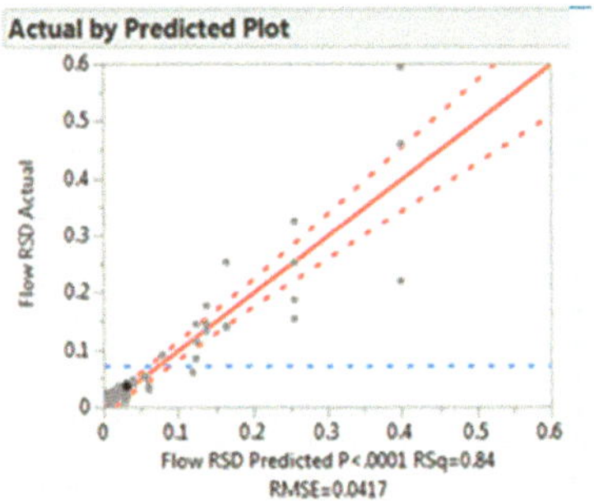

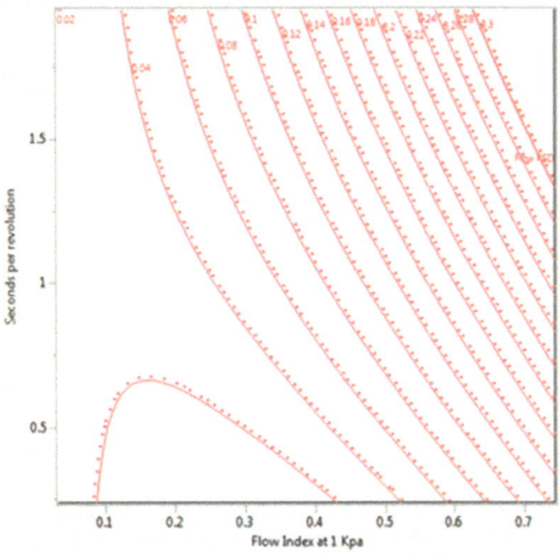

Summary of Fit

RSquare	0.842022
RSquare Adj	0.83259
Root Mean Square Error	0.041742
Mean of Response	0.072676
Observations (or Sum Wgts)	72

Analysis of Variance

Source	DF	Sum of Squares	Mean Square	F Ratio
Model	4	0.62222723	0.155557	89.2771
Error	67	0.11674108	0.001742	Prob > F
C. Total	71	0.73896832		<.0001*

Parameter Estimates

Term	Estimate	Std Error	t Ratio	Prob>|t|
Intercept	-0.064341	0.010601	-6.07	<.0001*
Flow Index at 1 Kpa	0.1889273	0.027612	6.84	<.0001*
Seconds per revolution	0.0564204	0.008212	6.87	<.0001*
(Flow Index at 1 Kpa-0.30083)*(Flow Index at 1 Kpa-0.30083)	0.5057237	0.094609	5.35	<.0001*
(Flow Index at 1 Kpa-0.30083)*(Seconds per revolution-0.86368)	0.233865	0.030841	7.58	<.0001*

Figure 13.35 Brahbender hopper powder flow RSD fraction model, response surfacc to powder flow index at 1-KPa, and number of seconds per feed screw rotation.

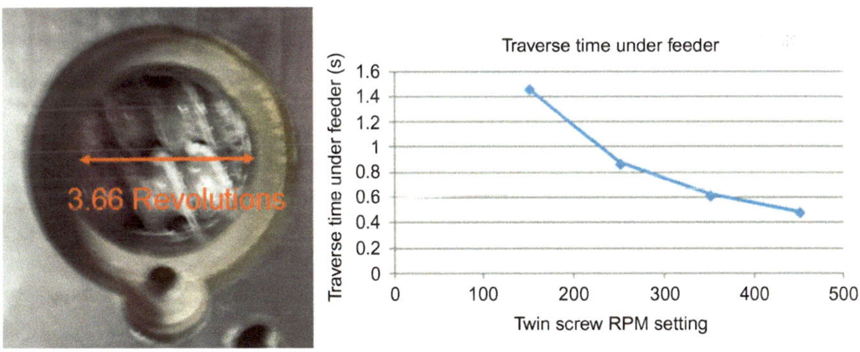

Figure 13.36 Impact of twin screw granulator RPM on residence time under powder and liquid feed.

revolutions of the impeller to traverse, resulting in a residence time of 0.5 and 1.5 s at 450 and 150 RPM, respectively (Fig. 13.36). As this residence time is decreased, more variable packets of powder then encounter the water addition nozzle, resulting in variable extents of moisture fraction, and thus more variable granulation.

The RSD should decrease the more powder discharge events can be averaged together from the hopper feeding the twin screw. If the measurement time is extended from 3 s to 12 s, a nonlinear trend is observed in the relative RSD that is measured.

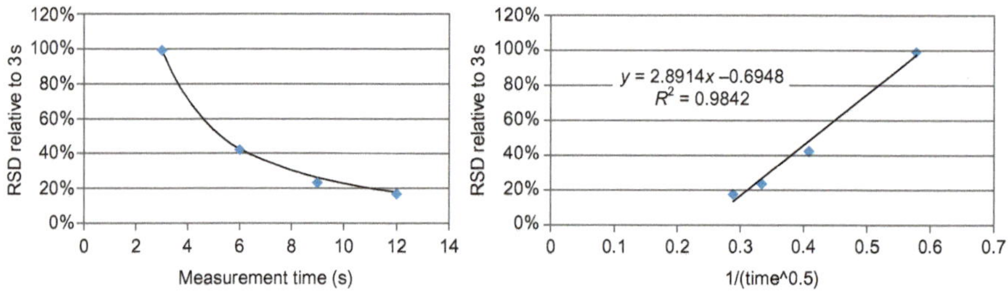

Figure 13.37 Impact of change in measurement time on calculated RSD relative to 3 s.

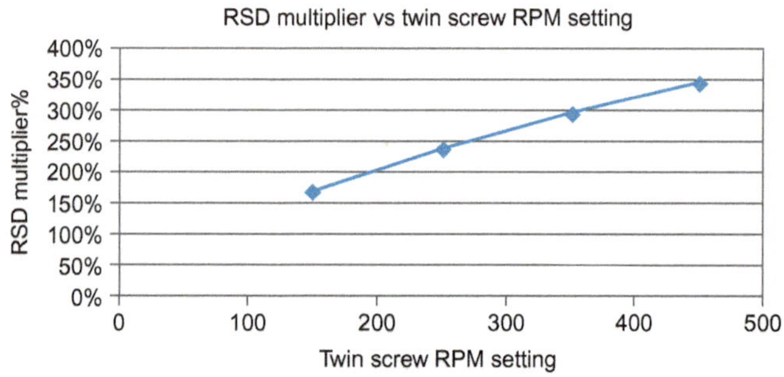

Figure 13.38 Impact of twin screw granulator RPM setting and RSD multiplier compared to 3-s data.

Theoretically this RSD should scale based upon the reciprocal of the square root of time, based on the theory of how standard deviation of a population mean tends to vary with increasing number of observations. Fig. 13.37 shows the impact of measurement time period and also the near-linear response if plotted versus the reciprocal of square root of time. This near-linear relationship can then be extrapolated to faster time periods, larger values of $1/(\text{time}^{0.5})$, to get an estimate of the increase in RSD expected as the twin screw RPM setting is changed (Fig. 13.38).

The result of input powder variability is then going to be water-wetting variability, and then variability in granulation extent in the resulting product granule. It's important to develop and include back-mixing zones that increase the powder residence time to seconds before and after the water addition zone to reduce the impact of this phenomenon for poorly flowing powders.

Fig. 13.39 shows two case study predictions assuming impeller configuration is set up with no back mixing elements, for a powder with a flow index of 0.8 at 1 KPa. The first case, shown on left sets the K-Tron feed setting to 50% (1.08 revolutions/s) and a twin screw speed of 150 rpm. For a water target of 20%, 99% of the material would be expected to have wetting between 15% and 25%. Case two on the right shows it's possible to get much more variability by reducing the K-Tron feed setting to 20% while increasing the twin screw speed to 450 RPM. In this second scenario the 99% limits of wetting is between 3% and 37%, and significant variation in granule properties is expected.

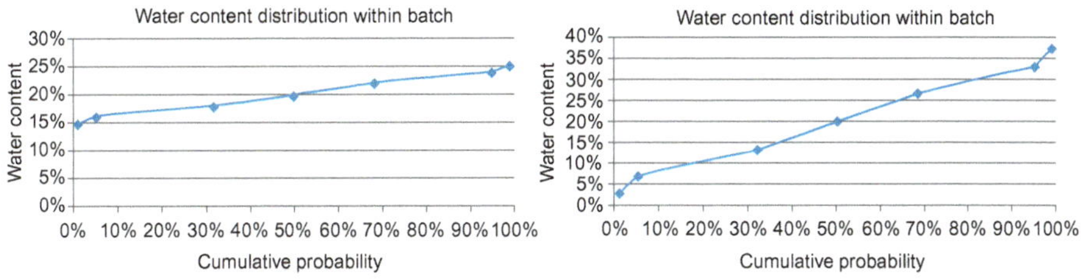

Figure 13.39 Model predictions of water distribution for case 1 (left) and case 2 (right).

In reality the twin screw granulator would not be set up with no back mixing elements, and operated in such an extreme case of slow K-Tron feeder speed and rapid screw RPM. The situation is unlikely to be as extreme as this, and the impact of powder feed variation will be more subtle, more similar to the case study shown on the left in Fig. 13.39. For drug products that are sensitive to granulation, it does illustrate the need to consider powder flow properties, it's impact on feed variability, the residence time distributions, the impact of back mixing, and the resulting granulation consistency. Models using the equations provided in this section can be used to estimate the worst case water-wetting consistency, before the addition of back mixing elements.

13.11 Conclusion

Continuous processing is rapidly becoming a normal means of processing pharmaceutical powder blends. A shear cell measurement of the powder can be highly useful in providing the formulators with an assessment of likely performance in the various secondary unit operations, and allow a "first intent" process selection early in the drug development process using the requirements outlined in Fig. 13.2. The selection between batch high shear granulation versus twin screw granulation is primarily based upon powder flow, and an assessment of how robust the product dissolution is to the granulation variation induced by flow variation in twin screw granulation.

Batch high shear granulation and twin screw granulation can both be successfully modeled using equations relating to the granulation work done per unit mass of dry powder. Models based on work per unit mass can and have been used to successfully control granulation processes in real time, even for drug products fairly sensitive to granulation extent. If an even finer degree of control or potentially more precise modeling is desired, then it's useful to measure the minimum amount of water needed to cause a significant change in impeller power during water addition, referred to as "X_{sat}" in this discussion. For high shear granulation, observation of X_{sat} as it varied with scale allow the generation of models that can predict how the water requirements will change with scale, and allows construction of granulation impeller blades designed to ensure similar water requirements across scale.

For high shear granulation, an equation (named SaWW) that integrates both granulation work and the amount of water in excess of X_{sat} is found to be useful in providing better models and reducing the number of dimensions that need to be considered when creating a linear regression response surface model. It appears likely the SaWW model shown as Eq. (13.7) is a good fundamental equation for modeling most granulation processes over moderate changes in water excess, and will reduce the resulting predictions to a single characteristic line that requires fewer experiments to define. If large changes in water amount are explored (e.g., moving from 25 to 40% water addition), it's possible there may be significant nonlinearity in the impact of water excess, in which case Eq. (13.9) should be explored.

Continuous twin screw granulation adds the complexity that the powder feeding the granulator does not necessarily feed in a continuous fashion, but rather in a variable fashion that can be predicted using the response surface models for each hopper type described in this chapter. A measure of powder flow using the Brookfield PFT shear cell flow index at 1 KPa was found to correlate to the resulting variability. Models for worst case water-wetting variation, assuming minimal back mixing are discussed. For drug products where dissolution is sensitive to variation in granulation extent, it is useful to consider optimizing the flow properties through API physical properties or through use of flow aids such as fumed silica, to reduce the variability in feed rate to the twin screw granulator. It's also useful to consider use of back mixing elements to reduce the severity of the feed variability.

References

Clancy, D., 2010. Method and Apparatus for Predicting Properties of Granulated Materials and Dosage Forms made Therefrom. US Patent, 20100318228.

Clancy, D., Campbell, G., Zhang, J., Gupta, M., Oh, C., 2011. Closing the gap in series scale up of high shear wet granulation process using impeller power and blade design. Powder Technol.184–192.

Djuric, D., 2008. Continuous Granulation with a Twin Screw Extruder. Heinrich-Heine-Universität Düsseldorf, Düsseldorf.

Keleb, E., Vermeire, A., Vervaet, C., Remon, J., 2002. Continuous twin screw extrusion for the wet granulation of lactose. Int. J. Pharm. 69–80.

Mollan MJ. Jr., P.a., 2004. Continuous Processing in Pharmaceutical Manufacturing. Pharmaceutical Manufacturing.

Trafton, A., 2012. Continuous Drug Manufacturing Offers Speed, Lower Costs. MIT News.

Vercruysse, J., Dias, C., Peeters, E., Fonteyne, M., Delaet, U., Assche, U., et al., 2012. Continuous twin screw granulation: influence of process variables on granule and tablet quality. Eur. J. Pharm. Biopharm. 205–211.

von Orelli, J., Leuenberger, H., 2004. Search for technological reasons to develop a capsule or a tablet formulation with respect to wettability and dissolution. Int. J. Pharm. 287 (1–2), 135–145.

Wallack, T., 2007. Novartis to Give MIT $65m to Find New Way to Produce Drugs. The Boston Globe.

Wilburn, K., 2010. The Business Case for Continuous Manufacturing of Pharmaceuticals. Massachusetts Institute of Technology, Massachusetts.

Appendix A DoE and Repeat Run Data Tables

Table 13.1 **Drug product "P" granulation DoE at 300-L scale, 10 granulation batch response surface design for granulation work and water, split plot design to 50 compression batches**

Granule batch	Tablet batch	Granulation elapsed time (s)	Power for 10-s at end of batch (% motor load)	Water delivered (% mass/mass)	Eq. (13.2) work (% load*s)	X_{sat} (%)	Eq. (13.8) X_s (%)	Eq. (13.7) SaWW (% load*s)	Tablet thickness (mm)	Milled granule tapped density at 1250 taps (g/cc)	Percent dissolved at 45-min	Dissolution RSD 45-min
1	A	481	41.9	29.9	4268.1	20.2	9.7	322.730	6.21	0.73	65	22.7
1	B	481	41.9	29.9	4268.1	20.2	9.7	322.730	6.34	0.73	88	7.2
1	C	481	41.9	29.9	4268.1	20.2	9.7	322.730	6.51	0.73	91	1.1
1	D	481	41.9	29.9	4268.1	20.2	9.7	322.730	6.67	0.73	89	1.7
1	E	481	41.9	29.9	4268.1	20.2	9.7	322.730	6.86	0.73	87	0.7
2	A	484	43.1	31.8	6364.2	20.2	11.6	573.387	6.21	0.81	5	41.4
2	B	484	43.1	31.8	6364.2	20.2	11.6	573.387	6.36	0.81	13	86.4
2	C	484	43.1	31.8	6364.2	20.2	11.6	573.387	6.51	0.81	31	49.6
2	D	484	43.1	31.8	6364.2	20.2	11.6	573.387	6.68	0.81	69	24.6
2	E	484	43.1	31.8	6364.2	20.2	11.6	573.387	6.85	0.81	77	2.4
3	A	442	47.3	31.8	4125.6	21.9	9.9	309.117	6.23	0.77	70	22.8
3	B	442	47.3	31.8	4125.6	21.9	9.9	309.117	6.35	0.77	89	1.3
3	C	442	47.3	31.8	4125.6	21.9	9.9	309.117	6.53	0.77	89	2.2
3	D	442	47.3	31.8	4125.6	21.9	9.9	309.117	6.70	0.77	89	2.4
3	E	442	47.3	31.8	4125.6	21.9	9.9	309.117	6.86	0.77	82	2.6
4	A	501	30.0	27.7	2796.6	20.5	7.2	144.777	6.21	0.73	88	5.7
4	B	501	30.0	27.7	2796.6	20.5	7.2	144.777	6.36	0.73	96	1.2
4	C	501	30.0	27.7	2796.6	20.5	7.2	144.777	6.55	0.73	96	1.3
4	D	501	30.0	27.7	2796.6	20.5	7.2	144.777	6.71	0.73	94	1.5
4	E	501	30.0	27.7	2796.6	20.5	7.2	144.777	6.89	0.73	90	5.3
5	A	664	33.9	27.7	5587.9	20.1	7.6	301.534	6.20	0.72	69	36.3

(Continued)

Table 13.1 **(Continued)**

Granule batch	Tablet batch	Granulation elapsed time (s)	Power for 10-s at end of batch (% motor load)	Water delivered (% mass/ mass)	Eq. (13.2) work (% load*s)	X_{sat} (%)	Eq. (13.8) X_s (%)	Eq. (13.7) SaWW (% load*s)	Tablet thickness (mm)	Milled granule tapped density at 1250 taps (g/cc)	Percent dissolved at 45-min	Dissolution RSD 45-min
5	B	664	33.9	27.7	5587.9	20.1	7.6	301.534	6.36	0.72	94	1.6
5	C	664	33.9	27.7	5587.9	20.1	7.6	301.534	6.50	0.72	94	1.5
5	D	664	33.9	27.7	5587.9	20.1	7.6	301.534	6.69	0.72	93	2.8
5	E	664	33.9	27.7	5587.9	20.1	7.6	301.534	6.87	0.72	80	8.7
6	A	413	33.5	31.8	2647.0	22.1	9.7	178.592	6.19	0.73	92	3.1
6	B	413	33.5	31.8	2647.0	22.1	9.7	178.592	6.34	0.73	96	0.8
6	C	413	33.5	31.8	2647.0	22.1	9.7	178.592	6.50	0.73	96	0.6
6	D	413	33.5	31.8	2647.0	22.1	9.7	178.592	6.69	0.73	93	2.4
6	E	413	33.5	31.8	2647.0	22.1	9.7	178.592	6.87	0.73	84	9.7
7	A	533	41.0	29.9	4934.7	20.7	9.2	337.302	6.20	0.73	60	41.5
7	B	533	41.0	29.9	4934.7	20.7	9.2	337.302	6.34	0.73	90	0.9
7	C	533	41.0	29.9	4934.7	20.7	9.2	337.302	6.52	0.73	88	1.5
7	D	533	41.0	29.9	4934.7	20.7	9.2	337.302	6.68	0.73	89	2.2
7	E	533	41.0	29.9	4934.7	20.7	9.2	337.302	6.87	0.73	84	3.3
8	A	413	30.2	30.1	2626.3	21.0	9.1	156.056	6.20	0.70	89	7.2
8	B	413	30.2	30.1	2626.3	21.0	9.1	156.056	6.37	0.70	94	2.5
8	C	413	30.2	30.1	2626.3	21.0	9.1	156.056	6.52	0.70	93	1.4
8	D	413	30.2	30.1	2626.3	21.0	9.1	156.056	6.71	0.70	87	7.7
8	E	413	30.2	30.1	2626.3	21.0	9.1	156.056	6.89	0.70	86	10.5
9	A	544	29.5	28.0	3612.5	20.5	7.5	190.096	6.21	0.70	90	10.9
9	B	544	29.5	28.0	3612.5	20.5	7.5	190.096	6.36	0.70	97	0.9
9	C	544	29.5	28.0	3612.5	20.5	7.5	190.096	6.53	0.70	97	0.8
9	D	544	29.5	28.0	3612.5	20.5	7.5	190.096	6.70	0.70	93	4.8
9	E	544	29.5	28.0	3612.5	20.5	7.5	190.096	6.88	0.70	83	6.2
10	A	456	39.3	30.1	3712.7	20.9	9.3	275.916	6.20	0.74	80	8
10	B	456	39.3	30.1	3712.7	20.9	9.3	275.916	6.36	0.74	91	3.8
10	C	456	39.3	30.1	3712.7	20.9	9.3	275.916	6.52	0.74	91	0.6
10	D	456	39.3	30.1	3712.7	20.9	9.3	275.916	6.68	0.74	89	1.9
10	E	456	39.3	30.1	3712.7	20.9	9.3	275.916	6.86	0.74	81	10

Table 13.2 **Drug product "D" 11 granulation batch factorial DoE at 65-L scale**

	DoE factors			Calculated DoE factors					Dried granule properties			Tablet properties		
Run ID #	Water addition (% w/w)	Wet massing time (min)	Water addition rate (g/min kg)	Work	X_{sat}	X_s	SaWW	In (SaWW)	Tapped bulk density (g/mL)	Median particle size	Compaction compressibility (%)	Tablet dissolution 15 min	Tablet dissolution 30 min	Tablet dissolution 45 min
1	40	0	29	5032.1	24.25	15.75	48207	10.78	0.76	396.6	20	35.7	72.0	86.0
2	33	2	24	5113.3	25.50	7.50	27550	10.22	0.72	194.0	18	62.0	93.0	99.0
3	40	0	19	7874.0	24.45	15.55	75101	11.23	0.77	421.3	21	28.7	63.3	79.0
4	26	0	29	624.2	23.21	2.79	257	5.55	0.61	165.1	18	69.7	99.3	103.0
5	33	2	24	4582.4	23.67	9.33	30046	10.31	0.72	199.2	18	58.0	89.0	97.0
6	26	0	19	1196.5	24.80	1.20	84	4.43	0.63	168.3	17	54.7	94.0	100.7
7	40	4	29	11870.8	22.99	17.01	158878	11.98	0.78	472.8	14	26.3	52.7	64.7
8	26	4	19	2424.8	25.26	0.74	844	6.74	0.67	152.0	17	86.0	99.0	101.0
9	26	4	29	1447.3	25.54	0.46	478	6.17	0.66	176.6	17	75.0	97.0	100.0
10	33	2	24	5170.4	24.08	8.92	32919	10.40	0.72	202.7	16	57.3	89.7	97.7
11	40	4	19	14713.2	25.26	14.74	159812	11.98	0.79	566.9	15	23.7	48.0	60.3

Table 13.3 Drug product "S" experiment at 65-L scale, four granulation batches each sampled five times at designated time points, resulting in 20-sample DoE

Granulation batch	Sample	Description	Water content added	Water addition time (s)	Granulation time (s)	Impeller load (kW)	Work (kJ/kg)	SaWW ($N = 1$) (kJ/kg)	SaWW ($N = 3$) (kJ/kg)	% Granules dissolved in 15/min
1	1	25% water sample 1	0.2540	320	360	0.808174	25.63106	0.219555	0.000556	90
1	2	25% water sample 2	0.2540	320	540	0.941444	39.00426	0.552105	0.001525	
1	3	25% water sample 3	0.2540	320	660	0.885915	49.55154	0.805422	0.002264	86
1	4	25% water sample 4	0.2540	320	960	0.808174	65.86184	1.174112	0.003339	84
1	5	25% water sample 5	0.2540	320	1240	0.808174	99.23494	1.869198	0.005366	87
2	1	35% water sample 1	0.3540	300	380	1.178368	31.57435	1.592449	0.033889	90
2	2	35% water sample 2	0.3540	300	540	1.178368	48.88172	3.153912	0.070921	90
2	3	35% water sample 3	0.3540	300	660	1.230196	60.52855	4.215445	0.096096	86
2	4	35% water sample 4	0.3540	300	960	1.256109	83.33616	6.310204	0.145776	84
2	5	35% water sample 5	0.3540	300	1200	1.282023	1305264	10.6802	0.249414	76
3	1	40% water sample 1	0.4106	320	380	1.337552	31.02979	2.069927	0.074342	95
3	2	40% water sample 2	0.4106	320	540	1.415293	50.81866	4.694684	0.186448	89
3	3	40% water sample 3	0.4106	320	660	1.415293	67.07937	6.882321	0.279885	78
3	4	40% water sample 4	0.4106	320	960	1.522649	93.87543	10.53338	0.435825	57
3	5	40% water sample 5	0.4106	320	1200	1.548562	151.172	18.53245	0.777474	39
4	1	45% water sample 1	0.4546	300	380	1.759573	36.7678	4.000549	0.226612	82
4	2	45% water sample 2	0.4546	300	540	1.8114	63.06521	8.894825	0.543823	52
4	3	45% water sample 3	0.4546	300	660	1.785487	83.94737	12.77302	0.795179	34
4	4	45% water sample 4	0.4546	300	960	1.759573	116.4073	18.73007	1.181271	13
4	5	45% water sample 5	0.4546	300	1200	1.574476	177.6654	29.6435	1.888599	11

Table 13.4 **Drug product "P" micronization and granulation DoE at 65-L scale illustrating the impacts of API raw material variation on granulation**

API batch	Micronization work (kJ/kg)	API D90 (microns)	Rheometer Work (mJ/30 grams)	Granulation sample number	Granulation work (kJ/kg)	Granulation work/ Rheometer Work	Milled granule tap density (g/cc)	Tablet dissolution at 45-min	Tablet dissolution RSD at 45-min
1	180	6.5	11.0	1	27.2	74117	0.67	86	10.6
1	180	6.5	11.0	2	44.0	120030	0.71	93	3.0
1	180	6.5	11.0	3	83.5	227782	0.73	92	1.9
1	180	6.5	11.0	4	126.4	344642	0.75	85	1.4
2	60	13.2	6.8	1	22.0	97018	0.69	89	8.7
2	60	13.2	6.8	2	34.8	153436	0.70	91	4.1
2	60	13.2	6.8	3	64.6	284842	0.74	87	1.4
2	60	13.2	6.8	4	91.5	403851	0.78	52	25.4
3	280	5.8	12.2	1	28.6	70446	0.67	87	11.5
3	280	5.8	12.2	2	45.2	111125	0.69	86	11.0
3	280	5.8	12.2	3	81.9	201398	0.72	92	3.4
3	280	5.8	12.2	4	112.1	275592	0.76	91	3.8

Table 13.5 Data from ten experimental granulation batches for drug product "P" followed by 30 runs at optimum work and water setting at 300-L scale

Batch ID	Water fraction	Granulation work	X_{sat}	X_s	SaWW	Dissolution mean at 45-min
1	29.93	4268	20.2%	9.7	322.7	91
2	31.81	6364	20.2%	11.6	573.4	31
3	31.81	4126	21.9%	9.9	309.1	89
4	27.74	2797	20.5%	7.2	144.8	96
5	27.74	5588	20.1%	7.6	301.5	94
6	31.80	2647	22.1%	9.7	178.6	96
7	29.93	4935	20.7%	9.2	337.3	88
8	30.14	2626	21.0%	9.1	156.1	93
9	27.95	3612	20.5%	7.5	190.1	97
10	30.14	3713	20.9%	9.3	275.9	91
11	30.15	3545	20.8%	9.4	236.9	91
12	30.15	3569	19.8%	10.3	290.7	95
13	30.15	3587	21.4%	8.7	236.3	95
14	30.15	3581	20.3%	9.8	268.4	94
15	30.15	3573	22.0%	8.1	215.7	92
16	30.15	3555	19.5%	10.7	282.4	95
17	30.15	3545	21.8%	8.4	216.6	93
18	30.15	3563	20.7%	9.4	255.3	94
19	30.15	3572	20.8%	9.4	255.4	96
20	30.15	3421	19.7%	10.4	269.2	96
21	30.15	3611	20.6%	9.5	278.6	98
22	30.15	3552	19.7%	10.4	277.1	98
23	30.15	3637	20.1%	10.0	279.0	99
24	30.15	3606	21.4%	8.8	235.6	99
25	30.15	3567	21.4%	8.8	241.5	97
26	30.15	3601	21.2%	9.0	245.0	99
27	30.15	3592	21.0%	9.2	262.6	98
28	30.14	3591	20.8%	9.3	256.3	100
29	30.14	3553	19.8%	10.4	292.7	94
30	30.14	3543	25.1%	5.1	124.5	89
31	30.14	3486	24.7%	5.5	114.3	83
32	30.15	3521	24.5%	5.7	135.7	84
33	30.14	3554	22.9%	7.3	162.2	89
34	30.14	3599	20.6%	9.5	228.6	94
35	30.16	3645	22.3%	7.9	219.3	93
36	30.15	3614	23.5%	6.7	173.9	94
37	30.15	3618	21.2%	9.0	259.7	93
38	30.15	3623	21.7%	8.5	231.7	90
39	30.16	3613	20.9%	9.3	254.0	91
40	30.15	3628	23.5%	6.6	173.4	86

Table 13.6 **Theophylline DoE on twin screw granulator at Ghent University recalculated using first principle equation**

	DoE parameters						Observed	Calculated parameters			Granule characteristics	
Run number	**Throughput (kg/h)**	**Screw speed (RPM)**	**Kneading elements**	**Angle of kneading**	**Barrel temp (°C)**	**Type binder addition**	**Screw torque (N m)**	**Power/mass (J/g)**	**Water dynamic viscosity (kg/m s)**	**Power/(mass* viscosity)**	**Yield (percent granules between 150 and 1400 microns)**	**Milled granules D50 (microns)**
1	17.5	775	4	60	32.5	Wet	1.5	25.0	7.37E-04	34.0	70.7	442
2	25	600	2	90	25	Wet	2.2	19.9	8.68E-04	22.9	55	352
3	25	950	2	30	40	Dry	2.1	30.1	6.35E-04	47.3	64.8	399
4	10	600	12	30	40	Dry	4.0	90.5	6.35E-04	142.4	84.3	567
5	25	600	12	30	40	Wet	7.3	66.0	6.35E-04	103.9	84.7	583
6	25	950	2	30	25	Wet	2.4	34.4	8.68E-04	39.6	66.1	435
7	25	600	12	60	25	Dry	5.6	50.7	8.68E-04	58.3	70.7	445
8	25	950	12	30	25	Dry	6.6	94.5	8.68E-04	108.9	82.1	542
9	25	600	2	90	40	Dry	1.9	17.2	6.35E-04	27.1	63.4	405
10	10	600	2	30	25	Dry	1.3	29.4	8.68E-04	33.9	65.9	423
11	10	950	2	90	25	Dry	0.9	32.2	8.68E-04	37.1	62.4	394
12	25	950	6	90	40	Wet	4.9	70.2	6.35E-04	110.5	81.8	544
13	10	950	12	30	25	Wet	4.5	161.2	8.68E-04	185.6	80.5	536
14	17.5	775	4	60	32.5	Wet	1.7	28.4	7.37E-04	38.5	68.9	430
15	17.5	775	4	60	32.5	Wet	1.4	23.4	7.37E-04	31.7	66.7	418
16	10	950	2	30	40	Wet	1.3	46.6	6.35E-04	73.3	72.6	458
17	10	600	6	90	40	Wet	4.4	99.5	6.35E-04	156.6	82.8	542
18	10	950	12	60	40	Dry	2.8	100.3	6.35E-04	157.8	82.1	533

Process modeling in the biopharmaceutical industry

14

M. Horner[1], *S. Joshi*[2] *and Y. Waghmare*[3]
[1]ANSYS, Inc., Evanston, IL, United States, [2]ANSYS Fluent India Pvt Ltd., Pune, Maharashtra, India, [3]Sanofi-Genzyme, Framingham, MA, United States

14.1 Introduction

Biologics represent a continually increasing proportion of pipeline and approved drug therapies (Oakley, 2015). As the industry is maturing and biosimilars are beginning to enter the market, the focus is shifting from product to process. One reason is that competition from generic biosimilars is forcing innovators to optimize their process to be more cost effective. In parallel, regulatory emphasis on Quality by Design (QbD) is promoting a focus on process understanding and robustness. These three drivers: a maturing industry, competition from generics, and increased regulatory expectations, are motivating manufacturers to incorporate process modeling tools into their development and manufacturing practices.

Process models are mathematical descriptions of the physical processes governing a unit operation. They provide a noninvasive method for generating performance data that may be difficult to collect experimentally. This additional engineering information minimizes the number of experiments required to develop a process and reduces the risk of failure during scale-up, thereby lowering development costs and shortening time-to-market. Yet, due to the inherent complexity of biologics processes and limited mechanistic understanding about the biology of living cells, these tools are penetrating the biologics industry at a much slower pace than the pharmaceutical industry. It is therefore imperative to understand the background and utilization of process models in the bioprocessing industry.

14.1.1 Manufacturing process overview

A typical monoclonal antibody manufacturing process is shown in Fig. 14.1 (Kelly, 2009). In the first step, cells from a single vial are grown to the appropriate cell density and volume during seed train expansion. These cells are used to inoculate the production bioreactor, where they grow and produce drug substance. The drug is harvested and cell debris removed during the harvest and clarification step. The clarified harvest is then processed through series of chromatographic purification steps to concentrate the drug and remove impurities. A viral filtration step is

Predictive Modeling of Pharmaceutical Unit Operations. DOI: http://dx.doi.org/10.1016/B978-0-08-100154-7.00014-4

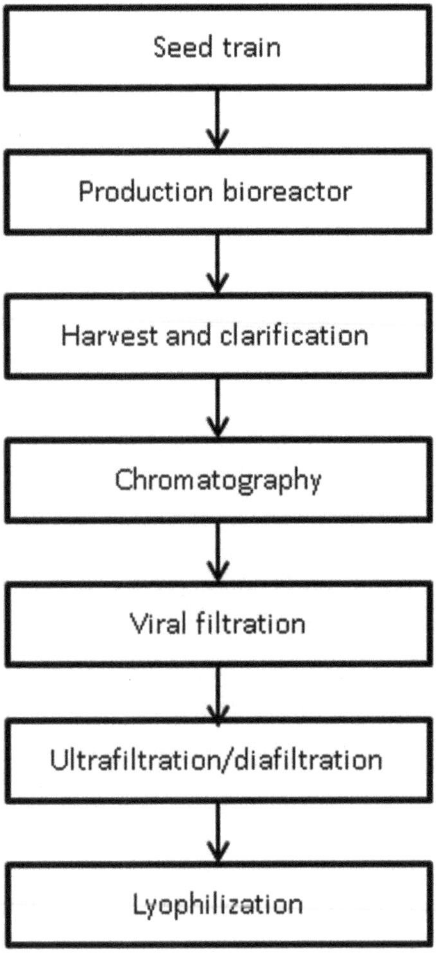

Figure 14.1 Flow chart illustrating the steps in a typical monoclonal antibody manufacturing process.

performed to ensure that residual virus particles are removed. The drug substance is then formulated in an appropriate buffer using ultrafiltration/diafiltration. And as a final step, the formulated drug product is freeze-dried into vials. The manufacturing process for other biologics, such as recombinant proteins, would typically involve one or more modifications to this process.

14.1.2 Current modeling techniques

Computer modeling enhances process understanding at each step in the manufacturing process, which can provide a variety of benefits to the organization. For example, a model can be used either to identify optimal process conditions or to optimize the design of the process equipment. Additionally, the ability of a model to provide an a priori prediction can be harnessed to forecast the behavior upon scale-up, which allows for modification of the process or process equipment to minimize the risk of failure at larger scales. And under the QbD paradigm, models occupy a central role in defining the permissible range of input variables and operating conditions, i.e., the design space, for the process.

An array of modeling techniques are currently used to predict the performance of bioprocess industry unit operations. Computational fluid dynamics (CFD) tools are well known for their ability to predict bioreactor performance, but are also applied to many other unit operations. Non-CFD-based heat and mass transfer models are used to model chromatography and lyophilization unit operations. Flow sheet models are used to model production capacity, identify bottlenecks, and perform economic analysis. And metabolic flux analysis models are used to understand and optimize the metabolic pathways of the cells, which are represented as individual microreactors that produce biological drug products (Koffas and Stephanopoulos, 2005).

14.1.3 Scope

The richness in different modeling techniques and the variety of unit operations used in the bioprocess industry prohibit an in-depth review in a single chapter. Therefore, the scope of this chapter is limited to modeling techniques that are based on first principles, with a focus on CFD since this is the primary method used for detailed modeling of bioprocess unit operations. The chapter begins with a review of the conservation equations for fluid flow, heat transfer, and mass transfer for single-phase flows and the extension of these equations to multiphase flow conditions. Methodologies for applying these equations to predict the performance of selected upstream and downstream unit operations are then described. Throughout the chapter, examples illustrate the application of process modeling to design challenges facing today's process development engineers.

14.2 Theoretical foundations

Continuum mechanics is the branch of mechanics that is concerned with the behavior of solids and fluids on a macroscopic scale. By neglecting the discrete nature of these materials at the molecular or atomic scale, matter can be treated as a space-filling medium with continuous properties. This permits the development of conservation equations for mass, momentum, heat, and species transport. This section provides an overview of these conservation equations followed by a brief introduction to the CFD modeling process.

14.2.1 Conservation equations

A set of conservation equations describes the processes of mass, momentum, energy, and species transport. Each equation is founded on first principles, e.g., the momentum equation is based on Newton's second law of motion, which states that the rate of change of momentum of a fluid element equals the sum of the forces acting on that element. Similarly, the energy equation is based on the first law of thermodynamics, which states that the rate of change of energy of a fluid element is equal to the rate of heat addition to the fluid element plus the rate of work done on the element. Conservation equations are, therefore, a statement about how conserved quantities are affected by physical transport processes.

More than one transport equation is sometimes required to describe the behavior of a system. This may be because changes in one variable (say, the temperature) give rise to changes in other variables (say, the pressure). The need to model an equation of state, chemical reaction, or phase change, are a few of the more common reasons for requiring more than one conservation equation. In these cases, the resulting set of governing equations is typically solved simultaneously because the solution of each variable is coupled to the solution of one or more other variables. But there are situations where transport equations can be solved sequentially. One example is the advection-diffusion problem, which occurs when the material properties of a fluid medium are independent of temperature or concentration. In this approach, the momentum equations are solved using a steady-state formulation, resulting in a single solution for the velocity field. This velocity field is then used as input for the convective terms of other transport equations. This approach is a common simplifying assumption in mixing, chromatography, and drug delivery problems, and can save significant time and computational resources because the velocity field is computed only one time, even if the scalar transport processes are transient.

The rest of this section introduces the conservation equations fundamental to process modeling. It will be shown that all conservation equations can be written as balances of a variable ϕ that include terms accounting for the rate of change of ϕ, the convection of ϕ, the diffusion of ϕ, and ϕ sources/sinks. Recognizing these relationships among conservation equations not only helps with understanding the fundamentals of transport theory, but also is of great importance when implementing these equations into a flow solver.

14.2.1.1 Continuity

The continuity equation is a mathematical expression of the conservation (or continuity) of mass. Because of its' relative simplicity, the derivation of the continuity equation will be provided in this section, while the derivation of the remaining conservation equations will be left to the reader (see Bird et al., 1960 for a complete treatise).

A conservation equation is typically derived using a control volume approach, which aids in determining the relationship between the time derivative of a

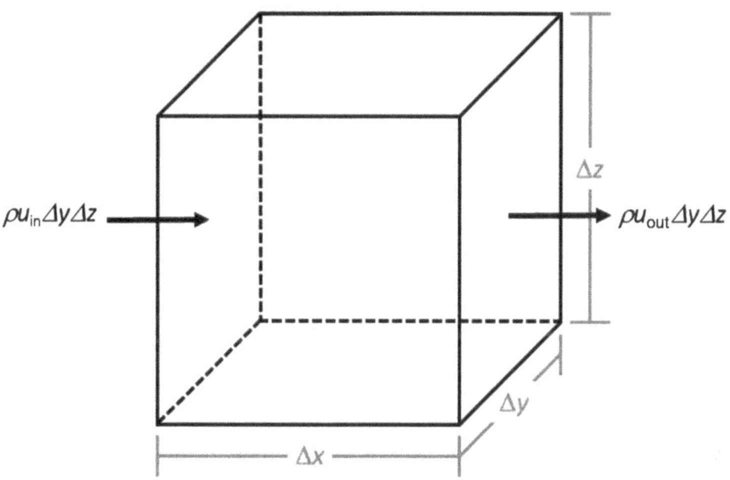

Figure 14.2 Control volume used to determine the mathematical form of each conservation equation in rectangular coordinates. The mass flux into and out of the control volume in the x-direction is shown. Similar relationships can be written for the mass flux in the y- and z-directions.

transported quantity and the rate of change of that quantity inside a fixed region of space. A typical control volume is shown in Fig. 14.2. In this figure, Δx, Δy, and Δz are the lengths of the sides of the control volume in the x-, y-, and z-directions, respectively. Similarly, u, v, and w are the components of velocity in the x-, y-, and z-directions, respectively.

The continuity equation is a balance of the net rate of mass accumulation in the control volume and the net flow rate (or flux) of mass through the surfaces of the control volume. The net rate of mass accumulation due to compressibility is

$$\frac{\partial \rho}{\partial t}\Delta V = \frac{\partial \rho}{\partial t}\Delta x \Delta y \Delta z, \tag{14.1}$$

where ρ is the fluid density and V is the volume of the control volume.

The flux of material through each control volume surface is defined as the normal component of the velocity on the surface times the mass of material flowing through that surface. As shown in Fig. 14.2, the flux of material into the control volume in the x-direction is $(\rho u_{in})^* \Delta y \Delta z$ and the flux of material out of the control volume in the x-direction is $(\rho u_{out})^* \Delta y \Delta z$. Calculating the flux for the remaining faces and collecting like terms

$$\rho(u_{out} - u_{in})^*(\Delta y \Delta z) + \rho(v_{out} - v_{in})^*(\Delta x \Delta z) + \rho(w_{out} - w_{in})^*(\Delta x \Delta y), \tag{14.2}$$

where the *in*/*out* subscripts refer to velocity vectors directed toward/away from the control volume.

Equating Eqs. (14.1) and (14.2) and dividing by the element volume:

$$\frac{\partial \rho}{\partial t} = \rho \frac{(u_{\text{out}} - u_{\text{in}})}{\Delta x} + \rho \frac{(v_{\text{out}} - v_{\text{in}})}{\Delta y} + \rho \frac{(w_{\text{out}} - w_{\text{in}})}{\Delta z}. \tag{14.3}$$

And in the limit of ΔV going to zero, Eq. (14.3) becomes

$$\frac{\partial \rho}{\partial t} + \frac{\partial(\rho u)}{\partial x} + \frac{\partial(\rho v)}{\partial y} + \frac{\partial(\rho w)}{\partial z} = 0, \tag{14.4}$$

which is the continuity equation for a compressible fluid. Restating using vector notation

$$\frac{\partial \rho}{\partial t} + \nabla \cdot (\rho \mathbf{u}) = 0, \tag{14.5}$$

where **u** is the fluid velocity in vector form.

14.2.1.2 Momentum

The momentum equations are a balance on the rate of change of momentum of a fluid element and the sum of the forces acting on that element. A separate momentum balance is performed in each of the three coordinate directions, resulting in a set of three simultaneously coupled differential equations for fluid flow. Taken together, the three momentum equations are referred to as the Navier–Stokes equations, which can be written as

$$\rho \frac{\partial \mathbf{u}}{\partial t} + \rho(\mathbf{u} \cdot \nabla \mathbf{u}) = -\nabla P + \mu \nabla^2 \mathbf{u} + \mathbf{S_M}, \tag{14.6}$$

where μ is the fluid viscosity. The convective (acceleration) terms are on the left-hand side of Eq. (14.6) and the right-hand side contains terms describing the pressure gradient, diffusion of momentum due to viscous forces, and additional source terms $\mathbf{S_M}$, such as gravity and other body forces, respectively.

Turbulence

Fluid flows are typically divided into two regimes: laminar and turbulent. Laminar flows represent a situation where the motion of fluid elements is well-ordered. Turbulent flows, on the other hand, are in a highly disordered (chaotic) state that can be thought of as a population of rotational structures, called eddies, of varying sizes and strengths (see Fig. 14.3 for an early study). Flow disturbances such as surface roughness or obstructions initiate the transition from laminar to turbulent flow. Once the flow is turbulent, energy passes sequentially from the largest to smallest scale eddies through what is called the turbulent energy cascade. Large eddies contain most of the kinetic energy of the flow, which is dissipated into internal energy, i.e., heat, by

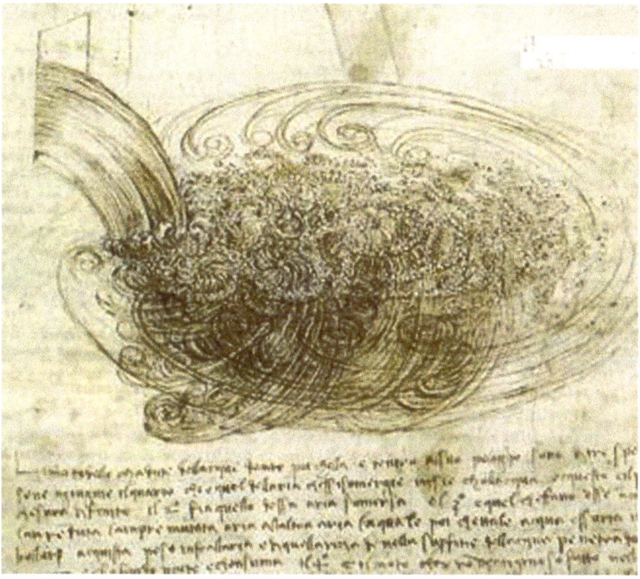

Figure 14.3 An early study of turbulent flow structures by Leonardo da Vinci (Royal Collection Trust/© Her Majesty Queen Elizabeth II 2016).

viscous stresses at the smallest scales. The inherent unsteady and aperiodic nature of a turbulent flow causes the spatial and temporal fluctuations in transport quantities that result in the enhanced mixing encountered in turbulent flows.

Dimensionless arguments are typically used to identify the flow regime (laminar or turbulent). The Reynolds number (*Re*) is a dimensionless number that quantifies the relative importance of the convective and viscous forces of a flowing fluid. For flow in a pipe, the Reynolds number is given by $(\rho^* V^* D/\mu)$, where V is the characteristic speed and D is the pipe diameter. The transition from laminar to turbulent flow begins to occur at $Re \approx 2000$ and pipe flow is accepted to be fully turbulent for $Re \geq 3000$. For mixing tanks, the Reynolds number is defined as $(N_i^* D_i^* \rho/\mu)$, where N_i is the rotational speed of the impeller and D_i is the impeller diameter. The transition to turbulent flow typically occurs over a much wider range of Reynolds numbers ($100 < Re < 10{,}000$), and it is generally accepted that the flow in a mixing tank is turbulent if $Re \geq 10{,}000$. The reader is referred to Hemrajani and Tatterson (2004) for an extensive discussion of the relationship between mixing tank design, process conditions, and turbulence.

From a modeling perspective, the Navier–Stokes equations contain all the information required to model a turbulent flow without any assumptions or simplification; this is referred to as direct numerical simulation (DNS) (Ahn et al., 2013; Moser et al., 1999; Moin and Mahesh, 1998; Le et al., 1997). But the grid resolution requirements for DNS are impractical even using today's high-performance computing technology; analysts therefore look to turbulence models to provide approximate solutions to industrially relevant flow situations. The two most common approaches for modeling turbulence are the Reynolds-averaging Navier–Stokes

(RANS) method and scale-resolving simulations (SRS). In RANS, time-averaging transforms the instantaneous flow equations into a mean flow representation. Reynolds stress terms, representing the transport of momentum due to turbulent fluctuations, are introduced as a result of the averaging process. These terms are modeled through a set of closure equations. The computational results from a RANS model provide information about the mean flow. SRS is required when the unsteady motion of turbulent structures needs to be resolved, e.g., when modeling noise and vibration. Larger eddies are resolved in SRS while the small-scale eddies are modeled. Therefore, the grid for an SRS model must be fine enough to resolve the larger scale eddies, whose structure is derived from the mean flow. There are many other considerations to take into account when modeling turbulence, such as the selection of the appropriate turbulence model, computational mesh requirements, and turbulence-related boundary conditions. Such details are beyond the scope of this chapter, therefore the reader is referred to other works (Pope, 2000; Wilcox, 1993; Tennekes and Lumley, 1972; Batchelor, 1953) for further information.

14.2.1.3 Heat transfer

Thermal energy comes from the internal kinetic energy of matter and is proportional to the temperature of an object or system. Heat transfer refers to the flow of thermal energy from matter occupying one region in space across a boundary to matter occupying a different region in space; the flow of heat is normally from a high temperature region to a low temperature region. The three primary mechanisms of heat transfer are conduction, convection, and radiation. Conductive heat transfer occurs through molecular vibration, convective heat transfer is due to bulk fluid motion, and radiative heat transfer occurs through electromagnetic waves. Conduction and convection are the primary modes of heat transfer in biopharmaceutical unit operations.

The energy equation may be written in the following form:

$$\frac{\partial}{\partial t}(\rho E) + \nabla \cdot (\mathbf{u}(\rho E + p)) = -\nabla \cdot \left(k_{\text{eff}} \nabla T - \sum_j h_j \mathbf{J}_j + \tau_{\text{eff}} \cdot \mathbf{u} \right) + \mathbf{S}_{\text{H}}, \tag{14.7}$$

where E is the energy, h_j is the enthalpy of species j, k_{eff} is an effective conductivity that includes a contribution due to turbulence, and $\mathbf{J}_j$ is the diffusion flux of species j. The left-hand side of Eq. (14.7) includes transient and convective terms and the terms on the right-hand side account for transport due to conduction, species diffusion, and viscous dissipation, respectively. Finally, the $\mathbf{S}_{\text{H}}$ term is used to account for heats of reaction, radiation, or other volumetric source/sink terms.

The energy, E, can be related to temperature through the enthalpy, h:

$$E = h - \frac{P}{\rho} + \frac{v^2}{2}. \tag{14.8}$$

The enthalpy of an incompressible fluid is given by

$$h = \sum_j Y_j h_j + \frac{P}{\rho}, \tag{14.9}$$

where Y_j is the mass fraction of species j. Finally, the enthalpy of each species is typically a temperature-dependent function of the specific heat at the local temperature:

$$h_j = \int_{T_{\text{ref}}}^{T} c_{p,j} dT. \tag{14.10}$$

14.2.1.4 Species transport

The mixing and transport of chemical species is described using conservation equations containing convection, diffusion, and reaction source terms for each component species. Multiple simultaneous chemical reactions can be modeled, with reactions occurring in the bulk phase (volumetric reactions) and/or on wall or particle surfaces (surface reactions).

A convection-diffusion equation is used to solve for the local mass fraction, Y_i, of each species i:

$$\frac{\partial}{\partial t}(\rho Y_i) + \nabla \cdot (\rho \mathbf{u} Y_i) = -\nabla \cdot \mathbf{J}_i + R_i + S_i, \tag{14.11}$$

where $\mathbf{J}_i$ is the diffusion flux, R_i is the net rate of production by chemical reaction, and the S_i term accounts for species sources/sinks. An equation of this form is typically solved for each of (N-1) species, where N is the total number of chemical species in the system. The mass fraction of the Nth species is determined by the fact that the total mass fraction over all species sums to unity. As a best practice, defining the Nth species as the one with the largest mass fraction in the system will typically minimize the error associated with this assumption.

The diffusive flux $\mathbf{J}_i$ is based on Fick's Law, which utilizes a dilute solution approximation to model mass diffusion due to concentration and thermal gradients:

$$\mathbf{J}_i = -\rho D_{i,m} \nabla Y_i - D_{T,i} \frac{\nabla T}{T}, \tag{14.12}$$

where $D_{i,m}$ is the mass diffusion coefficient and $D_{T,i}$ is the thermal diffusion coefficient.

14.2.1.5 Multiphase modeling

Multiphase flow refers to the simultaneous presence of multiple states of matter (i.e., phases) in a process. These simulations model the interaction of one or more phases with each other and with their environment. Many biopharmaceutical unit operations involve a mixture of multiple phases, for example:

- liquid–liquid mixtures: media feed mixing, acid/base addition
- liquid–gas mixtures: sparged bioreactors, surface aeration
- liquid–solid mixtures: solids suspension, chromatography column packing
- liquid–solid–gas mixtures: bioreactors with microcarriers, spray drying

In a general sense, a phase is defined as an identifiable class of material with a unique response to, and interaction with, both the mixture and external forces. Each phase may be comprised of one or more physical states of matter: gas, liquid, and solid. And each state of matter can have more than one phase assignment in a single simulation. For example, solid particles of similar composition, but with different diameters, may be considered as different phases if the particles in each size bin respond differently to the flow field. Thus, from a computational modeling perspective, a phase can be thought of as a material that has been assigned a unique set of material properties.

Types of multiphase models

Multiphase models can be classified as Euler–Lagrange or Euler–Euler. Euler–Lagrange models solve for the transport of the continuous phase(s) in the Eulerian frame and the dispersed phase(s) in the Lagrangian frame, while Euler–Euler models utilize the Eulerian frame for all phases. The Lagrangian multiphase model is an example of an Euler–Lagrange approach, while the volume of fluid (VOF), Eulerian, and discrete element method (DEM) are examples of the Euler–Euler approach. An overview of each of these methods is provided in the following sections.

Lagrangian The Lagrangian model assumes that a particulate flow is a dilute dispersion of solids, bubbles, or droplets. The suspending fluid is typically referred to as the primary (or continuous) phase and the particles are referred to as the secondary (or dispersed) phase. The flow patterns of the fluid phase are solved using the Navier–Stokes equations, and particle trajectories, $\mathbf{x}_p(t)$, are determined by integrating a force balance for each particle:

$$\frac{d\mathbf{u}_p}{dt} = \frac{(\mathbf{u} - \mathbf{u}_p)}{\tau_r} + \frac{(\rho_p - \rho)\mathbf{g}}{\rho_p} + \mathbf{F}, \tag{14.13}$$

which is sequentially coupled to the Lagrangian equation for particle motion:

$$\frac{d\mathbf{x}_p}{dt} = \mathbf{u}_p, \tag{14.14}$$

where $\mathbf{x}_p$ is the particle position vector, $\mathbf{u}_p$ is the particle velocity vector, $(\mathbf{u}-\mathbf{u}_p)/\tau_r$ is the drag force acting on the particle, τ_r is the particle relaxation time, $\mathbf{g}$ is the gravity vector, and $\mathbf{F}$ accounts for any additional acceleration terms acting on the particle, e.g., virtual mass effects. Particle–particle interactions are neglected in this model, it is therefore recommended that the volume fraction of the dispersed phase not exceed 10%. This approach is used in the biopharmaceutical industry to understand how bioreactor design affects mixing time and shear history on cells.

The dispersed phase can be extended to include the exchange of mass and energy with the fluid phase. This is accomplished via the inclusion of heat/mass exchange terms for the particulate phase. An example is spray drying, where momentum, heat and mass transfer terms account for drag forces on particles, heat transfer between the air and drying droplets, and solvent evaporation, respectively (Soltania et al., 2015; Huang et al., 2006). Another application that requires mass transfer modeling is the dissolution of solid particles in a buffer or media preparation operation. (Koganti et al., 2010).

Volume of fluid (VOF) The VOF model is a technique for tracking the motion of the interface(s) between two or more immiscible fluids. Because the fluids do not mix, a single momentum equation is solved in each element of the flow domain. Material properties are calculated as volume-weighted quantities in each element. For example, the mixture density is calculated as

$$\rho = \sum_{q=1}^{n} \alpha_q \rho_q, \tag{14.15}$$

where α_q and ρ_q are the volume fraction and density of phase q, respectively.

The evolution of the shape and position of the free surface is determined by solving a transient advection equation for each phase. For the qth phase, this equation takes the following form:

$$\frac{1}{\rho_q}\left[\frac{\partial}{\partial t}(\alpha_q \rho_q) + \nabla \cdot (\alpha_q \rho_q \mathbf{u}_q) = S_{\alpha_q} + \sum_{p=1}^{n}(\dot{m}_{pq} - \dot{m}_{qp})\right], \tag{14.16}$$

where $\mathbf{u}_q$ is the velocity of the qth phase, m_{pq} is the rate of mass transfer from phase p to phase q and m_{qp} is the rate of mass transfer from phase q to phase p. Eq. (14.16) is typically solved for (n-1) phases, where the volume fraction of the nth phase is determined by enforcing the following constraint in each element of the grid:

$$\sum_{q=1}^{n} \alpha_q = 1. \tag{14.17}$$

In other words, the total volume fraction of the mixture must sum to unity in each element. As a result, the volume fraction of each phase fits into one of three situations in each mesh element:

1. $\alpha_q = 1$: the element is filled with phase q
2. $\alpha_q = 0$: the element is devoid of phase q
3. $0 < \alpha_q < 1$: the element is partially filled with phase q

There is no interface in elements that are completely filled with any one of the n phases, but an interface is present if α_q is between 0 and 1. One application of the VOF model is to predict vortex formation in unbaffled bioreactors (Haque et al., 2006).

Eulerian The Eulerian multiphase approach permits the modeling of mixtures containing multiple interpenetrating, i.e., continuous, phases. This is accomplished by modifying the conservation equations for each phase to include the phase volume fraction (Anderson and Jackson, 1967). Correlations accounting for the exchange of momentum, heat, and mass between phases are also incorporated into the transport equations. One benefit of the Eulerian approach is that the volume fraction of each phase may vary from 0 to 1 at any point in space. This last point is critical in many biopharmaceutical manufacturing processes, e.g., near the spargers, impellers, and baffles of sparged bioreactors, where the concentration of liquid and gas can vary considerably.

A unique set of transport equations model the response of each phase in the mixture. For example, the continuity equation is modified as follows to account for the volume fraction of each phase q:

$$\frac{\partial}{\partial t}(\alpha_q \rho_q) + \nabla \cdot (\alpha_q \rho_q \mathbf{u}_q) = \sum_{p=1}^{n} (\dot{m}_{pq} - \dot{m}_{qp}) + S_C, \tag{14.18}$$

where the summation term on the right-hand side accounts for mass exchange between phases and S_C is a mass source/sink term. Similar to the VOF model, the sum of the volume fractions is constrained to be equal to 1 in all elements and at all times.

The momentum equation is adapted as follows to account for the presence of multiple phases:

$$\frac{\partial}{\partial t}(\alpha_q \rho_q \mathbf{u}_q) + \nabla \cdot (\alpha_q \rho_q \mathbf{u}_q \mathbf{u}_q) = -\alpha_q \nabla P + \nabla \cdot \boldsymbol{\tau}_q + \alpha_q \rho_q \mathbf{g} + \mathbf{S}_{M,q}, \tag{14.19}$$

where the pressure P does not have a subscript because this property is shared by all phases, i.e., the pressure has a single value in each element. The continuity and momentum equations are solved for all phases and momentum coupling between phases occurs through the pressure and the phase interaction forces. The energy and species transport equations are similarly modified to account for the effects of thermal and molecular transport in a multiphase system.

For systems where there is a high frequency of particle collisions and/or a high degree of particle–particle contact, the Eulerian–granular model extends the Eulerian multiphase model to include the effect of particle–particle interactions on the behavior of solid-fluid mixtures. Particle transport is assumed to be comprised of a mean (bulk) flow component and a fluctuating component, where fluctuations are attributed to random collisions between particles. An analogy with the thermal motion of molecules in a gas provides the basis for modeling the velocity fluctuations arising from particle–particle collisions. This requires the solution of an equation for the granular temperature, representing the solids fluctuating energy, and an equation for the solids bulk and shear viscosities. The suspension of microcarriers or other solid particles in mixing tanks is perhaps the most common use of the Eulerian–granular model in the biopharmaceutical industry (Gohel et al., 2012).

Discrete element method (DEM) Lastly, DEM is suitable for simulating mixtures containing a high volume fraction of granular materials. DEM uses Newton's laws of motion to simulate the effects of contact forces and body forces on particle motion, where contact forces are due to particle–particle or particle–boundary interactions and body forces are due to the presence of external fields, e.g., gravity. In contrast to the Eulerian–granular approach, each particle is modeled explicitly in DEM. An additional difference between DEM and the Eulerian–granular model is that the interaction between the particles and the fluid phase are neglected in a pure DEM model. To address this, DEM-CFD cosimulation is on the rise as is the implementation of DEM capabilities into mainstream CFD codes, the goal being to provide an even deeper understanding of the interaction between the motion of the granular phase and fluid, heat and mass transport.

DEM is covered in great detail in other chapters of this volume, and so, for the sake of brevity, it is left to the reader to further explore this topic.

14.2.2 Introduction to CFD

Industrially relevant applications rarely permit an analytical solution of the equations presented earlier in this section. Therefore, numerical methods such as CFD have been adopted to provide solutions to these complex problems. CFD provides a nonintrusive environment to virtually model, and then evaluate, product or process performance with minimal investment of engineering resources. Because of this, CFD software is used in a variety of industries to gain insights into product performance and/or process behavior that would be difficult to attain experimentally.

The CFD modeling process can be divided into three sequential stages: preprocessing, solution, and postprocessing. During preprocessing, the geometry of the manufacturing equipment is created in digital format using CAD or other geometry creation software. The geometry is then decomposed into an assembly of smaller volumes called elements. The collection of all elements is referred to as the computational mesh. The governing equations, material properties, and boundary conditions are then entered into preprocessing software. During the solution phase, the solver discretizes the governing equations, applies the model information, and then solves for flow variables at each mesh point. During postprocessing, results are extracted and analyzed using high-end graphical visualization tools and quantitative measures. The following sections provides a number of examples illustrating the ability of CFD to predict the performance of various biopharmaceutical unit operations.

14.3 Bioreactor operation and modeling

14.3.1 Introduction

The productivity of a biologics process depends on the ability to grow biological cells, such as mammalian, yeast, and bacteria cells, to high population densities in a controlled environment. A bioreactor provides such an environment by suspending cells in a well-mixed cell culture. Bioreactor types include agitator-driven bioreactors, airlift bioreactors, wave bioreactors, vibromixers, and others. This section will focus on agitator-driven bioreactors, which are the most widely used by today's biopharmaceutical manufacturers.

There are several demanding, and sometimes competing, requirements that must be considered when designing an agitator-driven bioreactor. For example, oxygen is to be supplied by airflow to support cell growth, but at the same time metabolic waste products, like carbon dioxide and acids, need to be removed. Impeller stirring is required to distribute air bubbles throughout the tank so that dissolved oxygen (DO) is available for cell growth, but excessive stirring leads to high shear that can damage cells (Werner et al., 2014). Cells are also very sensitive to changes in temperature and pH, which need to be maintained at specified levels. These factors, and others, lead to many challenges when designing a bioreactor.

14.3.2 Mixing in bioreactors: physics and key parameters

Several physical mixing phenomena happen simultaneously during operation of a bioreactor. These include liquid mixing, gas distribution, gas mass transfer, cell suspension and, sometimes, microcarrier suspension. These processes are directly or indirectly driven by the power supplied to the fluid by the impeller. This power results in bulk fluid motion and velocity fluctuations, which are characterized by velocity and turbulence, respectively.

Turbulent flow conditions improve the growth environment inside the tank in a number of ways. First, turbulence increases the interfacial area available for the transfer of oxygen from the gas phase to the liquid phase by breaking air bubbles into smaller bubbles and by increasing the bubble residence time inside the tank. Second, turbulent mixing, along with bulk fluid motion, help to homogenize the temperature and pH inside the tank. And while excessive power is favorable for better mixing, unreasonably high turbulence can be harmful to cells (Elias et al., 1995). These competing requirements necessitate the identification of optimum bioreactor operating conditions. The following sections introduce some of the key parameters that contribute to optimal bioreactor performance.

14.3.2.1 Blend time

Blend time, or macromixing time, is the amount of time required to bring the contents of a bioreactor to macro-level uniformity. In other words, blend time provides an estimated response time required for the tank to equalize the concentration of an externally added stream, e.g., after the addition of a media feed bolus. Long blend times are indicative of slow mixing and poorly mixed regions in the tank, which can harm the cells, e.g., if the pH is too high or too low (Bonvillani et al., 2006).

Blend time is typically measured experimentally using dye tracer and/or conductivity methods (Zhang et al., 2009). In these methods, the bioreactor is filled with water and the agitation rate is varied over a range of rotational speeds. In a dye tracer experiment, a visual method is used to determine the time required for a small quantity of dye solution to reach a uniform concentration inside the tank. In a conductivity experiment, one or more conductivity probes record the concentration of a salt tracer solution with respect to time. The blend time is defined as the time required for these measures to achieve 95% uniformity.

14.3.2.2 Mass transfer coefficient

For aerobic processes, sufficient levels of oxygen must be maintained in the liquid phase to support cell growth. A mass transfer coefficient quantifies the rate of mass transfer between the gas phase and the liquid phase as a function of process conditions. As shown in Fig. 14.4, oxygen molecules in an air bubble must overcome the gas–liquid boundary layer surrounding the bubble before entering the liquid phase (Stoker, 2011). Dissolved oxygen then travels from regions of high concentration near the bubble surface to regions of low concentration near the biological cells, where oxygen is consumed. The rate at which the oxygen transfer takes place is termed the oxygen transfer rate (OTR), which is calculated as (Oosterhuis and Kossen, 1984):

$$\mathrm{OTR} = k_L a\ (C^* - C), \tag{14.20}$$

where C^* is the solubility limit, C is the local DO concentration, k_L is the volumetric mass transfer coefficient, and a is the interfacial area of the gas phase. The combination of $k_L{}^*a$ (commonly referred as k_La) quantifies the oxygen transfer efficiency of a bioreactor and is used by industry to ensure that oxygen transfer is not a limiting factor during scale-up.

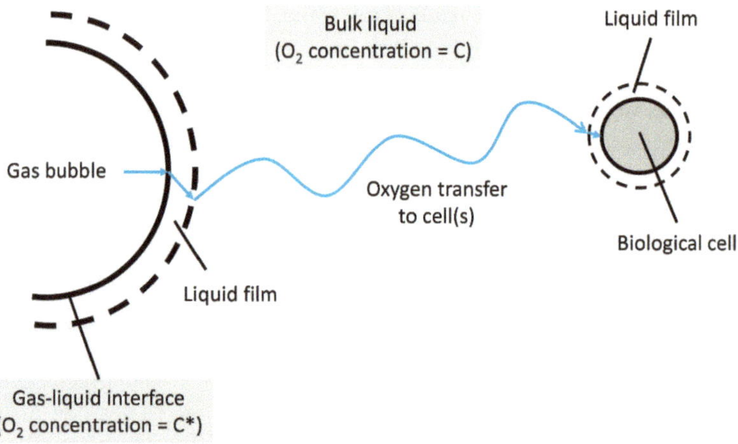

Figure 14.4 Barriers to mass transfer of oxygen from a gas bubble to a suspended cell.

There are several methods to experimentally measure k_La (Garcia-Ochoa and Gomez, 2009), the most popular being the unsteady DO-probe measurement (Wisee, 1951). In this method, an empty reactor is filled with water and then sparged with nitrogen to remove DO from the liquid phase. Airflow is then started and the oxygen concentration in the liquid is recorded in time. Plotting DO versus time yields a straight line with a slope of negative k_La. This method is beneficial because it is simple, there are no chemical additives required, and it can be applied to many different media types.

14.3.2.3 Just suspension speed

Just suspension speed is relevant when mammalian cells are attached to microcarriers. In this scenario, the speed of the agitator should be maintained at a level high enough to prevent settling of the microcarriers. The minimum rotational speed required to keep the solids suspended is termed the just suspension speed, N_{js}, which is typically defined as the impeller speed at which no particle remains stationary at the bottom of the tank for more than 1 or 2 s (Zwietering, 1958). Experimentally, just suspension speed is measured through a visual inspection method (Gohel et al., 2012; Zhu and Wu, 2002).

14.3.3 CFD modeling of mixing in bioreactors

Researchers and design engineers alike utilize a hierarchy of CFD models to study bioreactor performance. This hierarchy may be categorized based on the complexity of the physical model(s) employed. For example, the simplest analysis is single-phase, isothermal mixing. Simulation complexity increases with the inclusion of additional phases, biological reactions, heat transfer, and/or other transport phenomena. The additional complexity provides more information about process performance, typically at the cost of increased simulation time. In many cases, design engineers can rely on less complex physical models to characterize mixing. The following sections discuss the application and relative benefits of single-phase and multiphase approaches for characterizing the mixing environment in a bioreactor.

14.3.3.1 Single-phase analysis

Single-phase CFD studies provide an understanding of the fluid flow patterns inside a mixing tank due to the rotation of one or more impellers. Both steady and unsteady numerical approaches are available to model impeller rotation. The multiple reference frame (MRF) method is a steady-state approach in which the tank is decomposed into rotating and nonrotating (stationary) zones. In the rotating zone, impeller rotation is modeled using a frozen rotor approach. The MRF method is viable when rotating and stationary components, such as baffles, are not in close proximity and/or there are weak interactions between the impeller and fixed components. The sliding mesh method is a more rigorous approach because the transient motion of the impeller is explicitly modeled. This method utilizes more computational resources because the solution is unsteady, but is required when the impeller(s) and neighboring components are in close proximity. Either of these approaches can provide the following insights into mixing tank performance.

Flow patterns

One of the greatest strengths of CFD for mixing tank design is that it provides detailed visualization of the flow field throughout the entire tank interior. As shown in Figs. 14.5 and 14.6, these results can provide several insights into the mixing quality inside a bioreactor. For example, Fig. 14.5A shows how fluid enters the impeller region axially and exits radially toward the vessel wall. This motion sets up a highly organized recirculation pattern throughout the tank. And the close-up view of the region below the impellers in Fig. 14.5B suggests the presence of a low velocity zone near the tank bottom. These regions are important to identify as potential locations for increased blend times and solids build-up. In addition to bulk flow patterns, examining the velocity and pressure fields near an impeller can provide insights into impeller performance. For example, Fig. 14.6A shows a low-pressure region (blue color) in the wake of a Rushton turbine, which can lead to cavitation during gas sparging. Low-pressure regions can be eliminated using a curved-blade impeller (Fig. 14.6B). These impellers also tend to exhibit reduced wake formation versus a flat-blade Rushton impeller.

CFD postprocessing also enables visualization of other flow-related parameters. For example, turbulence dissipation refers to the rate at which turbulent kinetic energy is converted to thermal (internal) energy. This parameter is useful because a certain level of turbulence will improve heat and mass transfer, but an excess can damage biological cells. Fig. 14.7 shows contours of turbulence dissipation rate at

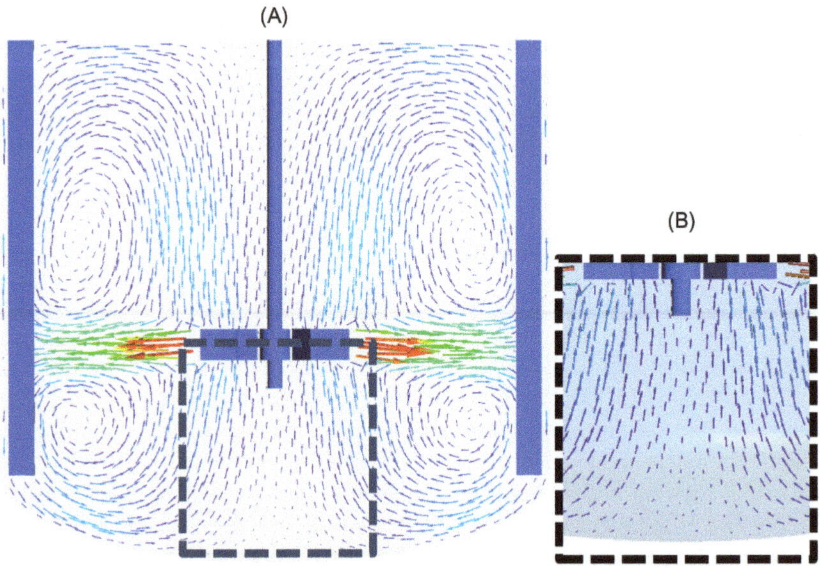

Figure 14.5 (A) Cross-sectional view of the velocity vectors inside a bioreactor reveals two recirculation regions separated by the impeller and (B) a close-up view of the region beneath the impeller illustrates the potential for low speed flow near the tank bottom.

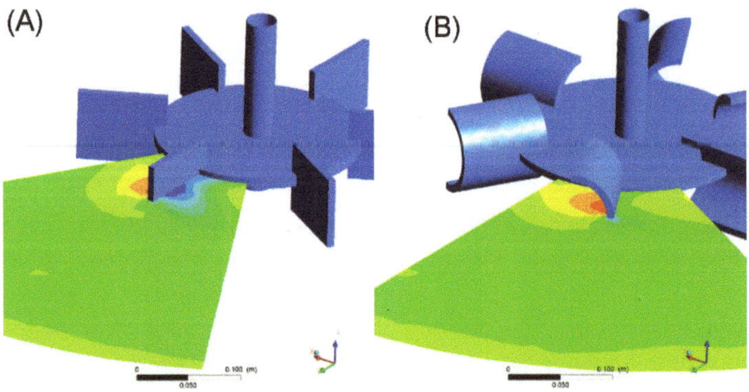

Figure 14.6 Pressure contours in the vicinity of a (A) Rushton impeller and (B) curved impeller (both impellers rotating in the clockwise direction).

different scales and operating conditions; this analysis helps to ensure similarity of the shear and mass transfer behavior during scale-up.

Blend time analysis

Blend time can be studied numerically in both single-phase and multiphase systems. But experimental data are typically collected for single-phase systems,

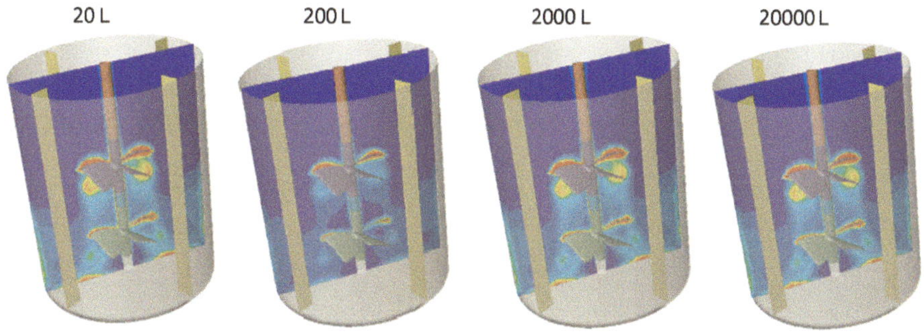

Figure 14.7 Comparison of turbulence dissipation rate simulation results showing the similarity of turbulence across four tank scales. The dissipation rate scale ranges from 0 (blue) – 0.01 (red) m^2/m^3 in all contour plots.

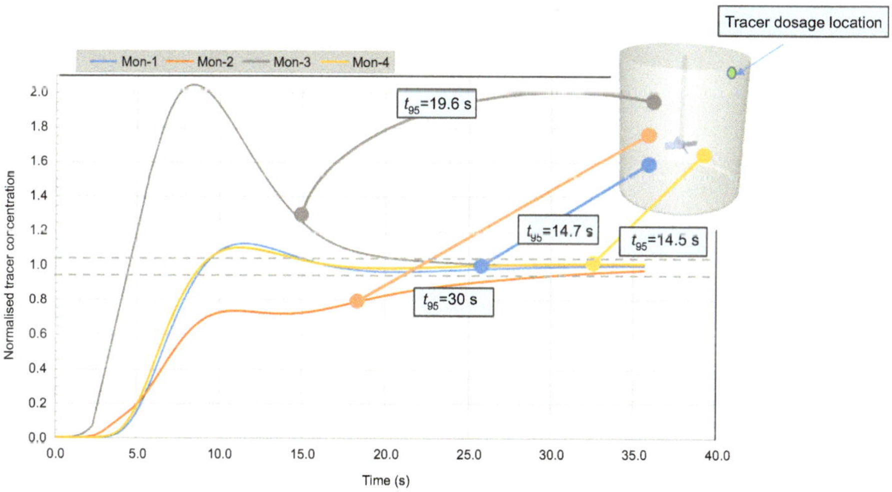

Figure 14.8 CFD analysis of blend time at various locations in a mixing tank.

hence, the corresponding single-phase CFD simulations are more frequently studied. As stated in Section 14.3.2.1, experimental techniques utilize a visual method or conductivity probe to track the dispersal of a tracer inside a bioreactor. In CFD, a bolus of passive tracer can be initialized at one or more feed locations and then advected using a scalar transport equation (see Fig. 14.8 for an example). Blend time is defined as the time when the tracer concentration reaches 90 or 95% of the final (homogenized) value. A range of blend times will be observed in this approach; as a conservative estimate, it is common practice to use the largest observed value of blend time as a prediction for the blend time of the bioreactor.

Impeller performance data

CFD simulations can provide quantitative insights into impeller performance through calculation of the flow number, N_Q, and the power number, N_P. These nondimensional numbers form the basis for several correlations that permit the comparison of various tank designs.

The flow number, N_Q, is a measure of the pumping capacity of an impeller, it is defined as

$$N_Q = \frac{Q_l}{ND^3}, \tag{14.21}$$

where Q_l is the net outward flow through a surface surrounding the impeller (i.e., impeller discharge), D is the impeller diameter, and N is the frequency of impeller rotation, in Hz.

Once the flow number is calculated for a given impeller type, Eq. (14.21) can be rearranged to calculate impeller discharge at any other rpm or impeller diameter without running additional CFD simulations. Impeller discharge can then be used to calculate the turnover time, t_{TO}:

$$t_{TO} = \frac{V}{Q_l}, \tag{14.22}$$

where V is the reactor volume. Note that turnover time can be used as an empirical estimate of blend time in the absence of CFD simulation or experimental data.

The power number, N_P, is a measure of the power requirements of an impeller, and is defined as

$$N_P = \frac{P_I}{\rho N^3 D^5}, \tag{14.23}$$

where P_I is the power applied to the impeller. Standard correlations are available to estimate N_P based on the Reynolds number. Thus, if CFD is not available, the power requirements can generally be obtained from one of these established correlations (Paul et al., 2004). It is important to note, however, that these correlations break down if they do not account for the presence and spacing of multiple impellers or the D/T or C/T ratios of single impellers, where C is the liquid height and T is the tank diameter. In such cases, the power drawn by the impeller is estimated from the torque as

$$P_I = 2\,\pi\,N\,\tau, \tag{14.24}$$

where CFD results for the pressure exerted on the impeller blades are used to estimate the torque, τ (Marshall and Bakker, 2004).

More complex parameters like the mass transfer coefficient, gas hold-up, and others can be estimated from N_Q, N_P, and the average turbulence dissipation rate (Tomáš et al., 2003). Therefore, single-phase CFD simulations can provide a wealth of information in a relatively short amount of time, while more accurate estimates of mass transfer require multiphase gas–liquid experiments and/or CFD simulation.

14.3.3.2 Multiphase analysis

In a bioreactor, the liquid phase is the primary phase that hosts the rest of the bioreactor contents. Except for very small bioreactors, where surface aeration is sufficient, oxygen is supplied to living cells through gas sparging. Hence, at least two phases—liquid and gas—are always present in a bioreactor. And in those cases where mammalian cells are attached to solid bead microcarriers, the solid beads constitute a third phase.

As mentioned in Section 14.2.1.5, multiphase flow models consist of a primary phase and one or more secondary phases. Broadly, there are two methods to model multiphase flows in a bioreactor:

1. Eulerian–Lagrangian (E–L): The Eulerian–Lagrangian method, also referred to as the discrete phase model, tracks the gas phase in the Lagrangian frame. This method is very fast to converge and provides a qualitative view of the gas distribution inside the tank. The primary limitation of this method is that the interaction between gas bubbles is not taken into account. Hence, predictions based on this model are assumed to lose accuracy in regions where the volume fraction of gas exceeds 10%.
2. Eulerian–Eulerian (E–E): The Eulerian set of methods provide the most accurate approach for modeling gas sparging and particle suspension. All phases are solved in the Eulerian frame and the interactions between each phase are modeled through drag forces. Other interaction forces are also available but are typically negligible for this class of applications. And unlike the E–L method, there are no volume fraction limitations in this approach.

   The two most common types of E–E simulations of gas sparging are classified based on how the bubble diameter is modeled:

   a. Constant bubble diameter: A single bubble diameter or distribution of bubble diameters are specified at the beginning of the calculation and remain fixed throughout the calculation, i.e., breakup and coalescence are not modeled. While this is an approximation, these simulations are useful for qualitative comparisons between different operating conditions and different geometries.
   b. Variable bubble diameter: Bubble diameters are calculated by modeling breakup and coalescence using the population balance method (PBM). This is by far the most accurate CFD method for bioreactor modeling (Werner et al., 2014). The primary limitation is the significant computational resources required to perform these calculations. But with the increasing availability of compute resources, the use of this method is now prevalent in industry.

In addition to information about the flow field, multiphase simulations provide following information specific to the distribution of the gas phase in the bioreactor.

Gas distribution

CFD simulations calculate the amount of gas present at all locations in the bioreactor as a standard output. Using postprocessing tools, one can visualize the gas distribution on two-dimensional (2D) planes or throughout the entire tank using three-dimensional (3D) rendering, as shown in Fig. 14.9.

Figure 14.9 A 3D rendering of the gas distribution inside a mixing tank.

Bubble size distribution

The PBM provides the user with an estimate of the bubble size distribution throughout the tank. Similar to the gas distribution, the bubble size distribution can be plotted at various locations. For example, the mixing analysis in Fig. 14.10 shows the presence of smaller bubbles near the impellers and larger bubbles in other regions of the tank.

Mass transfer rate (k_La)

As described in Section 14.3.2.2, k_La is the product of the local mass transfer coefficient, k_L, and the interfacial area available for mass transfer, a. k_L can be calculated using Higbie's penetration model (Dhanasekharan et al., 2005):

$$k_L = \frac{2}{\pi}\sqrt{D_{O_2}}\left(\frac{\varepsilon\rho_L}{\mu L}\right), \tag{14.25}$$

where D_{O_2} is diffusion coefficient of oxygen in liquid, ε is turbulence dissipation rate in the liquid phase, ρ_L is liquid density, and μ_L is liquid viscosity. The equation for interfacial area is given by

$$a = \frac{6\alpha_G}{d_{32}}, \tag{14.26}$$

where α_G is gas volume fraction and d_{32} is the Sauter mean diameter (SMD) obtained from the PBM. The combination of these two parameters provides an understanding of the ability of the bioreactor to support cell growth as a function of bioreactor design and process conditions.

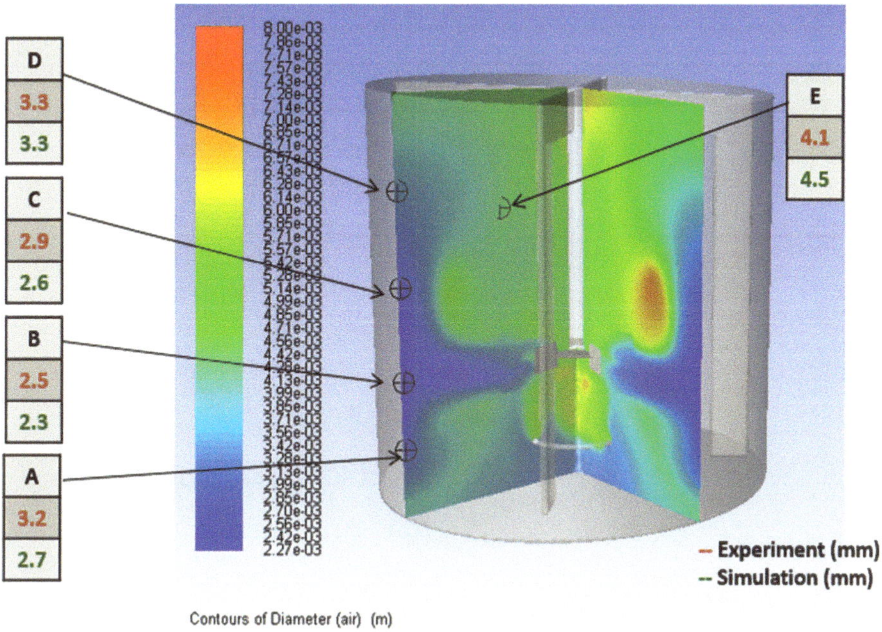

Figure 14.10 Comparison of experimental and CFD results for the bubble size distribution in a stirred tank using the PBM to model gas bubble breakup and coalescence.

14.3.4 Case study: Creating a design space for QbD using simulation

The concept of design space plays an integral part in the implementation of QbD for pharmaceutical products (Rathore et al., 2012). The design space of a process or unit operation is defined as the combination of input parameters and process parameters that ensure product quality. The design space for a particular unit operation is typically developed based on experimental inputs, requiring significant material costs and engineering resources. CFD simulations are increasingly being used to carry out virtual design of experiments (DOE), aka "design of simulations", studies to establish the design space. As an example, this section outlines a case study by (Rathore et al., 2012), where CFD is utilized to identify the design space for an oxygen mass transfer process in a bioreactor. Their DOE study aims to understand the effect of impeller speed, gas flow rate, and liquid height on k_La, the results of which are used to establish the design space.

14.3.4.1 Problem description

The geometry and computational grid used in this case study are shown in Fig. 14.11. The tank is a 3 L Brunswick BioFlo 110 reactor with a diameter of 12.5 cm and a 2 L working volume. The impeller is attached to a 1 cm central shaft and has three blades pitched at 45 degrees. The air sparger is a 4 cm ring with six

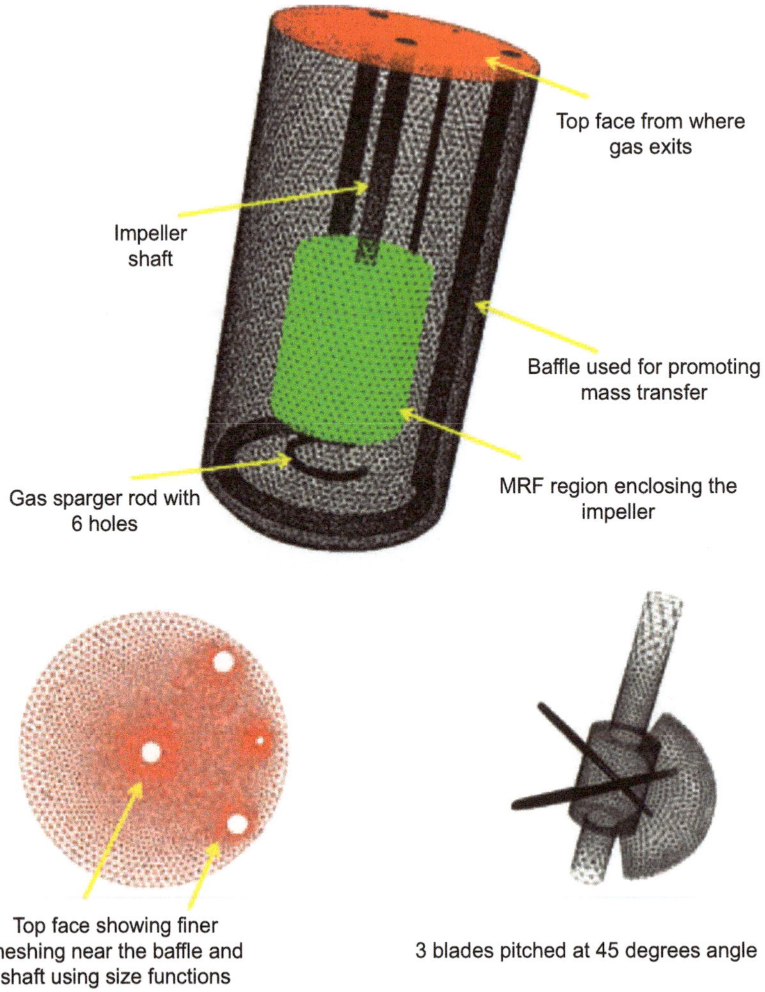

Figure 14.11 Geometry and mesh for the bioreactor simulations in (Rathore et al., 2012).

holes of 0.1 cm diameter each and is positioned 5 cm under the impeller. The geometry was discretized using a hybrid mesh consisting of a mixture of 843,008 tetrahedral, hexahedral, and wedge elements.

14.3.4.2 Model setup

The authors utilized the MRF (fixed rotor) approach to model impeller rotation. The dispersed $k-\varepsilon$ turbulent model was used to model turbulence. The E–E multiphase model with population balance was used to model gas–liquid transport. Only the bubble breakage and coalescence kernels were utilized in the population balance, i.e., bubble nucleation and growth were not included. A 3 mm bubble size was applied as a boundary condition at the sparger inlet. An isothermal assumption permitted the use of constant material properties for the air and water phases.

14.3.4.3 Results

Simulation results were analyzed for each operating condition to characterize bioreactor performance. Fig. 14.12 summarizes results for one set of operating conditions. Fig. 14.12A shows k_La contours along a tank midplane. The average k_La was calculated to be 0.0174 s^{-1}, which is in agreement with the reported experimental value of 0.0169 s^{-1}. Fig. 14.12B shows contours of SMD (d_{32}) on the same contour plane as was used in Fig. 14.12A. The volume-averaged value of d_{32} is reported to be 3.61 mm, suggesting that coalescence is more prevalent than bubble

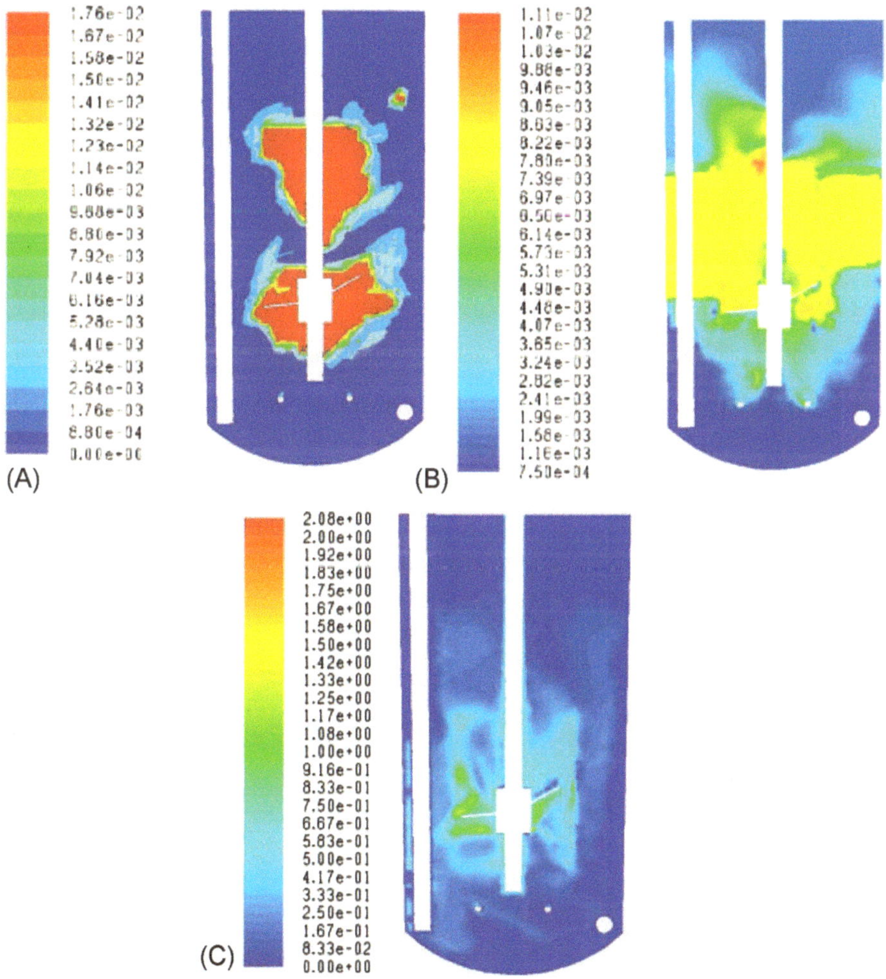

Figure 14.12 Contours of (A) mass transfer coefficient (k_La), (B) bubble size distribution, and (C) gas speed (Rathore et al., 2012).

breakup for this set of operating conditions. Lastly, Fig. 14.12C shows that the speed of the gas phase is highest in the vicinity of the impeller.

Upon completion of the initial simulation studies, the authors extended the study to investigate the relationship between operating conditions and k_La. A virtual DOE was performed, which was comprised of 18 simulations at different gas flow rates, agitation rates, and liquid levels. The data obtained from the DOE study was fit to an empirical expression of the following functional form:

$$k_La = f(\text{RPM}^*\text{liquid level}^*\text{gas flow rate}) \quad (14.27)$$

Statistical analysis suggested that gas flow rate had the greatest impact on k_La, while liquid level had limited impact. It is important to note, however, that the statistical model is only valid for the system in question and in the ranges of the independent parameters that were examined.

14.3.4.4 Estimating the design space

Design space is defined by ICH Q8 (ICH Harmonised Tripartite Guideline Pharmaceutical Development Q8(R2), 2009) as "the multidimensional combination and interaction of input variables (e.g., material attributes) and process parameters that have been demonstrated to provide assurance of quality." A process operating within the design space is considered to be operating under acceptable conditions, while any movement out of the design space is considered a change in process conditions. A regulatory post-approval change process would be initiated if such a change were desired.

The design space for a particular unit operation is typically developed based on experimental inputs, requiring significant material costs and engineering resources. However, a virtual design space can be established based on Eq. (14.27). One example is shown in Fig. 14.13, where Rathore et al. (2012) plotted acceptable operating condition combinations in white and unacceptable combinations in red. This information could then be used for process development, for continual process monitoring, and for evaluating potential new operating set-points that might enhance process performance without triggering a regulatory assessment. Therefore, combining CFD with statistical analysis provides a lower cost alternative that can yield a deeper and more robust understanding of process performance.

14.4 Liquid chromatography

14.4.1 Introduction

Liquid chromatography concentrates and purifies proteins, while removing impurities, from a cell culture harvest. This unit operation is the workhorse of purification in the biotechnology industry because it is flexible, robust, scalable, and economical. It is robust in that it can maintain product quality and impurity clearance requirements in spite of minor process disturbances, such as the natural variability in cell culture performance that occurs during production. This unit operation is routinely scaled up from column diameters as small as 1 cm to 1 m, which proves

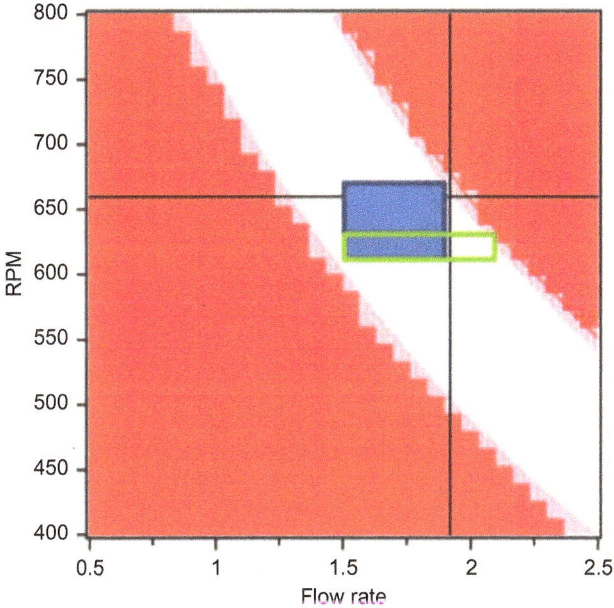

Figure 14.13 Contour plot showing the design space as a function of impeller agitation rate (RPM) and flow rate. The white region represents acceptable combinations of RPM and flow rate; operating in the red region will result in unacceptable mass transfer to the liquid phase (Rathore et al., 2012).

its highly scalable nature. And from an economic point of view, resins are very expensive, but the ability to reuse resin for up to hundreds of cycles makes it an economically feasible operation.

In a typical chromatography operation, resin beads (stationary phase) are first packed into a column, forming a packed bed. Next, the liquid media (mobile phase) is passed through the packed bed. Resin is comprised of micron to submillimeter diameter beads made up of structural materials, such as cellulose and ceramic. These materials have large surface area, high porosity and enough strength to withstand the high pressures and flow rates encountered during normal operation. In addition to these structural responsibilities, the external and internal bead surfaces are functionalized with ligands that can have attractive or repulsive interactions with the protein and/or impurities. These interactions can be modulated based on environmental factors such as pH, conductivity, etc. Additionally, a variety of resin chemistries are available, which allow for flexibility and optimal selection of a resin that addresses the specific needs of each drug molecule.

Liquid buffers are used in different steps of a chromatography operation to modulate the physicochemical environment in the column. For example, in a typical bind and elute operation, the impure load material (containing protein and impurities) is passed through the column. The protein of interest is preferentially adsorbed on the resin and impurities flow through the column. The protein is then eluted off the resin by changing column conditions, such as pH and conductivity, using a different buffer.

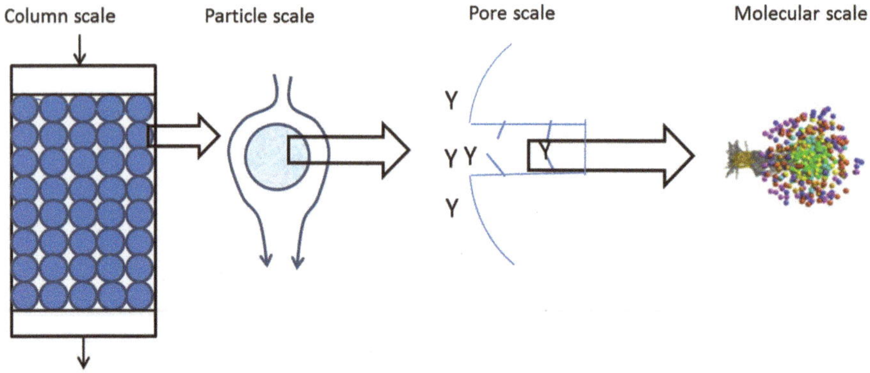

Figure 14.14 Illustration of the multiphysics, multiscale nature of chromatographic separation. *Source*: Molecular scale image from Hiranoa, A., Maruyamab, T., Shirakib, K., Arakawac, T., Kameda, T., 2014. Mechanism of protein desorption from 4-mercaptoethylpyridine resins by arginine solutions. J. Chromatogr. A 1373, 141−148.

As shown in Fig. 14.14, comprehensive modeling of the entire chromatography operation requires a multiphysics, multiscale approach. On a macroscopic scale, the flow through the packed column can be modeled using CFD (Malang et al., 2015). The mass transfer of protein to the external bead surface and subsequent diffusion through pores requires modeling at the particle and pore scales (Reck et al., 2015). Protein binding to the bead ligands requires molecular-level modeling (Hiranoa et al., 2014). And while examples can be found in the literature for modeling behavior at a particular scale, comprehensive models tying all these phenomena together are rare and are mostly academic (Wu et al., 2004). Industrial utilization of modeling is limited to primarily empirical or statistical models, such as transition analysis and multivariate analysis.

CFD models have been widely used to model liquid flow through packed columns. These models can help identify the sources of nonideal flow behavior, such as channeling, which can reduce separation efficiency. However, very few studies have examined the effect of column hardware, e.g., the liquid distributer and inlet/outlet geometry, on column flow patterns (Rousseau, 1987). Improper packing can also adversely affect column efficiency. For example, Dorn and Hekmat (2016) used CFD to investigate how resin properties such as size distribution, porosity, and heterogeneity in packing can influence peak broadening. CFD has also been used to develop a more complex model that incorporates fluid flow (axial dispersion effects), mass transfer and adsorption phenomenon (Wu et al., 2004). In this case, the authors showed that the separation efficiency of a two-component system decreased with increased axial dispersion and slower mass transfer rates. These examples show that CFD is a promising tool for achieving uniform flow in the column. And while there are currently very few examples illustrating how multiphysics CFD modeling (flow, mass transfer and adsorption) can offer deeper understanding of this process (Wu et al., 2004), the hope is that multiphysics modeling gains more momentum as computational power increases.

14.4.2 Non-CFD modeling of chromatography

In this section, a simplified mass balance is developed by assuming that the packed chromatography column can be represented by a single dimension along the column axis. Therefore, the mass balance equation has two independent variables: time, t and axial distance along the column, z. The concentration of component i in the mobile phase at distance z and time t is represented by $C_i(t,z)$. The equilibrium concentration in the stationary phase is given by $C_{s,i}$. The mobile phase flows through the column with velocity u. Nonidealities in the flow are characterized by axial dispersion D_i. The total interparticle and intraparticle void fraction in the packed bed is ε.

A material balance yields the following transport equation (Guiochon et al., 2006)

$$\frac{\partial C_i}{\partial t} + u\frac{\partial C_i}{\partial t} = D_i\frac{\partial^2 C_i}{\partial z^2} - \frac{1-\varepsilon}{\varepsilon}\frac{\partial C_{s,i}}{\partial t}, \tag{14.28}$$

where the first term represents the rate of accumulation of component i in the mobile phase, the second term is a convective term, the third term is a dispersive term, and the fourth term represents the amount of material adsorbed onto the stationary phase. This equation contains two unknowns C_i and $C_{s,i}$. Hence, an additional equation is needed to describe relationship between these two concentrations. In the equilibrium-dispersive model, the relationship between the mobile and stationary phase concentrations can be described by an equilibrium isotherm if the mass transfer is not rate-limiting:

$$C_{s,i} = q_i = f(C_i), \tag{14.29}$$

where $f(C_i)$ depends on the nature of the isotherm. For example, a linear isotherm can be described by

$$q_i = k\,C_i, \tag{14.30a}$$

where k is a partition coefficient. Alternatively, a Langmuir isotherm can be described by

$$q_i = \frac{a\,C_i}{1 + b\,C_i}, \tag{14.30b}$$

where a and b are two empirical constants, which are typically determined by fitting to experimental data.

Initial conditions ordinarily assume that the product concentration is zero throughout the column:

$$C_i(z, t = 0) = 0. \tag{14.31}$$

The inlet boundary condition can be given by

$$C_i(z=0,t) = C_i^0 p(t), \tag{14.32a}$$

where C_i^0 is the concentration at the inlet and $p(t)$ is a probability distribution function describing the injection profile. The probability distribution function can describe a variety of profiles, such as spike or step injections. For example, a step injection can be written as

$$C_i(z=0,t) = C_i^0 \quad \text{for} \quad 0 \le t \le t_p \tag{14.32b}$$

$$C_i(z=0,t) = 0 \quad \text{for} \quad t > t_p \tag{14.32c}$$

Eqs. (14.28)–(14.32a) constitute the equilibrium-dispersive model of chromatography. The solution of this system of equations is shown in Fig. 14.15. As illustrated, inclusion of the axial dispersion term results in peak broadening and using the Langmuir isotherm for equilibrium results in peak tailing.

In industry, it is common practice to use height equivalent of theoretical plate (HETP, H) to characterize peak broadening. The relationship between HETP and the dispersion coefficient is

$$H = \frac{2\,D_i}{u} \tag{14.33}$$

The equilibrium-dispersive model assumes that component i in the stationary phase is always in equilibrium with the mobile phase. In other words, the mass transfer rate and adsorption kinetics are assumed to be instantaneous. These assumptions can be relaxed to obtain more accurate results, but at a cost of more complex models. As an example, the lumped kinetic model assumes mass transfer is not rate-limiting. The unsteady state stationary phase concentration can be described by the following classical adsorption-desorption kinetics rate expression,

$$\frac{\partial C_{S,i}}{\partial t} = k_a\, C_i(q_{s,i} - C_{s,i}) - k_d C_{S,i}, \tag{14.34}$$

where k_a is the rate constant for adsorption, k_d is the rate constant for desorption, and $q_{s,i}$ is the maximum adsorption capacity.

14.4.3 Model applications

Bak et al. used the lumped kinetic parameter model to predict initial breakthrough of antibodies captured from a complex feedstock (Bak et al., 2007). They found that adsorption was well described by a Langmuir isotherm for all the adsorbents

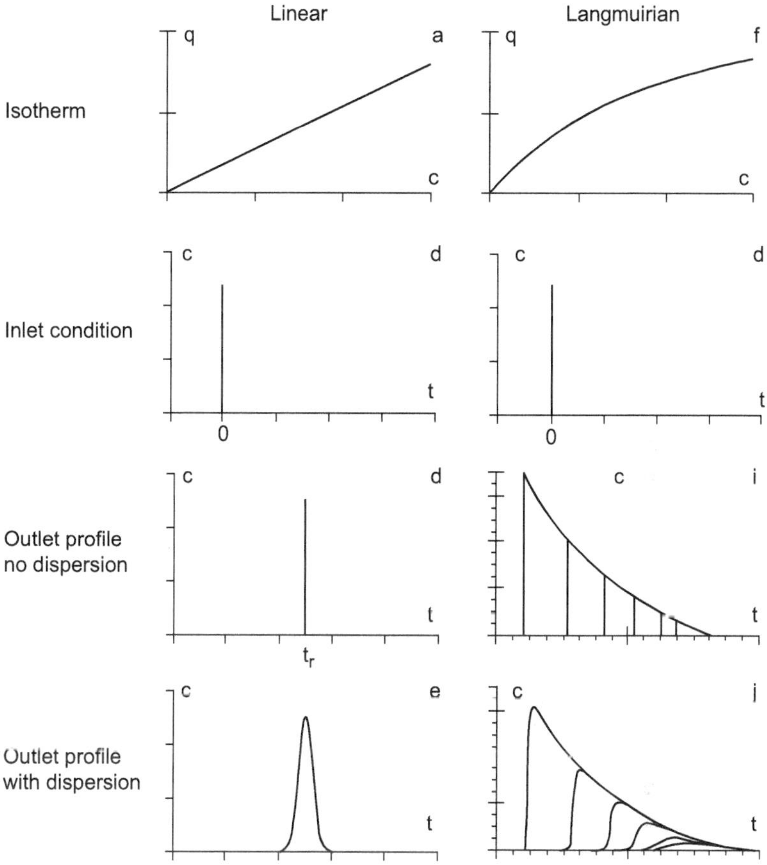

Figure 14.15 The relationship between equilibrium-dispersive model assumptions for the equilibrium isotherm and outlet concentration.
Source: Modified from (Guiochon et al., 2006).

studied. But the dynamic predictions from kinetic adsorption were in good agreement with the data only during the initial portion of the breakthrough. They attributed the discrepancy to the sensitivity of fitted parameters to the experimental noise.

Noriega et al. used the lumped kinetic parameter model to study the effect of regeneration condition on column performance (Noriega et al., 1997). They found that the forward adsorption rate constant, k_a, increased with increasing exposure time to cleaning buffer, but that the selectivity decreased with increasing exposure time. Therefore, this model enabled the authors to determine a mechanistic reason for decreasing selectivity, which was the loss of adsorbent capacity and not a change in adsorption kinetics.

14.4.4 Industry perspective

Knowledge of the governing principles of purification processes are well known by industry. The model equations describing the chromatography operation and the techniques to solve these equations are also well established. In spite of these facts, modeling is not routinely used during industrial purification process development. The main hurdle that limits the use of modeling is the large number of parameter values required as input to the model. Some of these parameters depend on the operating conditions and need to be estimated or measured for a particular scenario, e.g., parameters related to mass transfer depend on the flow rate, resin porosity, buffer viscosity, and size of the protein molecule. Parameters related to protein and ligand interactions are typically specific to the protein–ligand combination and are very difficult to estimate. As a result, a large number of experiments may be needed to estimate these parameters before a model can be effectively used to reduce the number of developmental experiments. This apparent dilemma can be tackled by practicing smart development strategies which take advantage of high throughput experiments, models and heuristic rules of thumb (Hanke and Ottens, 2014; Nfor et al., 2009).

14.5 Lyophilization (freeze drying)

14.5.1 Introduction

Lyophilization, also known as freeze drying, is frequently the final unit operation in the biologics manufacturing process. This operation removes water from the product so that it remains stable for an extended period of time (6–24 months) under ambient conditions. Lyophilization is one of the most energy intensive, and therefore expensive, unit operations. And the economic impact is magnified because the drug substance used during development has been processed through all the previous manufacturing steps; hence, any failure at this stage can be very expensive and is therefore highly undesirable.

In general, the fundamental physics of lyophilization are well understood and it is possible to carefully design this process to avoid failures during scale-up. The major challenge during development of a lyophilization process is the limited availability of the raw material (drug substance). Since this is the last step in the process, material generated in the bioreactor needs to be fully processed through the entire downstream train to make material for lyophilization testing. But yield losses during the various purification steps, and the large amount of resources needed for processing, typically limits development to batches of 10–100 vials. The process is later scaled up to manufacturing scale, which can range from 10,000–100,000 vials per batch. Scale-up is challenging because at the larger scales temperature differences between the wall and the center of the chamber are more drastic than at smaller scales, which exaggerates the vial-to-vial variation. Process modeling offers a solution to the aforementioned challenges by reducing trial-and-error and hence the number of experiments. This enables development with a limited amount of drug

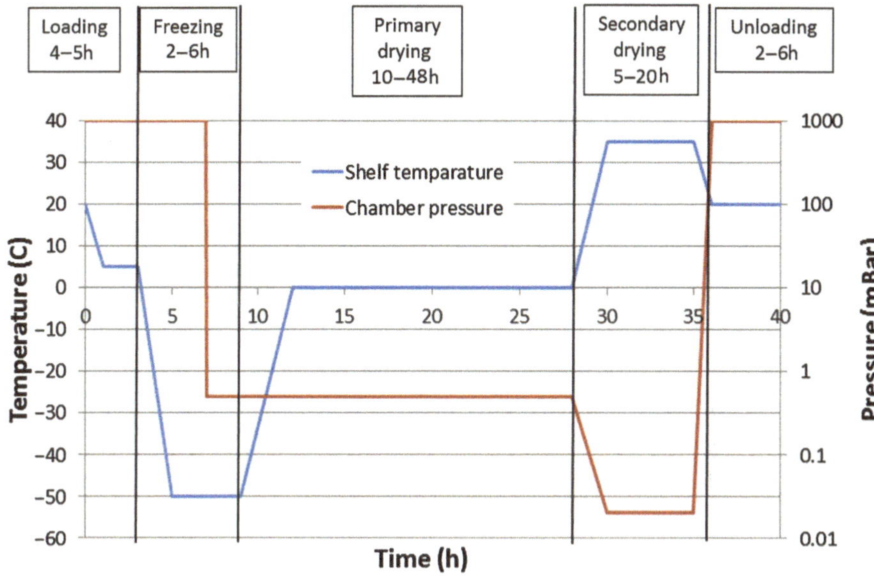

Figure 14.16 Temperature and pressure profiles of a typical lyophilization cycle.

substance. Models can also help to predict the effect of scale-up a priori, thus reducing the risk of failure.

The freeze drying process consists of a number of steps or cycles. Initially, the formulated drug substance is filled into small (5–30 mL) vials. The vials are half-stoppered and placed in the freeze drying chamber. Chamber temperature and pressure are manipulated through a series of temperature and pressure cycles, as shown in Fig. 14.16. First, the temperature is decreased below the freezing point and the material in the vial is allowed to freeze. Then, a vacuum is applied to the chamber and the temperature increased to initiate ice sublimation. This is called the primary drying process and can take several hours to a couple of days to complete. At the end of the primary drying cycle, the pressure is dropped further and the temperature is increased (typically in the range of 30–60°C) to drive off residual bound moisture from the cake by desorption. This process is called secondary drying and is the final processing step. It is important to note that the temperature of the material in the vial should be maintained below the glass transition temperature to avoid product damage. It is also important to note that not only the temperature and pressure set-points for each step, but also the rate at which the temperature and pressure are changed, both play a key role in the outcome of the process.

14.5.2 Non-CFD modeling of lyophilization

Non-CFD modeling of freeze drying often relies on a lumped-parameter approach to account for the simultaneous heat and mass transfer phenomena occurring in the vial.

This type of analysis begins by identifying the various transport resistances. For example, the heat provided by the shelf is conducted through the vial wall to the subliming ice. The rate of heat transfer depends on a heat transfer coefficient that accounts for both conductive and radiative heat transfer. And the ice sublimation process depends on the rate at which vapor can clear the vial to make room for new vapor. This clearance process involves water vapor leaving the dried cake, exiting the vial through the stopper, and ultimately depositing on the condenser. And while the heat and mass transfer steps can be discussed individually, they are not independent factors. Rather, they are coupled at steady state, such that the rate of heat transfer is exactly equal to the amount of heat needed to sustain the rate of mass transfer.

A simplified steady-state macroscopic heat and mass transfer model was proposed by Pikal et al. (1984). Their model accounts for the various heat and mass transfer resistances depicted in Fig. 14.17 as follows. First, the resistance of the dried product layer, R_P, is

$$R_p = (P_0 - P_v)/\dot{m}, \tag{14.35}$$

where P_0 is equilibrium vapor pressure of subliming ice, P_v is the water vapor pressure in the vial, and $\dot{m}$ is the rate of ice sublimation.

In the semi-stoppered case, the mass transfer resistance of the gap between the stopper and the vial, R_S, is

$$R_S = (P_V - P_C)/\dot{m}, \tag{14.36}$$

where P_C is the chamber pressure.

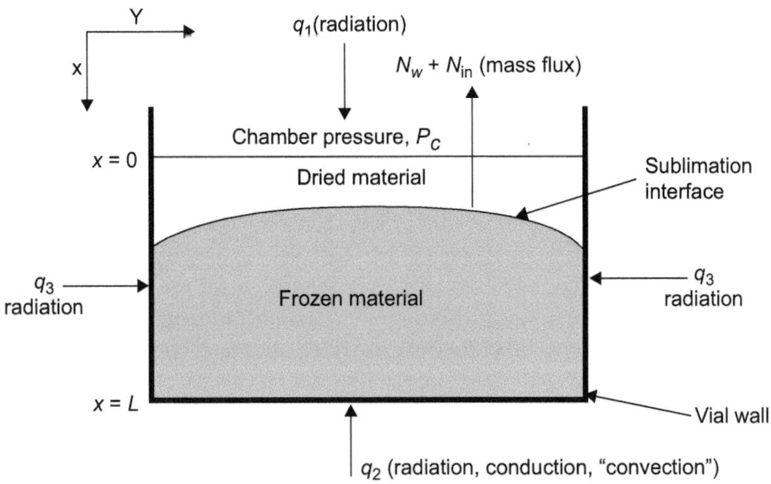

Figure 14.17 Schematic of the heat and mass transfer resistances in a freeze dryer (Pikal et al., 2005).

The resistance between the chamber and the condenser is

$$R_C = (P_C - P_{CD})/\dot{m}, \tag{14.37}$$

where R_C is the chamber resistance and P_{CD} is the condenser pressure.

Combining Eqs. (14.35) through (14.37) gives the rate of ice sublimation,

$$\dot{m} = (P_0 - P_{CD})/R_T, \tag{14.38}$$

where the total resistance, R_T, is the sum of the resistances of the dried cake, stopper, and condenser, i.e., $R_T = R_V + R_S + R_C$.

The rate of heat transfer from the shelf to the subliming ice, $\dot{Q}$, is given by

$$\dot{Q} = A_V K_V (T_S - T_P), \tag{14.39}$$

where A_V is the cross-sectional area of the vial, K_V is the lumped heat transfer coefficient, T_S is the shelf temperature, and T_P is the temperature of the product at the bottom center of the vial. It is important to note that K_V includes the effects of radiative heat transfer, conduction through the glass in contact with shelf, and conduction through the air trapped in the gap between the vial and the shelf. K_V is typically measured experimentally.

Empirically, the vial heat transfer coefficient is a combination of many factors (Pikal et al., 2005)

$$K_V = K_K + \frac{K_P P}{1 + K_D P}, \tag{14.40}$$

where K_K represents contributions from radiative heat transfer and direct contact conduction, K_D accounts for the conduction through the air between the gap in the vial and the shelf, and K_P is a constant that is independent of the vial size or type.

At steady state, the rate of mass transfer can be related to the rate of heat transfer as follows

$$\dot{Q} = \lambda \dot{m}, \tag{14.41}$$

where λ is the latent heat of sublimation.

Substituting Eqs. (14.38) and (14.39) into Eq. (14.41) gives

$$A_V K_V (T_S - T_P) = \lambda (P_0 - P_{CD})/R_T, \tag{14.42}$$

Using a thermodynamic relationship to express P_0 as a function of product temperature reduces Eq. (14.42) to a single equation with only one unknown, T_P. The final form of Eq. (14.42) typically requires a numerical solution to determine the product temperature. It is important to note that the various heat and mass transfer resistances depend on the components of the formulation and the geometry of the vial and process. Therefore, experimental measurements are usually required to establish these resistances for each situation.

14.5.3 Model applications

Lyophilization models have been shown to adequately predict cake temperatures once accurate input parameters are established. For example, Pikal et al. (2005) showed that unsteady heat and mass transfer modeling can yield reasonably accurate predictions of product temperature as a function of drying time, as shown in Fig. 14.18.

(Kodama et al., 2014) used lumped-parameter modeling to optimize the primary drying process. Their goal was to minimize the primary drying time by operating the shelf at the highest possible temperature without exceeding the maximum collapse temperature for the product. This was accomplished by generating contours of maximum product temperature as a function of shelf temperature and chamber pressure (see Fig. 14.19A). Corresponding curves were also created for the drying time as a function of shelf temperature and chamber pressure (see Fig. 14.19B). Using these curves, the optimum shelf temperature and chamber pressure can be easily fixed to obtain the fastest drying conditions. For example, as shown in Fig. 14.19, if the maximum allowed temperature for the product is −31.5°C, then operating the lyophilizer at −8°C shelf temperature and 10 Pa chamber pressure would result in the fastest primary drying time of 19.3 h.

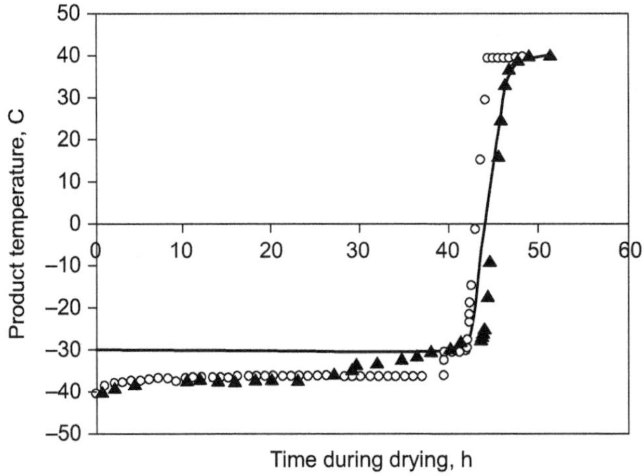

Figure 14.18 Comparison of product temperatures determined from experiment (solid triangles) and model (open circles). The solid line represents the shelf temperature (Pikal et al., 2005).

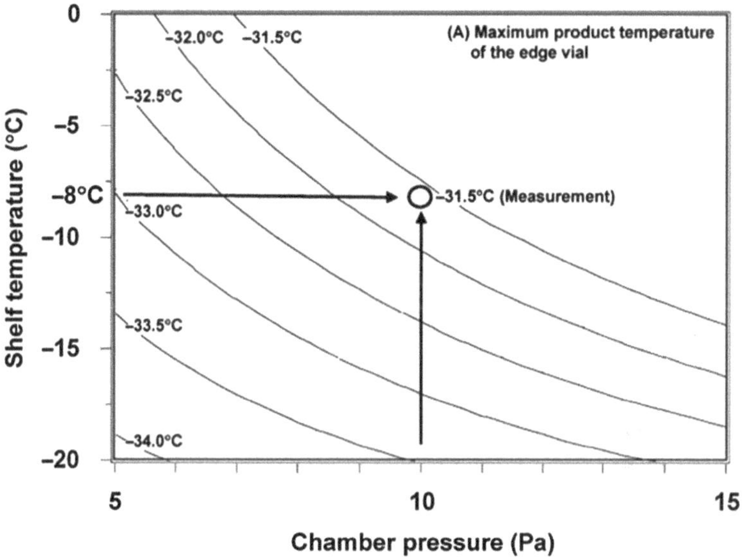

(A)

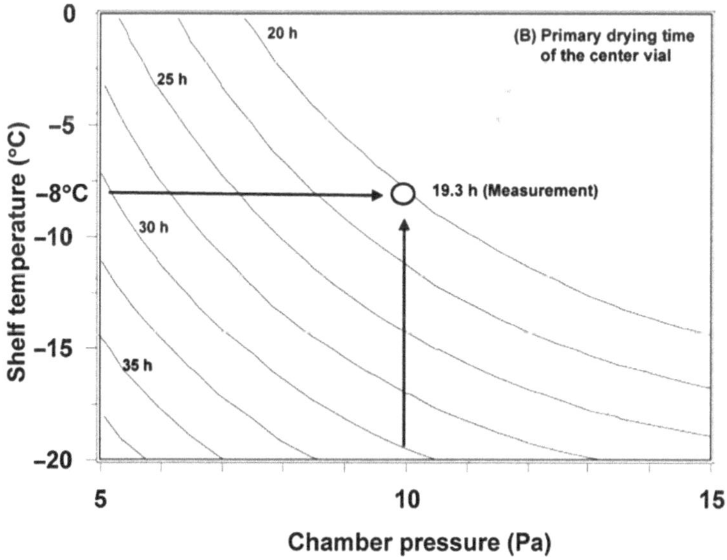

(B)

Figure 14.19 Contour plots showing the relationship between shelf temperature and chamber pressure on (A) the predicted maximum product temperature and (B) the primary drying time (Kodama et al., 2014).

As opposed to macroscopic lumped-parameter models, which assume a uniform state inside the vial, microscopic models have also been developed. These models account for the spatial variation of temperature, location of the subliming ice interface, moisture content and other parameters in the vial. For example, Sheehan and Liapis (Sheehan and Liapis, 1998) developed a 2D model which accounts for variation along the vial height, z, and radius, r. Their model predicted the temperature within the entire vial and the movement of the subliming interface in time. Their recommendation was an aggressive operational strategy utilizing high shelf heating and low side-wall heating to achieve greater uniformity in the temperature distribution and bound water content. Others have used the finite element method (FEM) to understand the heat and mass transport environment within the vial (Mascarenhas et al., 1997; Muzzio and Dini, 2011). For example, Muzzio et al. (Muzzio and Dini, 2011) used FEM to predict not only the temperature distribution but also the mean crystal size throughout the vial.

Modeling is also used to address challenges associated with scale-up of the lyophilization process. For example, the temperatures and pressures experienced by the vials varies to a greater extent at commercial scale because of the ~10–50x increase in shelf size relative to the lab scale. Additionally, the difference between the vial temperature in the center of the shelf and the vial immediately adjacent to the wall is greater at commercial scale due to increased distance from the wall. Pisano, Fissore et al. (2013) used mathematical modeling in conjunction with experimentally derived heat and mass transfer coefficients to scale up a primary drying cycle. The freeze drying cycles were initially developed at lab scale and then, using mathematical modeling, the temperature of the shelf was modified at larger scale to ensure the product temperature in all vials (including vials adjacent to the wall) was always below the critical temperature for cake failure. Chen et al. (2015) used modeling to predict the primary drying time at commercial scale while keeping the operating conditions, including shelf temperature, constant across scales. The authors demonstrated the applicability of their model for a variety of process development and manufacturing activities, including design space, parameter variation, and process deviation studies.

14.5.4 Industry perspective

Freeze drying process models have recently gained ground in the industrial setting, using both general-purpose CFD and application-specific software (Koganti et al., 2011). The lyophilization process lends itself to accurate modeling for the following reasons. The first is that the models are less complex because the mode of action is primarily governed by physics and not by chemistry or biology. Second, the majority of the model input parameters can be readily estimated using simple experiments. And finally, these process models are not computationally intensive and can be easily solved using standard personal computers. Industry currently uses the insights gained from modeling to design and optimize freeze drying cycles, saving significant time and material costs by minimizing the number of trial and error experiments.

14.6 Conclusions

The biopharmaceutical industry is a maturing industry, now confronted with increasing generic competition and greater regulatory expectations. These drivers are motivating manufacturers to incorporate process modeling tools into their development and manufacturing practices to reduce development costs and shorten time-to-market. This is because the enhanced process understanding provided by modeling minimizes the number of experiments required to develop a process and reduces the risk of failure during scale-up.

This chapter provided an overview of the current state of the process modeling field for bioprocess development, with an emphasis on mixing in bioreactors, chromatography, and lyophilization. This included a summary of the theory and application of both CFD and non-CFD models for the design, scale-up, and optimization of these three unit operations. Of course, many other successful applications of process modeling were not covered. These include the freeze/thaw process (Iannuccelli et al., 2011; Roessl et al., 2014), vial filling (Pordal et al., 2002), filtration (Bolton et al., 2005; Velayudhan and Menon, 2007), and ultrafiltration/diafiltration (Ng et al., 1976; Jaffrin and Charrier, 1994; Cheryan, 1998), to name only a few. In all of these cases, process models can help identify critical process parameters, support design decisions, mitigate risk, and optimize a process for peak performance. Process modeling can also reveal interdependencies between process parameters that may be either difficult or costly to identify experimentally.

Looking to the future, continued development of the physical modeling capabilities associated with turbulence and multiphase flow, along with prolonged increases in solver robustness and performance, will further enable the biopharmaceutical industry to predict the performance characteristics and robustness of their unit operations. Gains in the ability of numerical tools to accurately and efficiently solve large nonlinear problems with coupled physics will pave the way for the rapid evaluation of process sensitivities to variability in raw materials and process conditions, thus providing a more effective way of developing robust processes that deliver consistent product quality. Ultimately, process modeling will usher in an era of virtual design space analysis, which will significantly lower process development costs and strengthen the biopharmaceutical industry's ability to satisfy key regulatory initiatives such as QbD.

References

Ahn, J., Lee, J.H., Jang, S.J., Sung, H.J., 2013. Direct numerical simulations of fully developed turbulent pipe flows for Re,t = 180, 544 and 934. Int. J. Heat Fluid Flow. 44, 222–228.

Anderson, T., Jackson, R., 1967. A fluid mechanical description of fluidized beds. Ind. Eng. Chem. Fundamen. 6 (4), 527–539.

Bak, H., Thomas, O.R., Abildskov, J., 2007. Lumped parameter model for prediction of initial breakthrough profiles for the chromatographic capture of antibodies from a complex feedstock. J. Chromatogr. B. 848 (1), 131–141.

Batchelor, G., 1953. The Theory of Homogeneous Turbulence. Cambridge University Press, New York, NY.

Bird, R.B., Stewart, W.E., Lightfoot, E.N., 1960. Transport Phenomena. John Wiley & Sons, Hoboken, NJ.

Bolton, G., LaCasse, D., Lazzara, M., Kuriyel, R., 2005. The fiber-coating model of biopharmaceutical depth filtration. AIChE J. 51 (11), 2978–2987.

Bonvillani, P., Ferrari, M., Ducrós, E., Orejas, J., 2006. Theoretical and experimental study of the effects of scale-up on mixing time for a stirred-tank bioreactor. Braz. J. Chem. Eng. 23 (1), 1–7.

Chen, X., Sadineni, V., Maity, M., Quan, Y., Enterline, M., Mantri, R.V., 2015. Finite element method (FEM) modeling of freeze-drying: monitoring pharmaceutical product robustness during lyophilization. AAPS PharmSciTech. 16 (6), 1317–1326.

Cheryan, M., 1998. Ultrafiltration and microfiltration handbook. 2nd ed. CRC Press, Boca Raton, FL.

Dhanasekharan, K., Sanyal, J., Jain, A., Haidari, A., 2005. A generalized approach to model oxygen transfer in bioreactors using population balances and computational fluid dynamics. Chem. Eng. Sci. 60 (1), 213–218.

Dorn, M., Hekmat, D., 2016. Simulation of the dynamic packing behavior of preparative chromatography columns via discrete particle modeling. Biotechnol. Prog. 32 (2), 363–371.

Elias, C.B., Desai, R.B., Patole, M.S., Joshi, J.B., Mashelkar, R.A., 1995. Turbulent shear stress — effect on mammalian cell culture and measurement using laser doppler anemometer. Chem. Eng. Sci. 50 (15), 2431–2440.

Garcia-Ochoa, F., Gomez, E., 2009. Bioreactor scale-up and oxygen transfer rate in microbial processes: an overview. Biotechnol. Adv. 27 (2), 153–176.

Gohel, S., Joshi, S., Azhar, M., Horner, M., Padron, G., 2012. CFD modeling of solid suspension in a stirred tank: effect of drag models and turbulent dispersion on cloud height. Int. J. Chem. Eng. Article ID 956975, 9 pages.

Guiochon, G., Felinger, A., Shirazi, D.G., Katti, A.M., 2006. Fundamentals of Preparative and Nonlinear Chromatography. 2nd ed. Elsevier Academic Press, San Diego, CA.

Hanke, A.T., Ottens, M., 2014. Purifying biopharmaceuticals: knowledge-based chromatographic process development. Trends Biotechnol. 32 (4), 210–220.

Haque, J.N., Mahmud, T., Roberts, K.J., Rhodes, D., 2006. Modeling turbulent flows with free-surface in unbaffled agitated vessels. Ind. Eng. Chem. Res. 45 (8), 2881–2891.

Hemrajani, R.R., Tatterson, G.B., 2004. In: Paul, E.L., Atiemo-Obeng, V.A., Kresta, S.M. (Eds.), Handbook of Industrial Mixing: Science and Practice. John Wiley & Sons, Inc, Hoboken, NJ.

Hirano, A., Maruyama, T., Shiraki, K., Arakawa, T., Kameda, T., 2014. Mechanism of protein desorption from 4-mercaptoethylpyridine resins by arginine solutions. J. Chromatogr. A. 1373, 141–148.

Huang, L.X., Kumar, K., Mujumdar, A., 2006. A comparative study of a spray dryer with rotary disc atomizer and pressure nozzle using computational fluid dynamic simulations. Chem. Eng. Proc. 45 (6), 461–470.

Iannuccelli, M., Suzzi, D., Sirnik, B., Rinderhofer, A., Khinast, J., 2011. Numerical simulation of freeze-thaw biopharmaceutical processes. Chem. Eng. Trans. 24, 907–912.

ICH Harmonised Tripartite Guideline Pharmaceutical Development Q8(R2), 2009. Retrieved from <http://www.ich.org/fileadmin/Public_Web_Site/ICH_Products/Guidelines/Quality/Q8_R1/Step4/Q8_R2_Guideline.pdf>.

Jaffrin, M., Charrier, J., 1994. Optimization of ultrafiltration and diafiltration processes for albumin production. J. Memb. Sci. 97, 71–81.
Kelly, B., 2009. Industrialization of mAb production technology: the biorpocessing industry at a crossroads. MAbs. 1 (5), 443–452.
Kodama, T., Sawada, H., Hosomi, H., Takeuchi, M., Wakiyama, N., Yonemochi, E., et al., 2014. Optimization of primary drying condition for pharmaceutical lyophilization using a novel simulation program with a predictive model for dry layer resistance. Chem. Pharm. Bull. 62 (2), 153–159.
Koffas, M., Stephanopoulos, G., 2005. Strain improvement by metabolic engineering: lysine production as a case study for systems biology. Curr. Opin. Biotechnol. 16 (3), 361–366.
Koganti, V., Carroll, F., Ferraina, R., Falk, R., Waghmare, Y., Berry, M., et al., 2010. Application of modeling to scale-up dissolution in pharmaceutical manufacturing. AAPS PharmSciTech. 11 (4), 1541–1548.
Koganti, V., Shalaev, E., Berry, M., Osterberg, T., Youssef, M., Hiebert, D., et al., 2011. Investigation of design space for freeze-drying: use of modeling for primary drying segment of a freeze-drying cycle. AAPS PharmSciTech. 12 (3), 854–861.
Le, H., Moin, P., Kim, J., 1997. Direct numerical simulation of turbulent flow over a backward-facing step. J. Fluid Mech. 330, 349–374.
Malang, J., Kumar, P., Saptoro, A., 2015. Computational fluid dynamics-based hydrodynamics studies in packed bed columns: current status and future directions. Int. J. Chem. React. Eng. 13 (3), 289–303.
Marshall, E.M., Bakker, A., 2004. In: Paul, E.L., Atiemo-Obeng, V.A., Kresta, S.M. (Eds.), Handbook of Industrial Mixing: Science and Practice. John Wiley & Sons, Inc, Hoboken, NJ.
Mascarenhas, W., Akay, H., Pikal, M., 1997. A computational model for finite element analysis of the freeze-drying process. Comput. Methods Appl. Mech. Eng. 148 (1–2), 105–124.
Moin, P., Mahesh, K., 1998. Direct numerical simulation: a tool in turbulence research. Annu. Rev. Fluid Mech. 30, 539–578.
Moser, R.D., Kim, J., Mansour, N.N., 1999. Direct numerical simulation of turbulent channel flow up to Re, t = 590. Phys. Fluids. 11 (4), 943–945.
Muzzio, C.R., Dini, N.G., 2011. Simulation of freezing step in vial lyophilization using finite element method. Comput. Chem. Eng. 35 (11), 2274–2283.
Nfor, B.K., Verhaert, P.D., van der Wielen, L.A., Hubbuch, J., Ottens, M., 2009. Rational and systematic protein purification process development: the next generation. Trends Biotechnol. 27 (12), 673–679.
Ng, P., Lundblad, J., Mitra, G., 1976. Optimization of solute separation by diafiltration. Sep. Sci. Technol. 11 (5), 499–502.
Noriega, J.A., Tejeda, A., Magaña, I., Ortega, J., Guzmán, R., 1997. Modeling column regeneration effects on dye-ligand affinity chromatography. Biotechnol. Prog. 13 (5), 296–300.
Oakley, T., 2015. Device developer perspective. ONdrugDelivery, 4–6.
Oosterhuis, N., Kossen, N., 1984. Dissolved oxygen concentration profiles in a production scale bioreactor. Biotechnol. Bioeng. 26 (5), 546–550.
Paul, E.L., Atiemo-Obeng, V.A., Kresta, S.M. (Eds.), 2004. Handbook of Industrial Mixing: Science and Practice. John Wiley & Sons, Hoboken, NJ.
Pikal, M., Roy, M., Shah, S., 1984. Mass and heat transfer in vial freeze drying of pharmaceuticals: role of the vial. J. Pharm. Sci. 73 (9), 1224–1237.

Pikal, M., Cardon, S., Bhugra, C., Jameel, F., Rambhatla, S., Mascarenhas, W., et al., 2005. The nonsteady state modeling of freeze drying: in-process product temperature and moisture content mapping and pharmaceutical product quality applications. Pharm. Dev. Technol. 10 (1), 17–32.

Pisano, R., Fissore, D., Barresi, A.A., Rastelli, M., 2013. Quality by design: scale-up of freeze-drying cycles in pharmaceutical industry. AAPS PharmSciTech. 14 (3), 1137–1149.

Pope, S.B., 2000. Turbulent Flows. Cambridge University Press, New York, NY.

Pordal, H., Matice, C., Fry, T., 2002. Computational fluid dynamics in the pharmaceutical industry. Pharm. Technol. 26 (2), 72–79.

Rathore, A., Sharma, C., Persad, A., 2012. Use of computational fluid dynamics as a tool for establishing process design. Biotechnol. Prog. 28 (2), 382–391.

Reck, J., Pabst, T., Hunter, A., Wang, X., Carta, G., 2015. Adsorption equilibrium and kinetics of monomer-dimer monoclonal antibody mixtures on a cation exchange resin. J. Chromatogr. A. 1402, 46–59.

Roessl, U., Jajcevic, D., Leitgeb, S., Khinast, J., Nidetzky, B., 2014. Characterization of a laboratory-scale container for freezing protein solutions with detailed evaluation of a freezing process simulation. J. Pharm. Sci. 103 (2), 417–426.

Rousseau, R. (Ed.), 1987. Handbook of Separation Process Technology. 1st ed. John Wiley & Sons, New York, NY.

Sheehan, P., Liapis, A., 1998. Modeling of the primary and secondary drying stages of the freeze drying of pharmaceutical products in vials: numerical results obtained from the solution of a dynamic and spatially multi-dimensional lyophilization model for different operational policies. Biotechnol. Bioeng. 60 (6), 712–728.

Soltania, S., Gerde, P., Acevedo, F., Rasmuson, A., 2015. Counter-current spray drying with stream separation: computational modeling of a novel dryer design. Chem. Eng. Res. Design. 93, 163–173.

Stoker, E.B., 2011, 5 1. Comparative Studies On Scale-Up Methods of Single-Use Bioreactors. Retrieved from DigitalCommons@USU: <http://digitalcommons.usu.edu/cgi/viewcontent.cgi?article=1885&context=etd>.

Tennekes, H., Lumley, J.L., 1972. A first course in turbulence. The MIT Press, Cambridge, MA.

Tomáš, M., Linek, V., Prokopová, E., 2003. Gas hold-up, mixing time and gas–liquid volumetric mass transfer coefficient of various multiple-impeller configurations: Rushton turbine, pitched blade and techmix impeller and their combinations. Chem. Eng. Sci. 58 (9), 1839–1846.

Velayudhan, A., Menon, M., 2007. Modeling of purification operations in biotechnology: enabling process development, optimization, and scale-up. Biotechnol. Prog. 23 (1), 68–73.

Werner, S., Kaiser, S.C., Kraume, M., Eibl, D., 2014. Computational fluid dynamics as a modern tool for engineering characterization of bioreactors. Pharm. Bioprocess. 2 (1), 85–99.

Wilcox, D.C., 1993. Turbulence Modeling for CFD. DCW Industries, Inc., La Canada, CA.

Wisee, W., 1951. The measurement of the aeration of culture media. J. Gen. Microbiol. 5 (1), 167–177.

Wu, Y., Yu, H., Ching, C., 2004. A computational fluid dynamics study of binary adsorption separation in chromatography. Chem. Eng. Technol. 27 (9), 955–961.

Zhang, Q., Yong, Y., Mao, Z.-S., Yang, C., Zhao, C., 2009. Experimental determination and numerical simulation of mixing time in a gas–liquid stirred tank. Chem. Eng. Sci. 64 (12), 2926–2933.

Zhu, Y., Wu, J., 2002. Critical impeller speed for suspending solids in aerated agitation tanks. Can. J. Chem. Eng. 80 (4), 1–6.

Zwietering, T., 1958. Suspending of solid particles in liquid by agitators. Chem. Eng. Sci. 8 (3–4), 244–253.

Index

Note: Page numbers followed by "*f*" and "*t*" refer to figures and tables, respectively.

G

H

I

Q

R

Kolibri 360 GmbH
Ferdinand-Jühlke-Straße 7
99095 Erfurt, Deutschland
produktsicherheit@kolibri360.de